patisserie

patisserie

*An encyclopedia of cakes, pastries, cookies, biscuits,
chocolate, confectionery & desserts*

AARON MAREE

Angus&Robertson
An imprint of HarperCollins*Publishers*

An Angus & Robertson Publication

Angus&Robertson, an imprint of
HarperCollins*Publishers*
25 Ryde Road, Pymble, Sydney NSW 2073, Australia
31 View Road, Glenfield, Auckland10, New Zealand
77-85 Fulham Palace Road, London W6 8JB, United Kingdom

Distributed in the United States of America by
HarperCollins*Publishers*
10 East 53rd Street, New York NY 10022, USA

First published in Australia in 1994

National Library of Australia
Cataloguing-in-Publication data

Maree, Aaron
Patisserie: an encyclopedia of cakes, pastries, cookies, biscuits, chocolates,
confectionery and desserts.
Bibliography.
ISBN 0 207 18478 X
1. Pastry. 2. Cake. 3. Confectionery. I. Title.
641.865

Cover and internal photographs, unless otherwise credited: Andre Martin
Photographic stylists: Karen Carter and Melanie Feddersen
Assistant stylists: Megan Smith and Katie Mitchell
Back cover photograph: Prince Regent Torte, see page 224
Printed in Hong Kong

9 8 7 6 5 4 3 2 1
97 96 95 94

Contents

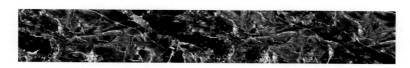

Acknowledgments

vi

Introduction

vii

How to Use This Book

viii

An A–Z of Pâtisserie

1

Bibliography

296

Acknowledgments

Ewald, Susan and Brittany Notter and the School of International Confectionary Arts,
Gaithersberg, America;

Deborah Mynott and Rod Slater, Cadbury Schweppes;

Ian Webb and David Fell, Cadbury Food Service Division;

Paul Frizell and Darryl Jackson, Sunny Queen Egg Farms;

Australian Dairy Corporation;

Joy Noble and the staff at Executive Chef Pty Ltd;

Peter Laing, lecturer, Mt Gravett Tafe College;

Ingo Schwarze, senior lecturer, Regency College, South Australia;

John Sexton, senior lecturer, Cotah, Queensland;

Jan Liddle and Paul Lawson, Glad Products of Australia;

John Dart, Trumps Nuts and Dried Fruits;

Josephine Ive and Geoff Taylor, friends to the end;

Juleigh and Ian Robins, Indigenous Food Suppliers, Robin's Food Store, Melbourne;

Serge Dansereau, Executive chef, The Regent of Sydney;

Robert Hill-Smith, Peter Sawrey, and S. Smith & Sons of the wine labels Yalumba, Heggies,
Eden Valley and Pewsey Vale, South Australia, for their information on dessert wines;

Bernadette Roach, McCormicks Foods;

Ian Elliott, CSR;

Dietmar Gasser, Executive chef, Park Royal Hotel, Brisbane;

Myles Seymour, Executive chef, Government House, Brisbane;

Rick Stephens, Executive chef, Raphael's Restaurant, Brisbane;

Maria Weisshauser, Executive pastrychef, Sheraton Mirage Resort, Gold Coast;

Staff at New York State Library, New York;

Jan Power for her kind words, kind heart and use of her library;

and Bob Hart for his teachings on food journalism and his belief in me.

Introduction

Many of today's recipes that are 'invented' are not the birth of a new recipe but the fruition of many ideas based on old traditions and methods.

J. Ive, March 17, 1993.

Welcome to the culinary delights of the *pâtisserie*. Literally translated, *pâtisserie* is the French term for the art of the pastry cook or a pastry cook's shop. Within this context, the book is a celebration of the art of the *pâtissier*, so let us imagine the pages are a shop filled with tempting results of the work of the pastry chef.

Pastry-making is an ancient art (mention of it is found in early Greek and Roman documents) but what we recognise as the art of the pastry chef in the late 20th century has its origins in the late 16th century. *Larousse Gastronomique* dates the impetus given to patisserie as coming from the time of the Crusades. Prior to that period, the Greek *oblios* (the ancestors of wafers and waffles) had given their name to the first French pastry chefs — hence *obloyers*. Towards the Middle Ages in France, the work of the pastry chef and the baker started to overlap. The Crusaders unwittingly began a culinary revolution when they returned to Europe with their precious discoveries: sugar cane and puff pastry. According to *Larousse*, this caused pastry cooks, bakers and restaurateurs to claim these new products as their own. To try to end the confusion, the status was given to the 'master *oubloyers* and the varlets of the *oubloiries*'.

Throughout the mid-1300s, *pâtisserie* meant the production of the following: wafres, estrées, supplications, nieules, echaudes, fritters, gohieres, popelins, marzipan, darioles, flanets, casse museaux, talmouses, ratons, tarts made with frangipane, pistachio, young pigeon, and lark. In 1440, the sole rights to meat, fish, and cheese pies were also handed to the *pâtissier* — this was the first time the word actually appeared in the history. Around this time, rights and duties were defined and rules established. A true *pâtissier* did not use spoiled meat, bad eggs, sour or skimmed milk, nor did he sell re-heated pies. The job description of the pâtissier and oubloyeru became one in 1556.

The 16th century pâtisserie product is certainly different from what we understand to be the produce of the modern pastry cook. Today's *pâtisserie* encompasses any sweet or savoury pastries and cakes, most of which are baked in a relatively hot oven, and which can be served either hot or cold. The modern Western pastry cook makes a variety of sweet things: hot or cold desserts, ice cream and confectionery, sugar-based products, candied fruits, almond paste, nougatine, sweetened creams and sauces, plus a wide variety of cakes.

In this book, I have attempted to present a summary of the many and varied types of pastries, cakes, and desserts which have been created over the centuries. In the A to Z format, you will find single entries, as well as entries followed by recipes of the classic dishes. If there is an omission, forgive me. To anyone nervous about attempting the more complicated-sounding recipes, remember that this type of cooking requires the maximum convenient coolness in ingredients, and the minimum handling of dough. For pastry generally, the oven is to be hot to begin with, then cooled accordingly. Any liquid is to be added carefully to prevent a soggy result. It also requires a love of the sweeter things in life. Being a pastry chef has been the greatest pleasure in my life (to date) and I hope that I will have imparted a little of that pleasure by the time you come to the end. Bon appetit!

Aaron Maree

How to Use This Book

Most ingredients or their equivalent are readily available at a supermarket. There are a few items which may involve a trip to the local delicatessen. If you have no luck at either, try a major food wholesaler or importer who will be able to help you source the item.

The style and type of cream varies throughout the world so when cream is listed in the ingredients, this refers to normal dairy cream, the sort you use for whipping. Where otherwise, it is stated as thickened.

All eggs in ingredients are the large size.

In most recipes there is a basic production method. The choice of using an electric hand beater, an electric mixer or food processor, is up to you.

I hope you enjoy the book, and have fun in the kitchen.

OVEN TEMPERATURES

Temperatures	Celsius °C	Farenheit °F	Gas Mark
Very slow	120	250	½
Slow	150	300	2
Moderately slow	160-180	325-350	3-4
Moderate	190-200	375-400	5-6
Moderately hot	220-230	425-450	7
Hot	250-260	475-500	8-9

A

ABAISSE

A term used in French cookery for a sheet of puff pastry which has been rolled very thinly. Occasionally it refers to a thin slice of sponge cake used in a dessert.

ABOUKIR

A Swiss dessert made up of thin sponge layers sandwiched with a rich chestnut- and alcohol-flavoured cream. Originally the sponge was cooked in a decorative tin or charlotte mould prior to being cut and decorated. Today it is customary to use a round sponge. It is decorated with a coffee-flavoured fondant which is drizzled over the top and sides, and finished with a sprinkling of finely chopped pistachio nuts.

ABOUKIR ALMONDS

A sugar-glazed petit four made by pressing two whole blanched and roasted almonds into the sides of a ball of green-coloured marzipan. It is then held with a dipping fork and dipped into a boiled sugar syrup and allowed to sit on baking paper (parchment) until firmly set. It is served as a petit four with coffee or as an afternoon tea fancy.

ACETIC ACID

A natural organic acid which is also known as vinegar. It is used in sugar and confectionery recipes, in pavlovas (as a stabiliser for the egg whites), and in royal icing, to assist the icing mixture to set firmly.

ACETOMEL

From the Latin words 'acetum' — vinegar, and 'mel' — honey, acetomel is a mixture of these two substances. A sweet/sour syrup, it was used in the past to preserve fruits such as pears, apples and quinces. It is rarely used today, although it is still available throughout parts of Europe.

ACIDULATED WATER

A mixture of water and fresh lemon juice which is used for soaking cut pieces of apple or pear so as to prevent oxidisation, which causes the flesh of the fruit to turn brown.

AERATION

The aeration of products such as cakes, creams and most pastry mixtures is one of the most important processes that pastry chefs need to attend to carefully. Without aeration, products would be flat, solid and indigestible. It is through aeration that recipes gain their volume, flavour and palatability. Basically, it is the process by which air or carbon dioxide gas is incorporated into substances such as cake or biscuit (cookie) mixtures, yeast doughs or liquids.

Air can be incorporated by whisking, creaming, beating, liquefying, laminating or puréeing a mixture, while carbon dioxide is added by using yeast or baking powder (soda). For aeration to occur, the aerating agent must produce a gas or pressure within the mixture, thus increasing that product's volume. This must then remain stable until the mixture can be heated via baking, causing the ingredients to coagulate or gel and ensuring that any lift or volume will remain within the product, so that it does not collapse.

There are five methods of aeration:

(I) PANARY — YEAST. Panary aeration is produced by the fermentation of yeast. In the presence of warmth, moisture and food, the yeast grows and produces carbon dioxide. This gas is trapped within the elastic gluten framework of the dough in which it is contained and this causes the dough to rise. When risen to the required extent, the dough is baked, which initially speeds up the fermentation process due to the increase in heat until the yeast is killed at 55°C (131°F).

(II) CHEMICAL — BAKING POWDER. Several different types of chemical aerating agents are used in the pastry kitchen. Baking powder (soda) is perhaps the most popular, others being ammonium bicarbonate, cream of tartar and bicarbonate of soda. When using these, the product must be handled gently and quickly as chemicals tend to produce a gas only once and when the product is deflated as a result of heavy handling or mixing, they will not re-react and the mixture will remain heavy and lacking in aeration. This work must be done quickly as these chemicals begin reacting immediately on coming in contact with liquid or warm moisture, and so will normally have begun working before the mixture reaches the oven.

(III) PHYSICAL/MECHANICAL — WHISKING AND BEATING. Much of what was once physical aeration is today mechanical, due to modern technology and the time-saving devices that are used in the pastry kitchen.

It is through beating a mixture by hand that air is incorporated and a new craftsperson should be taught this form of aeration before being introduced to modern machinery. Products such as sponges (sugar/egg), meringues (egg whites/sugar), buttercreams (butter/sugar) and even cream all call for a form of aeration by whisking or beating using a hand whisk or machine.

(IV) LAMINATION – ROLLING AND FOLDING. Puff pastry is the major example produced using this method. Lamination produces a build-up of alternate layers of fat and dough. When the product is baked, the steam produced by the fat separates the dough layers and forces them upwards.

(V) COMBINATIONS OF THE ABOVE. Quite often recipes call for more than one form of aeration. Danish pastry and croissant doughs utilise a yeast (panary) dough that is laminated with fat layers. In cake production, it is not uncommon to see the first half of a recipe call for the creaming of butter and sugar for lightness and then to have whisked egg whites folded through the mixture, or in certain recipes a combination of baking powder and whisked egg whites is used for extra lift.

AEROMETER

An instrument invented by the French chemist Antoine Baume (1728–1804) to measure the specific density of sugar syrups and sauces.

AFGHAN

These small chocolate biscuits (cookies) are filled with cornflakes and dusted with icing sugar or drinking chocolate, or iced with a water icing. Similar in texture to a chocolate shortcake, they can quite easily be made larger and, when baked, split and filled with cream and strawberries.

210 g (7 oz) unsalted (sweet) butter
¾ cup (4 oz) brown sugar
1 egg
2 cups (8 oz) plain (all-purpose) flour
4 tablespoons cocoa powder
2 teaspoons baking powder (soda)
⅔ cup (2 oz) desiccated (shredded) coconut
2½ cups (2½ oz) cornflakes (corn crisps)
drinking chocolate, for dusting

Preheat oven to 180°C (350°F).
Line two baking sheets with baking paper (parchment). Place butter and sugar in a mixing bowl and cream together until light and fluffy. Add egg and mix until well combined. Sift flour, cocoa powder and baking powder and add to the mixture, mixing in by hand. Lastly, add the coconut and cornflakes and mix lightly by hand until combined. Place heaped teaspoonfuls of mixture on the prepared sheets and bake for 10–12 minutes. Cool on sheet before dusting with drinking chocolate and serving.

Makes 36

AGAR-AGAR
(see also gelatine)

Made from reddish seaweed, agar-agar is dried, washed, pounded and then dried again before being bleached in the heat of the sun. After being boiled for 18–24 hours it is then filtered and allowed to cool. The gelatinous gel which has formed is then rolled thinly into sheets or strips which are further sun bleached and dried. Agar-agar is tasteless and odourless and will swell when soaked in cold water. When warmed, it will dissolve into a slimy brown liquid and will set strongly when cooled. It has almost triple the strength of gelatine. Agar-agar is principally used in the pastry industry for cream desserts, ice creams and sauces.

AGRAZ
(see also sorbet)

A favourite in Northern Africa, agraz is a sorbet made from grape juice, almonds, sugar and Kirsch. Usually made from unripe grapes, the sorbet has a very tart, almost acidic taste.

AKWADU

This rich but simple dessert from Ghana is usually served after a spicy meal. It is a banana-based dessert, but the bananas can be replaced by any fruit desired.

4 bananas
60 g (2 oz) unsalted (sweet) butter, melted
zest and juice of 2 oranges
zest and juice of 1 lemon
⅓ cup (2 oz) brown sugar
2 tablespoons sugar
⅔ cup (2 oz) desiccated (shredded) coconut

Preheat oven to 180°C (350 °F). Lightly grease a large pie dish. Chop bananas into fine slices and place in a bowl. Mix melted butter, orange and lemon zest and juice, sugars and coconut in a bowl. Mix bananas through the coconut mixture and place all the mix in a large pie dish. Bake for 15–20 minutes until the coconut is brown. Serve hot or cold.

Serves 4

ALBUMEN
(see also eggs)

Albumen, otherwise referred to as egg white, is a very important ingredient in the production of many pastries, and one of many proteins used in the baking industry. The albumen constitutes almost 60% of the total egg weight and after being separated from the egg yolk is used for whisking into a light white foam for meringues or for folding into cake or cream mixtures to make them rise or make them lighter. When heated, the egg white foam will coagulate. Egg white foam is poached in such desserts as Oeufs à la Neige.

In basic cake mixtures containing eggs the albumen constitutes a major part of the cake structure and assists with the binding of all the ingredients.

ALKAZAR

Alkazar (or alcazar) is a very rich almond- or marzipan-based cake which is lightened using a stiff meringue of egg whites. When the almond cake is baked, it is latticed across its top with marzipan and each of the holes caused by the lattice is filled with strawberry jam (jelly) or marmalade. When filled and finished, the cake is returned to a very hot oven and 'flashed' to brown the marzipan and form a skin on the jam so it will set.

Alkazar Step-by-Step

Step 1: Pipe the marzipan in diagonal lines across the cold cake.

Step 2: Pipe strawberry jam into the diamond-shaped holes. See page 2.

8 egg yolks
⅔ cup (5 oz) caster (superfine) sugar
8 egg whites
⅔ cup (5 oz) caster (superfine) sugar, extra
3 cups (11 oz) ground almonds
160 g (5½ oz) unsalted (sweet) butter, melted and cooled

To Decorate
250 g (8 oz) marzipan
⅔ cup (5 oz) caster (superfine) sugar
3 egg whites, lightly beaten
¾ cup (8 oz) strawberry jam (jelly)
apricot glaze (see page 10)
1 cup (4 oz) flaked almonds, roasted (see page 5)

Preheat oven to 180°C (350°F).
Grease a 23 cm (9 in) springform cake tin with butter
and line the base with baking paper (parchment).
Whisk egg yolks and sugar until thick and pale and the
mixture forms a ribbon (see page 236). Beat egg whites until
stiff peaks form and gradually beat in the extra sugar, a
spoonful at a time. Beat until sugar is dissolved. Take a
spoonful of the mixture and mix by hand into the beaten egg
yolks. Gently fold in ground almonds, melted butter and
remaining egg white mixture. Pour into the prepared tin.
Bake for 35–40 minutes or until the cake has shrunk slightly
away from the sides of the tin and the top springs back when
lightly touched. Cool on a cake rack for 15 minutes.

Decoration
Preheat oven to 220°C (425°F).
Blend marzipan and sugar with sufficient egg white to make a
soft paste that can be piped without losing its shape. Fill a
piping (pastry) bag fitted with a plain ½ cm (¼ in) nozzle with
the marzipan mixture and pipe a lattice pattern on top of the
cake. Pipe strawberry jam into the diamond-shaped spaces.
Bake for 5 minutes or until the marzipan browns slightly and
the jam forms a skin. Cool in the tin on a cake rack for
30 minutes. Remove cake from tin and chill.
When cold, brush the sides with apricot glaze and press
flaked almonds onto the glaze. Paint a little apricot glaze
onto the marzipan lattice using a fine brush.

ALL-IN METHOD

Also known as One-Stage Method, this method of production
generally refers to a mixture where the ingredients are all put
in together and mixed in the one bowl and are then usually
turned out directly into the cake tin or baking tray (*jelly roll
pan*), with little or no further preparation required.

ALLSPICE
(see also spices)

Found in Mexico, Central America and the West Indies, this
spice bears its name because it has the flavour or aroma of
'all spices', namely cloves, cinnamon, mace, juniper berries
and pepper. It should not be confused with mixed spice,
which is in fact an actual blend of different spices. Allspice is
a pea-sized fruit of the *Eugenia pimenta* and grows in small
clusters on the tree. It is always taken when unripe, as the
riper the fruit the less aromatic the finished product. The
green, unripe fruit become shrivelled brown berries once they
are cured. The best allspice is sun dried, but this method is
more hazardous than oven drying as the amount of time
required for drying means that it needs to be protected from
both weather and other foreign contaminants. The dried fruit
is reddish brown in colour.

ALLELUIA

A confectionery with a citrus flavour that is produced by
French pastry chefs for Easter. Legend has it that the cake
was named by Pope Pius VII, who was passing through the
town one Easter. Apparently he was captivated by the tale of
how the recipe had come into the hands of the town's pastry
chef: it had been handed to him by a dying soldier who had
found the recipe during a battle. The Pope gave the cakes a
ceremonial baptism and named the products Alleluias, a
name which has remained to this day.

ALLIGATOR PEAR
(see avocado)

ALLUMETTES
*(see also millefeuille, puff pastry,
royal icing)*

These are rectangular strips of puff pastry which are spread
with royal icing and baked till golden brown. When cooled,
they are served plain as a petit four or split and filled with a
variety of fillings and served as individiual pâtisseries or as a
dessert. Allumettes were created by Planta, a Swiss pastry
chef, when trying to use up leftover pastry and icing.

500 g (16 oz) butter puff pastry (see page 43)
1 quantity royal icing (see page 241)

Preheat oven to 180°C (350°F).
Line a baking sheet with baking paper (parchment).
Roll out puff pastry to a thickness of 4–5 mm (¼ in). Spread
rolled puff pastry with the royal icing, ensuring that a thin,
even covering is achieved. Cut puff pastry into rectangular
strips 10 x 5 cm (4 x 2 in) with a hot (dipped in warm water)
clean knife and place them on the prepared sheet. Bake in
preheated oven until the icing is lightly browned and the puff
pastry well risen, approximately 25–30 minutes.

ALMOND
(see also nuts)

The fruit of the almond tree is worthless in itself, but within it
is a hard shell containing a kernel which, according to its
variety, can either be sweet or bitter. Sweet almonds are the
ones most commonly used in the pastry and confectionery
industries due to their pleasant taste. Though primarily used
for the production of marzipan or almond paste, almonds
have many other uses in the pastry kitchen and come in a
variety of forms. They are available whole, blanched (without
their skins), splintered or slivered, flaked, chopped and as
almond meal or in ground form. Roasted flaked almonds are

among the most common finishes used on the outside of cakes or gâteaux because they are easy to place around the sides and they give a wonderful flavour to the cake.

Almonds originated in the north of Africa and central areas of Asia, but the bulk of the world's almonds today come from Mediterranean countries, especially Spain and Italy, where many of the almond-based recipes originated.

Roasted Flaked Almonds
2¼ cups (8 oz) flaked almonds
Preheat oven to 180°C (350°F).
Spread almonds thinly on a baking sheet. Bake for 4 minutes. Remove sheet and use a fork to turn the almonds. Return to oven and bake for a further 4 minutes. Remove and turn again. Continue this process until the almonds are golden brown. Cool on the sheet.

ALMOND MILK
(see also blancmange)

Historically, almond milk was a preparation of crushed almonds, wines and spices which was boiled until it became thick enough to set. This mixture was the forerunner of today's blancmange. The crushed almonds were used in place of the white meats of fish or pork, making the blancmange an instant dessert rather than a main course meal.

In more recent times, almond milk has been produced by mixing milk or water with marzipan and heating slightly until the mixture is smooth. This is used in custards, cakes and sauces and in a dome-shaped almond cake bearing its own name, Lait d'Amande ('milk of almonds').

ALMOND PASTE
(see also marzipan)

As well as being used to produce petits fours and to provide a smoothly finished cake covering, this confectionery paste is used as a modelling medium. Almond paste is a mixture of ground almonds and sugar, usually of equal weights, to which glucose is added to bind the mixture together. It can be prepared in two ways, either cooked or uncooked. The uncooked method is a simple cold mixture of the base ingredients, while in the cooked version the sugar and glucose are boiled with some water to form a sugar syrup which is then folded through the ground almonds. After being allowed to set for 24 hours it is kneaded before use to soften it.

These days, however, almond paste usually refers to an inferior product which is a substitute for the real almond paste, which is known as marzipan.

The substitute almond paste, which is cheaper, is made from apricot kernels, almond essence, sugar and glucose, a mixture which is also known as persipan. This type of almond paste is usually identified by the extreme aroma of the almond essence, a feature which marzipan does not have, being both subtle in flavour and having a smoother, more delicate almond scent.

Almond paste is usually sold in a natural colour, and may then be coloured with any food dye and used in just about every way that marzipan can. Usually, however, it cannot be used in baking as it tends to contain an extreme ratio of sugar, which will boil when used in a mixture that is baked.

ALMOND TORTE

A rich, sweet, heavy cake that is topped with a praline-encrusted buttercream.

1⅔ cups (6 oz) ground almonds
⅔ cup (2 oz) desiccated (shredded) coconut
1 cup (8 oz) sugar
200 g (7 oz) unsalted (sweet) butter, melted
4 eggs, beaten

To Decorate
1 quantity praline (see page 221), crushed
¼ quantity quick no-fuss buttercream (see page 43)

Preheat oven to 180°C (350°F).
Grease a 23 cm (9 in) springform cake tin lightly with butter. Dust with flour and shake out excess.
Line the base with baking paper (parchment).
Mix almonds, coconut, sugar and butter together and blend in the beaten eggs. Pour mixture into prepared tin.
Bake for 40–45 minutes or until cooked.
Cool in the tin on a cake rack.
When cold, remove from the tin and spread buttercream evenly over the top. Sprinkle praline over the buttercream.

AMANDINE

An invention of French pâtissier Ragueneau, these small almond tartlets have now reached world fame under a bevy of different names. Amandines are a sweet pastry base filled with a frangipane-style filling of eggs, sugar, butter and ground almonds. Topped with flaked almonds which brown to a golden colour through baking, they are always glazed with an apricot glaze and often iced with fondant with a final decoration of glacé (candied) cherries.

AMAREE COOKIES

This delightful cookie has a true festive Christmas flavour in the European tradition. It is a gingerbread-style biscuit (cookie) with a raw sugar crust and a base coated in rich dark chocolate, allowed to set in a bed of roasted sesame seeds. These were invented in 1990 by Australian pastry chef Aaron Maree.

180 g (6 oz) unsalted (sweet) butter, softened
1 cup (6 oz) soft (light) brown sugar
¼ cup (3 oz) golden syrup (light treacle)
1 egg
2 cups (8 oz) plain (all-purpose) flour
2 teaspoons baking powder
2 tablespoons cocoa powder
2 teaspoons ground cinnamon
raw cane sugar, for cooking
200 g (7 oz) dark (plain or semi-sweet) chocolate, melted (see page 62)
1¼ cups (7 oz) sesame seeds, roasted

Place butter, sugar and golden syrup in a mixing bowl and cream until light and fluffy. Add egg and mix until combined.

Sift flour, baking powder, cocoa and cinnamon together
and add in two batches to the creamed mixture
Mix well. Cover with plastic wrap (cling film)
and refrigerate for 45 minutes.
Preheat oven to 180°C (350°F). Line baking sheets with
baking paper (parchment). Remove the mixture from the
refrigerator. Take walnut-sized portions and roll into a ball.
Dip half of the ball into the raw sugar and place, sugar
uppermost, on the prepared sheets. Allow at least 5 cm (2 in)
between the cookies for spreading. Bake in the preheated
oven for 10–12 minutes. Remove from the oven and cool
slightly on the sheet before placing on a cake rack. When the
cookies are cool, dip the bases lightly in chocolate and then in
the sesame seeds. Place on a baking sheet to set.

AMARETTI

Amaretti, the Italian relative of the macaroon, are very crisp
little cookies. The mixture must sit for 6–8 hours before being
baked.

2 tablespoons plain (all-purpose) flour
1¼ cups (9 oz) caster (superfine) sugar
2¼ cups (8 oz) ground almonds
2 teaspoons ground cinnamon
zest and juice of 1 lemon
2 egg whites
icing (powdered) sugar, for dusting

Line baking sheets with baking paper (parchment).
Place flour, sugar, ground almonds, cinnamon, lemon zest
and juice in a mixing bowl and stir together. Place egg whites
in a clean mixing bowl and whisk until stiff peaks are formed.
Fold flour/sugar mixture into egg whites and gently stir
together. Take tablespoons of the mixture and spoon onto
prepared sheet, allowing room for spreading. Set the sheet
aside, uncovered, for 6–8 hours.
Preheat oven to 160°C (320°F).
Dust amaretti heavily with icing sugar before placing in
preheated oven. Bake until the amaretti take on a light brown
colour. Remove when brown and cool on the baking sheet.
Dust with icing sugar again before serving.

Makes 18

AMMONIUM BICARBONATE

Also known as ABC, ammonium bicarbonate is used in a
similar way to baking powder (soda) in cake mixtures and is
used in mass baking mixtures as a leavening agent. When it
becomes hot, it decomposes into ammonia and carbon
dioxide, which give it its raising qualities. Usually ammonium
bicarbonate is used only in thin biscuits and cookies, as it
may leave an unpleasant flavour when it is trapped in large
products such as cakes.

AMMONIUM CARBONATE

Also known as carbonate of ammonia, it is better known to
those in the pastry and baking industries as 'Vol'. Ammonium
carbonate is a white salt which traditionally was gathered
from the hooves and horns of animals. It offers bakers a light
and quick raising agent which, if used correctly, leaves little
trace of its use. It reacts in the baking process to the presence
of heat and will give off carbon dioxide, steam and the gas
ammonia. Ammonium carbonate must only be used in thin
products, as the flavour and odour of the ammonia remains
in the moisture retained by bigger or deeper baked goods. It
is often used in gingerbreads, lebkuchen and honey cakes, as
the overpowering flavours and spices cover any taste or
aroma of the ammonia.

ANGEL FOOD CAKE

An American favourite, this cake is so light that it is
considered to be 'food of the angels'. It is a stark white,
moist, fluffy cake decorated with white frosting and is one of
few cakes produced without any fat. Basically, it is made
from four ingredients: egg whites, flour, cornflour
(cornstarch) and sugar, and if made with the correct amount
of cornflour, it should simply melt in the mouth. It is famous
throughout the world.

ANGELICA

Angelica stalks, in crystallised or preserved form, are used by
the pastry chef for their flavour, colour and aroma. Angelica
is incorporated into cakes, biscuits (cookies), doughs,
puddings and other sweet recipes. It is highly regarded
worldwide but is used predominantly throughout Europe,
where it was introduced from Scandinavia into France by the
Vikings. There it was culitivated and promoted by the monks,
who used the angelica plant (a member of the *Umbelliforous*
plant family) both for its medicinal qualities and for its
aromatic power in foods. Angelica was later introduced into
Germany and the rest of Europe.
It is used sparingly today and often only as a garnish.

Crystallised Angelica
Produced in the same way as crystallised (candied) fruits, you
must first blanch the young angelica stems until they are
tender, peel them and return to the hot water until quite
green. The angelica is then given a sugar treatment for
2–3 days, until the green angelica is almost translucent. At
this stage the angelica is allowed to dry on a wire rack for
24 hours, before being coated or rolled in sugar and allowed
to dry further in a cool oven. The angelica is then stored in an
airtight container until required. Preserving the angelica will
allow it to be kept for 1–2 years, although it should never be
manufactured in such a quantity that it needs to be stored for
this length of time.

ANGOSTURA BITTERS

First produced in 1824 by an army doctor who was involved
in the war to liberate South America, these bitters were
named after the town of Angostura, in which the doctor was
working at the time. He initially produced them as a remedy
for a common cause of the death of his fellow soldiers. Bitters
are an aromatic liquid concoction of cloves, cinnamon,
quinine, nutmeg, rum, dried fruits and plant flowers and
other herbal and root extracts.

Today, bitters are used primarily in beverages but offer the pastry chef a pleasant aromatic ingredient which has not been tapped to its fullest. The special flavours of bitters marry perfectly with cakes, compôtes, cookies, puddings, creams and chocolate desserts in particular, providing a unique taste sensation.

ANISE/ANISEED

A member of the same plant family as angelica, anise has a very distinctive flavour. The seeds are crushed for their oil, which is used for its flavour alone in cakes, pastries and confectionery, and also liqueurs.

ANZAC

The Anzac biscuits (cookies) of today are far tastier and more glorified than the hard biscuit the soldiers of the Australia and New Zealand Army Corps ever enjoyed during the war. They were known originally as Anzac Tiles due to their shape, and the soldiers reportedly joked that they were their greatest protection as they were almost bulletproof.

The recipe for the so-called Anzac Tiles that follows is supposedly from the original biscuit manufacturer who exported the biscuits to the Anzac soldiers during the war.

1¾ cups (7 oz) plain (all-purpose) flour
3 cups (12 oz) wholemeal flour
5 tablespoons sugar
1 tablespoon milk powder (non-fat dry milk)
1 cup (8 fl oz) lukewarm water

Preheat oven to 180°C (350°F). Grease a baking sheet.
In a large mixing bowl, mix together flour, sugar and milk powder. Add the lukewarm water to the dry ingredients and work mixture into a dough. A little extra water may be required if the dough definitely will not come together, but the mixture should be quite hard. Remove mixture from the bowl, place on a lightly floured surface and knead well for several minutes. Wrap the dough in plastic wrap (cling film) and allow it to rest in a cool area for 1 hour.
Cut dough into small, even pieces. Take pieces one at a time, keeping the others covered to prevent drying out. Roll each piece of dough on a lightly floured surface to 5–6 mm (¼ in) in thickness. Using a pastry docker (see individual entry), docker the pastry well before cutting the rolled dough into 5 x 5 cm (2 x 2 in) squares. Place each square on prepared sheet and bake in the preheated oven for 15–18 minutes.
Cool and store for 24 hours before eating.
The following is a more palatable modern version.

1 cup (4 oz) plain (all-purpose) flour
1¾ cups (5 oz) rolled oats
1¼ cups (8 oz) caster (superfine) sugar
1 cup (3 oz) desiccated (shredded) coconut
125 g (4 oz) unsalted (sweet) butter
1 tablespoon golden syrup (light treacle)
6 teaspoons ground cinnamon
1 teaspoon bicarbonate of soda (baking soda)
2 tablespoons boiling water

Preheat oven to 180°C (350°F). Lightly grease baking sheets. Place sifted flour, rolled oats, sugar and coconut in a mixing bowl and lightly mix together. Place butter, golden syrup and cinnamon in a saucepan and bring to the boil. Add bicarbonate of soda to the boiling water and stir quickly into butter mixture. Pour immediately into dry ingredients and mix well. Spoon heaped teaspoonfuls of the mixture onto the prepared sheets, leaving 3–4 cm (1–1½ in) between biscuits to allow for spreading. Bake in prepared oven for 18–20 minutes. Remove sheets from the oven, slide a spatula or palette knife under biscuits to loosen them from the sheet and then allow biscuits to cool on the sheet.
If they will not loosen from the sheet, return to the oven for a minute and then try again.
When cool, store in an airtight container until served.

APPLE

The apple is one of the most versatile fruits. It is used fresh, dried, preserved and in its juiced form in cakes, puddings, whips, snows, compôtes, sauces and ciders. It is also the fruit most commonly eaten in its natural form.

Apples are cultivated in almost every country that has a temperate climate, growing well wherever there are mild summers, cool autumns and cold winter climates, as well as fertile, well-drained, slightly acidic soils. They are a close relative of the crab apple, from which they originally developed. Apples are a member of the 'pome' family of fruits, as are pears, the term pome referring to the separate compartments which make up the core and which contain the seeds. Popular varities of apples include Jonathon, Gravenstein, Granny Smith, Golden Delicious and Red Delicious. In some form or another, apples can be traced back some 2500 years and there are several thousand varieties of the fruit.

APPLE CHARLOTTE
(see charlotte)

APPLE CHUTNEY

5 green cooking apples, peeled, cored and chopped
4 tablespoons red wine vinegar
4 tablespoons water
¾ cup (4 oz) sultanas (golden raisins)
⅓ cup (2 oz) brown sugar
1 teaspoon mixed spice
1 teaspoon ground ginger

Place all ingredients in a saucepan and allow to come slowly to the simmer. Place lid on top of saucepan and simmer for 15 minutes. Stir occasionally to ensure the mixture is not catching on the base of the saucepan. Remove from heat and pour the mixture into a glass jar. Cool before covering and storing until required. Serve with very sweet desserts for a delicate harmony of different flavours.

BAKED APPLES

6 apples, cored
¾ cup (3 oz) ground almonds (almond meal)
¼ cup (3 oz) honey
1 tablespoon golden syrup (light treacle)
⅓ cup (2 oz) currants
⅓ cup (2 oz) brown sugar
zest of 1 orange
125 g (4 oz) unsalted (sweet) butter

Preheat oven to 180°C (350°F).
Place cored apples in a baking dish. Mix almonds, honey, golden syrup, currants, sugar and orange zest in a mixing bowl. Spoon filling mixture into the centre of the apples and pack firmly into each so that all of the mixture is used. Top each of the apples with a tablespoon of the butter and spread the remaining butter in the base of the baking dish.
Bake apples for 35–40 minutes or until they are soft when pierced with a knife or skewer. Serve immediately.

DUTCH APPLE TORTE

This tart combines two distinctive flavours — almonds and tart apples — in a casing of rich sweet shortbread. It's a treat to eat.

Base
2½ cups (10 oz) plain (all-purpose) flour
1 cup (5 oz) icing (powdered) sugar
200 g (7 oz) unsalted (sweet) butter, cut into small pieces
2 eggs, lightly beaten
30 ml (1 fl oz) water
¼ cup (3 oz) apricot jam (jelly)
½ vanilla génoise sponge (see page 134), cut horizontally

Filling
5 cooking apples, cored and thinly sliced
6 level teaspoons ground cinnamon
30 ml (1 fl oz) Calvados
⅓ cup (3 oz) sugar
½ cup (2 oz) ground almonds
1 cup (3 oz) desiccated (shredded) coconut

To Decorate
200 g (7 oz) apricot glaze (see page 10)
200 g (7 oz) fondant (see pages 118–119), melted
¾ cup (3 oz) flaked almonds, roasted (see page 5)

Preheat oven to 200°C (400°F). Grease a 23 cm (9 in) springform cake tin lightly with butter and line the base with baking paper (parchment).
Place flour and icing sugar in a bowl. Add butter and very lightly rub into flour and icing sugar until the mixture resembles fresh breadcrumbs. Add eggs and sufficient water to make a firm dough. Knead several times to ensure that all ingredients are thoroughly blended. Wrap in plastic wrap (cling film) and chill for 30 minutes.
Combine all the filling ingredients.

To Assemble
Roll out chilled pastry dough into a circle large enough to cover the base and sides of the prepared tin. Ease pastry into place and trim the edges. Spread the base with apricot jam and top with a layer of sponge. Spoon on apple filling. Roll out remaining pastry and cut to cover the top. Press and seal the edges. Bake for 40–45 minutes. Cool in the tin on a cake rack. Remove the springform rim when the tart is lukewarm. Brush the top and sides with the apricot glaze and allow to dry. Brush glaze with melted fondant and allow to dry. Press roasted flaked almonds around the top edges.

See page 9

APPLE FRITTERS

3 fresh apples, peel and cored
1¼ cups (5 oz) plain (all-purpose) flour
1 quantity batter (see page 21)
oil for deep frying, heated in deep fryer or deep frying pan
icing (powdered) sugar, for dusting

Prepare yeast batter as described.
Slice apples 2 cm (¾ in) thick. Coat both sides of apple slices lightly with the flour and then dip apple slices quickly into yeast batter, ensuring that the entire apple slice is completely coated. Carefully place the apple in the heated cooking oil and cook until both sides are golden brown. Remove from the oil, dust lightly with icing sugar and serve.

APPLE MERINGUE CAKE

This cake has an egg-rich butter cake base covered with a layer of finely sliced apples and topped with snowy white meringue. Serve it warm with crème Chantilly.

Base
2½ cups (10 oz) plain (all-purpose) flour
2½ level teaspoons baking powder (soda)
250 g (8 oz) unsalted (sweet) butter
1¼ cups (8 oz) caster (superfine) sugar
5 egg yolks
vanilla essence (extract), to taste
2 medium-sized cooking apples, peeled, cored and very finely sliced

Topping
5 egg whites
⅔ cup (5 oz) caster (superfine) sugar
crème Chantilly (see page 85), for serving

Preheat oven to 180°C (350°F). Very lightly grease a 23 cm (9 in) springform cake tin with butter and line base with baking paper (parchment).
Sift flour and baking powder. Beat butter and sugar until creamy, light and fluffy. Add egg yolks one at a time, beating very well after each one is added. Beat in vanilla essence.
Mix in sifted flour and baking powder by hand.
Pour into prepared tin and arrange the apples on top.
Bake in preheated oven for 45 minutes. Remove.

Dutch Apple Torte Step-by-Step

Step 1: Place the layer of sponge on the base of the pastry-lined tin.

Step 2: Fill the centre of the pastry with the apple filling and press down so that it is even with the top of the tin.

Step 3: Cover the top of the torte with thinly rolled pastry. See page 8.

Maintain oven temperature. Whisk egg whites until
stiff peaks form and gradually beat in the extra sugar,
a spoonful at a time. Beat until sugar is dissolved.
Pipe the meringue over the cake.
Return to the oven for a further 10–15 minutes.
Let stand for 5 minutes before removing the rim of the tin,
leaving the cake on the base. Place on a cake rack to cool.
Serve with crème Chantilly.

APPLE SHORTCAKE

Melting shortcake with a centre of moist, spicy, stewed apple.

300 g (10 oz) unsalted (sweet) butter
1½ cups (10 oz) caster (superfine) sugar
3 eggs
2½ cups (10 oz) plain (all-purpose) flour
1 teaspoon baking powder (soda)
1 teaspoon ground cinnamon
1 teaspoon mixed spice
1¼ cups (10 oz) lightly stewed apple (well drained)
½ cup (3 oz) icing (powdered) sugar

Preheat oven to 180°C (350°F). Lightly grease and line
an 18 x 28 x 2 cm (7 x 11 x ¾ in) baking tray
(jelly roll pan) with baking paper (parchment).
Cream butter and sugar until light and fluffy. Add eggs one at
a time, beating well after each one is added. Continue mixing
until well combined. Sift flour, baking powder and spices into
the creamed butter and egg mixture and continue mixing
until all is well incorporated. Spread half of this mixture
evenly over the base of the tray.
Spread the stewed apple evenly over the mixture, then
carefully cover the top of the apple with the remaining cake
mixture. Bake in preheated oven for 45–55 minutes.
Cool in the tray and dust with icing sugar.

APPLE SUGAR

This traditional sweet confectionery originated in the French
city of Rouen in the 15th–16th century. Apple sugar is a sugar
syrup made from apple juice and sugar which was originally
boiled to the hard crack stage then poured flat onto a marble
slab and cut into sticks which were then further coated in fine
sugar crystals.

Today, the same principles of production are retained,
although the recipe now includes stabilising agents (to prevent
the sugar dissolving in humidity) and glucose. It is
manufactured into the traditional sugar sticks as well as into
small drops (pastilles) and slabs. These are wrapped in rice
paper that is decorated with the famous Rouen landmark, its
clock tower, a design which was created for the sweet in the
mid-19th century.

APRICOT

Its natural flavour makes the apricot one of the most popular
fresh fruits to be used in the pastry kitchen but perhaps more
important is its use as a jam (jelly or conserve). Apricot jam
plays an important role in the finishing of many cakes as well
as being used as a spread to join cake layers together.

Apricots originated in China and have been cultivated in
the temperate zone for some 2000 years. They are available to
the pastry chef in a variety of forms: fresh, dried, preserved
and in conserves, as apricot jam and as a cordial drink.
Apricots contain a stone, to which the flesh does not cling.
Within this stone is a kernel which is used in the production
of almond paste; the kernel looks like that of the almond and
contains a rich oil which is used as a substitute for almond oil.

A good apricot should have an even orange tone to its skin,
be firm but not hard when pressed lightly, have a nice fine
'fur' or 'fuzz' to its skin and be sweet in taste, with no floury
aftertaste.

APRICOT GLAZE

¾ cup (8 oz) apricot jam (jelly)
3 tablespoons water
2 teaspoons lemon juice

Place all the ingredients in a saucepan and stir until
thoroughly blended. Cook over a high heat for 5 minutes and
force through a fine wire strainer. Brush over the cake while
still warm, then cool before finishing the decoration.

APRICOT AURORA

Place sponge finger biscuits (cookies) on the base of a
prepared and baked pie crust. Sprinkle orange liqueur over
the sponge finger biscuits and place a coffee-flavoured parfait
over the top of the soaked biscuits. Allow the coffee parfait to
freeze and then cover this with halved fresh apricots. Cover
the entire dessert with fresh whipped cream (crème Chantilly)
and sprinkle grated chocolate over the top of the cream.
Serve immediately.

APRICOTING

Apricoting is the process by which a cake or pastry is coated
with a boiled apricot glaze to give it a smooth, hard surface on
which softer compounds such as chocolate and fondant can be
spread without soaking into the cake.

Danish pastries are often apricoted simply to give them a
shiny appearance and an added sweet flavour.

APRIL FOOL

This day has close links with pastry chefs, not because
they are fools but because they make the gifts given to
people on April Fool's Day. Also known as All Fools' Day,
this special day has been celebrated on 1 April each year
since the 16th–17th century when the Gregorian Calendar
(1 January–31 December) came into being to replace the
inefficient Julian calendar.

The Julian calendar, which had been used for centuries,
celebrated the first day of the year on 1 April. Under this
calendar, Christians had always celebrated the beginning of
the year with the giving of gifts on 1 April, a ritual which
continued after the inception of the new calendar. As this
calender change was not a popular decision, the giving of gifts
became the giving of mock gifts and joke playing as a form of
protest.

The giving of useless and inexpensive gifts eventually gave way in some European countries to the giving of pastries and other sweetmeats. Because 1 April fell under the star sign of Pisces, the figure of the fish was popular. It was usually used in cakes baked in a fish shape or in marzipan figures, and in France was known as Poisson d'Avril (April Fish).

ARROWROOT
(see also cornflour, thickeners)

Arrowroot is a very fine white powder with no flavour and is used as a thickening agent for sauces and glazes where a clear finish is required, because cornflour (cornstarch) cooks to a cloudy or opaque finish in glazes. It is the starch extracted from underground stems known as rhizomes and is ground to a fine powder. The name arrowroot comes from the original use of the powder by American Indians to cure arrow injuries. At first the Indians used the 'arrow root' as a powder to dust over the wounds and cuts, and then, when some thickened on being dropped into water, it was used as a paste.

Over the centuries arrowroot has become indispensable in the kitchen as a thickener for sauces, jellies, soups and glazes. It is used more in sweet cookery than in savoury sauces.

ARROWROOT GLAZE
3 tablespoons arrowroot
2¾ cups (22 fl oz) fruit juice or cordial syrup

Mix arrowroot with a little of the juice or syrup to make a smooth paste. Place remaining liquid in a saucepan and slowly bring to the boil. When boiling, pour the liquid over the arrowroot mixture and stir until both are well combined. Return to the saucepan and allow to heat until the mixture thickens and clears. Strain (sieve) the mixture if necessary and use immediately, while still hot, for glazing. If the syrup or juice is not sweet enough, add some sugar to the unboiled juice or syrup before making the glaze.

This recipe can be adapted to suit whatever you are glazing. Blackcurrant cordial can be used for cherry or blackcurrant tarts, and pineapple, orange or lemon juice for tarts of those particular flavours.

ARTIFICIAL COLOURINGS
(see also food colourings)

Artificial colourings can either be produced from inorganic materials or prepared synthetically. The colours available are extensive and, as with natural colours and food additives, they must meet food and health regulations requiring them to be harmless to the skin, and in reaction to food, and non-toxic.

ATTA FLOUR
(see also flour)

Used throughout India and parts of Asia and China in the making of traditional breads and pancakes, atta flour is a coarse-grained flour made from the wheat grain. In its countries of origin the grain is crushed using a mortar and pestle or by stone grinding.

AVICE, JEAN

Jean Avice was a French pastry chef who worked in Paris at the beginning of the 19th century and is considered the greatest pâtissier of all time. The trainer of such other greats as Antonin Carême, Avice was said to create magic from everything he produced, turning his creations into works of art. He is attributed with the creation of the Madeleine (see page 170), having invented the recipe while in the employ of Prince Talleyrand. (Some argue, however, that Madeleines were known well before Avice's time.)

AVOCADO

The much-misunderstood avocado is a tropical fruit with a light yellow to green flesh which is smooth and buttery in texture and has a large central nut. Avocados originated in South America and have a firm outer skin, ranging from smooth to rough, and coloured from green to black depending on the variety. They are rare among the fruit species in that they contain a high amount of an unsaturated fat: they do not, however, contain cholesterol.

When avocados are cut in half, the smooth flesh will begin to be affected by oxidization, quickly turning brown and then black. You can use citrus juices to prevent this discolouration: brush the juice over the exposed flesh and then wrap the cut fruit so that it is airtight. Avoid cooking avocados — they become bitter in flavour.

AVOCADO MOUSSE

2 ripe avocados
⅓ cup (2 oz) icing (powdered) sugar
zest and juice of 1 orange
zest and juice of 1 lemon
⅓ cup (3 fl oz) cream
2 egg whites
6 teaspoons caster (superfine) sugar, extra

Cut avocados in half, remove the central nut and scoop the flesh from the skin. Place the flesh, icing sugar and orange and lemon zest and juice in a blender. Blend quickly until smooth, until the avocado is lump free. Add cream and blend again quickly, making certain the cream is just combined and the mixture is smooth and creamy in texture. Place avocado mixture in a mixing bowl. Place egg whites in a grease-free mixing bowl and whisk until light and frothy. Slowly drizzle the extra sugar into the stiff egg whites and whisk until sugar is dissolved. Fold egg whites into the avocado mixture and spoon the mousse into serving dishes. Serve immediately.

B

BABA AU RHUM

Similar to the savarin in consistency, a traditional Baba au Rhum (Rum Baba) simply has rum-soaked sultanas (golden raisins) folded through the savarin dough and is soaked in a similarly sweet syrup and then glazed with apricot jam (jelly) to prevent it going stale.

The Baba is said to have originated with Chevriot, a chef at the court of King Stanislas Leczinski of Poland, who invented it in honour of his king. When the King was exiled to the Duchy of Lorraine, he found the local pastries and cakes far too dry for his sweet palate and ordered the local pastry chefs to make the Baba into something richer and sweeter than the cake Chevriot had invented. Pastry chef Stohrer, in 1835, changed the recipe to that of a brioche dough which was folded through the rum-soaked sultanas, and after baking the pastry, he soaked it in a rich sugar syrup and rum.

The King, in exile, had little to do and turned to reading. His greatest hero was Ali Baba, from the story of Ali Baba and the Forty Thieves, and hence he named the dessert creation after his hero.

These days the sugar syrup is occasionally replaced by a dessert wine, sweet and full of flavour, making it slightly more expensive but worthy of being a King's dessert.

⅓ cup (2 oz) sultanas (golden raisins)
¼ cup (2 fl oz) dark rum
¼ cup (2 fl oz) milk
15 g (½ oz) fresh compressed yeast
2 cups (8 oz) plain (all-purpose) flour
½ teaspoon salt
3 eggs
125 g (4 oz) unsalted (sweet) butter
3 teaspoons sugar
1 quantity savarin syrup (see page 250)

Preheat oven to 180°C (350°F).
Lightly butter 10 dariole moulds.
Soak sultanas in rum until required.

Place milk and yeast together in a small bowl and mix to dissolve the yeast. Place flour, salt and eggs in a mixing bowl along with yeast liquid and mix well for about 5 minutes, or until the mixture is very smooth and elastic. Place the butter and sugar on top of the mixture. Place the bowl in a warm area for 20–25 minutes or until the dough is double in size. Mix the dough for a further 2–3 minutes or until the butter and sugar are well combined in the dough. Fold through the sultanas. Pipe or spoon the mixture evenly into the buttered moulds. Allow the babas to sit on a tray in a warm area for 30–35 minutes or until double in size. Bake in preheated oven for 15–18 minutes or until golden brown. Remove from the dariole moulds and cool slightly before soaking in savarin syrup. Serve immediately or glaze with apricot jam (jelly) for longer storage.

Makes 10

BABOVKA

A rich and traditional festive cake from Czechoslovakia.

220 g (7 oz) unsalted (sweet) butter
1 cup (8 oz) sugar
4 egg yolks
4 cups (16 oz) plain (all-purpose) flour
1 teaspoon baking powder (soda)
¾ cup (3 oz) chopped hazelnuts
3 tablespoons lemon juice
½ cup (4 fl oz) milk
4 egg whites
⅓ cup (3 oz) sugar
300 g (10 oz) dark (plain or semi-sweet) chocolate, grated
icing (powdered) sugar, for dusting

Preheat oven to 180°C (350°F).
Grease and line a 24 cm (10 in) springform cake tin.
Cream butter and sugar in a large mixing bowl until light and fluffy. Add egg yolks one at a time, beating well after each one is added. Add sifted flour and baking powder and chopped hazelnuts to the butter mixture and mix through with lemon juice and milk until all is well combined. In a clean bowl, whisk egg whites with the sugar until stiff peaks form and then fold through the first mixture. Spread a quarter of the mixture over the base of the cake tin and sprinkle a third of the grated chocolate over the top. Spread another quarter of the cake mixture over this and again sprinkle with the chocolate. Continue in this manner until all the mixture and the chocolate have been used and then place the cake in the preheated oven and bake for 50–55 minutes or until a knife inserted in the top of the cake comes out clean. Dust with icing sugar and serve hot or cold.

BAER RINGS

The secret of success with this recipe lies in using the correct kind of marzipan. You need one that consists of 66% almonds and 34% sugar.

330 g (11 oz) unsalted (sweet) butter
150 g (5 oz) marzipan (see page 177)
1 cup (6 oz) icing (powdered) sugar, sifted
1 egg
3½ cups (14 oz) plain (all-purpose) flour, sifted
zest and juice of 1 lemon

Preheat oven to 180°C (350°F).
Line baking sheets with baking paper (parchment).
Place butter, marzipan and icing sugar in a mixing bowl and
cream together until light and fluffy. Add egg and mix well.
Fold through the sifted flour and the lemon zest and juice.
Place mixture in a piping (pastry) bag fitted with a 1 cm
(½ in) star-shaped nozzle and pipe 5 cm (2 in) rings onto
prepared sheets. Bake in preheated oven for 10–12 minutes
or until lightly golden brown and cool on the sheets.

Makes 24

BAGEL

Bagels are the invention of a 17th century Viennese baker
who gave the King of Poland two crescent-shaped pieces of
bread dough that had been boiled and baked together to
thank him for protecting Austria from the Turkish invasion.
Today bagels are renowned as the Jewish bread rolls with
holes in the centre which are boiled in water before being
baked; the boiling gelatinises the starch, giving the rolls their
characteristic shiny glaze when baked, and also gives bagels
their traditional chewy texture. Bagels can be made from
either sweet or savoury dough.

BAIN MARIE

A container in which hot or warm water is stored for warming
food. Smaller containers can be set into the larger one and
the heat of the water or the steam given off keeps the food
warm. This form of food warming prevents the food burning
or drying out, as it is only warmed from the moist heat or the
water itself.

A double saucepan formed by placing a saucepan above a
pot of warm or boiling water is another version of the bain
marie.

BAISER (KISS)

Baisers are traditionally petits fours, but they can also be
made into desserts or used in pastry lines. A baiser is simply
two small meringue shells which have had their bases dipped
into chocolate and have been joined together with any sweet
pastry filling, such as whipped sweetened cream, crème
pâtissière, buttercream or even ice cream.

BAKE BLIND

An important process in baking tart or pastry cases (pie
shells). An uncooked pastry case or flan shell is lined with a
sheet of greaseproof (waxed) paper and filled with beans, rice
or baking beads and is then baked for 10–12 minutes, until
the pastry is golden brown and crisp. This is a way to prevent
the pastry rising without having to prick the pastry base, and

is useful where a wet filling is to be poured into the pastry
case, such as a quiche or custard tarts, or simply where the
pastry case is required unfilled for later use. Depending on
what the filling for the tart is to be, the paper and weights
may be removed and the pastry returned to the oven for a
further few minutes to continue baking and browning lightly.

BAKED ALASKA
(see also bombe)

This American invention was not created by a pastry chef but
by a certain Doctor Rumford, who was trying to prove to his
students that egg whites were a poor heat conductor. Today's
Baked Alaska, also known as Omelette à la Norvegienne, is a
liqueur-soaked, sponge-based dessert topped with fresh fruit
and ice cream and then smothered with Italian meringue. The
whole dessert is then frozen, and before being served, the
meringue is glazed (flamed) to a golden brown under a grill,
or using a blow torch, or by placing it in a hot oven.

BAKERS' CHEESE
(see cream cheese)

BAKERS' CHOCOLATE
(see also chocolate)

Also known as compound chocolate, bakers' chocolate is
similar to pure chocolate or couverture but does not contain
cocoa butter. The cocoa butter is replaced by a compound
fat or other type of fat. It is called bakers' chocolate because
they require a chocolate that is easy to use and does not need
to be tempered. It can be used in the same way as any other
chocolate, but it lacks the full flavour of chocolate and also
tends to be slightly oily on the palate.

BAKERS' FLOUR

Also known as strong flour, bakers' flour contains a high level
of protein or gluten, usually around 12–26%, which assists
with the development of the bread and doughs created from
this kind of flour.

BAKERS' THERMOMETER

A small thermometer used to measure the temperature of
bread dough and also to ensure that the temperature of the
bread flour and water used in the production of the dough is
correct. It measures temperatures from 0–50°C (32–122°F)
and is used in conjunction with a simple factor (see page 255)
to obtain a measurement. The thermometer takes the
temperature of the flour, which is then subtracted from the
simple factor (see page 255) and the amount remaining gives
the temperature that the water should be. This temperature
checking is used to give the final bread dough the perfect
temperature in the best time for proving in order to obtain a
perfect loaf of bread.

BAKING PAPER

In the past, baking paper (parchment) referred to
greaseproof or waxed papers, which, once they had been used
for baking, had to be discarded, as they would weaken.

Today most baking papers are silicon-based and can be used for baking many times. The paper does not decrease in quality when it is subject to heat and nothing sticks to the paper, so it only needs to be wiped before being reused. This paper is also perfect for work with chocolate and sugar because of its non-stick nature.

BAKING POWDER
(see also aeration, bicarbonate of soda)

A combination of two substances, baking powder is used in the majority of cakes and biscuits (cookies) to give them lift when baked. Produced by combining a ratio of one part bicarbonate of soda to two parts cream of tartar, baking powder is affected by heat and moisture, reacting to produce carbon dioxide gas, which is trapped within the protein structure of the product being baked. An amount of cornflour (cornstarch) prevents a chemical reaction during humid and wet weather.

BAKING SHEET

A thin, flat, usually rectangular sheet (tray) of metal, sometimes with no edges or sides or more commonly with a slight lip around three sides, onto which cookies, biscuits and unmoulded pastries can be placed for baking. The sheets are greased and floured, or covered with a sheet of baking paper (parchment), or left plain, and these days also come in non-stick coated surfaces. Usually only light products are placed on baking sheets as they are very thin and do not handle weight very well.

Baking sheets are also known as scone or biscuit (cookie) trays or oven slides. In some countries, they are also called baking trays.

BAKING SODA
(see also aeration, baking powder)

The American equivalent of baking powder, baking soda is a combination of cream of tartar and bicarbonate of soda or one other substance.

BAKING STONE

A small piece of stone or an unglazed stoneware tile which is used in the oven to absorb any moisture or steam given off by doughs that are baking so that they finish with a crisp outer crust.

BAKING TIN

Available in a wide variety of sizes and shapes, baking tins or pans are usually produced from aluminium or copper-plated tin. They are usually deep and able to take a grid or wire rack on their base, onto which roasts can be placed prior to roasting. Filled with water, baking tins can be used to bake egg custards or as bain maries, if they are required in the baking process.

BAKING TRAY
(see baking sheet)

BAKEWELL TART

A dessert tart made by lining a puff pastry case (shell) with jam (jelly), which is then topped with a rich egg, butter and almond filling. It is said to have been invented by mistake by a cook in the English town of Bakewell. History has it that a cook made her lord's favourite pie with puff pastry instead of sweet pastry, so to use up the leftover ingredients she beat the melted butter with sugar and eggs and almonds and poured the liquid filling into the puff pastry case. When it was baked, she served it to her lord, who loved the sweet dish and proclaimed it to be the Tart of Bakewell.

The tart has become synonymous with the name Rutland Arms Hotel, where it has been served since its invention and which has seen the Bakewell Tart become a national treasure.

BAKLAVA

This rich Easter cake of Middle Eastern origin consists of buttered layers of filo (phyllo) pastry which are interleaved with a sweet mixture of ground nuts (almonds, pistachios and walnuts), sugar and spices. After being covered in butter to make the thin filo layers crispy, a sweet honey/sugar syrup is poured over the baked filo pastry. When soaked, the baklava is cut into triangles and served hot or cold. Traditionally, and in accordance with the religious requirements of the Easter festival, the baklava is soaked in a rosewater-flavoured sugar syrup.

300 g (10 oz) unsalted (sweet) butter, melted
500 g (16 oz) filo (phyllo) pastry sheets

Filling
¼ cup (2 oz) caster (superfine) sugar
1¾ cups (7 oz) finely chopped macadamia
(Queensland) nuts
¼ cup (1 oz) ground hazelnuts (filberts)
¾ cup (3 oz) ground almonds
1 teaspoon ground cinnamon
1 cup (3 oz) desiccated (shredded) coconut

Syrup
1¼ cups (10 fl oz) water
1¾ cups (12 oz) caster (superfine) sugar
½ cup (4 fl oz) white wine
100 ml (3½ fl oz) dark rum
2 teaspoons ground cinnamon
zest of 3 oranges
2 tablespoons clear honey

Preheat oven to 160°C (320°F). Grease well a 30 x 28 x 5 cm (12 x 11 x 2 in) baking tray (jelly roll pan). Carefully open out sheets of filo pastry and cut in half crossways. Stack the sheets on top of each other and keep covered with a damp cloth when not in use. Place the sheets on the base of the tray, layering until the layer is 2 mm (¹/₁₂ in) thick, brushing every second sheet with melted butter. After every 10–12 sheets of filo, sprinkle the nut mixture evenly and gently over the pastry. Continue to layer and butter the remaining filo pastry until all the pastry and filling have been used up. Brush the top well with any remaining melted butter. With a sharp knife, cut into 5 cm (2 in) squares or diamond shapes.

Bake in preheated oven for 1 hour. Remove, and pour the cold syrup evenly over the top. Cool completely and then run a knife through marked slices and remove from tray.

Filling
Mix together sugar, nuts, cinnamon and coconut in a bowl.

Syrup
Place all ingredients in a saucepan and bring to the boil. Reduce the heat and simmer for 15 minutes. Set aside to cool.

Makes 12—18

See page 16

BALKA

Similar to the French brioche, Russian kulich or Italian panettone, the balka is a Polish yeast cake which is traditionally cone-shaped and is baked for Polish Easter festivities.

BALLER

This is most commonly referred to as a melon baller as it is mainly used for this purpose. This small hand-held utensil has a half-ball scoop at one end which is sharpened around the edge. When set into the side of melon flesh or potatoes or most vegetables and twisted while being pressed into the flesh it should result in a perfect ball being scooped out.

BANANAS

One of the world's most common fruits, bananas are a yellow fruit approximately 20–25 cm (8–10 in) in length, and with a characteristic curve. The outer skin is easily peeled from the fruit and the pulpy, cream-coloured inner flesh is eaten raw or cooked — baked, grilled or fried. Bananas grow in large clusters known as 'hands' and several hands of bananas grow per bunch of bananas. A bright red flower is to be found at the end of the bunch, where it remains until the bananas are ripe for picking, at which point it drops off the bunch. Banana trees rarely grow from seeds, growing instead from suckers, which are small trees that shoot from the root system of the old banana tree. This is why most banana tree colonies are to be found in small clusters. Bananas are a semi-tropical fruit, requiring a warm, frost-free climate, and are usually grown on hillsides or where there is good drainage.

It is believed that bananas originated in Africa or were brought by merchants from India to Africa on their travels. It was in Africa that they received the name 'banana'. Recorded as having been grown in India from 500 BC onwards or perhaps even before this, bananas were eventually introduced into the Mediterranean region around 700 AD, during the Mohammedan invasion, and to the Pacific Islands by sailors and merchants around 900–1000 AD.

During the early 19th century bananas found their way via merchants and travellers to England, where the Duke of Devonshire decided to grow and experiment with the different breeds of banana plants. The variety which resulted was given his family name, 'Cavendish', and today remains one of the most popular eating varieties in the world.

BANANAS AU RHUM

A quick dessert that tastes delicious.

4–5 ripe bananas
90 g (3 oz) unsalted (sweet) butter, melted
⅓ cup (2 oz) moist brown sugar
¼ cup (1 oz) flaked almonds
⅓ cup (1 oz) flaked coconut
juice and rind of 1 lemon
juice and rind of 1 lime
½ cup (4 fl oz) golden (dark) rum

Preheat oven to 180°C (350°F).
Chop bananas into 1 cm (½ in) thick discs and arrange over the base of a large baking dish. Sprinkle the top of the bananas with melted butter, sugar, almonds, coconut and lemon rind then pour in the juice of the lemon and lime. Stir bananas gently so that they are all coated in the juices. Place the baking dish in preheated oven for 10–15 minutes, stirring occasionally. Remove the bananas.
Place the rum in a small saucepan and heat gently.
Light the rum and pour the flaming liquid over the bananas. Serve immediately, before the flames die out.

Serves 6

BANANA MOUSSE

3 firm, ripe bananas, mashed
juice and zest of 1 lemon
1 tablespoon gelatine powder
3 tablespoons cold water
3 egg yolks
¼ cup (2 oz) sugar
3 egg whites
2½ cups (20 fl oz) cream, whipped

Stir lemon juice through the banana pulp. Soak gelatine powder in the cold water. Place egg yolks, sugar and lemon zest in a mixing bowl and whisk until light and fluffy. Place the firm gelatine in a saucepan and heat gently until clear and liquid; do not allow to boil or become too hot. Stir the gelatine into the whipped egg yolk mixture. Place egg whites in a clean bowl and whisk until they form stiff peaks. Fold mashed bananas into the egg yolk mixture, fold through the whipped cream and finally fold through the whisked egg whites.
Refrigerate for 1½ hours before serving.

BANANA SPLIT

A dessert which originated in America, the banana split consists of a banana cut lengthwise and placed flat in a long narrow glass dish. Three scoops of ice cream, traditionally vanilla, chocolate and strawberry, but today any flavour, are placed on top of the banana strips. Whipped cream is piped over the top of this and chocolate sauce (topping) is poured over this. Chopped walnuts or sliced almonds are used as decoration and a maraschino (glacé) cherry is placed on top of each of the ice cream scoops.

Baklava Step-by-Step

Step 1: Place sheets on the base of the tray, layering until the layer is 2 mm (¹/₁₂ in) thick, buttering every second sheet.

Step 2: After every 10–12 sheets of filo (phyllo), sprinkle the nut mixture evenly and gently over the pastry.

Step 3: Pour the topping over the baked and cut baklava. See page 14.

BANANA CAKE

As famous as the carrot and fruit cake, banana cake is a cheap, quick and tasty delight to have in the pantry.

2¼ cups (9 oz) plain (all-purpose) flour
2 level teaspoons baking powder (soda)
1 level teaspoon bicarbonate of soda
150 g (5 oz) unsalted (sweet) butter
⅔ cup (5 oz) caster (superfine) sugar
2 eggs
3 ripe bananas, mashed or puréed
¾ cup (3 oz) walnut pieces

To Decorate
1 quantity of lemon cream cheese frosting (see page 125)
marzipan bananas (see page 177)

Preheat oven to 180°C (350°F).
Grease a 23 cm (9 in) springform cake tin with butter
and dust very lightly with flour.
Sift flour, baking powder and bicarbonate of soda.
Beat butter and sugar until creamy, light and fluffy.
Add eggs, one at a time, to the egg mixture, beating well
until just combined, then fold in bananas, flour and
baking powder by hand. Lastly, fold in the walnuts.
Spoon the cake mixture into the prepared tin.
Bake for 40–45 minutes, or until a skewer inserted into
the centre of the cake comes out dry.
Turn the cake onto a cake rack and allow to cool completely.
When the cake is quite cold, cover the top and sides
with lemon cream cheese frosting and
decorate with marzipan bananas.

BANANA PASSIONFRUIT

Banana passionfruit (granadilla) is a vine fruit which grows 5–10 cm (2–4 in) in length and is shaped like an elongated egg. It is green skinned until it ripens, when it becomes pale yellow and very soft to touch. The flesh is similar to that of a passionfruit. It is usually orange and has a slight banana flavour, distinctly different from that of the ordinary passionfruit (purple granadilla). When added to pavlovas, cream desserts, bavarois or mousses, banana passionfruit has a strong impact. If ripened correctly, the fruit will be quite sweet.

BANBURY CAKES

Amongst the oldest known English cakes, these oblong-shaped sweet cakes, made of an outer crust of flaky puff pastry and filled with a sweet mincemeat, are said to have been baked especially for weddings. At some point during the Crusades soldiers brought back the idea for Banbury cakes from spiced sweetmeats they had enjoyed on their campaigns of the Holy Land. They are named after the Oxfordshire town of Banbury in England where they were first baked. Banbury cakes reached the height of their popularity in the mid-17th century but later had to compete with Eccles cakes, the only real difference between the two being that Banburys were oblong and Eccles were round or oval.

500 g (16 oz) fresh or frozen puff pastry (see page 228)
1½ cups (7 oz) currants
⅓ cup (2 oz) mixed (candied) peel
½ cup (3 oz) moist brown sugar
1 teaspoon ground cinnamon
grated rind and juice of 1 large lemon
½ cup (4 fl oz) water
6 teaspoons plain (all-purpose) flour
2 egg yolks, beaten
⅓ cup (3 oz) raw sugar

Preheat oven to 200°C (400°F).
Line a baking tray (sheet) with baking paper (parchment).
On a lightly floured surface, roll pastry out to 1–2 mm
(¹⁄₁₂ in) in thickness. Using a sharp knife, cut the pastry into
oblong shapes 10 x 5 cm (4 x 2 in). Place currants, mixed
peel, sugar, cinnamon, lemon juice, water and flour in a
saucepan over low heat. Stir the mixture continuously until it
thickens and comes to the simmer. Allow mixture to cool.
Using the two egg yolks, brush the edge of half of the oblong
shapes. Place a tablespoon of mixture in the centre of each
oblong. Place another oblong strip of pastry over the first and
press the edges together. Brush the top of each Banbury cake
with the remaining egg yolk and sprinkle the coarse grains of
sugar over the top. Place the Banburys on the prepared
baking tray (sheet) and bake for 20–25 minutes,
or until the pastry is crisp and golden brown.
Eat hot or cold.

Makes 12

BANNOCK
(see also girdle cakes, griddle cakes)

Originating in Scotland, Bannocks are a flat, round bread made of either oatmeal, wheat or barley and were developed from primitive unfermented doughs. Traditionally baked on a griddle over an open fire, they can be plain or contain sultanas (golden raisins) or other dried fruits and are risen with yeast or baking powder (soda). In the past, Bannocks were made using sour milk, which gave them a distinct flavour and aroma. The Bannock was the basis of the modern scone (biscuit).

BARA BRITH

The national fruit loaf of Wales, which, although said to have been invented in Wales by a cook who mixed wholemeal dough and dried fruits, is an almost exact replica of the Irish national bread Barm Brack; both have names that mean small loaves with a speckled or spotted crust, 'bara' meaning bread and 'brith' meaning speckled. Bara Brith is very lightly spiced but full of dried fruits.

BARBADOS SUGAR
(see also muscovada, sugar)

A highly flavoured, dark brown, almost black sugar, barbados sugar is used in gingerbreads and fruit cakes and is moist and soft in texture. Once considered to be too dirty to use, it is simply a sugar that contains a lot of molasses.

BARCELONA NUT
(see hazelnut)

BARLEY SUGAR
(see also confectionery)

A sweet confection of boiled sugar with the colour of barley, it should be a very light yellow colour and cut into thin 5 cm (2 in) strips and twisted.

BARM BRACKS

A fruit loaf common to Ireland, Barm Brack is said to derive its name from the Irish 'bairnin', meaning small homemade loaf of bread, and 'breach', meaning spotted or mottled in colour. Another possibility is that the name comes from 'barm', which is the name given to yeast made by the bakers themselves.

7 g (¼ oz) fresh compressed yeast
2½ cups (10 oz) plain (all-purpose) flour
¼ cup (2 oz) sugar
2 eggs
½ cup (4 fl oz) milk
300 g (10 oz) unsalted (sweet) butter
1¼ cups (6 oz) currants
2 tablespoons mixed (candied) peel

In a large mixing bowl, crumble yeast into the flour and sugar. Lightly whisk the eggs and add to the milk. Melt the butter. Add egg/milk mixture to the flour and then add the butter. Mix by hand to a soft dough. Mix for 2–3 minutes and then cover and leave in a warm place for 1–2 hours, or until the dough has doubled in bulk.
Preheat oven to 180°C (350°F). Grease a baking sheet.
Stir the currants and peel through the dough and, using a little flour, mould the dough into a large round shape and place on the prepared sheet. Allow to prove (rise) in a warm place for a further 45 minutes before placing in the preheated oven and baking for about 1¼–1½ hours.

BARQUETTE

A small boat-shaped piece of pastry into which sweet or savoury, hot and cold fillings are piped. Baked in thin aluminium Barquette moulds, the pastry case (pie shell) can either be of sweet or shortcrust pastry, depending on the use.

BA-TA-CLAN

This French almond-flavoured cake invented by 19th century pastry chef Lacam is baked in a brioche mould and covered with a white, vanilla-flavoured icing (frosting).

8 eggs, separated
1 cup (7 oz) caster (superfine) sugar
⅔ cup (5 fl oz) dark or white rum
2½ cups (10 oz) ground almonds
1 cup (4 oz) plain (all-purpose) flour
icing (powdered) sugar, for dusting
1 quantity basic frosting (see page 125)

Preheat oven to 180°C (350°F).
Grease and flour a large brioche mould.
Lightly whisk together egg yolks and sugar. Add rum and whisk in well. Stir in ground almonds and the sifted flour. In a separate bowl, whisk egg whites until they form stiff peaks and then fold these through the mixture. Pour the mixture into the greased tin and bake for 45–55 minutes.
When cool, cover with vanilla frosting and serve.

BATH BUNS

A round bun invented by Dr W Oliver in 1754 in the English city of Bath. Named after their inventor, these sweet yeast buns contain sultanas (golden raisins), currants and mixed (candied) peel and are topped with coarse sugar crystals before baking. The original Bath buns were made from a dough not dissimilar to that of brioche, which was introduced to Bath by the French, who visited for the healing powers of the Roman Baths.

BATH BISCUITS
(cookies)

Also known as Bath Olivers or Oliver biscuits, as they derived from the bun made famous by Dr Oliver.

2½ cups (10 oz) plain (all-purpose) flour
1 cup (5 oz) icing (powdered) sugar
1 teaspoon ground cinnamon
150 g (5 oz) unsalted (sweet) butter
1 egg
1 tablespoon water
¾ cup (4 oz) currants
1 quantity egg wash (see page 110)
caster (superfine) sugar, for decoration

Line baking sheets with baking paper (parchment). Place flour, icing sugar, cinnamon and butter in a bowl and lightly rub the butter through the other ingredients until the mixture resembles coarse breadcrumbs. Add lightly beaten egg and water and work the mixture to a dough. Finally, add currants and knead through the dough lightly.
Wrap in plastic wrap (cling film) and place in the refrigerator for 30 minutes.
Preheat oven to 180°C (350°F).
Remove the dough from the refrigerator and knead until ready to roll. Roll on a lightly floured surface to 4 mm (⅙ in) thickness. Cut small discs using a 10 cm (4 in) fluted round biscuit (cookie) cutter and place directly on the prepared sheets. Lightly egg wash each disc and sprinkle lightly with caster sugar. Bake in the preheated oven for 10–15 minutes or until lightly golden brown.
Remove and cool on sheets before serving.

Makes 18–24

BATTENBERG
(see also Tennis Cake)

Battenberg has always been a respected English favourite, originally named after the German royalty of that name.

At the beginning of World War I the Battenberg family changed its surname to Mountbatten. The name of the cake also changed, to Tennis Cake, as it resembled the design of a tennis court and was also served at tennis matches as a refreshment. It was better to change the name than lose the cake altogether because of the hatred of all things German at the time. Today, few know it as anything but Battenberg.

4 cups (16 oz) plain (all-purpose) flour
4 level teaspoons baking powder (soda)
500 g (16 oz) unsalted (sweet) butter
2½ cups (16 oz) caster (superfine) sugar
8 eggs
1 teaspoon vanilla essence (extract)
2–3 drops red (cochineal) food colouring
¾ cup (8 oz) apricot jam (jelly)

To Decorate
500 g (16 oz) marzipan (see page 177)
marzipan flowers and leaves (see page 179)

Preheat oven to 180°C (350°F).
Lightly grease two 20 x 10 x 5 cm (8 x 4 x 2 in) bar tins with butter and line with baking paper (parchment). Mix flour and baking powder and sift twice. Beat butter and sugar until creamy, light and fluffy. Add the eggs, one at a time, beating very well after each one is added. Gently mix in the sifted flour and baking powder by hand. Add the vanilla essence. Do not overmix. Spoon half the mixture into one of the prepared tins and add the red colouring drop by drop to the remaining half until the mixture is the desired colour. Spoon into the second tin. Bake for 40–45 minutes, or until a skewer inserted into the centre of the cakes comes out dry and the cakes have shrunk slightly away from the sides of the tins. Leave the cakes in the tins for 5 minutes before turning out onto a wire rack to cool.
When cold, cut each cake in half lengthways and then in half again. Brush each of the pieces with warmed apricot jam. Arrange the eight pieces to form a long cake with a chequerboard pattern of alternating colours. Spread apricot jam on all four sides of the cake. Roll out marzipan into a rectangle long enough to wrap around the cake, a little wider than the cake and about 3 mm (⅛ in) thick. Cover the cake with marzipan. Crimp the top edges and decorate with marzipan flowers and leaves.

See page 20

BATTER
(see also beer batter)

From the French 'battre', meaning 'to beat', a batter is a liquid mixture of flour, eggs, milk and, depending on the use, sugar, used for cakes, dessert and savoury puddings, biscuits (cookies), crêpes or pancakes and as a dip or coating for certain fried dishes.

Most batters require the flour to be beaten with the liquid ingredients until the mixture is smooth, at which stage it is allowed to sit and rest before being used. The stiffness or liquidity of the batter depends on how it will be used and the particular batter recipe. Thick batters are used for cake mixtures and fried foods while thinner batters are used for crêpes and blinis. All batters require a very hot oven for correct baking, as steam is required in order for them to rise. Batters such as Yorkshire batter are cooked within hot fat so as to puff immediately and become crisp.

In certain countries the term 'batter' is used to refer to most flour-based mixtures such as cake batters or pudding batters. Some of the most famous foods throughout the world are created from batters: France is renowned for its crêpes, Russia for blinis and the United Kingdom for Yorkshire pudding and Scotch pancakes, while America is renowned for its waffle and muffin batters and Australia for its pikelet batters.

BATTERBREAD
(see also bread)

A strange bread for the uninitiated, it is made from cornmeal and has a consistency not unlike that of custard. Batterbread is also known as spoonbread, as it is with this implement that the bread must be eaten. It is common in America and is traditionally served with certain savoury dishes.

BAUME, ANTOINE
(see also aerometer, saccharometer)

Antoine Baume was born in Senlis, France on 26 February 1728 and died on 15 October 1804, at 76 years of age. He was a French chemist who invented the hydrometer (saccharometer), which is used to measure liquids heavier or lighter than water. Used extensively in the petroleum and chemical industries, it also performs a vital role in the pastry industry, measuring the density of sugar syrups used in making ice cream and sorbets, for example.

BAUMKUCHEN
(see also tree cake)

Perhaps the oldest style of baking in history led to these wondrous cakes, which today are seen as the pinnacle of German baking, even appearing in the coat-of-arms of the Society of German Pastry Cooks. Well before the oven had been invented, people baked dough masses on spits or on sticks over an open fire. Over time the dough masses were made thinner and were eventually poured over the rotating stick or spit, becoming thicker as the stick was rotated and more mixture was poured over. Upon being sliced, the baked dough revealed its many layers, resembling the growth rings of a tree. Hence its German name Baumkuchen or Tree Cake.

3 tablespoons plain (all-purpose) flour
3 tablespoons cornflour (cornstarch)
250 g (8 oz) unsalted (sweet) butter
⅓ cup (2½ oz) caster (superfine) sugar
50 g (1¾ oz) marzipan, softened (see page 177)
8 egg yolks
8 egg whites
⅓ cup (2½ oz) caster (superfine) sugar, extra
2 tablespoons ground almonds

To Decorate
200 g (7 oz) no-fuss chocolate buttercream (see page 43)
cocoa powder, for dusting

Battenberg Step-by-Step

Step 1: Cut each cake in half lengthways and then in half again.

Step 2: Brush each piece with warm apricot jam.

Step 3: Join the pieces together, alternating colours.

Step 4: When all eight pieces of cake are joined together, brush apricot jam around the four sides.

Step 5: Wrap the marzipan around the cake and trim the edges.

Step 6: Pinch the top edge of the marzipan with your fingers for decoration. See page 18.

Preheat oven to 200°C (400°F).
Line four 18 x 28 x 6 cm (7 x 11 x 2½ in) baking trays
(jelly roll pans) with baking paper (parchment).
Mix the flours and sift twice. Beat butter, sugar and marzipan
until creamy, light and fluffy. Gradually add egg yolks and
beat well. Whisk egg whites until stiff peaks form and
gradually beat in the extra sugar, a spoonful at a time. Beat
until the sugar is dissolved. Fold in the sifted flours and
almonds, then the creamed butter and sugar, by hand.
Beat for 30 seconds to mix thoroughly. Spread the mixture
evenly onto the four prepared trays. Bake for 10–12 minutes
or until the tops of the cakes are slightly brown and spring
back when lightly touched. Do not overcook.
Cut four sheets of baking paper (parchment) larger than the
cakes and spread them out on a bench (counter) top. Working
very quickly, turn one cooked cake at a time onto a sheet of
baking paper. With one of the short edges of the cake facing
you, carefully roll the cake by turning over the first few
centimetres (inch) of paper. This will cause the cake to curl.
Keep rolling the cake tightly. Turn out a
second cake and where the first cake ends start the second
cake. Repeat with the other two cakes. Chill for 1 hour.
Cover with buttercream and dust with cocoa powder.

BAVAROIS
(see crème bavarois)

BAY

A small hollow or well in the centre of a dry mixture, such as
flour and other ingredients, into which liquid or softer items
are placed so that mixing can begin.

BEAT

Introducing air to a mixture by beating the ingredients
together, either by hand or by mechanical means.

BEAU RIVAGE
(see crème beau rivage)

BEER BATTER
(see also batter)

60 g (2 oz) fresh compressed yeast
1¾ cups (14 fl oz) beer
1½ teaspoons salt
3 cups (12 oz) plain (all-purpose) flour

Crumble yeast into the beer and add salt.
Whisk lightly until yeast is dissolved. Add flour and whisk
until all is incorporated smoothly and there are
no lumps. Allow the batter to sit covered in a warm
place for 1½ hours to ferment and rise.
Dip lightly floured fruits into the batter and when well
coated, place battered fruits in heated oil to fry until
golden brown on both sides.

BEE STING
(see also bienenstich)

The English version of Bienenstich, a traditional German
sweet yeast dough filled with a German-style custard. The
English variety is topped with a Florentine mixture and filled
with a plain thickened custard.

BEETROOT
(see also vegetables)

A member of the same family as sugar beet (a major source of
the world's sugar), beetroot has more sugar content than
nearly any other vegetable: 8%. Beetroots are purple bulbs
with green leafy stems. The purple flesh can be eaten raw or
cooked; if it is to be cooked it should be boiled with its skin
intact so that it retains its deep colouring.

BEETROOT CAKE

4 egg yolks
⅓ cup (2 oz) icing (powdered) sugar
4 egg whites
⅓ cup (2 oz) icing (powdered) sugar, extra
1¼ cups (6 oz) grated beetroot
1½ cups (6 oz) grated almonds
¼ cup (1 oz) plain (all-purpose) flour
1½ teaspoons baking powder (soda)
zest of 1 lemon
½ cup (4 fl oz) sugar syrup (see page 266)
zest and juice of 1 orange
250 g (8 oz) German buttercream (see page 43)
125 g (4 oz) dark (plain or semi-sweet) chocolate, grated

Preheat oven to 180°C (350°F).
Grease and line a 22 cm springform cake tin.
Place egg yolks and ⅓ cup (2 oz) icing (powdered) sugar in a
mixing bowl and whisk lightly together. Place the egg whites
and extra icing (powdered) sugar in a mixing bowl and
whisk to stiff peaks. Fold the beetroot, almonds, sifted flour
and baking powder and lemon zest into the egg yolk
mixture before carefully folding through the egg whites.
Bake for approximately 40–45 minutes in preheated oven.
Cool on a cake rack.
Mix sugar syrup with orange zest and juice.
When cool, cut the cake in half and brush the orange-
flavoured sugar syrup over both halves. Cover the
bottom half of the cake with a third of the buttercream
and then place the other half of the cake on top.
Cover the cake around the sides and over the top with
buttercream. Decorate the cake with chocolate shavings
and refrigerate for 1 hour before serving.

BEET SUGAR
(see also sugar)

Beet sugar is extracted from the root plant sugar beet, one of
the biggest sources of sugar in the world.

BEIGNET
(see also fritters)

This is the French word for a basic fritter and can be anything which has been dipped into a batter and fried. More specifically, though, a beignet is a small amount of choux pastry which is piped or spooned into hot oil or fat and fried so that it puffs and becomes light and golden brown. The German version, crullers, can be spooned or piped; but the Spanish churros are only piped to obtain length and shape. Eaten hot, rolled in cinnamon or vanilla sugar, beignets can also be served as a dessert with jam (jelly) and cream.

BELLE HELENE
(see pear belle hélène)

BERLIN DOUGHNUTS
(see krapfen)

BERLINGOT

While the origin of the name of this confectionery is still unknown and continuously disputed, some suggest that the name derives from the Italian sweet cake called Berlingozzo, which is traditionally flavoured with peppermint and shaped in a pyramid, these being two main features of the berlingot sweet. Today berlingots are commonly manufactured with fruit flavourings and a true berlingot is made by wrapping two colours (one usually white) together. The mixtures are extruded by machine and cut by rotating blades, but this can be done by hand. In England and many other countries berlingots are known as humbugs or bulls' eyes, or simply as boiled lollies or sweets.

BERNHARDT, SARAH

This famous French actress (1844–1923) inspired the equally famous Auguste Escoffier to create and name a number of dishes after her. Some have suggested that the relationship between Escoffier and Bernhardt was not simply based on a passion for fine food, but was indeed a romantic attraction; whatever the case, the food created in her honour remains popular today. Chocolate cream piped onto macaroon biscuits (cookies), a rich strawberry soufflé and a Curaçao-flavoured mousse are all named after Miss Bernhardt.

BERRY
(see also individual listings and summer pudding)

Among the most popular fruits in the world today, berries are used in dishes whole, chopped and puréed. Although similar in size, shape and usually colour, all varieties have their own very different flavours, for which they are renowned. Most berries are quite small in size, contain no stone and are usually round or oval in shape. Some, such as raspberries, grow on stalks, known as canes. Many berries are quite tart in flavour on their own and when puréed may or may not have sugar added, depending on the dessert they are to accompany.

Many famous desserts such as summer puddings, mousses and soufflés have berries as their base.

There are five major groups of berries:

(i) berries which grow on plants, e.g. strawberries;
(ii) berries which grow on trees, e.g. mulberries;
(iii) berries which grow on canes, e.g. raspberries;
(iv) berries which grow on bramble hybrids, e.g. loganberries and boysenberries; and
(v) berries which grow on bushes, e.g. black, red and white currants and gooseberries.

To avoid the disappointment of having berries become unavailable throughout the year, freeze excess stock while they are at their peak. Spread the berries onto a tray so they are not touching and freeze. When frozen, the berries can then be transferred to a bag, giving loosely packed frozen berries rather than a mushy mess. This also allows the chef to take as many or as few berries as are needed, without having to thaw the lot.

BETISE
(see also confectionery)

Betises are small sweets with a mint flavour, made from a boiled and poured sugar syrup. They have air injected into them, which produces microscopic air bubbles and makes them light to touch and light to eat. As with many famous confections and pastries, they are said to have originated as the result of a mistake. This one was made by an apprentice in 1850, who poured the boiled mixture of sugar, water, glucose and mint incorrectly onto the marble slab thus inviting tiny amounts of air into the solidifying syrup.

BETTLEMAN

As with its distant cousin, the bread and butter pudding, the bettleman was made in times of hardship to use what scraps were around and turn them into a tasty dish. The name 'bettleman' means beggar's pudding, which is literally what it was. It is made from stale bread and cake scraps which are grated into fine crumbs and allowed to soak in boiled milk. The mixture is then broken into pieces again and sweetened, mixed with spices, mixed (candied) peel, eggs, cherries and a stiffly whisked meringue mixture. It is then poured into a ramekin or large baking dish, covered with more crumbs and dotted with large chunks of butter, before being baked in a hot oven until golden brown.

BEUGNON
(see also fritter)

A traditional fried fritter dessert of France, the beugnon is made of a yeast-raised dough which is moulded into a ring shape and fried in hot oil. Many suggest that the beugnon was one of the original doughnuts, which, having made its way across the continents to America, gained its fame there in a much sweeter form. Beugnons, although invented after the savarin, are similar to it in that some recipes suggest soaking them in sweet syrups after cooking or simply rolling them in vanilla sugar.

BIALY
(see also bagel)

Made from bagel dough, the bialy does not have the traditional central hole, but instead has a small indentation which does not go the whole way through the dough. It also does not require boiling prior to being baked. Crunchy and dense in texture, the bialy is named after the city where it was first produced, Bialystok in Poland.

BIBER

A famed Swiss honey cake confection, the Biber is always decorated with the symbol of a bear standing upright. Legend has it that Saint Gall (650 AD) fed a bear with his last scraps of honey cake in reward for the work the bear had done for him. Bibers are the most famous of the countless recipes and versions of the gingerbread/honey cake. They are filled with a spiced filling and glazed with a potato glaze while still hot, giving them a distinct gloss.

BICARBONATE OF SODA
(see also baking powder, baking soda, raising agent)

Also known in some countries as baking soda, bicarbonate of soda is used with cream of tartar to form baking powder, a raising agent for cakes, pastries and breads. It can also be combined with other reactors, such as an acid-like sour milk, to act as a raising agent. On its own, bicarbonate of soda is used for making confectionery and some forms of gingerbreads as it rises by itself, although not much. It is often used for its darkening effect on mixtures such as chocolate cakes, gingerbreads, fruit cakes and even banana cakes.

BIENENSTICH

The German yeast cake otherwise known as Bee Sting. It is said that as the baker prepared the honey-rich topping for this cake, a bee was attracted by its aroma and flew in and stung the baker. This is one of the ultimate yeast cakes; it has a base of unsweetened dough filled with custard and is topped with a liberal coating of honey, butter and almonds.

Cake
30 g (1 oz) fresh compressed yeast
45 g (1½ oz) unsalted (sweet) butter, softened
3 tablespoons sugar
3 cups (12 oz) plain (all-purpose) flour
⅛ level teaspoon salt
cold water

Topping
125 g (4 oz) unsalted (sweet) butter
½ cup (4 oz) caster (superfine) sugar
2 tablespoons honey
1 cup (4 oz) flaked almonds

Filling
2 cups (16 fl oz) confectioners' custard (see page 77)

Using an electric mixer fitted with a dough hook, mix yeast, butter, sugar, flour and salt. Add sufficient cold water to make a soft dough. Beat slowly for 10 minutes.

Cover and leave for 20 minutes in a warm spot. Preheat oven to 180°C (350°F).
Lightly grease a 23 cm (9 in) springform cake tin with butter and line the base with baking paper (parchment). Place all topping ingredients in a saucepan and slowly bring to the boil. Boil for 2 minutes or until the mixture leaves the sides of the saucepan.
Uncover the dough and knead lightly to expel the air. Roll out into a 23 cm (9 in) circle and place in the prepared tin. Using a palette knife, spread the warm topping over the dough. Place the tin in a warm spot and allow to prove (rise) for 30–40 minutes or until the dough has tripled and almost fills the tin.
Bake for 45–50 minutes or until a skewer inserted into the centre of the cake comes out dry. Cool in the tin on a cake rack.
When cold, remove from the tin and cut in half horizontally. Spread the bottom layer with confectioners' custard and place the other layer on top. Chill for 1 hour.

BILBERRY

Also known as whortleberry, braeberry and huckleberry, depending on the country, the bilberry is said to be of Scottish origin and is grown on heathlands and moors. It is a small round, dark blue/purple (sometimes even black), tart-flavoured berry fruit of the myrtle family and traditionally grows wild. Its very tart, sharp flavour makes it a fantastic accompaniment to very sweet desserts. The berries can also be used by themselves in jams (conserves), or stewed, or made into wine, syrups and liqueurs, ices and sorbets, as well as compôtes. The berries freeze well on their own.

BINDING

Eggs, cream and some other liquids are used to hold mixtures together or set them firm by binding the ingredients together.

BIRCHER MUESLI

Invented by Dr Bircher Benner, who was in search of a healthy and complete breakfast meal, Bircher muesli is enjoyed today around the world and contains a mixture of oats, milk, fresh cream and fresh fruits. A specialty of European pastry chefs, it can be made fresh daily or stored for 2–3 days, the oats becoming more glutenous each day and the muesli gaining in flavour as it also becomes thicker.

1 cup (8 fl oz) fresh cream
2 tablespoons sugar
1¾ cups (5 oz) porridge oats
1¼ cups (10 fl oz) fresh milk
2 large apples, grated
1 large pear, grated
125 g (4 oz) blueberries, washed
6 medium sized strawberries, washed and chopped
1 medium sized orange, peeled and cut into pieces
⅓ cup (2 oz) almonds, chopped and roasted
1 ripe banana, cut thinly
1 tablespoon honey

In a large bowl, lightly whip the cream with the sugar. In a mixing bowl, soak porridge oats in milk and allow to sit for 30 minutes. Add grated apples, pear, blueberries, chopped strawberries, orange, almonds, banana and honey to soaked oats. Stir the cream and sugar through the oat mixture and serve immediately.

BIREWECK

An Alsatian favourite, the ball-shaped bireweck is a fruit dough made of sweetened dough mixed with Kirsch-soaked chopped crystallised (candied) fruits and fresh fruits.

BIRTHDAY CAKE

A cake given to somebody to celebrate the anniversary of their birth. Name day cakes are often given in European communities, some celebrating this on the naming day (christening) while others do so on the actual birth day. Birthday cakes can be of any size, shape or colour and, depending on the age and type of celebration, can be formal or novelty-style cakes.

BISCOTIN
(see also biscuit)

A small, thin, crisp biscuit (cookie) which is traditionally served with ices, ice creams and mousses or as a petit four with coffee or tea. These biscuits are not overly sweet, so they avoid competing with the dessert.

BISCOTTE
(see also zwieback)

Similar to a rusk, the French biscotte is a thin slice of bread, usually brioche, which is individually buttered, sprinkled with sugar and rebaked in the oven so that both sides of the slice are lightly golden brown. It is served with some desserts and for snacks or afternoon tea.

BISCOTTI

Similar in both name and nature to the French biscotte, this double-baked Italian delight is more like a solid biscuit or cookie than the biscotte. It is quite firm and is served with cappuccino; it is meant to be dunked into the frothy drink to soften the biscuit and add flavour to the coffee.

A long roll of the dough is baked lightly, then, while cooling, the dough is cut into slices diagonally across the roll. Each of these strips is then placed flat on a baking sheet and rebaked for 15−20 minutes or until crisp.

ALMOND BISCOTTI
3½ cups (14 oz) plain (all-purpose) flour
2 teaspoons baking powder (soda)
90 g (3 oz) unsalted (sweet) butter
1 cup (8 oz) sugar
3 eggs
zest of 1 orange
¼ cup (1 oz) almonds, chopped and roasted
1 egg white

Preheat oven to 175°C (350°F). Grease baking sheets.
Sift flour and baking powder into a large mixing bowl.
Cream butter and sugar until well mixed, but not light and fluffy (the mixture should just be incorporated).
Add eggs one at a time, beating well after each one is added.
Add orange zest and chopped almonds, then sifted flour and baking powder. Work mixture to a dough.
Cut it into two even pieces and roll each dough into a sausage shape approximately 20 cm (8 in) in length. Place sausage shapes on prepared baking sheets and brush the tops with the lightly beaten egg white. Flatten the sausage shapes slightly.
Place in preheated oven and bake for 20 minutes, or until lightly golden brown.
Allow each biscuit (cookie) roll to cool for 5 minutes and then, with a sharp serrated knife, cut the rolls diagonally into 10–12 pieces. Place each of the cut slices flat on the baking sheets again and, with the oven reduced to 160°C (320°F), bake the biscotti on both sides until lightly browned, 10–15 minutes either side.
Store cooled biscotti in an airtight jar and serve with coffee.

Makes approximately 30

BISCUIT
(see also biscotte, biscotti, casse museau, cookie)

Biscuit comes from the words 'bis', meaning twice, and 'cuit', meaning baked or cooked, and in days gone by referred to twice-baked pieces of dough or bread that were baked to a firm crispness so that they would keep on long voyages where there were no proper storage conditions. This style of biscuit is these days known as pulled bread or rusks. It was first mentioned in the journals of seafarer Tannhauser, who, in 1260, wrote, 'My water is cloudy, my wheat "piscot" hard'.

In most countries today, however, the word biscuit refers to both sweet and savoury, crisp and soft biscuits, leavened or unleavened, iced and decorated or those simply left plain, except in America, where a sweet biscuit is known as a cookie and a savoury biscuit as a cracker. 'Biscuit', in America, refers to what other countries call scones or small tea cakes.

Sweet biscuits are made from butter, sugar, eggs and flour and differ from each other only in the amount of flavouring and the amount of each of the basic ingredients. Shortbread biscuits and similar light-eating biscuits have a higher portion of fat than most other types.

Today's pastry chef has many kinds of biscuits:

(i) Rolled or moulded biscuits, made from a paste which is rolled or pressed into moulds to shape the biscuits. Such doughs tend not to spread when baked. Refrigerated biscuit doughs, which are moulded or rolled, refrigerated, cut and then baked are included in this category.

(ii) Forced or forcer biscuits, produced from a softish, light, smooth mixture which is forced out of a piping bag or cookie press to obtain its shape.

(iii) Drop or wafer biscuits, which include all those formed from liquified mixtures which bake solid and are then curled, curved, bent or rolled into their final shape before they set hard and crisp. Wafer and drop or liquid mixtures tend to produce the thinnest and most brittle of all biscuits and include tuiles, brandy snaps and wafers. Traditionally baked or cooked on a grill or flat iron, some are still produced in this way, while others are baked on floured or plain lined baking sheets.

(iv) Sliced biscuit mixtures, also known simply as slices or bars, usually consist of a short or sweet pastry base with a thin filling or topping. This category also includes slices which are not baked and those which are simply pressed or poured into the baking tray (jelly roll pan) and then baked. Many slices are marked fresh from the oven into the portions they are later to be cut into when they are cold, to prevent them breaking or cracking.

(v) Savoury biscuits, which can be made using any of the above methods for producing the base dough. Some crackers are simply a mixture of water, flour and a flavouring, which is rolled thinly and cut into shapes, while others are a shortcrust and require rolling or moulding into their shapes. The most common savoury biscuits are those served with cheese or which contain cheese and are served as or with hors d'ouevres.

(vi) The American biscuit, or scone or drop scone, is formed from a soft dough which is scarcely worked at all, and is sometimes so soft that instead of rolling the dough it is easier to drop it onto the sheet or griddle and allow it to cook. A perfect scone or biscuit is about 5 cm (2 in) in diameter and 3 cm (1¼ in) in height, with straight sides and a golden brown glazed top. Biscuits are cooked in a hot oven and are traditionally risen using baking powder (soda).

BISCUIT BASE
(see also crumbcrust)

The term biscuit base can refer to two different types of bases. The first is a base for cheesecakes and mousse-style desserts where leftover or unneeded biscuits (cookies) are crushed into small pieces, mixed with melted butter and pressed into the base of cake tins. The second is a disc of sweet or shortcrust pastry which is baked round and used to place underneath decorated cakes or gâteaux so that when a slice is cut from it, the slice is easier to serve because it is sitting on a stable base.

BISCUIT CUTTER

Made from thin metal with one end sharp and the other blunt, biscuit (cookie) cutters come in a myriad of styles, designs, shapes and prices. All good pastry chefs would have a selection of round, fluted, oval and other shaped cutters, as well as number cutters and perhaps alphabet cutters as well. Usually sold in sets of 4, 8, 12 or 24, it is worthwhile buying a good quality set of biscuit cutters that, with a little care, can be kept for life.

BISCUIT PRESS

A biscuit (cookie) press is a cylindrical hand-held machine which, in some cases, can look somewhat like a large pistol. At the far end of the long cylinder is a blunt end into which a selection of different-shaped discs can be placed, and at the other end is a removable hand piece. The biscuit dough is placed down the cylinder and the hand piece placed on the

end. With a small amount of pressure, the biscuit dough is forced out through the shaped disc in small enough quantities to make only one biscuit. This machine has been surpassed in many countries by the simpler, quicker and cleaner piping bag.

BISHOP'S CAKE
(see Tiffany cake)

BISHOP SAUCE

2 cups (16 fl oz) red wine
½ cup (4 oz) sugar
½ cinnamon stick
1 cup (8 fl oz) white wine
3 tablespoons cornflour (cornstarch)
zest of 1 lemon, finely chopped
zest of 1 orange, finely chopped

Place red wine in a saucepan with sugar and cinnamon stick and slowly bring to the boil. Mix white wine with cornflour and stir well until combined. When red wine mixture boils, stir white wine mixture through and slowly reboil, stirring continuously. Strain the sauce, add lemon and orange zest and serve immediately on hot or cold puddings.

BITTERS
(see Angostura bitters)

BITTERSWEET
(see also chocolate)

Usually dark chocolate which contains very little sugar, giving it a bittersweet flavour, it is fabulous for sauces and cakes, but is an acquired taste when eaten on its own.

BLAANDA BREAD
(see also bread)

Blaanda bread is an old recipe from England that dates back to around 1500 BC and is similar to many of the other flatbreads used through this period, such as the first griddle cakes, girdle cakes, Barm Bracks and Bara Briths. Made using wholemeal and oatmeal, the bread is heavy and dense and, as with most breads of its time, was flat and round so that it could cook quickly on the griddle. Before the griddle's appearance during the Iron Age, a fire would be started under a small rock outcrop and some of the rock above chipped away to form a flat heating surface for baking the Blaanda bread, or a flat rock would be placed, or held by sticks, over the fire.

1¾ cups (7 oz) wholemeal flour
1¼ cups (6 oz) oatmeal
75 g (2½ oz) unsalted (sweet) butter, chopped
1 teaspoon salt
water

Place the two meals together in a medium-sized bowl. Rub butter and salt through the meal mix until it is fine.

Add enough water to make the mixture form a firm dough. Cut dough in half and flatten both halves into discs. Bake the Blaanda bread on a flat griddle (or frying pan/skillet) over an open fire or gas flame until brown underneath, then turn the dough over and cook until golden brown on the other side.

BLACKBERRY
(see also berries)

A member of the large berry family and the fruit of the bramble, the blackberry is considered a nuisance in many areas as it grows quickly when allowed to grow wild and is a very prickly bush to try and remove. Berries grown in the wild, however, are the tastiest and are usually a sweeter, though smaller, fruit. The flavour can vary from small to large fruit and can be sweet to very sour, depending on the soil conditions. Blackberries are from reddish-purple to a rich black in appearance, but tend to leave a purple stain on skin and clothing.

Used for decoration and for their colour in mousses and desserts, they are also used in summer puddings, ice creams, sorbets, jams and jellies or in their very own blackberry pudding, which was the original format of the summer pudding.

BLACKBERRY PUDDING

The original summer pudding, this recipe has the fresh bread folded through the berries. Eventually a chef had the idea of using an outer crust of fresh bread to soak up the juices and simply packing down the fresh berries inside this crust.

Here is the simple recipe:

Take a large quantity of blackberries and stew lightly with a little sugar and water to soften them. While the berries are still over the heat, quickly mix through sufficient fresh breadcrumbs to achieve a pudding consistency, and then press the mixture into a pudding bowl. Allow to chill for 2–3 hours before serving with fresh cream.

BLACK BREAD
(see also bread, pumpernickel)

A common term, not for burnt bread but for the dark-coloured rye breads made throughout Scandinavia and northern Europe. Most contain a mixture of rye and barley flour and are made using sourdough. Pumpernickel is also a form of this bread.

BLACK BUN
(see scotch bun)

BLACKCURRANT
(see also berries)

Often confused with the small black currants which are dried grapes, these are in fact a berry which is dark purple/black in colour and a native shrub of northern Europe, although now grown throughout the world. Blackcurrants have always been

highly regarded for their medicinal properties and since the 13th century both the berry and its foliage have at times been used for making medicines. They are a very good source of vitamin C and are used in cordials and syrup drinks around the world for this purpose. They are also made into a liqueur called cassis.

The small berries are very aromatic and can range from extremely tasty to very sour and quite acidic. Fresh berries tend to have firm skins, which suits their use in pastries such as muffins, as their juices do not bleed into the mixture before baking.

Blackcurrants are available to the pastry chef or baker fresh, frozen, concentrated, puréed or in syrup or liqueur form, and all of these have their own special place in the pastry kitchen, from sorbets and mousses to muffins, summer puddings, jams and jellies, to fresh fruit tarts or soufflés.

BLACKFOREST GATEAU

Named after the majestic Black Forest in Germany, this has become one of the world's best-known cakes and is easily identified by its chocolate curls, red cherries and fresh cream.

Base
⅔ cup (3 oz) plain (all-purpose) flour
3 tablespoons icing (powdered) sugar
60 g (2 oz) unsalted (sweet) butter, softened
1 egg
2 teaspoons water
1 chocolate génoise sponge (see page 134),
cut into quarters horizontally

Filling
2 cups (16 fl oz) crème Chantilly (see page 85)
400 g (14 oz) canned sour black cherries,
drained and pitted
¼ cup (2 fl oz) Kirsch

To Decorate
crème Chantilly (reserved)
chocolate curls (see page 64)
icing (powdered) sugar, for dusting
12 glacé (candied) or maraschino cherries

Place flour and icing sugar in a bowl and very lightly rub in the butter until the mixture resembles coarse breadcrumbs. Add egg and sufficient water to make a firm dough. Wrap the dough in plastic wrap (cling film) and chill for 1 hour. Preheat oven to 180°C (350°F). Lightly grease the base of a 23 cm (9 in) springform cake tin with butter. Roll out the chilled dough to fit the prepared base. Bake for 5–10 minutes or until light golden brown. Cool.

To Assemble
Reserve a quarter of the crème Chantilly for decorating. Spread the cooled pastry base with four tablespoons crème Chantilly. Place one of the sponge cake layers on top. Spread with a quarter of the remaining crème Chantilly, cover with a third of the cherries and sprinkle on a little Kirsch. Repeat this until all but one of the sponge layers have been used.

Top with the remaining sponge layer.
Cover the top and sides with the remaining crème Chantilly.
Decorate the cake with chocolate curls.
Lightly dust with icing sugar and position the
glacé cherries around the edge. Chill.
Remove from the refrigerator 10–15 minutes before serving.

BLACK JACK
(see also caramel)

A colouring mixture produced from burnt sugar. The sugar syrup is heated at around 180°C (350°F) and allowed to go beyond the caramel stage, making it very bitter. It then has fresh water added to it and is allowed to reboil into a thick black syrup. Due to its pungent flavour and distinct blackness, only a small amount is ever added to pastry items but it is used in fruit cakes, gingerbreads and in the colouring of sugar or pastillage pieces.

BLANCH

A process whereby foodstuffs are placed in boiling water briefly, to partially cook them for reheating later, or in order to remove skins, as in the case of almonds and pistachios and some fruits such as peaches.

BLANCMANGE
(see also almond milk)

From the French 'blanc manger', meaning something white which is eaten, blancmange is one of the oldest dessert dishes, having survived the test of time in an almost original form. Blancmange actually started its life as a savoury dish in the Middle Ages, when it was a white jelly made from the meat of chicken and fish which was thickened with ground almonds so that it could hold its shape without the use of gelatine or setting agents, which at that time were virtually unknown.

Slowly, over the centuries, the dish contained more and more almonds and less of the savoury meats, the whiteness being supplied by milk and cornflour, which themselves eventually replaced the almonds. Cornflour being a thickener, the almonds were no longer needed for this purpose and were eventually left out of the recipe completely. Finally the dish became sweetened, first with honey and then by the use of sugar, until blancmange became the dessert as it is known today.

3¼ cups (26 fl oz) milk
½ cup (4 oz) sugar
zest of 2 lemons
⅔ cup (3 oz) cornflour (cornstarch)
1 cup (8 fl oz) milk, extra

Place the first amount of milk, with the sugar and lemon zest, in a saucepan and bring to the boil. Place the cornflour and the second amount of milk in a small bowl and whisk together so cornflour is diluted. When the milk boils, pour it into the cornflour mixture, stirring continuously. Return entire mixture to the saucepan and reboil slowly, stirring continuously so that the mixture does not stick to the base of the saucepan and burn. Allow mixture to thicken and then

remove from the heat and immediately pour into a decorative mousse or jelly mould. Allow the blancmange to set for 2–3 hours. To remove blancmange, dip the base of the mould into warm water for several seconds and invert onto a plate.

BLEACHED FLOUR
(see also flour)

With age, flour will naturally become bleached, through the process of oxidisation, but for some recipes in pastry cooking bleached flour is specifically required. To bleach flour, a bleaching agent is added to hide the natural colouring of the flour. When the carotene in plain flour is bleached, the flour should look clean and pure white, not its natural creamy colour.

BLENDING

This involves combining two or more ingredients, but not neccesarily to incorporate air, in which case the recipe would call for beating or whisking.

BLINI

This yeast-risen pancake made from buckwheat has been in existence in Russia for more than 1000 years and is an important feature of the Russian pre-Lenten festivities. Lent is a time of fasting where only basic foods and vegetables were allowed in the diet. Hence the period before this was one of bountiful eating.

Depending on the occasion, the meal and the toppings applied, blini can be either sweet or savoury, and can form either small or quite substantial meals.

¾ cup (6 fl oz) warm milk
30 g (1 oz) fresh compressed yeast
1 tablespoon sugar
1¼ cups (5 oz) buckwheat flour
2¾ cups (11 oz) plain (all-purpose) flour
4 egg yolks, lightly beaten
90 g (3 oz) unsalted (sweet) butter, melted and cooled
⅓ cup (2 fl oz) sour cream
2 cups (16 fl oz) milk, extra
½ teaspoon salt
4 egg whites
clarified butter, for serving

Place milk and yeast in a small bowl and whisk together until yeast is dissolved. Allow the bowl to stand in a warm place for 10–15 minutes so that the mixture can begin fermentation and double in bulk. Place half of the milk/yeast mixture in a large mixing bowl with sugar and add half the buckwheat flour and all the plain (all-purpose) flour. Beat with a wooden spoon or using an electric mixer until the ingredients are smooth. Cover the bowl and leave for up to 3 hours for the ingredients to prove (rise), or double in size. Then beat in the remaining buckwheat flour, cover again and allow to sit for 2 hours in a warm area. Add egg yolks, the remaining milk/yeast mixture, melted butter, sour cream, extra milk and salt to the batter and stir thoroughly. Place egg whites in a clean dry bowl and whisk them to stiff peaks. Fold egg whites through the batter and allow the mixture to sit for 20–30 minutes, covered, in a warm area.

In a hot frying pan (skillet), place 3 tablespoons of the batter mixture for each blini. Cook until the heated side begins to brown, brush the top with a little clarified butter and flip the blini over so the other side can cook. When golden brown on both sides, serve the blini immediately.

Makes 10–12

BLINTZ

Traditional blintzes are light and tasty Jewish pancakes, risen by using baking powder (soda). They are traditionally cooked only on one side, one side being left unbrowned and open, and served hot, with fresh cream or cottage cheese or jam (jelly) and hot butter.

BLITZEN KUCHEN
(see also lightning cake)

This 'blitzen' (lightning) 'kuchen' (cake) is quite simple. It was one of the first German cakes to be made with baking powder (soda) when it was invented. The speed at which it rose compared to yeast or other rising methods was truly like lightning. This recipe is for a rich, orange-flavoured tea cake which should be served warm from the oven.

125 g (4 oz) unsalted (sweet) butter, softened
1 cup (8 oz) sugar
zest and juice of 1 orange
4 eggs
1 cup (4 oz) plain (all-purpose) flour
1 teaspoon baking powder (soda)
¼ cup (1 oz) ground walnuts
¼ cup (2 oz) raw (crystal) sugar
2 tablespoons mixed (candied) peel

Preheat oven to 180°C (350°F).
Grease and line a 22 cm (9 in) round cake tin.
In a large mixing bowl, cream butter with sugar and orange zest and juice until light and fluffy. Add eggs one at a time, beating well after each one is added. Add sifted flour and baking powder and mix well with butter mixture.
Spread the mix into the prepared cake tin and flatten using a spatula. Sprinkle the ground walnuts, sugar and mixed (candied) peel over the top of the cake and bake for 40–45 minutes or until cooked.

BLOOD ORANGE
(see also orange)

From the outside, a blood orange looks like any other orange, but when cut open it is a deep red colour, with the same flavour as a normal orange. It makes a refreshing and different drink and is great to use in fruit salads, jellied desserts or in dessert sauces.

BLOOM
(see also bread, chocolate)

Bloom can mean one of two things, depending on the area of the pastry kitchen involved, and can mean either good workmanship or poor handling of ingredients. In the case of unglazed bread and cakes, it refers to the crust colour and is said to be the sign of a healthy loaf of bread, indicating correct handling of the product and its ingredients, and that the recipe is good.

In chocolate and sugar work (candy making), bloom indicates the poor handling of products. Fat bloom on chocolates or in chocolate goods shows poor tempering of couverture or pure chocolate, causing some of the fat to float to the surface of the setting chocolate product. This is detected by the appearance of a grey fat streak across the firm chocolate. In sugar work, the bloom is a result of crystallisation of the sugar and can mean poor cleaning of the sugar, poor handling of the poured or blown sugar, or poor handling of temperatures in the finished products. With a change from moist to dry conditions, the sugar piece will become wet and then dry and crystallise, showing a distinct bloom across the work.

BLOWN SUGAR
(see sugar)

BLUEBERRY
(see also berry)

A small ball-shaped berry which is dark blue/purple in colour and is seedless, has sweet juices and a mild, sweet flavour. The blueberry is common in all facets of baking and pastry making due to its firm skin, which prevents bleeding of the juices before baking. For this reason, blueberries are used in cakes, muffins, cheesecakes, soufflés and sauces and many other different styles of recipes.

Wild blueberries have been in use for centuries and are still very popular today. They have a firmer skin than the cultivated variety. The ancient Indians of North America and Canada ate the wild blueberries and believed them to have healing and medicinal qualities. They also sun-dried the blueberries for use throughout winter in soups and as a dried delicacy on their own.

BLUEBERRY SAUCE
300g (10 oz) fresh blueberries
30 ml (1 fl oz) Benedictine (or similar) liqueur
6 teaspoons sugar
30 g (1 oz) unsalted (sweet) butter
zest and juice of 1 lemon
zest and juice of 1 orange
1 cinnamon stick
2 cloves

Place all ingredients in a saucepan and slowly bring to the boil. Simmer for 5–10 minutes or until the blueberries begin to break down slightly and become pulpy. Remove cinnamon stick and cloves and serve hot or cold.

BLUEBERRY TORTE

1½ cups (6 oz) plain (all-purpose) flour
2 level teaspoons bicarbonate of soda
2 level teaspoons baking powder (soda)
175 g (6 oz) unsalted (sweet) butter
1½ cups (10 oz) caster (superfine) sugar
3 eggs
1 tablespoon lemon juice
375 g (12 oz) fresh blueberries
1¼ cups (10 fl oz) sour cream

To Decorate
1 quantity lemon cream cheese frosting (see page 125)

Preheat oven to 170°C (340°F).
Grease a 23 cm (9 in) springform cake tin lightly with butter and line the base with baking paper (parchment). Mix flour, bicarbonate of soda and baking powder and sift twice. Beat butter and sugar until creamy, light and fluffy. Add eggs one at a time, beating very well after each one is added. Gently fold in the sifted flour by hand. Fold in lemon juice, blueberries and sour cream. Pour into prepared tin and bake for 1½ hours, or until a skewer inserted into the centre of the cake comes out dry.
Cool in the tin on a cake rack.
When cold, remove from the pan, cover the top and sides with frosting and decorate with blueberries.

BLUEBERRY CORDIAL

600 g (20 oz) fresh blueberries
1¼ cups (10 fl oz) water
1 cinnamon stick
2 cloves

Place blueberries, water, cinnamon stick and cloves in a large saucepan and allow to come to the boil. Boil the liquid for 10 minutes or until the berries begin to break down. Remove cinnamon stick and cloves and purée the warm liquid in a blender. Allow the liquid to cool.
Using cheesecloth or muslin, strain the liquid to remove all but the pure watery liquid. Throw away the pulpy mass and return the liquid to the saucepan. For every cup of juice add ¼–½ cup of sugar, depending on taste and the sweetness of the berries. Reboil the sweetened juice until the sugar has dissolved, then cook for a further 3–4 minutes.
Allow syrup to cool, then bottle in sterilised bottles or jars.
To serve, simply add syrup to cold water, half and half.

BLUEBERRY PIE

375 g (12 oz) sweet (shortcrust) pastry (see page 272)
500 g (1 lb) fresh blueberries
¼ cup (1 oz) plain (all-purpose) flour
1 cup (8 oz) sugar
1 teaspooon ground cinnamon
30 g (1 oz) unsalted (sweet) butter
egg yolk for glaze

Preheat oven to 180°C (350°F).
Line a 22 cm (9 in) quiche or pie plate (dish) with ¾ of the thinly rolled pastry.
Wash blueberries in warm water and dry slightly by patting them between two towels. Place blueberries in a large mixing bowl and sprinkle flour, sugar and cinnamon over them. Shake the bowl so that all the blueberries are covered with the flour mix. Place blueberries in the pastry-lined pie dish and dot the top with pieces of the butter. Cover pie with the remaining pastry and press the pastry lid into the pastry sides. Glaze the top of the pie with the egg yolk by brushing over the top. Bake in preheated oven for 30–35 minutes. Remove and cool slightly before serving warm or cold.

BOILED SUGAR
(see sugar)

BOILED SWEETS

Boiled sweets are perhaps the most difficult confectionery to create due to the extreme temperature of the syrup that must be formed with your hands. If the syrup is produced correctly it should be quite hot, yet easy to stretch. When producing this kind of confectionery you should always work on a lightly oiled marble slab.

2 cups (16 oz) sugar
1 cup (8 fl oz) water
¼ cup (3 oz) liquid glucose (corn syrup)
5 drops of tartaric acid

Place sugar and water in a large heavy-based saucepan and dissolve slowly over gentle heat. When sugar is completely dissolved, allow the mixture to come to the boil. As the mixture boils, wash down the sides of the saucepan with a pastry brush dipped in warm water, to remove any mixture that has splashed up the sides of the pan. Add glucose to the mixture and stir in, using a clean spoon. Continue cleaning the sides of the saucepan and allow the syrup to return to the boil. Remove saucepan from heat and pour syrup directly into a large jar that has a tight-fitting lid. Store syrup in the container for 12–24 hours. Storing the syrup in this way helps all the sugar crystals to dissolve.
Pour syrup into a clean saucepan and bring it to the boil. Be sure to once again wash down the sides of the saucepan. Place a sugar (candy) thermometer in the boiling liquid. Once it has reached 120°C (250°F) there is no need to continue washing down the sides of the saucepan. Allow the mixture to reach 137°C (280°F) on the sugar thermometer and add the tartaric acid. Continue boiling the mixture until it reaches 154°C (310°F). Remove sugar thermometer carefully, then pour syrup onto the lightly oiled marble slab. Allow it to cool for several minutes until a slight skin forms. Using a lightly oiled metal scraper, scrape the outer edges of the syrup into the centre. Allow it to spread out again before scraping the outer edges into the middle once more. Repeat this process until the syrup becomes fairly cool and forms a firm ball. The syrup should

THE MOST COMMON TYPES OF BOMBES

Name	Ice	Filling	Decoration
Aboukir	almond/praline	praline	roasted flaked almonds and marzipan
Abricotine	apricots	Kirsch layered with apricot jam (jelly)	slices of fresh apricot
Alexandra	pineapple	vanilla with crystallised (candied) pineapple	glacé (candied) pineapple
Alsacienne	pistachio	half vanilla, half chocolate	chocolate filigrees
Benedictine	blueberry	benedictine-flavoured with vanilla ice cream	crushed crystallised (candied) violets
Bordelaise	apricot	strawberry	fresh strawberries
Bourdaloue	pear	anisette	slices of dried or fresh pear
Cardinal	redcurrant and raspberry	vanilla with praline	crystallised (candied) rose petals
Carnival	lemon with macedoine of glacé (candied) fruits	strawberry	strawberries dipped in chocolate
Cecilia	orange and chocolate	vanilla with a mixture of crytallised (candied) watermelon and tropical fruits	crème Chantilly and chocolate butterflies
Ceylon	tea	strong tea-flavoured sorbet	chocolate filigree designs
Chantilly	chocolate	Kirsch-flavoured	grated chocolate and crème Chantilly
Creole	pineapple	strawberry and pineapple	glacé (candied) pineapple
Cyrano	chocolate	cherries and Kirsch-flavoured	whipped cream and glacé (candied) cherries
Dauphine	lemon	almond and macaroon biscuits (cookies) with glacé (candied) fruit	crystallised (candied) lemon segments
Diable Rose	strawberry	Kirsch and chopped glacé (candied) cherries	chocolate filigree designs
Diplomate	vanilla	maraschino liqueur with fresh fruits, soaked in same liqueur	sponge pieces cut into 1 cm ($\frac{1}{2}$ in) squares
Figaro	chocolate	jaffa flavour (chocolate and orange)	crystallised (candied) orange segments
Florentine	raspberry	praline	praline pieces
Grand Duc	orange	orange liqueur	fresh orange segments
Hernani	coffee	pistachio	caramelised pistachios or pistachio praline
Italienne	walnut	vanilla	Italienne meringue flecked into peaks and flamed
Jaffa	praline	orange liqueur	chocolate-enrobed mandarin segments
Japonaise	peach	orange liqueur	Japonaise crumbs
Jubilee	vanilla	vanilla	served on a bed of cherry compôte flamed with Kirsch
Madeleine	almond	vanilla	crème Chantilly and glacé fruits soaked in Kirsch
Monte Carlo	orange	praline	sugar-glazed mandarin segments
Monte Cristo	raspberry	vanilla	fresh raspberries
Montmorency	vanilla	Kirsch with glacé cherries	fresh cherries
Neron	caramel	vanilla mousse and chocolate drops	Italian meringue and grated chocolate
Nesselrode	chestnut	vanilla	roasted and possibly sugar-glazed chestnuts
Nina	strawberry	crystallised (candied) violets folded through crème Chantilly	crystallised (candied) violets folded through crème Chantilly
Prince of Wales	chocolate	rich chestnut purée mixture	chocolate caraque
Princess Beatrice	pineapple	Curaçao	crystallised (candied) orange zest
Queen Victoria	pineapple	strawberry flavoured with Kirsch	fresh strawberries sugar glazed
Russe	praline	kummel	whipped cream and pieces of marron glacé
Sappho	strawberry	vanilla with wild strawberries	Kirsch-flavoured crème Chantilly
Sicilienne	lemon	praline	roasted almonds
Succès	apricot	crème Chantilly with diced apricots soaked in Kirsch	roasted almonds dusted with icing (powdered) sugar
Suisse	vanilla	strawberry	Kirsch-soaked strawberries
Tutti Frutti	strawberry	vanilla with medley of glacé (candied) fruits	crème Chantilly sprinkled with medley of chopped glacé (candied) fruits
Zanzibar	coffee	orange liqueur	coffee meringue

still feel fairly hot to touch, but should not burn. With lightly oiled hands and a scraper, pull the syrup into a long sausage shape. Take each end and stretch it to triple its original length. Fold the ends together and stretch it again. Fold the two ends back together and repeat the process several times until the mixture changes from a clear to a silky white colour. This should take 10–15 minutes. When the sausage shape reaches this colour, pull it one last time, a little longer than usual. Fold it in half and then in half again and twist each length around and around so that it forms a long fine rope.

Using lightly oiled scissors, cut this rope into 1 cm (½ in) lengths and allow the sweets to cool on the oiled marble until they are firm. Store the sweets in an airtight jar.

Note: Should the syrup crystallise or harden before it becomes a silky white colour, place it in a saucepan with ½ cup (4 fl oz) water and slowly mix until the hard sugar has dissolved. Boil the mixture to 155°C (310°F) and repeat the whole process.

BOMBE
(see also Baked Alaska)

Also known as iced bombes or bombes glacées, bombes are an ice cream dessert named after the spherical moulds they are made in. A true bombe has an outer crust of one or two flavours of ice cream. Inside this is a special bombe mixture which is soft frozen and can be flavoured with spices, fresh or dried fruits, nuts or alcohol. Today, it is generally accepted that a bombe is any ice cream or sorbet-crusted shape which contains a filling of either mousse, sorbet, custard or traditional bombe mixture. Bombes must contain the softer filling, otherwise they are simply ice cream cakes. Special spherical bombe moulds are available but pudding basins and large deep containers are also used.

Bombes have all of their colour and design on the inside and are rarely highly decorated as they must be served quickly or the ice cream will begin to melt. Traditional bombes have no decoration; they are simply unmoulded, masked in Italian meringue, then frozen. When the dessert is served, the meringue is browned or glazed using a blow torch or by placing it in a hot oven for several minutes. Bombes served in this way are set on a bed of sponge or cake when they are unmoulded, before being coated in the meringue. The most widely known of these meringue-covered bombes is the Bombe Alaska.

The most common bombes are listed in the table on the opposite page.

BOMBE CECILIA
500 g (16 oz) chocolate ice cream
1 cup (8 oz) sugar
½ cup (4 fl oz) water
5 egg whites
⅓ cup (3 oz) sugar
5 egg yolks
1¼ cups (10 fl oz) cream, lightly whipped
1¼ cups (5 oz) chopped peanuts
90 g (3 oz) crystallised watermelon (candied fruits)
½ génoise sponge (see page 134)

Line a large pudding basin, large soufflé ramekin or individual ramekins thinly with the chocolate ice cream and freeze until the chocolate ice cream is set firm. Place sugar and water in a saucepan and boil. Boil to 110°C (230°F). Whisk egg whites with sugar until they form stiff peaks. Slowly, while still whisking egg whites, drizzle boiled sugar slowly into the whipping whites. Whisk until all is added and then until the whites are cool. Whisk the egg yolks into the stiff whites. Fold whipped cream through the cold meringue then fold through the chopped nuts and chopped fruits. Pour bombe mixture into the centre of the chocolate lined mould/s and place a thin layer of sponge on the top which, when unmoulded, will become the base. Cover securely. Freeze for 6–8 hours or overnight before umoulding, decorating and serving.

BON BON
A name given to a wide range of sweets or candies.

BORDURE
A border or edge of pastry or bread placed around a dish as a decoration or to hold in the contents of the dish.

BOREK
A sweet or savoury Turkish dish made from layers of fine filo (phyllo) pastry and, in the sweet variety, layers of ground nuts and spices which are covered in a sweet syrup. Borek differs from the Greek baklava in that borek is traditionally fried individually and can range from small to large cigar shapes, both of which are soaked in the sweet syrup in the sweet variety.

BOUCHEE
(see also puff pastry, savoury pastries, vol-au-vents)

Translating into 'of the mouth' or 'small mouthfuls', this is exactly what a bouchée is; a small vol-au-vent shaped puff pastry, bite size and filled with either sweet or savoury fillings. Bouchées can also be made from choux pastry. Looking exactly like a profiterole or small choux puff, a choux pastry bouchée is simply the name given to a savoury-filled profiterole.

BOULANGER
The French name for baker is said to derive from that of a famous baker about whom little is known except that he was highly regarded and his name widely respected, eventually being used to identify all tradespeople in baking. Boulangers are rarely seen anywhere but in large hotels these days, the name generally referring to one who is a master of specialty doughs, croissants and Danish and breakfast specialities.

BOULE-DE-NEIGE
Literally translated, this means 'ball of snow' and refers to either one of two French specialties. The first and most famous is a petit four consisting of two snow white small

meringues sandwiched together with chocolate buttercream and then completely enrobed in vanilla buttercream and rolled in flaked or grated chocolate.

The second of the cakes with this name is a large cake consisting of multiple layers of vanilla génoise sponge sandwiched together with vanilla buttercream and allowed to set firm. When firm, it is cut to resemble a ball shape, covered in more buttercream and rolled in shredded (grated) or flaked coconut and allowed to firm again before being served.

BOURDALOUE

A French dessert of apples or pears poached in white wine, placed in a pastry-lined tart and then covered with crème frangipane. The name of the cake or tart apparently comes from the street name Rue Bourdaloue, the location of the shop where this dessert was created.

BOURDELOT
(see also baked apples, rabote, talibur)

First made in a French town in Normandy, this apple pastry is made using a fresh apple which has been cored and filled with a mixture of butter, spices, breadcrumbs or ground almonds and sultanas (golden raisins), to which a nip of Calvados is added. The apple is then wrapped in a square of puff or shortcrust pastry, which is joined by its corners at the top of the apple and glazed with egg yolk. It is baked for 25–30 minutes, until the apple is tender and the pastry baked and light. In different parts of Europe, it is known as rabote and talibur.

Brandy Snaps

BRANDY BUTTER

This is traditionally served with Christmas pudding and is also known as hard butter or hard sauce.

2 cups (12 oz) icing (powdered) sugar, sifted
3 tablespoons brandy
125 g (4 oz) unsalted (sweet) butter

Mix brandy and icing sugar together in a bowl. Place butter and icing mix ino a mixing bowl and whip until light and creamy. Serve brandy butter in a large bowl and place tablespoonfuls onto warm Christmas pudding or cake.

BRANDY SNAPS

These thin, wafer-like gingerbread biscuits (cookies) are flavoured with spices and generally curled while hot and pliable by being rolled around the handle of a wooden spoon.

¾ cup (5 oz) caster (superfine) sugar
½ cup (6 oz) golden syrup (light treacle)
90 g (3 oz) unsalted (sweet) butter
¾ cup (3 oz) plain (all-purpose) flour

Place sugar, golden syrup and butter in a saucepan and place over medium heat. Allow butter to melt and mix into all the other ingredients, but do not allow to boil. Remove from the heat when all ingredients are melted into a syrup, add flour and stir with a wooden spoon until all is combined. Pour mixture into a container and refrigerate for 1–2 hours, or until mixture is quite cool and firm.
Preheat oven to 180°C (350°F).
Lightly grease several baking sheets.
When mix is cold and hard, take one teaspoonful at a time and roll each into a small ball. Place balls on the sheet at regular intervals, leaving plenty of room between for spreading. When sheet is full, dip your fingers into cold water and flatten the balls so that they are quite flat.
Place the sheet in the oven and bake for 5–8 minutes or until all the biscuits are bubbling and have coloured slightly.
Remove sheet from the oven and cool slightly before attempting to remove the biscuits. When biscuits have firmed slightly, peel them from the sheet carefully, using a palette knife or spatula, and roll each one quickly around the handle of a wooden spoon or similarly sized object. Cool around the mould. When cold, slide from the mould and either leave plain or fill with freshly whipped cream.

Makes 2–3 dozen

BRAZIL NUTS
(see also nuts)

Brazil nuts are rarely used in pastry, but not because they are unworthy of the privilege. They are native to Brazil and the Amazon region and grow in almost triangular-shaped hard shells which themselves are the seed of a large fruit. Brazil nuts are a rich source of oil and can be used whole, grated, shaved or ground with sweet cakes, biscuits (cookies) and desserts, or with savoury items.

A few of the many different kind of breads now available.

BREAD
(see also flatbreads, griddle breads, quickbreads, sandwich, tomato bread, wholemeal bread)

Bread must surely be one of the oldest items ever made in the pastry and bakery trades. From early times, mixtures of wheat, water and flavourings have been kneaded together and baked in flat round form on hot rocks, griddles or in crude ovens. Many of these original breads are amongst the most famous of breads in existence today.

Every culture and nation has its own unique style, type or flavour of bread. Spoonbread and batterbreads come from America; India has paratha, chapattis, naan and puris bread; Ireland the Irish soda bread; Scotland its baps; Australia its damper; European countries are famed for rye, black bread, pumpernickel and sourdough breads, to name but a few; pitta bread comes from the Middle East; there are flatbreads, large loaves, quick breads and griddle breads, and the list goes on. Today all of these breads have reached far beyond their places of origin to gain world acceptance.

BREAD MAKING

Bread is relatively easy to produce yet the need to use yeast tends to scare many away from producing their own breads on a regular basis. For good bread, good fresh (compressed) or dried (freeze-dried) yeast should be used, along with a good quality flour; the only other factor which plays a major part in the final product is the mixing and handling of the bread dough. Careless and haphazard kneading of bread doughs is often the cause of fermentation problems and results in a poor quality loaf. An even distribution of all the ingredients, in particular the yeast and its foods, and the salt and sugar, is obtained by good and careful kneading, which also results in the formation of a good gluten structure, which ensures a perfectly risen dough.

Gluten is formed when the two proteins glidin and glutenin are mixed with a liquid. When it forms into a fine framework, gluten is elastic and strong, and the carbon dioxide gas given off by the fermenting yeast fills the fine gluten network causing the bread dough to rise like balloons. Once the bread dough has reached optimum fermentation or proving, then the bread is baked. Oven spring is the name given to the final rising of the bread dough in the oven before the yeast is killed and the fine dough framework is baked into a loaf of bread.

Another tricky area for bread makers is determining the length of time they should knead the bread dough for. This depends on whether the dough is made by hand or with a machine, the amount of dough being kneaded, the type or variety of the bread dough and, finally, on the quality of the ingredients used, especially the flour.

The best guide is to test for optimum gluten formation by kneading the dough for 5–8 minutes and then resting it for 30–40 seconds. Tear a piece of bread dough from the main dough and begin stretching it from the centre. If it can be stretched slowly until it becomes so fine that you could read print through it then it has reached optimum gluten strength and is ready for the next stage of the bread making process. Otherwise, keep kneading.

Major Bread Types and Varieties

BAGUETTE: A long, narrow baked loaf of bread measuring almost 60 cm (2 ft) in length. Made from a very soft white bread dough, the loaf is baked on narrow trays which contain small holes to enable the heat to circulate all around and to allow the steam from the dough to escape. Also called a French stick, the baguette is traditionally cut lengthwise and filled with savoury cold fillings for lunches.

BAPS (SCOTTISH): Baps at the breakfast table are to the Scots what croissants are to the French. Baps are large, fairly flat white breakfast buns which are dusted in flour before they are baked and are soft crusted due to their high fat content. They contain a small amount of sugar but are not overly sweet, and are generally eaten direct from the oven with butter and jam (jelly).

CHEESE BREAD: A white bread dough which contains 12–15% cheese, usually in a dried powder form.

COBURG LOAF: More commonly known simply as Cob loaf, a Coburg is traditionally a large loaf of bread which has a deep cross cut into the top prior to baking so that during baking the top will open up and create four high peaks on the crust. Made from white or milk bread doughs.

COTTAGE LOAF: Two different-sized Cob loaves joined together, with a smaller one sitting on top of the larger. Looks similar to a brioche but is made from ordinary white bread dough and dusted in flour.

FARL: A light Irish soda bread.

LEOPARD SKIN BREAD: Any bread that has been washed with a leopard skin wash, which is a mixture of fermented yeast and rice flour and water, and baked to give a decoative design and a crisp crunchy crust.

MALT BREAD: A wholemeal bread dough containing malt.

MILK LOAF: A loaf made from a richer, whiter and sweeter dough than normal bread. Either milk has been added in liquid form to the dry ingredients or the dry ingredients contain a percentage of milk powder.

PISTON OR TANK LOAF: Baked inside a double-sided tank tin, these decorative loaves are ribbed or fluted when baked and are made from milk or normal white bread dough. A saddle of venison pan can be used to give the loaf a single-sided effect. The name Tank Loaf relates to its resemblance to the corrugated sides of a water tank.

RYE BREAD: Rich, heavy and dense, and with an intense flavour, rye breads are traditional in European countries and usually contain a sour dough starter within the dough to make the rye flour edible. This sour dough itself imparts a special flavour.

VIENNA LOAF: A large loaf of white bread which is pointed at either end and almost oval in shape, with, traditionally, five slits diagonally across the top. It can be baked plain or washed with water and sprinkled with sesame seeds. It is baked on flat irons, trays or on 'Vienna slippers'

BREAD AND BUTTER PUDDING

2 slices of 1 or 2 day old bread
1 tablespoon butter
1½ cups (12 fl oz) fresh milk
1 cup (8 fl oz) fresh single cream
2 eggs
¼ cup (2 oz) sugar
2 tablespoons sultanas (golden raisins)
2 tablespoons currants

Preheat oven to 160°C (320°F).
Spread bread slices with butter. Remove crusts and cut bread into quarters. In a large bowl, whisk milk, cream, eggs and sugar until all are combined. Place bread slices in a pie dish or shallow ovenproof bowl and sprinkle sultanas and currants over them. Pour milk mixture over the top of the bread and dried fruits. Set the pie dish in a baking tin filled with hot water to reach half way up the pie dish sides. Bake till the top is golden brown and the custard has set firm.

Serves 4–6

BREADCRUMBS

Fresh, dried and powdered breadcrumbs are an important ingredient for the pastry chef. Not only can breadcrumbs be used to cover foods for frying or as a simple topping for some of the pastry dishes, but the breadcrumbs can also be used to replace more expensive ingredients such as ground nuts or desiccated (shredded) coconut.

There are three main ways to produce breadcrumbs, each method giving a different type of breadcrumb:

(i) Fresh bread can have the crusts removed and grated and the fresh breadcrumbs can be used as a topping for desserts, or sautéed or fried in a little butter to give colour and then mixed with some sugar, for example, to make a crunchy crumble topping.

(ii) Stale bread may be sieved or minced finely to produce a fine white crumb which is firm and can be used for the outside crust of dumplings, for example.

(iii) Golden-coloured breadcrumbs can be produced by baking bread scraps till golden brown and then crushing the crusts in a mortar and pestle or in a blender. These crumbs will last for months as long as they are stored in an airtight container or jar.

BREAD IMPROVER
(see also yeast food)

Bread improvers are commercially prepared mixtures of bread additives and modifying agents that assist in preparing the optimum volume of the bread dough. They enhance the flavour, texture and colour of the finished product by improving gluten development and increasing the activity of the yeast.

Bread improvers must be made up using a base carrier, which is usually malt or soy flour. They will also contain many other ingredients, including salt and sugar, potassium bromate (to assist with the formation and strengthening of gluten), and ascorbic acid, which can make the dough more elastic.

Each bread improver will be different, and the amount added to the dough depends on the size and type of dough, brand and type of flours used and the amount of proving or fermentation time needed. Generally, though, a little more is required by doughs with a short fermentation, while less is required by those with a long fermentation period.

BREAD ROLLS

6½ cups (26 oz) plain (all-purpose) flour
75 g (2½ oz) unsalted (sweet) butter, softened
1 teaspoon salt
3 teaspoons fresh compressed yeast
2 tablespoons sugar
2 teaspoons gluten flour
about 1¾ cups (14 fl oz) water

Place all dry ingredients in a mixing bowl and mix for 5 minutes. Add enough water so that a nice dough is formed. Mix for a further 10 minutes, then remove the dough from the bowl and allow to rest on a bench, covered, for 10 minutes.

When rested, scale dough into sizes required and mould into small balls. Knock them back (punch them down), and roll into required shapes. Place on a baking sheet in a warmed area so that they prove (rise) for a further 30–40 minutes, or until double in size, before baking. Preheat oven to 190°C (375°F). Bake rolls for 20–25 minutes or until golden brown.

BREADSTICKS
(see grissini)

BREAKFAST

Breaking the fast of the night was made into a formal and important meal of the day during the early 15th century, when specific foods were first made just for this meal, although an early morning meal had probably been in existence since time began, people having to eat when they awoke from a sleep. Until the 18th century, breakfast was taken between 4–6 am, and consisted of cold meats, ales, omelettes, breads and cakes.

Today almost every country has a famous bread-like product that is eaten with the morning meal, which may or may not also consist of a savoury dish. France enjoys the croissant with coffee, Scandinavia the Danish pastries and kringle, Germany the Kugelhupf, England the crumpet, Scotland enjoys baps with hot drinks and jam (jelly), while in America sweet or savoury muffins and biscuits are eaten.

The breakfast service is just as important to the pastry chef as any other in the day, as it is one of the few meals during which they are on duty. Most pastry chefs work through the night and early morning so that the breakfast pastries are fresh. Other foods the pastry chef may produce for the guest are Bircher muesli, sweet plaits and twists, breakfast buns, fruit salads and fruit compôtes. In large establishments the pastry chef may also be in charge of manufacturing the jams and preserves required for their breads.

BREAKFAST BUN

A small sweet yeast dough roll or bun, usually highly decorated or shaped and occasionally iced with bun wash or a fondant.

BRESTOIS

A specialty of the French town of Brest, from which it derives its name, this cake is made from a génoise sponge mixture to which almonds and orange and lemon zest have been added, giving the cake a rich and slightly heavy consistency.

Baked in brioche moulds, the cakes are cut when cold, filled with apricot jam (jelly), covered completely with boiled apricot glaze, then rolled in roasted flaked almonds.

BRETON

Created in 1850, this pastry table decoration was considered a food masterpiece for many years. It is an assembly of small almond-flavoured biscuits (cookies), each iced in a different colour and arranged in a tower formation or in the shape of a pyramid. The impetus for this creation by pastry chef Dubusc was apparently his desire to find an ingenious way to serve the biscuits or petits fours for coffee.

BRETON GATEAU

A large round butter cake of French origin, characteristically decorated with a heavy egg yolk glaze before baking and marked in a crisscross fashion using the prongs of a fork.

BRIOCHE
(see also torteil)

One of the most famed pastry products of French cuisine worldwide, the brioche has been baked since around 1404.

The origin of the name is much disputed, some saying that it comes from Jean Brioche, who claimed to have invented it, others that it is named after the guild of pastrycooks of St Brieuc, who were known as Briochins. Yet other stories refer to the doughs once being made from brie cheese and traditionally looking like an 'occhi' which was a fig, similar in shape to a brioche.

Whatever the origin of the name, the sweet yeast dough brioche is famed for its lightness, flavour and aroma. It consists of a large ball-shaped 'body' and a small 'head' of the same dough. Enjoyed in France for breakfast, brioches feature worldwide in many dishes and in many forms. As a dessert on their own, brioches can be served hot or cold and usually are sliced in half or hollowed out and filled with mousse, berries, ice cream or sorbet. They can also serve as a replacement for bread in 'brioche and butter' pudding.

Different sizes and styles make brioches the perfect breakfast bread.

Brownies, an ever-popular American treat.

4 cups (16 oz) plain (all-purpose) flour
¼ cup (2 oz) sugar
6 teaspoons fresh compressed yeast
4 eggs
½ cup (4 fl oz) milk
180 g (6 oz) unsalted (sweet) butter, softened
egg yolk, to glaze

Grease 18 individual brioche moulds well.
Place flour in a large mixing bowl and crumb through
the sugar and yeast with your fingers. Add lightly beaten
eggs and milk and form the mixture into a dough.
Knead dough for 5–8 minutes or until smooth and elastic.
Place butter on top of dough and cover the dough,
allowing it to rest in a warm place for 20–25 minutes.
Remove the well-risen dough and, with your hands, mix
butter through until completely incorporated into the dough.
On a flightly floured surface, knead the dough lightly.
Cut the dough into 27 pieces of equal size. Roll 18 of these
pieces into small balls and place these in the brioche moulds.
Cut each of the remaining 9 pieces in half and roll these into

small balls. Press a finger into the top of each of the eighteen
large balls already in the moulds and press the smaller balls
onto the top of each so that they sit in the indentation.
Glaze the top of the brioches with egg yolk and place them,
covered, in a warm area for 25–35 minutes
to prove (rise), until they are double in size.
Preheat oven to 180°C (350°F).
Bake in preheated oven for 20–25 minutes or
until golden brown.

BRIOCHE NANTERRE

Made of four sections and characteristically cut on top with
scissors, brioche Nanterre is one of the many variations of the
traditional brioche dough.

Cut the dough into four equal parts and roll each into a ball.
Place all four balls in one well-greased loaf tin, so that they sit
close together. Allow the brioche to prove (rise) until double
its original size and then, with scissors dipped into oil, snip
the top of the loaf in two rows down its length. Glaze with egg
yolks and bake for 25–30 minutes at 180°C (350°F).

BRIXSCALE

Replacing the baume scale in the 1960s, the Brixscale measures the density of sugar syrups using a saccharometer.

BROWNIES

A rich American chocolate slice, which can come in two varieties, each either with nuts or plain. A true brownie is dense and heavy and is produced from eggs, flour, sugar, chocolate and a lot of butter and should not require frosting or icing, as this takes away from the pure chocolate quality and also makes it far too sweet. The second variety is a much lighter, almost cake-like, product which is still rich in chocolate but not as dense.

RICH AMERICAN BROWNIE
180 g (6 oz) unsalted (sweet) butter
330 g (11 oz) dark (plain or semi-sweet) chocolate
3 eggs
1¼ cups (9 oz) caster (superfine) sugar
¾ cup (3 oz) plain (all-purpose) flour
2¾ cups (12 oz) chopped walnuts

Preheat oven to 175°C (345°F).
Lightly grease and line a 25 x 30 x 3 cm (10 x 12 x 1¼ in) baking tray (jelly roll pan) with baking paper (parchment). Melt butter and chocolate together in a double boiler or bowl placed over a saucepan of boiling water. Place eggs and sugar in a mixing bowl and whip until they are light and fluffy and pale in colour. Add melted chocolate to whisked egg and sugar mixture and stir well to combine. Add sifted flour and chopped walnuts to the chocolate mixture and stir well. Pour into prepared tray and smooth out using a spatula or palette knife. Bake in preheated oven for 30–35 minutes or until a thin skewer inserted into the centre comes out clean. Remove from oven and cool in the tray before cutting into squares and serving.

Makes 20—25

See page 37

LIGHT CHOCOLATE BROWNIE
3 cups (12 oz) plain (all-purpose) flour
2½ teaspoons baking powder (soda)
4 level teaspoons bicarbonate of soda
½ cup (2 oz) cocoa powder
125 g (4 oz) unsalted (sweet) butter
2 cups (12 oz) soft (light) brown sugar
2 eggs
150 g (5 oz) dark (plain or semi-sweet) chocolate,
melted (see page 62)
1 cup (8 fl oz) milk
1 teaspoon vanilla essence (extract)
1 quantity chocolate frosting (see page 125)

Preheat oven to 180°C (350°F).
Grease and line a 25 x 30 x 3 cm (10 x 12 x 1¼ in) baking tray (jelly roll pan) with baking paper (parchment).

Sift flour, baking powder, bicarbonate of soda and cocoa powder twice. Beat butter and sugar until they are well combined in a soft paste. Add eggs one at a time, beating well after each one is added. Add melted chocolate to butter mixture and beat in well. Mix in the sifted dry ingredients alternately with the milk and vanilla essence, by hand. Pour into prepared tray and bake in preheated oven for 35–40 minutes, or until firm to the touch. Cool in the tray. When cold, cover the top with the chocolate frosting. Cut into small squares to serve.

Makes 36

BROWN BETTY
(see also cobbler, crumble, streusel)

Known by this name throughout America, this dish is usually made of apples, though it can be made from pears, apricots or peaches. It has a similar basis to apple crumble, apple streusel and cobbler dishes. A fruit compôte or base of stewed fruits, covered with a firm but crumbly topping, the Brown Betty was first introduced to America in the late 1800s and is a dessert which can be served hot or cold, on its own or with a custard-based sauce, ice cream or cream.

2½ cups (5 oz) soft fresh brown (wholewheat) breadcrumbs
½ cup (3 oz) light brown sugar
1 teaspoon ground cinnamon
1 kg (2 lb) cooking apples, peeled, cored
and chopped into 1 cm (½ in) pieces
60g (2 oz) unsalted (sweet) butter, cut into small pieces

Preheat oven to 180°C (350°F). Lightly butter a pie dish. In a mixing bowl, stir together fresh breadcrumbs, sugar and cinnamon. Scatter ⅓ of this crumb mixture over the base of the pie dish. Place half the chopped apples on top of the crumb mixture and scatter half the chopped butter over the apples. Cover with another ⅓ of the crumbs and top again with the apples and butter. Cover the apples with the remaining crumb mixture and bake in preheated oven for 25–30 minutes or until the apples are tender and the crumbs on top are brown and crisp.

BROWN SUGAR
(see also sugar)

Brown sugar is sugar that has some molasses remaining after it has been cleaned, the molasses clinging to the individual sugar crystals. Depending on the individual producer's way of refining or cleaning and purifying sugars, and the amount of molasses present, different brown sugars will vary in flavour, aroma and colour. There are two ways of producing the brown sugar: mix a small amount of molasses with refined white sugar or simply partially refine the original sugar.

Brown sugar is used today for any number of recipes. It can replace its white counterpart in almost any recipe, offering a new flavour, colour and characteristic to the dish. It has not always been popular, though, and was once thought of as dirty sugar and sold cheaply to pâtissiers for use in gingerbreads, fruit cakes and honey cakes, where its flavour was best put to use.

BROWN LUMP SUGAR
(see also sugar)

This is simply brown sugar which has been pressed into cube shapes and dried.

As with white sugar cubes, these can be rubbed over the skin of citrus fruits such as lemon to impart flavour into gingerbreads and sauces.

BUCHE DE NOEL
(see also Yule Log)

French name for a traditional Christmas cake which is decorated as a Christmas log.

caster (superfine) sugar
1 vanilla génoise sponge, uncooked (see page 134)

To Decorate
1 quantity no-fuss chocolate buttercream (see page 43)
225 g (7½ oz) marzipan
dark (plain or semi-sweet) chocolate, melted (see page 62)
marzipan holly and berries (see page 179)

Preheat oven to 180°C (350°F). Lightly grease a 20 x 30 cm (8 x 12 in) baking tray (sheet) with butter and line with baking paper (parchment). Spread a tea towel on a bench (counter) and cover with greaseproof (waxed) paper. Sprinkle the paper with caster sugar.

Pour uncooked génoise sponge mixture into prepared tray and bake for 15–18 minutes or until the top of the sponge springs back when lightly touched. Turn out onto the greaseproof paper and remove the baking paper (parchment).

Trim the crusty edges of the sponge with a knife. Cover the sponge with another sheet of greaseproof paper and position with a long side nearest you.

Grasp the furthest ends of the tea towel and carefully roll the sponge around the top sheet of paper. Cool.

When sponge is cold, unroll and remove the paper and spread the sponge with half the buttercream. Roll up the sponge again and refrigerate for 30 minutes.

Using a sharp knife, cut a 5 cm (2 in) slice off the end of the log and, using a little buttercream, attach it to the log to resemble a broken branch. Roll the marzipan thinly.

Cut 3 discs the same diameter as the log. With melted chocolate, pipe growth rings onto each disc and leave to dry. Using a little buttercream, attach discs to the ends of the log and the broken branch. Pipe the remaining buttercream onto the log, using a star nozzle to make the bark texture.

Decorate with marzipan holly and berries.

See page 40

BUCHTELN
(see also Chelsea bun)

These famed Austrian jam (jelly) sweet buns are similar to the English Chelsea bun, but contain only jam.

60 g (2 oz) fresh compressed yeast
1 teaspoon sugar
¼ cup (2 fl oz) milk
4 cups (16 oz) plain (all-purpose) flour, sifted
¼ cup (2 oz) sugar
¼ teaspoon salt
1 teaspoon ground cinnamon
1 cup (8 fl oz) milk, warmed
125 g (4 oz) unsalted (sweet) butter, melted
2 eggs
zest and juice of 1 lemon
¾ cup (8 oz) apricot jam (jelly), sieved and warmed
210g (7 oz) unsalted (sweet) butter, melted (extra)

Preheat oven to 180°C (350°F).

Place yeast, the first amount of sugar and milk together in a bowl and whisk lightly to dissolve the yeast. Allow to sit in a warm place for 10–15 minutes or until double in size and frothy. In a large bowl, place sifted flour, sugar, salt and cinnamon and, with your fingers, mix lightly. Make a well in the flour mix and pour in the milk, butter, eggs, the yeast mixture and lemon juice and zest. Work mixture into a dough and then remove from the bowl and knead the dough on a bench (counter) top for 5–8 minutes or until smooth and elastic. Cover the dough in a bowl and place in a warm area for 30–35 minutes or until double in bulk.

Remove dough to a lightly floured surface and knead lightly to remove all of the air. Roll dough into a rectangular shape approximately 15 x 30 cm (6 x 12 in), about 3–4 mm (⅙ in) thick. Spread dough with the warmed and sieved jam, then, beginning with the long side furthest from you, roll the dough like a Swiss roll toward you, forming the rolls tightly as you do so. Cut the long roll at every 3 cm (1¼ in).

Dip each of the cut rolls halfway into the butter and place them, cut side uppermost, in a lightly buttered pie dish, leaving 1–2 cm (½ –1 in) between them. Place dough in a warm area for 20–30 minutes, or until double in bulk, and then bake in the preheated oven for 30–35 minutes or until golden brown.

Serve warm or cold with butter.

BUCKWHEAT
(see also flour)

A member of the grain or wheat family, buckwheat is really the fruit of a herbaceous plant.

The ancient Greeks used buckwheat to make dessert fritters, flavouring and sweetening them with natural honey. Buckwheat is most noted, though, for its use in blini, or buckwheat pancakes, in Russia. When used as a ground flour, buckwheat can also be made into pastas, breads, biscuits (cookies), cakes and pastries. As a grain, it can be made into a porridge or eaten on its own, steamed.

Buche de Noël Step-by-Step

Step 1: Place the chocolate-decorated marzipan discs on the ends of the log.

Step 2: Using a star nozzle, pipe bark texture onto the cake, piping only in one direction.

Step 3: When the cake is covered with buttercream, decorate with marzipan holly and berries. See page 39.

BUGNE
(see also fritter)

Bugnes are large fritters, traditionally eaten on Shrove Tuesday and other festive occasions. They are produced from a batter of flour, sugar, eggs and butter and are served hot with a rich vanilla crème anglaise or hot treacle, or simply dusted in icing (powdered) sugar and eaten on their own.

4 cups (16 oz) plain (all purpose) flour, sifted
½ teaspoon ground cinnamon
125 g (4 oz) unsalted butter, softened
¼ cup (2 oz) sugar
4 eggs, beaten
¼ cup (2 fl oz) orange juice
icing (powdered) sugar, for dusting

Sift flour and cinnamon into a large mixing bowl and make a well in the centre. Add butter and sugar and mix into the flour with the fingertips. Add lightly beaten eggs and the orange juice, and knead the mixture to a firm dough. Knead for a further 3–5 minutes. Wrap the dough with plastic wrap (cling film) and rest it in the refrigerator for 3–4 hours, or overnight.
Preheat a deep fryer or saucepan of oil to 180°C (350°F). On a very lightly floured surface, roll the mixture to a thickness of 3–4 mm (¼ inch). Cut the rolled dough into strips 4 cm (1½ in) wide, and cut each of them to 10 cm (4 in) in length. Leaving 1 cm (½ in) from each end, cut a slit down the centre of each strip. Thread one end of each strip through the central slit and pull slightly to make a type of knot. Place the bugnes into the frying oil one at a time and cook till golden brown on both sides. Remove from the oil and allow to drain on absorbent paper, then dust with icing (powdered) sugar or cover the bugne with vanilla sugar or cinnamon sugar and eat immediately.

BUN
(see also bread, Chelsea bun, fruit bun)

Made from a yeasted dough similar to bread, bun doughs contain a higher percentage of sugar and fat than normal bread. The term bun is given to the sweeter doughs, while small rounded plain bread is referred to as bread rolls or simply dinner or lunch rolls.
Buns often contain spices and dried fruits and the majority are either iced with fondant or washed with a sweet bun wash or sugar syrup. Some buns are even cut and filled with jam and cream, while others are famous for their name alone, such as Bath buns, or for their finished decoration, such as Hot Cross buns. Bun doughs are occasionally rolled flat and filled with sugar, butter and fruits and then rolled like a Swiss roll or roulade and cut and arranged to create specialties such as Chelsea buns.

BUN WASH

A liquid glaze of sugar syrup that may or may not contain a small amount of gelatine for extra shine and gloss and is brushed over hot sweet buns on removal from the oven.

1¼ cups (10 oz) sugar
⅔ cup (5 fl oz) water
1 teaspoon gelatine powder

Place all three ingredients in a saucepan and slowly bring to the boil. Allow to boil for 3–4 minutes and then remove from the heat. While syrup is hot, brush it over the top of the hot buns as they are removed from the oven to give a high gloss finish to the products. Allow buns to cool before serving.

BURANELLI

These tie- or knot-shaped deep-fried pastries are also known as Cenci alla Fiorentina, crullers or klenater, as well as many other names. The only difference is in how they are served and whether they are rolled in caster (superfine) sugar, cinnamon sugar, or icing (powdered) sugar, or served hot with a sauce.

180 g (6 oz) unsalted (sweet) butter, softened
1½ cups (12 oz) sugar
zest and juice of 1 orange
7 eggs yolks
5 cups (20 oz) plain (all-purpose) flour
1 teaspoon ground cinnamon

Preheat oven to 175°C (345°F).
Line a baking sheet with baking paper (parchment). Place butter, sugar, orange zest and juice in a large mixing bowl and cream until light and fluffy. Add egg yolks slowly to the creamed mixture and continue mixing until all are well combined. Add sifted flour and cinnamon to the butter and mix until well combined. Take large tablespoonfuls of the finished mixture between lightly floured hands and roll long sausage shapes. Place on the prepared sheet and shape each sausage shape into an S shape. Bake for 15–20 minutes or until golden brown.

BUTTER
(see also buttercream, margarine)

One of the most used ingredients in pastry, butter has a low melting point and is invaluable for the manufacture of cakes, biscuits (cookies), buttercreams and truffle fillings, giving the pastry products a distinct flavour, richness and light texture.
A substance obtained from churning fresh cream, it is believed that butter was first made by mistake by nomads who had collected the milk from their goats and cattle, separated the cream from the milk and somehow churned the cream or constantly mixed the cream until it became butter.
Being more scientific, cream is made up of many fat particles suspended in water and when churned or mixed, these fat globules link together and produce butter. The other product produced along with butter is buttermilk, the liquid left when the cream has turned to butter. Most ordinary butters are made up of 80% milk fat, around 16% water, 3% salt and 2% non-milk solids.

Butter plays an important part in the production of cakes and pastries and plays many roles in producing the cake batter. As well as imparting its richness and flavour, butter also assists in the following ways:

(a) By softening the cake structure, the butter makes cakes tender and light to taste.
(b) Aeration is an important factor for the lightness of cakes and butter allows the cake mixture to increase in volume by influencing the amount of air beaten into the cake batter.

In today's kitchens there are three major types of butter available:

(i) Unsalted (sweet) butter: Used in recipes where the flavour of butter is wanted without a salty aftertaste, usually sweet recipes such as buttercreams and truffles. If salt is required for recipes using unsalted (sweet) butter, the salt should be added at the discretion of the pastry chef.
(ii) Salted butter: Used in the production of large cakes and pastries where the major flavour is not that of the butter and where the salt content will not overpower but instead will simply harmonise with the other flavours present. Salt added to butter also prolongs the life of the butter.
(iii) Clarified butter: Known as ghee, which is its Indian name and in which cuisine it is most used. Clarified butter is simply butter which has had the water and non-fat milk solids removed. This is easily done by hand: Chop the salted or unsalted (sweet) butter into small pieces and melt it slowly in a large saucepan. On the top of the melted butter a froth should form. Using a ladle, scoop away this scum. Into a fresh bowl, ladle the pure yellow liquid which remains, without including the white, milky liquid which should have settled to the base of the saucepan. The pure yellow liquid is the clarified butter. Clarified butter can also be bought in containers in some countries and in large industrial-sized drums in others.

BUTTERCAKE

Good-tasting buttercakes can be served plain for morning teas, sliced and dressed with jam (jelly) and whipped cream for high tea, or lightly toasted and topped with maple syrup for brunch or supper. This rich cake keeps well and is ideal for cake decorators who want to avoid the expense of using solid fruit cakes.

2½ cups (10 oz) plain (all-purpose) flour
1 level teaspoon baking powder (soda)
180 g (6 oz) unsalted (sweet) butter
1 cup (7 oz) caster (superfine) sugar
3 eggs
1 cup (8 fl oz) milk
icing (powdered) sugar, for dusting

Preheat oven to 180°C (350°F).
Lightly grease a 23 cm (9 in) springform cake tin with butter and line base with baking paper (parchment).
Sift flour and baking powder. Beat butter and sugar until creamy, light and fluffy. Add eggs one at a time, beating very well after each one is added. Mix in sifted dry ingredients alternately with the milk. Pour mixture into the prepared tin. Bake for 1–1½ hours or until a skewer inserted in the centre of the cake comes out dry. Cool in the tin for 5 minutes then turn out onto a cake rack. When cold, dust with icing sugar.

BUTTERCREAM
(see also butter)

Buttercream is produced by creaming butter and incorporating as much air as possible. When the butter has changed from yellow to a creamy white colour, sweeteners and other ingredients are added for flavour and bulk. There are many varieties of buttercream used in the pastry kitchen, and these differ according to personal, regional and national tastes, and availability of certain products. Most buttercreams contain sugar, icing sugar or fondant and either egg yolks, egg whites or the entire egg, and can be flavoured as desired. Buttercreams range from the very quick to those with more complicated methods, and from the very light and airy to those which are rich and heavy in flavour and texture.

It is best to use buttercream as soon as it is made, when it is light, airy and fresh. Never make more buttercream than is required just to save time on the next cake. It is quicker to make it fresh than to reconstitute chilled buttercream and better results are obtained for the finished product. If buttercream has to be stored, it should be kept in an airtight container in the refrigerator. Never store buttercream for more than two weeks in the refrigerator. Remove from the refrigerator when required and stand at room temperature for one hour to soften. Beat in a mixing bowl until light and fluffy.

The following are the main ingredients contained in the buttercreams produced by different countries:

FRENCH BUTTERCREAM: butter, fondant and eggs;
GERMAN BUTTERCREAM: butter, custard and flavouring;
ITALIAN BUTTERCREAM: butter, Italian meringue and flavouring;
RUSSIAN BUTTERCREAM: butter, icing sugar and flavouring;
DANISH BUTTERCREAM: butter, icing sugar and cream.

Each of the recipes for buttercream that follow makes enough to decorate a single cake.

FRENCH BUTTERCREAM
(A heavier, richer style of buttercream)
450 g (14 oz) unsalted (sweet) butter
160 g (5 oz) soft fondant (see page 118)
2 eggs

Place butter and fondant in a mixing bowl and beat until white, fluffy and smooth. Add eggs, one at a time, beating very well after each one is added.

CHOCOLATE FRENCH BUTTERCREAM
For a chocolate variety of French buttercream, melt 100 g (3½ oz) dark (plain or semi-sweet) chocolate and add it to the buttercream before adding the eggs. Ensure that the chocolate is only warm before adding it to the mixture or loss of aeration will occur from melting of the butter.

QUICK NO-FUSS BUTTERCREAM

400 g (13 oz) unsalted (sweet) butter
1 cup (5 oz) icing (powdered) sugar
3 eggs
2 teaspoons vanilla essence (extract)

Beat butter and icing sugar together until blended and add eggs, one at a time, beating very well after each one is added. Add vanilla essence to the mixture and beat on medium speed for 20 minutes until mixture is light and creamy.

CHOCOLATE NO-FUSS BUTTERCREAM

As with Quick No-fuss Buttercream, but when butter, icing sugar, eggs and vanilla have been mixed together, add 100 g (3½ oz) melted dark (plain or semi-sweet) chocolate to the mixture and allow to mix through before beating the buttercream for 20 minutes on medium speed.

ORANGE NO-FUSS BUTTERCREAM

As with Quick No-fuss Buttercream, but when butter and icing sugar are placed in the mixing bowl, add zest of 2 oranges, and ¼ cup (2 fl oz) of orange juice. Let these mix together for 5 minutes on a medium speed before adding the eggs and 1 teaspoon of vanilla essence. When all ingredients are incorporated, beat on medium speed for 20 minutes.

LEMON NO-FUSS BUTTERCREAM

As with Quick No-fuss Buttercream. Depending on personal taste, this recipe can be made tarter, by adding more lemon juice. This recipe gives just a nice hint of lemon. When icing sugar and butter are placed in the mixing bowl, add zest of 2 lemons and 2 tablespoons of lemon juice. Allow mixture to beat together for 5 minutes on medium speed before adding the eggs and 1 teaspoon of vanilla essence. Allow buttercream to beat for a further 20 minutes on medium speed before using.

GERMAN BUTTERCREAM

(A light, sweet buttercream)
300 g (10 oz) unsalted (sweet) butter
⅓ cup (2 oz) icing (powdered) sugar
¾ cup (6 fl oz) milk
¼ cup (2 oz) caster (superfine) sugar
¼ cup (2 fl oz) milk, extra
3 tablespoons custard powder
2 eggs
5 teaspoons caster sugar (extra)

Beat butter and icing sugar until light, fluffy and pale yellow. Place milk and caster sugar in a saucepan and bring to the boil. Blend the extra milk with custard powder and eggs and pour the hot milk over this mixture, whisking all the time. Return mixture to the saucepan and cook over medium heat until thickened, and just on the boil. Place custard in a shallow dish and sprinkle with the extra caster sugar to prevent a skin forming. Chill quickly. When custard is cool, beat it into the creamed butter and icing sugar mixture, a spoonful at a time. Beat for a further 10 minutes before using.

CHOCOLATE GERMAN BUTTERCREAM

For a chocolate variety of German buttercream, add 125 g (4 oz) melted dark (plain or semi-sweet) chocolate to the hot custard mixture before chilling. Continue as for plain German buttercream.

ITALIAN BUTTERCREAM

(A very light, sweet buttercream)

1¼ cups (8 oz) caster (superfine) sugar
100 ml (3½ fl oz) water
8 egg whites
400 g (13 oz) unsalted (sweet) butter

Place sugar and water in a saucepan and bring to the boil. Continue to boil, cooking the sugar until it reaches 115°C (240°F) on a sugar (candy) thermometer. Whisk egg whites until soft peaks form and beat in hot sugar syrup, a little at a time. When all sugar syrup has been added, continue to beat the mixture until it is quite cool. Beat butter until it is light and creamy, then fold it into the egg white mixture.

Note: Due to the lightness of this buttercream it is best used when made. It does not store well and will not reconstitute into a light buttercream.

BUTTERFLY CAKE
(see also queen cake)

A small patty cake or queen cake is used to produce these delicate tea-time favourites, which originated in England. The top of the small cake is cut out with a small sharp knife so that a cone shape is removed. Into the recess is piped a small amount of fresh cream. The removed cone shape is cut in half and inserted into the cream to represent the wings of a butterfly.

BUTTERMILK
(see also milk)

This is the liquid that remains after cream is turned to butter. Used for its rich flavour in cakes, pancakes, scones (biscuits) and biscuits (cookies), buttermilk is also a delicious drink. In some countries buttermilk is now manufactured, by adding a bacterial culture to skim milk. This thickens the milk and gives it the rich tangy traditional flavour of buttermilk.

BUTTER PUFF PASTRY
(see also puff pastry, rough puff pastry)

When making this pastry, keep the bench well floured and cool at all times. If the butter becomes very soft and hard to work, simply place the dough in the refrigerator for 30–40 minutes to allow it to chill and become firm.

2½ cups (10 oz) plain (all-purpose) flour
¾ cup (6 fl oz) cold water
500 g (16 oz) unsalted (sweet) butter
1¼ cups (5 oz) plain (all-purpose) flour

Place flour and water in the mixer and form a dough. Remove dough from the mixer, wrap in plastic wrap (cling film) and refrigerate for 30 minutes. Place butter and flour in a mixing

Butterscotch

bowl and bring both to a dough by hand. Stop mixing when they are combined. Do not cream the butter or aerate the mixture at all. Wrap butter mixture and chill for 30 minutes. On a cool and lightly floured surface, roll both doughs out to the same size, approximately 40 x 20 cm (16 x 8 in). With the butter layer on the bench surface, lay the dough layer on top. Mark the dough into three sections and fold one of these over the other, then fold the other end to cover the first two (this is called a threefold). Place this on a clean cool tray in the refrigerator to chill and rest for 15 minutes.

Remove dough to a cool lightly floured surface and with the open ends of the dough facing vertically towards and away from you, roll dough so that it is three times its original length. Do not roll across the closed sides as this ruins the puff of the pastry. Mark the pastry into halves and then into halves again. Fold both ends in towards the centre and then fold one side over the other. (This is called a fourfold or bookfold.) Place the dough ino the refrigerator for a further 30 minutes to chill and then repeat the last two folds again, first the threefold and then the bookfold.

Once this is done the dough is ready to chill for 40 minutes before rolling to 2–3 mm (⅛ in) thickness and using for whatever puff pastry product you wish to make.

BUTTERSCOTCH
(see also confectionery)

A toffee confectionery which originated in Scotland in the 1700s, possibly by mistake, when an apprentice is said to have dropped the butter he held in one hand into the caramel he had removed from the stove for his master. Instead of throwing the mixture away, he quickly stirred to see if his master would notice the difference. The more he stirred the more intense became the colour and aroma of the caramel, so he poured it onto a tray and allowed it to harden.

Butterscotch is made by boiling water, glucose and sugar together until brown and then stirring butter into the caramel. As well as the toffee confectionery, butterscotch sauce is a delicious favourite for rich puddings, ice cream and waffles, puddings and cakes.

½ cup (4 fl oz) water
3 cups (24 oz) sugar
¾ cup (9 oz) liquid glucose (corn syrup)
180 g (6 oz) unsalted (sweet) butter

Grease an 18 x 28 x 2 cm (7 x 11 x ¾ in) baking tray (jelly roll pan).

Combine water, sugar and glucose in a large saucepan and stir over low heat until sugar has dissolved. While mixture is boiling, brush down the sides of the saucepan with a pastry brush dipped in warm water. This should clean any splashes or granules of sugar. When mixture has come to the boil, place a sugar (candy) thermometer in the pan and allow the mixture to boil to 150°C (302°F). When it has reached this temperature, the mixture should be a pale amber colour. Remove pan from the heat and allow the bubbles to subside before adding the butter. Stir butter into the mixture with a long-handled wooden spoon, taking care not to splash yourself with the hot mixture. Continue to stir until butter is combined. Pour the stirred mixture into the prepared tray and cool slightly before scoring the top with a lightly oiled knife. Once cold, break the butterscotch into the marked pieces.

Makes 48

BUTTERSCOTCH SAUCE

1½ cups (12 oz) sugar
180 g (6 oz) unsalted (sweet) butter
2¼ cups (18 fl oz) cream

Place half the sugar in a hot saucepan. Stir over high heat until caramel is formed. In another saucepan, place the second half of the sugar and the butter. Add cream and bring this to the boil. While stirring, add the caramel to the cream mixture.

Cool and serve with puddings and ice creams.

CABINET PUDDING
(see also puddings)

An English translation of the French Diplomate Pudding, this is a baked or steamed, even frozen, dessert of breadcrumbs, egg and dried fruits.

The original recipe from the early 18th century contains dried bread scraps, currants, egg and lemon rind. Today, however, any dried fruits are used and the bread scraps can be bread or sponge crumbs. Either way, this is a rich dessert, which can be served hot or cold.

2 cups (16 fl oz) single cream
4 eggs
½ cup (4 oz) sugar
zest of 2 lemons
1⅔ cups (8 oz) currants
4 cups (8 oz) fresh breadcrumbs or 1 cm (½ in) cubes
of sponge cake

In a large bowl, mix cream, eggs, sugar and lemon zest together and whisk till all are incorporated and the sugar dissolved. Allow to rest for 30 minutes.
Preheat oven to 150°C (300°F).
Spread currants over the base of a large pudding basin or individual ramekins. Spread breadcrumbs or sponge cubes over the currants. Pour liquid egg/cream mixture over the sponge/breadcrumbs and allow to rest for 5 minutes, so the mixture can soak in. Place pudding bowl or ramekins in a baking tin half filled with warm water. Place in oven and bake for 35–40 minutes or until a knife inserted into the centre of the dish/es does not reveal any liquid custard.
Serve in their dishes or unmould and serve hot or cold.

CACHOUS

Very hard tiny silver balls, made from sugar candy, which are used in cake decorating. Cachous are available in most cake decorating stores. While edible, they should be used sparingly on cakes due to their hard nature.

CAFE LIEGEOIS
(see also sundae)

This dessert originates from a coffee drink which was originally called Café Viennois. The name was changed to Liègeois at the begininning of World War II because it sounded German, and by the end of the war a dessert had been invented in Belgium (although some say it was invented earlier than this) with almost the same ingredients as the American-style iced coffee. The Belgian dessert is a coffee-flavoured ice cream whipped with cold strong black coffee and served with crème Chantilly and chopped nuts.

CAKE
(see also gâteau, torte, layer cake)

A true cake should be finished on removal from the oven or require only a dusting of icing (powdered) sugar or a basic icing to cover it. In modern kitchens the word 'cake' tends to refer to almost all sweet baked items, including tortes and gâteaux. Produced with or without any fat, a cake can also be in loaf or round shape but is rarely layered, and even then only one layer is allowed for a true cake.

Cakes can be produced using several different methods: creaming butter and sugar; whisking yolks and whites; flour batters; the egg and sugar method; or by rubbing fat into flour. The basic ingredients, though, are much the same, most cakes being a mixture, in differing amounts, of flour, baking powder (soda), eggs, sugar and butter. Cakes are not meant to be highly decorated — this is left to gâteaux and tortes — and should stand on their taste alone.

The methods used for making cakes are explained below.

Sugar Egg Method
Used to produce sponges or sponge sheets, and Swiss rolls, the recipe consists of virtually equal quantities of three ingredients — sugar, eggs and flour — with some recipes calling for the addition of melted fat or butter. The eggs and sugar are whisked to a very stiff foam or sabayon and the sifted flour and melted butter is then lightly folded through so as not to collapse the aerated foam.

Egg Yolk/Egg White Method
Some of the lightest cakes are made in this manner, which requires no baking agent such as baking powder (soda) at all and is more stable than the usual sugar/egg mixture. The egg yolks are whisked in one bowl with sugar until they reach a stiff and light sabayon, while in another bowl the whites and sugar are whisked to produce a light stiff foam. Flavourings, nuts, fruit purées and grated vegetables are then folded through the egg yolk mixture, followed by the egg whites, which give it lightness. Savoy cakes and many sponge bases, such as that for Dobos Torte, are made using this method.

Flour Batter Method
This old method is not often used today as it takes time and care. It involves whipping the fat and flour together to make a smooth creamed mixture, then whipping the eggs and sugar together separately to form a stiff sabayon. The milk or liquid content is also kept separate. Then the egg mixture is slowly incorporated into the flour/fat, then the liquid is slowly added. Any other dry ingredients and the raising agent are added after the milk. Then the cake is baked.

TRADITIONAL CAKES

Name	Base	Finish
Carrot Cake	cinnamon-flavoured; baking powder (soda) or egg white risen cake with grated fresh carrot	cream cheese frosting and marzipan carrots
Banana Cake	creamed butter and sugar cake with walnuts and fresh bananas	cream cheese frosting with marzipan bananas
Fruit Cake	butter and sugar creamed cake with higher proportion of dried fruits than base mixture; highly spiced	tea: none; weddings, Christmas or christenings: decorated with royal icing
Dundee Cake	similar base to fruit cake	top is decorated with a pattern of whole blanched almonds
Simnel Cake	similar base to fruit/Dundee cake, but with layer of marzipan in centre	decorated with a thick layer of marzipan, the name written in chocolate and small Easter eggs
Hummingbird Cake	oil and fresh fruit add the moisture to this basic cake	cream cheese frosting and fresh mango
Angel Food Cake	egg whites with flour/cornstarch and no fat	vanilla frosting
Devil's Food Cake	rich chocolate cake from butter/sugar method	chocolate frosting
Shortcake	butter/sugar creamed heavy cake mixture, either spread into tin or dropped in spoonfuls onto baking sheet	icing (powdered) sugar dusted, if individual, and filled with fresh fruit and cream; large shortcakes can be split in half and decorated with frosting or buttercream
Tea Cake	butter/sugar creamed method; plain cake with little flavour on its own; very buttery	top is heavily dusted or coated in a mixture of cinnamon, sugar and coconut; eaten warm or spread with butter in slices.
Madeira Cake	creamed butter and sugar, lemon-flavoured cake	dusted with icing sugar
Sponge Cake	whisked sugar/egg method with flour folded through lightly; some contain butter, others do not	if served for morning/afternoon tea, sponges are usually split and filled with fresh jam (jelly) and cream and dusted lightly with icing sugar
Upside Down Cake	usually very moist cake base from butter/sugar method; the cake mixture is poured into tin over the top of fruit which has been placed on base	turned upside down after baking to reveal a base of baked fruit, it is glazed with apricot jam (jelly) and served in slices or as a dessert (in larger portions)

Five-Minute Method

Becaue it uses a light (soft or cake) flour, this method works only for certain recipes.

Basically, the butter and sugar are mixed together, but not creamed, with the eggs. To this mixture is added any other liquid and most of the flour. The mixture is then whipped or creamed for around 5 minutes in the mixer, then the remaining flour and raising agents are added.

The All-In Method

Traditionally, only heavy recipes, such as gingerbreads and honey cakes, were made using this method. However, other much lighter cakes can also be produced in this fashion, muffin cake mixtures being amongst them. All ingredients are placed in the bowl at once and stirred or blended lightly, then poured into a container and baked.

Egg/Flour Method

Not many cakes come into this category, but the famed Othellos are among them. The egg yolks and flour are whipped together until there is no gluten left in the flour; sometimes a little water is needed to assist. This whipping can take 5–10 minutes in a mixer. The egg whites are then whipped up and folded through the first mixture.

CAKE FLOUR
(see also flour)

This is the American name for soft flour, a lighter style and lower-gluten content flour which keeps cake mixtures light rather than tough and strong. Used for almost all cakes when it is available or simply for those recipes which are meant to be super light, such as pancakes, waffles and similar products.

CAKE FORK

Small decorative forks used specifically for eating cake. An old tradition, they are still used in those establishments offering traditional morning or afternoon teas.

CAKE HOOP
(see also cake tin)

A metal or aluminium ring without a base, which holds cake mixture if placed flat on a baking sheet.

CAKE RACK

Also known as a cake cooler, cake wire, cooling wire, wire rack or just a wire, it is an oblong, round or square wire frame which is latticed with fine but strong wire. The entire frame is raised several centimetres (¼–1 inch) from the bench surface by small stands or legs placed in each corner. A cake rack allows cool air to circulate around a hot cake, fresh from the oven, so that it cools evenly and does not sweat as a result of sitting directly on a flat surface or in its tin.

Wire racks are also used in savoury cooking as roasting trays so the meats do not cook in their own fat.

CAKE TIN
(see also cake hoop)

Traditionally made of tin, although now usually made of aluminium, these are fixed-base containers 5–10 cm (2–4 in) in depth and of varying diameters. They can be small, large or minute, and round, square, rectangular, hexagonal, teardrop or heart-shaped. They are also manufactured in novelty designs, and can be plain, fluted or ribbed. Basically, they are any containers used for baking cake mixtures. Produced from any number of metals, they are now available in non-stick surfaces.

Round cake tins are also available in springform style, which consists of a cake hoop with an attached clip, into which is inserted a cake base. Once the cake is baked, the hoop can be opened out so that the cake can be slipped out without damage.

Smaller cakes can be made from moulded tins that have separate moulds for each small cake; these include patty tins, cupcake and muffin pans or trays.

CANDIED FRUITS
(see fruit)

CANDIED PEEL
(see citrus peel)

CANDY FLOSS
(see cotton candy)

CANDY SUGAR
(see also sugar)

CANE SUGAR
(see also sugar)

Cane sugar is the sucrose produced from natural sugar cane.

Large sugar crystals are manufactured by allowing a concentrated sugar syrup to cool slowly so that it will crystallise around fine threads which have been inserted into the syrup. Candy sugar can be either white or brown and is used in preference to normal sugar when making preserved and bottled fruits and in liqueurs, as it dissolves slowly and allows time for the fruit flavours to be infused.

Made from either cane or beet sugar, this candying sugar is first mentioned in 12th century writings as a healing medicine flavoured with rose and citrus oils.

CANNELER

Also referred to as a cannelle knife, this is a small V-shaped piece of metal attached to the end of a handle. It is dragged down the sides of fruits and vegetables to make large strips, or so that when fruit is sliced it shows a decorative fluting effect.

CANNELONS
(see also puff pastry)

Traditionally made of puff pastry, cannelons use the same principle as cream horns except that the puff pastry is wrapped around a cylinder rather than a cone shape before baking, so that it comes out hollow and in a cigarette shape. It is then filled from either end with one of two mousse or ice cream-style fillings and dusted in icing (powdered) sugar before being served.

CANNOLI

1 cup (4 oz) plain (all-purpose) flour
6 teaspoons sugar
⅛ teaspoon salt
1 egg yolk
30 g (1 oz) unsalted (sweet) butter
2 teaspoons dark or light rum
8 tablespoons milk
a little egg white
oil, for deep frying

Filling
1⅔ cups (8 oz) cream cheese
6 teaspoons sugar
1 egg yolk
2 tablespoons mixed (candied) peel
2 tablespoons chopped glacé (candied) cherries
icing (powdered) sugar, for dusting

Sift flour into a large bowl and mix well with sugar and salt, egg yolks and butter. Add rum and milk and knead the mixture to a smooth, elastic soft dough. Allow dough to rest, covered, for 30–40 minutes and then cut into 10–12 equal portions. On a very lightly floured surface, roll each piece into a disc of 10 cm (4 in) diameter.
Wrap each around a metal cylinder or cream horn mould and brush egg white where they meet so that they stick.
Place each cannoli in the oil at 180°C (350°F) and deep fry till golden brown, and then slip each off its mould and remove to a plate or tray of absorbent paper.

Filling
Beat cream cheese with sugar and egg yolk until creamy. Add mixed peel and glacé cherries and fill each cannoli with a little of the mixture. Dust heavily with icing sugar and serve.

CANNOLLE

During the One Hundred Years War, the town of Rochechouart, France, was under siege for months. In late 1371 it achieved freedom at the hand of General du Guesclin. In the joyousness of the occasion and in retaliation for the siege, the townsfolk raided the English camp, where they found fresh butter, wheat, sugar and eggs. The town pastrycooks decided to make an honorary dish in celebration of the day and produced these dry biscuits (cookies) which they named after the English leader who had been defeated, Sir Robert Cannolles.

CANTALOUPE
(see rockmelon, melon)

CAPE GOOSEBERRY

Cape gooseberries are most commonly known as physallis, which is their true botanical name, but also as yellow ground cherry, tomatillo or golden berry. They are small, yellow, ball-shaped tart gooseberries that grow inside a fine papery husk. Until opened, the husk makes them look as if they are enclosed in a Chinese paper lantern, and indeed China may be where the fruit originated as for centuries it has been depicted there in paintings as a floral tree with a berry. Their common kitchen name of Cape gooseberry comes from the fact that since the late 1800s they have been extensively cultivated in the Cape of Good Hope in South Africa. Once removed from their husks, the berries can be made into sauces, sorbets, jams (conserves), ice creams and, if left in the opened husk, which is then held above the fruit, they can be coated in fondant, chocolate or sugar-glazed as petits fours.

CARAC

Traditionally made as a small tartlet or as a slice (bar), carac consists of a sweet pastry base on top of which is placed a rich chocolate filling topped with green fondant. Each tartlet or slice has a chocolate dot in the centre, which simply signifies that it is a carac.

> 3½ cups (14 oz) plain (all-purpose) flour, sifted
> 1¼ cups (7 oz) icing (powdered) sugar, sifted
> 270 g (9 oz) unsalted (sweet) butter
> 1 egg
>
> **Ganache Filling**
> 1 cup (10 fl oz) cream (single, light)
> 30 g (1 oz) unsalted (sweet) butter
> 300 g (10 oz) dark (plain or semi-sweet) chocolate,
> melted (see page 62)
>
> **Icing Glaze**
> 1 cup (6 oz) icing (powdered) sugar, sifted
> 2 tablespoons milk
> 1–2 drops green food colouring
> dark (plain or semi-sweet) chocolate, melted

Place sifted flour and icing sugar in a bowl and, using your fingertips, lightly rub the butter through the dry ingredients until the mixture resembles fresh breadcrumbs. Add egg and continue mixing to a soft dough. Wrap dough in plastic wrap (cling film) and refrigerate for 1 hour.
Preheat oven to 200°C (400°F). Lightly grease baking sheets. On a lightly floured surface, roll dough out to 3–4 mm (⅛ in) in thickness and cut two rounds for each carac with a 5 cm (2 in) plain round biscuit (cookie) cutter. Bake in preheated oven for 8–10 minutes, or until lightly browned on the edges. Cool on the sheet.

Ganache Filling
Place the cream in a small saucepan with the butter and bring to the boil. Add the melted chocolate to the boiled mixture and stir until a smooth, rich dark chocolate cream is formed. Place in the refrigerator to firm.

Icing Glaze
Place the sifted icing sugar in a bowl and mix in the milk to make a thin icing. Add one or two drops of green food colouring to give a subtle colour.

To Assemble
Divide the baked rounds into two even piles; half will form the base of the carac, half the top. Take the tops and dip each one into the green icing. Allow to set. Take the ganache from the refrigerator when firm and place in a piping (pastry) bag fitted with a plain 5 mm (⅕ in) nozzle. Pipe a small amount of ganache onto the bases. Press the tops and bottoms together. To finish, pipe a small dot of melted chocolate into the centre of each top.

Makes 12–18

CARAMBOLA

This attractive green star-shaped fruit has a soft (but waxy) smooth skin covering a watery flesh and is ripe when it turns yellow, otherwise being quite tart and acidic despite its sweet aromatic flavour. The fruit has five prominent angles, which, when cut, make up the star shape which gives the fruit its other name (star fruit). It is used mainly as a garnish or as one fruit in a complex fresh fruit flan.

CARAMEL
(see also black jack, praline, sugar)

Caramel is brown sugar liquid, manufactured in either of two ways, and is used as a flavouring, an ingredient and as decoration by the pastry chef. Caramel also forms the basis of many other methods and styles of preparation within the

Caramel threads (see page 50)

pastry kitchen, being the base for praline or croquant, cake decorations and spun sugar, for example. It can be made by two methods: the 'dry' method, which involves heating sugar until it reaches melting point, at which temperature it will also begin to brown, or the 'wet' method, which is to add water to the sugar and boil the liquid until it reaches above 154–6°C (310–13°F), at which point dehydration causes the sugar to turn brown.

2½ cups (17 oz) caster (superfine) sugar
100 ml (3½ fl oz) water
2 level teaspoons liquid glucose (corn syrup)

Grease a marble slab or stainless steel tray
very lightly with butter.
Place all ingredients in a saucepan and bring to the boil.
As mixture boils, wash down the sides of the saucepan with a
pastry brush dipped in fresh clean water. Do not stir at any
time. Cook until the syrup turns a golden brown. Remove
from the heat immediately and dip the base of the saucepan
in cold water for 4 seconds to stop any more cooking.
Pour onto the prepared surface and cool. Break into small
pieces or crush finely. Store in an airtight container.

There are four different types of caramel:

(i) Pale caramel: Almost clear, or very lightly coloured, this caramel is used for spinning angel hair and for plate decorations. It is also used to coat fruits, choux pastries and for Italian meringue. It is made only in small amounts, as reheating any excess will colour the caramel.

(ii) Medium caramel: Light brown to golden in colour, this is used to make praline decorations and for a small amount of spun sugar. Allowed to cool and then mixed with extra water or cream, it is used as a flavouring and sauce for puddings and ice creams.

(iii) Brown caramel: A deep brown colour, this is occasionally used for decorations and to bind nuts for petits fours, although at this colour and temperature it begins to take on a distinct flavour as well.

(iv) Black caramel: Also known as Black Jack, this caramel is allowed to go beyond brown and burn. Mixed with extra water, it is made into a thick black syrup which is used lightly to colour fruit cakes, plum puddings and gingerbreads.

CARAMEL CAGES

Caramel cages are a quick and relatively easy decoration to use over the top of individual desserts or entire dessert plates.

Once caramel has been made, slow the cooking process by dipping the saucepan into cool water for a few seconds. Dip a spoon into the caramel and stir lightly (without incorporating air) until the caramel is cool and thick enough to drip in a continuous ribbon from the spoon.

Have a ladle or bowl turned upside down and lightly oiled with olive oil. Moving fairly quickly, dribble the caramel from the spoon over the upturned mould in one direction, and then in the other direction, to crisscross the caramel. If more caramel is required, stir the spoon in the caramel again and then allow the caramel to continue drizzling around and

around the base to firm up the entire structure. When enough caramel is on the top and the sides and around the base, let it cool for several seconds and then carefully twist and remove the caramel cage from the upturned mould.

Place immediately over the dessert or plate and serve. Prolonged sitting while so fine will cause the caramel to quickly dissolve.

CARAMEL THREADS
(see also spun sugar)

To make caramel threads, allow a basic caramel to cool and thicken slightly.

Cover the prongs of a fork with caramel, then allow the caramel to drip in a fine, continuous stream and, using oiled fingers, pinch the bottom of the caramel stream and quickly pull away from the stream. Repeat until a collection of threads are held between the fingers. Drape these threads over the cake to be decorated before making more threads.

See page 49

CARAMELISATION

This occurs when fructose, maltose or dextrose is heated to or beyond 170°C (340°F), at which stage it becomes caramel and undergoes a distinct colour change, to a golden or amber brown. As distinct from making caramel, caramelisation refers to the process whereby products actually become brown. This process occurs in all products containing sugars that are heated, whether it be a loaf of bread, biscuits (cookies) or cakes. Caramelisation can also be achieved when sugar is sprinkled onto such items as crème brulée and glazed under a griller or salamander. This effect can also be achieved on biscuits or pastries where icing sugar or refined sugar is dusted or sprinkled onto the item and a hot poker or iron is set on top of this to brown or caramelise the sugars.

CARAMELISED NUTS

Also known as praline, which refers to not only caramel-covered almonds, but any type of nut. Used for decoration, flavourings and also as petits fours with coffee on their own, they are produced by simply heating a small amount of sugar in a copper bowl and tossing nuts into the molten sugar until they are covered, allowing them to cool and then crushing them or using them whole.

CARAQUE
(see also chocolate)

Caraque is the French name for fine curls of chocolate removed using a scraper when the chocolate is just on the verge of setting. They should be 8–10 cm (3–4 in) in length and quite fine; they are not considered to be caraque if they are thick or in short, stubby curls.

CARAWAY

A common European flavouring which is added to bread and cake doughs, and rye breads, for a distinct yet subtle flavour. The part of the caraway which is used is often referred to as a seed but is in fact the fruit of the caraway plant. It is also used for its flavour in certain confectionery items and in the manufacture of liqueurs.

For a delicate flavour to bread doughs or plain-flavoured buttercakes, simply add 1–2 teaspoons of caraway to the dough or cake batter before the final mixing.

CARDAMOM
(see also spices)

Originating in India, cardamom grows in a long yellow three-sided pod which contains several rows of the brown cardomom seeds. The pod has no flavour or value but the seeds are aromatic and, when dried, can be used whole or ground in cakes, pastries and savoury dishes.

Mentioned in writings as far back as seven centuries before Christ, cardamom is said to have grown in the gardens of the King of Babylon and is known to have begun its culinary journey when used for its aroma in perfumes and essences. These perfumes were then used as liquid ingredients to flavour cakes, although eventually the cardamom was used in a raw ground form by itself.

CARDAMOM COOKIES

180 g (6 oz) unsalted (sweet) butter, softened
⅔ cup (4 oz) firmly packed brown sugar
¼ cup (2 fl oz) cream
1½ cups (6 oz) plain (all-purpose) flour
½ teaspoon baking powder (soda)
½ teaspoon salt
2 teaspoons ground cardamom

Preheat oven to 180°C (350°F).
Line baking sheets with baking paper (parchment).
Place softened butter and brown sugar in a mixing bowl and cream until light and fluffy. Slowly add cream and mix until incorporated. Sift flour, baking powder, salt and cardamom together and mix with the butter mixture. Remove the dough and wrap in plastic wrap (cling film). Roll the dough into rolls and refrigerate for 1 hour or until firm.
Cut thin slices from the firm dough and place on the prepared sheets. Bake the cookies for 8–10 minutes in the preheated oven.

CARDINAL SAUCE

The name 'cardinal' is a name given to any dish which is naturally coloured red by means of such ingredients as raspberries, redcurrants or strawberries. It can be used to refer to cakes, biscuits (cookies), sauces, sorbets and ice creams.

300 g (10 oz) fresh raspberries
⅓ cup (2 oz) icing (powdered) sugar
1 tablespoon liquid glucose (corn syrup), warmed
juice of 1 orange

Purée raspberries in a blender. Add icing sugar, glucose and orange juice to the purée. Purée again and then allow the mixture to sit for 1–2 hours in the refrigerator.

Strain the sauce to remove the raspberry flesh, first through a fine sieve and then through muslin (cheesecloth). Refrigerate sauce for 12–24 hours before serving.

CAREME

'The Chef of Kings and the King of Chefs' is a description which will long be associated with Carême, considered the greatest of chefs not only for his innovations in cooking but also for his superb architectural mind, as far as centrepieces and decorations were concerned, and his writings and philosophy of cooking. Marie-Antoine Carême was born in Paris in 1784 to a very large and poor family and subsequently was put on the street at the age of ten and told to fend for himself. Fortunately, he was quickly taken in and housed by the owner of a lower-class restaurant.

In 1798, at fifteen years of age, Carême applied for a job at Bailly, at that time the leading confectionery house of Paris. He was accepted for the position and over the years that he worked there was given time to research and experiment. The owner of the pastry shop, Bailly, realised Carême's genius and assisted in every way possible to further his career and satisfy his thirst for knowledge. Carême, at this time, was also reading and studying drawings from architectural books. These would later become the basis for his centrepieces and magnificent displays.

Famed for his eye for detail, precise work, displays, and methods way before his time, Carême invented recipes which are still popular today, such as vol-au-vents, bouchées, sauces both sweet and savoury, meringues, soufflé Rothschilds, as well as being the impetus for many other dishes.

In his final years Carême worked for Baron de Rothschild, before dying in Paris 1833. It was said of his death that the great Carême had been 'burnt out by the flame of his own genius'.

CARMINE
(see also colourings)

Used to colour marzipan, jams, jellies, custards, pastes, prepared mixes, sauces and syrups, carmine, also known as carminic acid, is a natural red food colouring used in many pastry applications and confectionery work, or simply for highlighting centrepieces of sugar or pastillage.

CAROB
(see also chocolate)

A replacement or substitute for chocolate, carob, also known as St Jacob's bread, has a flavour to which one's palate must adjust if used to chocolate. Grown on a tree in a large pod, the carob is native to Syria. As story has it, when St Jacob was walking alone in the forest he began eating what he thought were locusts and then realised they were the carob pods, which led to the other name by which the carob tree is known, locust bean tree.

Carob pods can be eaten raw, by themselves, but these days they are mainly dried and made into a chocolate substitute. Completely unrelated to the cocoa tree and to chocolate, the carob pod does, however, look similar in size to a cocoa pod, being 25–30 cm (10–12 in) in length and containing reddish brown seeds. Carob powder can also be used as a replacement for cocoa, if so desired.

CARROT CAKE

Connoisseurs of the perfect Carrot cake will like this recipe. It makes a cake that's moist, light and of just the right consistency.

½ cup (2 oz) plain (all-purpose) flour
1 level teaspoon baking powder (soda)
7 egg yolks
¾ cup (6 oz) caster (superfine) sugar
175 g (6 oz) carrots, finely grated
½ cup (2 oz) ground almonds
½ cup (2 oz) ground hazelnuts
½ cup (2 oz) dry breadcrumbs
7 egg whites
1 quantity lemon cream cheese frosting (see page 125)
¾ cup (3 oz) flaked almonds, roasted (see page 5)
marzipan carrots (see page 177)

Preheat oven to 180°C (350°F).
Lightly grease a 23 cm (9 in) springform cake tin
with butter and line with baking paper (parchment).
Sift flour and baking powder. Beat egg yolks and sugar until light, fluffy and almost white. Gently fold in carrots, almonds, hazelnuts, breadcrumbs and sifted flour and baking powder, by hand. Whisk egg whites until stiff peaks form and very gently fold into the beaten egg yolks.
Pour into prepared tin and bake for 45–50 minutes, or until the cake has shrunk from the sides of the tin.
Cool in the tin on a cake rack.
When cake is completely cold, turn out onto the cake rack, cover the top and sides with frosting and press flaked almonds around the sides.
Decorate with marzipan carrots and greenery, such as parsley, dill or fennel, for carrot leaves.

CARTRIDGE PAPER
(see baking paper, parchment)

Cartridge paper is also known as baking parchment. It is used to absorb fat, often being crushed slightly and placed on a tray so that freshly fried products can be rested on it to drain for several minutes.

CASSADEILLES

Traditionally made from rich butter puff pastry, Cassadeilles are turnovers filled with walnuts that have been flavoured with anise. Served hot before the Christmas dinner, they are a true winter warmer treat.

¾ cup (3 oz) finely ground walnuts
¼ cup (2 oz) sugar
1 tablespoon brown sugar
1 egg yolk
75 g (2½ oz) unsalted (sweet) butter
2 tablespoons anise liqueur
450 g (14 oz) puff pastry (see page 228)
1 egg white
icing (powdered) sugar, for dusting

Preheat oven to 200°C (400°F).
Mix ground walnuts, sugars, egg yolk and butter in a mixing bowl with anise liqueur. On a lightly floured surface, roll the puff pastry to 2–3 mm (⅛ in) in thickness. Cut puff pastry into discs using a 7 cm (3 in) round cutter. Into the centre of each disc place a small ball of the walnut mixture. Brush the edges of the puff pastry with the egg white and fold one side over to join the other. Pinch edges so that they join firmly. Place the Cassadeilles on a baking sheet lined with baking paper (parchment) and bake for 25–35 minutes in preheated oven. Remove when baked, dredge heavily with icing sugar, and serve immediately.

CASSATA
(see also ice cream)

Cassata is Italian for 'case or chest' and refers to two famous desserts, Cassata Gelata, the iced dessert, and Cassata alla Siciliana, a rich cheesecake. The iced cassata dessert is an exact replica of the French bombe and is usually made oval or round with an ice cream outer casing and an internal filling of soft cream filled with glacé (candied) fruit and roasted nuts. Traditionally, the cassata was moulded into brick- or chest-shaped moulds which were lined with ice cream and filled with a bombe paste containing different fruits and nuts. In more modern times, they occasionally have an outer coating or decoration of meringue, cream or chocolate.

Cassata alla Siciliana is also named because of its resemblance to a case or chest. It originated in Sicily around the 9th century, when the Saracens invaded the small island. Having travelled far and wide in their campaigns, the Saracens brought with them a vast array of sweets ideas, to which the Sicilians eventually added their own touch. A festive cake baked at Christmas and Easter, this delicacy is also served at Italian wedding feasts and at Holy Communions, where it has come to represent the beginning of a new way of life.

Cassata alla Siciliana is a rich combination of génoise sponge, coated in both Italian cheese and chocolate, with glacé fruits featuring throughout the cake.

CASSE MUSEAU
(see also biscuit)

Meaning 'jaw or tooth breaker', these French delights are hard, dry biscuits (cookies) made of almonds and cheese and served as both sweet and savoury biscuits. The name 'jaw breaker' actually refers to their use at the Festival of Rogation procession, where it was customary for people to throw biscuits at each other, attempting to get them in each other's mouths, but often simply breaking each other's jaws.

CASTLE PUDDING

A steamed pudding which can also be baked, this is made of a light buttery sponge mixture and cooked in a dariole mould that has a small amount of red jam (jelly) in its base. When cooked and inverted, the jam sauce runs over the pudding.

CASTER SUGAR
(see also sugar)

Known also in America as superfine sugar, this is exactly what caster sugar is, very finely ground sugar. It is used extensively in pastry cooking because it dissolves quickly when mixed with butter or other ingredients. This is the best sugar to use when making dry caramel because it melts quickly, but it is no good for sugar-boiling liquids or wet caramel because, being so fine, it picks up dirt easily and can cause sugar mixtures to crystallise.

CAT'S TONGUE

Called 'Langue de Chat' in French, these biscuits (cookies) are long and thin, hence their name.

165 g (6 oz) unsalted (sweet) butter, softened
1¼ cups (7 oz) icing (powdered) sugar, sifted
4 egg whites
¼ cup (2 oz) caster (superfine) sugar
1¼ cups (5 oz) plain (all-purpose) flour, sifted
icing (powdered) sugar, extra, for dusting

Preheat oven to 200°C (400°F).
Line baking sheets with baking paper (parchment).
Place softened butter and icing sugar in a mixing bowl and cream together until light and fluffy and almost white. Whisk egg whites in a clean bowl until they form stiff peaks. As they stiffen, slowly add the caster sugar, a tablespoon at a time. Continue whisking after each one is added. Fold stiff egg whites into the creamed butter mixture and then add sifted flour. Place mixture in a piping (pastry) bag fitted with a 1 cm (½ in) piping nozzle and pipe 7 cm (3 in) lengths onto prepared sheet. Allow 5 cm (2 in) between tongues for spreading. Bake in preheated oven for 5–8 minutes before removing to a cake rack to cool completely. Dust lightly with icing sugar before serving.

Makes 36

CENCI ALLA FIORENTINA

Similar to the French bugne, Cenci alla Fiorentina are made from fritter dough which is cut into strips. The centre is then split and one end is threaded through it. They are dusted with sugar and can be served as a dessert or eaten on their own.

CENTIGRADE

Centigrade is the name of the heat measuring scale invented by Anders Celsius (1701–1744) to replace the Fahrenheit scale, making measurement much easier. Freezing point is 0°C and boiling point 100°C, and the temperatures below, in between and above these points are determined accordingly.

CENTREPIECE
(see also chocolate, pastillage, sugar)

In pâtisserie terms, a centrepiece is any ornament produced from any of the confectionery mediums: chocolate, marzipan, croquant, caramel, pastillage or similar substances. Pastry centrepeices are used to decorate everything from a platter of petits fours, gâteaux, sweets and pralines to entire festive tables for smorgasbords or buffets. Centrepieces are usually produced by copying a design or stencil. For pastillage and chocolate, the design can simply be cut out around a cardboard stencil. Other centrepieces, such as piped chocolate work, are usually made by piping onto baking paper (parchment) which is set over a drawn stencil. With all types of centrepieces much care is needed to ensure that every section of the design is matched and looks perfect, and to ensure purity of style.

See page 54

CHALLAH

Challah is a sweet, white plaited bread invented in Israel and still eaten today on special Jewish holidays. It contains sweet dried raisins or sultanas (golden raisins) and should be served warm, either plain or with jam (jelly).

1 cup (8 fl oz) water
10g (⅓ oz) fresh compressed yeast
4 cups (16 oz) plain (all-purpose) flour
¼ cup (2 oz) ground matzoh meal
1 teaspoon salt
6 teaspoons sugar
3 eggs
2 tablespoons (1 fl oz) olive oil
⅓ cup (2 oz) sultanas (golden raisins)
1 egg yolk, lightly beaten with a pinch of salt

Preheat oven to 180°C (350°F).
Warm the water slightly, add yeast and stir till dissolved.
In a large mixing bowl, place flour, matzoh, salt and sugar.
Make a well in the centre and pour in yeast liquid. Cover the liquid with a small amount of flour then cover the whole bowl and put in a warm place for 15 minutes.
Add eggs and oil to flour mixture and mix to a firm dough. Knead the dough for 5–8 minutes or until it is smooth and elastic. Knead in sultanas and when they are mixed through the dough, place dough in a bowl, cover it, and place it in a warm place for 50 minutes or until double in bulk.
When risen, knock back (punch down) the dough and knead it lightly before returning it to the bowl and allowing to prove (rise) for a further 50 minutes.
On a lightly floured surface, knead the risen dough and cut it in half. Roll each of the dough pieces into equal length sausages, pinch the ends of both together and then twist the two together quickly to form a braid, pinching the opposite ends together. Glaze the braid with the egg yolk mixture and place the loaf on a large baking sheet. Cover dough for a further 30–40 minutes or until double in size.
Bake the proven dough in the preheated oven for 40–45 minutes or until golden brown.

Centrepieces Step-by-Step

Step 1: Trace the design with chocolate onto the baking paper (parchment).

Step 2: First join two of the hardenend chocolate designs together with melted chocolate. Once firm, join the third piece vertically, with melted chocolate. When this has hardened, stand it upright, and, with more melted chocolate, join the fourth piece. See page 58.

CHAMPAGNE PASTRY
(see also sablé, sweet pastry)

A rich but light-to-eat pastry similar to sable paste and used for biscuits (cookies) and for lining the bases of tarts and pies. Made by creaming butter and sugar and then adding the flour and cornflour (cornstarch), champagne pastry is so named because that is the colour it should have.

CHANTILLY
(see crème Chantilly)

CHANTRENE PASTRY
(see also shortcrust)

A quick, easy and light pastry used in the same way as all shortcrust doughs. The lemon juice in the dough is not only for flavour but to allow the gluten structure to relax after kneading so that little if any shrinkage will occur when the pie crust is blind baked.

4 cups (16 oz) plain (all-purpose) flour
pinch of salt
250 g (8 oz) unsalted (sweet) butter
2 egg yolks
juice of 1 lemon juice
iced water

Place flour, salt and butter together in a bowl and, using fingertips, lightly rub the butter through the flour until the dough resembles fresh breadcrumbs.
Add egg yolks, lemon juice and enough iced water to bring the mixture to a firm but softly textured dough.
Knead dough for 3–5 minutes, or until soft, smooth and elastic. Wrap the dough in plastic wrap (cling film) and refrigerate for 20–25 minutes before rolling on a lightly floured surface and using for quiche or pie bases.

CHAPATTI
(see also flatbread)

An unleavened Indian bread served not only with dips and sauces but with almost all meals throughout the country, chapatti is often also used as the plate on which the food is served. Traditionally, the chapatti dough was made from buffalo's milk, although today any milk is fine. When the dough has been rested, it is fried in oil or butter (ghee) and puffs and becomes crisp. Thought to be one of the oldest forms of bread that is still popular, it is made exactly the same way that all bread doughs first were. A flat dough is made into a thin disc and baked or fried. Chapattis must be made fresh before every meal, as they go stale quickly. Some Indian households make their own chapattis using the traditional atta flour, but it is quite common practice to buy the chapatti from market vendors on the way home.

1¾ cups (7 oz) atta flour
1 teaspoon salt
1 tablespoon ghee (clarified butter)
1 cup (8 fl oz) warm water

Place atta flour in a mixing bowl with the salt and rub in the ghee. Make a well in the centre and add the water all at once.
Form a dough and knead for at least 6–8 minutes. Wrap dough in plastic wrap (cling film) and chill overnight.
Shape the dough into 10–12 small balls. On a lightly floured board, roll out each one to a 15 cm (6 in) circle.
Heat a frying pan (skillet) until quite hot.
Place chapattis in pan and cook for 1 minute, then turn to cook other side. Remove and serve immediately.

CHARLOTTE

Derived from the old English word 'charlyt', the charlotte of modern times refers to two major and equally famous desserts.
Following the original meaning of 'charlyt' (dish of custard filling), the first charlotte, Charlotte Russe, is a cold dish of a mousse or light bavarois mixture held within the confines of sponge finger biscuits (cookies). Invented by Marie-Antoine Carême, Charlotte Russe was first made to rectify a mistake made by the great Carême himself. Not having enough gelatine to set his bavarois mixture, Carême decided to hold it together with the biscuit crust. Originally named Charlotte à la Parisienne by Carême, the name was changed many years later to Charlotte Russe when it was fashionable to serve food in the Russian style or with a Russian name.
A wide variety of biscuits (cookies), can, in fact, be used to line the charlotte mould, including ordinary biscuits, wafers in all shapes and sizes, macaroons and layer cake base; however, the pieces must be shaped so that they form a decorative and accurate pattern and fit closely together in the mould.
The second charlotte is a fruit charlotte, the most famous being Apple Charlotte. It is made in a similar way to the cold charlotte, the apple mixture being held in place by an outer crust of sliced and buttered bread or brioche, but is served warm. It should always be served fresh. Fruit or Apple Charlotte first appeared in cooking journals around late 1800s and was named in honour of the wife of George III of England, Queen Charlotte.

APPLE CHARLOTTE
½ large thickly sliced sandwich loaf, crusts removed
180 g (6 oz) unsalted (sweet) butter, for frying
120 g (4 oz) butter
6 cooking apples, peeled, cored and sliced
juice of 1 lemon
¼ teaspoon ground cinnamon
½ cup (4 oz) sugar
200g jam (jelly)

Preheat oven to 190°C (375°F). Grease 6–8 dariole moulds.
Cut out 6–8 heart-shaped croûtes from the bread slices, with a biscuit (cookie) cutter. Cut remaining slices into fingers about 1 cm (½ in) wide and slightly longer than the depth of a 1.8 litre (3 pint) charlotte mould.
Melt 180 g (6 oz) butter in a frying pan (skillet).
Add bread hearts and fingers and fry until golden.
Arrange the hearts, overlapping, in the bottom of the greased charlotte mould and stand most of the

fingers around the side, again overlapping.
Melt the remaining 120 g (4 oz) butter in a saucepan.
Add apples, lemon juice and cinnamon. Cover and cook
gently until apples are pulpy. Stir in sugar and jam
until well mixed. Spoon the apple mixture into the
mould and cover with the remaining bread fingers.
Bake in preheated oven for 10–15 minutes.
Cool slightly, then turn out the charlotte onto a
heated serving plate. Serve hot or chilled.

Serves 4–6

CHARLOTTE RUSSE

Sponge Fingers
1 cup (4 oz) plain (all-purpose) flour
5 egg yolks
½ cup (4 oz) caster (superfine) sugar
5 egg whites
(or 1 packet savoiardi, sponge finger or
lady finger biscuits/cookies)

Filling
6 level teaspoons gelatine powder
90 ml (3 fl oz) cold water
2¼ cups (18 fl oz) milk
1 vanilla bean
6 egg yolks
¾ cup (6 oz) caster (superfine) sugar
1 cup (8 fl oz) thickened (double or heavy) cream, whipped
¾ cup (7 fl oz) passionfruit (purple granadilla) pulp

To Decorate
½ cup (4 fl oz) passionfruit (purple granadilla) pulp
ribbon to tie around cake

Preheat oven to 180°C (350°F).
Line a baking sheet with baking paper (parchment).
Sift flour twice. Beat egg yolks and sugar until thick, light
and fluffy and the mixture forms a ribbon (see page 236).
Whisk egg whites until stiff peaks form. Fold sifted flour into
the egg yolks. Very gently fold in beaten egg whites.
Fill a piping (pastry) bag fitted with a plain 1 cm (½ in)
nozzle with the mixture and pipe 10 cm (4 in) lines onto
prepared sheet, leaving 4 cm (1½ in) between lines.
Bake for 10–15 minutes or until the top springs back
when lightly touched. Cool on the sheet on a cake rack.

Filling
Mix gelatine and water in a small bowl. Stand bowl in a pan of
hot water to dissolve the gelatine. Place milk and vanilla bean
in a saucepan and bring slowly to the boil. Beat egg yolks and
sugar together and very slowly beat in the boiling milk.
Return the mixture to the milk saucepan and cook over very
low heat until the mixture thickens, stirring all
the time. Remove from heat and mix in dissolved gelatine.
Cool until slightly thickened. Remove vanilla bean.
Mix whipped cream and one third of the passionfruit pulp
together and fold into the thickened mixture.

To Assemble
Line the base and sides of a 23 cm (9 in) springform
cake tin with the sponge fingers, trimming them to fit.
Pour the mousse filling into the tin. Tap the tin lightly
on the bench (counter) to bring any large air bubbles to
the top. Chill for 1–2 hours or until completely set.
To serve, remove the tin and tie a ribbon around the side.
Spoon the reserved passionfruit pulp on top.

CHEESECAKE

Recipes that date back to the Greek and Roman Empires
prove that people have long enjoyed the flavours and taste
sensations of cheesecakes. The Romans obtained their recipes
or ideas for this cake after invading the Greeks' territory.
Most historians, though, grant the Romans the privilege of
having invented it. The recipe spread to Britain centuries
later when soldiers returned home from the Crusades with
many recipes and new food ideas. British cooks were
responsible for the success of the cold cheesecake, while it was
the Germans who made the baked cheesecake famous.

COLD-SET CHEESECAKE
The cheesecake has evolved into many forms over the
centuries and this one, with a filling of sweetened cream
cheese, eggs and cream, has become very popular because it is
so easy to prepare.

Base
250 g (8 oz) sweet plain biscuit (cookie) crumbs
100 g (3½ oz) unsalted (sweet) butter, melted

Filling
375 g (12 oz) cream cheese
⅔ cup (5 oz) caster (superfine) sugar
4 eggs
5 level teaspoons gelatine powder
4 teaspoons water
juice and grated rind of 2 lemons
1¼ cups (10 fl oz) thickened (double or heavy)
cream, whipped
ground cinnamon, for dusting

Line a 23 cm (9 in) springform cake tin with plastic wrap
(cling film). Mix crumbs and butter and press into the tin,
using the back of a spoon to make a firm, flat base. Chill.
Beat cream cheese and sugar until light and creamy,
then beat in eggs one at a time. Mix gelatine and cold
water in a small bowl and let stand for 3 minutes.
Heat lemon juice until just boiling and add soaked gelatine.
Remove from the heat and stir until the gelatine dissolves.
Add the rind. When cool, beat gelatine mixture into the
creamed ingredients. Gently fold whipped cream in
by hand. Pour over the chilled base and refrigerate
for at least 2 hours or until set. Turn the cake out
and peel off the plastic wrap.
Lightly dust the top with cinnamon.

BAKED CHEESECAKE
A classic German version of the original invention, this delight has a rich flavour of cream cheese and is thickened with a little custard powder, but remains light in texture.

1¼ cups (10 fl oz) milk
30 g (1 oz) unsalted (sweet) butter
250 g (8 oz) cream cheese
6 teaspoons sugar
½ cup (4 fl oz) milk, extra
½ cup (2 oz) custard powder
6 egg whites
⅓ cup (2 oz) caster (superfine) sugar
½ cup (2 oz) flaked almonds, roasted,
to decorate (see page 5)

Preheat oven to 180°C (350°F).
Grease a 23 cm (9 in) springform cake tin lightly with butter and line the base with baking paper (parchment). Place milk, butter, cream cheese and sugar in a saucepan and bring slowly to the boil. Blend the extra milk and custard powder and beat into the mixture as it heats. Cook until thickened, stirring all the time. Remove from heat and cool slightly. Whisk egg whites until stiff peaks form, then gradually beat in caster sugar, a spoonful at a time. Beat until sugar is dissolved. Fold by hand into the custard mixture and pour into the prepared tin. Bake for 35–40 minutes or until just cooked. Cool in the tin on a cake rack. When cold, run a knife around the edge of the tin to loosen the cake. Press flaked almonds around the side of the cake.

CHEESE SAVOURY DOUGH
A quick dough that you can cut into strips. It is ideal as an accompaniment to dips or as a snack.

3¼ cups (13 oz) plain (all-purpose) flour
pinch salt
¼ teaspoon cayenne pepper
180 g (6 oz) unsalted (sweet) butter
2¾ cups (11 oz) grated cheddar cheese
3 eggs

Preheat oven to 180°C (350°F).
Place flour, salt, cayenne pepper and butter in a mixing bowl and lightly rub together until the mixture resembles fresh breadcumbs. Add grated cheese to the mixture and mix until the cheese is evenly dispersed. Add eggs and work the ingredients to a dough. Do not overmix; as soon as dough is formed, remove it from the bowl and work lightly to ensure all the flour and other ingredients are combined, then wrap the dough in plastic wrap (cling film) and refrigerate for 30 minutes. Cut dough in half and, on a lightly floured surface, roll each half to 2–3 mm (⅛ in) in thickness. Place the dough sheets on large baking sheets. Using a sharp knife and a ruler, score the top of the sheets into fingers. Bake the scored dough sheets for 12–15 minutes. Cool and then snap into fingers and serve or store in an airtight container.

CHEESE PUFFS
These small light puffs of cheese are made using only a few ingredients, making them a great last minute recipe for an impromptu party. Flavour the recipe with any herb or spice for a different effect every time.

4 cups (16 oz) grated mild cheese
2 eggs, lightly beaten
1 cup (4 oz) plain (all-purpose) flour
6 teaspoons baking powder (soda)
2 tablespoons chopped fresh herbs

Preheat oven to 180°C (350°F). Lightly grease baking sheets. Place cheese, eggs, flour and baking powder in a mixing bowl and combine with the herbs. Taking small dessertspoonfuls at a time, roll the mixture into balls and place on the prepared sheets. Bake in the preheated oven for 10–12 minutes, or until golden brown.

Makes 36

CHEESE STRAWS
(see also puff pastry)
These are long straws of cheese-laminated puff pastry. When making anything with puff pastry save all the scraps and re-roll them flat.

Preheat oven to 180°C (350°F).
Sprinkle the top of the dough with grated Parmesan cheese and fold the dough into a bookfold (both ends into the centre and then fold in half). Roll the dough flat again to about 2–3 mm (⅛ in) in thickness. Brush the top of the dough with egg yolk and sprinkle with more grated Parmesan. Cut the dough into strips 2 cm (¾ in) wide and cut these to 15 cm (6 in) in length. Twist each by holding both ends and twisting in opposite directions. Place straws on a baking sheet lined with baking paper (parchment) and bake in preheated oven for 10–15 minutes, or until crisp and golden brown. Serve immediately as an hors d'oeuvre or with dips.

CHEF PATISSIER
The head of the pastry section, or chief pastry cook, within large pastry establishments and hotels. The chef pâtissier usually must have had 5 years' experience after his/her apprenticeship and have 2–3 years international experience. A master or specialist in certain areas, the chef pâtissier must as well know every section within the pastry area: cakes, pastries, doughs, petits fours, chocolate and so on. At the same time, he or she must be capable of producing centrepieces and theme showpieces from sugar, chocolate, or pastillage. The business side of the pastry section — budgeting, stock ordering, staff control, menu planning and liaison with other kitchen sections — also falls within the chef pâtissier's domain. Above all, the chef pâtissier must be an authority on all things to do with pastry, as he or she is seen as the leader of the section and also the trainer of apprentices who work within that section. A flair for creativity and imagination assist greatly in this role.

CHELSEA BUN
(see also buchteln, buns)

These are an English specialty from the town of Chelsea, which has been renowned for these buns since the late 17th century. This bun is said to have been highly sought after by both nobility and royalty. A yeast dough is rolled with dried fruits and spices. It is then cut into small buns which are baked together in a round cake tin then glazed with jam (jelly). Served with coffee, the individual buns are split and served with butter or jam.

1 cup (8 oz) plain (all-purpose) flour
6 teaspoons (1 oz) sugar
60 g (2 oz) unsalted (sweet) butter
15 g (½ oz) fresh compressed yeast
1 egg
water
⅓ cup (2 oz) currants
2 tablespoons mixed glacé (candied) peel
2 tablespoons light brown (moist) sugar
½ teaspoon ground cinnamon
icing (powdered) sugar, for dusting

Grease a 20 cm (8 in) round tin and line with baking paper (parchment). Place flour and sugar in a mixing bowl and mix together. Add butter and yeast and lightly rub the butter through the mixture until it resembles fresh breadcrumbs. Make a well in the centre of the mixture. Add egg and water and turn the mixture into a dough. Knead the dough for 5–8 minutes until smooth and elastic. Allow dough to rest for 30–40 minutes, or until double in size. Knock back (punch down) the dough and, on a lightly floured surface, roll the dough to 30 x 30 cm (12 x 12 in). Brush the top of the flat dough with milk and sprinkle with the currants, mixed peel, sugar and then the spice. Starting with the side furthest from you on the bench, roll the dough tightly toward you like a Swiss roll. When the dough is completely rolled, cut it into seven portions of about 4 cm (1½ in) in width. Place six of the cut buns around the edge, cut side up, and the last one in the centre, again with cut side up. Place the tin in a warm area and allow the buns to rise until double their size. Preheat the oven to 180°C (350°F). Bake the buns in the preheated oven for 35–40 minutes, or until golden brown. Place a cake rack over the top of the buns and invert the tin so the buns turn out. Dust lightly with icing sugar and serve immediately.

CHEQUERBOARD
(see also Battenberg)

These brown and white chequered biscuits (cookies) originated in Holland, and are also known as Dutch cookies. They are made of two doughs, the white dough usually being flavoured with cinnamon and the chocolate dough with lemon.

White Dough
1¾ cups (7 oz) plain (all-purpose) flour
½ cup (3 oz) icing (powdered) sugar
¼ teaspoon ground cinnamon
150 g (5 oz) unsalted (sweet) butter
1 egg yolk

Chocolate Dough
1½ cups (6 oz) plain (all-purpose) flour
½ cup (3 oz) icing (powdered) sugar
¼ cup (1 oz) cocoa powder
zest of 1 lemon
150 g (5 oz) unsalted (sweet) butter
1 egg yolk
2 egg whites

Grease baking sheets.
To prepare the white dough, sift flour, icing sugar and cinnamon together into a mixing bowl. Add butter and crumb lightly through the dry ingredients until it resembles fresh breadcrumbs. Add egg yolk and continue mixing until a dough is formed.
To make the chocolate dough, sift the flour, icing sugar and cocoa together. Add lemon zest and butter and repeat the procedure for the white dough.
Wrap each dough in plastic wrap (cling film) and refrigerate for 1 hour. Knead each dough lightly so that it is soft enough to roll. On a lightly floured surface, roll both doughs into squares of equal length and width and 1 cm (½ in) in thickness. Cut four 1 cm (½ in) wide strips from the chocolate dough and five 1 cm (½ in) strips from the white dough.
Knead any scrap pastry from both doughs into one ball. Roll the scrap pastry (it should now be milk chocolate in colour) so that it is 2–3 mm (⅛ in) thick, the same length as the white and chocolate strips and as wide as possible. Lightly brush the top with egg white.
Starting from the outer edge, place side by side one strip of white pastry, one strip of chocolate pastry and one strip of white pastry. Brush lightly with egg white. Repeat the process on top of this layer, but alternating the colours so that a chocolate strip is placed on top of a white strip and vice versa. Brush this layer with egg white. Create a third layer, repeating the process and again alternating the colours. Brush this layer with egg white. Lightly brush egg white around the sides of the layers. Press the outer sides of the milk chocolate pastry around the chequerboard layers so that the layers are completely covered by the milk pastry.
Place in refrigerator for 1 hour.
Preheat oven to 180°C (350°F).
Remove the chequerboard from the refrigerator and cut it into 2 mm (⅛ in) thicknesses. Place each biscuit (cookie) piece on prepared sheet and bake for 8–10 minutes, or until the white pieces are lightly browning around the edge. Remove from oven and cool slightly before eating.

See page 59

Chequerboard Step-by-Step

Step 1: Place side by side on top of the milk chocolate pastry a strip of white pastry, a strip of chocolate pastry and another strip of white pastry.

Step 2: Repeat the process, alternating the strips. See page 58.

CHERRY

A small ball-shaped red fruit with a central stone which is easily removed using a cherry pitter. Cherries have a short season and are therefore often used tinned or preserved, or as glacé or crystallised (candied) cherries and, when in season, are also made into chutneys, liqueurs, jams (jellies), ice creams and sorbets. Cherries play a major role in several desserts, Black Forest Gâteau and Cherries Jubilee in particular, and give the liqueur Kirsch its distinctive flavour.

CHERRIES JUBILEE

300 g (10 oz) fresh cherries, pitted and cut into pieces
1 cup (8 fl oz) water
2 tablespoons sugar
1 small cinnamon stick
1 tablespoon arrowroot
3 tablespoons water, extra
½ cup (4 fl oz) Kirsch

Place cherries, water, sugar and cinnamon sticks in a saucepan and bring slowly to the boil. Simmer gently for 5 minutes then remove cinnamon stick and strain the cherry mixture, returning the juice to the saucepan and leaving the cherries aside.
Bring cherry juice to the boil. Mix arrowroot with the extra water and slowly pour this into the cherry juice, stirring continuously until the mixture comes back to the boil.
When boiled, add the cherries and Kirsch and stir through.
Cool slightly before serving warm on ice cream and cakes.

CHESTNUT
(see also marrons, nuts)

A very popular, but slightly floury-tasting, sweet nut of Europe and the United Kingdom. The chestnut tree is part of the beech tree family, and the brown glossy skinned nuts are grown inside green spiny shells. The outer shell or skin is easily peeled away; however, to remove the brown skin, the nut must be roasted and then once it is almost black the skin can easily be flaked away. Chestnuts are sold whole around the world, but are also available tinned in purée form, the purée commonly being used in making cakes, pastries and petits fours. One of the most famous sweetmeats of all times is marrons glacés, or glazed chestnuts.

CHIBOUST
(see crème Chiboust)

CHICHIFREGI
(see also fritters)

Small French fritters sold at market stalls and consisting of yeast-raised dough which is fried and coated in sugar. Chichifregi are traditionally made in a fluted shape.

CHIFFON

A light dessert filling made from a flavoured custard base set with gelatine and lightened with egg whites. The base can be fruit purée, chocolate or any flavour at all, mixed with a light egg yolk custard, and stiffened with a small amount of gelatine, through which egg whites are folded. Chiffon differs from crème Chiboust in that it contains a higher ratio of egg whites, making it much lighter. Chiffon should also be set in a sweet pastry base as a flan or as a traditional chiffon pie. Most common chiffon mixtures are lemon, orange chocolate and banana.

CHINESE FIVE SPICE
(see also spices)

A mixture of five spices — anise, fennel, ginger, cloves and cinnamon — which is often used in Chinese savoury cookery, but occasionally in European pastries as well.

CHINESE FORTUNE COOKIES

3 egg whites
½ cup (3 oz) icing (powdered) sugar, sifted
45 g (1½ oz) unsalted (sweet) butter, melted
⅔ cup (2½ oz) plain (all-purpose) flour, sifted

Preheat oven to 180°C (350°F). Grease baking sheets well. With the tip of your finger, mark three 8 cm (3 in) circles onto each sheet.
Place egg whites in a mixing bowl and whisk until they just begin to turn frothy. Continue mixing and add sifted icing sugar and melted butter. Add flour and mix with a spatula until the paste is smooth and lump free. Allow the mixture to rest for 15 minutes. Place 1½ teaspoons of mixture on each marked circle on the sheet and, using a small spatula or palette knife, spread to fill each circle. Bake one sheet at a time in the preheated oven and only bake for 5–8 minutes, or until the cookies begin to brown slightly around the edges. Remove the sheets and, working quickly, slide a palette knife underneath the cookies to remove them from the sheet. Place a written fortune in the centre of each. Fold the cookie in half and then in half again over the edge of a sharp edged object.
Cool on a cake rack and then serve.

Makes 18–24

CHOCART
(see also puff pastry)

Made from puff pastry, chocarts are small turnovers filled with a fruit (usually apple) purée which is sweetened and flavoured with lemon and spices. Baked and eaten fresh while still hot, chocarts have been produced in France for centuries.

CHOCOLATE
(see also carob, caraque, bakers' chocolate, cocoa, cocoa butter, couverture, ganache)

One of the most-loved flavours in the pastry chef's domain, chocolate is enjoyed throughout the world. Chocolate offers the budding pastry chef many new ideas in addition to its existing uses in cooking, modelling, piping and baking. One must know exactly how to handle the product, from the tempering of couvertures through to storage temperatures, and that when mixing chocolate into batters or mixtures it must be worked quickly or it will set and become lumpy, a problem occurring daily in mousses, creams and sauces.

History, Cultivation and Production

Its origins can be traced to the ancient forests of Central and South America, where the 'cacao' tree was cultivated by the Mayan Indians, the Incas of Peru and the Aztecs of Mexico. The word 'chocolate' actually comes from the Aztec word 'xocoatl', a drink they prepared from the seeds of the cacao tree. The beans had ceremonial significance and in certain regions the drink could only be consumed by those of high rank. Cocoa beans were frequently used as money by indigenous people or offered as a tribute during festivities.

Some people say Christopher Columbus introduced Europe to the wonders of chocolate. Historians, however, claim it was Hernan Cortés, the Spanish conquistador who conquered Mexico in 1519–21. Cortés was treated to this royal drink of the realm by the Aztec Emperor Montezuma. When Cortez brought the cocoa beans back to Spain, the flavour of the drink was improved for European tastebuds by heating it and sweetening it with sugar.

Following their conquest of Mexico, the early Spanish kept the cultivation and preparation of cocoa a secret. Until 1700 Spain controlled the supply of cocoa beans through their plantations in Central and South America, and remained the chief producers and exporters of cocoa until 1891. By the turn of the century, though, the French had established their own cocoa plantations on Martinique, from which they provided cocoa for the French market. The Dutch probably introduced cocoa trees into Indonesia and Sri Lanka, while the Portuguese planted them in West Africa. Today, major cocoa-producing areas include West Africa, Ghana, Central and South America, the Far East and Southeast Asia.

Cocoa and chocolate are obtained from the cocoa bean. Sorting and cleaning are the first steps in processing cocoa beans. The premium grade beans undergo extensive quality control checks before they are blended and then automatically cleaned and destoned. The cleaned beans are treated (to allow the shell to be removed from the nib) by passing them through a multi-stage winnowing process. The nib is then kibbled, roasted and ground to produce cocoa mass. Cocoa mass, with the fine chocolate flavour so characteristic of chocolate products, is the most essential ingredient in producing cocoa powder and chocolate.

Cocoa powder is made by extracting, under pressure, some of the cocoa fat (cocoa butter). This is also used in chocolate making. Once the cocoa butter is removed, a solid block of cocoa called 'presscake' remains. Once the pressing cycle is completed, the hard cocoa cake is ejected from the press pots and the cocoa cakes are ground into a fine, high grade cocoa powder.

Definitions

One of the most commonly asked questions is What is the difference between chocolate and compound chocolate (coating)? The answer is simple. Chocolate is produced from cocoa mass, cocoa butter and sugar, and may, depending on the style of chocolate, contain milk solids and milk fat. Compound chocolates, on the other hand, are produced from cocoa powder, vegetable fat and sugar. As with chocolate, milk solids and milk fat may also be used. The difference between the two types, therefore, is basically the replacement of cocoa mass and cocoa butter in chocolate with cocoa powder and vegetable fat in compound chocolate.

Although the products have similar texture and colour, they are produced by different recipes, and have different handling characteristics. In the case of chocolate, once the product has been melted, it may be necessary to temper it for further application. This process is not necessary for compound chocolate.

Tempering

This is the process of working chocolate so that all the fats in the cocoa butter are melted and distributed evenly throughout the chocolate. Tempering involves bringing the liquid chocolate to a precise temperature so that the cocoa butter achieves a perfect crystallisation, ensuring that the chocolate will taste and look as it should, with an attractive gloss, colour and crispness. Improper tempering yields a chocolate that will not set and makes unmoulding difficult.

Fat Bloom

This is a white spotty or streaky brown appearance on the surface of the chocolate. This bloom is seldom noticed until the chocolate has set. It can be caused in any of the following ways:

- Destroying the temper; or
- Over-heating; or
- The addition of fats which do not mix with the cocoa butter (e.g. vegetable fats).

Fat bloom alters the appearance of the chocolate, but does not affect the taste of flavour.

REMEDY: Retemper or reheat the chocolate and use it again. A short-term solution is to brush the chocolate with milk before serving.

Sugar Bloom

This occurs when moisture condenses on the surface of the chocolate and sugar crystals are formed on top. It can be caused by:

- Effects of moisture or steam when chocolate is incorrectly melted over a pan of water; or
- Cooling in a damp place (such as a refrigerator).

Humidity deposits cause the sugar bloom effect, which occurs when water dissolves part of the sugar at the chocolate surface. Unlike fat bloom, sugar bloom affects the quality of the chocolate and gives it a sandy feeling.

REMEDY: None. Avoid humidity and condensation. In summer, pack chocolate in foil, especially if put in the refrigerator.

Conditioning

There are certain procedures which will help protect the moulded chocolate after it has been cooled so it is not damaged by humidity or heat:

- 22–27°C (72–81°F) is the recommended room temperature when enrobing, dipping or chocolate depositing is being carried out.
- The ideal air temperature for cooling chocolate is 10–12°C (50–54°F) for moulds, and 15–18°C (59–64°F) for dipping and enrobing.

- When melting or tempering, always stir gently, never vigorously (air bubbles will enter).
- Avoid steam, water and humidity deposits on chocolate.
- Moulds: once set, a chocolate mould may be placed for a few minutes only in the refrigerator to assist release from the mould. Once cooled, the chocolate should be brought back to room temperature.
- Centres: to retain their shape or texture, the centres being used for dipping or enrobing may need to be stored at a special temperature or humidity prior to covering. However, before enrobing, make sure the centres are brought back to room temperature.

Melting

- Careful handling will prevent problems. Do not overheat and do not hurry the process along.
- Blocks of chocolate can be grated in a food processor or chopped into chunks before melting.
- Chocolate should be heated to a temperature of 45°C (113°F). The use of a chocolate thermometer is recommended to take the guesswork out of melting.

Methods of melting include:

DOUBLE SAUCEPAN: Break chocolate into pieces in a bowl. Place it over a pan of hot, simmering water once the pan has been removed from the heat. Take care to avoid contact with the water or steam. Allow chocolate to soften for 10 minutes. Do not stir until quite soft. Use immediately. Avoid working more chocolate than required.

MICROWAVE: Chocolate heated in a microwave does not melt or change its shape in the traditional way. Instead it takes on a shiny appearance, which indicates it is ready. Break chocolate into a small bowl. Heat uncovered to prevent moisture forming. Microwave conditions vary greatly, so it may be necessary to experiment, depending on the type of microwave used. However, short sharp bursts are suggested, with regular gentle stirring depending on the thickness of the chocolate block. Lumps of chocolate may appear, but it will be soft right through when ready. Remove from microwave. Leave chocolate to continue melting, occasionally stirring gently, to produce a smooth, glossy liquid chocolate. Do not reheat as it is likely to crystallise and burn.

Tempering

For this to occur, the chocolate needs to go through a distinct temperature cycle of pre-cooling and heating to form the fat crystals which start the solidification process. Chocolate melts at 35°C (95°F) and is suitably fluid between 31–32°C (88–90°F) (dark/plain) or 30–31°C (86–88°F) (milk). Should the chocolate be warmed up beyond 32°C (90°F) (plain) or 31°C (88°F) (milk), the whole tempering process must begin again. Do not temper a batch of chocolate bigger than you can handle. For example, start with a 1 or 2 kg (2 or 4 lb) batch.

Milk Chocolate

Melt chocolate (see above). When all the chocolate has melted and has risen to a temperature of 45°C (113°F), remove bowl from heat and partially immerse in cold water. Stir the chocolate as it cools and avoid contact with water or condensation. Scrape chocolate from sides of bowl frequently. This will ensure even cooling and stop lumps developing.

When the chocolate has cooled to 26–27°C (79–81°F), it will start to thicken. Place a small sample on a cold surface

(marble slab, cold bench/countertop) to test the colour and temper. It may be necessary to adjust the cooling time. Slowly warm the cooled, thickened chocolate by placing it in a warm

Chocolate collar — Step 1: Spread the chocolate thinly and evenly over the strip of baking paper (parchment).

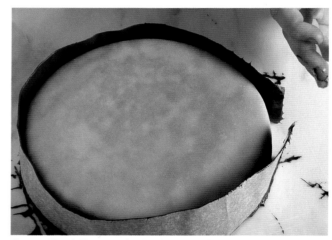

Step 2: Carefully wrap the chocolate-coated strip around the outside of the strip. See page 64.

Plain curls (see page 64)

water bath at 33–35°C (91–95°F). Mix thoroughly to ensure an even temperature throughout. Stir constantly yet gently until it reaches a final temperature of 30–31°C (86–88°F). Test by lifting out some of the chocolate on a palette knife. (If the temperature exceeds 31°C (88°F) for the whole batch, it will be necessary to start again from the initial cooling process.) The chocolate is now ready for use. Keep a chocolate thermometer in the bowl, as any variation in temperature will result in a lack of gloss, streaks or an unfinished product. While you are working on it, keep the chocolate fluid in a water bath at 33–35°C (91–95°F). Stir occasionally to ensure none of the cocoa butter separates. To top up the batch, small pieces of untempered chocolate that have been melted and cooled to 33°C (91°F) may be added.

Note: If tempering dipped centres, they should be set within a few minutes. Moulded pieces take slightly longer to set depending on size. Slow setting indicates unsuccessful tempering. Do not refrigerate to hasten setting. The ideal temperature for desserts which are to be dipped or have the chocolate poured over them is 20–24°C (68–75°F).

Dark Chocolate

Follow same procedures used for milk chocolate, except as follows: after melting, cool the chocolate to 27–28°C (81–82°F); reheat to 31–32°C (88–90°F); do not exceed 32°C (90°F) or you will need to retemper the batch.

Chocolate Substitutes

Compound chocolate, also called chocolate coating, is designed to replace couverture chocolate for coating as it has the advantage of not needing to be tempered. Made from a vegetable oil base with sugar, milk solids and flavouring, compound chocolate contains cocoa powder, but no cocoa butter. Its flavour is inferior to couverture, but it sets faster in hot weather, so it is the choice of many cooks for sweetmaking in summer, and is also used for chocolate decorations. For dipping, compound chocolate is melted exactly like other chocolate.

Problems and Remedies

SCORCHING/BURNING: This is caused by excessive heat (above 49°C/120°F) and damages the components of the chocolate,

resulting in a gritty taste and texture. When melting milk chocolate avoid even localised heat or overheating, as it causes the milk solids in the chocolate to coagulate.
REMEDY: None.

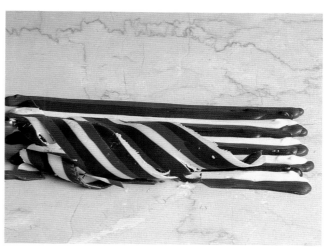

Triple curls (see page 64)

Marbled curls (see page 65)

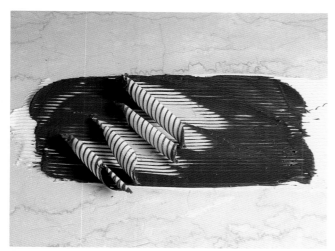

Two-tone curls (see page 64)

Chocolate shavings (see page 65)

THICKENING: This may be caused by:
- Uneven heating or over-heating;
- Addition of other ingredients with a high water content; or
- Spilled water or excessive steam from a saucepan.

REMEDY: Irreversible. As an alternative, use the mixture for chocolate shavings, curls, or as a flavouring.

BUBBLES: These occur when tiny pockets of air are caught up in the liquid chocolate. Often caused by stirring too vigorously during the melting process.

REMEDY: Tap the mould gently with a wooden spoon before the chocolate sets, or use a small brush to pop the bubbles out.

LACK OF GLOSS: This may be caused by:
- Incorrect melting or tempering;
- Storing chocolate in the refrigerator or near steam; or
- Finger marks.

REMEDY: Re-melt and start again.

SLOW SETTING: Chocolate in an unstable condition will not set properly. This indicates that it has not been correctly tempered. (Chocolate which has not set within a few minutes will not set without refrigeration. This will, however, cause it to have a dull, matt finish).

REMEDY: Retemper the chocolate before using.

ADDING WATER: Even small amounts of water will thin chocolate and ruin it completely. Steam, condensation, water in a sugar syrup, all cause it to thicken and develop coarse crystals. (Adding ingredients with a high water content should be avoided unless they are heated with the chocolate right from the start). Avoid all contact with water/moisture.

REMEDY: None.

THINNING: Should only be achieved by adding small amounts of cocoa butter. Always measure the amount of cocoa butter to chocolate used.

Centrepieces

Whether crowning a cake or sitting by itself on a dessert buffet, there is nothing quite so dramatic as a beautifully produced chocolate centrepiece. Serve it by itself with coffee and simply allow your guests to sample the fine threads and lattices of chocolate in front of them. Take care and time when producing all centrepieces. The designs that follow are meant as a guide only. There is an endless number of designs you can experiment with to create the most fantastic chocolate centrepieces.

Approximately 360 g (12 oz) of melted dark (plain or semi-sweet) chocolate is needed for a centrepiece to crown a 23 cm (9 in) cake.

Cut four strips of baking paper (parchment) large enough to cover the shape of your centrepiece. Using the designs on page 54, place one sheet of baking paper over one of the designs. Pipe the design with the chocolate, using a paper piping (pastry) bag (see page 205) which is cut so that it has a thick nozzle. Pipe four copies of the design and allow them to set in the refrigerator on a tray. Once set, take two of the designs and place them flat on a tray so that they touch each other (one will have to be turned upside down so that they are facing each other). Join them using a small amount of melted chocolate on the two points that are touching, and allow this to set.

When this has set, pipe a small dot of chocolate on the previous joins and sit another of the piped pieces vertically onto this. Using your fingertips, hold the centrepiece together until it has set firm and does not need to be held up.

Once firm, stand the centrepiece up so that it is resting on the base of all three joined pieces. Carefully pick up the fourth piece and with a little melted chocolate piped onto the same points, join it to the other three pieces. Allow this to set hard before placing on top of a cake.

Note: When making a centrepiece for the first time, make 2–3 more designs than the four required, to allow for breakages and so that you can choose the best piped designs. If you need to store a centrepiece for a considerable time, strengthen the piped designs by turning each one over, once it is set, and piping the design over the top. By piping over the flat side (which was attached to the paper), you will enhance the appearance of the centrepiece. Allow the second side to set firm before joining the centrepiece as described.

Collars

Chocolate collars add a special and decorative finish to any cake. Measure the height of the cake to be decorated and cut a strip of baking paper (parchment) 1 cm (½ in) higher than the depth of the cake. This strip should also be long enough to wrap easily around the circumference of the cake with 1 cm (½ in) to spare on each end: for a 23 cm (9 in) cake, make a strip 25 cm (10 in) long.

To make a collar that will wrap around a 23 cm (9 in) cake, spread 300 g (10 oz) of melted dark (plain or semi-sweet) chocolate over the paper, spreading thinly and evenly. As soon as the paper is covered, very carefully pick it up lengthways and wrap it around the cake, paper face out. You can cut off any excess if it is too long for the cake. Smooth the paper around the cake and chill in the refrigerator for 5–10 minutes, until the collar has set firm. Peel the paper off.

Plain Curls

About 500 g (16 oz) of dark (plain or semi-sweet) chocolate will make enough curls to cover a 23 cm (9 in) cake.

Pour melted dark (plain or semi-sweet) chocolate onto a marble slab or a stainless steel bench (counter) top and, using a palette knife, spread it out thinly. As the chocolate begins to set, hold a large knife at a 45° angle to the bench or surface and pull gently through the chocolate. It is essential to work quickly or the chocolate will harden and splinter.

Two-tone Curls

Approximately 250 g (8 oz) combined weight of white chocolate and dark (plain or semi-sweet) chocolate will make enough curls to cover a 23 cm (9 in) cake.

Pour melted white chocolate onto a marble slab or stainless steel bench (counter) top and, using a palette knife, spread it out thinly. Make ridges in one direction with a comb scraper or fork. Cool and harden. Pour melted dark chocolate over the top of the ridges of white chocolate. Spread thinly until the white chocolate is completely covered. As the chocolate begins to set, hold a large knife at a 45° angle to the bench or surface and pull gently through the chocolate.

Triple Curls

Approximately 210 g (7 oz) each of white, milk and dark (plain or semi-sweet) chocolate will make enough curls to cover a 23 cm (9 in) cake.

Melt each kind of chocolate separately and pour each into a separate paper piping (pastry) bag. Pipe rows of dark chocolate onto a marble slab or stainless steel bench (counter) top. Leave enough room between each row of dark chocolate to pipe the other two chocolates. Working quickly, pipe in the rows of milk and then white chocolate, making certain that each chocolate is touching the other as it sets. Allow the chocolate to firm slightly before holding a large knife with a flexible blade at a 45° angle to the bench or surface and pulling through the chocolate to produce the curls.

See page 63

Marbled Curls

Approximately 100 g (3½ oz) each of white, milk and dark (plain or semi-sweet) chocolate will make enough marbled curls to cover a 23 cm (9 in) cake.

Drizzle melted white chocolate in a very abstract fashion onto a marble slab or stainless steel bench (counter) top. Over the top of the white chocolate, drizzle the milk chocolate in a different pattern. Allow the white and milk chocolate to set together. Pour dark (plain or semi-sweet) chocolate over the top of the white and milk chocolate to create the finished marble effect. Spread it thinly.
Allow it to set but not completely harden before holding a large knife with a flexible blade at a 45° angle to the bench (counter) top and pulling through the chocolate to produce curls.

See page 63

Chocolate Shavings

Approximately 250 g (8 oz) of milk, dark (plain or semi-sweet) or white chocolate will make enough shavings to cover a 23 cm (9 in) cake.

Pull a vegetable peeler smoothly and evenly across the surface of a block of chocolate. This will produce small shavings which are great for spreading on cakes or for rolling truffles in.

See page 63

Chocolate Squares

approximately 400 g (14 oz) of melted dark (plain or semi-sweet) chocolate

Use a palette knife to spread the chocolate evenly onto a sheet of baking paper (parchment) 30 x 30 cm (12 x 12 in). Leave in a cool place to set for 5–10 minutes. Mark 5 x 5 cm (2 x 2 in) squares onto the chocolate and, using a clean. sharp knife, cut the chocolate where it has been marked. If the chocolate has set too hard and is shattering at the slightest touch, use a hot sharp knife for cutting.

Makes 20–30 squares

Note: Chocolate Squares can be used to decorate the top or sides of any cake.

Modelling Chocolate

About ⅔ cup (8 oz) liquid glucose (corn syrup) and 300 g (10 oz) melted dark (plain or semi-sweet) chocolate will cover a 23 cm (9 in) cake.

Place the syrup in a saucepan and heat until it liquefies. Remove from the heat and mix in the chocolate. Continue to stir until the mixture leaves the sides of the pan. Pour into a container lined with plastic wrap (cling film) and allow to set at room temperature. Do not chill.
When the chocolate has set, roll out onto a lightly floured surface until it is very thin (approximately 3–4 mm / ⅛ in thick) and fits the cake to be decorated. Stretch the chocolate in your hands so it is about one and a half times the surface area of the cake. Holding the piece of chocolate in the centre, allow it to fall over the cake so that it looks ruffled. Smooth down the sides of the chocolate against the cake. If the chocolate tears, tuck the torn area under and drape another piece of chocolate over the torn area.
Alternatively, the cake can be covered smoothly by simply placing the chocolate layer on top of the cake, smoothing over and cutting away any excess chocolate from around the sides of the cake. When the cake is completely covered with the modelling chocolate, dust lightly with cocoa powder.
Modelling chocolate will store in a cool dry place for up to 6 months, if not subject to dramatic changes in temperatures.

Chocolate Piping

Before piping directly onto any finished pastry item, practise on a piece of baking paper (parchment).

To pipe, spoon a small amount of melted chocolate into a small paper piping (pastry) bag. Make sure no lumps are present. Fold over the ends of the bag. Cut the tip of the bag to the desired size. Practise designs on the paper and allow the chocolate to set. These designs can then be carefully peeled from the paper and placed on top of a cake.
To make unusual decorative designs for special occasions, draw an outline of the figure required and place a sheet of baking paper over the top. Using a thin-tipped paper piping (pastry) bag filled with chocolate, trace the drawn design on the top sheet. Allow this outline to set firm, then use the piping bag filled with chocolate of another colour to fill in all the gaps inside the design. Take extra care that you do not go over the top of the outline of the design. Once you have completely filled the gaps, allow chocolate to set till firm, then peel from the paper.

CHOCOLATE FONDUE

½ cup (5 oz) liquid glucose (corn syrup)
⅔ cup (5 fl oz) thickened (double or heavy) cream
2 tablespoons Grand Marnier liqueur,
or your favourite liqueur
250 g (8 oz) dark (plain or semi-sweet) chocolate, chopped
selection of fresh fruits (perhaps strawberries, grapes,
pineapple, mandarin or orange segments), marinated
for 1 hour in 2 tablespoons Grand Marnier liqueur
or your favourite liqueur

Dark Chocolate Truffles

Gently heat glucose, thickened cream and your choice of liqueur in a saucepan and stir until boiled. Remove saucepan from the heat, add chopped chocolate and stir until all the ingredients are combined. Serve immediately with a selection of marinated fresh fruits.

Note: You can replace the dark (plain or semi-sweet) chocolate with white or milk chocolate in this recipe. You can also make one mixture from all three types of chocolate by pouring them into one dish and allowing them to become a marbled mass.

Serves 6—8

CHOCOLATE PATE

⅓ cup (2½ fl oz) water
¾ cup (6 oz) caster (superfine) sugar
1 tablespoon cocoa powder
180 g (6 oz) unsalted (sweet) butter
½ cup (2 oz) chopped brazil nuts
½ cup (2 oz) chopped pistachio nuts
⅓ cup (2 oz) chopped glacé pineapple
⅓ cup (2 oz) chopped glacé apricots
125 g (4 oz) shortbread biscuits (cookies), finely crushed
180 g (6 oz) dark (plain or semi-sweet) chocolate, melted (see page 62)
2½ tablespoons Grand Marnier
zest of 1 orange
zest of 1 lemon
1 egg
2 egg yolks

Line a 23 cm (9 in) springform cake tin with plastic wrap (cling film). Place water and sugar in a saucepan and slowly bring to the boil. Boil for 5 minutes. Cool slightly. Cream cocoa powder and butter together until light and fluffy. Mix chopped nuts, fruit and crushed biscuits together. Add chocolate to boiled sugar syrup and stir until smooth. Add Grand Marnier, lemon and orange zests and mix. Fold in the egg and egg yolks. Fold in butter/cocoa mixture and mixture of fruit, nuts and biscuits. Stir well until combined. Pour mixture into the prepared tin. Press firmly into the tin and smooth the top. Refrigerate for 24 hours before unmoulding. Serve in very fine slices.

Serves 20

CHOCOLATE TART

Base
180 g (6 oz) unsalted (sweet) butter
½ cup (3 oz) icing (powdered) sugar
2 cups (8 oz) plain (all-purpose) flour
3 tablespoons cocoa powder
1 egg

Filling
90 g (3 oz) unsalted (sweet) butter
90 g (3 oz) dark (plain or semi-sweet) chocolate
3 eggs
⅓ cup (1½ oz) plain (all-purpose) flour
⅔ cup (5 oz) caster (superfine) sugar

Topping
90 ml (3 fl oz) thickened (double or heavy) cream
210 g (7 oz) dark (plain or semi-sweet) chocolate, melted (see page 62)

Preheat the oven to 140°C (280°F). Lightly grease a 24 x 4 cm (10 x 1½ in) round quiche dish or cake tin.

Base
Rub the butter into the dry ingredients until the mixture resembles fine breadcrumbs. Add the egg and work the mix to a dough. On a lightly floured surface, roll the dough thinly and large enough to fill the greased tin. Line the tin with the pastry and place in the refrigerator till filling is ready.

Filling
Place the butter and chocolate in the top of a double boiler and melt together. Place the eggs, flour and sugar into a mixing bowl and whisk on high speed for 8 minutes. Fold melted chocolate mixture in. Pour the mixture into the pastry-lined tin and bake for 35—45 minutes.

Topping
While the tart is baking, place the cream in a saucepan and slowly bring to the boil. Remove from the heat and add the chopped chocolate, stirring until all the chocolate has dissolved. Leave the mixture in the saucepan, covered, until the tart has baked and cooled.
When the tart is baked, cool it in the tin. As it cools, the crust will sink. As it does, help it to flatten by pressing it down gently. When cold and with crust flattened, pour the chocolate topping over the top of the tart. Refrigerate for 1 hour before serving.

CHOCOLATE TRUFFLES

1 cup (8 oz) thickened (double or heavy) cream
630 g (21 oz) milk chocolate, chopped finely
90 g (3 oz) unsalted (sweet) butter, softened
300 g (10 oz) milk chocolate, coarsely grated
360 g (12 oz) milk chocolate, melted
flaked almonds, roasted (see page 5), for rolling, or icing (powdered) sugar, for dusting

Place cream in a saucepan and allow it to come to the boil. Remove saucepan from the heat and add finely chopped chocolate. Allow mixture to stand for several minutes before stirring to a smooth paste, free of chocolate lumps. Add butter immediately and stir slowly until it is completely incorporated into the chocolate mixture. Pour mixture into a bowl and cover tightly with plastic wrap (cling film). Refrigerate until firm (12 hours or overnight). Remove mixture from the refrigerator. Using a melon baller which has been dipped in warm water, place balls of the mixture on a tray lined with plastic wrap (cling film). When all the balls have been arranged on the tray, place in the freezer for 20 minutes to allow the balls to firm.

Place coarsely grated milk chocolate on a tray, and the melted milk chocolate beside the tray. Remove the tray of chilled balls from the refrigerator. Dip your fingers into the melted milk chocolate, then roll one ball at a time between your fingers to coat it with chocolate before dropping it into the grated chocolate. Roll the balls around in the tray to cover completely. Place the truffles on a serving dish or in an airtight storage container, and refrigerate until required.

Before serving, dust lightly with icing sugar.

Makes 36

CHOCOLATE TUILES

6 egg whites
1 cup (7 oz) icing (powdered) sugar, sifted
½ cup (2 oz) plain (all-purpose) flour, sifted
1 tablespoon cocoa powder, sifted
75 g (2½ oz) unsalted (sweet) butter, melted

Preheat oven to 180°C (350°F).
Lightly grease a baking sheet.
Mix egg whites with sifted icing sugar until incorporated. Add flour and cocoa and lightly whisk until a smooth paste is formed. Allow batter to rest for 15 minutes. Stir in melted butter and mix well. Place tablespoons of the batter on the prepared sheet and spread into 5–8 cm (2–3 in) circles. Bake for 10 minutes in preheated oven. Remove the tuiles from the sheet by sliding a flat knife underneath each one. Press each tuile immediately around a rolling pin or a cylindrical object so that it hardens into a semi-circular shape. If the tuiles become cold and firm before you have finished shaping them, reheat them on a baking sheet in the oven for 1–2 minutes, or until they become soft and malleable.

Makes 18–24

CHOCOLATIER

A professional chocolate maker who specialises in the production of quality chocolates and chocolate goods, a chocolatier is trained under apprenticeship or by taking courses (of a month, six months or a year) under a master chocolatier in Europe. To handle chocolate without fear of the tempering process, to understand the temperatures and to work skilfully with chocolate is not simply a matter of training, but requires a love of chocolate and many years of practice working with the medium.

CHOUX PASTRY
(see also churros, croquembouche, éclairs, profiteroles)

A cooked panade of water, butter and flour which is made light by adding eggs and then baked, choux pastry was invented around 1540 by Popelini, Catherine de Medici's pastry chef, who, it is said, accidentally dropped the flour into some boiling water. Out of curiosity, he added some eggs to the ball of dough which had formed and eventually perfected a recipe for choux. The name choux pastry refers to the cabbage-like look of the finished product if it is made correctly.

The water and butter must be boiling rapidly when the flour is added so that all the starch cells in the flour burst open, allowing them to accept more liquid (in the form of the eggs), which in turn will help them rise because of the increased amount of steam being given off. Choux pastry rises via steam and therefore the oven door must be kept shut so that the internal steam can be kept in and help the pastry rise.

A good choux pastry recipe should not contain added sugar, allowing the natural sugars in the flour to brown the crust; this enables the choux to be baked for a lengthier time so that the internal mixture dries out. If the internal stucture does not dry out, the steam coming from it will soften the outer crust and then the whole choux pastry will be soggy and moist. Another way of preventing this is to cut or punch a hole in the baked products as soon as they are removed from the oven to allow the steam to escape.

The most popular choux pastry products are:

(i) Eclairs: Long, thin, bone-shaped strips of choux pastry, traditionally coated with chocolate fondant and filled with crème Chantilly.

(ii) Profiteroles: Small choux puffs filled with crème pâtissière.

(iii) Choux buns: Also known as choux puffs or cream puffs. Large profiteroles which are filled with fruit and sweetened cream and dusted with icing (powdered) sugar.

(iv) Swans: Shell-shaped bodies and heads are piped from the choux pastry in the shape of a 2. When baked, the bodies are cut in half, the bottom halves are filled with cream and the heads are inserted upright, while the top halves of the bodies are split to look like wings.

(v) Crumble Puffs: Streusel or crumble mixture is sprinkled on top of the choux pastry before baking, for extra flavour and sweetness.

Choux Pastry

1½ cups (12 fl oz) water
150 g (5 oz) unsalted (sweet) butter
1¼ cups (5 oz) plain (all-purpose) flour
5 eggs

Preheat oven to 180°C (350°F).
Line baking sheets with baking paper (parchment).
Place water and butter in a saucepan and bring to the boil.
Add flour while the liquid is still boiling and stir until the mixture leaves the base and sides of the pan. Remove from the heat, cool slightly and then begin to add eggs slowly, stirring well after each each one is added, until all the eggs are combined and the mixture is smooth. Pipe mixture onto prepared sheets.
Bake in preheated oven for 45 minutes.
(Do not open the oven for the first 15 minutes.)

CHRABELI

This sweet Mediterranean bread-like biscuit is made from a meringue and flour mixture. With a dry and lightly golden casing, the inside texture is like bread. It is wonderful as an accompaniment to desserts and coffee, and delicious as a snack. The unbaked mixture must dry for 8–10 hours before being baked.

5 egg whites
1½ cups (8 oz) icing (powdered) sugar
2¼ cups (9 oz) plain (all-purpose) flour

Preheat oven to 200°C (400°F). Line baking sheets with baking paper (parchment) and lightly dust with cornflour (cornstarch).
Place egg whites and icing sugar in a mixing bowl. Using an electric mixer, whip until the mixture is stiff and fluffy. Fold flour through by hand, stopping as soon as all ingredients are combined. Allow mixture to sit, covered with a damp cloth, for 1 hour.
Knead the dough on a lightly floured surface, keeping dough and your hands lightly floured to prevent stickiness. Take heaped tablespoons of the mixture and form into pear shapes. Using scissors or a knife, make three cuts down one side of each shape and then place them on the prepared sheet.
Bend the pieces slightly to open up the three cuts.
Allow the chrabeli to sit uncovered at room temperature for 8–10 hours to dry out and then bake in preheated oven for 8–10 minutes or until slightly browned.

Makes 28

CHRISTENING CAKE
(see fruit cake)

Traditionally, this is a highly decorated cake made in honour of the newborn baby on the day of its christening.

CHRISTMAS CAKE

1½ cups (6 oz) plain (all-purpose) flour
4 level teaspoons ground cinnamon
300 g (10 oz) unsalted (sweet) butter, softened
2 cups (10 oz) light brown sugar
6 eggs
4 tablespoons golden syrup (light treacle)
1½ cups (8 oz) seedless (dark) raisins
3 cups (18 oz) sultanas (golden raisins)
⅔ cup (4 oz) mixed (candied) peel
⅔ cup (4 oz) glacé (candied) red cherries
1 cup (4 oz) slivered almonds

To Decorate
1 egg white
300 g (10 oz) marzipan
1 quantity royal icing (see page 241)

Preheat oven to 170°C (340°F). Lightly grease a 23 cm (9 in) springform tin with butter and line with 5 layers of greaseproof (waxed) paper, bringing the level of the paper 2.5 cm (1 in) above the rim of the tin.

Mix flour and cinnamon together and sift twice. Beat butter and sugar until creamy, light and fluffy. Add eggs and golden syrup and beat well. Mix dried fruit, peel, cherries and nuts into the mixture alternately with sifted flour. Spoon into prepared tin. Bake for 3–4 hours, or until a skewer inserted into the centre of the cake comes out dry.
Cool the cake in the tin for 24 hours.
Wrap the cake so that it is airtight and store in a cool, dry place until required.

To Decorate
Remove greaseproof paper before decorating. Brush the top and sides of the cake with the egg white. Roll out the marzipan on a lightly floured surface and cover the cake. Trim edges. With a palette knife, spread the royal icing over the top and sides of the cake and decorate in a Christmas theme with holly.

CHRISTMAS LOGS (DUTCH)

6 eggs
⅔ cup (5 oz) caster (superfine) sugar
1 teaspoon vanilla essence (extract)
1¼ cups (5 oz) plain (all-purpose) flour
30 g (1 oz) unsalted (sweet) butter
375 g (12 oz) plain marzipan (see page 177)
½ cup (5 oz) apricot jam (jelly)
½ cup (2 oz) sultanas (golden raisins)
⅓ cup (2 oz) glacé (candied) cherries, finely chopped
¼ cup (1 oz) slivered almonds, soaked overnight in 90 ml (3 fl oz) sherry or port

Meringue
3 egg whites
1½ cups (8 oz) icing (powdered) sugar, sifted

Preheat oven to 180°C (350°F). Lightly grease a 25 x 30 x 3 cm (10 x 12 x 1 in) baking tray (jelly roll pan) with butter and line with baking paper (parchment).
Place eggs and sugar in a mixing bowl and whip until very thick and frothy. Add vanilla. Fold flour and melted butter through egg mixture. Take care not to lose too much air from the mixture. Pour mixture into prepared tray and bake in preheated oven for 15–18 minutes or until the top of the sponge springs back when lightly touched.
On a lightly floured surface, roll the marzipan to the size of the sponge sheet. Turn the cake out onto a sugar-dusted surface or sugar-lined paper. Remove baking paper from the underside of the cake and trim the crusty edges of the cake with a sharp knife. Cover the cake with the apricot jam. Place the rolled marzipan over the top of the jam-covered cake. Sprinkle the soaked sultanas, cherries and almonds over the surface of the marzipan. Working quickly, grasp the furthest end of the baking paper and pull it towards you or, if working on the sugar-dusted surface, simply roll the sponge sheet into a Swiss roll shape. When rolled, cool completely then place on a baking tray.

Christmas Pudding Step-by-Step

Step 1: Place the pudding mixture in the centre of the square pudding cloth.

Step 2: Carefully and firmly tie the top of the cloth so that no water will penetrate.

Step 3: Carefully remove the pudding from the cloth. See page 71.

Meringue
Preheat oven to 200°C (400°F).
Whisk egg whites until light and fluffy and stiff peaks have
formed. Slowly begin adding sugar, a little at a time, until all
has been dissolved and a stiff meringue has formed. Spread
meringue mixture over the sponge roll. Using a fork, mark
lines along the length of the roll to resemble bark.
Place covered roll in preheated oven for several minutes
to brown lightly. Dust lightly with icing sugar
and serve immediately.

Serves 12

CHRISTMAS ICE PUDDING

This is a frozen ice cream dessert full of brandied fruits or
fruit mince and flavoured with chocolate, nougat or chestnut
purée. The iced puddings originated in hot countries where
the traditional hot Christmas pudding was not viable, in the
19th century.

½ cup (3 oz) sultanas (golden raisins)
½ cup (3 oz) raisins, chopped
¼ cup (2 fl oz) Grand Marnier
2½ cups (20 fl oz) thickened (double or heavy) cream
210 g (7 oz) sweetened condensed milk
150 g (5 oz) dark (plain or semi-sweet) chocolate, melted
⅓ cup (2 oz) glacé (candied) cherries
¼ teaspoon ground cinnamon
¼ teaspoon ground nutmeg
¼ teaspoon ground cloves
½ cup (2 oz) flaked almonds, roasted (see page 5)
90 g (3 oz) dark (plain or semi-sweet) chocolate,
melted, for curling decoration

Soak sultanas and raisins overnight in the Grand Marnier.
Lightly whip cream, add condensed milk and chocolate.
Stir quickly to ensure chocolate blends smoothly with the
other ingredients and does not set solid or in lumps.
Stir soaked fruit, glacé cherries, spices and almonds into the
cream mixture. Pour mixture into a large pudding bowl and
freeze for 12 hours. To remove the pudding from the bowl,
place a hot cloth around the outside of the bowl and turn it
upside down onto a serving dish. Sprinkle the pudding
with chocolate curls (see page 64) to serve.

CHRISTMAS PUDDING

Christmas pudding as we know it today, developed from the
ancient 'figgy', a mixture of meat and figs which eventually
had the meat replaced by oats and became a sweet pottage or
porridge. Some time around the 17th century, the porridge
was thickened with ground almonds, fruits, nuts and flour
and was then boiled within a cloth, and hung and dried for
several months to mature before serving. Until recently, it
was a tradition to put small objects inside the pudding
mixture and these indicated whether good or bad luck would
greet the finder in the year ahead. To find the ring meant
marriage, a thimble or a button meant the girl and boy would
stay single, while a small coin meant becoming rich.

1½ cups (9 oz) raisins
1½ cups (9 oz) sultanas (golden raisins)
1⅔ cups (8 oz) dates
1 cup (5 oz) currants
¾ cup (4 oz) mixed (candied) peel
1 cup (4 oz) slivered almonds
250 g (8 oz) unsalted (sweet) butter
1¼ cups (8 oz) caster (superfine) sugar
1 teaspoon ground cinnamon
1½ cups (6 oz) plain (all-purpose) flour
½ teaspoon bicarbonate of soda
1½ cups (6 oz) dry breadcrumbs
1 teaspoon vanilla essence (extract)
5 eggs

Mix raisins, sultanas, dates, currants, mixed peel and
almonds in a large bowl. Cream butter and sugar until light
and fluffy. Add eggs, vanilla essence and cinnamon to the
butter mixture and mix well. Add fruits and almonds and
combine by hand. Sift flour and bicarbonate of soda onto
mixture and lastly add the breadcrumbs, folding all
ingredients together until well combined.
Stir mixture well for 5 minutes.
Cut a 70 x 70 cm (28 x 28 in) sheet of calico material and
place it in hot water to moisten the cloth. Place mixture in the
centre of the material and gather the excess material together
tightly in a firm cluster to totally enclose the mix. Tie the top
of the material, very tightly, as close to the pudding mix as
possible, with strong string, so that no water will enter from
the top. Place pudding in a large pot of boiling water and boil
for 4½ hours. During this time, keep the pot full of water and
do not allow it to go off the boil. When finished boiling,
remove the pudding from the water and hang it for up to
6 weeks in a well ventilated area
so that it does not touch anything. This allows
the pudding to mature and develop a fuller flavour.
When you want to serve the pudding, place it in
a large pot of boiling water and boil it for 2 hours.
Remove the pudding from its cloth and serve
immediately with rum sauce or brandy butter.

See page 70

CHRISTOPSOMO

Served at Christmas, this traditional festive bread of Greek
origin is decorated on top with a cross of nuts.

CHURROS
(see also choux pastry)

Named after a Spanish long-haired sheep, churros resemble
the long tufts of hair on the sheep. Churros are made from
choux pastry (cream puff paste) which is piped in straight
lines into hot fat and fried. Once they are golden brown, the
churros are rolled in cinnamon-flavoured sugar and served
immediately as a dessert or as a snack with coffee.

CIGARETTE

These are also known as Cigarettes Russes, or Russian Cigarettes. Made from tuile or langue de chat mixture, the cigarette shapes are formed while the baked tuiles are still warm, by rolling them around a thin wooden handle. When cool, they are removed and filled or left plain or, more traditionally, half dipped into melted chocolate. They are served as a petit four with coffee or with light mousse desserts or fresh fruits.

CINNAMON
(see also spices)

Cinnamon is the crushed, ground or rolled bark of a laurel tree which grows in India and surrounding areas. It is one of the oldest spices known to have been used in cooking, having been used for trade purposes by the Egyptians some 2000 years before the birth of Christ. Since those times cinnamon has been used to spice and flavour sweet and savoury dishes and is also considered a herbal remedy by many cultures including the Chinese, who burn cinnamon quills for their incense.

Cinnamon can be bought in ground powder form or in sticks or quills, which have a more intense flavour and are produced by peeling the bark from the tree and rolling it. Good cinnamon should be reddish brown, although this can depend on the variety and region where the cinnamon is grown.

CINNAMON SUGAR
(see also sugar)

1 teaspoon ground cinnamon
4 tablespoons sugar

Mix the two ingredients together and sprinkle on top of biscuits (cookies) before and after baking, or on top of pastries after glazing with egg wash and before baking.

CINNAMON TOAST
(see also bread)

Use only fresh white bread and butter both sides of each slice. Dust each buttered side heavily with cinnamon sugar and then grill each side of the bread until golden brown.

Cinnamon toast can be served fresh with ice cream or maple syrup or cut into fingers and served with light mousse-style desserts or syllabubs.

CISELER

The name for the small hole that is cut or marked into the top of small or large pies and pastries to prevent the pastry splitting or breaking open due to the rising of steam from within.

CITRIC ACID
(see also lemon)

A naturally occurring acid in citrus fruits and certain varieties of berries which is extracted and sold in both dry crystal form and liquid form. It is added to sugar syrups to prevent crystallisation and is also used in the production of jams, jellies and cordials, as well as being used in royal icing to ensure a dry crisp product that will set immediately.

CITRUS
(see also grapefruit, lemon, lime, orange)

The family name for fruits such as oranges, lemons, grapefruit, mandarins, limes and tangerines. All citrus fruits contain highly aromatic oils within their skins which can be removed for use in sauces by rubbing sugar cubes over the skin. Citrus fruits tend to have a high level of vitamin C and are also among the most popular flavours used within the pastry domain, with lemons and oranges being the most commonly used for both their zest and juice.

CITRUS PEEL

The zest or rind of the citrus fruits which have been boiled and crystallised in sugar syrup and chopped into fine pieces for use in fruit cakes, fruit desserts and fruit minces, among other recipes. Also known commonly as mixed peel, in which the zests of several varieties of citrus fruit are mixed together after crystallising. It is often used as a decoration and although commonly found in chopped form, can also be made or bought in long thin slivers for dipping into chocolate or for extra decorative effect. Citrus peel is one of the most common forms of crystallised fruit and is used in many recipes.

2 oranges
2 lemons
1 cup (8 oz) white granulated sugar
⅔ cup (5 fl oz) water
2 tablespoons liquid glucose (corn syrup)

Make sure that the oranges and lemons have clean skin. Using a sharp knife carefully remove the skin. Try not to take too much of the white pith with it. When all the rind has been removed from the fruit, cut away any excess pith from the rind. Cut each of the strips of rind 1–2 mm (⅛ in) thick or as thin as possible. Put sugar, water and glucose into a saucepan and bring to the boil. Add rind of the fruit and boil for a further 20 minutes. As the mixture boils, wash down the sides of the saucepan with a pastry brush dipped in warm water. Place the peel on a wire rack and allow it to drain and dry overnight. Once dried, the peel can be cut into small pieces and used in cakes or puddings, fondues, dipped in chocolate or eaten by itself.

Makes 1 cup of peel

CLAFOUTIS

A well-known French dessert from Provence, its name originating from the Provençale dialect, in which 'clafir', means to fill. It is made from a rich batter poured over fresh fruits, traditionally sour black cherries. The dessert should be served warm with its golden brown crust dusted in icing sugar.

400 g (13 oz) fresh or tinned sour black cherries (drained)
2 cups (16 fl oz) milk
1 cup (8 fl oz) cream
¾ cup (3 oz) plain (all-purpose) flour, sifted
1 cup (6 oz) icing (powdered) sugar
4 eggs

Preheat oven to 180°C (350°F).
Lightly grease an earthenware baking dish or flan dish. Sprinkle the base of the dish with chopped cherries. Place milk and cream in a saucepan and bring slowly to the boil. When boiled, pour the liquid over the sifted flour and icing sugar and beat until cool and lump free. When the mixture is cool, add eggs one at a time and then pour mixture over the cherries and bake for 30–35 minutes, or until firm and golden brown. Dust with icing sugar and serve immediately.

CLARIFY
(see also butter)

'Clarify' means to clear and is a process used on butter and also stocks and sauces. Clarification of a liquid involves removing any unwanted fats or impurities. In the case of stocks and clear sauces this is done by folding egg whites through them. To clarify butter, melt it and use a ladle to remove the clear yellow fat.

CLARET ICE

This is not a churned sorbet but broken ice particles of claret wine served as a dessert or as a refresher between courses.

1 cup (8 fl oz) claret red wine
1 cup (8 fl oz) sugar syrup (see page 266)
zest and juice of 3 lemons
zest and juice of 3 oranges

Stir all ingredients together, pour into a flat baking dish and place in the freezer. As the mixture becomes icy, stir it occasionally to keep the ice crystals small. When frozen, break the ice into small pieces and serve in a champagne glass which has been frosted on the rim with sugar.
Serve as a dessert or between courses as a refresher.

CLOTTED CREAM
(see also cream)

An English specialty of the West Counties, clotted cream is produced by heating fresh milk and skimming the cream from the top to produce a rich thick, yellow cream which has a fat content of around 50% and is traditionally served with scones (biscuits) in Devonshire teas. Clotted cream does not require whipping as it is thick enough to scoop.

CLOVES
(see also spices)

Originating in Africa and Madagascar, cloves come from the French word 'clou', which literally refers to the clove's shape, a nail. Cloves are in fact the dried flower calyx of *Eugenia caryophyllata*, a small tree. The flower buds are beaten from the tree by hitting the tree with wooden paddles, the red coloured calyx falling to the ground onto mats. The calyx is taken and dried and becomes hard and black/brown in colour. To produce 1 kg (2 lb) of ground cloves it takes an average of 10–15 000 whole dried cloves. Having a sweet, spicy flavour, cloves are used whole or ground in fruit compôtes, pies, syrups, and ground cloves are used in many cake and pastry doughs, batters, gingerbreads, and fruit mince.

COAT
(see also mask)

To give a dessert or cake a total covering of icing, fondant, chocolate or marzipan, modelling pastes or buttercreams or a combination of these as a final finish or as a preparation for a final coating.

COBBLER
(see also brown betty, crumble, streusel)

An English traditional dessert similar in many ways to the American Brown Betty or the crumble or streusel, cobbler consists of a fruit base which is topped with a scone (biscuit) dough. The dough can be in small balls, so that there is a single piece for each portion, or it can cover the dish completely, in which case it will be cut when served.

COBBLER APPLE
6 large cooking apples, peeled, cored and sliced
⅔ cup (5 oz) sugar
¾ cup (6 fl oz) water
2 cloves
½ teaspoon ground cinnamon
2¼ cups (9 oz) plain (all-purpose) flour
2 teaspoons baking powder (soda)
1 tablespoon sugar
¼ teaspoon ground cloves
125 g (4 oz) unsalted (sweet) butter
2 eggs, lightly beaten

Preheat oven to 180°C (350°F).
Place apples in a casserole dish and sprinkle sugar and water over them, then add cloves and ground cinnamon. Place dish in preheated oven and bake for 25–30 minutes, or until apples are soft. Sift flour and baking powder into a mixing bowl with sugar and cloves. Rub the butter into the dry ingredients until the mixture resembles fresh breadcrumbs. Add lightly beaten eggs and mix to a dough consistency. Break off small pieces of the dough and place on top of the apple mixture so that it is well covered. Place the cobbler in the oven and bake for 25–30 minutes or until the dough pieces are risen, brown and crisp.

COBURG
(see bread)

COCHINEAL
(see also colourings)

One of the most common colourings used in cake and pastry production or for colouring of centrepieces and displays, cochineal is a red food colouring produced from a small Mexican beetle. The beetles, which live on cacti, contain a pigment known as carminic acid, which, when the beetles are dried and crushed, produces the cochineal colouring.

COCOA
(see also chocolate, drinking chocolate)

Cocoa powder is produced from presscake, the paste left over once cocoa butter has been pressed from crushed cocoa beans, and contains 5–20% cocoa butter or fat, depending on how much pressing the press cake has undergone. Derived from the Aztec word 'xocoatl', cocoa is actually a word invented by accident when its botanical name *cacao* was misspelled.

Cocoa powder is used in baking pastries, biscuits (cookies), cakes and for making drinks. On its own, it is very bitter, and sugar or a sugar-based mixture needs to be added for edibility; however, some people do like the flavour of the bitter raw cocoa and it is therefore occasionally dusted raw onto the tops of cakes and desserts or used to coat sweet truffles for a bittersweet effect.

When using cocoa in cake batters, the cocoa should be sifted with the flour several times before its incorporation into the batter. If cocoa is being added on its own to a cake batter, it can also be reduced to a paste, for easier, more complete distribution, by mixing it with some boiling water. It is hard to get a powder to dissolve completely into a cold cake batter.

COCOA BUTTER
(see also chocolate)

Cocoa butter is the natural fat derived from the pressing of cocoa beans when producing cocoa mass or cocoa powder and is a creamy yellow colour when solidified, or transparent when warmed above 32°C (90°F). Cocoa butter is returned in the chocolate-making process to help produce chocolates with a rich, pure chocolate flavour. The use of cocoa butter in chocolate requires the chocolate to be tempered, as the cocoa butter naturally contains two crystals with different setting points. In order to integrate them, the chocolate containing the cocoa butter must be warmed to a certain temperature, cooled, then rewarmed to around 32°C (90°F) so that it can set and have a crisp break and gloss finish.

Cocoa butter is the most expensive fat in the world. As well as being used in the production of chocolates and chocolate confections, it is also used in manufacturing of cosmetics.

COCONUT

A firm, large, woody, ball-shaped nut, the coconut is the fruit of the tall coconut palm tree, which originated in Malaysia and today grows in most of the world's tropical regions.

Coconut shells are opened in one of two ways: by hitting the shell hard with a mallet or hammer, or by piercing three soft holes in the end of the coconut. The milk is then drained from it and the coconut placed in a hot oven until it cracks open, at which point the pure white flesh can be scraped out and used.

The coconut milk is used in some dishes to enhance the flavour, while the white flesh is usually dried and grated into three forms of coconut for use in baking: desiccated (finely grated), shredded (long thin threads) and flaked or shaved (large white sheets of the coconut, removed with a vegetable peeler). The coconut can also be pressed to extract an oil known as coconut butter or copha, a hard white fat which becomes transparent when heated and is used to set biscuits (cookies) and slices firm without baking.

COCONUT ICE

A rich sweet form of confectionery or candy which consists of two coconut-rich layers, one pink and the other white, which set firm and are served in only very small slices.

4 cups (32 oz) sugar
1¼ cups (10 fl oz) milk
2½ tablespoons liquid glucose (corn syrup)
2⅔ cups (8 oz) desiccated (shredded) coconut
2–3 drops pink food colouring

Lightly grease an 18 x 28 x 2 cm (7 x 11 x ¾ in)
baking tray (jelly roll pan).
Place sugar, milk and glucose in a large, heavy-based
saucepan. Stir over low heat until sugar is dissolved.
Bring to the boil and continue to boil until mixture reaches
112°C (235°F) on a sugar (candy) thermometer.
Remove saucepan from the heat and divide the mixture
between two bowls. Add half of the coconut to each bowl.
Beat the first mixture until it is thick and creamy and
very white. Press it into the prepared tray.
Colour remaining mixture with the food colouring and
beat until it is thick and creamy. Press on top of the first
mixture. When the combined mixture is cold and set, cut it
into squares before removing from the tray.
Store in an airtight container.

Makes 36

COCONUT MACAROONS

3⅓ cups (10 oz) desiccated (shredded) coconut
2 cups (14 oz) caster (superfine) sugar
210 ml (7 fl oz) egg white
juice of 1 lemon
200 g (7 oz) dark (plain or semi-sweet) chocolate, melted

Preheat oven to 180°C (350°F).
Line a flat baking sheet with baking paper (parchment).
Place coconut and sugar in a large saucepan and mix with a
wooden spoon. Add egg whites and lemon juice and stir the
mixture to a moistened paste. Place saucepan over low heat
and stir continuously until the mix reaches 40°C (104°F).
Remove pan from the heat and continue mixing until the mix
becomes cool again. Place mixture into a piping (pastry) bag

which has been fitted with a 1.5 cm (⅝ in) star piping nozzle (tube). Pipe mixture onto the sheet in rosette shapes, leaving 1–2 cm (½–1 in) between them. Bake for 10–15 minutes or until the mixture is just beyond golden brown. Cool on the sheet before dipping the bases into chocolate. Allow the chocolate to set before serving.

COCONUT CAKE

100 ml (3½ fl oz) coconut cream
1 cup (7 oz) caster (superfine) sugar
¼ cup (2 fl oz) rum
4⅓ cups (13 oz) desiccated (shredded) coconut
100 ml (3½ fl oz) milk
3 tablespoons cornflour (cornstarch)
3 egg yolks
2 cups (16 fl oz) milk, extra
3 egg whites
⅓ cup (2 oz) caster (superfine) sugar, extra
1 vanilla génoise sponge (see page 134)
shredded coconut, extra, for decorating

Place coconut cream, sugar and rum in a saucepan and bring to the boil. Pour over the coconut and allow to soak for 1 hour.
Pour 100 ml (3½ fl oz) of milk into a saucepan and bring to the boil. Mix cornflour and egg yolks in a bowl. Pour hot milk in, beating all the time. Return mixture to the saucepan and cook for 2 minutes, stirring all the time. Keep custard mixture warm. Whisk egg whites until stiff peaks form, then gradually beat in the extra sugar, a spoonful at a time. Fold into warm custard.
Cut the sponge horizontally into thirds. Spread the bottom layer with half the soaked coconut and spoon on one third of the custard. Top with a layer of sponge. Repeat with the remaining coconut and another third of the custard.
Top with a layer of sponge. Cover the top and sides of the cake with the remaining custard and the shredded coconut.

COCONUT MILK

The interior liquid from the coconut, drained from the nut via three small holes at one end and used for making cakes and batters, where a richer flavour of coconut is required. Further coconut milk can be derived from desiccated (shredded) coconut by soaking it in boiling water and then rinsing and draining it and reserving the liquid.

COEUR A LA CREME

300 g (10 oz) bakers' cheese or cream cheese
1 tablespoon icing (powdered) sugar
zest and juice of 1 lemon
1 cup (8 fl oz) cream, lightly whipped

Line small heart-shaped moulds with muslin (cheesecloth). Place bakers' cheese, sugar and lemon zest and juice in a food processor and blend until smooth. Add cream and blend lightly until just incorporated taking care not to curdle the cream. Pour mixture into the lined heart-shaped moulds. Allow the ramekins to set in the refrigerator overnight before turning them out onto a plate to serve and peeling away the muslin. Pour raspbery purée (recipe below) around the crème and serve immediately.

Raspberry Purée
300 g (100 oz) fresh or frozen (thawed) raspberries
30 g (1 oz) caster (superfine) sugar

Place raspberries and sugar in a food processor and blend until a smooth liquid. Serve either as is or press the purée through a muslin cloth to remove the seeds.

COFFEE

Coffee is one of the most widely known and used commodities in the world today and offers the budding pastry chef a vast array of ideas and flavours with which to play. According to legend, around 1000 AD a shepherd in Ethiopia noticed that his flock of goats were more lively and playful after having fed on the local plants, so he too sampled what they were eating and liked the beans so much he took them to a local monastery. They produced a drink by roasting the seeds of the fruit, crushing them and adding water, and enjoyed it very much, as it kept them awake during their prayers.

Coffee never really became popular until the 15–16th centuries, when coffee houses began opening throughout European countries. Coffee houses became very fashionable; not being seen at a coffee house said something about one's social status. This push towards coffee houses also saw the success of the ice cream, chocolate and many other pastry products, not to mention a dramatic increase in sales of confectionery, cakes and pastries, as it was just as fashionable to have coffee and cake as it was to be seen at the coffee houses.

A plant grown in tropical climates, it takes an average of 4 years for coffee trees to begin to produce the beans, which are contained within the red cherry-like fruit. To harvest the coffee beans, the fruit, each containing two coffee beans, is placed into a pulper and the flesh is washed away using high pressure water, leaving the green coffee beans behind. These beans are then fermented, dried and hulled, graded according to size and then sold to buyers throughout the world.

While each type of coffee bean has its own characteristics according to climate, soil conditions and plant variety, the majority of the flavour differences come from the actual roasting of the beans. The beans are roasted by the individual buyers and can take from 13–18 minutes to roast, depending on the preferences of the buyer and the flavour, taste and aroma being sought. All coffee bean varieties differ to some extent in colour, hardness, size, age and water content, so roasting must be varied accordingly.

Perhaps more widely used by pastry chefs is instant coffee, which allows for a smooth, even incorporation of the coffee into the dessert or cream without the customary coffee grains. Instant coffee is made by spraying brewed coffee into hot air so that the water is evaporated, leaving only the concentrated coffee granules, or it can be freeze dried by lowering the temperature and then raising it dramatically so that the coffee crystals go instantly from ice to vapour.

Coffee is used to make coffee-flavoured chocolate cakes, coffee cakes, tiramisu and coffee mousses. These are famous around the world, offering a slight pick-me-up to accompany the delicious flavour.

COFFEE TRUFFLES

1 cup (8 fl oz) thickened (double or heavy) cream
90 g (3 oz) unsalted (sweet) butter
3 tablespoons instant coffee granules
600 g (20 oz) white chocolate, chopped finely
1½ cups (9 oz) icing (powdered) sugar, sifted
375 g (12 oz) white chocolate, melted

Place cream and butter in a saucepan and allow to come to the boil. Quickly whisk coffee granules into the boiling mixture and, when dissolved, remove the saucepan from the heat, immediately adding the chopped chocolate. Allow to sit for several minutes, then stir the mixture until it is smooth and free of any chocolate lumps. Pour the warm mixture into a bowl and cover with plastic wrap (cling film). Refrigerate for 12 hours.
Remove the mixture from the refrigerator and, using a melon baller dipped in hot water, place balls of mixture on a tray lined with plastic wrap (cling film). Place the tray in the freezer for 20 minutes to allow the balls to firm. Sift the icing sugar onto a baking tray (sheet). Melt the second amount of the white chocolate. Dip your fingers into the cooled melted chocolate and then roll each ball in your fingers to coat it with chocolate. Quickly drop each ball into the sifted icing sugar. Shake the tray to ensure that each truffle is completely coated in icing sugar.
After coating all the truffles, place them on a serving platter if they are to be served immediately, or store them in an airtight container and refrigerate.

Makes 36

COLD SOUFFLES
(see iced soufflés)

COLETTE
(see also petits fours)

This petit four consists of a chocolate base, almond cream filling and a chocolate disc for a lid. When set firm, the whole petit four is dipped into chocolate, which is allowed to firm before serving.

COLIFICHETS
(see also petits fours)

A dry crisp biscuit (cookie)/cake mixture used as a petit four throughout France.

COLLEGE PUDDING
(see also steamed puddings)

A quick, easy steamed pudding famous throughout the colleges of England, whence its name came. Jam (jelly) is placed at the bottom of a greased dariole mould which is filled with steamed pudding mixture. The mixture is baked, and when inverted, it is coated in a rich jam sauce.

COLOMBO DI PASQUALE

The Colombo di Pasquale was invented in Milan around 1170 by a peasant girl who gained her freedom by giving the King this sweet bread in the shape of a dove, her symbol of freedom. A Milanese specialty, the sweet dough is shaped like two doves and is covered with sugar and nuts, although now it is often baked simply as a twisted loaf and, as with German stollens, basted with butter and dusted heavily with icing sugar just before it finishes baking.

4 cups (16 oz) plain (all-purpose) flour
3 teaspoons gluten flour
1 tablespoon golden syrup (light treacle)
¼ cup (2 oz) sugar
1 teaspoon salt
40 g (1½ oz) fresh compressed yeast
2 egg yolks
1 cup (8 fl oz) milk
125 g (4 oz) unsalted (sweet) butter, melted
⅓ cup (2 oz) glacé (candied) cherries, chopped
⅓ cup (2oz) whole almonds, blanched
125 g (4 oz) unsalted (sweet) butter, melted, extra
¾ cup (4 oz) icing (powdered) sugar

Preheat oven to 180°C (350°F).
Place flour, gluten flour, golden syrup, sugar and salt in a bowl and stir to combine. Add yeast and crumb through the dry ingredients well. Mix egg yolks with milk and melted butter and pour this into the dry ingredients.
Work mixture to a dough and knead on a bench (counter) surface for 5–8 minutes or until smooth and elastic.
Place dough in a bowl and cover and set in a warm place for 35–45 minutes, or until double in size.
Remove dough and knead the chopped cherries through while knocking out the air from the dough. Cut dough in half and roll both pieces into thin sausage shapes, about 40 cm (16 in) in length. Pinch pieces together at one end, twist the two pieces together, then pinch the other end together.
Press blanched almonds into the dough, covering it evenly. Place dough on a baking sheet and allow to prove (rise) for 30–40 minutes, or until again double in volume. Bake for 25 minutes and then baste the dough with the extra melted butter and dust heavily with icing sugar. Return to oven for a further 10 minutes, remove and again dust heavily with icing sugar. Cool before cutting, and use the Colombo di Pasquale within 2–3 days.

COLOURINGS
(see also artificial colourings, cochineal, food colourings)

These are taken from natural sources such as fruit and vegetables as well as trees, roots, shrubs and, in the case of cochineal, animals. Food colourings can also be synthetically produced. Colourings should be used sparingly in all facets of cookery, and preferably not at all, but natural colourings react with some substances when mixed together, so synthetic colours are required. It is imperative when using colourings that the colour complements the natural flavours of the product and that it is subtle rather than highly coloured and gaudy. The higher the content of colourings used in or on products, the more the imperfections within a dessert or centrepiece are likely to be revealed.

Colourings are available to the pastry chef in flavoured liquid form, as concentrates, oil-based liquid, pastes and in powder form, the form used being a matter for the individual pastry chef. The type of colouring used also depends on what it is being used for; water-based colourings do not colour buttercreams or oils well and may tighten chocolate if used to colour white chocolate, while some colourings are affected in acidic mixtures and others change colour when in the presence of lemon juice, making them useless for royal icing, for instance. Colours should only be added to cake batters, icings and other mixtures drop by drop, as more colouring can be added, but too much colour at once cannot be removed.

Natural colourings

Many fruits, vegetables, roots, leaves and even animals provide the multitude of colours required in the kitchen to make and decorate different recipes.

Here are the basics and their origins:

(i) Green: Produced from plants such as nettles or spinach, which are blanched and squeezed to extract the colourings.
(ii) Pink or red: Obtained by drying, crushing and boiling a Mexican beetle.
(iii) Yellow: Produced from either saffron or turmeric roots.
(iv) Orange: Prepared by fermenting the fruit and seeds of an African plant.
(v) Brown and black: Produced by overcooking a caramel mixture to dark brown or black and adding more water, reboiling and producing a thick brown or black syrup.
(vi) Light brown to dark brown: Cocoa powder can be mixed with water or cocoa butter for use in cocoa painting or in cake batters.

COMB SCRAPER

Available in many shapes and sizes, a comb scraper is made from either metal or a flexible plastic and is merely a scraper with jagged teeth which is dragged through mixtures such as icings or chocolate to create ridges or rows in the mixture; for example, when making dual-coloured chocolate curls or wavy designs on icings.

COMPOTE DES FRUITS
(see fruit)

COMPOUND CHOCOLATE
(see chocolate)

CONCENTRATE

A mixture of fruit liquid or any substance produced by reducing the liquid or water content by evaporation or similar processes. Concentrates are made of liqueurs, fruit juices and purées, milk and soups, and are a method of carrying more of the product for later rehydration through remixing with water. Some concentrates are used as additives, only a small amount being required to produce a full flavour.

CONCHING
(see chocolate)

CONCORD CAKE

A famed modern cake invented by the French patissier Gaston Lenôtre. It consists of chocolate meringue layers sandwiched together and covered with a chocolate mousse mixture. The final decoration consists of small strips of chocolate meringue mixture placed on the outside of the cake, then the cake is dusted with icing sugar.

CONDE

The term 'à la Condé' is used to describe desserts and dishes named after the great French general, Condé, and considered to be comparable to him in greatness. In pastry circles, the name refers to both a hot dessert pastry made from puff pastry, royal icing and almond, known simply as Condé cake, and to a rice-based cold dessert, Riz à la Condé, which is made from milk, rice, poached fruit and gelatine set in a fruit purée sauce.

CONDENSED MILK
(see also milk)

A very sweet milk which was used widely throughout England during wartime, as it kept well. It was used in place of fresh milk on cereals. Today it has a permanent place in confectionery and pastry making, where it is caramelised or made into slices. It is also used in the production of iced dishes, as its high sugar content stops it setting too hard. Condensed milk is a form of preserved milk. The water content of the milk is evaporated and sugar — around 40% — is added to the milk as a preservative and a sweetener, ensuring that a can of condensed milk will rarely go off.

CONFECTIONER
(see confiseur)

CONFECTIONERS' CUSTARD

2 cups (16 fl oz) cream
2 cups (16 fl oz) milk
1½ cups (10 oz) caster (superfine) sugar
100 ml (3½ fl oz) cream, extra
100 ml (3½ fl oz) milk, extra
1 cup (4 oz) cornflour (cornstarch)
3 eggs
4 level teaspoons gelatine powder
2 tablespoons water

Place cream, milk and sugar in a saucepan and bring slowly to the boil. Blend together the extra cream, extra milk, cornflour and eggs. Pour the boiled mixture over the cold mixture and stir continuously until all is combined. Return to the saucepan and cook over medium heat until the custard boils and thickens, stirring all the time. Mix gelatine and water in a small bowl and stand in a pan of hot water until the gelatine dissolves. Mix into hot custard. Sprinkle the surface of the custard with caster sugar to prevent a skin forming, or place greased greaseproof (waxed) paper directly on the custard. Allow custard to cool or use according to the requirements of the individual recipes.

Makes about 4 cups (32 fl oz)

CONFECTIONERS' SUGAR
(see also icing sugar, sugar)

This sugar is ground as fine as sugar can be ground and is used in the production of icings, frostings and sweet fondants or glazes. It can also be substituted for sugar crystals where it is necessary for them to dissolve completely, such as in making meringues. Known in America as powdered sugar.

CONFECTIONERY
(see also barley sugar, butterscotch, coconut ice, marshmallow, boiled sweets, sugar, turkish delight)

From the Latin word 'confect', which means that which is produced with skill, confectionery is definitely the trade of a skilled craftsperson, but it is also fun for those who simply wish to dabble and make the occasional confectionery. Confectionery in its many forms has been in production from very early times, one of its earliest forms being produced by the Babylonians, who boiled honey with rosewater or herbs and spices to make sweet syrups. It is known that the Arabs used sugar for medicinal purposes as early as the 8th or 9th century and that even before this the Romans were making sweets from dates stuffed with pine kernels and pepper and dipped into boiling honey.

During the Crusades, and somewhat earlier, doctors would use sweet mixtures of honey, rosewater, orange oil and herbs to make their potions. It is thought that many confections resulted from this practice and that, indeed, this is why many medicines today are sweetened and flavoured, and produced as lozenges or pastilles for sucking. For many centuries sweets and confectionery were considered to be part of the apothecary's trade and were sold or handed out by doctors and chemists, remaining very much a valued or exclusive product enjoyed only by kings, noblemen and the wealthy.

It was also during the Crusades that sugar, and with it an interest in confectionery making, was spread throughout Europe and the rest of the known world. Sugar mixed with ground almonds was soon a favourite of the Venetians, the bread-shaped logs being named Marcus Pane or Marci Pane (after the patron saint of Venice), later becoming known as marzipan. By this time there was considerable trade in confectionary of all sorts: sweets made from boiled sugar, marzipans, caramels, toffees and fudges, nougats, fondants, pralines, fruit confectioneries, crystallised (candied) jellies and other jelly products.

It is not difficult to master the art of confectionery making. By following a few simple rules, one can achieve success every time. Sugar or candy thermometers are essential for perfect results, but these must be cared for and kept clean. As well, bowls and ingredients used in the manufacture of confectionery must be spotlessly clean. In the case of sugar mixtures, the bowls must be washed down during the boiling process to ensure that the sugar crystals splashed up the sides do not reboil into the mix. If confectionery recipes are followed precisely, it is not difficult to achieve results similar to those of qualified tradespeople.

CONFISEUR

The European name for those who works with confectionery. In a large pastry firm or within the pastry section of an hotel, the confiseur prepares fondants, sugar mixtures, syrups and marzipans, and produces the artistic centrepieces and displays which are made from sugar, chocolate or pastillage for functions, buffets and celebrations. With the increase in pre-prepared goods (such as marzipans and chocolates) now available, the confiseur's position has been eradicated in many businesses and the few duties which would be undertaken by him/her are now handled by the chef pâtissier. While confiseurs may produce centrepieces using chocolate, they would normally not touch chocolate, as this is the job of the chocolatier. Confiseurs will, however, produce the centres for the chocolates.

CONFITURE
(see also conserves, jams, preserves)

The French word for jam.

CONGRESS TARTS

Small sweet pastry cases which have jam (jelly) piped onto their bases and are filled with an almond mixture similar to frangipane. Thin slices of sweet pastry are then placed diagonally across the top of each tart and they are baked to a golden brown. When baked, they are glazed with apricot glaze and fondant which has been thinned with Kirsch.

CONSERVE
(see also jam)

A conserve is a jam which contains large chunks of the fruit which was boiled to make the jam.

CONVE CAKE
(see also Twelfth Night cake)

A form of galette with a rich flavouring of lemon, the Conve, or Twelfth Night, cake originates from the Dauphine region of France.

CONVERSATION CAKE

As with many pastry items, the Conversation cake or gâteau was named after a play that was successful at the time of its creation. Titled 'Les Conversations d'Emilie', the play was written by Madame d'Epinay. Apart from its name, its relevance to the play or its characters is unknown. Perhaps a pastry chef simply wished to immortalise the play. Conversation cake is the French equivalent, and the predecessor, to the English congress tart, a puff pastry tartlet (base and lid) which is filled with a flavoured almond filling and has its top coated in a thin layer of royal icing. The top of the tartlet is then covered with diagonally crisscrossing lines of thin pastry strips.

Filling

150 g (5 oz) unsalted (sweet) butter
⅔ cup (5 oz) sugar
2 egg yolks
⅓ cup (1½ oz) plain (all-purpose) flour
½ teaspoon ground cloves
1⅓ cups (5 oz) ground almonds
500 g (16 oz) butter puff pastry (see page 41)
beaten egg wash (see page 110)
100 g (3½ oz) royal icing (see page 241)

Preheat oven to 180°C (350°F).
Lightly grease a muffin pan with 5 cm (2 in) diameter cups.
Cream butter and sugar until light, creamy and smooth.
Add egg yolks and combine well. Add sifted flour, cloves and ground almonds and mix thoroughly.
Roll puff pastry to 2–3 mm (⅛ in) in thickness and cut out ten to twelve 10 cm (4 in) circles using a plain round biscuit (cookie) cutter. Press these bases into the muffin pan.
Fill each of these pastry cups with almond filling.
Reroll the scrap pastry on a well floured surface to 2–3 mm (⅛ in) in thickness and cut out 5 cm (2 in) discs for the lids, using a pastry or biscuit (cookie) cutter. Brush these on one side with egg wash and place over each tartlet, washed side up, pinching the edges together. Spread a small amount of royal icing over each tartlet lid and, using a knife, mark a diagonal crisscross lightly through the royal icing, not cutting the pastry. Bake tartlets in preheated oven for 30–35 minutes, or until golden brown.

COOKIE
(see also biscuit)

The word cookie derives from the Dutch word 'koekje', which is still used in Jamaica and means little cakes. It is used in the USA to describe what in most other countries are called biscuits. Soft, thick and light home-baked cookies are indeed small cakes, whereas many of the thin varieties and savoury lines are known in the USA as crackers. 'Biscuit' is used in the USA to refer to what others call scones.

Choc Chip Cookie

125 g (4 oz) unsalted (sweet) butter
½ cup (4 oz) sugar
½ cup (3 oz) soft (light) brown sugar
2 eggs, lightly beaten
2¾ cups (11 oz) plain (all-purpose) flour
2 tablespoons baking powder (soda)
1 cup (4 oz) chocolate chips (drops)
½ cup (2 oz) walnuts, chopped

Preheat oven to 175°C (350°F).
Grease baking sheets well.
Cream together butter and both sugars until light and creamy. Add eggs gradually, beating well after each one is added. Mix in sifted flour and baking powder and then add chocolate chips and chopped nuts. Mix well.
Shape small balls of the mixture and place on the prepared sheets. Allow room for spreading. Bake in preheated oven for 10–12 minutes. Remove from the sheets carefully and cool on wire racks.

Makes 48

COOKIE CUTTER
(see biscuit cutter)

COOKIE PRESS
(see biscuit press)

COPHA
(see also coconut, fats)

Copha (a trademark name), also known as white vegetable shortening or coconut butter or fat, is not available in all countries. It is in fact the buttery fat expelled by crushing coconut flesh. Set firm, the fat is white and opaque, while when melted, it is clear and transparent. It is usually used in cakes, slices and mixtures which solidify in the refrigerator, and do not require cooking.

CORNBREAD
(see also bread, cornmeal, polenta)

Cornbread is an American favourite made from cornmeal, or polenta. Cornmeal does not have a gluten structure so it needs to be risen either by using baking powder or, if yeast is the desired raising agent, the cornmeal needs to be added to a dough which has already been produced.

90 g (3 oz) polenta (cornmeal)
1 cup (8 fl oz) boiling water
5¾ cups (23 oz) plain (all-purpose) flour
1 teaspoon gluten flour
⅓ cup (3 oz) sugar
4 teaspoons salt
90 g (3 oz) unsalted (sweet) butter
50 g (1¾ oz) fresh compressed yeast
2 eggs
¾ cup (6 fl oz) milk

Preheat oven to 180°C (350°F).
To make the polenta cake, mix the polenta with its own weight of boiling water. Stir the polenta as the water is added to ensure it is all moistened.
Place the flours, sugar, salt, butter and yeast in a mixing bowl and crumb through (rub in) the butter and yeast until the mixture resembles fine breadcrumbs. Add eggs and milk, and bring the mixture to a dough and knead lightly.
Add the polenta cake and continue kneading the dough

for a further 5–6 minutes. Cut dough into 100 g (3½ oz) pieces and roll each into a ball. Allow the balls of dough to prove (rise) for 30–40 minutes.

Knock back (punch down) each of the doughs and reroll into tight bread rolls. Sit them on a baking sheet which has been lightly dusted with polenta. Place the sheets of rolls in a warm area and allow them to double in size (30–40 minutes) before baking in preheated oven for 25–30 minutes. Remove and serve immediately with soups or (in slices) with pâtés.

Makes 14–18 rolls

CORNE D'ABONDANCE
(see Overflodigshorn)

CORNET
(see also piping bag)

A cornet is a cone-shaped piece of paper (otherwise known as a piping bag), usually made from greaseproof (waxed) paper or silicon paper, used for piping mixtures such as buttercreams, chocolate and royal icing.

CORNFLOUR
(see also arrowroot, thickeners)

Cornflour (or cornstarch, as it is known in the USA) is a white powder, finer than flour, which is extracted from the starch endosperm of either wheat or corn and contains no gluten. It is used to thicken sauces and glazes, sweets and jellies, as it gelatinises when heated in liquid, gives shortness to cakes and biscuits (cookies), or is mixed with equal quantities of plain (all-purpose) flour to soften the flour for cake manufacture. It is only used to thicken sauces where clarity is not required, because it causes sauces to go slightly milky or opaque; arrowroot is used for clear sauces. Due to its water retention properties, cornflour is also used to dry out products such as fondant centres, liqueur centres and jubes or jellies. American cornstarch is available in both fine and coarse grains, the latter being called pearl starch.

The first reported use of wheat starch was given by Marcus Porcius Cato (234–149 BC), who described the use of the starch in stiffening monks' clothes. It was produced by soaking the wheat for several days, then wrapping it in a cloth and rinsing or pressing out the starch. Starch was later produced in England and shipped elsewhere. It was used for stiffening frills, ruffles and dresses, but was banned in 1596 by Elizabeth I.

By 1850 it was back in use throughout Europe in baking — the starch was browned in the oven, boiled with water and the glaze produced brushed over gingerbreads and honey cakes — and also in cosmetics and perfumery. It has been in use ever since.

CORNISH PASTIES

These were invented by the housewives of Cornwall, England, during the 1800s as an easy way for their mining husbands to carry a sustaining meal without too much bother. A true Cornish pastie is a pastry disc filled with a mixture of meat and vegetables which is then folded over and the pastry pinched at the top to enclose the filling in an envelope of pastry. The idea of the pastie is that the pastry should so firm that it can be carried in a pocket, which is one of the reasons for its traditional long shape. The pastie should not leak juices, should taste good and, according to folklore, should nevertheless be able to withstand a fall down a mine shaft without breaking open — if not, the woman was not a good cook. Originally the pastie was considered to be a complete meal, being long enough to contain the traditional filling of vegetables and meat at one end, and a sweet concoction of stewed fruits at the opposite end, separated by a wall of pastry.

Pastry
4 cups (16 oz) plain (all-purpose) flour
250 g (8 oz) unsalted (sweet) butter
2 egg yolks
¾ cup (6 fl oz) water
juice of ½ lemon

Filling
300 g (10 oz) fillet steak
1 large potato, cut into cubes
1 carrot, cut into cubes
1 turnip, cut into cubes
1 onion, finely diced
3 tablespoons chopped spring onions
salt and pepper
¼ cup (2 fl oz) beef stock or
1 stock cube and ¼ cup (2 fl oz) water

Preheat oven to 180°C (350°F).

To make pastry, place flour in a large mixing bowl with butter and rub the butter into the flour until well combined and the mixture resembles fresh breadcrumbs. Add egg yolks, water and lemon juice and mix to a dough.

Knead lightly and then wrap the pastry in plastic wrap (cling film) and refrigerate for 30 minutes. Remove and, on a lightly floured surface, roll dough out thinly (2 mm/¹⁄₁₂ in) and, using a small plate or saucepan lid, cut out circles 15 cm (6 in) in diameter. Cover these and rest them while the filling is being made.

To make the filling, clean the meat of any sinew, cut it into cubes 1 x 1 cm (½ in) and add to the cubes of potato, carrot, turnip and onion. Add the chopped spring onion, salt and pepper for flavouring, and the beef stock, and allow the mixture to sit for several minutes, giving it an occasional stir.

Place a good tablespoon of the filling into the centre of each disc of pastry. With the disc sitting on the bench surface, brush completely around the filling with the egg wash and bring the edges of the pastry together above the filling. Pinch all around the edges tightly and crimp with your fingers to seal the edges well. Place the pasties on a baking sheet lined with baking paper (parchment) and bake in preheated oven for 30–35 minutes or until the pastry is brown and crisp.

Serve immediately or when pasties cool.

CORNISH SAFFRON CAKE
(see also saffron)

200 ml (7 fl oz) lukewarm milk
½ teaspoon saffron threads, crumbled
15 g (½ oz) fresh compressed yeast
3 cups (12 oz) plain (all-purpose) flour
3 eggs
125 g (4 oz) unsalted (sweet) butter, softened
¼ cup (2 oz) sugar
⅓ cup (2½ oz) dried sultanas
2 tablespoons mixed (candied) peel

Place milk and saffron in a saucepan and allow to come to the simmer over gentle heat. Remove from heat and allow to sit for 1 hour before using.
Dissolve yeast in the saffron milk. Place flour in a large bowl. Make a well in the centre of the flour and add the dissolved yeast mixture and the eggs, butter and sugar.
Mix ingredients to form a soft dough and mix for 3–4 minutes. Place the dough back in the bowl with the butter and sugar on top of it. Cover and place in a warm area for 30–40 minutes or until the dough is double in bulk. Knock back (punch down) the dough, cover and refrigerate for 24 hours.
Preheat oven to 180°C (350°F).
Grease a 22 cm (9 in) springform cake tin and line the base with baking paper (parchment).
Mix sultanas and mixed (candied) peel into dough and combine. Place dough in prepared pan. Cover with a clean dry cloth and stand the tin in a warm area until dough has reached the top of the tin or is double in bulk. Bake in preheated oven for 35–40 minutes or until a skewer inserted comes out clean and dry. Allow cake to cool in the tin for a few minutes before turning out onto a cake rack.
Serve warm slices with jam (jelly) and Cornish clotted (thickened) cream.

CORNMEAL
(see also cornbread)

Cornmeal, known in Italy and various other countries as polenta, is a yellow gritty powder similar to semolina. It is used extensively in cooking in South America, and is known to have been served at the court of Montezuma. It was made into a paste (much as it is today) and baked on an open flat grill to make breads, tortillas and bases for sweet and savoury recipes. For centuries, cornmeal porridge was a staple food of the Italians, and it is known that the Greek and Roman civilisations also ate it, experimenting by cooking the yellow powder in wines, mead and milk.

Usually yellow, but also available white, cornmeal these days is milled in factories, where the skin and germ are removed to allow it to be stored for longer periods; stoneground cornmeal, which retains the skin and germ, does not store well. Cornmeal is most well known for the deliciously flavoured cornbread that is produced from it. To regenerate cornmeal for cooking, soak it in triple its weight of boiling water to produce a firm solid mass called polenta cake.

CORNSTARCH
(see cornflour)

CORN SYRUP
(see glucose)

CORNUCOPIA
(see Overflodigshorn)

COTIGNAC

Cotignac is thought to have its origins in early Greece, where it was produced by mixing honey with quince paste. It is a sweetened paste made of quinces which have been dried, and turn pink as a result of natural oxidation. Although the Greeks may have been the inventors of this preserved paste, the French loved the sweetmeat, and records show that it has been eaten in France since before the time of Joan of Arc. No connection is known between the quince paste and the martyr, but her effigy decorated a famed brand of cotignac for many centuries.

COTTON CANDY
(see also sugar, spun sugar)

Often eaten at fairs or fêtes, cotton candy or candy floss, also known as fairy floss, was first presented to the general public at the 1900 Paris Exposition, when a hand driven crankshaft machine produced the first cotton candy on a stick. Today, high-revolution machines produce the confection at high speed and in large quantities. Coloured sugar is inserted into a hot central core which melts the sugar and spins the molten sugar at a high revolution against cool walls which hold the wisps of sugar for collection on a stick or fork.

COTSWOLD CAKE

This cake is taken from an Irish recipe which was made famous in the Cotswolds district of England. It uses potato, as many people have often had to do because of its cheapness and availability.

90 g (3 oz) unsalted (sweet) butter
⅓ cup (3 oz) sugar
125 g (4 oz) potatoes, boiled and sieved (mashed)
½ teaspoon vanilla essence (extract)
1 egg
1 egg yolk
1 cup (4 oz) plain (all-purpose) flour
1½ teaspoons baking powder (soda)
icing sugar, for dusting

Preheat oven to 180°C (350°F). Grease and line a 28 x 30 x 3 cm (11 x 12 x 1 in) baking tray (jelly roll pan).
Cream together butter, sugar, potatoes and vanilla until almost white. Add egg and egg yolk and beat until combined. Sift flour and baking powder and gently fold into mixture. Spread mixture evenly into the tray and bake in preheated oven for 35–40 minutes. Turn out onto a cake rack, dust with icing sugar and leave to cool.

COUCOULELLI

This is a diamond-shaped cake made with flour, spices, wine and olive oil, and is a traditional festive cake of the Corsicans.

COUKE
(see couque)

COULIS
(see also purée)

A coulis is a thin purée of fruit which is sweetened and thinned to a sauce consistency using stock or sugar syrup.

The fruit flesh can be either raw or cooked before puréeing and can be served as a sauce or as an accompaniment for hot or cold desserts.

COUPE

This is the name of both the dessert and the dish in which it is served. A coupé, also known as a sundae, can be complex or quite simple and, as well as the more famous coupé combinations listed, can be virtually any combination of ice cream, fruit and a sauce, all served in a towering glass dish. A list of common coupés follows:

Name	Ice	Fruit Base	Liqueur	Sauce	Decoration
Andaluz	lemon	orange segments	Curaçao	—	whipped cream and orange segments
Aurora	strawberry	half a fresh peach, lightly poached	—	strawberry	whipped cream and crystallised rose petals
Black Forest	vanilla	Morello cherries	Kirsch	cherry	whipped cream, chocolate curls; served with a langue de chat
Carême	vanilla	apricots	Grand Marnier	apricot	crushed nougat, macaroons and crème Chantilly
Cleopatra	praline	raspberries	Eau de Vie	raspberry	whipped cream and meringue mushrooms
Edna May	vanilla	cherries	Kirsch	raspberry	raspberry, whipped cream and redcurrants
Japonaise	peach	raspberries	Eau de Vie	—	roasted slivered almonds
Josephine Baker	chocolate	diced pineapple	Cointreau	orange	pistachios and grated chocolate
Kirsch	vanilla, chocolate	cherries	Kirsch	Kirsch jelly	chocolate and glacé (candied) cherries
Madeleine	vanilla	diced pineapple	maraschino	maraschino	whipped cream
Mal Maison	vanilla	peeled and stoned grapes	Curaçao	orange	whipped cream
Metternich	raspberry	diced pineapple	Curaçao	—	vanilla whipped cream
Mont Blanc	vanilla	strawberries	—	strawberry	meringue pieces, whipped cream and cocoa
Monte Carlo	vanilla	fruit salad	Eau de Vie	strawberry	decorate with whipped cream and pistachios
Monte Cristo	pistachio	fruit salad	Grand Marnier	—	whipped cream and chopped pistachios
Mozart	almond/ praline	sliced peaches	—	raspberry	whipped cream and roasted almonds
Niçoise	orange	fruit salad	Grand Marnier	—	chocolate pieces
Sarah Bernhardt	chocolate and vanilla	apricots	—	chocolate	whipped cream, grated chocolate and chopped pistachios
Savoy	coffee	fruit salad	anisette liqueur	—	anisette-flavoured whipped cream
Singapore	vanilla	pineapple	Curaçao	pineapple	whipped cream and crystallised pineapple
Tutti Frutti	raspberry, pineapple, mango	fruit salad	Curaçao	raspberry	whipped cream
William	lemon	poached pears	poire William	—	whipped cream and praline

COUQUE

Derived from a Dutch word 'koekje', meaning cake, couque, which is also spelt couke, is a Flemish specialty which is served for breakfast. It is an enriched brioche dough dotted with sultanas (golden raisins), currants and mixed (candied) peel. Individual couques are served warm with butter.

COUVERTURE
(see also chocolate)

Couverture is a pure form of chocolate which contains at least 30% cocoa butter, the percentage of cocoa butter varying according to the different uses to which it will be put. Couverture requires tempering because of its cocoa butter content and is used for enrobing, moulding and in cakes, fillings, gianduja and so on.

Couverture for coating cakes and enrobing — 36% cocoa butter.

Moulding couverture for Easter eggs — 38–40% cocoa butter.

COVENTRY PUFFS

These originated in the English city of Coventry sometime during the 1500s. Given at Easter as a present from godparents to their godchildren, they consist of a three-cornered puff pastry turnover filled with rich mincemeat. They are shaped to resemble the three spires of the Coventry Cathedral.

CRACKERS
(see also biscuits)

American savoury biscuits which are also known as water crackers or water biscuits because they are made from flour and water.

CRAMIQUE

A famed Belgian brioche-style bread which is rich, sweet and filled with raisins. It is similar to a Russian kulich.

CRANBERRY
(see also berry)

Cranberries are crimson-red small berries which grow on small shrubs. They are members of the heather family, and are grown throughout the United Kingdom, America and parts of Europe. They are a much-loved fruit in the USA and are made into jams, jellies and pies and used in muffins and cakes. Being quite sour, they need to be cooked in sweet dishes or with sugar if used in pies. Cranberry sauce is a traditional accompaniment to turkey at Christmas and is one of the few savoury uses for this berry.

CREAM

In basic terms, cream is the fat part of milk. In unhomogenised milk, cream will float to the top of the lighter milk, where it can be skimmed away, leaving what is known as skim milk. In different countries cream comes in varying fat percentages, resulting in differing thicknesses as well. See the following chart for the different fat content of varying styles and types of cream, although, again, this varies from country to country. A list of creams follows:

NATURAL CREAMS

Type	Milkfat	Uses
Rich cream (double cream)	48%	fruit pies, sauces, puddings
Cream — pure and whipping	35%	mousses, cakes, soups
Reduced cream	25%	drinks
Single cream	21%	pouring (UK)
Light cream	18%	pouring
Extra light cream	12%	pouring

TREATED CREAMS

Type	Milkfat	Uses
Thickened	35%	whipping, cakes, pie-filling, mousses, cheesecakes, fresh fruits
Scalded or clotted	48%	Devonshire teas, scones
Cultured or sour cream	35%	European-style cakes requiring 'tart'
Light cultured cream	18%	European-style cakes requiring 'tart'
Canned reduced cream	25%	fruit pies
UHT	35%	as for natural cream
Aerosol/pressure pack	25%	as for thickened cream
Crème fraîche	48%	sauces, soups

CREAM BUN
(see also fruit bun)

A round bun made of a sweetened fruit bun dough. After baking, the bun is split, filled with jam (jelly) and cream and dusted with icing sugar. They are popular in England, Australia and the USA.

CREAM CHEESE

Also known as bakers' cheese and quark, cream cheese is produced by adding rennet to unpasteurised milk and is popular for making light fillings for Danish pastries and in the manufacture of cheesecakes, parfaits and light mousses. Cream cheeses are soft unripened cheeses, rich and smooth, and include such cheeses as neufchâtel and mascarpone.

CREAM HORN
(see also puff pastry)

A hollow cone of puff pastry made by wrapping 2 cm (¾ in) strips of puff pastry around a metal cornet mould or cream horn mould. These moulds are thin hollow metal shapes which allow the heat to reach both sides of the pastry and cook it all in equal time. Cream horns are filled with jam (jelly) and cream or mousses.

CREAM IMITATIONS

A substitute for real cream, cream imitations consist of milk solids blended with vegetable fats, rather than the butterfat or real cream. They are more stable than cream when whipped, and more heat resistant, and are often preferred for use in cake decorating. However, they tend to leave a fatty film on the roof of one's mouth and do not have the true rich flavour of cream. The other advantage of these creams is that they have a much longer storage life than real cream and therefore are preferred by many small business operators. Many styles, varieties and brands are available in all countries.

CREAM PUFF
(see also choux pastry, profiterole)

A large choux pastry bun or an enlarged profiterole, cream puffs are filled with jam (jelly) and cream or flavoured mousses and dusted with icing sugar. They are served at morning teas.

CREAM OF TARTAR
(see also baking powder)

A major component of baking powder (soda), where it is used in a ratio of 2 parts cream of tartar to 1 part bicarbonate of soda, cream of tartar is the common name for potassium bitartare, which is a by-product of wine making. It is the residue left in wine vats which is dried and crushed to form cream of tartar, used in cakes to assist rising, and to prevent crystallisation of sugar syrups when making confectionery. When mixed with water or moisture in the presence of bicarbonate of soda, cream of tartar gives off the gas carbon dioxide, making it a valuable addition to cakes and quickbreads.

CREAMING

This involves beating together ingredients such as butter and sugar until they become light and fluffy and almost white in colour. Mixtures of butter or fat and flour can also be creamed together.

CREME ANGLAISE

A rich, smooth French custard-style sauce, crème anglaise is made using eggs, sugar and milk or cream and is not actually a custard, as it is not thickened using a thickening agent but is naturally thickened by the coagulation of the eggs. This recipe can be varied by adding a small amount of chocolate to the boiling liquid or by substituting orange zest for the lemon. Once cool, fruit purées such as raspberry, strawberry, rhubarb and so on which have themselves been strained can be added.

1 cup (8 fl oz) cream
1 cup (8 fl oz) milk
5 egg yolks
⅓ cup (2 oz) sugar
zest of 1 lemon

Place cream and milk in a saucepan and allow to come to the boil. In a mixing bowl, whisk egg yolks, sugar and lemon zest together lightly. Remove boiled liquid from stove and slowly whisk into the egg yolk mixture. Pour entire mixture back into the saucepan once all the liquid has been added. Use a wooden spoon to stir the crème anglaise while it heats over a gentle flame. Do not allow the crème anglaise to boil or even simmer; heat only until it has thickened sufficiently to cling smoothly to the wooden spoon. Remove from the heat and continue stirring while the saucepan is set into iced water. Stir until the crème anglaise is cool. If required, strain the anglaise through muslin (cheesecloth) or a fine strainer.

CREME BAVAROIS

This cold pudding is a light cream of egg yolks, sugar, milk and fresh cream to which a small amount of gelatine is added, and which occasionally has egg whites folded under the light custard. Bavarois flavours should be fresh and sharp in the mouth, preferably obtained by using fruit purées, but flavours such as coffee and rich chocolate are also now commonplace. As proof of the chef's light-handed touch, the bavarois should be light, creamy and quite openly porous, showing the incorporation of air. They are generally served as unmoulded desserts on their own, but are also used as fillings for cakes, charlottes and other pastry lines. The bavarois is considered to be the greatest and finest of all custard-based desserts, when produced correctly.

RASPBERRY CREME BAVAROIS
3 tablespoons gelatine powder
3 cups (24 fl oz) milk
1¼ cups (8 oz) sugar
6 egg yolks
⅔ cup (5 fl oz) strawberry liqueur
3 cups (24 fl oz) whipped cream
1 cup (8 oz) raspberries, puréed

Place gelatine in a small bowl and cover with enough cold water to soak up gelatine (about 5 tablespoons). Place milk in a saucepan and allow to come slowly to the boil. Place sugar and egg yolks in a large mixing bowl and whisk together until light and fluffy. Slowly pour boiling milk into whisked egg yolk mixture and immediately add soaked gelatine and stir until gelatine has dissolved. Add liqueur and then place custard mixture in refrigerator to cool, stirring occasionally to ensure it does not set solid. Cool until cold to the touch. Lightly whip cream until it forms soft peaks, and fold with raspberry purée into the cooled custard. Pour immediately into clean dry dariole moulds. Refrigerate until firmly set, about 2 hours.

Serves 10–20

CREME BEAU RIVAGE

Crème Beau Rivage is a traditional English baked custard which has been flavoured with praline dust.

125 g (4 oz) unsalted (sweet) butter
1½ cups (7 oz) fresh praline, finely ground to a powder
6 eggs
2 egg yolks
⅓ cup (3 oz) sugar
1½ cups (12 fl oz) milk

Preheat oven to 150°C (300°F).
Lightly butter 8 dariole or ramekin moulds and
sprinkle each well with the powdered praline.
Lightly whisk eggs, egg yolks and sugar together until light
and creamy. Slowly add milk and whisk until all is
incorporated. Fill each of the praline-lined moulds
with the egg mixture. Place the ramekins in a large baking tin
and half fill the dish with warm water.
Bake for 35–40 minutes or until the crèmes are firm.
Cool in refrigerator for 2–3 hours. Unmould by running a
sharp knife around the top of the mould to loosen the crème
and then turning the mould upside down and shaking it
lightly. The crème should drop from the mould.
Serve with extra praline powder and fresh cream.

CREME BRULEE

Crème brulé is a smooth, lightly baked custard topped with a crisp layer of sugar, which should be crack hard when served. There are many variations on this recipe, some producing a thin custard, others a thick one, and some modern variations have a brandy snap or lace sugar biscuit (cookie) sitting on top rather than caramelising the sugar prior to service for the crisp crust.

While many declare this to be a cream of French origin, the English university of Cambridge has served this as Cambridge cream for many years, their university kitchens being acclaimed as the best producers of crème brulée in the world.

2 cups (16 fl oz) thickened (double or heavy) cream
7 egg yolks
¼ cup (2 oz) sugar
⅓ cup (3 oz) sugar, extra

Preheat oven to 180°C (350°F).
Place cream in a saucepan and bring slowly to boiling point.
Place egg yolks and sugar in a mixing bowl and whisk together
until light and fluffy. Slowly pour heated cream
into egg yolk mixture and mix thoroughly. Pour cream
mixture into 4 ramekins or small ceramic pots or one large
ovenproof dish. Place dish/es into a large baking tin
and half fill the dish with hot water.
Place baking tin in preheated oven and cook for
35–40 minutes. Remove dishes from the oven and from the
baking tin of water and cool for 1 hour. Sprinkle the extra
sugar over the top of each dish and place under the grill until
the sugar has caramelised. Serve hot or cold.

CREME CARAMEL

Of the crème family of desserts this is perhaps one of the most exacting and more difficult, but most rewarding when a good product is achieved. A smooth baked custard cream, this dish is turned out of its mould to serve and should be covered with the thick smooth caramel sauce which lined the mould. The trick to this dessert is to not overcook the custard and not use too high a temperature, as the baked custard will bubble and not be smooth if you do this.

1¼ cups (10 oz) sugar
½ cup (4 fl oz) water
1 teaspoon liquid glucose (corn syrup)
6 eggs
2 egg yolks
⅓ cup (3 oz) sugar
1½ cups (12 fl oz) milk

Preheat oven to 150°C (300°F).
Place sugar, water and glucose in a saucepan and
slowly bring to the boil. Boil until sugar mix
becomes a light golden brown colour (caramel).
Pour approximately 2–3 mm (⅛ in) of caramel into the base
of 8 dariole moulds or ramekins, ensuring that it covers the
entire base of the mould. Allow the caramel to harden.
Lightly whisk eggs, egg yolks and sugar together until light
and creamy. Slowly add milk and whisk until all is
incorporated. Fill each of the caramel-based moulds with the
mixture. Place the ramekins in a large baking tin and
half fill the tray with warm water. Place in oven and
bake for 35–40 minutes or until the crèmes are firm.
Cool by refrigerating for 2–3 hours. Unmould by running
a sharp knife around the top of the mould to loosen the crème
and then turning the crème upside down and
shaking lightly. The crème should drop from the mould
and the caramel sauce spread over the top.

CREME CHANTILLY

This is a basic sweetened, lightly whipped cream served with desserts and used in desserts themselves to fold under mousses and crèmes. The name Chantilly comes from the House or Château of Chantilly, which had a reputation in the 17th century for fine food, recognised now in the names of several dishes.

2¼ cups (18 fl oz) cream, well chilled
⅓ cup (3 oz) pure icing (powdered) sugar, sifted
1 teaspoon vanilla essence (extract)

Place all the ingredients in a mixing bowl and beat
until the cream holds stiff peaks. Chill.

CREME CHIBOUST

A rich but light crème of custard folded through meringue and set slightly with a small amount of gelatine, this delight was first invented to accompany Gâteau St Honoré, both having been invented by French pâtissier Chiboust in 1846 in honour of the patron saint of pastry cooks and bakers, St Honoré.

4 level teaspoons gelatine powder
¼ cup (2 fl oz) water
2⅓ cups (19 fl oz) orange juice
½ cup (4 fl oz) cream
4 tablespoons caster (superfine) sugar
½ cup (2 oz) cornflour (cornstarch)
6 egg yolks
1 cup (7 oz) caster (superfine) sugar, extra
2 tablespoons water, extra
6 egg whites

Place gelatine and water in a small bowl and stand it in a pan of hot water to dissolve. Place orange juice and cream in a saucepan and bring to the boil. Beat sugar, cornflour and egg yolks together and pour hot cream and orange juice in, beating all the while. Return mixture to saucepan and cook over medium heat until thickened. Cool slightly and stir in dissolved gelatine. Cool. Place extra sugar and extra water in a saucepan and bring to the boil. Cook to 130°C (266°F) on a sugar (candy) thermometer. Whisk egg whites until stiff peaks form and pour the hot syrup in. Beat until mixture is cold. Gently fold in cooled custard by hand. Use immediately.

CREME FRAICHE

A thick, tart-flavoured crème which is used on both savoury and sweet dishes, crème fraîche harmonises particularly well with very sweet desserts.

1 cup (8 fl oz) fresh cream
⅔ cup (5 fl oz) fresh cultured plain yoghurt
1 teaspoon fresh lemon juice
1 teaspoon sugar

Mix all ingredients in a glass bowl and allow to sit at room temperature (no more than 25°C/77°F) for 5–6 hours. Place the crème fraîche in the refrigerator for 2 hours. Whisk the crème lightly before serving.

CREME PATISSIERE

This is one of the more famous of the custards used by the pâtissier. Crème pâtissière is a smooth custard cream made from milk, cream, eggs and sugar (to taste) and is thickened with cornflour (cornstarch). It is used to fill choux pastries, as a base for fruit tarts and in various gâteaux.

1 cup (8 fl oz) fresh cream (single or light)
1 cup (8 fl oz) milk
½ cup (4 oz) sugar
⅓ cup (3 fl oz) cream, extra
⅓ cup (3 fl oz) milk, extra
⅔ cup (3 oz) cornflour (cornstarch)
2 eggs, lightly beaten

Place cream, milk and sugar in a saucepan and bring to the boil. Blend together the extra cream, extra milk, cornflour and eggs and pour the hot mixture in, stirring all the time. Return to the saucepan and cook over medium heat until custard boils and thickens, stirring all the time. Remove from heat and scrape down the sides of the saucepan. Cool at room temperature or use according to the particular recipe instructions. To prevent a skin forming on the cooling custard, sprinkle a small amount of sugar over the surface. This will dissolve and form a syrup which can be whisked into the custard after cooling. Alternatively, place a sheet of greased greaseproof (waxed) paper directly on top of the custard. Store custard which is not required immediately in an airtight container for 2–3 days.

CREOLE SWEET BLACKBREAD

Also called Creole gingerbread, this black bread is served in chunks with desserts and eaten instead of traditional biscuits (cookies) or wafers.

½ cup (5 oz) golden syrup (light treacle)
½ cup (4 fl oz) buttermilk
60 g (2 oz) unsalted (sweet) butter
½ teaspoon bicarbonate of soda
1 tablespoon boiling water
1½ cups (6 oz) plain (all-purpose) flour
1 teaspoon ground ginger
¼ teaspoon ground cinnamon

Preheat oven to 180°C (350°F). Grease and line a 25 x 30 x 3 cm (10 x 12 x 1 in) baking tray (jelly roll pan). Place golden syrup, buttermilk and butter in a saucepan and heat until butter is melted. Dissolve bicarbonate of soda in the boiling water and add to the liquid mixture, then add sifted flour and spices, stir into the mixture and work into a stiff batter. Pour batter into prepared tray and bake for 30–35 minutes, or until light brown. Remove and cool before cutting into pieces.

CREPE
(see also pancake)

A very thin, unleavened style of pancake, crêpes are often served as a dessert, but can also be filled with savoury fillings. They derive from the early unleavened breads, which are simply thickened crêpe batters, and have remained at the forefront of great desserts for centuries. Crêpes may be enjoyed on their own with citrus juice and sugar, or with thick sauces, or stacked on top of each other with chocolate layered in between (a crêpe cake).

2 cups (16 fl oz) milk
5 eggs
2 tablespoons olive oil
1¼ cups (5 oz) plain (all-purpose) flour

Place milk, eggs and oil in a bowl and whisk together. Slowly sprinkle the flour over the liquid and whisk until all of the flour is incorporated. Pour crêpe mixture through a fine sieve and allow it to rest for 30 minutes before using. To cook the crêpes, pour a small amount of mixture into a hot

Croissants and Danish pastries (see page 88)

frying pan (skillet) and tilt pan until the surface is covered.
Allow to cook for 2 minutes or until lightly
browned before flipping quickly and cooking for
1 minute on the reverse side. Serve immediately.

CREPES SUZETTE

Crêpes and pancakes which are served with a sweet buttery
sauce of orange juice, sugar and orange zest. Orange liqueur
is used to flame the dish or simply flavour the sauce. A chef
working in America for magnate John Rockefeller falsely
claimed to have invented Crêpes Suzette. He claimed to have
served the crêpes to the Prince of Wales, who was dining with
a friend by the name of Suzette in Monte Carlo. At the time in
question, 1896, the chef would not have been old enough to
have done this. In fact, as early as 1893 similar recipes to the
Suzette were being produced in Paris, leading to the belief
that the first recipe for Crêpes Suzette came from Marie's
Restaurant in 1898.

It is also said that chef Henri Carpentier, who was serving
King Edward VII of England and his guests, was preparing
their dessert, when he accidentally added the wrong liquid, a
liqueur, which was immediately set alight. With due aplomb,
the chef took the flaming mixture to the King's table and
declared his new dish was in honour of the Princess Suzette,
who was dining with the King.

8–10 crêpes (see page 86)
4 cubes sugar
zest and juice of 1 lemon
zest and juice of 3 oranges
60 g (2 oz) sweet (unsalted) butter, softened
¼ cup (2 oz) sugar
3 tablespoons orange liqueur
3 tablespoons brandy

Rub one side of each of the sugar cubes up against the sides of
the lemon and oranges to extract the oils and flavour from the
skins. Place butter in a large frying pan (skillet). As butter
melts, add sugar cubes, allowing them to melt into the butter.
Add the rest of the sugar and allow mixture to come to a
slight boil and begin to caramelise. As soon as the mixture
appears to be caramelising, add the zest and juice of
the lemon and oranges. Stir in well. Add orange liqueur
and allow mixture to simmer gently.
Place the crêpes in the sauce. When covered with the syrup,
fold each in half and then half again, forming a triangle.
When all the crêpes have been folded in the syrup, add the
brandy. Warm it a little then tip the pan towards the
naked flame of the gas so that the brandy ignites.
Take the whole flaming pan immediately to the table,
and when the flames have died, serve the crêpes.

CRIMPING

Crimping is a decorative finishing process for the edges of
pies, pastry, marzipan or almond paste. It is easily done by
using the thumb and index fingers to pinch the pastry or
paste inwards. There are crimping tools available for a more
professional finish.

CRISPBREAD
(see grissini)

CROISSANT
(see also yeast doughs)

One of the world's finest pastries, the renowned French
croissant was in fact first invented in Budapest, Hungary,
during the siege of that city by the Turks in 1686. The bakers
and pastry chefs, who worked through the night, were able to
send a warning that the Turks had tunnelled through
underground passages into the city. Thus the attack was
overpowered. In appreciation for their great bravery and
assistance, the bakers were granted the right to use the
crescent emblem, the symbol of the Ottoman Empire, in their
confections in whatever way they chose. They made their
design with a rich yeast dough, and so the croissant was born.
To this day, the croissant is a feathery, light, butter-rich
yeast pastry which is laminated with butter. It is served
throughout France for breakfast, plain or with jam (jelly),
and can also be filled with savoury fillings.

1¾ cups (14 fl oz) cold milk
1 egg
3 teaspoons sugar
30 g (1 oz) fresh compressed yeast
6 cups (24 oz) plain (all-purpose) flour
1 teaspoon salt
500 g (1 lb) unsalted (sweet) butter
1¼ cups (5 oz) plain (all-purpose) flour, extra

In a bowl, mix cold milk with egg, sugar and yeast and stir
until well combined. Add flour and salt to the liquid and
mix until a dough is formed. Knead the yeast dough for
5 minutes on a lightly floured surface and then allow to rest,
covered, for 10 minutes. Mix butter and extra flour together
lightly and quickly until both are combined. Do not cream
the butter, simply mix lightly until a dough is formed.
Refrigerate for 10 minutes. Roll dough into a large square.
Press the chilled butter mixture into the centre of the dough
square. Pull each of the four corners up and over the butter
mixture so that it is totally enclosed within the dough.
Refrigerate the dough for a further 30 minutes.
On a lightly floured surface, roll the dough out to triple its
original length, then mark and fold it into thirds. Rest dough
in the refrigerator for 20 minutes, then once again roll out to
triple its original length and fold into thirds. Rest dough
another 20 minutes in the refrigerator, then form a
further threefold and place back in refrigerator.
Roll dough out to 5 mm (¼ in) in thickness and form a long
oblong shape. Cut straight down the centre of the dough and
then cut each half into individual triangles. Roll the
croissants, starting at the large end and rolling towards the
pointed end, curving the croissants so that they are
crescent-shaped. Place on a baking sheet.
Place the sheets of croissants in a warm place for
30–40 minutes or until double in size. Bake at
200°C (400°F) for 35–40 minutes, or until golden brown.
Allow croissants to cool slightly before serving.

See page 87

CROQUANT
(see also praline)

Croquant is the German name for the French praline and English grillage and is a mixture of caramelised sugar, glucose and lemon juice into which flaked or nibbed almonds are added. The mixture can be rolled thinly while warm and cut into shapes using a lightly oiled knife. If the Croquant is made using flaked hazelnuts and, when cool, ground to a fine paste, the mixture is known as nougat, a brown fine paste used in pâtisserie for flavour and to join cakes together.

CROQUEMBOUCHE
(see also choux pastry, profiteroles)

A traditional French wedding cake of choux pastries (profiteroles), each filled with crème pâtissière, joined together in a pyramid shape with caramel, and decorated with spun sugar. The caramel gives this tower of sweetness its name: 'croque-en-bouche' means crack-in-the-mouth, and 'croque' is a shortened version of 'croquant', the crisp caramelised almond sugar with which this cake is quite often decorated.

Pastry
1½ cups (12 fl oz) water
150 g (5 oz) unsalted (sweet) butter
1¼ cups (5 oz) plain (all-purpose) flour
5 eggs, lightly beaten

Filling
2 cups (16 fl oz) crème pâtissière (see page 86)

To Decorate
1 quantity of caramel (see page 49)

Preheat oven to 200°C (400°F).
Line a baking sheet with baking paper (parchment).
Place water and butter in a saucepan and bring to the boil over medium heat. Remove from heat and add the flour all at once, beating all the time. Cook until the mixture leaves the sides of the saucepan, stirring all the time. Remove from heat and gradually add eggs until the mixture is smooth, soft and shiny. Use a piping (pastry) bag fitted with a plain nozzle to pipe small mounds, about 2½ cm (1 in) high, on prepared sheet. Bake for 20–25 minutes or until profiteroles are puffed, brown and crisp. Cool profiteroles on the sheet on a cake rack. Use the piping bag to fill each profiterole with crème pâtissière.

To Assemble
Dip profiteroles into the caramel and position them side by side to form a ring. Keep adding profiteroles, reducing the number on each layer and stepping each ring in from the previous one to make a cone-shaped pyramid. Dip a fork into the remaining caramel and spin fine threads of caramel (see page 49) over the top of the croquembouche.

See page 90

CRULLER
(see also choux pastry)

A sweet, light puffy American pastry similar to a doughnut in look and shape, but usually produced from deep-fried sweet dough which is risen from baking powder or produced using spiced choux pastry. Cruller dough is twisted to give it shape. As soon as the crullers are golden brown, they are rolled in icing (powdered) sugar.

CRUMBCRUSTS
(see also biscuit base)

A traditional base for cold cheesecakes, crumbcrusts are a quick alternative for the base of most set sweet pies (cold and hot), chiffons, cheesecakes and ice cream cakes. Crumbcrusts are an economical way for the pastry chef to use waste or unused biscuits, biscuit pastry, macaroons and crackers. Made from crushed biscuits (cookies) and a small amount of sugar which are bound together with a little butter, crumbcrusts are spread on the base and sometimes up the sides of the pie or cake tin, which is then filled.

CRUMBLE
(see also brown betty, cobbler, streusel)

Similar to the German streusel, this mixture of flour, butter and sugar is traditionally served on top of stewed fruits for fruit crumbles. In the European tradition, it is used on top of slices, cakes and muffins for a sweet, crumbly, textured finish.

1 cup (4 oz) plain (all-purpose) flour
125 g (4 oz) unsalted (sweet) butter
½ cup (4 oz) sugar
¼ cup (1 oz) ground almonds (almond meal)
1 teaspoon ground cinnamon

Place all ingredients in a bowl and lightly rub together until the mixture resembles fresh breadcrumbs.
Sprinkle mixture over stewed fruits or on top of cakes, slices or muffins before baking.

CRUMPETS
(see also yeast doughs)

Crumpets are small, thick round tea cakes of yeast batter which are baked on a frying pan (skillet) or griddle in small egg rings. Crumpets are baked on one side only, giving a flat golden brown base and a top which is dotted with holes. They are usually served at breakfast time, toasted, and with sweet toppings such as butter, jam (jelly) and honey.

4 cups (16 oz) plain (all-purpose) flour
1 tablespoon baking powder (soda)
1 teaspoon salt
1 teaspoon sugar
3 cups (24 fl oz) warm water
25 g (¾ oz) fresh compressed yeast

Place flour, baking powder, salt and sugar in a large mixing bowl. Place the yeast in the warm water and whisk lightly

Croquembouche Step-by-Step

Step 1: Dip the profiteroles into the caramel and cover evenly.

Step 2: Make a small ring of filled and dipped profiteroles on a serving platter.

Step 3: Fill the middle of the ring with profiteroles.

Step 4: Build up the stack, one layer at a time, starting on the outside edges and then filling in the centre.

Step 5: Dip a fork into the remaining caramel and spin caramel threads over the croquembouche.

Step 6: Spin the caramel threads over the croquembouche until the desired decoration is achieved. See page 89.

until it is dissolved. Make a well in the centre of the dry ingredients and pour in the yeast liquid. Mix by hand or whisk until all the ingredients have formed a thick batter. Beat until smooth.

Lightly grease a frying pan (skillet) and heat to 150°C (300°F). Lightly grease egg rings and place them in the heating frying pan. When the pan is the correct temperature, pour the batter into the egg rings, filling them half way. Cook the crumpets for 12–15 minutes, or until the tops of the crumpets are firm and set and full of small holes.

Remove the egg rings and place the crumpets on a cake rack. Cool, then toast and serve.

CRYSTALLISED FRUIT
(see fruit)

CUBE SUGAR
(see also sugar)

Considered the best type of sugar for boiling for pulled sugar and caramel, cube sugar is made from top quality sugar liquor. Being small and slightly rough, the sugar cubes also provide an easy way of extracting essential oils and essences from citrus fruits. Rub the sugar cubes over the surface of the orange, lemon or lime fruit zest, and the sugar absorbs the oils and some of the colourings and can then be dissolved directly into custards, sauces and syrups. Plain sugar cubes are also used when making large decorations, usually architectural structures. The cubes are joined by royal icing and can be used to create virtually any design required.

CUP CAKE
(see also patty cake, queen cake)

These small cakes (the size of a cup) are often baked in paper cases in patty tins (muffin pans) and used to produce butterfly cakes and jelly cakes (see individual listings). A popular party food for young children, plain cupcake batter can be altered by adding dried fruits or chocolate chips and decorating with frostings, water icings. They are usually simply adorned with cachous or hundreds and thousands.

CURD
(see also lemon curd)

In pastry terms, the word 'curd' does not directly relate to the curd which is produced when an acid is added to milk, but instead refers to a rich smooth custard of citrus flavourings of British origin. Lemon, orange or mandarin curds are made by heating butter, eggs, sugar and citrus juices.

ORANGE CURD
3 x 60 g (2 oz) eggs
1 cup (8 oz) sugar
zest and juice of 2 oranges
125 g (4 oz) unsalted (sweet) butter

Whisk eggs sufficiently to break them down, then add orange zest and juice and the sugar to the lightly whisked eggs. Mix well. Chop butter into small pieces and add to the other ingredients. Place the bowl over a bain-marie or saucepan of simmering water and stir until the butter has melted. Keep stirring until the mixture thickens and coats the back of a metal spoon. Pour the warm mixture into tartlet cases or over the top of desserts.

CURDLE

Often when butter and sugar are beaten together and eggs or liquids are either added too fast or in too large a quantity, the mixture will curdle, or split into many small pieces of fat, too small to absorb the liquid being added. Often the curdle is caused because ingredients are not all the same temperature. It can be fixed by simply warming the mixture slightly and rewhipping to peak volume. If not fixed immediately, a curdle will cause a recipe to lose its volume and any aeration that was produced by beating the butter and sugar. A curdled cake mixture can be fixed by adding a small portion of the flour and other dry ingredients, although the mixture should first be warmed and rewhipped to peak volume if a top quality cake is desired.

CURRANT
(see also dried fruit)

A small dried stoneless form of black grape, currants are more than 50% sugar. They are used for their sweetening effect in cakes, pastries and desserts. Currants are often used in conjunction with other dried fruits such as sultanas and mixed (candied) peel in sweet buns, cakes, biscuits (cookies) and fruit mince.

CUSTARD
(see also sauces)

Custard is a thick mixture of milk or cream, sugar, eggs and a thickening agent, usually custard powder but traditionally cornflour, which is cooked in a saucepan. A good custard should be smooth, not too thick or sweet and pleasant to the taste. Custards are used in buttercreams, as bases in cakes, soufflés and cream desserts and as sauces to accompany puddings and desserts.

If a custard is too thick, it can be thinned down with extra milk. If it is lumpy, however, it should be strained or recommenced. Custards should be stirred continuously while on the stove so that they do not stick to the base and burn.

They should be used immediately, although they can be stored in the refrigerator for 1–2 days.

CHOCOLATE CUSTARD
⅔ cup (5 oz) caster sugar
6 tablespoons cocoa, sifted
3 tablespoons cornflour (cornstarch), sifted
2 cups (16 fl oz) milk
1¼ cups (10 fl oz) thickened cream
1 teaspoon vanilla essence (extract)
2 eggs

Place all ingredients in a saucepan and whisk together to remove any lumps. Gently heat for about 5 minutes or until the mixture begins to thicken. Continue to stir and increase the heat to allow the mixture to come to the boil. Remove from heat and strain into a serving bowl or individual bowls.

Makes about 4 cups

CUSTARD POWDER
(see also custard, thickeners)

A powder-thickening agent made up of colourings, cornflour or arrowroot, usually with a vanilla flavouring. Some custard powders are pre-sweetened and some simply need to be mixed with water. The typical and most common custard powders need to be added to heated liquids such as milk or cream and cooked, to remove the floury taste of the powder from the sauce.

CUT-IN

This method is often used to cut fats into dry ingredients and involves using a continual cutting motion. It is suited to doughs which must have only a little handling if they are to retain their lightness. With pastry doughs, this is sometimes performed using a pastry cutter, although more often it is simply done using a knife. Scones (biscuits) are the most common dough made using this method.

DACQUOISE
(see also Japonaise/Le Succès)

A traditional French cake which is very similar to the succès or the japonaise, this consists of three layers of japonaise base, made using only the meringue and ground almonds. When baked and cooled, these are joined together using flavoured buttercream. More traditionally, small, individual dacquoises can be served for afternoon tea and are made by piping oval-shaped discs of the base which, when baked, are filled with the buttercream. The most common flavour is coffee and, no matter what the flavour, dacquoises are always dusted with icing (powdered) sugar.

4 egg whites
⅔ cup (5 oz) caster (superfine) sugar
1 cup (3½ oz) ground almonds
⅓ cup (1½ oz) cornflour (cornstarch)
1 tablespoon icing (powdered) sugar

Coffee Buttercream
375 g (12 oz) unsalted (sweet) butter, softened
½ cup (3 oz) icing (powdered) sugar
2 eggs
2 tablespoons instant coffee powder
1 tablespoon warm water
2 teaspoons vanilla essence (extract)
roasted flaked almonds for decoration
icing (powdered) sugar for decoration

Preheat oven to 180°C (350°F).
Line three baking sheets with baking paper (parchment) and draw a 20 cm (8 in) circle on each.
Whisk egg whites until stiff peaks form and gradually beat in sugar, a spoonful at a time. Beat at top speed for 5–8 minutes or until sugar is completely dissolved.
Mix almonds, cornflour and icing sugar, then very gently fold in the beaten egg whites by hand.
Place mixture in a piping bag fitted with a 1 cm (½ in) plain round nozzle and pipe the dacquoise mixture

into the marked circles, starting from the centre and working outwards. Bake for 25–30 minutes.
Cool on the sheets on a cake rack.

Coffee Buttercream
Spread the first disc evenly with the coffee buttercream.
Add the second disc and again cover with the buttercream.
Spread a little of the coffee cream around the edges, then press the roasted flaked almonds onto the sides.
Leave the top plain and simply dust lightly with the icing sugar.

DAMPER
(see also quickbread, scones)

A quickbread, this baked dough mass is a traditional Australian bread which was made by a member of the First Fleet who settled in Sydney. Australia's first baker, William Bond, used a camp oven or small cast iron pot which he heated in the fire's coals. When the dough was placed inside the pot he would 'damp down' the pot with hot coals, placing them under and over the pot. This practice of damping down is said to be the reason for the name of damper, but other stories refer to the quickbread being named after its biggest fan, explorer William Dampier.

Damper was originally a simple mixture of flour, baking powder (soda) and water, butter being added to the dough if it was available. If camp oven pots were not available, the dough mass would be sat directly on the coals on the fire and the blackness scraped away after it was baked. Another method of baking was to place the dough pieces on the end of sticks and cook the dough in the flames, similar to the way medieval baumkuchen was cooked.

DANISH PASTRY

When a strike was called by the bakers of Copenhagen some 100 years ago, bakers and pastry chefs were called in from Austria and Germany. In Denmark they produced featherlight, crisp, layered pastries in different shapes, sizes and styles, and filled them with sweet fillings. The pastries, which were made from yeast doughs laminated with butter, were an instant success, and when the Danish bakers returned to work, they named these pastries 'Wienerbrod' or Vienna breads. It is estimated that over 100 varieties and designs of these pastries are made today, including the traditional snail or cinnamon scroll, windmills or pinwheels, bear claws, crescents, squares and triangles, and many others.

DANISH PASTRIES/CROISSANTS
1½ cups (12 fl oz) milk
1 egg
1 tablespoon sugar
2 teaspoons salt
30 g (1 oz) fresh compressed yeast
5¾ cups (23 oz) plain (all-purpose) flour
500 g (1 lb) unsalted (sweet) butter
125 g (4 oz) plain (all-purpose) flour, extra
apricot jam (jelly) for glazing
water icing (see page 288), for glazing

Danish Pastries

In a bowl, mix cold milk with egg, sugar, salt and yeast, and stir until well combined. Add flour to make a dough that is the same consistency as the butter. Should the dough be too firm, add a little extra milk to soften; if dough is too soft, add more flour to increase its stiffness. Knead dough lightly for 1–2 minutes only, then allow it to rest for 5 minutes.

Roll dough into a ball and, using a sharp knife, cut a cross in the top to create 4 sections. Pull each of these four sections out slightly in a cross shape and, using a floured rolling pin, pin each of these 4 sections into round but elongated flaps, leaving a definite thick square of dough still in the centre. The 4 flaps should be so thick that when they are placed on top of each other, they create a thickness the same as the central square of dough.

Mix the butter and extra flour together until well combined. Add to the centre of the dough and fold all 4 corners of the dough over to cover the butter. Roll the dough out to triple its original length, mark into thirds and fold the first end in and then the second end over this.

Rest dough in the refrigerator for 20 minutes then roll to triple its original length and give another three-fold.

Rest a further 20 minutes in refrigerator then repeat this process twice more, so that the the dough has been given four threefolds. Roll the dough out to 5 mm (¼ in) thickness and cut into required shapes.

Preheat oven to at 200°C (400°F).

Fold the Danish pastries and fill as required.

Place the pastries on a baking sheet and prove (rise) for 30–40 minutes, or until double in size, in a warm area (not hot, or the butter layers will melt and leak out of the pastry. Bake for 20–30 minutes. Cool.

Glaze pastries with boiled apricot jam and water icing.

FILLINGS

100 g (3½ oz) marzipan
⅓ cup (3 oz) sugar
100 g (3½ oz) unsalted (sweet) butter
1¼ cups (10 fl oz) custard (pre-prepared)

Cream the marzipan, butter and sugar together until a smooth paste has been achieved, then add the custard and pipe into the unbaked Danish pastries.

100 g (3½ oz) unsalted (sweet) butter
½ cup (3 oz) brown sugar
2 tablespoons golden syrup (light treacle)
1 teaspoon ground cinnamon

Cream all ingredients together until light and creamy. Spread very thinly on the unrolled Danish pastries before baking.

375 g (12 oz) cream cheese
⅔ cup (5 oz) sugar
75 g (2½ oz) custard powder
juice and zest of 1 lemon

Cream all ingredients together, then pipe into the unbaked Danish pastries.

DARK CHOCOLATE
(see also chocolate)

Referred to in many countries as bittersweet chocolate because of its lack of sugar, dark chocolate has the strongest flavour of all the chocolates produced.

DARIOLE
(see also moulds)

Dariole moulds are small cylindrical aluminium moulds with slightly sloping sides, in which puddings are traditionally steamed or baked and mousses set.

DATES
(see also dried fruits)

Dates are the fruit of the date palm. They grow in large bunches, which can contain several hundred dates per bunch and may weigh up to 18–20 kilograms (40–45 pounds) each. Fresh dates are smooth skinned with a tan-coloured flesh which has a smooth and buttery flavour. Dates are native to the Mediterranean region, and areknown to have grown there since 3000 BC. Turkey and Iran are the areas in the region most famous for their dates.

Dates can be eaten fresh from the tree, but most commonly are dried in the sun and boxed for shipment around the world. The best quality dates from any one season are packed separately and called confectionery dates, and are used in all forms of confectionery and pastry making. They are coated in sugar syrup or boiled honey, stuffed with marzipan and coated in sugar, and are delicious when freshly dried.

A good quality dried date should be firm and reddish in colour, while the flesh should be reddish and clear. Fine quality dates will already be stoned before purchase.

DATE PUDDING

2½ cups (12 oz) chopped dried dates
2 cups (16 fl oz) water
125 g (4 oz) unsalted butter
1½ cups (12 oz) sugar
4 eggs
3 cups (12 oz) plain (all-purpose) flour
2 teaspoons baking powder (soda)
2 teaspoons vanilla essence (extract)
2 teaspoons bicarbonate of soda

Preheat oven to 180°C (350°F). Grease two 28 x 20 x 6 cm (11 x 8 x 2½ in) baking dishes with butter.

Place dates and water in a pan and simmer until soft. Cream butter and sugar until very light and very pale. Add eggs and beat well. The mixture should become very light and almost liquid. Add flour, baking powder and vanilla essence and beat well. Add bicarbonate of soda to the dates, allow to bubble, then pour onto the sponge mixture. Mix well. Pour into prepared baking dishes and bake in preheated oven until sponge is well risen and brown and firm to the touch.

Serve with butterscotch or treacle sauce (see page 45).

DAY/NIGHT MOUSSE CAKE

This cake takes its name from the contrasting layers of white and dark mousse fillings.

1 chocolate génoise sponge (see page 134)

Filling (White Mousse)
4 level teaspoons gelatine powder
2 tablespoons water
100 g (3½ oz) white chocolate, chopped
3 egg yolks
⅔ cup (5 fl oz) cream (single or light)
¼ cup (2 oz) sugar
⅔ cup (5 fl oz) thickened cream (double or heavy), whipped
3 egg whites

Filling (Dark Mousse)
4 level teaspoons gelatine powder
2 tablespoons water
100 g (3½ oz) dark (plain or bittersweet)
chocolate, chopped
3 egg yolks
⅔ cup (5 fl oz) cream (single or light)
¼ cup (2 oz) sugar
⅔ cup (5 fl oz) thickened cream (double or heavy), whipped
3 egg whites

To Decorate
400 g (13 oz) marzipan
100 g (3½ oz) dark (plain or semi-sweet) chocolate,
melted (see page 62)

Cut sponge in half horizontally and place one half in the base of a 23 cm (9 in) springform cake tin. Mix gelatine and water in a small bowl. Stand bowl in a pan of hot water until gelatine is dissolved. Place chocolate in the top half of a double boiler and melt slowly over hot water, stirring occasionally. Remove from heat and allow chocolate to cool slightly. Place egg yolk mixture, cream and sugar in a heatproof bowl and whisk until blended. Stand bowl on a wire rack over a saucepan of simmering water. Do not let the bottom of the bowl touch the hot water. Beat mixture until it thickens. Mix gelatine into the egg yolks, making sure that both are the same temperature. Blend in melted chocolate. Cool over ice, stirring occasionally. When cooled and thickened, remove from ice and fold in the whipped cream by hand. Whisk egg whites until soft peaks form, then gently fold into the chocolate mixture.

Pour half the white chocolate mousse into the prepared tin and freeze for 10 minutes, or until slightly firm. Repeat this procedure with the remaining mousses. Place the second layer of sponge on top and freeze the cake for 20 minutes, or until set, then refrigerate for 2 hours.

Roll out the marzipan thinly. Cover the top and sides of the cake with the marzipan and trim the edges. Using a pastry brush, paint thinly with melted chocolate.

Store in refrigerator until ready to serve.

See page 98

DEATH BY CHOCOLATE

400 g (13 oz) dark (bittersweet) chocolate, melted
375 g (12 oz) unsalted (sweet) butter, melted
1⅓ cups (13 oz) sugar
6 eggs

Soft Butter Frosting
½ cup (4 fl oz) milk
¼ cup (2 oz) caster (superfine) sugar
125 g (4 oz) dark (bittersweet) chocolate, chopped
1 egg yolk
125 g (4 oz) unsalted (sweet) butter, softened

Preheat oven to 120°C (250°F). Line a 20 cm (8 in) springform cake tin with several layers of aluminium foil (to prevent any leakage of liquid). Place chocolate, butter and sugar together in a large bowl and stir together until well combined. Whisk eggs into the chocolate mixture. Pour liquid mixture into prepared tin and bake in preheated oven for 3 hours. The mixture will be firm. Allow the Death by Chocolate to sit for 1 hour, then cover, still in the tin, and freeze for 24 hours.

Soft Butter Frosting
Bring the milk and sugar to the boil in a small saucepan. Remove from the heat and add the chopped chocolate, stirring until smooth. When cool, whisk in the egg yolk. Allow the mixture to cool completely.
Whisk the butter until light and fluffy and then, in four amounts, slowly add the liquid chocolate mixture to the butter, beating well between each addition. When all the chocolate mixture is incorporated into the butter, spread the frosting over and around the Death by Chocolate and refreeze until required. Thin portions of this cake should be served direct from the freezer, allowed to thaw for 10 minutes and eaten immediately. (Warmth changes the texture and flavour of this cake, so eat it while it is cold.)

DECORATION

The topic of decoration in pastrycooking could fill a book of its own and many a book has been devoted to this topic over the centuries.

The most important things one needs to remember when decorating are the following points:

(i) Do not colour too brightly; colours used in a flavour-based dessert must look realistic and not be gaudy or unbelievably coloured;

(ii) Decorative centrepieces must look elegant, attractive and harmonise with the foods they are embellishing;

(iii) Themed decorations should blend in with the style and mood of the food;

(iv) Small dainty decorations often look more attractive than large decorations;

(v) A small decoration or centrepiece executed well is better than a large centrepiece roughly produced;

(vi) Only use natural-looking colours and in food products keep them realistic; and

Day/Night Mousse Cake Step-by-Step

Step 1: Layer the mousses alternately, chilling each layer separately.

Step 2: When all the mousse mixture has been used, place a layer of sponge on top.

Step 3: Chill the cake until firm. Cover the cake with a thin layer of marzipan. Use a pastry brush to paint thinly with melted chocolate. See page 97.

(vii) Remember to decorate simply but elegantly, as people are attracted via their eyes, then their nose and finally their taste buds.

Remember that all decoration does not require the artistic flair or intensive labour expended by an international pâtissier, confiseur or chocolatier. With a little thought and imagination, one can give a simple but elegant garnish to cakes, desserts and pastries using roasted nuts, fresh fruits such as fanned strawberries, or with the zest of lemons or oranges. Even the simplest piped rosette of buttercream or piped design of chocolate can look magnificent atop a dessert if produced with care and attention to detail.

DEEP-FRYING

This is a method of cooking foods such as doughnuts, fritters and dumplings by placing them in hot oil or fat and allowing them to cook until golden brown, then turning them over and cooking them on the reverse side.

DE MEDICI, CATHERINE
(see also ice cream)

Catherine de Medici (1519-1589) had a great influence on the development of pâtisserie, not because she cooked herself, but simply because her wealth and marriage to Henri de Valois, later Henri II of France, made it possible for her chefs to indulge their creativity: it was rare for any worker to have the spare time or money to practise dishes until they were perfect or, indeed, to have the excess food with which to practise. It was her Italian chefs who brought to France the idea of ice cream, which was celebrated in the tea and coffee houses and became very fashionable. And it was her chefs who became famous for introducing frangipane tarts, among other delicacies.

DEMERARA SUGAR
(see also sugar)

A pale, golden brown sugar made from white sugar which has molasses added to it, used (for its delicate malt flavour as much as for its dark colour) in fruit cakes and gingerbreads. The name demerara comes from the name of the Guyanan port from which it was originally exported. In those countries where it is not available, it can be replaced by brown sugar.

DEPOSIT

The term for placing cake batters into cake tins by hand. For a trained pastry chef, who uses his hands in a cupped fashion and squeezes the mixture through his fingers into the cake tin, depositing is the quickest method of moving large amounts of mixture from bowl to tin. It is also a more precise way of depositing smaller mixtures into cupcake papers or patty tins (muffin pans).

DESDEMONAS
(see also Othellos, Iagos, Rosalinds)

These are small round cakes served for afternoon teas or, if made small enough, as petit fours. They are made from a mixture known as Othello sponge mixture, the same basic cake that is used for Othellos, Iagos and Rosalinds. All of these were made by an English pastry chef in honour of the Shakespearean characters, but each has its own filling and fondant covering. Desdemonas, in keeping with the pure character of this lady, are covered in a white fondant.

DESSERT

The final, and most important, course of a meal. This is the last chance a chef has to make his customers truly happy with their dining experience. Dessert covers any type of sweet dish which is served at the end of a meal: mousses, slices of cake, soufflés, hot and cold dishes. Almost everything the pastry chef creates could be titled a dessert. In producing the dessert, the pastry chef should consult with the chef to see how large the preceding meal is and of how many courses it consists, especially if there is a set menu, so that the pastry chef can construct a dessert which is appropriately light or heavy, small or large and aptly decorated.

DESSERT WINES

Dessert (or sticky) wines are quite sweet on the palate and should be served with, or even in, dessert. Good dessert wines are sweet to very sweet white table wines which are rich to luscious and weigh on the palate. They should finish with a crisp, cleansing, dry sensation as the result of a balanced acid and/or alcohol content and can rightly be labelled as auslese wines. Other varieties are beerenauslese, trockenbeerenauslese, sauternes and botrytis-affected, the major grape varieties being riesling, semillon and more recently sauvignon blanc. They can be made with or without the use of oak maturation: all dessert wines will benefit from ageing in the bottle. True dessert wines contain 100 g (3½ oz) of residual sugar per litre (32 fl oz) in the finished wine, whereas sweet white wines of a light medium variety contain only 20 g (⅔ oz) of residual sugar per litre (32 fl oz) in the finished wine. There are two major (and completely different) categories of dessert wine: botrytis and eis.

Botrytis cinerea, or noble rot, is a mould which, encouraged and assisted by weather conditions, attacks the bunches of grapes on the vines. The mould causes perforations in the skin of the grapes through which water can be absorbed, via fog and humid conditions, or expressed, via heat and evaporation. Therefore, on a warm autumn afternoon, when moisture has evaporated from the grapes and they appear shrivelled and raisiny and are filled with sweet fruit sugar, they are ripe for picking. Once picked, they are pressed. The juice is inoculated with yeast and fermentation commences. Fermentation is stopped at the desired residual sugar content level by passing the wine through a chiller, killing the active yeast. The wine is clarified/stabilised, stored in oak barrels or stainless steel and, when required, filtered, bottled, labelled and released onto the market.

Botrytis wines are expensive for the following reasons: they are hand picked to ensure careful bunch selection; being raisiny, the shrivelled fruit only yields small amounts of juice; wood, if used, is expensive; and half bottles (375 ml/12 fl oz) are expensive but more practical than full bottles.

The vehicle that causes the concentration of sugar levels in eis wine is, as the name implies, ice. Simply put, the ice sitting on the grape freezes the water inside. The remaining portion of the grape is a concentrated pulp of sweet fruit sugar. When the grapes are pressed, the juice flows but the solid little block of ice remains behind with the seeds and skins. Eis wine is highly regarded throughout Canada and Germany and tends to be even more expensive than botrytis wines due to the very low level of actual wine obtained from a grape crop.

DEVIL'S FOOD CAKE

In total opposition to Angel Food cake, this 'food for the devil' cake is rich, very dark and is iced with an equally rich frosting.

3 cups (12 oz) plain (all-purpose) flour
2½ level teaspoons baking powder (soda)
4 level teaspoons bicarbonate of soda
½ cup (2 oz) cocoa powder
125 g (4 oz) unsalted (sweet) butter
1½ cups (9 oz) soft brown sugar
2 eggs, lightly beaten
150 g (5 oz) dark (plain or semi-sweet) chocolate,
melted (see page 62)
1 cup (8 fl oz) milk
1 teaspoon vanilla essence (extract)

To Decorate
1 quantity chocolate frosting (see page 125)

Preheat oven to 180°C (350°F).
Grease a 23 cm (9 in) springform cake tin lightly with butter and line the base with baking paper (parchment). Sift flour, baking powder, bicarbonate of soda and cocoa powder twice. Place butter and sugar in a bowl and beat until light and fluffy. Add eggs, one at a time, beating well after each one is added. Add chocolate. Mix in flour, milk and vanilla essence alternately, by hand. Pour into prepared tin and bake for 45–55 minutes or until a skewer inserted into the centre comes out dry. Cool in the tin on a cake rack. When cold, cover the top and sides of the cake with chocolate frosting.

DIABETIC SUGAR
(see also sugar, sweeteners)

There are many diets and medical conditions experienced by people today, and it is up to pastry chefs to become familiar with the needs and requirements of their customers. As diabetics are usually unable to sample any of the products produced by pastry chefs, chefs should look at using diabetic substitutes in place of sugar. Diabetic sugars, for instance, are available from chemists and wholesalers in tablet and liquid form.

DICE

To dice food is to cut it into small cubes or squares as evenly as possible.

DIGESTIVES

A traditional English biscuit (cookie) which is spread with butter or used on cheese platters.

3 cups (14 oz) wholemeal (wholegrain, whole wheat) flour
¾ cup (4 oz) oatmeal
1 tablespoon baking powder (soda)
¾ cup (4 oz) soft (light) brown sugar
180 g (6 oz) unsalted (sweet) butter
1 tablespoon honey
⅔ cup (5 fl oz) milk

Preheat oven to 180°C (350°F).
Line baking sheets with baking paper (parchment). Place flour, oatmeal, baking powder and sugar in a mixing bowl. Add butter and rub through the dry ingredients until the mixture resembles fine breadcrumbs. Add honey and milk and continue mixing until a dough is formed. If dough is sticky, add more flour; if dry, add more milk. Roll out on a lightly floured surface to 4 mm (¼ in) thickness. Prick well with a fork and then, using an 8 cm (3 in) plain biscuit (cookie) cutter, cut out rounds. Place directly on prepared sheets and bake in preheated oven for 15 minutes. Remove and cool on the sheet before serving.

Makes 36

DILUTE

To dilute is to reduce the strength of a liquid by adding more liquid, usually water.
If diluting sauces, extra milk or cream may be added to lessen the richness of the sauce or, if the sauce was based on water, water is used; otherwise wine can be used. Sugar syrups are diluted by adding water.

DIPLOMAT PUDDING

Based on the baked custard range of English puddings such as queen pudding, bread and butter pudding and so on, this consists of either sponge fingers or cut sponge or brioche pieces flavoured with crystallised (candied) angelica, cherries and currants and set in an egg custard, which may be flavoured with Kirsch. In the unbaked version, the fruits and Kirsch-soaked sponge finger pieces are folded through a light gelatine-set cream, cut, sliced and served as per the original.

1½ cups (15 fl oz) (dairy) sour cream
1½ cups (12 fl oz) milk
½ cup (4 oz) sugar
6 eggs
¼ cup (2 fl oz) Kirsch
½ génoise sponge, cut into 1 cm (½ in) pieces
⅓ cup (2 oz) chopped glacé (candied) cherries
⅓ cup (2 oz) currants, poached in boiling water
2 tablespoons chopped crystallised (candied) angelica

Place cream in a bowl with milk, sugar, eggs and Kirsch, and whisk until all ingredients are combined. Place the sponge cubes in a large loaf tin or terrine mould 25 x 10 x 10 cm (10 x 4 x 4 in) and sprinkle chopped cherries, drained currants and angelica over the sponge cubes. Pour cream mixture over and allow to sit for 5 minutes so the sponge can soak it up.

Place the terrine mould in a large baking dish half filled with water and bake for ¾–1 hour at 150°C (300°F) or until the custard is set firm. When the pudding is cooked, allow it to cool in the refrigerator for 2 hours before cutting 1 cm (½ in) thick slices and serving on a lemon sauce.

DIPPING FORK

A thin 2-, 3- or 4-pronged fork onto which petit fours, chocolates, nuts, centres, caramels are placed so that they may be dipped into fondants, caramel or chocolate. The thin prongs of the fork allow the dipping medium to flow between them to cover the centre being dipped and also allow any excess mixture to remain on the centre. The forks are usually sold in a set of one of each of the three — a 2-, a 3- and a 4-pronged.

DOBOS TORTE

This torte was invented in 1884 for the Hungarian National Exhibition by Budapest chef Josef Karl Dobos, who won a gold medal for his thin layers of baumkuchen mixture, joined by and covered with a rich chocolate German buttercream and given a topping of caramel.

8 egg yolks
¾ cup (4 oz) icing (powdered) sugar
8 egg whites
¾ cup (4 oz) icing (powdered) sugar, extra
1½ cups (6 oz) plain (all-purpose) flour

Filling
250 g (8 oz) unsalted (sweet) butter
⅔ cup (2½ oz) cocoa powder
125 g (4 oz) dark (plain or semi-sweet) chocolate, melted (see page 62)
⅔ cup (2½ oz) cornflour (cornstarch)
100 ml (3½ fl oz) milk
5 egg yolks
2 cups (16 fl oz) milk, extra
1½ cups (11 oz) caster (superfine) sugar

Topping
1 cup (7 oz) caster (superfine) sugar
30 g (1 oz) unsalted (sweet) butter
flaked almonds, roasted (see page 5), for decoration

Preheat oven to 180°C (350°F). Line 5 baking sheets with baking parchment and draw a 23 cm (9 in) circle on each. Beat egg yolks and icing sugar for about 20 minutes or until thick and fluffy. Whisk egg whites until stiff peaks form, then beat in the extra icing sugar, a spoonful at a time. Sift flour onto the beaten egg yolks. Spoon beaten egg whites onto the mixture and fold in very gently by hand. Spread mixture evenly into the 5 circles on prepared sheets and bake in preheated oven for 10–12 minutes, or until lightly browned, when top of each cake springs back when lightly touched. Turn the cakes out onto cake racks to cool.

Filling
Cream the butter until light, fluffy and almost white. Beat in the cocoa and melted chocolate. Blend the cornflour, 100 ml (3½ fl oz) milk and egg yolks. Place the extra milk in a saucepan and bring to the boil, stir in the sugar and then pour into the egg yolk mixture, stirring all the time. Cool. When completely cold, beat into the chocolate mixture.

Topping
Place the sugar in a heavy saucepan and heat until it melts and caramelises, stirring occasionally. Add the butter and stir until melted and mixed, then pour onto one of the cakes. Spread the caramel quickly and evenly. While it is still soft, cut cake into 12 equal wedges with a hot, oiled knife.

To Assemble
Spread the cooled filling over the remaining cakes, reserving enough to cover the sides. Stack the cakes on top of each other. Cover the sides with the filling mixture and place the caramel-topped wedges on the top. Press flaked almonds around the sides. Cut the cake into 12, each portion topped with a caramel wedge, and serve immediately.

See pages 102–3

DOCKER

An instrument used in pastry cooking for the mass pricking of pastry sheets and bases, for which a fork is completely inadequate. A docker consists of a roller with a handle and a central shaft containing many blunt ended spikes. Pricking the base of pastries allows the steam to escape so that bubbles do not form under the pastry when baking.

DOLLY VARDEN CAKE

Inspired by a character in a Charles Dickens's *Barnaby Rudge*, the Dolly Varden cake is a base cake of any flavour baked in a special Dolly Varden cake tin or an ordinary pudding bowl. When the cake is baked and turned out, a doll is inserted into the top of the cake and then the entire cake and doll are decorated to look like a lady wearing a long crinoline dress.

DOUBLE CREAM
(see also cream)

A thick cream which has a fat content of around 48%.

DOUBLE SAUCEPAN
(see also bain-marie)

A set of two saucepans, one fitting snugly on top of the other. The base saucepan is half filled with water and the top saucepan filled with chocolate or any other ingredient or mixture which needs to melt or cook gently, such as custards, sauces and creams. Double saucepans are usually made from stainless steel, although glass and aluminum are also available, and, as with bain-maries, provide a method of cooking or melting without using direct heat.

Dobos Torte Step-by-Step

Step 1: Melt the sugar in a saucepan and add the butter when the sugar is dissolved and golden brown in colour. When the butter is melted and mixed, pour the caramel onto one of the cakes.

Step 2: Spread the caramel quickly and evenly. Allow this to cool slightly. While the caramel is still soft, use a hot, oiled knife to cut the disc into 12 wedges. This must be done quickly.

Step 3: Take another layer of the cake and spread a quarter of the cooled filling over the top.

Step 4: Top with a layer of sponge spread with the filling. Repeat until all the layers of sponge are used.

Step 5: Cover the top and sides of the cake with the remaining filling. Press almonds around the side. Place the caramel-topped wedges on top of the cake. See page 101.

DOUGH
(see also yeast dough)

Any mixture which is a mass of liquid and flour and usually holds its own shape when removed from a bowl or mixing basin. Doughs are both sweet and savoury and vary in texture and consistency from tough to malleable to soft and able to be rolled. The general description encompasses both leavened and unleavened doughs.

DOUGHNUT

Doughnuts are sweet cakes that are raised either with yeast or baking powder (soda) and are deep fried and then iced with water icing or fondant or simply coated in boiling honey or icing sugar. They are not strictly an American invention; many countries have long had sweet yeast doughs which are fried, such as the German Berliner, but it is the Americans who are recognised for giving the doughnut its hole. Official records credit John Blondel with the invention and patent of the doughnut cutter with a hole in the late 1870s. However, although he may have patented the cutter, it is reported that the doughnut had been around long before his cutter.

There are at least two stories about the origins of the doughnut with a hole: a Native American brave is reported to have taken a wild shot, shooting out the centre of a piece of dough a squaw had in her hand. Shocked by the incident, she dropped the dough piece into the hot fat over the fire, frying it. Another story tells of a Massachusetts man inventing the doughnut when he finally tired of the soggy centres in his wife's fried cakes: in frustration, he ripped the centres out and refried them, thus creating the doughnut.

YEAST DOUGHNUTS
4 cups (16 oz) plain (all-purpose) flour
1 teaspoon salt
75 g (2½ oz) sugar
30 g (1 oz) fresh compressed yeast
1 cup (8 fl oz) water
1 egg
1 egg yolk
60 g (2 oz) unsalted (sweet) butter

Heat the frying oil or fat to 160°C (320°F).
Sift flour and salt into a bowl with the sugar. Dissolve yeast in water and when dissolved, mix in egg and egg yolk.
Crumb (rub in) butter lightly through flour using fingertips.
Add yeast liquid to flour and work mixture to a dough.
Remove from bowl and lightly knead on a floured surface.
Cut dough into 24 even pieces and roll each into a ball. Press the two fingers closest to your thumb into the centre of each ball. When the fingers are through the dough, roll your fingers in a circular motion to make a hole in the dough.
Place doughnut on a floured sheet of baking paper (parchment) and allow to prove (rise) in a warm place until double in size. Carefully dip each into the frying fat and cook on both sides until golden brown. Remove to a tray of absorbent paper so they can drain, then ice doughnuts or roll them in ground cinnamon sugar, or simply dip them in boiled honey and cool them before eating.

BAKING POWDER DOUGHNUTS
30 g (1 oz) unsalted (sweet) butter
½ cup (4 oz) sugar
3 cups (12 oz) plain (all-purpose) flour
½ teaspoon salt
1 tablespoon baking powder (soda)
¼ cup (1 oz) milk powder (non-fat dry milk)
1 egg
¾ cup (6 fl oz) water

Preheat deep fryer to 170°C (340°F).
Place butter and sugar in a bowl and cream lightly until blended, but not light and fluffy. Sift flour, salt, baking powder and milk powder into butter mixture and combine together with egg and water. Form mixture into a dough and work until smooth. Roll dough on a well floured bench (counter) top to 1 cm (½ in) thickness. Allow dough to rest for 5 minutes. Using a floured 7 cm (3 in) scone (biscuit) cutter, cut out as many discs as possible. Using a 3 cm (1¼ in) scone cutter, remove the centre of each of the discs. Rest doughnuts, covered, for a further 5 minutes. Carefully place each in the heated frying fat and cook until golden brown on each side. Remove when cooked and place on absorbent paper until cool. Roll in ground cinnamon sugar or ice using fondant or water icing.

DRAGEES
(see also cachous)

This name refers to two types of sweet products: cachous, the small balls of silver or gold colour used for decorating cakes, and sugar-coated almonds served as petit fours.

DRAIN

To allow a product to release excess liquids such as water or fat, either by sitting it on absorbent paper or by allowing it to sit in a strainer until the excess amount has drained away.

DREDGER
(see also sieve)

Less precise than a sieve, a dredger is a cylindrical tin into which dry powders such as icing (powdered) sugar, cocoa powder or ground cinnamon sugar are placed. A tight-fitting lid, containing many large holes through which the powder is dusted, is placed over the top. A dredger is useful for covering or dusting large areas quickly, but not for a fine precise cover over small pastries or plates.

DRIED FRUIT
(see fruit)

DRINKING CHOCOLATE
(see also chocolate, cocoa)

Produced by most chocolate manufacturers as a side line product, drinking chocolate is a mixture of cocoa and sugar to which it is only necessary to add hot water (or milk) or cold milk to make a chocolate drink.

Dual Torte Step-by-Step

Step 1: Grease the bar pan and line the base and sides with flaked almonds.

Step 2: Spread the chocolate mixture over the bottom and around the sides of the pan.

Step 3: Pour the white cake mixture into the centre of the chocolate mixture and spread evenly. Bake. See page 106.

DROP SCONES
(see also girdle cakes, griddle cakes, scones)

Also known as biscuits (in the USA) and batter scones or griddle cakes, drop scones are a traditional scone mixture of flour, eggs, milk and butter. Instead of being worked to a dough and rolled flat, the mixture is simply spooned or dropped as a moist batter onto a griddle plate. Drop scones are served with jam (jelly) and butter for morning teas.

DUAL TORTE

The flavour and colour of chocolate and almond blend beautifully in this two-toned torte.

¾ cup (3 oz) flaked almonds

Chocolate Torte
2 egg whites
¼ cup (2 oz) caster (superfine) sugar
½ cup (3 oz) icing (powdered) sugar
1 cup (3½ oz) ground almonds
¼ cup (1 oz) cocoa powder

White Torte
¾ cup (3 oz) plain (all-purpose) flour
⅛ level teaspoon baking powder (soda)
125 g (4 oz) unsalted (sweet) butter
1¼ cups (4 oz) ground almonds
2 eggs
1 egg yolk

Preheat oven to 180°C (350°F). Grease a 20 x 10 x 5 cm (8 x 4 x 2 in) bar tin generously with butter. Line the base with flaked almonds.

Chocolate Torte
Whisk the egg whites until stiff peaks form, then beat in the caster sugar a spoonful at a time. Beat until the sugar is dissolved. Fold in the icing sugar, almonds and cocoa powder. Spread the mixture over the flaked almonds in the tin and up the sides as well.

White Torte
Sift flour and baking powder. Beat butter, sugar and almonds until creamy, light and fluffy. Add eggs, one at a time, then the egg yolk, beating very well after each one is added. Gently fold in sifted flour by hand. Pour into the centre of the tin. Bake for 50–55 minutes or until the top of the cake springs back when lightly touched. Cool in the tin for 5 minutes before turning the torte out onto a cake rack.

See page 105

DUCATS
(see also yeast doughs)

An Austrian dessert, these delicate little yeast-risen cakes are served with hot custard and a sprinkling of ground cinnamon sugar.

2½ cups (10 oz) plain (all-purpose) flour
¼ cup (2 oz) sugar
zest of 1 lemon
¾ cup (6 fl oz) milk
10 g (⅓ oz) fresh compressed yeast
1 egg
45 g (1½ oz) unsalted (sweet) butter, melted
125 g (4 oz) unsalted (sweet) butter, melted, extra

Place flour, sugar and lemon zest in a bowl and combine. Make a well in the centre. In a small bowl, mix milk and yeast until yeast is dissolved. Pour this liquid, along with the egg and melted butter, into the well in the flour. Slowly mix flour into the liquid and bring the mixture to a dough. Knead dough on a floured bench for 5–8 minutes, or until smooth and elastic. Place dough in a bowl, cover, and leave in a warm area for 25–30 minutes, or until double in size. Lightly grease a 20 x 25 x 3 cm (8 x 10 x 1¼ in) baking tray (jelly roll pan) or cake tin. Remove the dough and knead lightly to knock out the air. Cut dough into 24 small pieces, rolling each into a ball shape. Dip the base of each ball into the extra melted butter, then place the balls side by side in the prepared tray. When the tray is full, brush the tops of the ducats with any leftover melted butter, then place the full tray in a warm place for 35–40 minutes, or until double in size. Bake at 200°C (400°F) for 20–30 minutes or until golden brown.
Serve 4 ducats per person with ground cinnamon sugar and custard or crème anglaise.

DUMPLINGS

Dumplings are a traditional English pudding. Golden syrup (light treacle) dumplings are enjoyed throughout the world, while steamed or boiled savoury dumplings are famed throughout Asia and China, and are also served elsewhere with stews and other dishes. Dumplings are a light mixture of flour or potato with eggs and sugar. They are either steamed or poached in boiling sweet syrups or stock.

30 g (1 oz) unsalted (sweet) butter, softened
375 g (12 oz) cream cheese
2 eggs
1 tablespoon sugar
zest and juice of an orange
75 g (2½ oz) white bread, grated

Sweet Crumbs
90g (3 oz) unsalted (sweet) butter
6 teaspoons sugar
1 tablespoon brown sugar
¾ cup (3 oz) biscuit (cookie) crumbs
1 teaspoon ground cinnamon

Place butter and cream cheese in a bowl and mix well.
Add eggs, one at a time, beating well after each one is added.
Add sugar, lemon zest and juice and grated white bread,
then beat thoroughly. Allow mixture to rest,
covered, for 30 minutes.
Stir mixture several times before taking tablespoonfuls and
shaping into dumplings. Drop dumplings into simmering
water and cook them for 15–20 minutes.
Remove dumplings gently and allow to drain well
before rolling in the sweetened crumbs.

Sweet Crumbs
To make sweet crumbs, melt the butter in a small frying pan
(skillet) or saucepan and add both sugars, stirring until
dissolved. Stir in biscuit crumbs and cinnamon.
Allow to brown slightly, then remove and cool.

DUNDEE CAKE
(see also fruit cake)

From the city of Dundee in Scotland, the Dundee cake was
first made in the early 1800s when a marmalade factory
operated close to the city. The excess citrus peelings had no
value to the factory, so a clever cook gathered them up and
used them in this rich fruit cake, which is decorated with
blanched almonds.

3 cups (12 oz) plain (all-purpose) flour
4 level teaspoons baking powder (soda)
275 g (9 oz) unsalted (sweet) butter
1¾ cups (10 oz) soft (light) brown sugar
5 eggs

6 teaspoons apricot jam (jelly)
1 cup (3½ oz) ground almonds
2 cups (11 oz) seedless raisins
1½ cups (9 oz) sultanas
½ cup (3 oz) mixed (candied) peel
2 tablespoons milk
1½ cups (8 oz) blanched almonds, for decoration

Preheat oven to 180°C (350°F). Lightly grease a 23 cm (9 in)
springform cake tin with butter and line the base
and sides with baking paper (parchment).
Mix flour and baking powder and sift twice. Beat butter and
sugar until creamy, light and fluffy. Add eggs, one at a time,
beating very well after each one is added. Beat in apricot jam.
Mix in sifted flour and baking powder alternately with the
almonds and dried fruit, by hand. Pour mixture into
prepared tin and brush lightly with milk. Arrange almonds
on top and press into the cake. Bake for 1½ hours, or
until a skewer inserted into the centre of the cake comes
out dry. If the cake is browning too quickly and
the mixture is not cooked, cover the top with
brown paper or aluminium foil. Cool in the tin for
15 minutes before turning out onto a cake rack.

DUST
(see also dredger)

Bread dough can be dusted with flour before baking
(a characteristic of the Scottish baps), or a bench (counter)
top can be dusted with flour before dough is rolled on it.
Foods can also be dusted with icing sugar before being served,
to enhance their appearance.

EASTER

Named after the goddess of spring, Eostre, whose festival fell in spring, Easter is also the celebration of the death and resurrection of Christ, one of the oldest festivals celebrated by Christians. Chocolate eggs are the most commonly given gift at Easter. As well as Easter eggs, hot cross buns, marzipan chickens and rabbits and Easter breads are all part of the Easter festivities.

EASTER BREAD

Easter bread is the predecessor of the hot cross bun. It is not known whether the cross on Easter bread relates to the cross on which Christ died or resembles the four quarters of the moon. In fact, during medieval times, crosses were cut into the top of all breads as it was believed that the first bun or loaf from each batch being placed outside the house warded off evil spirits. Fishermen took their loaf on board their vessels in hope of a better catch and safe sailing, and it is said that some homes excavated in England had several generations of the crossed bun stored. Easter bread was not supposed to go mouldy; it would become stale, but keep forever.

30 g (1 oz) fresh compressed yeast
1 cup (8 fl oz) milk
4 cups (16 oz) strong (bread) flour
⅛ teaspoon salt
100 g (3½ oz) unsalted (sweet) butter, melted
3 egg yolks
¼ cup (2 oz) sugar
grated zest of 1 lemon
½ cup (3 oz) sultanas (golden raisins)

Preheat oven to 200°C (400°F).
Lightly grease a baking sheet.
In a small bowl, dissolve yeast in milk. Sift flour and salt into a large mixing bowl. Make a well in the centre and pour in milk and yeast mixture. Cover with a little of the flour and leave to stand in a warm place for 20 minutes.

Place butter, egg yolks, sugar and lemon zest in the centre of the flour and yeast mixture. Knead mixture to a dough, adding a little extra milk should the dough be too firm. Knead till dough is smooth and elastic. Cover dough and place it in a warm area for 45–55 minutes, or until double in bulk.
Knead dough lightly to expel the air, then knead in the sultanas. Cut dough into halves and roll into balls. Place the balls on prepared sheet and press flat. Stand them in a warm area, covered, for 35–40 minutes, or until double in bulk. Bake for 25 minutes.

EASTER EGGS

The Easter egg is the symbol of resurrection, renewed life and immortality — and is said to represent the empty cave from which Christ had risen. During the fast of Lent, eating eggs was prohibited, so they were a treat to be looked forward to at Easter!

Plastic Easter egg moulds are the best to use, as they are quite inexpensive and are available in all specialty and hobby kitchen stores. With a little care and attention, they can last forever. Always wash moulds immediately after use with warm water and a soft cloth. Do not use any abrasive washing materials and detergents and dry the moulds with tissues or absorbent paper, rubbing the inside with cotton wool until the mould really shines again. Store the clean moulds in a cool area away from direct sunlight. After a period of storage, always clean the moulds with cotton wool before using again.

Melt about 300 g (10 oz) dark (plain or semi sweet) chocolate (see page 62) for each Easter egg. Place the mould on a flat surface. If the mould will not stand by itself, sit it on a towel or in a bowl. Using a soup ladle or a large spoon, pour enough chocolate in the mould to reach the rim. Allow the egg to sit for several minutes until the chocolate begins to look dull around the edge of the rim, indicating that it is beginning to set. Tip the mould upside down and allow the excess chocolate to drain back into the pot. Turn mould back up the right way and scrape off any drizzled chocolate. Allow the mould to stand in a cool area until the chocolate has set hard, but do not set in the refrigerator at this stage.
When solid, fill the mould again with chocolate to the rim and repeat the process. When drained and cleaned after the second time, turn the mould upside down on a sheet of baking paper (parchment) so any excess chocolate can be caught to form a lip. Place in the refrigerator for 2–3 minutes, or until you can see that the chocolate has left the sides of the mould. Tap the sides of the mould very gently and the egg shell should drop from the mould casing. If it does not, return the mould to the refrigerator for several minutes and try again.
Make the second half of the egg in exactly the same way and, when it has set, sandwich the halves together using a little melted chocolate piped onto the lip which has formed. Wipe away any excess chocolate.
The egg is now ready to be wrapped or decorated with flowers, piped chocolate or with a simple bow placed around the edge.

ECCLES CAKES

These oval-shaped puff pastries, first made in the town of Eccles in Lancashire, England, are filled with a rich currant mixture. The top has three cuts made in it and is then sprinkled with sugar. Eccles cakes differ from Banbury cakes in that they are richer in butter and are oval in shape.

Eccles comes from the Greek word 'ecclesia', meaning assembly. In English it means church. It is thought that these small pastries were so named because they were made for the priests and those who lived in the church by the parishioners, to celebrate the dedication of the churches to the community. These celebrations were banned by an Act of Parliament in 1650, and being caught eating a currant pie or Eccles cake meant certain imprisonment. It is possible that they date back to the building of Eccles Cathedral in 1111 AD.

500 g (1 lb) fresh or frozen puff pastry (see page 228)
1½ cups (7 oz) currants
⅓ cup (2 oz) mixed (candied) peel
½ cup (3 oz) moist brown sugar
finely grated zest of 1 lemon
1 teaspoon ground mixed spice (apple pie spice)
½ cup (4 fl oz) water
2 tablespoons unsalted (sweet) butter, softened
6 teaspoons plain (all-purpose) flour
2 egg whites for glaze
⅓ cup (3 oz) sugar for sprinkling

Preheat oven to 200°C (400°F).
Line a baking sheet with baking paper (parchment).
On a lightly floured surface, roll the pastry out to 1–2 mm (1/12 in) in thickness. Cut into 8 cm (3 in) rounds.
Place currants, mixed peel, sugar, lemon zest, spice, water, butter and flour in a saucepan over low heat.
Stir the mixture continuously until it thickens and comes to the simmer. Allow mixture to cool. Place a tablespoonful of the mixture in the centre of each pastry disc. Moisten edges of rounds with water and draw them up to meet in the centre and completely enclose the filling. Press well together and turn over so the join is underneath. Roll out lightly until currants just show through the dough. Make certain that the Eccles are round or oval in shape. Place on prepared sheet. Make 3 slits in the top of each cake, brush lightly with the excess beaten egg white and sprinkle with sugar. Bake in preheated oven for 15 minutes, or until golden brown. Remove from baking sheet and cool on a cake rack.

ECLAIR
(see also choux pastry)

One of the most popular choux pastry products in the world, éclairs are more commonly known as chocolate éclairs. They are long lengths of choux pastry topped, traditionally, with melted chocolate or chocolate fondant, then split and filled with a vanilla-flavoured crème pâtissière. They can, however, be changed quite easily depending on the flavour of the topping (maybe coffee or vanilla) and the filling (maybe chocolate mousse, crème Chantilly or coffee-flavoured creams). Served from an afternoon tea trolley or as a sweet snack, éclairs should have a crisp crust and not be too large.

EGGS
(see also albumen)

Eggs are among the most important ingredients used in pastry work. They give us the smooth creaminess of custards, crème anglaise and mousses, help bind cakes together and make the light airiness of sponges possible. Eggs also provide pastries with colour, and add important food value to many of the goods created by the pastry chef. In cooking, no part of the egg is more important than the other; whites offer a light leavening agent for cakes and heavenly light meringues and a clarification process for jellies, while yolks assist in binding foods and provide a thickening agent in crème anglaise.

The egg has been used as food since around 3000 BC. The hen's egg is most commonly used today because of the laying consistency of the hen. In cooking, though, goose, duck and quail eggs are still quite commonly used. The modern-day hen is a descendant of the red jungle fowl, which was native to India and nearby regions. It was domesticated around 2000 BC. At that time, the hen was an important bargaining chip in trading. It was introduced throughout Europe and the Middle East by traders and merchants, and eventually into the Americas by Christopher Columbus.

The three major constituents of an egg are the egg shell, which makes up 12% of the total egg, the egg white, which is 58% of the egg, and the egg yolk, which is 30%.

The amount of these components in each egg varies with the size of the egg, which can range from 40 g (1½ oz) through to 70 g (2½ oz).

Egg White
Around the egg yolk is a clear liquid and a thicker jelly-like liquid, both of these forming the egg white.

The thicker of the two white liquids acts as a cushion for the egg yolk, while the thinner liquid holds the other in place. Egg whites are mainly used in cooking for their aeration properties, being able to be whisked to a light foam, and tripling their own volume when beaten well. With the addition of sugar they form a stable meringue and, with cooking, will coagulate, trapping the air inside them and giving lift to the baked product. Egg white will coagulate at around 60°C (120°F), supporting and stabilising items such as cakes.

Egg Yolk
Egg yolks are round and yellow and, if fresh, should sit high in the cracked egg when tipped onto a flat surface. The colour of the yolk, be it pale yellow, bright yellow or orange, only indicates what form of food the chicken has eaten, not the freshness or nutritional value of the egg. The egg yolk is held in place in the centre of the egg by a cord known as the 'chalazae', which helps keep the yolk stable, and prevents it hitting the outer walls of the shell and breaking.

Egg yolks are used in buttercreams, cakes, sabayons and for thickening crème anglaise. Due to their fat content, egg yolks should never come into contact with egg whites that are being whisked to a light foam, as they will inhibit the aeration process.

Dried Eggs
Dried eggs have little place in the modern pastry section, though they are sometimes used. The eggs are merely dehydrated and should be reconstituted according to the manufacturer's instructions; this is usually 3 parts water to 1 part egg powder.

Meringue powder, also known as dried egg white, is another product which should only be used if the fresh product is not available. It is made from the dried albumen, which is crushed into a powder, and is rehydrated by adding water according to manufacturer's instructions. These dried egg powders usually contain starches and stabilisers to help give a firm meringue when whisked, so packages should be read for ingredients before use. This form of egg white can be used for meringues, icings and cakes, depending on the quality and the brand used.

Egg Pulp

Commonly used in bakeries and large production kitchens, egg pulp, or frozen egg pulp, is a frozen egg liquid which can be used in the same way as normal eggs although it cannot, of course, be separated. It is popular in the pastry section and bakeries, as it saves space otherwise taken up by egg cartons and because bakers then do not have to spend time cracking eggs. The use of egg pulp does mean, however, that recipes need to be rewritten to give a liquid volume amount instead of the number of eggs.

EGG CUSTARD, BAKED

As well as being amongst some of the world's favourite and most traditional puddings, baked custards and their derivatives are also amongst the cheapest. Served both hot and cold, they include crème caramels, queen of puddings, bread and butter custard and baked egg custard.

2 eggs
1¼ cups (10 fl oz) fresh milk
1 cup (8 fl oz) fresh single cream
¼ cup (2 oz) sugar

Preheat oven to 160°C (320°F).
In a large bowl, whisk eggs with milk, cream and sugar until well mixed. Pour the mixture into a single large ramekin dish or into 4 individual ramekin dishes. Place the dish/es in a baking tin half filled with warm water, then in the oven.
Bake until the top is lightly golden brown and the custard is set firm.

Serves 4–5

EGG WASH

This is used in recipes to give a glossy sheen to baked products and is also used to join layers of pastry together so that they do not separate in the baking process, allowing their filling to pour out.

1 egg
2 tablespoons water

Lightly beat egg with a fork or small whisk, then add water.
Whisk together. The egg wash is now ready to use.
This quantity should be ample to glaze the top of any cake.
If not used immediately, it should be stored, covered, in the refrigerator, but for no longer than 2 days.

ELASTICITY
(see also bread making)

The more a dough is worked or kneaded, the more the gluten will be developed within the dough and thus the more elastic the dough will be. Elasticity within a dough is important; it means that when the carbon dioxide is released during fermentation, the dough has the ability to expand. Without elasticity, the dough would simply tear or collapse in releasing the gases.

ELDERBERRY
(see also berry)

Elderberries are a dark purple, almost black colour and grow on the elder tree, a member of the honeysuckle family. As well as growing wild, this tree is cultivated for both its berries and flowers, which are used to make jams, jellies and syrups and for flavouring cordials and making wine.

ELDERFLOWER CORDIAL

4 cups (32 fl oz) water
3 cups (24 oz) sugar
1 lemon, sliced
20 heads of elderflowers

Place water, sugar and lemon in a large saucepan and bring to the boil. Allow the mixture to cool slightly and add the elderflowers. Allow mixture to sit for 24 hours.
Place the mixture back on the heat and return to the boil.
Strain mixture into bottles, diluting it when required as a drink. Keeps for 6 months, bottled.
It can also be used in small amounts in syrups that are used to soak cakes or savarins and give them a different flavour.

ELISEN
(see also gingerbread)

A gingerbread of German origin raised using egg whites.

EMPRESS RICE
(see also rice dishes)

Also known as Imperial Rice and Riz à l'Impératice, this moulded rice dish was first made for Empress Eugénie, Napoleon III's consort. The dessert consists of a crème bavarois base and cooked rice which is unmoulded when set.
It is served with raspberry coulis.

EMULSIFIER

A substance which, when mixed with fat and water, will allow the two to combine and form a stable emulsion that does not separate on sitting.

EMULSION

A stabilised mixture of two ingredients that normally would not combine. Such mixtures as oil or fat and water are brought together into a stable emulsion by the addition of an emulsifying agent.

ENGADINER

A traditional Swiss rich nut tart.

300 g (10 oz) prepared sweet pastry (see page 272)
125 g (4 oz) dark (plain or semi sweet) chocolate,
melted (see page 62)
1½ cups (12 oz) sugar
2 tablespoons honey
1 cup (8 fl oz) cream
125 g (4 oz) unsalted (sweet) butter
2 ½ cups (10 oz) finely chopped walnuts

Preheat oven to 180°C (350°F).
On a lightly floured board, roll the pastry to 2–3 mm (⅛ in) in thickness and line a 23 cm (9 in) flan tin (pie pan) with the pastry. Place a sheet of baking paper (parchment) in the base of the lined flan, fill with rice or beads and blind bake for 12–15 minutes, or until the pastry is a light golden brown around the edges and lightly baked though on the base. If necessary, remove the paper and contents and bake the base for a further 5 minutes. Allow pastry to cool, then brush with melted chocolate.
Place a large saucepan over the heat and heat slowly. Sprinkle in a small amount of the sugar and allow to melt before adding more. As each amount of sugar dissolves or melts, add more slowly, but quickly enough to make sure that the sugar does not become too dark. Add the honey, cream and butter to the caramelised sugar and stir using a long-handled wooden spoon to ensure hands and fingers are not scalded by the steam coming from the pan. Stir continuously to ensure that no lumps of sugar are still present.
Add chopped walnuts and stir well.
Allow mixture to cool slightly before pouring into the chocolate-lined pastry case (pie shell). Allow to refrigerate overnight before serving.

Note: This mixture is meant to be soft and may even be runny when serving the tart.

ENGLISH PLUM CAKE
(see also fruit cake)

A rich yeast dough which is packed full of dried fruits and peel. The fruit cake originated as an adaptation of this cake.

ENROBE

To coat products in chocolate, sugar or fondant with a mechanical enrobing machine.

ENROBER

A mesh band (with fillings for chocolates placed on it) which travels through a slot where a continuous stream of chocolate, fondant or sugar drops onto it. Excess coating passes through the fine mesh band and is reused by being pumped into the holding tank and dropped once again over more centres.

EN SURPRISE
(see surprise, en)

EPIPHANY CAKE
(see Twelfth Night cake)

ESSENCE

Essences are used in foods that have little flavour, either to enhance what natural flavour they do have or to give them another flavour. Essences are concentrated and aromatic liquids, so they should only be added to recipes in small amounts or they may overkill the recipe. Essences are the concentrated oils of plants, roots, leaves and flowers and the fruit itself and are obtained using three basic methods: extraction; infusion; and reduction.
Extraction is carried out by crushing or squeezing the flowers, nuts, fruits or their skins (roses, citrus fruits).
Reduction involves boiling the flavours out of the products and then reducing the resultant liquid by continuing to boil it until the water is evaporated and only the essence remains.
Infusion means heating liquids, steeping the flowers and leaves in the hot liquids and allowing them to sit and infuse for several hours or days (orange flower water, rose water, lavender syrups and so on). The liquid can then be distilled for a stronger, more enhanced flavour.

EVAPORATED MILK
(see also milk)

Similar to condensed milk, except not sweet, this form of preserved milk has much of the water content removed through evaporation.

EVE'S PUDDING

The English cousin of the French Tarte Tatin and the American Upside Down Cake, this pudding is traditionally only made with apples, as these were the fruits which Eve handed to Adam in the Garden of Eden.

5 cooking apples, peeled, cored and finely chopped
¾ cup (4 oz) demerara sugar
180 g (6 oz) unsalted (sweet) butter
⅔ cup (5 oz) sugar
3 eggs, beaten
2 cups (8 oz) plain (all-purpose) flour
½ teaspoon ground cinnamon
⅛ teaspoon ground cloves
2 teaspoons baking powder (soda)
¼ cup (2 fl oz) milk

Preheat oven to 180°C (350°F).
Place chopped apples in the base of a deep pie dish (pan) and sprinkle with demerara sugar. Place butter and sugar in a mixing bowl and cream until light and fluffy. Add eggs one at a time, beating well after each one is added. Add sifted flour, spices, baking powder and milk and mix together well. Spread this mixture over the apples and bake at 180°C (350°F) for 45–50 minutes.
Remove and serve immediately.

F

FAHRENHEIT SCALE

Named after its German physicist inventor, Gabriel Daniel Fahrenheit, the Fahrenheit scale is a measurement of heat which has freezing point at 32°F and boiling point at 212°F. In most modern appliances, the Celsius scale is used in preference to the Fahrenheit scale.

FAIRY BREAD
(see also bread)

Fresh slices of bread which are buttered and covered on one side with hundreds and thousands.

FAIRY FLOSS
(see cotton candy)

FAIRY TOAST

Very similar to Melba Toast, this thin bread is said to have been so light the fairy could fly away with it. It is made for serving with very light dips. It is produced by toasting both sides of a very thin piece of bread and then, using a sharp knife, cutting the toast in half and toasting each half on the cut side. Cut these pieces into 8 triangles.

FAR BRETON

This sweet prune dish derives its name from its place of origin, Breton. The word 'far' is an old French term for a porridge made from wheat, which, simply by adding fresh or dried fruits, can be made into a dessert.

2 cups (8 oz) plain (all-purpose) flour
½ teaspoon ground cinnamon
¼ cup (2 oz) sugar
4 eggs
1¾ cups (14 fl oz) milk
1¼ cups (7 oz) stoned (pitted) prunes, chopped finely
1¼ cups (7 oz) sultanas (golden raisins)

Preheat oven to 160°C (350°F).
Grease a large deep pie dish (pan) with butter.
Place flour, cinnamon and sugar in a large bowl and make a well in the centre. Add lightly whisked eggs and milk and whisk to a smooth batter. Sprinkle prunes and sultanas into the pie dish and pour the sweet batter over them.
Bake in preheated oven for 1–1½ hours or until firm to the touch. Remove, dust with icing (powdered) sugar and serve.

FARAREER

A Greek dessert made of twisted filo pastry which resembles a bird's nest, it is baked till crisp, then soaked in a rosewater- and lemon-flavoured honey syrup.

FARCEMENT

A thin batter mixture which is baked into a cake and served traditionally with crème anglaise. The cake, made from grated potato, dried fruits, eggs, flour and spices, is steam baked in a charlotte mould, tipped out while warm onto a serving platter and flooded with the crème anglaise. Rich and sweet, the pudding can also be made without sugar and served with meat as a fruit custard.

FARINAGE
(see also flour)

From the French word 'farine', meaning flour, farinage refers to any dessert or product made using flour, including semolina, cornflour (cornstarch) and cornmeal, and grits, pastas and dumplings.

FARL BREAD
(see also quickbread)

The traditional quickbread of Ireland, farl is aerated with bicarbonate of soda or baking powder (soda) and buttermilk or (dairy) sour cream. It is shaped like a large cob loaf and has two deep cuts made in its top before baking. The traditional farl was baked over a hot fire on a griddle or in a large pot which had the lid placed on and hot coals or hot peat placed on the lid to provide even and thorough heat for baking, similar to the way in which camp ovens are used in outback Australia for dampers.

FASCHINGSKRAPFEN
(see also berliners)

This fried dough product is similar to the Berlinerkrapfen and is eaten during the festival of Fasching, a period of festivities which begins after the Epiphany or Twelfth Night, on 6 January, and goes through to Shrove Tuesday. Supposedly invented around 1615, the Faschingskrapfen is a ball of yeast dough which is proven (risen) until light and fluffy and then fried on both sides so that a band of white encircles the entire ball. Once fried, it is rolled in vanilla sugar. It differs from the Berliner in that it is filled with apricot jam (jelly).

FATS

A fat differs from an oil in that at room temperature a fat should be solid, whereas oils are almost always liquid. Fats are extracted from animals or vegetables and include copha (white vegetable or coconut fat), butter, margarine, lard and suet.

FEATHERING
(see also marbling)

Feathering is used on water icing, fondant or chocolate to produce effective decorations on any cake.

Cover the top surface of the cake with a thin layer of the desired topping and smooth. Pipe different coloured topping in lines or circles over the first layer. Draw a toothpick or knife through the toppings from one side of the cake to the other. When 6–7 lines have been drawn in one direction, turn the cake around and repeat the process.

Approximately 200 g (7 oz) of topping is sufficient to decorate one 23 cm (9 in) cake.

FERMENTATION
(see also bread)

In yeast-based products, fermentation occurs when the yeast breaks down the sugars within the dough (added and natural) to produce the carbon dioxide and alcohol which lift or raise the dough.

FIG

Originating in Asia several thousand years ago, figs are available today in some 150 varieties. They are suitable for poaching, baking, preserving, for making into jams, conserves, pickles, ice creams, sorbets or for eating on their own. Figs are grown in tropical regions and are pear-shaped, green- to purple-skinned fruit which split when ripe. Fresh figs should be served at room temperature, as chilling reduces their flavour. Dried figs are also quite popular and can be used chopped and diced in many recipes for confectionery, cakes and pastry fillings.

FILBERT
(see hazelnut)

FILO PASTRY
(see also baklava, pastry)

Filo (phyllo) is a paper-thin pastry used in Greek and Mediterranean cooking for many dishes including the sweet cake baklava. It consists of a simple dough of flour, water, oil and eggs which is kneaded until smooth and elastic and allowed to rest. It is then pulled by hand into very thin layers. The Hungarians stole the recipe and used it to produce the now famous Viennese strudel, which is made from the same pastry recipe and filled with sweet or savoury fillings.

Filo, phyllo or phillo pastry is time consuming to produce and is often bought as a pre-prepared product these days. Due to its thinness, it should be well wrapped at all times. When being used, it should be brushed with a covering of oil or butter before it dries out.

FINAL PROOF
(see also bread, fermentation, proving)

The final proving (rising) period for yeast goods is usually the longest. By this stage the doughs have risen once or twice and have been shaped or moulded and placed in tins or trays. The final proof is the rising period that takes place before the goods are placed in the oven. As the products will be feathery light when removed from their proving position, they should be treated with great care — sudden gusts of cold air or a sharp knock against something will quickly flatten them.

FINANCIER

A cake base commonly made for petit fours from a light sponge mixture with egg whites and ground almonds folded through it. The cake batter is often baked into flat sheets and cut out when cold using an oval-shaped cutter. It makes a firm base cake, and can also be baked thinly, layered, then weighted with jam (jelly) between its layers and cut out for use as a petit four glacé.

FLAKY PASTRY
(see also puff pastry)

Flaky pastry is a member of the puff pastry family, and, as with rough puff pastry, uses a quick method of production. It is made in a ratio of three-quarters fat to flour, the fat usually being rolled into the dough in chunky-sized pieces and laminated, rather than two separate doughs being made from the fat and the flour and then laminated. It can be used in the same way as puff pastry to make turnovers, Eccles cakes, Banbury tarts, millefeuille and vol au vents.

FLAMBE

A form of showmanship which is usually performed when a chef is working on the guéridon trolley, where cooking is done at the table. A basic flambé is also created in many households every Christmas when the Christmas pudding is flamed in brandy.

High alcohol content spirits or liqueurs must be used to flambé. They need to be warmed slightly before they are ignited and then poured over the dish. In the case of Crêpes Suzette, a sweet sauce is made and the warm spirits or liqueurs added and flamed almost instantly as the crêpes are added or while stirring them. Adding sugar or sugar cubes to a flambé will lengthen the flame time.

FLAMING

This refers to two processes. The first is the flaming of a dish, which involves pouring alcohol over it and setting it alight, while the other term refers more to the gratinating or physical flaming of a particular dish (or dessert, or confection). Marzipan confections and desserts covered with sabayons are often flamed by being placed under a salamander or grill or by being flamed with a gas torch, giving only a subtle colouring where required for decorations or to bring the flavour out of a dish. Iced bombes are also flamed using gas torches. This can also be referred to as 'flashing' the product.

Another way to flash a product is to place it in a very hot oven for 2–4 minutes, or until it has become golden brown.

FLAN

There are slight differences between pies, tarts and flans and. According to some, the rules are that a pie is a pastry-covered dish which has no pastry base, a tart can be sweet or savoury and has both a pastry base and a lid, while a flan is an open tart. The open-topped flan is usually quite flat and wide and is traditionally no deeper than 1½–2 cm (½–¾ in). Flans can be sweet or savoury, the most famous of the savoury flans being quiche. Sweet flans can have any filling, from a fruit mince to a liquid clafoutis filling which is poured over fresh fruits and baked. For added decoration, flans can also have finely cut strips of pastry laid across in a diagonal fashion for a decorative effect, although if more than 50% of the top is covered with pastry, it is considered to be a tart.

FLAN NORMANDE
300 g (10 oz) sweet pastry (see page 272)
4 cooking apples, peeled, cored and finely sliced
2 eggs
1 egg yolk
⅛ teaspoon ground cinnamon
1 cup (8 fl oz) milk
75 g (2½ oz) sugar
apricot glaze (see page 10)

Preheat oven to 180°C (350°F).
On a lightly floured surface, roll the pastry to fit a 22 cm (9 in) tart or flan ring which is set on a baking sheet.
Blind bake the flan shell until the pastry is just cooked, not golden brown. Fill the interior of the lined flan ring with the finely sliced apple, overlapping the slices as they are placed in a circular pattern around the flan.
Whisk together eggs, egg yolk, cinnamon, milk and sugar until sugar is dissolved and eggs are well combined. Pour the custard mixture over the apples and place the flan in the oven for 35–40 minutes, or until custard has set firm.
Remove the flan and glaze immediately with apricot glaze.
Cool before cutting into fine slices. Serve with ice cream.

FLAN RING

A ring of metal which is placed straight on a baking sheet and lined with pastry, to which a filling of either a liquid or a firm paste is added. Some chefs prefer to use rings because they allow the pastry to be heated from the base directly through the hot baking tray, not through a heavier layer of metal. However, even small cracks or breaks in a slightly too-dry pastry will result in liquid fillings pouring through the pastry onto the baking sheet. Flan rings are available in a range of diameters from 5–6 cm (2–2¼ in) through to 30–40 cm (12–16 in), and vary from 3–8 cm (1–3 in) in depth.

FLAPJACK
(see also pancakes)

The two forms of flapjacks both originated in th USA. The first is a sustaining treat made from rolled oats, treacle and brown sugar, while the other is similar to a pancake, and is also known as a griddle cake or a hot cake.

FLAPJACK FINGERS
Popular with the pioneers of North America.

⅓ cup (4 oz) golden syrup (light treacle)
180 g (6 oz) unsalted (sweet) butter
1 tablespoon clear honey
½ cup (3 oz) soft (light) brown sugar
¼ cup (2 oz) raw sugar
6 cups (20 oz) rolled oats

Preheat oven to 180°C (350°F).
Grease and line an 18 x 28 x 2 cm (7 x 11 x ¾ in) baking tray (jelly roll pan) with baking paper (parchment).
Place golden syrup, butter, honey and brown sugar in a saucepan and heat until butter is melted. Pour this mixture over raw sugar and oats and stir until well combined.
Press mixture into the prepared tray and score lightly into serving portions with a knife. Bake in preheated oven for 20–25 minutes. Cool and cut.

Makes 20–24

FLASH
(see flaming)

FLATBREADS
(see also bread)

Flatbreads are among the world's most traditional and oldest bread. Some are leavened, others unleaved. The first flatbreads were baked on hot rocks, then, during the Iron Age, they were cooked on cleaned and oiled iron plates. The iron plate is still often used today for camping and is known by different names in different countries. The Welsh call it a bakestone, the Northern English a girdle, and the Irish a griddle, all these names deriving from the word 'gredil', a Norman word which literally means the 'flat iron plate'. Some of the breads cooked on the flat irons, or in modern day frying pans, are very flat and crisp, while others have some body to them and are chewy. The varieties are endless and range from chapattis and tortillas to soft crumpets and pancakes. The most popular flatbreads are listed below:

Pita	A flat disc of thin bread often referred to as pita bread.
Paratha	Brushed with oil, a paratha is then rolled and folded so that fine layers are produced.
Naan	Traditionally baked on the hot walls of the Tandoor oven, this is a flat and blistered bread.
Ingera	African in origin, ingera is a flat yeast-raised pancake-like bread made from millet.

Matzoh	During Jewish Passover, the fermentation of doughs is not allowed. Matzoh is a cracker-like flat bread which can also be crushed and used as flour during this time.
Chapatti	A ghee-rich flour dough, the chapatti dough is first heated on a hot flat iron and then cooked over a naked flame, producing the blistering from steam.
Peru-narieska	A Scandinavian flatbread made from potato.
Tortilla	A flat pancake-like bread made from cornmeal and common in South America. Taco shells and corn chips are made from the same basic mixture.

FLEURON
(see also puff pastry)

A small puff pastry crescent which is cut from fresh puff pastry and used garnish desserts or savoury dishes. The crescents should be quite small, as they are meant simply to garnish, not to add any substance to the meal.

FLOATING ISLAND
(see oeufs à la neige)

FLOODING
(see runouts)

FLORENTINE

A very thin biscuit (cookie) made from dried fruits and nuts, the Florentine is almost a confection: it contains only butter, sugar and cream, which must caramelise for the biscuit to set firm. The base or underside of the biscuit is covered with dark (plain) chocolate which is given a wavy texture by a comb scraper.

90 g (3 oz) unsalted (sweet) butter
⅓ cup (2 oz) brown sugar
¼ cup (2 fl oz) fresh cream
¾ cup (3 oz) flaked almonds
2 tablespoons sultanas (golden raisins)
1 tablespoon chopped glacé (candied) cherries
2 tablespoons mixed (candied) peel
1 egg yolk
125 g (4 oz) dark (plain or semi-sweet) chocolate melted

Preheat oven to 180°C (350°F).
Line a large baking sheet with baking paper (parchment).
Place butter, sugar and cream in a saucepan and bring slowly to the boil, stirring occasionally and getting the sugar to dissolve before the mixture boils. Allow the mixture to boil for 1–2 minutes, then remove from the heat and add almonds, sultanas, cherries and peel. Mix and combine the mixture thoroughly. When mixture has cooled slightly, add lightly whisked egg yolk and stir through quickly to combine well. Place teaspoonfuls of the mixture well apart on the prepared sheet. Bake in the preheated oven for 12–15 minutes, or until golden brown.
Leave on the sheets until firm, pushing them back into shape using a scone cutter if they are not round. When cool and firm, brush or spread the bases with melted chocolate and use a fork or comb scraper to wave the chocolate.

FLORENTINE TORTE

A chocolate-filled sponge which has a similar topping to a Florentine biscuit, although it is more traditional to place a disc of cut praline with almonds and perhaps chopped fruits on top.

2 quantities praline (see page 221), hot
1 chocolate génoise sponge (see page 134)
1 quantity no-fuss chocolate buttercream (see page 43)
roasted flaked almonds (see page 5), for decorating

Line a baking sheet with baking paper (parchment).
Grease the ring of a 23 cm (9 in) springform cake tin and place on the sheet.
Pour the hot praline into the ring and spread evenly to the edges. Cool slightly and remove the ring. While still warm, cut into 12 equal wedges with a hot, oiled sharp knife. Cool.

To Assemble
Cut the sponge into quarters horizontally. Spread the first layer with chocolate buttercream and place the next layer on top. Repeat until all layers have been used. Cover the top and sides with buttercream and press almonds around the sides of the cake. Decorate the top with praline wedges.
Chill for 1 hour before serving.

See page 116

FLOUR
(see also individual listings)

Basically flour is a white powder obtained from crushing and sifting cereals, oats, nuts and roots. Wheat, a member of the cereal family, is the most common form. Consisting primarily of starch and protein, flour is available in many forms — gluten increased, soft flour, all-purpose flour, self-raising flour and also wholemeal or wholewheat flour, in which the whole grain is crushed to produce the flour. Flour gives doughs and batters their bulk, holds together other ingredients and also provides elasticity.

Flour has been made in all parts of the globe for many centuries. The Aztecs crushing corn for cornmeal to make into flat doughs, while other cultures crushed grains of wheat between stones and used this for their first forms of bread and cakes. Eventually the mill or millstone was invented. The grains were placed in a trough and a heavy stone wheel was rolled over them until they were crushed. Initially turned by slaves, the stone was later drawn by horse or cattle, and eventually, after the invention of the windmill at the beginning of the 14th century, by windpower. The windmill was replaced by the steam engine. Then came the milling factories, which crush the wheat with heavy rollers, and are still used for processing wheat into flour today.

Florentine Torte Step-by-Step

Step 1: Pour the florentine topping into a greased cake ring and spread to the edges of the ring.

Step 2: While still warm, cut the florentine topping using a hot, oiled knife.

Step 3: When cold, arrange the florentine topping portions on the top of the finished cake. See page 115.

THE MOST COMMON TYPES OF FLOUR

Type	Characteristics
Plain	This general, all-purpose flour is suitable for most uses. It is a blend of soft and hard wheats. The low gluten content gives a light, short texture which makes it excellent for baking cakes, biscuits, pastries and scones.
All-purpose	This is used for all types of cooking in America and has no raising agent. It is milled from a blend of medium to strong wheats.
Self-raising (rising)	This flour contains leavening agents, which contain an alkali (such as bicarbonate of soda), and an acid (such as cream of tartar). The name of the aerators must be on the label.
Atta	This finely ground wholewheat flour is used to make Indian flatbreads.
Wholemeal	This consists of the whole wheat grain and is available both finely or coarsely milled. It does not keep as well as other flours. This type of flour makes a dense and more crumbly loaf with an earthy taste. Often it is used half and half with other flours, to create a less heavy product.
Cake	This is the 'high ratio' flour used commercially in cake mixes. It is treated to produce a starchy soft flour with a high absorbency for fat, sugar and liquid. It yields good volume, a tender crumb and very fine texture.
Bread (strong)	This mixture of soft and hard wheat has a higher gluten content than plain flour. Strong flour is the one to use when baking breads, buns and pizzas, because the gluten strands stretch and become flexible and elastic during kneading.
Buckwheat	Also known as saracen corn or beechwheat, this is used to make blini, the traditional small yeast pancakes of Russia, and is added to other flours in breadmaking.
Chickpea (besan)	Used for batters, especially for pakoras, the small Indian fritters, or to thicken soups, stews and gravies.
Cornflour	Pure cornflour is made from the heart of the maize kernel, which is ground to a very fine, silky powder. Some cornflour is made from wheat, and this is stated on the packet.
Rice	This is made from very finely ground polished rice grains. It is used as a thickening agent.
Roti	This has a granular texture and is cream colour. It is made from part of the wheat grain and is used for unleavened breads.
Rye	This is used for breads and crispbreads. Coarsely ground whole rye flour is used in pumpernickel, more finely ground is used in black bread, and a blend of rye and wheat flours is used in lightly coloured rye breads.
Potato	This has much the same qualities as arrowroot and can be used in the same way.
Gluten	This is made from wheaten flour which is mixed with water, then washed and dried. This results in a flour which is 70% protein (gluten).

FLOWERS

Before considering using leaves, flowers or petals from any plant, first do some research to determine that they are in fact safe to eat and will not poison anyone. Once this is established, flowers can be used to flavour and colour all types of recipes — jams, jellies, biscuits (cookies), breads and mousses. Whether taken from the garden or bought, it is important to ensure they are free from bugs and insecticides before cooking begins. The safest way to prepare flowers is to cold wash them then quickly dip their heads into boiling water for several seconds, then cold wash again. Then pick off the petals and remove the stamens.

The safest and most commonly used flowers in cooking are listed below. They are used in jellies, jams, syrups, sorbets, ice creams, wines, cakes and mousses, as well as in biscuit doughs and for decoration on dessert plates. You can even crystallise the petals.

Apple	Elderberry	Lemon
Borage	Geranium	Marigold
Carnation	Hibiscus	Nasturtium
Chrysanthemum	Honeysuckle	Pansy
Daisy	Jasmine	Rose
Dandelion	Lavender	Violets

WHITE CHOCOLATE AND ROSE PETAL MOUSSE

2 teaspoons gelatine

1½ tablespoons water

1½ tablespoons liquid glucose (corn syrup)

2 eggs

*250 g (8 oz) white cooking chocolate,
melted (see page 62)*

2½ cups (20 fl oz) cream, very lightly whipped

zest and juice of 1 lemon

*petals of 3 medium roses, different
colours, washed*

Line a 25 x 30 x 3 cm (10 x 12 x 1¼ in) baking tin with plastic wrap (cling film). Soak gelatine in water. Gently heat glucose and gelatine until melted. Add egg yolks to gelatine mixture. Stir in melted chocolate and immediately add this warm mixture to the cream, then add lemon juice and zest and rose petals. Pour the mixture into the prepared tin and refrigerate until firm. Cut the firm mousse into 5 cm (2 in) squares and serve 2 squares per serve on the raspberry sauce.

RASPBERRY PURÉE
300 g (10 oz) raspberries
30 g caster (superfine) sugar

Place raspberries and sugar in a food processor and blend until a smooth liquid. Serve either as is or press the purée through a muslin cloth to remove the seeds.

ROSE PETAL COOKIES
¾ cup (4 oz) icing (powdered) sugar
2 cups (8 oz) plain (all-purpose) flour
200 g (7 oz) unsalted (sweet) butter
petals of 2 red or yellow perfumed roses
finely grated zest of 1 lemon

Sift icing sugar and flour together and place in a bowl. Cut butter and rose petals into small pieces and lightly rub through the dry ingredients until the mixture resembles fine breadcrumbs. Add lemon zest and continue to blend the mixture with the fingers until it forms a solid or heavy dough. Remove from the bowl and lightly knead into a ball shape. Place the mixture in the centre of a sheet of baking paper (parchment) and fold both ends of the paper over to meet on one side so that the dough is enclosed in the centre and the ends are open. While holding the bottom piece of paper with one hand, use the other hand to press a plastic dough scraper firmly into the base of the pastry until the mixture tightens and forms a roll. Wrap completely in the baking paper and place in the refrigerator for 1 hour.
Preheat oven to 175°C (345°F).
Line baking sheets with baking paper.
Remove the dough from the refrigerator and cut into very thin slices. Place each disc on the prepared sheet.
Bake in the preheated oven for 8–10 minutes, or until very lightly golden brown.

Makes 24

See page 120

FLUMMERY

A light fruit-flavoured dessert which is thickened with gelatine or starch and has egg whites, cream or ice cream folded through it to make it light and fluffy. It originated in Wales when fruit jelly was made using oatmeal rather than cornflour as the thickening agent. It is very similar to Scandinavian grits.

FOBOIS
(see also chocolate)

A modern piece of equipment used in chocolate work to make chocolate look like a sheet of wood with the grain texture marked in it. A fobois consists of a curved piece of rubber into which are cut semi-circular grooves. These grooves when rolled backwards and forwards and pulled at the same time give the first layer of chocolate poured (usually white or a mixture of white and milk) the appearance of a wood grain. This is allowed to set firm and then a dark chocolate is spread over the top.

When firm, the chocolate is used for decorations. If it has been rolled onto a strip of paper before setting, it can be wrapped around a cake. A mixture of tuile or hippen paste can be used in exactly the same manner to create a wood grain effect.

FOCACCIA

An Italian semi-flat bread which is full of olive oil and parmesan cheese. Focaccia is traditionally served cut in half with fillings in the middle, but it can also be cut into fine finger-shaped pieces for buffets and functions.

FOLD

The art of combining two or more ingredients or mixtures together very lightly so as retain the air volume which has been beaten into the mixtures. Flour is usually folded into a sponge or sabayon base and egg whites into a cake batter, both procedures requiring an extremely light hand and the utmost care.

FONDANT
(see also sugar)

A carefully measured mixture of water, sugar and glucose syrup which is boiled to the soft ball stage and then poured out onto a marble slab. Using a spatula or wooden spoon, it is then worked into a white opaque paste which becomes firm but brittle. It is then reheated with a little water over a bain-marie to form a smooth, white, shiny liquid paste which is used to decorate cakes and petit fours. The fondant, which can be flavoured with essences or oils, can also be poured into a starch tray containing cornflour (cornstarch), allowed to set firm overnight and then dusted off and dipped into melted chocolate.

3 cups (24 oz) granulated sugar
¾ cup (6 fl oz) water
2 tablespoons liquid glucose (corn syrup)
cornflour (cornstarch) for starch tray

Place ingredients in a heavy-based saucepan and slowly bring to the boil, initially stirring with a wooden spoon to ensure the sugar does not burn on the base of the pan.
As you bring the mixture to the boil, periodically wash down the sides of the saucepan with a pastry brush dipped in clean warm water. Once the mixture comes to the boil, insert a sugar (candy) thermometer and continue boiling until it reaches 115°C (240°F). Remove the saucepan from the heat and sit it in a basin of cold water for 4–5 seconds to stop the mixture cooking.
Pour the syrup onto a marble slab and allow it to cool slightly for a few minutes. With a dampened metal scraper, turn the sides of the mixture into the centre so that it cools evenly.
When syrup has cooled and begun to thicken, continue working mixture in a figure 8 motion, stirring continuously until the mix becomes very thick and white, and possibly quite crumbly. This process could take 5–8 minutes of stirring.

Slightly moisten your hands with warm water and form the mixture into a ball, wetting your hands again if the mix does not re-form easily. Work the mixture between your hands for several minutes until it is smooth.

The fondant mixture should be placed in a covered bowl for 4–5 hours, during which time it should soften lightly. If it does not soften, place the mixture in a bowl over hot water and add 2–3 tablespoons of water. Stir until soft and liquid and then use immediately. Vary the consistency of the fondant by adding more sugar syrup if a more liquid fondant is required. When ready to use, place the bowl containing the fondant over a saucepan of boiling water and allow fondant to melt slowly over the steam. If the mixture does not melt, add a tablespoon of water, leave it over the heat and stir until a smooth paste forms. Do not allow mixture to heat above 35°C (95°F).

To Mould Fondants

To mould individual fondants, you will need a starch tray. Sift enough cornflour into a 25 x 30 x 3 cm (10 x 12 x 1¼ in) baking tray (jelly roll pan) to fill it completely. Using a ruler, scrape across the top of the tray to level off the cornflour. Press the pointy end of an egg into the cornflour at regular intervals to make 18 round hollows. Do not make too many hollows—they weaken the surface.

Pour the warm melted fondant into a piping (pastry) bag or simply spoon it into the hollows. Fill right to the top of each. When all the hollows have been filled, lightly dust more cornflour over the top of each and place the tray in a cool dry place for 8 hours to allow the fondant to harden. Use a fork to dig out the fondants, and remove the cornflour with a fine pastry brush. The fondants can be served as they are. Alternatively they can be dipped into chocolate and allowed to set before serving.

FONDUE

Sweet fondues developed from the savoury version. A chocolate (or any sweet) fondue is a thick mixture of sweet creams or chocolates which are placed in a pot and set in the middle of a table for serving with fresh fruits or sometimes biscuits (cookies) such as langue de chat or tuiles. The fruit is picked up using a long-handled fork, dipped into the fondue and then eaten with its delicious coating of fondue. The flavour of the fondue should complement the flavour of the fruit used.

The rules of eating fondue are that if you drop your fruit into it, you must kiss the person sitting opposite you.

½ cup (6 oz) liquid glucose (corn syrup)
⅔ cup (5 fl oz) thickened (double or heavy) cream
2 tablespoons Grand Marnier liqueur
(or your favourite liqueur)
250 g (8 oz) dark (plain or semi-sweet) chocolate, chopped
selection of fresh fruits (perhaps strawberries, grapes, pineapple, mandarin or orange segments), chopped and marinated in 2 tablespoons of Grand Marnier
(or your favourite liqueur) for 1 hour

Gently heat glucose, thickened cream and liqueur in a saucepan and stir until boiled. Remove saucepan from the heat, add the chocolate and stir until all the ingredients are combined. Serve immediately with a selection of marinated fresh fruits.

Note: You can replace the dark chocolate with white or milk chocolate in this recipe. You can also make one mixture from all three types of chocolate by pouring them into one dish and allowing them to become a marbled mass.

Serves 6—8

See page 121

FOOD COLOURING
(see colouring)

FOOL

Fools are usually made with cream, while snows are made with egg whites. A fruit fool is basically a sweetened fruit purée which has fresh whipped cream folded through it. To improve the intensity of the flavour in the fruit, a little lemon juice can be added.

Apple Fool
6 cooking apples, peeled, cored, and finely sliced
¾ cup (6 oz) sugar
100 ml (3½ fl oz) water
zest and juice of 1 lemon
2 cups (16 fl oz) cream, lightly whipped

Place the finely chopped apples in a saucepan and add sugar, water, lemon juice and zest. Allow the apple mixture to come to gentle simmer, then place the lid on and continue to simmer, covered, for 4–5 minutes. Remove from the heat, place the apple mixture in a food processor and purée finely. Cool. Whip the cream until firm peaks hold, then fold through the cold apple mixture. When combined, pour the apple fool into glass bowls or dishes and served well chilled.

FRAISIER

This gâteau is filled with crème Chantilly encased with strawberries and is covered on top with a layer of pale green marzipan decorated with melted chocolate and royal icing.

1 vanilla génoise sponge (see page 134),
baked in a 20 cm (8 in) square tin
1 quantity crème Chantilly (see page 85)
500 g (16 oz) small strawberries, hulled and halved
1 cup (7 oz) apricot glaze (see page 10)
250 g (8 oz) marzipan, tinted green (see page 177)

To Decorate
royal icing (see page 241) in a piping (pastry) bag
dark (plain or semi-sweet) chocolate,
melted (see page 62), for piping

Rose Petal Cookies Step-by-Step

Step 1: Fold the baking paper (parchment) over the dough.

Step 2: Hold the bottom piece of the baking paper (parchment) with one hand, and, with the other, using a plastic dough scraper or spatula, press firmly into the base of the pastry.

Step 3: Continue pressing until the mixture tightens and forms a roll. See page 118.

Fondant Step-by-Step

Step 1: Sit the saucepan of mixture in a basin of cold water for a few seconds, to stop it cooking.

Step 2: Pour the syrup onto a marble slab and allow it to cool slightly.

Step 3: Stir the mixture in a figure 8 motion with a wooden spoon until it becomes thick and white.

Step 4: Form the mixture into a ball with moistened hands. See page 118.

Trim the crusty edges of the sponge and cut it in half
horizontally. Spread the bottom layer with all the crème
Chantilly. Press strawberries into the sides of the crème
layer. Place the second layer of sponge on top of the crème
Chantilly and coat with warm apricot glaze.
Roll out the marzipan into a 20 cm (8 in) square
and place on top of the cake. For extra effect, texture
the marzipan with a patterned rolling pin.
Decorate the gâteau with piped royal icing
(see page 241) and melted chocolate.

See page 124

FRANGIPANE
(see also almonds)

This almond cream, used to fill dishes such as pithivier and
jalousies and in German strudels, was created by the
pâtissiers of France and named in honour of the Italian
Frangipane. Marquis Frangipani was a 16th century
nobleman who invented a perfume scented with almonds, an
aroma which pleased the pastry chefs of Paris, who used
drops of it in crème Frangipane. Today the cream is a fine
mixture of butter, ground almonds, eggs and flour. It is
baked in a sweet pastry crust lined with apricot jam (jelly).

Base
1¼ cups (5 oz) plain all-purpose flour
1 cup (6 oz) icing (powdered) sugar
180 g (6 oz) unsalted (sweet) butter, cut into small pieces
2 eggs, lightly beaten

Filling
200 g (7 oz) unsalted (sweet) butter, cut into small pieces
1 cup (7 oz) caster (superfine) sugar
3 eggs
1 egg yolk
¼ cup (1 oz) plain (all-purpose) flour
2 cups (7 oz) ground almonds
1 cup (7 oz) apricot jam (jelly)

To Decorate
apricot glaze (see page 10)
200 g (7 oz) fondant (see page 118)
flaked almonds, roasted (see page 5)

Preheat oven to 180°C (350°F).
Lightly grease a 23 cm (9 in) springform cake tin with
butter and line the base with baking paper (parchment).
Place flour and icing sugar in a bowl. Add the butter and very
lightly rub it into the flour and icing sugar until the mixture
resembles fresh breadcrumbs. Add eggs and
knead lightly to make a firm dough. Wrap in
plastic wrap (cling film) and chill for 30 minutes.

Filling
Beat butter and sugar until light and creamy. Gradually beat
in eggs and egg yolk, then fold in flour and almonds.

To Assemble
Roll out the pastry into a 35 cm (14 in) circle. Gently ease the
pastry into the base of the tin and up the sides.

Spread apricot jam over the base and spoon on the filling.
Trim the pastry so it is level with the top of the frangipane
filling. Bake for 45–50 minutes, or until cooked.
Cool in the tin on a cake rack. When cold, brush the
top of the torte with apricot glaze and allow it to dry.
Brush melted fondant over the glaze, press
flaked almonds around the top edges and allow to dry.

FRENCH PASTRIES
(pâtisseries françaises)

A generalised term which covers those pastries common to
France. Each of the French pastries uses one of the major
pastry doughs, whether it be puff pastry, choux pastry, sweet
pastry (sablé) or shortcrust pastry. Eclairs, choux buns,
millefeuilles, tartes aux fruits and crullers are all pâtisseries
françaises. The pastries may be sweet or plain, but are never
savoury and are usually served with coffee at morning or
afternoon tea.

FRENCH TOAST

6 thickly cut slices of bread
60 g (2 oz) unsalted (sweet) butter
3 eggs
1 cup (8 fl oz) milk
⅓ cup (3 oz) cinnamon sugar (see page 72)

Butter the six slices of bread well. Whisk eggs in a small
bowl so that they are well broken up, then add milk.
Whisk so that both are combined.
Heat a frying pan (skillet) to 180°C (350°F) and lightly
butter the base. Dip the bread slices into the
egg/milk mixture one at a time, ensuring that they are
well soaked in the liquid, but not crumbly. Place the slices
in the frying pan and cook until golden brown on both sides.
Remove to a serving plate, sprinkle with the
cinnamon sugar and serve hot with ice cream,
whipped cream and chocolate sauce or maple syrup.

FRIANDISES

Friandises (literally 'small delicacies') are served for morning
and afternoon teas, much in the same way as French pastries,
and, like petit fours, include many small cakes and pastries.
Unlike petits fours, which must be 3 x 3 cm (1¼ x 1¼ in),
however, they do not have to be of a specific size. They
should, nonetheless, still be dainty enough to serve as
accompaniments to tea or coffee. Japonaise, sponge cakes,
meringues, Othellos and caramelised or chocolate-coated
fruits are all classified as friandises. Friandises should be
light in texture as well as small in size so that at the end of a
meal a selection of such items can be offered to the guests in
place of a dessert.

FRIED YEAST GOODS
(see also fritters)

When making doughs for fried yeast goods such as for
berliners or doughnuts, it is important to remember that the
dough should be well developed before proving (rising). If it is

not worked enough, once it is proved and fried it will absorb fat rather than simply being fried in it. This, of course, can only be done in accordance with the recipe's requirements: if a well developed dough is not called for, the only assistance which can be given is to ensure the fat or frying oil is fresh, clean and at the correct temperature for frying.

Sweet products, or products intended for consumption as sweets, should never be fried in oils or fats which have been used for savoury recipes, as these flavours may be absorbed. Once cooked, always allow fried items to sit on absorbent paper for several minutes.

FRITELLE

Fritelles come from the French island of Corsica, and are made using a leavened yeast dough made from chestnut flour, eggs, olive oil and fennel. The dough is allowed to prove (rise) and is then fried. When golden brown, fritelles are coated in sugar, split and filled with jam (jelly). They are served warm as a snack, or with pouring cream as a dessert.

FRITTER
(see also batter, beignet, beugnon, bugne)

Fritters, or similar products, are found under different names in almost every country of the world; some are more famous than others. The original fritter may have been invented by accident or could have been some industrious cook's solution to the fact that the high water content of apples made it a hazardous venture to fry them on their own. Regardless, it is believed that the Crusaders brought the idea home with them following their attacks on the Saracens.

Fritters are always served hot. They are usually either rolled or dusted in sugar, cinnamon sugar or icing (powdered) sugar and served with a crème anglaise or bitter berry sauce to offset the sweetness. They come in a number of different varieties:

Yeast dough fritters are similar to berlinerkrapfen, faschingskrapfen and doughnuts. They are proved (risen) and fried, then rolled or coated in a sweet sugar mixture.

Yeast batter fritters consist of fruits or flowers which are rolled in flour, coated in a thick yeast batter and then fried until they are golden brown. Fruits can include bananas, apples, cherries and plums. Marrow or squash flowers and elderflowers are the two most popular varieties of flowers used nowadays.

Fritters made from choux pastry include churros, the Spanish delicacy, and crullers, which are perhaps better known as beignet soufflé or souffléd fritters due to the puffing action of the choux pastry.

Those fritters which are produced from a waffle or similar type of batter are not as common as the other varieties, but in some countries are served not only as a dessert but also as a breakfast pastry. Waffle batters tend to be fried in specially made deep moulds which are plunged into the hot fat. The batter is then cooked till it is crisp.

The way to produce perfect fritters is to use a good recipe, good oil at the right temperature and to cook quickly. A good fritter should be light, crisp and have only a thin batter covering the filling. Always serve fritters as soon as they are cooked. Do not allow them to cool and then reheat them — they will not taste nearly so good.

Fritter Batter
60 g (2 oz) fresh compressed yeast
2 cups (16 fl oz) beer
3 cups (12 oz) plain (all-purpose) flour
1½ teaspoon salt

In a large bowl, dissolve yeast in beer by lightly whisking. Add flour and the salt and stir to a thick paste. Place the bowl in a warm area for 2 hours to ferment, during which time the mixture should double in bulk. When ready, coat the items to be fried in flour, then dip them into the fritter batter with your fingers to obtain a complete coating. Place in a fryer at 180°C (350°F) and cook on either side until golden brown. Dust with icing sugar and serve immediately.

FROSTED FRUIT
(see also fruits)

Soft-skinned fruits can be dipped into or painted with egg whites and then dipped or rolled in fine or granulated sugar. After being allowed to sit for several hours, the egg white will dry, leaving a crisp crust of sugar. This gives a decorative effect to fruits being used as decorations on cakes or being served as petits fours.

2 egg whites
fresh fruits of your choice, dry and with a skin
(perhaps gooseberries, strawberries or grapes)
1 cup (7 oz) caster (superfine) sugar

Lightly whisk egg whites in a small bowl. Dip pieces of fruit into the egg whites separately and very lightly. Allow excess liquid to drain from the fruit so that only a very light coating remains. Roll fruit immediately in the sugar and place on a piece of baking paper (parchment) to dry.
Serve in small paper cups.
If you put the fruit in the refrigerator, the sugar dissolves.

Makes 24 strawberries or fruit of similar size

FROSTING
(see also icings, individual listings)

One form of frosting is the decorative edges applied to the rims of glasses, bowls and coupé dishes. The rim of the article is painted with or dipped into lightly whisked egg white and then dipped into fine or granulated sugar. It is then allowed to dry, the frosting becoming firmly attached to the glass rim and serving only as decoration.

The second and more popular type of frosting is the American sweet light icing used on cakes and pastries. A basic frosting is made from icing (powdered) sugar, liquid glucose (corn syrup) and water, with other ingredients added for flavour according to the recipes used. There are, however, many different styles of frostings, some being made as mentioned, others made using a meringue base.

Frosting mixtures should be kept well covered at all times, either with a damp cloth or by being stored in airtight containers, as they form a skin very quickly once mixing has finished.

Fraisier Cake Step-by-Step

Step 1: Place the strawberries around the edge of the cake and fill the centre with the cream.

Step 2: Place the top layer of sponge on top of the strawberries and coat with apricot glaze.

Step 3: Place the thinly-rolled and marked layer of green marzipan over the apricot glaze. See page 120.

Basic Frosting
60 g (2 oz) unsalted (sweet) butter
3 cups (18 oz) icing (powdered) sugar, sifted
1½ tablespoons liquid glucose (corn syrup)
¼ cup (2 fl oz) water
1 teaspoon vanilla essence (extract)

Place butter, icing sugar and glucose in a mixing bowl and blend together slowly. When all ingredients are thoroughly mixed, slowly add water and vanilla, little by little, combining well before more is added. When all ingredients are mixed together, beat for 15 minutes on top speed, or until the frosting is white, light and fluffy. This mixture is enough to cover one 23 cm (9 in) round cake. Remember, keep the mixture well covered at all times, either with a damp cloth or by storing it in an airtight container.

Chocolate Frosting
½ cup (2 oz) cocoa powder
3 cups (18 oz) icing (powdered) sugar, sifted
1½ tablespoons liquid glucose (corn syrup)
75 g (2½ oz) unsalted (sweet) butter
¼ cup (2 fl oz) water

Place cocoa, icing sugar, glucose and butter in a mixing bowl and blend slowly. When combined, slowly add the water, beating well after each amount of water is added. When all ingredients are combined, beat on top speed for 15 minutes or until the mixture is light and fluffy. This mixture is enough to cover one 23 cm (9 in) round cake. Remember, keep the mixture well covered at all times, either with a damp cloth or by storing it in an airtight container.

Citrus Frosting
60 g (2 oz) unsalted (sweet) butter
3 cups (18 oz) icing (powdered) sugar, sifted
1½ tablespoons liquid glucose (corn syrup)
rind and juice of 2 lemons or 2 oranges

Place butter, icing sugar, glucose and rind in a mixing bowl and blend slowly. When ingredients are combined, add the juice slowly, beating well after each addition of liquid to ensure all is combined before adding more. When all ingredients are thoroughly mixed, beat for 15 minutes on top speed or until the frosting is white, light and fluffy. This mixture is enough to cover one 23 cm (9 in) round cake. Remember, keep the mixture well covered at all times, either with a damp cloth or by storing it in an airtight container.

Cream Cheese Frosting
While still classed as a frosting for its softness and airy lightness, this variation using cream cheese does not form a crust or skin when exposed to the air, but instead remains moist and luscious in and out of the refrigerator.

2½ cups (14 oz) icing sugar
150 g (5 oz) cream cheese, softened
100 g (3½ oz) unsalted (sweet) butter, softened
2 tablespoons milk
1 teaspoon vanilla essence (extract)

Place icing sugar, cream cheese and softened butter in the bowl of a mixer and combine well. When these are mixed together, add the milk and vanilla essence and mix on top speed for 5 minutes, until the mix is light and fluffy. This mixture is enough to cover one 23 cm (9 in) round cake. Remember, keep the mixture well covered at all times, either with a damp cloth or by storing it in an airtight container in the refrigerator. Never store frosting for longer than 10–14 days, as taste and texture will alter.

Variation: Lemon- or Orange-flavoured Cream Cheese Frosting
Simply add the rind of two oranges or lemons to the mixture and substitute orange or lemon juice for the milk. Follow method as described.

FRUCTOSE
This is the natural sugar found in fruits. As well as giving fruits their sweetness, fructose enables fruit to keep while in storage and prevents their going soft. As diabetics are able to eat fruit sugar, it is important for the pastry chef to know about this sugar.

FRUIT
(see also individual listings)
Fruit is one of the most important ingredients the pastry chef uses, as it provides fresh, natural flavours, colours and aromas. Almost every fruit available is suitable for use in some form of pâtisserie, whether sweet or sour, large or small, be it a cake, a cream or filling, or simply a garnish or decoration.

Fruit falls into the following main categories: berries, citrus, pomme and tropical. Fruits are naturally sweet because of the fruit sugar or fructose they contain. They are not only used for their sweet and juicy flesh, which can be preserved, bottled, juiced, made into jellies, confectionery, or simply as a drink, but the fruit skins, rinds or zests can also be used for flavourings, as mixed (candied) peel or as petits fours if candied or boiled in syrup.

Many fruits need careful handling. Fruits from the pomme group, which includes quinces, apples and pears, must be treated with care or they will bruise, brown and soften very easily, while many other fruits will also deteriorate quickly once cut. Cut fruit, particularly apples, will oxidise quickly when exposed, turning brown and losing nutritional value. To prevent this in apples and various other fruits, rub the fruit with a cut lemon or soak it in lemon juice or lemon water. Most fruits tend to deteriorate quickly once they have ripened. There are four main forms of preserving fruit:

(i) Bottling or preserving in an alcoholic sugar syrup;
(ii) Crystallising, candying or glacéing;
(iii) Dehydrating; and
(iv) Making the fruit into a compôte.

Bottling or Preserving
To prolong or lengthen the life of fruit by bottling it in a sugar, vinegar, alcohol or combination syrup. The fruits are usually washed, peeled, placed in a large preserving jar or bottle and covered with either a sugar-rich or alcohol-rich

syrup. The more sugar, the less alcohol is required. Occasionally fruits are pickled, for which a syrup of vinegar is used.

Preserving fresh fruit will extend its life for up to 1–2 years, depending on the fruit, the syrup used and how sterile the conditions are kept. All tools and jars must be impeccably clean for preserving or bacteria can set in. Boil the bottles in water and allow them to drip dry. Use firm clasps and a rubber sealing ring between each bottle and its lid to ensure that it is airtight.

BOTTLED PEACHES

20 firm peach halves
1½ cups (12 oz) sugar
¾ cup (6 fl oz) water
3¾ cups (30 fl oz) brandy
1 tablespoon fresh lemon juice

Wash or boil the preserving bottles in boiling water and allow to drip dry on a clean towel. Wash the fruit and stack inside the clean, dry bottles. Ensure the bottles are full of fruit, but do not pack the fruit down firmly; simply place each piece on top of the other.
Place sugar, lemon juice and water in a saucepan and bring to the boil. Wash the sides of the saucepan down with a wet pastry brush and boil the mixture to 112°C (234°F). Remove from heat, add brandy and cool the liquid before slowly pouring it over the fruit, ensuring that the liquid reaches the top of each bottle. Cool before placing rubber ring, lid and clips in place on each bottle and storing in a cool dark place until required.
This mixture makes enough for two 1 litre (32 fl oz) bottling jars or preserving bottles. The size of the fruit will determine whether any liquid will be left over, or whether more will be required.

CRYSTALLISED (CANDIED) FRUIT

These fruits are quite often purchased pre-prepared, as most recipes do not require large amounts of crystallised (candied) fruit. It is nice to make one's own, however, and a pâtissier should at least know how to crystallise fruit or flowers. This type of fruit is mainly used in the confectionery and pastry trades as decoration or filling, or it is dipped into chocolate as a petit four. It is also used in recipes such as the American Tiffany cake or chopped into pieces for use in cakes and biscuits (cookies) and soufflés. Cherries and pineapples are the most commonly crystallised fruits and are usually known as glacé cherries and glacé pineapple, the term 'glacé' referring to their iced or glazed appearance.

The process of crystallising fruit involves continually dipping it into an increasingly denser sugar syrup, then leaving it to dry and crystallise. As long as it is stored correctly in a cool, dry area, this protects the fruit and prolongs its life. The fruit to be crystallised must have a clean dry surface and should be dipped into dry sugar before being saturated in the sugar solution.

Flowers and their petals may be treated in the same manner as fruit, although the sugar solution should be warm, not hot.

750 g (1½ lb) fresh fruit (oranges, lemons,
pineapple or grapefruit)
2 cups (16 fl oz) water
1⅔ cups (14 oz) sugar
½ cup (6 oz) liquid glucose (corn syrup)

Clean fruit and cut into fine slices ready for boiling. Place water in a saucepan and bring to the boil. Place the sliced fruit into the boiling water for 1 minute before removing and cooling on a wire rack. Place sugar and glucose in the cooking water and bring to the boil. Place the cooked fruit in a glass or ceramic casserole dish or tray and pour the boiling liquid over the top. Leave the mix for 24 hours.
Drain the liquid from the fruit, place the liquid in a saucepan and bring it to the boil. Pour the boiled liquid over the fruit and leave for 24 hours. Repeat this process for the next three days, simply draining the fruit, boiling the syrup and pouring it back over the fruit. At the end of this time, the fruit may remain in the syrup if to be used as soft crystallised fruit on cakes or tarts, or it can removed from the liquid, drained on a wire rack and allowed to dry.
Store the dried fruit in an airtight container in the refrigerator for 1–2 weeks.

DRIED FRUIT

For centuries fruits have been dried as a means of preserving them. The Canadian Indians dried berries for medicines and to give flavour and added nutrition to stews and soups in winter, when fruit was no longer abundant or unavailable.

Fruit is still dried for these reasons. Fruits with a short life-span are either sun-dried or dehydrated by machinery for use throughout the year. As much as 80% of the water in fruit is extracted in this process, making the dried fruit very sweet. It can easily be rehydrated by simply poaching it in boiling water or wine. The fruits most commonly dried are grapes — in the form of currants, sultanas and raisins — apples, pears, apricots and peaches. Virtually all fruits can be dried, except those where the water content is the greatest percentage of the fruit, such as strawberries and watermelons.

To regenerate dried fruits such as currants or raisins for fruit cakes or fruit mince, allow the fruit to poach lightly in boiling water, so that it has a slightly juicy flavour, rather than a firm dryness.

See page 128

GLACE FRUIT
(see crystallised fruit)

FRUIT COMPOTE

A common breakfast dish, fruit compôte is also served for dessert with fresh cream or ice cream. As a method of preserving fruits, compôtes will not last as long as dried or bottled fruits — they should be eaten within days of being made. A compôte differs from stewed fruits in that the fruits should be lightly poached then cooked in a sweet syrup so they retain their original shape.

1¼ cups (10 oz) sugar
½ cup (4 fl oz) water
2 cloves
2 cinnamon sticks
zest and juice of 1 lemon
1 kg (2 lb) peaches, pears, apricots, nectarines, apples

Place sugar, water, cloves, cinnamon sticks and lemon juice and zest in a large saucepan and bring slowly to the boil. Allow to boil for 2–3 minutes. Brush the sides of the saucepan down with a pastry brush dipped into clean water.
To prepare the fruits, peel and core or destone them and slice them into manageable pieces. Place the fruit in the sugar syrup and allow to boil for 5–6 minutes, or until fruit is tender. The fruit should be quite soft but not completely mushy. Remove from heat and cool before storing in the refrigerator or serving immediately.

SUGAR-GLAZED FRUIT

2 cups (16 oz) granulated sugar
250 ml (8 fl oz) water
1 tablespoon liquid glucose (corn syrup)
fruit of your choice, washed and dried (perhaps grapes,
small berries, fresh cherries or mandarin segments)

Place the sugar, water and glucose (corn syrup) in a saucepan and slowly bring to the boil. While the mixture is boiling, brush down the sides of the saucepan with a pastry brush dipped in warm, clean water to remove any sugar crystals left on the sides. Boil the mixture to 140°C (290°F), measured with a sugar (candy) thermometer. Remove immediately from the heat and dip the saucepan into a bowl of cold water for several seconds. Using a toothpick or fork, dip each piece of fruit into the sugar mixture. Do not pierce the skin of the fruit, or the sugar glaze will begin to dissolve. If you are glazing grapes, select a small bunch still joined to the stem and pick them up by the stem. Once the fruit is dipped, allow the excess syrup to drain off, then place the fruit on baking paper (parchment) to set hard.

Makes 24–30 glazed grapes or fruit of similar size.

FRUIT CAKE

(see also English plum cake, Dundee cake,
simnel cake, wedding cake)

Fruit cakes come in many forms, including Dundee, simnel and sultana (golden raisin) cakes, and vary in the amount of fruit and nuts they contain. Thin slices of this rich delight are often served with tea or coffee for morning teas. Originating from the English plum cake, which was a small amount of dough to which butter, eggs and fruits were added, the fruit cake evolved when the dough was replaced by flour, butter, sugar and more dried fruits. (The English plum cake is rarely made now, having been superseded by the fruit cake.)
Fruit cakes store exceptionally well and should be made at least 1 month before the date they are required, to give the fruit time to mature and develop its full flavour. They can be sprinkled with a nip (30 ml/1 fl oz) of brandy once a month to

enhance their flavour. They should be wrapped tightly to prevent air getting in. Fruit cakes are frequently used when highly decorated cakes are desired, as they will not deteriorate while the decoration is being completed, which, for cakes such as wedding cakes, can take several weeks.

QUICK FRUIT CAKE

2¼ cups (9 oz) plain (all-purpose) flour
1½ teaspoons baking powder (soda)
2 teaspoons ground cinnamon
1 teaspoon ground cloves
250 g (8 oz) unsalted (sweet) butter
1¼ cups (8 oz) caster (superfine) sugar
4 eggs
1½ tablespoons marmalade
½ cup (3 oz) sultanas (golden raisins)
⅓ cup (2 oz) mixed (candied) peel
⅓ cup (2 oz) seedless raisins
¾ cup (3 oz) roughly chopped walnuts,
almonds and hazelnuts
icing (powdered) sugar for dusting

Preheat oven to 180°C (350°F). Lightly grease a 23 x 10 x 10 cm (9 x 4 x 4 in) loaf tin with butter and line with baking paper (parchment).
Mix flour, baking powder, cinnamon and cloves and sift twice. Beat butter and sugar in a bowl until creamy, light and fluffy. Add eggs one at a time, beating very well after each one is added. Beat in marmalade. Dust dried fruit and nuts with a little of the sifted flour mixture to stop them sinking to the bottom of the cake. Mix fruit and nuts with the remaining sifted flour. Add to the butter mixture.
Spoon the mixture into the prepared tin and bake for 2 hours, or until a skewer inserted in the centre of the cake comes out dry. Cool in the tin for 20 minutes before turning out onto a cake rack. Dust with icing sugar.

FRUIT MINCE

Fruit mince is a thick, rich mixture of dried fruits and butter, sugar and alcohol. It is used as the base for many pastry dishes. Beginning its life as a form of porridge, which was eventually filled with fruits and then completely replaced by those fruits, it then became known as 'figgy', figs being the major fruit used in the mix. Figgy formed the basis for many recipes, including fruit mince and Christmas puddings.
Fruit mince can be used in pastries such as Banbury tarts or Eccles cakes in place of their traditional fillings, or it can be used in large pies or cobblers. In its more traditional role, it is made into small fruit mince tarts for Christmas.

FRUIT MINCE TARTS

These were originally made in the shape of a cradle, symbolising the birth of Christ, and are associated with present-giving, symbolising those offered the baby Christ by the Three Wise Men. The top of the fruit mince tart was always slit and an effigy of the baby Christ was inserted into the top of the tarts. Today the tarts are simply glazed or sprinkled with sugar.

Sugar-glazed Fruit Step-by-Step

Step 1: Dip the saucepan into a bowl of cold water for several seconds to prevent any further cooking.

Step 2: Using a toothpick or fork, dip each piece of fruit into the sugar mixture.

Step 3: Place the dipped fruit pieces onto baking paper (parchment) to set hard. See page 127.

Fudge Step-by-Step

Step 1: Boil the mixture until it reaches 118°C (245°F), or turns a light golden brown colour.

Step 2: Beat the mixture vigorously until it loses its shine.

Step 3: Spread the mixture in the prepared tray. See page 130.

3 cups (12 oz) plain (all-purpose) flour
1¼ cups (7 oz) icing (powdered) sugar
300 g (10 oz) unsalted (sweet) butter,
cut into small pieces
1 egg
1 tablespoon water

Fruit Mince

2¼ cups (12 oz) raisins
1½ cups (8 oz) mixed (candied) peel
1½ cups (8 oz) sultanas (golden raisins)
1½ cups (8 oz) currants
410 g (13 oz) grated green apples
75 ml (2½ fl oz) Grand Marnier
2½ cups (13 oz) brown sugar
rind and juice of 1 lemon
rind and juice of 1 orange
1 teaspoon ground cinnamon
1 teaspoon ground ginger
125 g (4 oz) unsalted (sweet) butter, melted
milk, for brushing
caster sugar, for sprinkling

Preheat the oven to 175°C (350°F). Lightly grease a
small patty tin (muffin pan) or individual tartlet moulds.
Place flour, icing sugar and butter in a large mixing bowl and
rub butter through the dry ingredients until the
mixture resembles fresh breadcrumbs. Add egg and water
and mix the ingredients to a dough. Wrap the mixture in
plastic wrap (cling film) and chill for 30 minutes.
On a lightly floured surface, roll the dough to 2 mm (¹⁄₁₂ in) in
thickness and cut out circles from it large enough to cover the
base and sides of each mould. Cut another circle for each
tart, for its lid. Spoon the fruit mince into the pastry cases
and press the lids on top. Brush the top of the tarts with milk
and sprinkle with caster sugar. Bake in preheated oven for
15–20 minutes, or until pastry is an even golden brown.
Remove and dust with icing sugar before serving.

Fruit Mince

Place all the ingredients in a bowl or container with a lid. Mix
the ingredients together. Place the lid on the bowl and place
the mixture in the refrigerator for 24 hours. Stir the mixture,
re-cover it, then return it to the refrigerator
for a further 24 hours. The mixture is now ready for use,
although it can be kept, in the refrigerator, for 3–4 weeks.
The mixture will develop an intense flavour
if continually stirred.

FRUIT SALAD

A salad or mixture of fruits which are chopped into small
cubes and mixed with a little sugar syrup.

FRUIT SUGAR
(see fructose)

FRUIT TARTS
(see tarte aux fruits)

FUDGE

A very sweet mixture of sugar, water, liquid glucose (corn
syrup), chocolate, milk or butter, or, depending on the
individual recipes, a combination of these. The combined
ingredients are boiled until they reach approximately 130°C
(266°F), at which point the syrup formed is cooled, then
beaten vigorously until firm. It is then spread into a tray to
cool. In general, fudge should be smooth, although there are
recipes for a crystallised form of fudge, which is quite gritty.
Various other fudges fall somewhere in between.

White Chocolate Fudge

2 cups (16 oz) sugar
1¼ cups (10 oz) thickened (double or heavy) cream
100 g (3½ oz) white compound chocolate
2 tablespoons liquid glucose (corn syrup)
1 tablespoon unsalted (sweet) butter

Lightly oil an 18 x 28 x 2 cm (7 x 11 x ¾ in) baking tray
(jelly roll pan) or line it with aluminium foil.
Place all ingredients in a large heavy-based saucepan.
Heat slowl,y while stirring with a wooden spoon. Bring the
mixture to the boil. Place a sugar (candy) thermometer in
mixture, still stirring continuously. Allow mixture to boil until
it reaches 118°C (245°F), or until it turns a light
golden colour. Remove the saucepan from the heat and
continue stirring while the mixture cools.
When lukewarm, beat the mixture vigorously until it loses its
shine. Spread into the prepared tray. Flatten the mixture
against the bottom of the tray, then refrigerate until it is set.
Cut into portions to serve.

Makes 30 medium portions

See page 129

FULL PROOF
(see also proving, bread)

The point at which a yeast dough cannot expand further or
contain any more gases without deflating or collapsing. It has
reached the maximum capacity to which it can prove (rise).

Preheat oven to 180°C (350°F).
Remove dough and knead until it is ready to roll.
On a lightly floured surface, roll to ½ cm (⅕ in) in thickness.
Using a 5 cm (2 in) round biscuit (cookie) cutter, cut out discs of pastry and place directly on the prepared sheets.
Spoon, pipe or spread a small amount of the topping mixture over the discs. Bake in preheated oven for 8–12 minutes, or until lightly golden brown.
Remove and cool on a wire rack.

Topping

Lightly whisk the egg whites to a soft foam. Slowly add the icing sugar, whisking continuously until the mixture forms a thick paste. Add the almonds. Allow to rest 5 minutes before using. Excess topping may be refrigerated for up to 10 days.

Makes 36

GALICIEN

A decorated sponge cake created in Paris by the 18th century pâtissier Frascati. The cake, which consists of a plain sponge filled with a nut-flavoured buttercream, is iced green and decorated with whole and chopped pistachios.

GANACHE
(see also chocolate)

Known by Germans as Parisien cream, ganache is said to have been invented between 1880–90. It is a mixture of boiled cream and chopped chocolate, the ratio of the two ingredients varying according to its use. Ganache can be made using white, milk or dark chocolate, with the addition of flavours such as alcohol, liqueurs, essences, extracts or natural fruit juices or concentrates. Flavours are more easily defined when added to a ganache of white chocolate, as it is quite neutral and complements citrus, berries and flavours such as coffee particularly well.

Ganache is one of the most important recipes for the pastry chef, being the basis of many desserts and useful in pralines, as cake coverings and as a form of whipped buttercream.

The basic ratios in which ganache can be prepared are:
FOR LIGHT, RICH MARQUISE FILLINGS: 1 part cream to 1 part melted chocolate;
FOR TRUFFLE FILLINGS: 1 part cream to 2 parts melted chocolate;
FOR CAKE GLAZE OR COATING: 1 part cream to 3 parts melted chocolate; or
FOR A CREAMIER FLAVOUR: beat a small amount of unsalted (sweet) butter in once it has cooled, but before it has set.

⅓ cup (3 fl oz) fresh cream
20 g (¾ oz) unsalted (sweet) butter
300 g (10 oz) dark (plain or semi sweet) chocolate, chopped

Place cream and butter in a saucepan and bring to the boil.
Add chocolate and stir until it melts. The ganache can be used immediately as a cake covering. If the ganache is to be used as a whipped covering, allow it to cool and firm and then whip with an electric beater.
It will be lighter in colour than the poured ganache.

GALETTE
(see also Twelfth Night cake)

A traditional French flat cake, the galette is one of the many forms of Twelfth Night or Epiphany cakes which are served on January 6. The galette is made from different pastries, fillings and designs according to the particular region in France where it is made. In its original form, many centuries ago, it was made from a paste of cereals, oats and wheat which was flavoured with honey and baked on flat stones over a fire. As it evolved over the centuries, it was also made of flour doughs and potatoes.

One of the most famous of the galettes is the Galette de Rois, which strongly resembles a pithivier in looks, being puff pastry filled with almond cream. As with most other galettes, it contains a Twelfth Night token which makes the finder king for a day. Some galettes, particularly the biscuit (cookie) form of galette (which has a topping, usually meringue and almonds, resembling a crown, to make everyone king for a day), still resemble flat cakes.

GALETTES ALMONDINES
2½ cups (10 oz) plain (all-purpose) flour
¾ cup (4 oz) icing (powdered) sugar
½ cup (2 oz) ground almonds
150 g (5 oz) unsalted (sweet) butter
1 egg, lightly beaten
1 tablespoon water

Topping
2 egg whites
1¾ cups (10 oz) icing (powdered) sugar
1⅓ cups (5 oz) slivered almonds

Line baking sheets with baking paper (parchment).
Place flour, icing sugar, almonds and butter in a bowl and lightly rub butter through until the mixture resembles coarse breadcrumbs. Add lightly beaten egg and water and work the mixture to a dough.
Wrap in plastic wrap (cling film) and place in the refrigerator for 30 minutes.

GARAM MASALA
(see also spices)

A combination of traditional Indian spices which can be used for both sweet and savoury recipes.

GATEAU
(see also cake/torte, layer cake)

A gâteau is traditionally a multi-layered cake filled with either a crème, a buttercream or fresh cream. The difference between a gâteau and a cake or torte is that a gâteau is decorated so that the portions into which it is to be served are defined.

As with tortes and cakes, many classic gâteaux have a characteristic decoration, flavour and overall appearance.

GATEAU A LA BROCHE

A French version of the German baumkuchen, this is made from a thick batter which is poured slowly onto a cone-shaped rotating spit which is wrapped in aluminium foil so that when the cake is baked it can easily be pulled from the cone. The cake is jagged in appearance and is usually flavoured with honey, rosewater or orangeflower water and spices.

GARNISH

A simple decoration added to a dessert or cake to complement the overall theme.

GAUFRETTES
(see also waffles)

Gaufrettes are thin Belgian waffles which are baked in a large clover shape of four individual heart-shaped pieces. The waffle is cut into these individual pieces and served with cream, ice cream and syrup.

GELATINE
(see also agar agar)

The most commonly used setting agent in pastry work, gelatine is produced by boiling calves' heads, bone, gristle or leather. By the time it reaches the pastry chef, in either a powdered or leaf form, it is odourless. Powdered gelatine should be sprinkled over cold water and, once the gelatine has absorbed the water, it should be placed in or over hot water to melt gently into a clear liquid. It is then ready to add to the recipe. Gelatine leaves simply need to be soaked in cold water before being added to the hot liquid.

CLASSIC GATEAUX

Name	Base	Finish
Gâteau Pithivier	crème frangipane and puff pastry	scored on top of pastry before baking to give decoration; glazed with apricot jam (jelly) and cut into portions
Gâteau Schwarzwalder (Black Forest)	chocolate génoise sponge, Kirsch-flavoured sour cherries and fresh cream	a layered gâteau which has sour black cherries and fresh cream with Kirsch between the layers; outside is decorated with fresh cream and chocolate shavings; rosettes of fresh cream and maraschino cherries define portions
Gâteau Paris Brest	choux pastry, fresh cream and fresh fruit	a large ring of choux pastry sprinkled with flaked almonds before baking; cut in half and filled with fresh fruit and cream and dusted with icing sugar before being cut into portions and placed back into a wheel shape
Gâteau Florentine	chocolate génoise, praline-flavoured chocolate buttercream and praline disc	sponge layered with cream and masked top and sides, the sides decorated with roasted almonds; praline disc is cut into portions while still warm and placed on top of cake
Gâteau Saint Honoré	sweet paste, choux ring, crème Chiboust and caramel	base of sweet paste topped with choux ring and filled with crème Chiboust and fresh fruit; profiterole dipped in caramel sits on top of each portion; spun caramel decorates top
Gâteau Tompouce	puff pastry, chocolate bavarois and fondant	two puff pastry discs with a filling of chocolate bavarois; top disc is covered with a feathered fondant and the sides covered with roasted flaked almonds; rosettes of chocolate buttercream and chocolate filigree usually mark portions
Gâteau Millefeuille	puff pastry, strawberry jam (jelly), diplomat cream, fondant and flaked almonds	four discs of puff pastry are each layered with jam and diplomat cream; top layer is covered with boiling jam and fondant, and is then feathered; flaked almonds around sides; fresh strawberries usually mark portions
Gâteau Eugènie	vanilla génoise, strawberry bavarois and fresh strawberries	sponge layered with strawberry bavarois and, when set, covered with more bavarois; allowed to set then decorated into portions with strawberries (often glazed in sugar syrup)
Gâteau Alexandra	chocolate almond cake, chocolate fondant, apricot jam (jelly) and chocolate buttercream	whole almond chocolate cake glazed with boiled apricot jam when baked and when cool covered with chocolate fondant; when set, portions are marked with rosette of chocolate buttercream and filigree pieces
Gâteau Flamand	sweet pastry base, almond meringue cake filling, Kirsch-flavoured fondant and glacé cherries	sweet pastry flan filled with almond meringue cake filling; when baked is covered with Kirsch-flavoured fondant and portions marked with cherries and angelica

Genoise Step-by-Step

Step 1: Beat the sugar and eggs until light and fluffy and the ribbon stage is achieved.

Step 2: Add the sieved flour to the egg mixture and slowly and carefully fold through. Be careful not to beat out too much air.

Step 3: After folding in the melted butter, pour the sponge mixture into a lightly greased and floured 23 cm (9 in) springform cake pan. See page 134.

To set liquids, mousses or creams, four leaves of gelatine or 3 teaspoons of gelatine powder per 500 ml (16 fl oz) should suffice. Desserts served in warm areas or for outdoor functions should have a little more gelatine, to help the dessert hold. Gelatine can be used to set virtually any liquid; however, kiwi fruit, pineapple and pawpaw all contain enzymes which prevent the gelatine setting, unless the fruit is cooked first.

GELATINISATION

This refers to the process of setting with gelatine and also to the use of starch as a thickening agent. Starch cells begin to gelatinise when the starch is mixed with a liquid and heated; at a certain temperature the starch cells burst and, as they cool, they thicken the liquid.

GELATO
(see also sherbert, sorbet)

Gelato is the true Italian version of sorbet. Like sorbet, it is a mixture of water, fruit juices, sugar and egg whites, but it is slightly icier.

1¼ cups (12 oz) sugar
1 cup (8 fl oz) orange juice
4 cups (32 fl oz) water
3 egg whites
½ cup (3 oz) icing (powdered) sugar

Place sugar, orange juice and water in a large saucepan and slowly bring to the boil. Allow to boil for 12–15 minutes, uncovered. Cool, then pour the mixture into a large baking tray (jelly roll pan) and allow to freeze for 24 hours.
In the large bowl of an electric mixer, place egg whites and icing sugar and whisk to a firm meringue with stiff peaks.
Remove frozen ice, break it up finely, add to the stiff meringue and whisk thoroughly so that both combine.
Pour mixture back into the tray and allow to freeze for 6 hours before serving.

GELEES D'ENTREMETS
(see jelly)

GEM IRON

An iron pan in which gem scones are baked. The solid cast iron pan consists of a number of deep rounded grooves.

GEM SCONE
(see also scone)

A very light scone (biscuit) which is traditionally baked in a gem iron and is more like a soft cake than the English scone. It is made of creamed butter and sugar to which flour is added; the method for making English scones involves fat being rubbed into the flour.

GENOA CAKE

One of two celebrated cakes which originated in the city of Genoa. The Genoa cake is a heavy, butter-rich fruit cake which contains ground almonds and dried fruits. The mixture is traditionally baked in a round tin with fluted edges.

GENOESE
(see génoise)

GENOISE

Génoise sponges take their name from the city of Genoa, in which they are said to have been invented. The basis for many a French gâteau, the génoise or genoese sponge is a light mixture of eggs and sugar whisked together to form a sabayon which then has flour and a small amount of butter folded through it. The sponge should be feathery light; if the eggs and sugar are whisked correctly, the flour only needs to be folded through lightly for success to be assured. The génoise mixture must be treated with care as it will lose aeration quickly with rough handling or heavy handedness when folding the flour through.

VANILLA GÉNOISE SPONGE
1¼ cups (5 oz) plain (all-purpose) flour
8 eggs
⅔ cup (5 oz) caster (superfine) sugar
1 teaspoon vanilla essence (extract)
25 g (¾ oz) unsalted (sweet) butter, melted

Preheat oven to 180°C (350°F). Lightly grease a 23 cm (9 in) springform cake tin with butter. Dust with a little plain flour and shake the tin to remove any excess.
Sift flour three times. Place eggs, sugar and vanilla essence in the mixing bowl of an electric mixer and beat on the highest setting for 10–12 minutes, or until the mixture forms a ribbon (see page 236). Lightly sprinkle half the sifted flour over the mixture and very gently fold it in by hand.
Repeat with remaining flour and fold in melted butter.
Pour the mixture into the prepared tin and bake in preheated oven for 30–35 minutes or until the sponge has shrunk slightly away from the sides of the tin and the top springs back when lightly touched. Cool in the pan for 5 minutes before turning out onto a cake rack.

CHOCOLATE GÉNOISE SPONGE
This is made in the same way as the basic génoise recipe, but with the following changes: add ¼ cup (1 oz) cocoa powder, sifting and adding it with the flour, omit the vanilla essence (extract) altogether, and use 30 g (1 oz) unsalted (sweet) butter instead of the amount specified in the basic recipe.

See page 133

GERMAN BUTTERCREAM
(see buttercream)

GIANDUJA

A sweetened chocolate mixture made from ground roasted almonds or hazelnuts and icing (powdered) sugar which is mixed to a firm paste with chocolate or couverture. Gianduja is used as a base for many decorations and petits fours.

2¼ cups (8 oz) ground almonds
1½ cups (9 oz) icing (powdered) sugar
375 g (12 oz) dark (plain or semi-sweet) chocolate, melted (see page 62)

Lightly roast almonds and, while still warm, place them in a food processor with icing sugar. Reduce the mixture to a paste, as fine as possible. Add melted chocolate and work the mixture to a dough. If it is too soft, allow it to rest in a cool place for a few minutes. When firm like marzipan, roll the gianduja (on a surface that has been lightly dusted with icing sugar) to 1 cm (½ in) in thickness. Cut out using cutters and dip the shapes into more melted chocolate or allow to firm in the refrigerator and eat them as is.

GINGER

Ginger is thought to have originated many thousands of years ago in Asia. Although it grows best in tropical climates, it has been spread globally by traders and merchants. The dried underground stems of the ginger plant are used either fresh, once the skin has been peeled away, or in powdered form. Ginger has a strong flavour and aroma that is quite unmistakable and has been used in medicines for around 5000 years. The powdered form is not as strong as fresh ginger, making it more suitable for cakes and pastry fillings. Ginger is used in drinks such as ginger ale, and in gingerbreads, cakes, puddings and confectionery.

GINGERBREAD

Gingerbreads are popular throughout Europe, each country having its own variety of gingerbread or honey cake. As with so many other pastry lines, gingerbread was brought to Europe by the Crusaders, who discovered the delicately ginger-flavoured sweetmeat on their travels. It evolved from flat griddle cakes which were sweetened with honey, the cakes eventually becoming so full of brown sugar and ginger that the gingerbread was born.

There are two major styles of gingerbread. The first, which is popular throughout England, is soft and cake-like, and is usually topped with a lemon icing. The second is the flat cake or biscuit (cookie) style common to the mainland of Europe and known as pain d'Epice or elisen in France, speculaas in Holland and lebkuchen in Austria. As far afield as China, there is a ginger-flavoured honeybread, known as mikong. As in the past, gingerbread is baked into shapes, traditionally in commemoration of a saint or a religious figure, the best known being St Nicholas.

2¼ cups (9 oz) plain (all-purpose) flour
2 cups (8 oz) dry cake crumbs
90 g (3 oz) unsalted (sweet) butter, softened
⅓ cup (3 oz) caster (superfine) sugar
1½ teaspoons mixed spice (apple pie spice)
3 teaspoons ground ginger
½ cup (6 oz) golden syrup (light treacle)
1 tablespoon baking powder
1 egg

Place all ingredients in a mixing bowl and mix until a dough is formed. Knead the dough lightly and then wrap in plastic wrap (cling film) and place in the refrigerator for 1 hour.
Preheat oven to 175°C (350°F).
Lightly grease baking sheets.
Remove the dough from the refrigerator and knead lightly until it can be rolled. On a lightly floured surface, roll the dough to a thickness of 3–4 mm (⅙ in). Cut the dough into any shape desired with fancy biscuit (cookie) cutters.
Place the gingerbread shapes on the prepared sheets and bake in the preheated oven for 10–12 minutes.
Cool on the sheets before removing and decorating.

Gingerbread Glaze

A quick glaze which gives a true shine to the baked gingerbread when it cools. To make this, one needs to make up quite an amount of the starch glaze or the liquid will evaporate and burn.

Simply place some cornflour (cornstarch) in the oven at a moderate heat (180°C/350°F) and allow to brown slowly. When brown, place it in a saucepan and add four times as much water as there is cornstarch. Allow the mixture to boil for 10–15 minutes.

Brush onto the baked gingerbreads as they come out of the oven. Coat the gingerbread lightly with the glaze and allow it to cool before eating.

Gingerbread House

4¼ cups (17 oz) plain (all-purpose) flour
6 teaspoons ground cinnamon
6 teaspoons ground ginger
6 teaspoons mixed spice (apple pie spice)
6 teaspoons bicarbonate of soda
1¼ cups (7 oz) caster (superfine) sugar
250 g (8 oz) unsalted (sweet) butter
75 ml (2½ fl oz) fresh and thickened (double or heavy) cream
¼ cup (3 oz) golden syrup (light treacle)
1 egg
300 g (10 oz) dark (plain or semi-sweet) chocolate, melted (see page 62)
royal icing (see page 241)
sweets or candies, for decorating
icing (powdered) sugar, for dusting

Preheat oven to 180°C (350°F).
Line a baking sheet with baking paper (parchment).
Begin by drawing the template for the house. On a piece of paper, draw a square 13 x 13 cm (5 x 5 in), and a triangle with a base 12 cm (4½ in) and sides 13 cm (5 in).
Place all the dry ingredients in a large mixing bowl and mix together by hand. Add the butter in small pieces and, using your fingers, rub the dry ingredients through until they are finely dispersed and the mixture resembles fresh breadcrumbs. Add cream, golden syrup and egg, and work by hand until the dough is formed.
Remove dough from the bowl and lightly knead.
Allow the gingerbread to rest for 5 minutes.
Divide dough into four even pieces. Roll each piece out

Gingerbread house Step-by-Step

Step 1: Brush the base of each gingerbread shape with melted chocolate.

Step 2: Use a small amount of royal icing to join the square shape to the triangular shape of gingerbread.

Step 3: Join the second triangular shape to the other side of the square shape with royal icing.

Step 4: Join the second square shape to the triangular shape.

Step 5: Pipe royal icing over the roof to cover the join before fixing the door.

Step 6: Decorate the gingerbread house with sweets and candies. See page 135.

very thinly onto a lightly floured surface. Place the templates over the top of the dough and, using a sharp knife, cut out shapes. You will need two triangular shapes and two square shapes from the rolled dough. From one of the shapes, cut out a door and a window. Keep these pieces for later use.

Place each piece on the prepared sheet and bake in the preheated oven for 18 minutes. When the shapes are baked, allow them to cool on a cake rack until cold. Using a pastry brush, brush the bottom of each shape with the melted chocolate (Step 1). Allow this to set hard. Using a large chopping board as your work surface, hold one of the triangular shapes upright and pipe a small line of royal icing down one of its edges. Press one of the square shapes into the iced triangular edge (Step 2). Pipe royal icing down the side of the second triangular shape and press it onto the opposite side of the square shape (Step 3). Pipe down the outward facing edges of both triangles and press them onto the second square shape (Step 4). Allow this to sit for at least 1 hour (preferably longer) to stop the house collapsing.

When it has set, place on a serving platter. Pipe extra royal icing down the sides of the roof to look like snow, then cover the join (Step 5). Fix the door to the house with royal icing. Decorate and lightly dust with icing sugar before serving (Step 6).

See page 136

GINGERBREAD SQUARES

Of the two forms of gingerbread, this soft luscious cake is clearly closer to the original.

125 g (4 oz) unsalted (sweet) butter
1¼ cups (8 oz) caster (superfine) sugar
1 cup (12 oz) golden syrup (light treacle)
2 eggs
1 tablespoon bicarbonate of soda, dissolved in
1 tablespoon boiling water
6 teaspoons ground ginger
1 teaspoon mixed spice (apple pie spice)
2¾ cups (11 oz) plain (all-purpose) flour
1 cup (8 fl oz) milk
1 quantity lemon cream cheese frosting (see page 125)
ground cinnamon, for dusting

Preheat oven to 175°C (350°F).
Grease a 25 x 30 x 3 cm (10 x 12 x 1¼ in) baking tray (sheet) and line with baking paper (parchment).
Place butter and sugar in a mixing bowl and cream until light and fluffy. Scrape down the bowl, add the golden syrup and continue creaming the mixture until completely combined. Add eggs one at a time, mixing well. Add bicarbonate of soda mixed with boiling water, along with ginger, spice, half the flour and half the milk. Mix well before adding the remaining flour and milk. Continue mixing until smooth. Pour the mixture into the prepared tray and bake in preheated oven for 45–50 minutes, or until a skewer inserted into the centre comes out clean. Cool in the tray before icing with lemon cream cheese frosting. Dust lightly with cinnamon and cut into small squares.

GINGERNUT BISCUITS

2½ cups (10 oz) plain (all-purpose) flour
1 teaspoon bicarbonate of soda
1 teaspoon baking powder (soda)
6 teaspoons ground ginger
1 teaspoon mixed spice (apple pie spice)
1 cup (6 oz) soft (light) brown sugar
60 g (2 oz) unsalted (sweet) butter, softened
⅓ cup (4 oz) golden syrup (light treacle)
2 tablespoons water

Sift flour, bicarbonate of soda, baking powder, ginger and spices into a mixing bowl. Add brown sugar and stir through well. Lightly rub butter into the dry ingredients and then add golden syrup and water. Mix until a dough is formed. Cover the mixture with a damp cloth and leave for 2 hours.
Preheat oven to 180°C (350°F).
Line baking sheets with baking paper (parchment).
On a lightly floured surface, roll the dough out to about 2 mm (1/12 in) in thickness. Cut out the gingernuts using a 6 cm (2½ in) fluted round biscuit (cookie) cutter. Place on prepared sheets and bake in preheated oven for 10–12 minutes. Remove the gingernuts, place on a cake rack to cool, then serve.

Makes 24

GIRDLE SCONES
(see also drop scones, griddle cakes)

One of the earliest forms of quickbread, the girdle scone is the Scottish and northern English variety of what is also known as a griddle scone, a far breton and damper, amongst a variety of other names. Girdle scones are placed flat and round onto the girdle and are marked into pieces. When golden brown on one side, the mixture is turned so it can rise and cook on the other.

GHORAYABAH
(see also kourambeithes)

Ghorayabahs are one of the original versions of the modern Greek kourambeithes. These melt-in-the-mouth Arabian delicacies are often filled with nuts and spices.

GLACE FRUITS
(see fruit: crystallised fruit)

GLACIER

Still seen in large establishments and hotels, the glacier is the person responsible for the preparation of sorbets, ice creams, ice cream cakes, parfaits, bombes and, if the glacier is skilled enough, ice carvings and iced displays. The glacier is normally a fully trained pastry chef as well, so he or she does not have to rely on anyone else to produce any related pâtisserie items that may be required. The glacier can also be of assistance to others during busy periods.

GLAZE
(see also bun wash, egg wash)

To glaze is to coat a product to give it a shiny or glassy appearance. Hot sweet buns are glazed with a bun wash or sugar syrup, biscuits (cookies) and gingerbreads with potato or gingerbread glazes and, before being baked, the tops of pastries are coated in egg yolk. A glaze of sweetened and boiled apricot or strawberry jam (jelly) may be used on fine pastries such as Danish and puff pastries before fondant is applied.

GLUCOSE
(see also sugar)

Glucose is a thick, clear form of sugar which is produced by the breakdown of starch cells that have been treated with acids or enzymes and then fermented to form sugars. The thickness of the liquid glucose depends on how much the starch cells have broken down. It can be produced from corn, starch, potatoes, grapes and honey, corn being the one most commonly used, and in the USA it is in fact known as corn syrup. When mixed with maple syrup, it is called pancake syrup. Glucose is regularly used in confectionery to give elasticity to the caramel or sugar piece and to help prevent crystallisation. It can also be added to chocolate to produce a modelling paste.

GLUTEN FLOUR
(see also flour)

A product of wheat flour, gluten flour is added to weak flours to increase their gluten content or to bread doughs and pastries that require a strong gluten framework. It is made by soaking flour with water and drying the mixture. This gives a product which is 70% protein or gluten. It can be bought from many health food stores. For breadmaking, if a weak, plain or all-purpose flour is being used, 1 teaspoon of gluten flour should be added for every cup of flour used. Gluten itself is not actually produced until a liquid such as water is added to the two gluten-forming proteins, gliadin and gludanin, so in reality there is no such thing as gluten flour, only gluten-forming flour.

GLYCERINE

A clear, sweet, syrupy liquid, glycerine is extracted from animal fats and vegetable oils, and is a by-product of soap manufacturing. It is used in small amounts in certain cake, pastry and icing mixtures, and is able to draw moisture from the air, thus keeping these products moist and giving them a long shelf life.

GOD CAKES

These three-cornered puff pastry tartlets filled with fruit or fruit mince originated in Coventry and evolved from Coventry puffs, a form of turnover. They were given as gifts by godparents to their godchildren one week before Easter.

GOLDEN SYRUP
(see also sugar)

Golden syrup is used to make sauces for rich puddings and to flavour biscuits (cookies), cakes and fillings. Known in the USA as light treacle, it is a light golden colour and is quite thick. It is a by-product of the sugar-refining process. The syrup is filtered and concentrated, but still retains a small amount of molasses, which gives it its colour and flavour.

GOLDEN SYRUP CAKES

60 g (2 oz) unsalted (sweet) butter
¼ cup (2 oz) sugar
⅓ cup (4 oz) golden syrup (light treacle)
2 eggs
2 tablespoons milk
1½ cups (6 oz) plain (all-purpose) flour
1½ teaspoons baking powder (soda)

Preheat oven to 180°C (350°F).
Grease a 20 cm (8 in) springform cake tin.
Place butter, sugar and golden syrup in a saucepan and, while whisking lightly, allow the mixture to heat until the ingredients have melted and mixed together.
Remove from heat and allow the mixture to cool.
Lightly whisk eggs and milk together and, when the syrup mixture is cool enough, whisk through the egg mixture.
Sift flour and baking powder in and stir until a smooth batter is formed. Pour into the prepared tin and bake in the preheated oven for 35–40 minutes.
Pour an orange-flavoured water icing over the cake when cool and serve in slices with whipped cream.

GOLDEN SYRUP DUMPLINGS

1 cup (4 oz) plain (all-purpose) flour
45 g (1½ oz) unsalted (sweet) butter
1 egg, beaten
5 tablespoons milk

Syrup
½ cup (3 oz) demerara sugar
¼ cup (3 oz) golden syrup (light treacle)
2 cups (16 fl oz) water
30 g (1 oz) unsalted (sweet) butter
juice and zest of 1 lemon
1 teaspoon ground cinnamon

Sift flour and rub in butter. Add egg and milk and mix to make a soft dough. Divide dough into 6 pieces and roll into balls.
In a large saucepan, heat sugar, golden syrup and water, stirring until sugar dissolves. Add butter and lemon juice and zest and bring to the boil. Place the dumplings in the hot syrup, cover and simmer gently for 10–15 minutes.
Serve dumplings immediately, spooning the syrup over them and sprinkling with a little cinnamon.
Serve with custard or cream.

GOMME SYRUP

This is a basic stock syrup, made of water and sugar, used to sweeten fruit salads, thin sauces and fruit purées and glaze hot sweet buns.

GOOSEBERRY
(see also Cape gooseberry, kiwi fruit)

Originally from North Africa, the gooseberry is cultivated in many countries, most of which have a cool climate, but it also grows wild. It is widely used throughout northern Europe. It has a green, white or red fruit, which can be quite tart, and is often used in sorbets and jams (conserves) for this reason. Gooseberries are also used in tarts, sauces and jellies, can be poached, and can be eaten fresh as well.

GRAHAM FLOUR
(see also flour)

Developed by American dietician and nutritionist Sylvester Graham (1749–1851), this coarse wholemeal flour is used in the production of many goods, but most commonly graham crackers and graham bread.

GRANITA
(see also sherbert, sorbet)

Granita is an early form of sorbet that was popular in Paris during the 19th century, and still remains popular today. Granita is a true water ice, made from sugar syrup, fruit juices and flavouring and water, and is frozen into large crystals. There is no meringue or egg white added to the mixture. Granita is served between meals as a refresher.

GRANULATED SUGAR
(see sugar)

GRAPES

As well as being the world's most widely grown fruit, grapes are also one of the oldest: grape fossils that date back to the Bronze Age have been found, and they were certainly used in wines from early biblical times. The grape is a small, oval or round fruit which grows in clusters or bunches on a climbing vine. When picked, grapes can be green, yellow or deep purple. The fruit has a firm, almost clear, inner flesh which contains up to four seeds. If grapes are used in tarts or other goods, the seeds should be removed. This can be done by slicing the grape in half and digging out the seeds with the point of a knife.

As well as being made into wines, they are used fresh by the pastry chef in tarts, cheese platters and for decoration. Fresh grapes should be firm and brightly coloured, should not be too bunched on the vine and should have a uniform size and shape. In their dried form, as sultanas (golden raisins), currants or raisins, they are used in fruit cakes, fruit mince and many other dishes.

GRAPE TART

300 g (10 oz) sweet pastry (see page 272)
4 eggs
½ cup (4 oz) sugar
¾ cup (6 fl oz) fresh cream
¼ cup (2 fl oz) sauterne
500 g (1 lb) seedless green grapes
icing (powdered) sugar, for dusting

Preheat oven to 180°C (350°F).
Grease a 20 cm (8 in) flan ring and a baking sheet.
On a lightly floured surface, roll the pastry to 3 mm (⅛ in) in thickness and carefully line the flan ring and baking sheet base. Whisk eggs, sugar, cream and sauterne in a bowl until the liquid is smooth and the sugar is dissolved. Place the grapes over the base of the flan and fill with the liquid mixture. Bake in preheated oven for 25–30 minutes or until the custard mixture is firm. Remove, dust immediately with icing sugar, and serve.

GRAPEFRUIT

Grapefruit belongs to the citrus family, and requires hot, dry growing conditions. It originated in the West Indies, and was initially only cultivated in a minor way after being introduced into the USA in 1823 by Napoleon's chief surgeon, who took it with him to Florida. During the latter half of the 19th century it was cultivated on a large scale.

Ripe grapefruit should be a straw yellow colour, have a smooth skin and be about the shape and size of a slightly squashed baseball. Grapefruit are usually seedless, although the pink-fleshed varieties do contain seeds, and are fairly tart, one of the reasons they haven't been as popular as the orange, or even the lemon. They are commonly served on their own, or as slices soaked in a little sugar syrup. They can also be sliced and grilled with a little cinnamon and brown sugar sprinkled on top.

GRATER

A hand-held or mechanically operated kitchen utensil used to shred products finely. Hand-held graters can have either flat or rounded grating surfaces in a range of different sizes. Mechanical ones usually take the form of a rotating grating blade that attaches to the top or side of an electric mixer or processor. They can grate larger quantities much more quickly than you can by hand.

GREASEPROOF

Paper which is impregnated with paraffin wax making it impervious to grease and water. It is also airtight when wrapped around food. Similar to American waxed baking paper.

GRIDDLE CAKES
(see also bannocks, blini, pancakes and pikelets)

These cakes include a range of products, including bannocks, scones, drop scones, pancakes, blini and pikelets, to name but a few. They are derived from the original flatbreads which were baked on a hot iron or griddle over an open fire. These days they are cooked in an open frying pan (skillet), and are produced from thick batters of varying consistencies, depending on the particular type of griddle cake or recipe being used. Some have a plain flavour and can be used as bread, and others are sweet.

GRISSINI
(see also bread)

These thin Italian breadsticks from Turin, which were referred to as 'petits batons de Turin' by Napoleon, are made using a dough of flour, yeast, water and olive oil rolled out (traditionally to the length of the pastry chef or baker's lower arm).

Grissinis' flavour and character, as well as their crispness, result from baking them on the surface of a wood-fired oven. They are like rusks, but have a characteristic nobbled shape and are normally served with savoury dishes. It was traditional for a basket of these to sit on each table in Turin to be eaten as a digestive after the meal.

GRITTIBAENZ

This bread loaf, made in the shape of St Nicholas, first appeared in the early 1800s and is the German version of the Swiss St Nicholas loaf. It is served at Christmas and bought for children over the festive period. It should be made from one complete piece of dough, to prevent breakages, and is formed from a long sausage shape with one end rolled into a ball shape. The other end is cut partway down the centre to form legs; arms are then cut out below the head, which has currants or sultanas (golden raisins) pressed in for eyes and a small cut made for the mouth. Although they are a very basic shape, children love them.

GRITS

Originally grits, or 'grutze', was a pauper's dish which was made from fruit juice boiled with the grits or husks of the granulated meal of wheat and oats; the mixture would thicken and, on cooling, set firmly. It is still made to this recipe in country areas of many parts of Europe. Eventually other forms of starch, such as tapioca and sago, even semolina, were also used, and these days it is common to use cornflour (cornstarch).

The dish can be made so clear that it looks like jelly, and is also called red fruit pudding, as raspberries are often one of the main ingredients.

600 g (20 oz) fresh raspberries
⅓ cup (3 oz) sugar
2 cups (16 fl oz) water
4½ tablespoons cornflour (cornstarch)
⅓ cup (3 fl oz) sauterne
2 tablespoons dark rum

Place fresh raspberries, sugar and water in a saucepan and slowly bring to the boil. Simmer until the raspberries become very soft. Remove from heat and purée in a food processor.

Cool, then pass through a fine sieve to remove the seeds.

Place purée in a saucepan and bring to the boil. Mix cornflour with the sauterne and rum and add to the purée, whisking well so that the mixture does not become lumpy. When mixture returns to the boil remove from heat and pour into small glass bowls. Cool and set before serving.

GUGELHUPF

This cake is often served at the European breakfast table, and has a variety of spellings — gugelhopf, kugelhoff, kugelhopf, kugelhupf — reflecting its popularity throughout Europe. It is a yeast-raised cake which is served thinly sliced, often spread with nougat. Unlike brioche, savarin and babas, to which this is similar, gugelhupf is made from a starter dough of yeast, flour and water which is prepared the previous day. It is then mixed with a batter of creamed butter and sugar.

Story has it that Eugène, the pastry chef to Prince Schwarzenberg, Napoleon's ambassador to Austria, was having trouble with the recipe he was using for this cake and gave it to Antoine Carême, who made the dough lighter, added rum-soaked raisins and more dried fruits. The cake is baked in a fluted ring mould.

Starter Dough
(make the day before)
40 g (1½ oz) fresh compressed yeast
(or 2 tablespoons active dry yeast)
1 cup (8 fl oz) lukewarm milk
2¼ cups (9 oz) plain (all-purpose) flour

Cake
250 g (8 oz) unsalted (sweet) butter
⅔ cup (5 oz) caster (superfine) sugar
8 egg yolks
2¼ cups (9 oz) plain all-purpose flour
1 cup (5 oz) sultanas (golden raisins)
⅓ cup (2 oz) blanched almonds, chopped
icing (powdered) sugar, for dusting

Starter Dough
Mix yeast and milk. Place flour in a bowl and make a well in the centre. Pour yeast mixture into the well and gradually mix in flour. Cover the bowl with plastic wrap (cling film) and leave in the refrigerator for 8 hours.

Cake
Preheat oven to 180°C (350°F). Grease a gugelhupf pan or any fancy fluted mould thoroughly with butter and lightly dust with plain flour. Shake out any excess. Beat butter and sugar until creamy, light and fluffy. Add egg yolks one at a time, beating very well after each one is added. Mix in the starter dough, flour, sultanas and chopped almonds. Pour into prepared mould, filling it only two thirds full. Cover with a clean, dry cloth and stand it in a warm place for 30 minutes. Bake for 35–40 minutes or until a thin skewer inserted into the centre of the cake comes out dry. Cool in the tin for 5 minutes before turning out onto a cake rack. Serve dusted with icing sugar.

GULAB JAMUN

This delicately flavoured sweetmeat from India is soaked in rosewater syrup.

½ cup (2 oz) plain (all-purpose) flour
½ teaspoon baking powder (soda)
¼ cup (1 oz) milk powder (non-fat dry milk)
¼ teaspoon ground cinnamon
30 g (1 oz) unsalted (sweet) butter, softened
¼ cup (2 fl oz) cold water
juice of 1 lemon
oil for frying

Syrup
½ cup (4 oz) sugar
1¼ cups (10 fl oz) water
1 stick cinnamon
1 cardamom pod, bruised
1 clove
2 tablespoons rosewater

Sift flour, baking powder, milk powder and cinnamon into a large bowl. Add butter and rub in until the mixture resembles breadcrumbs. Add water and lemon juice and work mixture to a dough. Some extra water may be required, but add this slowly. On a lightly floured surface, knead dough gently and then allow to rest.

Cut dough into 12 small pieces and roll each into a small ball. Heat some oil in a frying pan (skillet) and fry each of the small dough pieces until golden brown. Drain them on absorbent paper and cool slightly. Place all ingredients for the syrup in a saucepan and allow to boil for 3 minutes. Place the fried dough pieces into a large dish and pour the hot syrup over them.

GUM ARABIC

Used in confectionery as a glaze, gum arabic is obtained from the sap of acacia trees, which are found in Africa, India and Australia. It is sold in granular, block or powder form, and is water soluble, requiring twice its own weight in warm water. On dissolving, it becomes a clear liquid which is used to glaze marzipan goods, biscuits (cookies), buns and sweets.

GUM PASTE

Also known as sugar paste or modelling paste, this mixture of icing (powdered) sugar, cornflour (cornstarch) and gum tragacanth is used to model centrepieces or decorations for wedding cakes. The beauty of working with this modelling medium is that it dries so quickly. However, this also means that it should be worked fairly rapidly. Unused paste should be kept covered or an inferior decoration will result.

HAARLEM

A Dutch specialty, this cake can be used for any celebration. Itd is made up of a plain sponge which is soaked with a lemon-flavoured syrup and filled and covered with fresh fondant-based buttercream.

HALVA

Halva is a confection made in Mediterranean countries from sugar, butter, semolina and roasted nuts or sesame seeds. The flavourings used differ from country to country, but traditionally halva is flavoured with rosewater and a little saffron, cinnamon, or cardamom.

HAMBURGER BUNS
(see also buns)

2 cups (16 fl oz) milk
30 g (1 oz) fresh compressed yeast
6 teaspoons sugar
1 teaspoon salt
2 eggs
7 cups (28 oz) plain (all-purpose) flour
½ cup (4 oz) unsalted (sweet) butter

Line baking sheets with baking paper (parchment). Place warmed milk, yeast, sugar, salt and eggs in a large bowl and lightly whisk together until the yeast is dissolved. Allow the mixture to sit for 30 minutes.
Add flour and chopped butter and work to a dough (a little extra flour may be required to form a soft but not sticky dough). Knead the dough for 5–8 minutes by hand, or until dough is smooth and elastic. Allow dough to prove (rise), covered, for 45 minutes.
Knock back (punch down) the dough and knead it lightly to expel all the air. Cut dough into 10 evenly sized pieces and roll each into a ball. Place all the pieces together and allow them to prove (rise) for 10–15 minutes.
Preheat oven to 180°C (350°F).

Flatten the balls and place them on the prepared sheets. Place in a warm area, covered, for approximately 35–45 minutes, or until the buns are double in size. Bake buns in preheated oven for 20–25 minutes, or until golden brown. Serve immediately, or cool and serve cold. The buns can be frozen until required. Heat the frozen buns slightly to make them soft and crunchy once they have thawed.

HANDING-UP

The process of moulding dough into ball shapes, or placing it into tins, before the second proving (rising).

HARD BALL DEGREE
(see also sugar)

This is a confectionery term referring to the stage when sugar syrup reaches 120–30°C (250–65°F) and a small amount of the syrup forms a hard ball when dropped into cold water.

HARLEQUIN CAKES

These are small yellow and pink biscuits made from apricot and strawberry jam (jelly) baked onto the biscuits, then covered with a thin water icing.

HAZELNUTS
(see also nuts)

Hazelnuts, the fruit of the hazel bush or tree, are round brown-skinned nuts with cream-coloured interiors. They are rich with oil. They are also known as filberts (in the USA) or cobnuts.
The bush is cultivated, but also grows wild. It was discovered, and enjoyed, by the Chinese between 3000–2500 BC and later spread to Europe and the Mediterranean.
Hazelnuts grow in shiny brown shells and are easily removed once the shells are opened. Pastry chefs usually use them roasted, as this brings out their flavour, or ground, in place of flour in cakes and fillings. The French name for hazelnuts, filberts, comes from the abbot St Philbert, who held festivities near the time when hazelnuts ripened.

HAZELNUT AND HONEY TORTE

Base
1¼ cups (5 oz) plain (all-purpose) flour
½ cup (3 oz) icing (powdered) sugar
100 g (3½ oz) unsalted (sweet) butter,
cut into small pieces
1 egg, lightly beaten
2 teaspoons water

Filling
9 eggs
2 cups (16 fl oz) fresh cream (single or light)
1 cup (8 fl oz) honey
⅓ cup (2½ oz) caster (superfine) sugar

To Decorate

2¼ cups (10 oz) chopped hazelnuts (filberts), roasted
apricot glaze (see page 10)

Place flour and icing sugar in a bowl and very lightly rub in
the butter until the mixture resembles coarse breadcrumbs.
Add egg and sufficient water to make a firm dough.
Wrap in plastic wrap (cling film) and chill for ½–1 hour.
Preheat oven to 170°C (340°F).
Grease a 23 cm (9 in) springform cake tin.
Roll out chilled dough into a 27 cm (11 in) circle and
line the base and sides of the prepared tin. Beat eggs,
cream, honey and sugar until thoroughly mixed, then pour

into prepared tin. Bake for 40 minutes. Remove from oven
and lightly press roasted hazelnuts into the surface
of the filling. Bake for another 15 minutes, or
until golden brown and firm to the touch. Cool in
the tin for 5 minutes before removing the rim of the tin.
Cool on a cake rack. When cold, brush the top
with apricot glaze.

HEDGEHOG

A rich mixture of cocoa, sugar, coconut, broken biscuits
(cookies) and egg, set into a tray (jelly roll pan) and refrigerated. Hedgehog can be iced and decorated or left plain.

Hazelnut and Honey Torte

Hedgehog

3¾ cups (14 oz) plain sweet biscuits (cookies) crumbs
210 g (7 oz) unsalted (sweet) butter
1 cup (7 oz) caster (superfine) sugar
⅔ cup (2 oz) desiccated (shredded) coconut
½ cup (2 oz) cocoa powder, sifted
3 eggs, lightly beaten
1 quantity chocolate frosting (see page 125)
chopped nuts or chocolate chips (drops), for decoration

Lightly grease a 19 x 28 x 2 cm (7½ x 11 x ¾ in)
baking tray (jelly roll pan).
Place crushed biscuits in a mixing bowl. Place butter, sugar,
coconut and cocoa in a saucepan and melt over low heat.
Bring to the boil and boil for 2 minutes.

Remove from heat and cool. Add the eggs
Whisk in biscuits and stir with a wooden spoon until all
ingredients are well combined. Pour into prepared
tray and place in the refrigerator to cool. Remove from
refrigerator and spread with the chocolate frosting.
Sprinkle with chopped nuts or chocolate chips.
Cut into squares.

Makes 16—20

HEFETEIG

This rich yeast cake was first made in Germany and Austria.
Though it is possible to beat it by hand, an electric mixer
makes light work of this recipe.

30 g (1 oz) fresh compressed yeast
(or 3 tablespoons active dry yeast)
butter
60 g (2 oz) unsalted (sweet) butter
¼ cup (2 oz) caster (superfine) sugar
3½ cups (14 oz) plain (all-purpose) flour
⅛ level teaspoon salt
¼ cup (1 oz) milk powder (non-fat dry milk)
lukewarm water
150 g (5 oz) canned or fresh apricot halves

To Decorate
apricot glaze (see page 10)
1 cup (3 oz) flaked almonds

Place yeast, butter, sugar, flour, salt and milk powder in the bowl of an electric mixer fitted with a dough hook and blend for 1 minute. Gradually add water in small amounts until the ingredients come together to form a soft dough. Add a little more water if necessary. Mix for 5 minutes. Cover and leave in a warm place to prove (rise) for 20 minutes.
Preheat oven to 180°C (350°F). Lightly grease a 3 cm (9 in) springform cake tin with butter. Line the base with baking paper (parchment).
Gently knead the dough for 30 seconds to expel the air. Roll out dough into a 27 cm (11 in) circle and line the base and sides of the prepared tin. Top dough with the apricot halves. Cover the tin with a clean dry cloth and leave in a warm place to prove (rise) for another 30 minutes. Bake for 40–45 minutes or until a skewer inserted into the centre of the cake comes out dry. Cool in the tin on a cake rack. Turn the cake out of the tin and brush the top with apricot glaze. Press flaked almonds into the glazed top.

HERALDIC DEVICES
(see also tarts)

Decorated in the manner of a soldier's shield, these tarts or cakes consist of 3–4 open-faced pastry tarts, each filled with a different coloured jam (jelly) or fruit paste, and with pastry pieces that resemble the soldier's coat of arms or some form of religious symbol placed on top. They were originally served before doing battle, at the soldiers' farewell feast, or as a form of rejoicing over a victory.

HERBS
(see also individual listings)

Herbs are the flowers or leaves of aromatic plants and shrubs which, either dried or fresh, give a delicious flavour to foods. They are usually used by the pastry chef or baker in breads, such as onion and sage bread or tomato and basil bread, to complement the main flavour of the doughs. Otherwise they are rarely used, unless added to savoury pastries such as meat pies, sausage rolls or savoury hors d'oeuvres.

HIGH RATIO CAKE

This refers to cakes in which the batter contains a high ratio of sugar and liquids in relation to the amount of flour used.

This form of cake batter results in finished products with a long shelf life and a fine crumb. They are usually moister than ordinary cakes, too.

HIGH RATIO FLOUR
(see also flour)

Used in high ratio cake mixes, this specially prepared flour is able to absorb a vast amount of liquid, fat and sugar. Also known as special cake flour, it cannot be used in the same manner as ordinary flour. It is usually finer than ordinary flour and because it is treated with chlorine, the protein content of the flour is denatured (changed from its original structure).

HIPPEN DECORATING PASTE

1¾ cups (7 oz) plain (all-purpose) flour
1 cup (3½ oz) finely ground almonds
1 cup (7 oz) caster (superfine) sugar
5 eggs, lightly beaten
125 g (4 oz) unsalted (sweet) butter, melted

Preheat oven to 180°C (350°F).
Mix flour, almonds and sugar together and add eggs and butter. Whisk until the mixture becomes a smooth paste. Hippen decorating paste is usually piped into designs such as butterflies or filigree decorations straight onto baking paper (parchment) or silicon paper. It is then baked in the preheated oven for 5–8 minutes, or until lightly browned.
The designs are peeled from the paper and draped over rolling pins or similar objects to give them more character.
The paste is still quite flexible for about 1 minute after baking, but if it has become too brown, it loses its flexibility.

HOLLANDER

This torte made with walnuts is delicious served warm.

Base
1 cup (4 oz) plain (all-purpose) flour
½ cup (3 oz) icing (powdered) sugar
135 g (4½ oz) unsalted (sweet) butter, cut into small pieces
1 x 60 g (2 oz) egg, lightly beaten
1 tablespoon water
1 cup (3 oz) walnut halves

Filling
200 g (7 oz) unsalted (sweet) butter
⅔ cup (5 oz) caster (superfine) sugar
3 eggs
1¾ cups (7 oz) plain (all-purpose) flour
2½ cups (7 oz) ground walnuts
2¼ cups (7 oz) walnut halves, extra
strawberry glaze (see page 263)
crushed nuts, for decoration

Lightly grease a 23 cm (9 in) springform cake tin with butter. Line the base with baking paper (parchment).

Pastry Base

Place flour and icing sugar in a bowl and very lightly
rub in butter until the mixture resembles breadcrumbs.
Add egg and sufficient water to make a firm dough.
Wrap in plastic wrap (cling film) and chill for 1 hour.
Preheat oven to 180°C (350°F).
Roll out chilled dough into a 27 cm (11 in) circle
and line the base and sides of the prepared tin.
Sprinkle the pastry base with walnut halves.

Filling

Beat butter and sugar until creamy, light and fluffy. Add eggs
one at a time, beating very well after each one is added.
Mix flour and ground walnuts in by hand. Pour into
prepared tin, decorate the top with the extra walnut halves
and bake for 35–40 minutes, or until the top springs back
when lightly touched. Cool in the tin on a cake rack.
Brush with strawberry glaze and press crushed nuts
around the top edges.

HONEY
(see also sugar)

Honey, the original sweetener, has been in use for thousands of
years. In early times, it was mixed with snow to make the first
sorbets; when these sorbets were left to thaw, the first alcoholic
mead was produced. The Romans stuffed dates with sweet fillings
and then dipped these into boiling honey, the Germans made a
prized honey cake, and the French made nougat. The Belgians
made gingerbread, the Austrians produced lebkuchen and the
Turks halva, and the Greeks soaked their baklava in honey, all
using the delicately flavoured honey from their own regions.

Honey is a prized commodity around the world, not only as a
sweetener but also for its wonderful flavour, which varies
according to the type of plants or flowers from which the bees
collect their nectar. The difference in nectar also determines the
colour, aroma and texture of the finished honey. Light, creamy
honey should be used in lighter styles of cake and biscuits
(cookies), while the darker varieties should be used for
gingerbreads, nougats and biscuits such as honey jumbles or
lebkuchen, where a fuller flavour is required. The depth of
colour in a honey is related to its mineral content: the higher the
mineral content, the darker or deeper the colour of the honey.

Honey plays an important role in breadmaking, being a key
source of food for yeast. Breads made using honey are better
quality breads, both in texture and storage life.

HONEY ROLL

1 cup (12 oz) clear honey
90 g (3 oz) unsalted (sweet) butter
2 cups (8 oz) plain (all-purpose) flour
1 teaspoon ground cinnamon
½ teaspoon ground ginger
2 eggs
1 teaspoon bicarbonate of soda
¼ cup (2 fl oz) water
whipped cream or buttercream (see page 43) for filling

Preheat oven to 180°C (350°F).
Lightly grease a 25 x 30 x 3 cm (10 x 12 x 1¼ in) baking tray
(jelly roll pan) and line with baking paper (parchment).
Place honey and butter in a saucepan and allow to melt
together, stirring until well combined; do not allow to
become too hot. Sift flour and spices into the honey/butter
mixture and stir, combining well. Add eggs one at a time,
beating well after each one is added, and beat until smooth.
Place mixture in the bowl of an electric mixer.
Add bicarbonate of soda to the water and when dissolved,
immediately add to the mixture. Beat on medium
for 2–3 minutes. Scrape the mixture down and
spread onto the prepared baking tray.
Place in preheated oven and bake for 25–30 minutes,
or until evenly cooked. When baked, carefully remove
the honey cake from the baking tray by turning it
upside down onto a lightly sugared sheet of baking paper
(parchment). Cool. Use a sharp knife to remove the edges of
the cake and lightly spread the top of the cake with whipped
cream or buttercream. Starting at the short end furthest
from you, roll the cake up like a Swiss roll (jelly roll).
Wrap tightly and place in the refrigerator for 20 minutes,
then cut into slices.

HONEYDEW MELONS
(see also melons)

Members of the melon family, honeydew melons have a white
to pale green skin which is quite smooth. They are oval to
round in shape and have a soft, light green flesh which is
watery and quite sweet. The centre of the honeydew melon is
hollow and contains many white seeds. The melon can be cut
into segments and eaten as is, although the skin itself is
inedible, or it can be balled, using a melon baller, or cut into
pieces for fruit salad. It is often used as a puréed sauce with
desserts and also in sorbets (due to its high water content).

HONIG CAKE

The intense flavour of this German favourite is enlivened by a
sweet honey glaze.

½ cup (6 oz) honey
2 tablespoons golden syrup (light treacle)
30 g (1 oz) unsalted (sweet) butter
4 tablespoons walnut oil
½ cup (4 oz) caster (superfine) sugar
3 cups (12 oz) plain (all-purpose) flour
3 tablespoons ground cinnamon
2 teaspoons baking powder
1⅓ cups (5 oz) ground almonds
2 eggs, lightly beaten

Honey Glaze
2 tablespoons clear honey
1 tablespoon lemon juice
1 cup (6 oz) icing (powdered) sugar

Grease a 28 x 18 x 2 cm (11 x 7 x ¾ in) baking tray
(jelly roll pan) and line with baking paper (parchment).

Hungarian Chocolate Torte Step-by-Step

Step 1: Cover the glazed torte with thinly rolled marzipan. Mould the marzipan around the top and sides of the cake and trim any excess from the base.

Step 2: Spread melted chocolate onto a strip of baking paper (parchment) about 1 cm (½ in) higher than the cake is deep.

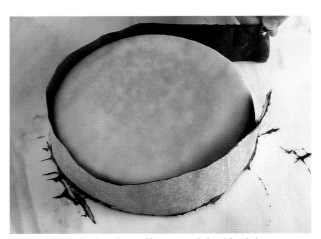

Step 3: Wrap the chocolate collar around the side of the marzipan-covered cake.

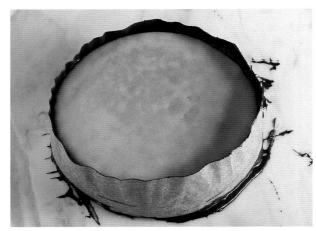

Step 4: Make sure that the collar fits evenly, then chill until the chocolate sets. When firm, carefully remove the baking paper (parchment).

Step 5: Cover the inside of the cake with the smallest chocolate curls.

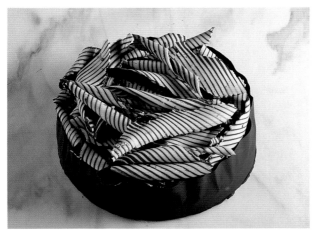

Step 6: Cover the top of the cake with the largest and neatest chocolate curls. See page 151.

Place honey, syrup, butter, oil and sugar in a saucepan and bring the mixture to the boil, stirring occasionally to make sure mixture does not burn. Boil for 2 minutes. Remove and cool. Sift flour, cinnamon and baking powder into a bowl with the almonds and eggs. Add cooled butter/honey mixture and work with a wooden spoon until it forms a dough. Remove from the bowl and lightly knead. Press into prepared tray and smooth. Place in refrigerator for 2 hours to allow dough to rest.
Preheat oven to 180°C (350°F).
Remove dough from the refrigerator and place directly in preheated oven. Bake for 30–35 minutes, or until a skewer inserted into the top comes out clean. Remove and glaze immediately with the honey glaze. Cool before cutting into squares. If the glaze doesn't set after 1 hour, place in the refrigerator to set.

Honey Glaze
Place the honey and lemon juice in a bowl and stir until combined. Add the sifted icing sugar and stir until no lumps remain.

Makes 20—25

HOT CROSS BUNS

These are small sweet yeast buns made with dried fruit and served at Easter. Before being baked they have a cross made from a paste of flour and water marked on the top. It is washed with a sweet syrup once baked. Different cultures have different stories to explain the significance of the cross. Most explanations relate to the religious significance of the Easter period. The Anglo-Saxons baked the sweet fruit buns in honour of their goddess Eostre, the goddess of spring, from whom the name Easter is derived. Another belief is that it simply marks the four quarters of the moon, and yet another is that it is a leftover from the medieval practice of marking a cross on top of bread loaves to ward off evil spirits. Condemned by the Puritans, this practice was ceased, but was eventually brought back to the buns served at Easter, described as as a sign of the Crucifixion.

1 cup (8 fl oz) water
2 tablespoons milk powder (non-fat dried milk)
3 cups (12 oz) plain (all-purpose) flour
¼ cup (2 oz) caster (superfine) sugar
½ teaspoon ground cinnamon
½ teaspoon ground cloves
60 g (2 oz) unsalted (sweet) butter
30 g (1 oz) fresh compressed yeast
1 egg
½ cup (2½ oz) currants
2 tablespoons sultanas (golden raisins)
30 g (1 oz) mixed (candied) peel

Cross Mix
1 cup (4 oz) plain (all-purpose) flour
3–4 tablespoons water

Glaze
2 tablespoons water
1 tablespoon powdered gelatine
2 tablespoons caster (superfine) sugar

Lightly grease 25 x 30 x 3 cm
(10 x 12 x 1¼ in) baking tray (jelly roll pan).
Mix water with milk powder and lightly whisk until well combined. Place flour, sugar and spices in a bowl, add butter and yeast and, using your fingers, mix all the ingredients together until they resemble fresh breadcrumbs. Add milk mixture and egg and work the ingredients to form a dough. Remove from the bowl and work dough quickly on a lightly floured surface for 5 minutes. Lightly knead in currants, sultanas and mixed peel. Return dough to the bowl and cover with a damp cloth. Place the bowl in a warm place for 40 minutes, or until the dsough has doubled in size.
Preheat oven to 180°C (350°F).
Remove the risen dough from the bowl and work it into a solid mass again, ridding it of any air. Cut dough into 18 small pieces and roll them into balls. Place the balls on the prepared tray in a warm area for 30–40 minutes, or until they are again double in size.
Pipe the cross mixture over the buns and place in the preheated oven for 30–35 minutes, or until golden brown. Remove and glaze immediately with the glaze mixture.

Cross Mixture
Mix flour and water together until the mix is stiff enough to hold its shape when piped. If the mixture is too thin, it will spread before going into the oven.

Glaze
Place water, gelatine and sugar in a saucepan and bring to the boil. Remove from heat and brush over the hot buns.

HOT WATER CRUST

This pastry is used for pork pies and savoury terrines.

100 ml (3½ fl oz) milk
100 ml (3½ fl oz) water
210 g (7 oz) unsalted (sweet) butter
4 cups (16 fl oz) plain (all-purpose) flour

Place the milk, water and butter in a saucepan and bring slowly to the boil. Pour the hot liquid over the flour and mix to a solid paste. Remove and work the dough by hand.

HUCKLEBERRY
(see also berry)

A small blue/red berry which is similar to the blueberry and common in the USA.

HUMMINGBIRD CAKE

No one is sure who named the hummingbird cake, but it is most appropriate, as the cake is made with the fruit that hummingbirds love.

2 cups (8 oz) plain (all-purpose) flour
1¼ cups (8 oz) caster (superfine) sugar
1 teaspoon salt
2 teaspoons ground cinnamon
2 teaspoons baking powder (soda)
2 x 60 g (2 oz) eggs
100 g (3½ oz) canned crushed pineapple, drained
2 over-ripe bananas, peeled and mashed
¼ cup (2 fl oz) pineapple juice
⅔ cup (5 fl oz) light polyunsaturated (safflower) oil

Filling
cream cheese frosting (see page 125)

Preheat oven to 180°C (350°F).
Lightly grease a 23 cm (9 in) round deep cake tin with butter and line base with baking paper (parchment). Place all dry ingredients in a mixing bowl and mix thoroughly. Add eggs, pineapple, bananas, pineapple juice and oil and mix thoroughly. Pour the mixture into the prepared tin and bake for 35–40 minutes, or until a skewer inserted into the centre of the cake comes out dry and the cake has shrunk slightly away from the sides of the tin. Let stand for 10 minutes before turning out onto a cake rack to cool.
Cut the cake into halves horizontally and spread one third of the cream cheese frosting on top of the bottom layer. Top with the second layer, then cover the top and sides of the cake with the remaining frosting.

HUNDREDS AND THOUSANDS

Small confections of sugar in a combination of many bright colours. They are used sparingly in cake decorating, on fairy bread and to decorate other confectionery and small cakes.

HUNGARIAN CHOCOLATE TORTE

5 egg yolks
⅓ cup (2½ oz) caster (superfine) sugar
400 g (13 oz) dark couverture chocolate, melted (see page 62)
2 cups (7 oz) ground almonds
100 ml (3½ fl oz) brandy
5 egg whites
¼ cup (2 oz) caster (superfine) sugar, extra
1¼ cups (5 oz) plain (all-purpose) flour

To Decorate
apricot glaze (see page 10)
250 g (8 oz) marzipan
dark (plain or semi-sweet) chocolate, melted,
for chocolate collar (see page 62)
chocolate curls (see page 64)

Preheat oven to 180°C (350°F).
Lightly grease a 23 cm (9 in) springform cake tin with butter and line the base with baking paper (parchment). Beat egg yolks and sugar until thick and almost white and the mixture forms a ribbon (see page 236). Very gently fold in chocolate, almonds and brandy by hand. Beat egg whites until soft peaks form, then beat in the extra sugar, a spoonful at a time. Beat until sugar is dissolved. Very gently fold in beaten egg yolks and flour, by hand. Pour into prepared tin and bake for 40–45 minutes, or until the top of the cake springs back when lightly touched.
Cool in the tin, on a cake rack.
When completely cold, turn the cake out and cover the top and sides with apricot glaze. Roll out the marzipan into a circle large enough to cover top and sides of cake. Place marzipan over cake and mould to fit neatly. Trim excess marzipan and make the chocolate collar (see page 64). Chill the torte until the chocolate collar is firm. Remove the baking paper from the collar before decorating the top of the cake with chocolate curls.

See pages 148–9

HUSH PUPPIES

A name given to American cornmeal cakes. They are said to have been given this name because they were thrown at puppies to quiet them after they began howling when they smelled the cornmeal cakes being cooked.

HUTZELBROT

A rich Christmas loaf made from an egg-rich yeast dough and filled with spices, dates, pears and dried fruits.

IAGOS

(see also Desdemonas, Othellos, and Rosalinds)

These are small round cake served for afternoon teas or, if small enough, as petits fours. They are made from a mixture known as Othello sponge mixture, the same basic cake as is used in Desdemonas, Othellos, and Rosalinds, which were made by an English pastry chef in honour of each of these characters. Each has its own filling and fondant covering: Iagos are filled with coffee-flavoured buttercream and coated with a coffee-flavoured fondant.

ICE CARVING

An art form in itself, ice carving is a form of sculpture in which large blocks of ice are chiselled or shaved into magnificent creations such as swans and eagles. The ice for larger ice sculptures must be made especially for the ice carver, as it must be clear and free from internal imperfections. The larger pieces are purely display pieces, but smaller pieces are used as service dishes for desserts, ices or sorbets.

ICE CREAM

(see also cassatta, de Medici, sorbet)

As with various other ice confections, ice cream began its life thousands of years ago as a crude form of sorbet made from snow and honey. The flavourings became more elaborate, with flowers, spices, herbs and fruits being added to the honey and snow. Eventually somebody added milk to the mixture and the first 'sharbert' was made — and the quest for a creamier ice cream began.

Marco Polo brought back from China a recipe for a snow-based dessert which consisted of goats' milk, fruit, honey and ice. The Italians changed the recipe, using cream instead of the milk and then, with the invention of churning, added whipped cream and a small amount of buttermilk. The snow was eventually dropped altogether and the cream liquid was instead frozen in the ice during winter. A crude form of vanilla anglaise was made, using eggs, milk, cream, sugar and flavourings.

By the early 1500s Bernardo Buontalenti had discovered the freezing effects of salt and ice, and when Catherine de Medici moved to France in 1533 to marry King Henri II of France, her court chef took with him the recipe and method for making ice creams. While for many years it was a well guarded secret of the King's court, and was only served at special occasions, the samples that were tried proved popular and, eventually, with the invention of better freezing churns, ice cream spread to coffee houses.

It could still only be served during winter, as there were still no freezing storage facilities other than snow. Several centuries later, with the inventions of better 'sorbetières' and of freezing facilities, ice creams went into production at the first factory in Baltimore, USA, sometime in the mid to late 1800s.

Ice cream has seen such popularity that many people do not appreciate the labour and skill behind homemade ice cream. It is still an integral part of a pastry chef's training to know how to make a perfect non-solid freezing ice cream that doesn't have too much air incorporated and will scoop nicely. It is a skill which comes with both pracrice and a good recipe.

For a good ice cream base, use the crème anglaise recipe on page 84, and allow this to freeze in an ice cream churn or maker.

ICE CREAM BROWN BREAD

7 slices of brown (wholemeal) bread
⅔ cup (6 oz) demerara sugar
4 egg yolks
⅓ cup (2½ oz) caster (superfine) sugar
1 cup (8 fl oz) cream
chocolate sauce, for serving

Cut the crusts from the bread and break it into small pieces. Place it on a tray and cover with the demerara sugar. Place the sugared bread under a griller or salamander until the sugar caramelises, stirring the bread mixture to ensure all the sugar is caramelised. Remove the bread and cool.
Whisk egg yolks and sugar in a large bowl until they form a thick sabayon (are light, white and fluffy). In a separate bowl, whisk the cream until it holds soft peaks.
Fold cream through egg yolk mixture and fold caramelised brown bread through the mixture. Pour into a large container and freeze overnight before serving. It can be frozen into terrine moulds or round cake tins for easier serving. To serve, simply cut slices and serve with a chocolate sauce.

ICE CREAM CAKE

Served as both a dessert and special occasion cake, an ice cream cake usually consists of many layers of differently coloured and flavoured ice creams or sorbets. The name is not used to refer to bombes or cassatas. Ice cream cakes can be log-shaped, domed or a normal cake shape. They may be quite simply decorated, or covered with whipped cream and decorated like normal cakes. Some companies make different shapes using their own brand of ice cream.

ICE CREAM MAKER

There is a wide variety of ice cream makers available. They can be large or small, expensive or inexpensive, motorised or battery-operated, and have varying capacities. Most good ice cream makers for the professional pastry kitchen are expensive, heavy-duty and churn about 1½–2 litres (48–64 fl oz) safely at a time. There are also machines which can freeze many litres at a time, but these are quite impractical for small pastry kitchens or home use. The Italian varieties are the best, coming, as they do, from the home of the first churn invented for ice creams and sorbets.

Used for both sorbets and ice creams, an ice cream maker or churn consists of a motor which lowers the temperature in the freezing compartment to freezing point. At the same time, it turns the churn to stop the ice cream and sorbet freezing into a solid lump and to incorporate a small amount of air into the mixture. When sufficiently frozen, the churn blades are removed and the ice cream scooped out for serving immediately or for further freezing while another batch is frozen.

ICED SOUFFLES
(see also soufflés)

Cold or iced soufflés are also called chiffon soufflés, as the mixture is very similar to that of a chiffon, a light, cream-based dessert. Traditionally, sugar and water are boiled in a saucepan to 115°C (240°F) and poured into egg yolks while they are being whisked. To the solid sabayon base which is formed, flavourings, egg whites and whipped cream are added. The mixture is poured into ramekins which have paper collars around their edges for support, as the mixture must protrude above the ramekin by several centimetres (an inch or so). The soufflé is then frozen or refrigerated, depending on whether gelatine has been used or not. When set and cold, the paper collar is removed and the dessert dusted with icing sugar, cocoa or a mixture of these, and served with a warm sauce or with biscuits.

The paper collars, which should be approximately 6–7 centimetres (2½–3 inches) higher than the dish lip, are tied tightly with string (or use rubber bands) to the sides of the dish.

½ cup (4 oz) caster (superfine) sugar
⅓ cup (2½ fl oz) water
8 egg yolks
2½ cups (20 fl oz) fresh cream, whipped
100 ml (3½ fl oz) Grand Marnier
fresh orange sements, for garnish
icing (powdered) sugar, for dusting

Place sugar and water in a saucepan and slowly bring to the boil. Boil sugar to 116°C (241°F) using a sugar (candy) thermometer. Place egg yolks in the bowl of an electric mixer and begin whisking eggs until light and fluffy. When sugar is the correct temperature, slowly begin drizzling the hot molten sugar into the whisking egg yolks. Do not stop until all has been added, then continue whisking the egg yolk mixture until cold. While the yolks are whisking and cooling, whip cream to soft peaks. Add liqueur to the cold egg yolk mixture, then fold through the cream.

Pour the mixture into individual soufflé dishes which have paper collars around the sides. Fill the dishes to 3 cm (1¼ in) higher than the actual dish. Freeze the soufflés for 4–5 hours, or overnight. To serve, place the orange segments on top of the soufflés, remove the paper collars and dust with icing sugar.

ICE, TO

To cover a product with a sweet mixture of icing (powdered) sugar in either its raw state or mixed to a thin or thick paste with milk or water.

ICING
(see also frosting, water icings)

Icing is a generalised term for mixtures of icing (powdered) sugar and water, but it also refers to fondants, fudge icings, frostings and royal icing, to name a few. They are all made using icing sugar in some way, and are all used to decorate cakes. Icings can be flavoured with the addition of coffee, passionfruit, citrus juice and zest.

ICING SUGAR
(see also sugar)

Also known as pure icing sugar, this is a pure form of sugar which has simply been ground to a powder dust so that it dissolves instantly. It is used to make icings for cakes, fondants for pastries and decorating, or on its own as a dusted decoration. Its use in making pastry is varied and in most cases it can be replaced by ordinary or caster (superfine) sugars in recipes. It is used in some shortbread and biscuit (cookie) doughs so that sugar spots do not show, and in sponge mixtures such as savoy sponges for the same reason. As pure icing sugar contains no additives, it needs to be kept airtight when stored. It should be sifted frequently because it absorbs moisture easily, causing the formation of hard, unusable lumps.

Non-lumping sugar (soft icing mixture) is a form of icing sugar which contains a starch or drying substance — cornflour (cornstarch), phosphate or silicate — to prevent the sugar absorbing moisture and forming lumps. Due to these drying agents, this form of icing sugar should not be used in all recipes, but in biscuit (cookie) mixtures it increases the shortness of the product.

INDIANER

Indianers, made famous by the house of Demel in Vienna, are baked or fried doughs which are filled with cream and topped with chocolate.

In Vienna an 'indianer' was a tightrope walker and story has it that in 1850 a baker saw his wife looking up at a tightrope walker who was crossing the town square on a high wire. Jealous, the baker yelled at her, to which she responded by taking aim with a lump of dough. She missed her husband, but the dough fell into the hot fat on the fire. When the dough was cooked the baker decided to fill it with cream, and named it after the man who was the cause of the fight.

Indonesian Layer Cake Step-by-Step

Step 1: Spread the coffee-flavoured cake layer with a quarter of the reserved buttercream mixture.

Step 2: Continue layering the cake slices with the buttercream.

Step 3: When all layers are joined, cover the sides with extra buttercream. Decorate with almonds and dust the top with icing sugar. See page 155.

INDONESIAN LAYER CAKE

In this multi-layered cake, half of the butter, sugar and egg mixture is not included in the baked cake, but is used to fill and cover the finished cake.

¼ cup (1 oz) plain (all-purpose) flour
⅓ cup (1½ oz) cornflour (cornstarch)
300 g (10 oz) unsalted butter
⅓ cup (3 oz) caster (superfine) sugar
8 egg yolks
8 egg whites
⅓ cup (2½ oz) caster (superfine) sugar, extra
2 teaspoons instant coffee powder
3 teaspoons hot water

To Decorate
1 cup (4 oz) flaked almonds, roasted (see page 5)
icing (powdered) sugar, for dusting

Preheat oven to 180°C (350°F).
Line four 20 x 30 cm (8 x 12 in) baking sheets (with edges on all sides) with baking paper (parchment). Mix flours and sift twice. Beat butter and sugar until creamy, light and fluffy. Add egg yolks one at a time, beating very well after each one is added. Beat egg whites until stiff peaks form, then gradually beat in the extra sugar, a spoonful at a time.
Beat until the sugar is dissolved. Gently fold in the sifted flours and half of the creamed butter and sugar by hand. Reserve the other half of the creamed butter and sugar for the filling. Divide the cake mixture in half. Leave one half plain. Mix the coffee dissolved in water into the other. Divide cake mixture in half again and pour all three mixtures on the prepared sheets. Bake in the preheated oven for 10–15 minutes, or until the tops of each cake spring back when lightly touched. Carefully remove the baking paper and allow cakes to cool.
Spread the reserved butter and sugar mixture between the layers of the cake, alternating the coffee and plain. Press down gently to even the layers. Cover the sides with the butter and sugar mixture. Press the flaked almonds into the sides and dust the top with icing sugar.

See page 154

ITALIAN BUTTERCREAM
(see buttercream)

ITALIAN ICES
(see sorbet)

ITALIAN MERINGUE
(see also meringue)

A meringue mixture made from whisked egg whites, to which a boiled sugar syrup is slowly added while whisking continues. The meringue is whisked until it cools to form a stable and firm meringue. Italian meringue mixtures can be piped and baked in a cool oven like normal meringues or, because of their stability, used in sorbets and parfaits.

JACOB'S BATON

These are long thin sticks of choux pastry filled with vanilla-flavoured cream and topped with plain fondant. Jacob's batons must not be more than 3 cm (1¼ in) in width, otherwise they are considered to be éclairs.

JAGGERY
(see palm sugar, sugar)

JALEBIS

Jalebis are Middle Eastern sweet treats made by peddlars or market stallholders throughout the Middle East and India. Thin batter is drizzled into very hot oil and fried until crisp, then soaked in a sweet syrup. They are sold and eaten immediately.

JALOUSIE

Jalousies are rectangular pastries made from a base and lid of butter puff pastry which is filled with frangipane cream or light almond cake mixture. The lid of the jalousie is cut with a lattice cutter or slit with a knife so that it opens slightly when draped over the base and filling. The almond filling is traditionally left plain and the baked jalousie is glazed with apricot glaze or dusted with icing sugar. Occasionally, though, fresh berries or poached fruits are added to the almond filling or substituted for it.

JAM
(known as jelly in the USA)

Jam (jelly) is a sweet spread for breads, toast and crumpets, which is made from boiled fruits and sugar. Equal quantities of fruit and sugar, plus water (one third the weight of fruit), are considered to be the proper base for a good product. The thickness of the jam depends on the amount of pectin within the fruits and also on the amount of sugar boiled with the fruits. In fruits where the level of pectin is not very high, lemon juice or pectin can be added to increase the stability of the jam. Such fruits include pears, pineapples, figs and some berries. Nearly all over-ripe fruits will be low in pectin. Jam differs from conserve in that the fruit is broken down during the cooking process or is pre-mashed before being boiled, while conserves must still retain some whole fruit.

JAPONAISE
(see also Malakoff torte)

A light mixture of whipped egg whites into which ground hazelnuts or almonds are folded. The mixture is then piped or spread into flat discs and baked for 20–25 minutes, until firm. The torte is formed by joining two of these discs together with buttercream and covering them with roasted flaked almonds.

The discs are also used as bases and tops for many of the world's most famous cakes. When used as bases for fruit flans, the discs are simply brushed with melted chocolate before the cream and fruit are stacked on top.

Meringue Base
4 egg whites (60 g/2 oz eggs)
⅔ cup (5 oz) caster (superfine) sugar
⅔ cup (3½ oz) roasted almonds, ground
⅓ cup (1½ oz) cornflour (cornstarch)
1½ tablespoons icing (powdered) sugar

To Decorate
250 g (8 oz) quick no-fuss buttercream (see page 43)
2 cups (7 oz) flaked almonds, roasted (see page 5)
icing (powdered) sugar, for dusting

Preheat oven to 180°C (350°F).
Line two baking sheets with baking paper (parchment)
and draw a 23 cm (9 in) circle on each.
Whisk egg whites until stiff peaks form, then gradually beat in
sugar, a spoonful at a time. Beat at top speed on the mixer for
15 minutes, until sugar is dissolved. Mix almonds, cornflour
and icing sugar, then very gently fold in beaten egg whites by
hand. Divide the mixture in half and carefully spoon into the
marked circles, keeping the meringue within the edges.
Bake for 30–35 minutes. Cool on the trays on a cake rack.
When the meringues are cold, spread one with buttercream
and top with the second meringue. Cover the top and
sides with buttercream. Press flaked almonds
on the top and sides and dust lightly with icing sugar.
Chill for 1 hour before serving.

JELLY

One of the world's most popular desserts, jelly is liked and used in almost every country and in every culture, either as a dessert or as a sweetmeat confection. While there are numerous varieties, styles and recipes for jellies, they are all basically a flavoured base liquid which is set using gelatine.

Gelées d'entremets is a term used to refer to dessert jellies in general, which includes wine-, fruit-, water- and liqueur-based jellies, and those made using spiced tea. A dessert jelly should be crystal clear when set and therefore also clear before being set; if a jelly mixture is not clear, whisked egg whites can be folded through it as it simmers. Usually, if the fruit juice or base liquid is boiled with the sugar and skimmed, the mixture becomes fairly clear naturally. Occasionally the clarification process will be required.

JELLIES

As well as the gelatinous dessert of clear liquid, jellies also refer to two other sweet treats made by the pastry chef. The first of these two jellies is the American-style spread often wrongly referred to as jam. While jams still contain a certain amount of the puréed or mashed fruits, jelly is a clear, almost translucent spread made from the juices of fruits mixed with sugar. As with jams, jellies are best made with fruits which have a high pectin content, although again, lemon juice can be added to increase the pectin content. The most common jellies are apple, cranberry, guava and gooseberry, all these fruits being high in pectin.

The second form of jelly is a sweetmeat or petit four, which is made by gelatinising fruit juices and, once set, cutting the jelly into pieces that are then rolled in sugar.

APPLE JELLIES
1 cup (8 fl oz) clear apple juice
⅓ cup (2 oz) gelatine powder
3 teaspoons Calvados (apple brandy)
1½ cups (12 oz) caster (superfine) sugar
¼ cup (3 oz) clear honey
white granulated sugar, for rolling

Place half the apple juice in a small bowl and sprinkle gelatine over the juice. Allow to soak for 30 minutes. Place the remaining juice, Calvados, sugar and honey in a saucepan and slowly bring the mixture to the boil. Add the soaked gelatine to the boiling liquid and stir until completely dissolved. Insert a sugar (candy) thermometer into the boiling liquid and allow liquid to boil until it reaches 112°C (233°F). Pour the mixture into a clean 28 x 18 x 2 cm (11 x 7 x ¾ in) baking tray (jelly roll pan) and cool before placing the tray in the refrigerator for 24 hours.
Cut the firm jelly into small oblong-shaped pieces and roll each piece in granulated sugar. Serve and eat immediately.
Do not sugar coat any pieces which are not to be served immediately. Store in an airtight container in a cool place.

Makes 40

JELLY CAKES

These are made by dipping small sponge cakes into a jelly mixture which has only partially set. Once completely covered in jelly they are covered with desiccated coconut. After setting firmly in the refrigerator, they are either eaten as is or split and filled with cream.

JELLY ROLL

The American version of the famed English Swiss roll.

JELLY ROLL PAN

Same size as the Swiss roll tray, usually 25 x 30 x 3 cm (10 x 12 x 1¼ in).

JESUITE

A puff pastry delight so-named because its shape resembled that of the hats worn by the Jesuits. Shaped into triangular puffs, jésuites are filled with almond or marzipan paste and are covered with a royal icing mixture before baking so that they become crisp and golden brown once baked.

JOHNNY CAKE

One of the many American products made using cornmeal.

1½ cups (6 oz) plain (all-purpose) flour
3 teaspoons baking powder (soda)
1 teaspoon salt
1½ cups (10 oz) yellow cornmeal (polenta)
2 x 60 g (2 oz) eggs, lightly beaten
⅓ cup (4 oz) golden syrup (light treacle)
1¼ cups (10 fl oz) milk
90 g (3 oz) unsalted (sweet) butter, melted

Preheat oven to 180°C (350°F).
Grease a 25 x 30 x 3 cm (10 x 12 x 1¼ in) baking tray (jelly roll pan) and line with baking paper (parchment). Into a large mixing bowl, sift the flour with the baking powder and salt. Add cornmeal, egg, golden syrup, milk and butter. Stir until all ingredients are well combined. Pour the mixture into the prepared tray and bake in preheated oven for 30–35 minutes. Cool before serving in buttered slices.

JUGGERY

A traditional dessert of India, this tapioca dessert is made with treacle, coconut and cream.

JUMBALS

An English honey dough which is rolled into long finger-shaped pieces and baked. When still warm, it is covered with a lemon icing, which brings out its flavour magnificently. The jumbal was first invented in the 17th century. It was flavoured with caraway and occasionally made with a gingerbread-style dough.

JUNKET
(see also mousses)

Junket is a light mousse-style dessert made of milk and a flavouring. It is set firm using either rennet or a junket tablet. A very old type of dessert, junkets are no longer very popular. Originating in England, the first junket was possibly made by mistake. Junket tablets are a mixture of the enzyme rennin, which is extracted from calves' stomachs: when mixed with the warm milk, rennet allows the milk to set. It is thought that a shepherd who had freshly milked his cattle may also have had meat or the carcass of a calf at hand and somehow mixed the stomach juices with the milk. When the milk set, the shepherd tried to kill the flavour with sugar and thus created junket.

Junket tablets are available from many specialist delicatessens, in a variety of flavours.

157

KAKADU PLUMS

A native fruit from the Kakadu region of the Northern Territory of Australia. The Kakadu plum looks somewhat like a green olive and has a light citrus flavour. It is the world's richest source of vitamin C and can be used in both fresh and frozen form for sorbets, sauces, jellies and cakes.

KALTSCHALE

Meaning 'cold cup', kaltschale is a Russian dessert of fresh fruits covered with a sweet red berry purée. The fresh fruits are soaked for 24 hours in a mixture of sugar, white wine and citrus juices before being covered with the purée. They are served in a bowl that is placed inside a bowl of ice to keep the dessert cold.

KATAIFI
(see also pastry)

A sweet sugar-soaked Greek pastry consisting of rolls of pastry. The rolls of kataifi are filled with a nut and spice filling and baked with butter, to keep them moist. When they are golden brown, they are soaked immediately with citrus-flavoured sugar syrup to which a few drops of rosewater have been added.

KAYMAK

A thickened, and sometimes sweetened, cream mixture which is served with desserts.

Turkish in origin, kaymak is traditionally made using fresh cream which is boiled until it reduces to about two thirds its original liquid content and becomes very thick. Kaymak may be sweetened before boiling and spiced after boiling, but this depends on the dessert with which it is to be served. Occasionally it is also aerated by being whisked lightly during the boiling process. It is served warm or cold.

KIPFERLN

Also known as Viennese horns or Vanilla kipferln, these shortbread-style biscuits (cookies) are a tradition in Germany and are said to symbolise the goat's horn, a long-standing symbol of fertility in German folklore. Initially they were only ever made at Christmas, then later at all festive and holiday occasions. Now they are served with coffee all year round. They were in fact invented in Austria and have been made since the early 13th century.

250 g (8 oz) unsalted (sweet) butter, softened
½ cup (4 oz) caster (superfine) sugar
2¾ cups (11 oz) plain (all-purpose) flour, sifted
½ cup (2 oz) ground hazelnuts (filberts)
½ cup (2 oz) ground almonds
caster (superfine) sugar, extra, for decoration

Preheat oven to 160°C (320°F). Lightly grease baking sheets. Place softened butter and caster sugar in a mixing bowl and mix until well creamed (light, fluffy and pale). Add flour, hazelnuts and almonds and mix until combined. Take each heaped tablespoon of the mixture, shape it into a ball and then roll it into a sausage shape, tapering the ends slightly. Bend this to form a horseshoe and place on the prepared sheet. Bake in preheated oven for 10–15 minutes, or until lightly golden brown. Remove from the oven and roll each kipferl carefully in caster sugar. Place on a cake rack until cold. Roll once more in caster sugar before serving.

Makes 30

KIRSCH OR KIRSCH WASSER
(see also spirits)

A clear alcohol distilled from cherries, Kirsch is one of most frequently used spirits in pastrycooking. It is traditionally sprinkled over fresh fruits and berries and used to soak the layers of sponge which form the basis of many cakes, the most famous being the Schwarzwalder or Black Forest gâteau. Kirsch is often used for flaming desserts, especially where guéridon work is still performed.

KISSEL

This differs from kaltschale only in that this white wine and red berry purée is thickened with cornflour (cornstarch) or arrowroot. It is served warm over the top of any desserts, creams or on its own. In some areas of Russia, it is traditionally folded through lightly whipped cream and allowed to cool, making a crude form of bavarois.

KIWI FRUIT

This fruit is now named after its surrogate home of New Zealand. It was taken there by New Zealand farmers who, around the turn of the century, found this exciting fruit on the banks of the Yangtze River in China. Also known as the Chinese gooseberry, this fruit has a cinnamon-coloured, thin, fuzzy skin which covers a bright green flesh.

Used in sauces for their colour, kiwi fruit are also used in fruit salads and displays. However, if used in mousses or jellies, the fruit must first be puréed and cooked or the enzymes in them will prevent the gelatine used in these desserts setting.

KLOBEN

These European yeast cakes, which can either be shaped in a slight crescent or left straight, are filled with a sweet combination of dried fruits and mixed (candied) peel, and coated with an apricot glaze.

KLOSSE

A potato dumpling dessert from Austria, klosse is a mixture of puréed cooked potatoes, eggs, flour, cornflour (cornstarch) and breadcrumbs which is heavily spiced with ginger, cinnamon and cloves. The dumplings are lightly poached in a syrup of sweet wine and spices. When cooked, they are rolled in a buttery breadcrumb coating and served with crème anglaise or a golden syrup (light treacle) sauce.

KLOUSKIS

A Polish version of the Austrian klosse, these potato dumplings are made with flour, eggs and spices. Klouskis are lighter than klosse, being risen with yeast and allowed to prove (rise) several times before being boiled or poached in the sweet wine syrup.

KNEADING
(see also bread)

This is the single most important process of breadmaking. Unless a dough is kneaded correctly, the gluten strands will not develop sufficiently to hold the gas produced by the yeast. However, some doughs, such as shortcrust and sweet pastries, should be kneaded as little as possible, as these pastries need to be kept short and should not have the gluten developed at all. A quick knead to bring the ingredients together is all that is required.

Bread and yeast doughs, on the other hand, are kneaded until the dough is smooth and elastic, which usually takes 5–8 minutes by hand or 3–4 minutes by machine, using a dough hook. The time required, of course, depends on the amount of dough, the type of flour and the type of machine being used (if done mechanically).

KNOCK BACK
(see also bread)

A term used to describe the process of forcing the air out of a yeast dough. It is also called 'punching down'. When a yeast dough has been allowed to sit, it will fill with air. It then requires de-gassing. A firm knock will allow the air to escape from the dough and with a further short amount of kneading, all air will be expelled. Knocking back can be performed by hand or by machine, depending on how much dough is involved.

KNODEL

Knodels are potato or plain flour dumplings which are risen by yeast or egg whites. Knodes are traditional dumplings of Germany and are served with sauce as a dessert, or on top of a stewed fruit compôte.

KOSHER FOODS

Pastry plays an important part in Jewish laws about kosher food. The principles of kosher food must be understood and obeyed by pastry chefs and home cooks alike, even when only dealing with the manufacture of pastries and cakes.

Firstly, lard must never be used, as it is a by-product of pork, a meat which is prohibited in the Jewish diet. Secondly, milk and meat products must never be eaten in the same meal, which means that meat stews or pies cannot be topped with pastries containing butter, cream or milk. And finally, for foods to be sold as manufactured kosher (clean) foods, their production must be supervised by a recognised rabbi.

KOUNAFA

An Arabian dessert consisting of long thin strips of buttered filo pastry layered with a sweet mixture of chopped nuts, sugar and spices. Once the mixture has baked and is removed from the oven, it is soaked in a citrus and rosewater syrup.

Depending on the area in which the kounafa is produced, there are different ways of preparing the dish. Some prefer the pastry strips to be woven and latticed, with the nuts left whole, while in other areas the nuts are omitted and ricotta or cream cheese and dried fruits are used in their place.

KOURAMBEITHES

Originating in the Arabian homelands as ghorayabah, this shortbread was claimed by the Turks as theirs and was known by them as kourabiye. The Greeks, however, eventually laid claim to it as well, making the shortbread famous as kourambeithes. Although traditionally fried, kourambeithes today are baked in the oven and can be served with dessert or as a midday snack.

These lightly spiced hazelnut shortbreads, served warm from the oven and rolled in their sugar coating, should melt in the mouth. They can also be kept, in an airtight container.

210 g (7 oz) salted butter
1 cup (5 oz) icing (powdered) sugar, sifted
1 egg yolk (60 g/2 oz egg)
3 cups (12 oz) plain (all-purpose) flour
1½ teaspoons baking powder (soda)
1 teaspoon ground cinnamon
2½ cups (9 oz) hazelnuts, finely chopped
icing (powdered) sugar, for dusting

Preheat oven to 160°C (320°F). Grease baking sheets. Place butter and sugar in a mixing bowl and cream together until light, white and fluffy. Beat in egg yolk. Sift flour with baking powder and cinnamon and mix lightly into the butter mixture together with the chopped hazelnuts.

Allow the dough to rest for 15 minutes.

Take teaspoonfuls of dough and roll into balls. Place on

prepared sheets. Bake in preheated oven for
15–20 minutes, or until very pale golden. Cool.
While biscuits are barely warm, dust with icing sugar.
Cool and store in an airtight tin.
Roll in icing sugar again before serving.

KRANSEKAGE
(see also Overflodigshorn)

Kransekage is a type of almond confectionery made famous
by Danish pastry chefs. It is made from a stiff marzipan
macaroon mixture which is piped or rolled into different-
sized rings. The rings are lightly baked then decorated with
royal icing and stacked together to create large, tall stacks,
long, curved horns, or a range of other shapes. Some of these
shapes are served as wedding cakes, others just as snacks.

KRAPFEN

Originating in Germany, krapfen, also known as Berliners or
Berlinkrapfen, are yeast-raised doughnuts which do not have
a hole. Risen till double in size, the krapfen are inserted
carefully into the frying fat and one side is fried till golden
brown. After being turned over they rise again slightly and
cook on the second side. If prepared correctly, the krapfen
should have a single white band running around the centre.
When cooked, they are rolled in sugar and (when cool enough
to handle) injected with jam (jelly).

¾ cup (6 fl oz) milk
20 g (¾ oz) fresh compressed yeast
2 tablespoons caster (superfine)
½ teaspoon salt
2 egg yolks (60 g/2 oz eggs)
1¾ cups (7 oz) plain (all-purpose) flour
45 g (1½ oz) unsalted (sweet) butter, softened
caster (superfine) sugar, for coating
⅔ cup (7 oz) plum jam (jelly)

Preheat a deep fryer of oil to about 170–190°C (340–375°F).
Place milk in a large mixing bowl and add yeast.
Whisk lightly so that the yeast will dissolve into the liquid.
Add sugar, salt and egg yolks to liquid mixture and
whisk to combine well. Add flour slowly to the mixture,
working slowly until all is mixed thoroughly
into the liquid and a dough is formed.
Knead dough by hand for approximately 5 minutes, or until
smooth, soft and elastic. Cover dough and allow it to sit in a
warm area for 1 hour, or until double in bulk.
Add butter to the risen dough and knead in until it is
completely combined. Cut dough into 40 g (1½ oz) amounts,
roll each into a small ball and allow to sit on a lightly
cornfloured (cornstarched) cloth. Cover rolls with
another cloth and allow to rise for a further
40 minutes, or until double in bulk.
Pick each up carefully and dip into the hot oil or fat.
Fry until golden brown, turning the doughnuts 2–3 times
during cooking. Remove from the fat and immediately roll in
sugar. Using a small pointed metal nozzle, pipe jam into the
centre of the doughnut, roll in sugar again and serve.

KUGELHUPF
(see gugelhupf)

KULICH

A traditional Russian Easter cake, kulich is made from a
brioche dough containing dried fruits which have been
plumped up by being soaked in wine or vodka. It is topped
with a white icing or fondant and usually sprinkled with nuts.
It is traditionally baked in a tall cylindrical mould so that the
finished product resembles a tall candle. Otherwise it is
baked in a gugelhupf mould. In certain parts of the country,
this sweet cake is served with savoury foods and in others it is
flavoured with cardamom or caraway and eaten as a
breakfast bread. More commonly, it is served with breakfast
jams or as a snack throughout the day.

15 g (½ oz) fresh compressed yeast
(or 6 teaspoons active dry yeast)
200 ml (7 fl oz) lukewarm milk
2¾ cups (11 oz) plain (all-purpose) flour
3 x 60 g (2 oz) eggs
135 g (4½ oz) unsalted (sweet) butter
¼ cup (2 oz) caster (superfine) sugar
½ cup (2½ oz) mixed dried fruit
2½ tablespoons dried apricots, chopped
1 tablespoon mixed (candied) peel, chopped

To Decorate
water icing (see page 288)
chopped nuts, for decoration

In a small bowl, dissolve yeast in milk. Place flour in a large
bowl. Make a well in the centre of the flour and add dissolved
yeast and the eggs. Mix ingredients together. Knead on a
lightly floured surface, or in the bowl, for 10 minutes. Place
butter and sugar on top of the dough in the bowl. Stand the
bowl in a warm place for 20 minutes to double in bulk. Knock
back (punch down) the dough and beat in the butter and
sugar until combined. Cover and refrigerate for 24 hours.
Preheat oven to 180°C (350°F). Lightly grease a kulich or
fluted round tin with butter and cut a circle of baking paper
(parchment) to line the base. Mix dried fruit, apricots and
mixed peel into the dough and knead for 1 minute. Place in
prepared tin, filling it only two thirds full. Cover with a clean
dry cloth and stand the tin in a warm place until the dough
reaches the top. Bake in preheated oven for 35–40 minutes,
or until a skewer inserted into the centre of the cake comes
out dry. Turn out onto a cake rack to cool.
When cold, drizzle water icing over the top
and sprinkle with chopped nuts.

KYOGASHI

Japanese sweets made for weddings and special festivities,
their variety and colours being determined by the season in
which they are served.

LADIES' FINGERS

Small extremely sweet bananas which measure 10–12 cm (about 4 in) in length.

LADYFINGER

Also known as the savoiardi biscuit or sponge finger, this is a thin and delicate treat. It has a sugar or icing (powdered) sugar coating for added sweetness, and a crisp sweet crust. Ladyfinger also refers to a dessert from the Middle East and Mediterranean, made of filo (phyllo) pastry roll with spiced sweet or savoury fillings.

LAMINATION

The process of layering and stacking fat and dough through the continued rolling and folding of the two substances. Lamination in Puff and Danish pastries (to achieve light, flaky layers) occurs when the fat is enclosed between the dough layers and the layers of the mixture are rolled and folded over. The fat layers produce steam which causes the dough layers to rise. This action produces a perfect number of layers.

LAMINGTON

A truly Australian pastry or small cake named in honour of Lord Lamington, Governor of Queensland from 1895–1901. The Lord's cook is credited with having created the cake by dipping a square of buttercake into a chocolate icing mixture, coating it in a chocolate icing glaze and then rolling it in desiccated (shredded) coconut. They are traditionally served for morning or afternoon teas, either plain or split in half and filled with jam and cream.

Base
180 g (6 oz) unsalted (sweet) butter
¾ cup (6 oz) caster (superfine) sugar
3 x 60 g (2 oz) eggs
2¼ cups (9 oz) plain (all-purpose) flour
3 teaspoons baking powder
½ cup (4 fl oz) milk

Line an 18 x 28 x 3 cm (7 x 11 x 1¼ in) lamington cake tin with baking paper (parchment).
Preheat oven to 180°C (350°F). Place butter and sugar in a mixing bowl and cream till light and fluffy.
Add eggs one at a time and incorporate well.
Sift flour and baking powder together.
Add half flour and half milk to the creamed mixture and stir until combined. Add remaining flour and milk and stir until smooth.
Spread cake batter into prepared tin and bake for 35–45 minutes or until a skewer inserted into the cake comes out clean.
Allow cake to cool before cutting into 5 x 5 cm (2 x 2 in) squares.

Icing
4 cups (24 oz) icing (powdered) sugar, sifted
4 teaspoons cocoa powder, sifted
45 g (1½ oz) unsalted (sweet) butter
½ cup (4 fl oz) boiling water
desiccated (shredded) coconut for coating

Place all ingredients in a mixing bowl and combine well. Place bowl over a pot of simmering water and stir until mixture feels warm. If mixture runs off completely when you dip the first square, it is too thin. If cake is breaking in the mixture, it is too thick.
The perfect consistency is that which allows the lamington square to be immersed into the dip mixture briefly and leaves an even coating. Dip the lamington into the desiccated (shredded) coconut, covering it completely. Place on a wire cooling rack for 30–40 minutes to dry. Serve.

LANCASHIRE CAKES

First produced in the county of Lancashire in England, these pastries are thought to be a derivative of the Eccles and Banbury cakes. Lancashire cakes differ in that instead of using puff pastry to wrap the fruit filling, a yeast-risen dough is used, making a fruit filled bun, which is sprinkled before baking with lump or raw sugar.

LANGUE DE CHAT
(see also cat's tongue)

A famed light and delicate crisp French biscuit (cookie) often served with tea or coffee, or with light desserts such as mousses, sabayons and zabaglione. It is similar to a sponge finger and a savoiardi biscuit, and is used as an ingredient in several dishes.

LARD

Lard is an odourless white fat obtained from the abdomen of the pig. It was used in baking before and in the early part of the 20th century. It is used less in baking these days as butter and margarines are preferred, but it is sometimes requested in pastries and is preferred in frying because of its high smoking temperature.

LARDY CAKE

Popular in certain parts of England, lardy cakes are made from a sweet, rich dough filled with dried fruit, lard and sugar. They are similar to Chelsea buns. Once made only in areas where lard was commonplace, lardy cakes are now made everywhere, and with butter.

LAS PALMAS

No one knows for certain why this cake should be named after Las Palmas in the Canary Islands, but the rich coconut flavours do evoke images of a tropical paradise.

2¼ cups (9 oz) plain (all-purpose) flour
3 teaspoons baking powder
3 x 60 g (2 oz) eggs
1⅓ cups (10 oz) caster (superfine) sugar
½ cup (4 fl oz) milk
50 g (1¾ oz) unsalted (sweet) butter

Topping
200 g (7 oz) unsalted (sweet) butter
2 cups (6 oz) desiccated coconut
1⅔ cups (10 oz) soft light brown sugar
30 g (1 oz) glucose(corn syrup)
½ cup (4 fl oz) milk
vanilla essence (extract) to taste
200 g (7 oz) dark chocolate, melted

Preheat oven to 180°C (350°F).
Grease a 23 cm (9 in) springform pan lightly with butter and line sides and base with baking paper (parchment). Sift flour and baking powder twice. Whisk eggs and sugar until thick, light and fluffy and the mixture forms a ribbon. Heat milk and butter and gradually add to eggs, beating all the time. The mixture will become thinner. By hand, fold in the sifted flour and baking powder and pour into the prepared pan. Bake for 35–40 minutes, or until the top of the cake springs back when lightly touched and the cake has shrunk away from sides. Cool in the pan on a wire rack. Place all the topping ingredients in a saucepan and slowly bring to the boil. Cook slowly for 15 minutes and then pour over the cooked cake. Set oven temperature to 160°C (325°F) and bake for a further 15 minutes.
Cool in the pan on a wire rack.
When completely cold, remove from the pan.
Turn base of cake uppermost and pour melted chocolate over the top. Spread the chocolate, allowing it to run down the sides of the cake. Chill. When chocolate is set, turn the cake upright and serve on a platter.

LA STUPENDA

This dessert was created by executive chef of The Regent Hotel of Sydney, Serge Dansereau, in honour of Dame Joan Sutherland, (La Stupenda), on the occasion of her last performance at the Sydney Opera House. It consists of japonaise biscuits, raspberry and mango coulis, a garnish of chocolate curls, sablé biscuits and a filling of passionfruit. The combination floats on a bed of crème anglaise.

Japonaise
3 egg whites
⅓ cup (2½ oz) caster (superfine) sugar
¾ cup (80 g) ground hazelnuts (filberts)
1 tablespoon plain (all-purpose) flour

Preheat oven to 180 C (350°F).
Brush baking trays (sheets) with melted butter and lightly dust with flour. Beat egg whites with an electric mixer until firm, adding sugar halfway through. As soon as egg whites are stiff, stop mixing. With a wooden spoon, quickly fold in the ground hazelnuts mixed with flour. Place the japonaise mix in a piping bag with a 1 cm (½ in) tube, and pipe out spirals to make 16 flat biscuits about 6 cm (2½ in) in diameter. Bake in preheated oven for about 15 minutes, until biscuits are light fawn in colour.

Raspberry Coulis
Blend some raspberries with a little sugar syrup, then add a few drops of lemon juice and pass the mixture through a muslin cloth. (Use frozen raspberries for a richer colour.)

Mango Coulis
Peel ripe mangoes, dice and blend, adding a little sugar syrup. Pass the mixture through a muslin cloth.

Sablé Biscuits (for stars)
¾ cup (3 oz) plain (all-purpose) flour
60 g (2 oz) unsalted (sweet) butter, softened
2 tablespoons (1 oz) icing (powdered) sugar
1 egg

Mix soft butter with icing sugar. While mixing, add the egg and finally add the flour. Put this mixture in the fridge to cool for 5–6 hours before use.

Passionfruit Mousse
300 g (10 oz) white chocolate
3 leaves gelatine
⅗ cup (5 fl oz) passionfruit juice
4 egg whites
2 tablespoons caster (superfine) sugar
300 ml (10 fl oz) fresh, lightly whipped cream

Melt chocolate over a double boiler. Soak gelatine in cold water to make it soft. Strain and set apart. Heat passionfruit juice and add the strained gelatine. Mix until gelatine is melted. Remove from heat. Beat egg whites with sugar until stiff. Fold half the egg whites quickly with melted and cooled chocolate and add whipped cream and juice. Then add the second half of the egg whites. Put mousse in the fridge for 12 hours before use.

Chocolate Decorations
Melt 100 g (3½ oz) dark chocolate in a double boiler. When completely melted, add 1 teaspoon of oil. Palette the chocolate on a marble slab until about 2 mm (1/12 in) thin and when set, using a metal scraper at a 45° angle, push scraper forward, about 4.5 cm (1¾ in). Leave for 1 hour to set.

Crème Anglaise
1 cup (8 fl oz) milk
1 vanilla pod, halved lengthwise
2 tablespoons caster (superfine) sugar
7 egg yolks
few drops vanilla essence (extract)

Cut vanilla pod in half and boil with milk. In a bowl, whisk the sugar and the egg yolks until mixture is fluffy, thick and nearly white. Remove vanilla pod from milk and add hot milk slowly. Pour mixture back into the saucepan and cook on low heat. Stir continuously with a wooden spoon, moving it around the bottom of the pan to prevent the egg yolks coagulating.
As the sauce heats, the egg yolks will thicken the cream. As soon as the cream starts to coat the spoon, remove from the heat. Pour into a bowl to hasten the cooling and to stop the egg yolks scrambling.
Sieve into another bowl immediately. Leave this bowl in iced water until mixture is cool. Stir from time to time.
To serve the dessert, cut the japonaise biscuits into two round sizes one of 6 cm (2½ in) and one of 4 cm (1½ in) in diameter. Spread some passionfruit mousse onto each of these and top the larger japonaise with the smaller.
Pipe some passionfruit mousse onto the two biscuits in a circular motion and place the whole thing onto the plate to be served. Decorate the mousse-topped japonaise with the two sauces, the chocolate decorations and the sable stars.
Chill well and serve.

Serves 8

See page 167

LATTICE CUTTER

A small tool in the shape of a rolling pin on an extended handle, it is a combination of many discs which, when placed side by side, do not match up evenly, so when it is pressed and rolled into pastry sheets or strips it leaves a lattice effect. When pressed hard enough, the lattice cutter cuts the pastry so that when that pastry is pulled apart, it gives a lattice pattern to the pies or strudels over which it is draped.

LAVOCHE BREAD
(see also unleavened bread)

Extremely thin sheets of a bread-type dough made from flour, sesame or poppy seeds, salt and a liquid — usually milk or water. The mixture is baked into sheets of golden brown crisp bread which may or may not have a slight leaven to puff it. Lavoche dates back 3000 years and is a form of the earliest known bread, which was baked flat onto rocks, then onto griddle plates and, even later, baked in ovens.

LAWTONBERRY

A black berry, this sweet fruit is a cross between the blackberry and the loganberry and is used in the same ways as most other berries: in sorbets, summer puddings, mousses, creams and sauces.

LAYER CAKE
(see also cake, gâteau)

Any cake consisting of two or more layers of cake product joined with a cream or filling. Originally a layer cake consisted of two or more sponge cakes baked individually and joined with jam and cream. As tastes changed, a smaller-sized cake was preferred, so one cake was cut into two, three or more layers, and these layers were joined with cream, ganaches, buttercream, custard, jam and various spreads.

LEAVEN
(see also baking powder, sour dough, yeast)

A leaven (leavening) agent or raising agent is any substance which causes the expelling of a gas, which causes lift or rising within a mixture. The most commonly used are yeast, baking powder and sour dough.
Yeast lifts a bread dough by reacting with three major factors: food, warmth and moisture. Yeast ferments and gives off carbon dioxide gas in these conditions. Baking powder is added with the flour in a recipe. When it comes into contact with a liquid, it also gives off carbon dioxide gas.
Sour dough is the remaining portion of dough from a previously made loaf of bread. It is kept from day to day and continually refreshed by a piece from the last dough of the day. The dough is mixed with a small amount of water and flour and allowed to ferment overnight for use the following day to flavour and raise bread.

LEBKUCHEN

A traditional Christmas biscuit from Austria and Germany consisting of a rich spiced dough which is baked into different shapes and dipped in chocolate. Almost like gingerbread, the original lebkuchen was a spiced almond and sugar mixture spread onto a thin wafer and baked. The most famous lebkuchen comes from Nuremberg, Germany, where pastrycooks have specialised in the delicacy for centuries.

60 g (2oz) unsalted (sweet) butter
6 teaspoons milk
⅔ cup (8 oz) honey or golden syrup (light treacle)
2 cups (8 oz) plain (all-purpose) flour
2 tablespoons cornflour(cornstarch)
1 teaspoon mixed spice
½ teaspoon ground cardamom
½ teaspoon ground cinnamon
2 tablespoons cocoa powder
1 teaspoon bicarbonate of soda (baking soda)
2 tablespoons cornflour (cornstarch), extra
1 tablespoon caster (superfine) sugar
1 tablespoon icing (powdered) sugar
2 tablespoons unsalted (sweet) butter, melted
300 g (10 oz) dark (plain or semi sweet) chocolate, melted

Preheat oven to 180°C (350° F).
Place butter, milk and honey in a saucepan and heat slowly, stirring constantly, until mixture comes to boil. Sift flour, cornflour, spices, cocoa and bicarbonate of soda and add to butter mixture. Stir until smooth, then cover with plastic

wrap (cling film) and leave in a cool place for 2 hours. Place cornflour, caster sugar and icing sugar in a bowl and mix well. Put to one side. Line baking trays (sheets) with baking paper (parchment). Remove mixture from the saucepan and knead lightly on a floured surface. The mixture will feel stiff and gelatinous. Work quickly and lightly, being careful not to overwork the dough.

(Roll any scrap pastry once only, otherwise the mixture will become overworked.) Bake in the preheated oven for 10–12 minutes. Remove and immediately brush rounds lightly with the extra butter, then dust with the cornflour, icing sugar and caster sugar mixture. When completely cold, dip bases in the melted chocolate. Allow to set before serving.

LECITHIN

An emulsifiying agent, lecithin is useful in confectionery and chocolate work as a stabiliser. Lecithin is produced from peanuts, soya beans or corn and is available commercially. It is also found naturally in egg yolks.

LECKERLI

There are two different types of this traditional Swiss confection. Baseler leckerli is a sweet mixture of honey and flour with spices, nuts and candied peel which is baked and covered with a fondant or water icing glaze. Zurich leckerli is a mixture of almonds, sugar and egg whites which is allowed to dry and then is cooked quickly to brown the top.

Leckerli is said to have originated in Basle, Switzerland, around the start of the 17th century. The Baseler variety is generally preferred.

BASELER LECKERLI

1⅓ cups (16 fl oz) clear honey
1 teaspoon ground cinnamon
1 teaspoon ground cloves
1 teaspoon ground ginger
75 g (2½ oz) mixed (candied) peel
¼ cup (1 oz) slivered almonds
5 cups (20 oz) plain (all-purpose) flour
1½ teaspoons bicarbonate of soda (baking soda)

Icing

1 cup (6 oz) icing (powdered) sugar
2 tablespoons lemon juice
1 teaspoon clear honey

Preheat oven to 180°C (360°F).
Line two 28 x 30 x 3 cm (11 x 12 x 1¼ in) baking trays (sheets) with baking paper (parchment).
Place honey, almonds, spices and mixed peel in a large saucepan over moderate heat and stir continually as honey warms and thins. Remove from heat when honey is thin. Sift bicarbonate of soda (baking soda) with flour and add to honey mixture. Stir all ingredients together. Spread mixture between two trays and bake for 35–45 minutes. Remove from oven and immediately score into squares. Place icing sugar, honey and lemon juice in a small bowl

and place over a pot of boiling water. Stir until the icing mixure is combined and slightly warm. Brush warm icing mixture over top of baked leckerli.

ZURICH LECKERLI

3 cups (10 oz) ground almonds
1 teaspoon ground cinnamon
½ teaspoon ground cloves
1⅔ cups (10 oz) icing (powdered) sugar
3 egg whites

Preheat oven to 200°C (400°F).
Line a 28 x 30 x 3 cm (11 in x 12 in x 1¼ in) baking tray (sheet) with baking paper (parchment).
Place ground almonds, cinnamon, cloves and sugar in a large mixing bowl and combine. Lightly whisk egg whites and stir into almond mixture. Combine until the mixture forms a dough. Press mixture flat into baking tray. Leave mixture sitting uncovered for 24 hours. Score top of mixture with a sharp knife, marking it into 24 even squares. Place tray in the oven and cook for 10–15 minutes, until top is golden brown. Remove. Cool before cutting into the marked squares. Serve with coffee.

LEMON
(see also citrus/pectin)

A member of the citrus family, the lemon is the second most popular fruit used in cooking: the orange is first. It is popular for its highly flavoured zest (extracted from the skin) and essential oils, as well as for its juice, which is tart and acidic but refreshing in cakes, tarts and sorbets. Lemons originated in India and Malaysia many centuries ago — the Hindu name is 'lemoen'. Taken by traders first to the Middle East in the 14th century, the lemon next reached the shores of the Mediterranean. On its arrival in Greece, Alexander the Great suggested that he had discovered the lemon. It found little popularity as a fruit in Europe but was used as a palate cleanser in sorbets and in cakes. In his voyage of 1492, Christopher Columbus took lemons across the Atlantic to Haiti, whence they spread into mainland America.

The pectin and citric acid of the lemon is essential in the setting of jams and jellies. Wrap the lemon skin and seeds in a muslin cloth and cook in the fruit mixture. Remove the muslin bag before pouring the jam into its jars.

The citric acid content of the juice helps set royal icing. Finely sliced lemons are an attractive garnish and can also be glacéed, crystallised or frosted with egg white and sugar. The only unpleasant part of the lemon is the white pith under the skin, which becomes bitter if cooked.

This fruit has more uses than these: it is also essential to the pastry chef for cleaning copperware. Combined with a little salt, lemon cleans copper miraculously within seconds.

LEMON ASPEN

This small fruit, native to the rainforests of Australia, resembles grapes and has a colour similar to the lemon, but has an intense eucalypt, honey and lemon flavour. It is used in cakes and desserts, and can be mixed with other fruits for stewing, which will bring out its delicate flavours.

LEMON CURD

An English specialty, this is made with the juices of limes, grapefruit, oranges or mandarins and is perfect for pouring into tartlet cases. The highly flavoured tart is served as a dessert on a raspberry sauce. This recipe will not set completely solid, only firm. Lemon curd is often spread on fresh buttered bread.

3 eggs
zest and juice of 2 lemons
1 cup (7 oz) caster (superfine) sugar
150 g (5 oz) unsalted butter

Whisk eggs enough to break them down. Add sugar, then lemon juice and mix well. Chop butter into small pieces and add to mixture. Place the bowl over a bain marie or saucepan of simmering water and stir until the butter has melted. Keep stirring until the mixture thickens and coats the back of a metal spoon. Pour into tartlet cases and place in the refrigerator to firm. Store unused curd in a jar.

LEMON MERINGUE PIE

One of the world's most popular lemon desserts, this can be made as small individual pies, or one large pie. It starts with a sweet pastry base, which may or may not be lined with chocolate to avoid the moisture softening the base. The interior of the pie crust is filled with lemon curd then topped with meringue. Generally the crust and filling are already made and chilled, and when the dessert is to be served, the meringue is placed on top and grilled or flamed until golden brown.

LEMON POSSIT

A English dessert made from sweetened cream which has been reduced by boiling, and intensely flavoured with lemons. It is a sweet, yet tart, rich dessert with a velvet-smooth texture.

3 cups (24 fl oz) double cream
1¼ cups (10 oz) sugar
juice of 3 lemons
6 champagne flutes

Place all ingredients in a saucepan and mix lightly. Bring mixture to the boil and, at rapid boil point, reduce heat slightly so that it boils gently. Do not just simmer. Boil for 20 minutes. Remove from heat and cool slightly before dividing equally among 6 champagne flutes. Place the glasses in the refrigerator for 2 hours for the mixture to firm. Pour a light layer of single cream onto the top of the mixture before serving.

LEMON SNOW

1 cup (7oz) caster (superfine) sugar
2 cups (16 fl oz) boiling water
2 lemons, juice and finely grated zest
2 tablespoons cornflour(cornstarch)
2 egg whites

Place caster (superfine) sugar and water in a saucepan and bring to the boil. Mix cornflour with lemon zest and juice till smooth. When water boils, remove pan from the heat and whisk in lemon cornflour mixture. Return to heat and stir constantly until it reboils. Remove and cool. In a separate bowl, whisk the egg whites until stiff peaks form. Gently fold egg whites through the cooling lemon mixture. Refrigerate the mixture until cold. Serve.

LEMON TORTE

The lemons give the rich filling a delightful sharpness. It is ideal for a late spring outdoor lunch or a summer barbecue.

Base
1¼ cups (5 oz) plain (all-purpose) flour
½ cup (3 oz) icing (powdered) sugar
100 g (3½ oz) unsalted (sweet) butter, cut into small pieces
1 egg, lightly beaten
cold water if required

Filling
rind and juice of 5 medium-sized lemons
11 eggs
2¼ cups (17 oz) caster (superfine) sugar
1½ cups (12 fl oz) cream (single or light)
apricot glaze (see page 10)

To Decorate
220 g (7 oz) fondant, melted (see page 118)
flaked almonds, roasted (see page 5)

Preheat oven to 170°C (350°F). Grease a 23 cm (9 in) springform pan lightly with butter. Line the base with baking paper (parchment). Place flour, icing (powdered) sugar and butter in a bowl and very lightly rub in the butter until mixture resembles coarse breadcrumbs. Add egg and enough water to make a firm dough. Wrap in plastic wrap (cling film) and chill for 1 hour. Roll out chilled dough into a 27 cm (11 in) circle and line base and sides of the prepared pan with dough.

Filling
Beat lemon rind and juice, eggs, sugar and cream until thoroughly mixed. Pour into the pan. Bake for 45–50 minutes or until golden brown and firm to the touch. Cool in the pan on a wire rack.

To Decorate
When cold, remove from pan, brush the top with apricot glaze and allow to dry before applying the melted fondant. Allow fondant to dry. Sprinkle with almonds.

LEOPARD SKIN LOAF

A loaf of bread which has been brushed with a preparation of liquid yeast and rice flour (a wash) before it is baked. During baking the wash becomes crisp and blotchy and when the loaf is removed from the oven it resembles the leopard's skin. The wash is also used to flavour the bread.

LIER

A thickening agent of egg yolk or cream used in anglaises and sauces.

LIGHTNING CAKE
(see Blitzkuchen)

An orange-flavoured buttercake with nuts. An American favourite, named because it rises as quick as lightning, because of the baking powder.

LIME
(see also citrus)

A member of the citrus fruit family, limes are smaller and more rounded than lemons and their skin and flesh is green. Originally from China and Persia, limes grow well in warmer climates and areas free from frost. There are several varieties.

Limes can be used in virtually all recipes where lemons are required. Most people opt for the lemon as more limes than lemons would have to be juiced and grated. However, limes offer recipes their own flavour and make an attractive garnish when their skin is finely grated or peeled.

LINZER LEAVES

A relative of the Linzer torte, these are a European Christmas favourite, sold in many Kafe und Konditorei to be enjoyed with a cup of coffee. They are usually coated in the finest European chocolate.

2¼ cups (9 oz) plain (all-purpose) flour
1 tablespoon ground cinnamon
1 cup (7 oz) caster (superfine) sugar
1⅓ cups (5 oz) ground almonds
210 g (7 oz) unsalted (sweet) butter, cut into small pieces
1 egg, lightly beaten
juice of 1 lemon
6 teaspoons milk
milk chocolate, melted, to decorate

Preheat oven to 180°C (350°F). Line base of baking trays (sheets) with baking paper (parchment). Place flour, cinnamon, sugar and ground almonds in a bowl and mix lightly. Very lightly rub butter into flour until the mixture resembles fresh breadcrumbs. Add egg, lemon juice and enough of the milk to make a firm dough. Wrap in plastic wrap (cling film) and place in the refrigerator for 1 hour. Remove the pastry and knead lightly. Roll on a lightly floured surface to 4 mm (⅙ in) thin sheet and then, using a 5 cm (2 in) round biscuit (cookie) cutter, cut leaf shapes from the dough. Place on prepared trays and, using a sharp knife, make a line down the centre and out to the sides to resemble leaf veins. Bake for 10–12 minutes, or until cooked. Cool in the tray. Dip one side of each leaf into the melted chocolate. Make sure chocolate is set before serving.

Makes 36

Linzer Leaves

La Stupenda (see page 162). Photograph courtesy Serge Dansereau and the Sydney Regent Hotel.

LINZER TORTE

Originating in the Austrian city of Linz, the rich sweet pastry base is spread with redcurrant jam and decorated with strips of dough arranged in a lattice pattern.

2¼ cups (9 oz) plain (all-purpose) flour
¾ cup (6 oz) caster (superfine) sugar
2 cups (7 oz) ground almonds
190 g (6 oz) unsalted (sweet) butter, cut into small pieces
1 egg, lightly beaten
juice of 1 lemon
1 tablespoon milk
⅓ cup (4 oz) redcurrant jam
beaten egg wash (see page 110)
apricot glaze (see page 10)
fondant (see page 118)

Preheat oven to 200°C (400°F). Grease the base of a 23 cm (9 in) springform pan lightly with butter. Place flour, sugar and almonds in a bowl and mix lightly. Add butter and very lightly rub into flour until the mixture resembles fresh breadcrumbs. Add egg, lemon juice and sufficient milk to make a firm dough. Wrap in plastic wrap (cling film) and chill for 15 minutes.

Roll out three-quarters of the dough into a 23 cm (9 in) circle and cover the prepared base. Brush top with red currant jam. Roll out half the remaining dough thinly. Cut into narrow strips with a fluted roller cutter and arrange in a lattice pattern on top of the jam. Shape the remaining dough into a long sausage to fit around the edge of the pastry base. Trim ends and place neatly in position. Brush with egg wash, making sure that none of the egg drips on the jam. Bake for 35–40 minutes, or until the pastry is a light brown. Brush with apricot glaze and let dry before applying fondant glaze.

LIQUEURS

Liqueurs are often served with desserts, but they are also used in small amounts by the pastry chef as a flavouring in many finer recipes and preparations because of their premium flavour and quality.

While liqueurs are often used in sauces, fondants, sugar syrups or chocolate mixtures for petits fours, the pastry chef must remember that, with alcohol contents ranging from 20–60 %, only a small amount of liqueur is needed. The most popular of the liqueurs used in pastry follow:

167

Calvados
An apple-flavoured brandy used in sorbets, syrups and soufflés, and often served chilled with an apple dessert.

Cassis
A French blackcurrant liqueur used in mousses, glazes and many berry desserts.

Cointreau
A brand name product, it is one of the most popular orange-flavoured liqueurs.

Crème de Cacao
A chocolate-flavoured liqueur produced from cocoa beans. It is often used to highlight chocolate flavours, and sprinkled on thin sponge cake layers before joining them with plain buttercreams.

Crème de Menthe (mint-flavoured)
A strong refreshing green liqueur made from mint and peppermint, it is used mostly in sauces, but occasionally in mousses or ice creams as a colouring.

Curaçao Liqueur
An orange-flavoured liqueur used more than the Grand Marnier and Cointreau as it is not as expensive. It has a gin or brandy base, and is flavoured with oil from the rinds of young, green, Seville oranges.

Drambuie
Drambuie is made from a Scottish recipe. Its ingredients are Scotch whisky, honey, heather, herbs and berries. It has a magnificent flavour, and is used in ice creams, soufflés (both iced and hot) and with fruit.

Grand Marnier
An orange liqueur used when an orange flavour is required in syrups, sauces, desserts and cakes. Superb in chocolate desserts or served chilled with hot chocolate desserts. Also flamed over crêpe desserts.

Maraschino
A cherry liqueur made in Dalmatia, Eastern Europe, from maraschino cherries. It is a clear liqueur with a strong aroma and is used in cakes, fruit salads and buttercreams, or to soak or preserve glacé (candied) cherries.

Tia Maria
A coffee-flavour liqueur originally from Jamaica. It is based on a mixture of rum and spices.

LIQUORICE

A black mass confectionery made from the rootstock of the liquorice, a small shrub. The grey to brown roots are crushed for the black sweet liquid, which is then mixed with sugar and other ingredients to make the confectionery. Egyptian Empire papyrus documents detail the crushing of the liquorice root and its use as a medicine, so we know that the plant has been used for centuries. Also, the root was cut and chewed for its refreshing flavour.

In the 19th century the juice was made into two forms of confectionery. The soft and pliable liquorice is made into different shapes, straps and bands; firm liquorice is made into pastilles and sticks for sucking on. Both types contain varying amounts of pure liquorice juice, sugar, gums and flavourings.

Liquorice is made by the confectioner or pastry chef but is rarely used for anything except confectionery, because similar-tasting liqueurs are preferable.

LOAF SUGAR
(see sugar)

LOAF TINS

These are five-sided containers (base and four walls), oblong in shape and produced in an array of sizes. Ranging from small to large and from shallow to deep, the most common sizings would be 5 cm (2 in) in depth and 15–30 cm (6–12 in) in length. Loaf tins are used for baking breads, brioches, cakes and marquises.

LOGANBERRY
(see also berries)

A cross between the raspberry and the blackberry, the loganberry is a reddish-purple berry with a refreshing but slightly tart flavour. It is used in sorbets, ice creams, cakes, muffins and pies.

LOLLIPOP

A boiled sugar syrup is cooked to 155°C (310°F) then poured in small droplets onto baking paper (parchment) or into oiled moulds. A small skewer is then pressed into the droplet. An early 19th century creation, they are also made with fine pulled sugar of differing colours coiled into a circle. A firm wooden or plastic stick is pressed into the mixture before the sugar sets.

See page 167

LUCULLUS
(see also savarin)

This dessert was named after a famed and wealthy Roman General, Lucius Licinius (110–56 BC). It is said to be as magnificent as he, and should stand as tall.

It has a savarin base soaked in a sweet liqueur syrup and placed on a wafer-thin sweet pastry base. The middle of the savarin is filled with a raspberry soufflé mixture then returned to the oven to cook. It is usually served on a raspberry sauce flavoured with the same liqueur in which the savarin is soaked.

LYCHEE

A Chinese native fruit similar to a rambutan, it is a small grape-like fleshy fruit which grows inside a hairy, thick, red, yellow or orange pod. The opaque white flesh is sweet and wrapped around a central seed. It is usually served in its own juice or in a syrup.

M

MACADAMIA NUTS
(see also nuts)

This native Australian nut is also known as the Queensland nut, after the state in which it was first discovered. Dr John Macadam found it in the Queensland rainforests in 1857. The nuts, which are encased within a firm shell, are prized in cooking for their buttery, smooth flavour, and are also pressed for their oil. Macadamia nuts are now also produced in the Hawaiian islands, where their commercial viability was recognised after the crop was trialled during the 1930s.

Macadamias are expensive because of the difficulty of cracking the solid shells, and should simply be used to enhance the flavour of dishes both sweet and savoury. In pastry making they are mainly used in cakes, ice creams, biscuits (cookies) and confectionery. They are available in many styles — raw, salted, roasted, whole, crushed, chopped, ground and flaked.

MACADAMIA PIE

270 g (9 oz) sweet pastry (see page 272)
180 g (6 oz) unsalted (sweet) butter
¾ cup (6 oz) caster (superfine) sugar
3 eggs
½ cup (2 oz) plain (all-purpose) flour
180 g (6 oz) ground macadamia (Queensland) nuts
10–12 whole macadamia (Queensland) nuts
icing (powdered) sugar, for dusting

Preheat oven to 180°C (360°F).
Grease a 20 cm (8 in) pie dish (plate) well.
On a lightly floured surface, roll the pastry to fit the pie dish and line the pie dish. Place butter and sugar in a mixing bowl and cream until light and fluffy. Add eggs one at a time, combining well after each one is added. Add flour and ground macadamias and combine well, then add the whole macadamia nuts. Spread mixture in the pie dish and bake in preheated oven for 35–40 minutes, or until baked.
Remove, dust with icing sugar and cool.
Serve in slices with cream or ice cream.

MACAROONS
(see also coconut macaroons)

Macaroons are neither biscuit (cookie) nor cake. They are in fact a confection of almonds or coconut which is mixed with sugar and egg white and heated slightly. It is then spooned or piped into small rounds which are baked until golden brown so that the crust becomes firm but the inside remains soft.

The almond macaroon is a flat cookie-style confection which can be served with mousses or dipped into liqueurs or syrups to soften it. It is used as the base for many desserts and can also be crushed and used in recipes. The coconut macaroon is a thicker mixture and is spooned or dropped onto baking sheets. When baked, its base can be dipped into chocolate. While the invention of the almond macaroon is attributed to the 17th century Italians, the origin of the coconut macaroon is uncertain. The word macaroon is derived from the Greek word 'makaria', which means content, or pleasure.

MACERATE
(see also marinate, steep)

To allow a substance or article to soak in a flavoured syrup, sauce or marinade. Macerating involves a shorter period of soaking than marinating. It is usually fruits that are macerated, in alcohol, to increase their flavour and juice.

MADEIRA

From the island of Madeira, this sweet or fortified wine looks similar to a sherry but has a richer flavour. Traditionally served in small glasses with high tea or afternoon tea, it was originally also used in the well-known Madeira cake. Now it is simply served as an accompaniment to it.

MADEIRA CAKE

3 cups (12 oz) plain (all-purpose) flour
3 teaspoons baking powder (soda)
360 g (12 oz) unsalted (sweet) butter
1¾ cups (12 oz) caster (superfine) sugar
6 eggs
1¼ cups (4 oz) ground almonds
grated rind and juice of 2 lemons
icing (powdered) sugar, for dusting

Preheat oven to 170°C (340°F).
Lightly grease a 20 x 10 x 5 cm (8 x 4 x 2 in) loaf tin with butter and line with baking paper (parchment).
Mix flour and baking powder and sift twice. Beat butter and sugar until creamy, light and fluffy. Add eggs one at a time, beating very well after each one is added. Gently fold in by hand sifted flour and baking powder, almonds and lemon juice and rind. Do not over mix. Pour into prepared tin.
Bake for 50–55 minutes, or until a skewer inserted into the centre of the cake comes out dry and the cake has shrunk slightly away from the sides of the tin.
Cool for 5 minutes before turning out onto a cake rack.
When cold, dust with icing sugar.

MADELEINES

Traditionally, madeleines are small, light scalloped sponge cakes flavoured with orangeflower water or rosewater. They are baked in special madeleine moulds or trays that give them their scalloped shape. The little cakes are served with tea or coffee. Many recipes exist for these little cakes, which can be prepared in a range of flavours. Lemon, orange, lime, coffee, cinnamon or chocolate are the main ones used.

It is suggested that King Stanislas's female cook, who was named Madeleine, made them for a dinner the King was having with Voltaire in 1730. They were flavoured with orangeflower water, and the King loved them so much, he sent a package of the delicate little cakes to his daughter, Marie Leczinski, who suggested naming them after the cook.

Others credit either Madeleine Paulmier of Commercy or the pastry chef Avice with having invented them.

CHOCOLATE ORANGE MADELEINES

Rosewater is the essence of these Madeleines.

150 g (5 oz) unsalted (sweet) butter, softened
1¼ cups (7 oz) icing (powdered) sugar, sifted
3 eggs
1½ cups (6 oz) plain (all-purpose) flour, sifted
2 tablespoons cocoa powder, sifted
1 teaspoon baking powder (soda)
1 tablespoon orange juice, freshly squeezed
1 teaspoon rosewater
finely grated rind of 1 orange
extra icing (powdered) sugar, for dusting

Preheat oven to 180°C (350°F).
Lightly grease a madeleine tray (pan).
Cream unsalted butter and sifted icing sugar until they are light and fluffy. Add eggs, one at a time, to the creamed mixture, combining well after each one is added. Add plain sifted flour, cocoa powder and baking powder to the mixture with the freshly squeezed orange juice, rosewater and orange rind. Mix until all ingredients are completely blended.
Place mixture in madeleine moulds so that they are three-quarters full. Bake in preheated oven for 15–20 minutes, or until each madeleine is springy to the touch. When baked, turn out immediately and dust lightly with icing sugar. Serve warm.

Makes 24

MAI LANDERLI

These are traditional lemon-flavoured German Christmas cookies.

2½ cups (10 oz) plain (all-purpose) flour
1 teaspoon baking powder (soda)
½ cup (3 oz) icing (powdered) sugar
¼ cup (2 oz) caster (superfine) sugar
150 g (5 oz) unsalted (sweet) butter
5 egg yolks
zest of 1 lemon
1 egg, lightly beaten
icing sugar, for dusting

Preheat oven to 180°C (350°F).
Line a baking sheet with baking paper (parchment).
Place sifted flour, icing sugar, baking powder and sugar in a mixing bowl and lightly rub butter through until the mixture resembles fresh breadcrumbs. Add egg yolks and lemon zest to the mixture and continue to combine until a dough is formed. Wrap dough in plastic wrap (cling film) and allow to rest in the refrigerator for 30 minutes.
Remove and knead lightly, then, on a lightly floured surface, roll out to 3 mm (⅛ in) in thickness. Cut biscuits out using a star-shaped cutter, and place on the prepared sheet.
Brush the top of each biscuit with lightly beaten egg, then bake in the preheated oven for 8–10 minutes.
Remove when baked and cool on the tray.
Dust lightly with icing sugar before serving.

MAIDS OF HONOUR

These are small English almond cheesecakes baked in puff pastry cases. It is said that in 1514, Anne Boleyn, at that time maid of honour to Henry VIII's sister Mary, was enjoying a picnic with the King and guests in Richmond, Surrey. When the King tasted the small cheesecakes, he demanded to know what the delightful cakes were called. As they as yet had no name, the King declared that they were as sweet as his sister's maid of honour, and thus they were named.

MAIZE

(see also cornmeal, polenta)

Also known as corn, maize is a member of the cereal family and consists of cobs made up of many white or yellow corn pieces or ears. These ears of corn are ground and used as polenta or cornmeal, cornflour (cornstarch) or semolina. Glucose or corn syrup can be produced from them as well. Maize is used in the production of porridges, cornbread and pancakes, as a thickening agent, and in the form of corn oil. It was first introduced into Europe by Cortés, who brought it back with him from his travels to the Americas.

MALAKOFF

Malakoff is the name given to a cake in which nuts are used in some form, or are a major part of its decoration.

MALAKOFF TORTE

A rich torte with a base of japonaise meringue joined together with a strong coffee cream. Allowed to sit overnight or for 24 hours, the cake is soft, rich and delicious.

Japonaise Base

4 egg whites
⅔ cup (5 oz) caster (superfine) sugar
⅔ cup (2½ oz) roasted almonds, ground
⅓ cup (1½ oz) cornflour (cornstarch)
1½ tablespoons icing (powdered) sugar

Mai Landerli

Coffee Cream
300 g (10 oz) unsalted butter
⅓ cup (2½ oz) sugar
¼ cup (1 oz) roasted almonds, ground
2 tablespoons instant coffee powder
1 tablespoon warm water
¼ cup (2 fl oz) cream

Preheat oven to 180°C (350°F).
Line 3 baking trays (sheets) with baking paper
(parchment) and draw a 20 cm (8 in) circle on each.
Beat egg whites until stiff peaks form and gradually beat in
sugar, a spoonful at a time. Beat at top speed for
5–8 minutes or until sugar is completely dissolved.
Mix almonds, cornflour and icing sugar, then very gently
fold in beaten egg whites by hand. Divide the mixture
evenly among the three sheets, and spread within the
edges of the drawn circles. Bake for 30–35 minutes.

Cool on the trays on a cake rack.
When the meringues are cold, spread one with the coffee
cream, place the next base on top, spread with more cream
and then place the last base on top of this, using a
small amount of the coffee cream on the top layer.
Do not cream or decorate the sides, but sprinkle chopped,
lightly roasted hazelnuts over the top of the cake.
Decorate with 12 rosettes of the coffee cream.
Place the cake in the refrigerator for 24 hours, then serve.

Coffee Cream
Place the butter and sugar in the bowl of an electric mixer
and beat until light and fluffy. Add the coffee to the warm
water to dissolve and cool slightly. When this is cool,
add the ground roasted almonds, coffee and cream
to the whipped butter. Stir until all ingredients are
well combined, then use immediately.

MALT
(see also sugar)

Malt has been produced from barley since the Bronze and Neolithic periods. These days it is produced from both barley and wheat by soaking the grains and allowing them to germinate or sprout. After germination, they are dried and crushed into a fine powder known as malt powder. This powder can then be converted to malt syrup by soaking and heating the powder and allowing it to ferment. Malt powder is used in drinks and for baking some cake and biscuit (cookie) mixtures, while malt syrup is generally used in the bread trade, where it assists with the development of the dough and fermentation of the yeast.

MALTAIS

This classic French petit four is made from a sweet paste of mixed (candied) peel and almond meal which is rolled thinly. Discs of the mixture are cut and allowed to dry for 24 hours. They are then spread half with white Kirsch-flavoured fondant and half with a fondant flavoured with pink orange blossom. After being allowed to dry again, they are served with coffee.

MALTAISE, A LA

A term describing pastry mixtures that are made using oranges or that have oranges as their predominant flavour.

MANDARINS
(see also citrus)

Mandarins are members of the citrus family, and are one of the five most popular citrus fruits used in pastry work, the others being oranges, lemons, limes and grapefruit. Mandarins are the best of these fruits to use for chocolate dipping or sugar glazing, as they are the only citrus fruit whose segments peel apart easily for dipping. They taste and look similar to oranges, but have a slightly sweeter flavour, and their skin is easier to remove. The firm skin surrounding each segment prevents the juice bleeding into mixtures, tartlets, and petits fours.

MANGO

Originally from India, the mango is today grown in many tropical areas. A thin-skinned, sweet-fleshed fruit with a yellow to red skin, it has a large, firm flat seed in its centre which must be cut away from the flesh. It is very much enjoyed eaten on its own, and is used in cakes, mousses and fillings, as well as for making pickles, chutneys and jams (conserves).

MANQUE

A member of the sponge cake family, 'manque' is French for mistake or failure, and is one of the many dessert or pastry creations which have been produced as a result of errors or mistakes made by pastry chefs. French pastry chef Felix was apparently attempting to make a savoy sponge mixture when, in his haste, he made a mistake and was unable to get the egg whites to whisk stiffly. Frustrated, he simply added the other ingredients, plus almonds and butter, and baked the cake. When the cake was cold, he filled it and covered it with a praline mixture. The result was such a success with his customers that it remained on the menu.

MAPLE SYRUP
(see also sugar)

A sweet sap obtained from one of some 200 varieties of maple tree, it has been used since the Indians first found the syrup by accident. While out hunting, one of a party of Indians is said to have shot an arrow into the maple tree. When collecting the arrow, he found that it was covered in a rich syrup. Maple syrup is tapped from the tree trunks during spring and is only collected for a short 6–8 weeks of the year. The golden syrup is then reduced to give it its sweet flavour, colour and aroma. Maple syrup is traditionally an accompaniment for pancakes, but it can also be used as a flavouring in many tarts and cakes or as a substitute for golden syrup (light treacle) or corn syrup.

MARASCHINO
(see also liqueurs)

This cherry liqueur was made originally in Trieste, Italy, from maraschino cherries. It is a clear liqueur with a strong aroma and is used in cakes, fruit salads and buttercreams, or to soak or preserve glacé (candied) cherries.

MARBLE
(see also chocolate, feathering)

A decorative effect given to cakes and decorations such as chocolate or fondant. Whereas feathering refers to organised fine piped lines that are dragged into a design using a toothpick, marbling involves mixing two or three colours together in any manner and then mixing them with a finger or toothpick to marble the colours together.

MARBLE CAKE

2¼ cups (9 oz) plain (all-purpose) flour
2 teaspoons baking powder (soda)
160 g (5½ oz) unsalted (sweet) butter
1 cup (7 oz) caster (superfine) sugar
3 eggs
1 cup (8 fl oz) milk
red (cochineal) food colouring
3 tablespoons cocoa powder blended with
2 tablespoons water to form a paste
½ quantity quick no-fuss buttercream (see page 43)

Preheat oven to 180°C (350°F).
Grease a 20 x 10 x 5 cm (8 x 4 x 2 in) loaf tin very lightly with butter and line the base with baking paper (parchment).
Mix flour and baking powder and sift twice. Beat butter and sugar until creamy, light and fluffy. Add eggs one at a time, beating very well after each one is added. Gently fold in by hand the sifted flour and baking powder alternately with the

milk. Divide mixture among 3 bowls. Add a few drops of red food colouring to one, mix the blended cocoa and water into another, and leave the remaining mixture plain.

Place a spoonful of each mixture in turn into the prepared tin. Bake for 50–55 minutes, or until a skewer inserted into centre of the cake comes out dry and the cake has shrunk slightly away from the sides of the tin. Cool in the pan for 5 minutes before turning out onto a cake rack. When cold, cover top with buttercream.

MARBLE SLAB

A stone slab which can be used for pastry, chocolate and sugar work, as the marble is non-porous, and tends to keep a constant coolness, unless directly heated. Marble slabs will not absorb flavours, fat or moisture, and they clean easily. When pouring sugar onto them, ensure they are lightly oiled, but for chocolate work, make certain they are spotlessly clean.

MARGARINE
(see also fats)

Under the directive of Napoleon III, who wanted cheaper food products for his army, scientists and chemists were asked to invent new food products for him to take on campaigns. The winner of the competition was Mège-Mouriès, who invented a butter substitute made from the fat of animals and milk. Mège-Mouriès found such success with his product that he patented it in the late 1860s, and began production in his own factory soon thereafter, selling the first margarine commercially by the middle 1870s. Initially it was not a great commercial success but once it was allowed to be coloured, the sales rose dramatically.

The name 'margarine' comes from the Greek word 'margaron' (pearl), which refers to the microscopic pearl-like crystals called margarites within the mixture. Margarine by law must contain 80% fat, no more than 3% salt and no more than 16% water or moisture, although this can differ from country to country.

Margarine can be used in place of butter in some cases, although it is better to use the real article for the fullest flavour and quality, especially in pastries. Industrial margarines with a high melting point are produced specifically for use in pastries and doughs in large volume bakeries and pastry kitchens, but these tend to leave a film of fat on the roof of one's mouth after eating. The best use to which these fats can be put is margarine sculpting.

MARGARINE SCULPTING
(see also centrepieces)

A decorative and cheap method of producing centrepieces and table decorations. A skilled pastry artist can produce any design imaginable using margarine as the modelling medium. Because it has a high melting point, margarine does not melt in one's hands and can easily be coloured for decorative effects. When using margarine for large major works that would usually be very heavy, the pastry chef can begin with a base of fine wire mesh or styrofoam and simply paste the margarine around the outside.

MARGUERITE CAKE

This is traditionally made in a round cake tin which has flowers or small mounds moulded into the base for decoration.

180 g (6 oz) unsalted (sweet) butter, softened
¼ cup (2 oz) caster (superfine) sugar
finely chopped zest and juice of 1 orange
5 eggs, separated
⅓ cup (2½ oz) caster (superfine) sugar, extra
1 cup (4 oz) plain (all-purpose) flour
1⅓ cups (5 oz) ground almonds
½ cup (2 oz) cornflour (cornstarch)
⅛ teaspoon ground cinnamon
icing (powdered) sugar, for serving

Preheat oven to 180°C (350°F). Lightly grease a 20–22 cm (8–9 in) springform cake tin or moulded marguerite cake tin and line with baking paper (parchment).

Place butter, sugar, orange juice and zest in the bowl of an electric mixer. Beat until light and fluffy. Add egg yolks one at a time, beating well after each one is added. In a separate bowl, whisk eggs until light and fluffy and stiff peaks form. Gradually add the sugar while still whisking and continue whisking until all sugar is incorporated and dissolved.

Fold egg whites into butter mixture along with the sifted flours, almonds and cinnamon. Pour batter into prepared tin and bake in preheated oven for 70–80 minutes.

Remove and cool. Invert cake, dust with icing sugar and serve.

MARINADE
(see also macerate, steep)

The liquid in which a product is marinated.

MARINATE
(see also macerate, steep)

To soak a product in a liquid so that the flavour of the liquid is imparted to that product.

MARMALADE
(see also citrus, jam)

Marmalade was originally made from quinces. In the 17th century the quince was dropped and oranges and lemons used instead to make the bitter tart jam (conserve). The name 'marmalada' (meaning quince) remained, however, and was eventually changed to marmalade. The first citrus marmalade is accredited to a Scottish greengrocer's wife from Dundee who, in 1790, made the spread from citrus peelings. In 1981 the European Economic Community (now the European Union) ruled that the name marmalade must refer to the spread made with citrus fruits, not to the quince product made under the same name.

To make marmalade, the fruit flesh is boiled with sugar and water until the jam-setting consistency is reached. It is important, though, to cook the pips and pith in with the mixture as these are a prime source of pectin, which assists in the setting of the product.

Marquise Step-by-Step

Step 1: After having whipped the chocolate filling until it is a thick, smooth, spreading consistency, line the base and the two longest sides of the pan with strips of cake.

Step 2: Place half the filling mixture into the lined pan.

Step 3: Use a palette knife to spread the filling into the corners. Smooth the surface.

Step 4: Place another strip of cake on top of the filling mixture. Remove the baking paper (parchment) and press the cake onto the filling.

Step 5: Place the other half of the filling mixture in the pan.

Step 6: Repeat Step 3, and then place the last strip of cake on top of the filling. Press so that it is firmly held by the mixture. Remove the paper and chill. See page 176.

5 large bitter oranges
3 lemons
8 cups (64 fl oz) warm water
8 cups (56 oz) caster (superfine) sugar

Clean and peel the fruit. Reserve the pith in one small bowl and place the coloured rind or zest in another.
Cut fruit into pieces and place the pips in the pith bowl. Wrap the pith and pips in a small piece of muslin cloth and tie this at one end. Place the cut fruit, the bag of pith and pips and the finely chopped zest in a large saucepan or stock pot and bring to the boil with the water. Reduce heat slightly and allow the mixture to gently simmer until it has reduced in volume by half. Remove the muslin bag and squeeze firmly to remove any juices.
Weigh the hot liquid, and for every 500 g (1 lb) pulp, add 500 g (1 lb) sugar. Place sugar and pulp back over the heat and bring back to the boil. Boil for a further 15–20 minutes, or until the mixture jells when a teaspoonful is dropped into cold water.
Pour the marmalade directly into glass jars which have been washed in boiling water and drip dried. Cover and store at room temperature for 1–2 days before eating.

MARQUISE

A thickened mixture of light mousse or a filling of butter consistency which is placed inside a lining of cake, sponge or biscuits (cookies). The term is also used to refer to the finished item. Chocolate marquise is the most common and is a filling of rich chocolate and cream whipped until it is of butter texture and spread inside a thin coffee-flavoured sponge. Savoiardi biscuits soaked in coffee or liqueur can also be used. The filling mixture can also be made using nougat paste (hazelnut paste) or white chocolate, and flavoured using spices or fruits.

CHOCOLATE MARQUISE TORTE

Prepare the filling the day before, cut the baking paper (parchment) accurately, and allow enough time for chilling.

Filling
2¾ cups (22 fl oz) fresh cream (single or light)
180 g (6 oz) white chocolate, chopped
375 g (12 oz) dark (plain or semi-sweet) chocolate, chopped

Cake
3 tablespoons instant coffee powder
¼ cup (2 fl oz) water
6 egg yolks
180 g (6 oz) dark (plain or semi-sweet) chocolate, chopped
6 egg whites
½ cup (4 oz) caster (superfine) sugar
cocoa powder, for dusting

Filling
Make the filling the day before you make the cake.
Heat cream in a small saucepan. Remove from heat and add all the chocolate. Stir until chocolate melts.
Cool, cover and refrigerate for 24 hours.

Cake
Preheat oven to 180°C (350°F). Line a 35 x 30 cm (14 x 12 in) baking sheet with baking paper (parchment). Dissolve instant coffee in water and blend into egg yolks. Place chocolate in a bowl and melt over hot water. Cool slightly and mix into the coffee mixture. Beat egg whites until stiff peaks form, then gradually beat in sugar, a spoonful at a time. Beat until sugar is dissolved. Take a spoonful of beaten egg whites and mix by hand into the coffee mixture. Gently fold in the remaining beaten egg whites. Spread the mixture very thinly on the prepared sheet and bake for 10–12 minutes, or until the top of the cake springs back when lightly touched. Turn out onto a cake rack to cool.

To Assemble
Line a 7 x 25 x 5 cm (3 x 10 x 2 in) bar or loaf tin with baking paper.
Cut three rectangles of cake the same size as the base of the tin and two rectangles to line the two long sides of the tin. Line base and sides with the rectangles of cake. Whip the chilled chocolate filling until it thickens. Carefully spoon half the mixture into prepared tin. Use a small palette knife to spread mixture into corners. Smooth. Top with another rectangle of cake and carefully spoon the remaining filling into tin. Top with remaining rectangle of cake and press down lightly. Refrigerate for 4 hours.
To serve, turn out the torte onto a serving platter, peel off the baking paper and dust the top with cocoa powder.
Cut with a hot knife, using a smooth cutting action.

See pages 174–75

MARRON
(see also chestnut)

A variety of chestnut used to flavour cakes, mousses, biscuits (cookies) and confectionery. Marrons glacés are made by poaching or boiling the chestnuts in a sweet sugar syrup, and soaking them over a period of time in an increasingly thicker solution of sugar, in much the same way that fruit is crystallised. Marrons glacés are said to have been enjoyed by Louis XIV, who ate them after dinner.

MARSHMALLOW
(see also confectionery)

A confectionery item, marshmallow was originally made from the roots of the medicinal plant, marshmallow. When boiled, the roots made a soft spongy product which was also called marshmallow. These days, marshmallow is produced from sugar, water and gelatine, the mixture being boiled, cooled and whisked until it is smooth, white, light and fluffy.

¼ cup (1½ oz) gelatine powder
1½ cups (12 fl oz) warm water
3 cups (21 oz) caster (superfine) sugar
¾ cup (6 fl oz) warm water
2 teaspoons lemon juice
1 teaspoon rosewater
desiccated (shredded) coconut, plain or toasted, for rolling

Sprinkle gelatine over the cold water. Place sugar and warm water in a saucepan over gentle heat. Bring to the boil and add soaked gelatine. Boil steadily for 20 minutes. Remove saucepan from the heat and stir the mixture occasionally while it becomes lukewarm. Pour the liquid into a mixing bowl and add the lemon juice and rosewater. Whisk until it becomes pure white and triples in volume. Pour the whisked marshmallow into an 18 x 28 x 2 cm (7 x 11 x ¾ in) tray (jelly roll pan). Alternatively, it can be poured into shaped moulds in a starch tray or piped into shapes.
Refrigerate overnight.
Remove the marshmallow from the refrigerator and use a sharp hot knife to cut it into small squares. Roll each square in the coconut. Store in an airtight container.

Note: To remove the marshmallows from the moulding containers (but not the starch tray), the bottom of the containers may need to be quickly dipped into warm water.

Makes 30—36

MARZIPAN
(see also almond paste, overflodigshorn, rout biscuits)

Also known as almond paste, marzipan is a sweetened mixture of ground almonds, liquid glucose (corn syrup) and icing (powdered) sugar. Good quality marzipan is usually produced in Europe and should contain a high ratio of almonds to sugar. There should not be a strong smell of almond essence — marzipan should not contain this at all. In many countries inferior products such as almond paste are produced from apricot kernels, almond essence, sugar and glucose. This mixture cannot be used for baking because of its high sugar content.

Marzipan was first invented during the 1300s when, in the midst of a famine, an order of nuns helped the local townsfolk out by making the closest thing to bread they could. Their creation, using of sugar and almonds, is now famous around the world. The name 'marzipan' is said to derive from the name St Marks Bread, the almond loaf having been made in his honour. In Italian, this translates as San Marco Pani and so eventually over time the paste came to be known as marzipan. Another theory, however, is that the name derives from coins called 'mataban'. The term 'mataban' was eventually used to refer to the weights used when purchasing sweets individually, then to refer to the individual sweets themselves, the name having changed slightly from mataban to mazapan and eventually to marzipan.

Marzipan can be used in baking to give a subtle almond flavour to cakes, biscuits (cookies), mousses, breads or confectionery. The Scandinavians are famous for their wedding cakes of kransekage, a mixture of marzipan, sugar and egg whites.

Marzipan is used on wedding cakes to prevent the oils in the outside covering of fondant or icing being absorbed into the cake.

Marzipan Storage
Marzipan can absorb moisture or dry out, so careful storage is essential. If it absorbs moisture it will begin to dissolve, and if it dries out, it will begin to ferment. Marzipan should be covered in plastic wrap (cling film) and placed in an airtight container. Store at room temperature in a dark place for up to 3 weeks.

To Tint or Colour Marzipan
When modelling either fruit or vegetables there are two ways of colouring them. The European way is to mould or shape the plain (white or clear) marzipan into its final form, then allow it to set and dry out overnight. It then forms a skin which will absorb the colours painted on later by hand. The American method is to mould the product from a basic colour suitable to that fruit or vegetable and perfect the colour later by painting in the details.

To create a basic coloured marzipan using the American method, flatten the piece of marzipan to be coloured and add a drop of food colouring to the centre. Fold the marzipan to enclose the colouring. Lightly knead the marzipan until the colouring is completely absorbed. Using the same method, continue to add food colouring drop by drop until the required colour is achieved.

When you use food colouring to create different coloured marzipans, be careful not to get it on your clothes, as it stains.

Marzipan Bananas
Approximately 300 g (10 oz) marzipan will make 12 bananas. Roll a small piece of yellow-tinted marzipan in the palm of your hand until it forms a ball. Roll into a sausage shape, using slight pressure on one side while rolling, to taper the sausage. Bend slightly to resemble a banana. Square off the thickest end by pinching it between three fingers. Use the back of a spoon or knife to smooth the curved surface of the banana. Allow to dry for 1 hour before painting with green food colouring and melted dark (plain or semi-sweet) chocolate (see page 60).

Marzipan Carrots
Approximately 250 g (8 oz) marzipan will make 12 carrots. Roll a small piece of orange-tinted marzipan between the palms of your hands until it forms a ball. Roll back and forth to taper the ball at one end. The narrow end should be short and blunt, not pointed. Place the carrot on a bench (counter) top and use the back of a knife to lightly score marks all over the carrot.

Marzipan Cherries
Approximately 150 g (5 oz) marzipan and 100 g (3½ oz) dark (plain or semi-sweet) chocolate will make 12 finished cherries.
For each bunch of cherries, roll two small pieces of red-tinted (use cochineal) marzipan into balls and set them close together on a flat surface. Into the top of each ball press a toothpick, to make small depressions where the stalk will go. On a piece of baking paper (parchment), pipe large V shapes of melted dark chocolate (see page 62). The V will form the stalk of each bunch and should be large enough at the open end to be inserted into the holes in the red balls.
Allow the chocolate to set in the refrigerator, then peel it from the paper. Insert the chocolate pieces into the tops of the balls and press in slightly.

Marzipan

Marzipan strawberries

Marzipan cherries

Marzipan frogs

Marzipan lemons, bananas, oranges, cherries and strawberries (see pages 177, 179)

Marzipan Flowers

Approximately 150 g (5 oz) marzipan will make 12 flowers. Roll out a small piece of appropriately tinted marzipan to a thickness of 2 mm (1/12 in). Cut out required shapes using a fluted round cutter. Place a piece of marzipan in the palm of the hand and use a marzipan tool or a smooth round object to shape a flower. Only a slight amount of pressure is needed. The marzipan will curl at the edges to form a flower.

Marzipan Frog

Approximately 125 g (4 oz) of marzipan will make one frog. A small amount of white and dark chocolate is also required. Roll 100 g (3½ oz) of green-tinted marzipan into a sausage shape about 1½ cm (½ in) wide and 5 cm (2 in) long. Place three fingers one third of the way along the sausage and roll the marzipan so that three indentations are formed and the marzipan is lengthened by 2 cm (¾ in). On the other end of the sausage, roll the marzipan so that there are two indentations, stretching the marzipan out a further 2 cm (¾ in). Cut down the middle of both stretched ends, leaving a whole piece of unrolled sausage shape in the centre. Spread apart the two halves of the longer rolled end and sit the rest of the piece upright. Bend the two long pieces of marzipan up so that they look like bent frogs' legs and sit them either side of the body. Set the two short halves on each side between the legs. To make the head of the frog, take the rest of the green-tinted marzipan and roll it into a ball. Using your thumb, make two large indentations for the eyes at the top of the ball and push out the bottom of the ball for a mouth. Sit the head on top of the body. Using a sharp knife, cut the mouth slightly so that it is open. Using melted white chocolate, pipe two balls of chocolate into the eye sockets. Dot each eyeball with a little melted dark chocolate.

Marzipan Holly and Berries

Approximately 200 g (7 oz) marzipan will make 12 holly leaves and berries. Roll out a small piece of green-tinted marzipan to a thickness of 2 mm (1/12 in). Use a holly-shaped cutter or a plain round cutter and a small, sharp kife to cut the holly leaf. Roll small pieces of red-tinted marzipan into balls for the holly spray.

Marzipan Leaves

Approximately 200 g (7 oz) marzipan will make 12 leaves. Roll a small piece of green-tinted marzipan between the palms of the hands to form a ball. Roll between the base of the hands to taper one end. One end should be pointed. Place the tapered marzipan onto a bench (counter) top and flatten two sides to shape a leaf, leaving a central vein. Use a sharp knife to remove the leaf from the bench, and mark veins down the sloping sides.

Marzipan Oranges and Lemons

Approximately 200 g (7 oz) marzipan will make 12 of each fruit. To make an orange, roll a small piece of orange-tinted marzipan into a ball. Roll the ball back and forth over the rough side of a fine grater to give it the texture of an orange. Press a clove into one side for the stalk. To make a lemon, roll a small piece of yellow-tinted marzipan into a ball. Roll it between the palms of your hands so that both ends of the ball are slightly tapered. Roll the piece of marzipan over the rough side of a fine grater to give it the texture of a lemon. Using a toothpick, insert two small holes into both ends of the lemon. Allow the lemon to dry for 1 hour before painting both of the tapered ends with a touch of light green food colouring.

Marzipan Pumpkins

Approximately 400 g (13 oz) marzipan will make 12 pumpkins and their stalks. Roll a small piece of orange-tinted marzipan into a ball shape. Hold the ball between your thumb and finger and, using the handle of a knife or the side of a pen, mark five lines from top to bottom around the sides of the ball. Place the balls on a flat surface and, using your thumb, press down slightly on the top of each ball to give a slight indent where all the lines meet. For the stalk, press a little piece of green marzipan which has been rolled into a sausage shape into the top of the indentation. To make the pumpkin into a jack-o'-lantern, press 2 triangles of dark brown marzipan into the orange marzipan for the eyes, and make a jagged mouth with a sharp knife.

Marzipan Strawberries

Approximately 200 g (7 oz) marzipan will make 12 strawberries and their stalks. Roll a small piece of pink- or red-tinted marzipan (2–3 drops of red, or cochineal, colouring) into a ball shape and then slightly taper one side of the ball by rolling it back and forth between the palm of your hand. It should look like a flattened pear. Press a toothpick into the larger end of the tapered ball to make a small hole. Roll the piece of marzipan gently back and forth over the rough side of a fine grater to give it the markings of a strawberry. Take a small piece of green-tinted marzipan, pinch it into a four-pointed star, flatten it and attach to the top of the strawberry for the hull.

Marzipan Icing

To cover a 23 cm (9 in) cake, roll out 500 g (16 oz) marzipan on a floured surface, rolling it 3–4 cm (1–1½ in) wider than the top of the cake. This will cover the top and sides of the cake. The cake will have been covered with a cream or glaze. Slide both hands underneath the piece of marzipan to pick it up. Slowly place in the centre of the cake, letting it fall from your hands as you pull them away. Smooth the top and sides of the marzipan to remove any air bubbles and stretch downwards to fit. If air bubbles remain, prick carefully with a toothpick or pin to expel the air.

Baking with Marzipan

Marzipan used in baking must have a higher proportion of almonds than sugar. If the proportion of sugar is too high, the marzipan will boil instead of bake. The preferred ratio is 66% almond to 34% sugar. This rule does not apply to simnel cake.

MARZIPAN — ALMOND HORNS

A traditional petit four of the Scandinavian countries, these almond horns can be finished in a number of ways. Coated entirely in chocolate, left plain or drizzled with chocolate or royal icing, they are delicious and can be used on all sorts of occasions.

540 g (18 oz) marzipan (almond paste)
1¼ cups (9 oz) caster (superfine) sugar
4 egg whites
2¼ cups (8 oz) flaked almonds
210 g (7 oz) dark (plain or semi-sweet) chocolate,
melted (see page 62)

Preheat oven to 180° (350°F). Line a baking sheet with a single sheet of baking paper (parchment).
Place marzipan and sugar in a bowl and mix until they form a solid mass. Slowly add egg whites until a stiff piping consistency is achieved (this may require more or less than the amount of egg white stated, depending on the brand of marzipan used). When mixture is ready (better too stiff than too wet), take small tablespoonfuls and, on a flat surface, roll them into the flaked almonds until sausage shapes are formed. Alternatively the mixture can be rolled into a sausage shape and left plain. Place sausage shapes directly on the baking sheet, making certain they are in straight lines.
When the sheet is full, bake in the preheated oven for 8–10 minutes, or until golden brown.
Remove and cool on the baking sheet.
When cool, dip the bases into melted chocolate (see page 62) and allow to set before eating.

Note: The sausage shapes can sit close together as they
should not spread if the correct marzipan is used.
If uncertain as to the correct marzipan, place a
single biscuit on the baking sheet and bake it.
If this doesn't bake correctly as indicated, the mixture
will not be any good for this type of biscuit (cookie).

MASCARPONE
(see also cream cheese, tirami-su)

Deriving from the Spanish term 'mas que bueno', which means very tasty or delicious, mascarpone is a member of the cream cheese or soft unripened cheese family. It is an Italian cheese which is used in desserts for a rich, creamy texture. It is famous for its inclusion in tirami-su. Looking almost like stiffly whipped smooth cream, mascarpone is soft and buttery, and can be served on its own (rather like whipped cream or ice cream), with brioche slices and fruits or with any dessert, as desired. The neutral flavour of mascarpone allows it to blend well with spices, herbs, fruits and liqueurs.

MASK
(see also cake decorating)

To completely coat or cover a cake or pastry with a sauce, buttercream, layer of marzipan or fondant, chocolate or jelly.

MATCHES
(see allumettes)

MATZOH
(see also flatbread)

Matzoh is a thin flat unleavened crispbread that plays a major role in the Jewish faith. During certain times, the fermentation of breads is forbidden. This is a way of commemorating the exit of the Israelites from Egypt, that was so speedy that the breads were left behind. Matzoh cakes or crackers are also crushed into various grades to use as flour for making cakes and slices during Passover.

MEASURING JUG OR GLASS

Made from glass, plastic or metal, measuring jugs vary in size and are marked in different measurements from country to country. They are used to measure the correct amount of hot or cold fluids for any given recipe.

MEAT PIE

The meat pie is said to be the cousin of the Châteaubriand, which was invented for the Vicomte de Châteaubriand and consisted of fillet steak wrapped and baked in a pastry casing. Over the centuries, a cheaper, more varied meat filling was used instead, and the pastry was baked in a pie shape.
The basic meat pie consists of a shortcrust base filled with a meat filling and traditionally topped with a thin layer of well-puffed puff pastry. Usually well seasoned, it provides a quick and easy meal, allowing one to have a meal of meat, and perhaps vegetables, in a handy pastry casing while on the run or in a hurry. Fillings can range from mince meat, pork, steak and kidney and any other combination desired, and they can range in size from small individual pies through to the family pie of about 22–23 cm (9 in) in diameter.

MELBA, DAME NELLIE

Dame Nellie Melba (1861–1931) was a great Australian opera singer. She was born Helen Porter Mitchell in Melbourne, the city after which she took her stage name. Escoffier met her, and named Melba Toast after her, as the thin slices of toast were all she would eat before her performances. The equally famous Peach Melba is also named after her. It consists of a blanched, skinned peach which is set on top of vanilla ice cream and covered with a rich red berry sauce of raspberries or strawberries.

PEACH MELBA

Dip a peach into boiling water and remove the skin. Place it on a slice of vanilla ice cream which is sitting on a thin sablé biscuit and pour Melba sauce over it. Peach Melba can be decorated with a little spun sugar or served plain.

Melba Sauce
250 g (8 oz) raspberries
250 g (8 oz) strawberries
210 g (7 oz) icing (powdered) sugar
¼ cup (3 oz) liquid glucose (corn syrup)
juice of 1 lemon

MELBA TOAST

Toast one side of a slice of bread, remove the crusts and then slice the toast through the middle to create two slices from the one. Toasted the uncooked sides. Melba toast is great for dips and hors d'oeuvres.

MELON

(see also honeydew melon, rockmelon, watermelon)

The most popular melons served or used in pastry are the rockmelon (or cantaloupe), the honeydew melon and the watermelon. Each of these consists of a firm outer skin which protects soft, watery flesh of differing colours. The rockmelon has an orange-coloured flesh, and contains its seeds in an otherwise hollow centre. The honeydew melon has a green, lime-coloured flesh and as with the rockmelon, contains its seeds in its hollow centre. The watermelon has the thickest skin of the three, having a bright green casing which holds the red- or pink-coloured flesh. The seeds are scattered throughout the watery flesh.

Melons are eaten raw, in fruit salads or, owing to their high water content, made into sorbets. They can also be used for savoury dishes, the most notable being melon and Parma ham.

Melons are known to have been grown for several thousands of years. Although natives of Asia, evidence exists that melons were familiar to both the Roman and Egyptian civilisations.

MELON BALLER

A small utensil with a semi-circular, sharp-edged metal scoop at the end of a handle. The scoop is pressed into the flesh of the melon and turned quickly so that a full scoop or ball is removed from the melon.

MELTING CHOCOLATE
(see chocolate)

MELTING MOMENTS

The name of these biscuits (cookies) says it all.

250 g (8 oz) unsalted (sweet) butter, softened
½ cup (3 oz) icing (powdered) sugar, sifted
2 teaspoons vanilla essence (extract)
2 cups (8 oz) plain (all-purpose) flour, sifted
glacé (candied) cherries, for decoration

Preheat oven to 160°C (320°F). Grease baking sheets.
Cream butter and icing sugar in a mixing bowl until almost white, light and creamy. Add vanilla and mix in well.
Add sifted flour and mix until well combined. Place mixture in a piping (pastry) bag fitted with a 1 cm (½ in) star-shaped nozzle. Pipe small rosettes or stars onto the prepared sheet.
Decorate each cookie with half a glacé cherry.
Bake in preheated oven for 10–15 minutes, or until golden brown. Cool on the sheet. Remove to a cake rack when cold.

Makes 36

MEN'S TORTE
(see also wine cream)

This alcoholic torte was once thought to be suitable only for men.

1 chocolate génoise sponge (see page 134)

Filling
2½ cups (20 fl oz) dry white wine
¾ cup (6 oz) caster (superfine)
⅔ cup (3 oz) custard powder
½ cup (4 fl oz) water
2 eggs, lightly beaten

To Decorate
250 g (8 oz) marzipan
200 g (7 oz) dark (plain or semi-sweet) chocolate, melted (see page 62)
12 maraschino cherries
¾ cup (3 oz) flaked almonds, roasted (see page 5)

Line base and sides of a 23 cm (9 in) springform cake tin with baking paper (parchment). Slice sponge into quarters horizontally and place the top layer in the prepared tin.
Place wine and sugar in a saucepan and bring to the boil.
Blend custard powder and water and stir into lightly beaten eggs. Pour in hot wine syrup, beating all the time. Return mixture to the saucepan and heat, stirring all the time until the custard boils and thickens. Pour a third of the custard into the prepared tin and top with a layer of sponge.
Repeat with custard and other layers of sponge. Press down lightly to spread filling evenly and chill for 2 hours.
Roll marzipan into a 23 cm (9 in) circle and cover with chocolate. With a hot knife cut it into 12 wedges. Cut chilled torte into 12 wedges and top each with a marzipan wedge. Support each wedge with a maraschino cherry and tilt. Press flaked almonds around the side of the torte.

MERINGUE
(see also Pavlova)

Some claim that this light aerated foam of egg whites and sugar was first invented in honour of a Napoleonic victory at the Italian town of Marengo in 1881. Others insist that it was the invention of a Swiss pastry chef who worked in Meiringen. It is quite possible that both tales are true, as there are Italian meringues and Swiss meringues, of equal fame.

Meringue is a mixture produced by whisking egg whites until they form stiff peaks and then slowly incorporating sugar, still whisking until all is incorporated. Until the 19th century — and the wonders of Marie-Antoine Carême (the founder of haute cuisine) — meringue was simply a light mixture which was baked in a long slow oven so that it dried out. Carême, however, decided to pipe it into shapes, thus inventing the piped meringue shell and the vacherin.

Meringue in its various forms is the basis of many light mixtures, from mousses to cakes, decorations and cake bases such as japonaise, dacquoise and succès. It is also used to decorate the outside of cakes which are then flamed, and is poached to create Oeufs à la Neige.

There are three major types of meringue:

(i) Swiss or plain meringue is a simple mixture of egg whites and sugar;

(ii) Italian meringue is made by whipping the egg whites until stiff peaks form and then adding a boiled sugar syrup to the mixture. This creates a more stable meringue which will hold the longest before breaking down; and

(iii) The last variety of meringue is a mixture of egg whites and sugar, warmed over a bain-marie and whisked until light, known as the cooked meringue. This is used mainly for the outside of bombes.

4 egg whites
⅔ cup (5 oz) caster (superfine) sugar
3 tablespoons (1½ oz) cornflour
1 tablespoon (¾ oz) icing (powdered) sugar

Preheat oven to 150°C (320 °F). Line a baking tray (sheet) with baking paper (parchment). Beat egg whites in a mixing bowl until stiff peaks form, then gradually beat in sugar, a tablespoonful at a time. Beat at top speed on an electric mixer until sugar is dissolved. Fold sieved cornflour and icing sugar through meringue mixture. Either spoon or pipe meringue mixture onto the tray and bake for 1 hour. Turn oven off and leave meringue to cook further in cooling oven.

M'HENCHA

Made from filo (phyllo) pastry, this North African dessert is closely related to many Mediterranean desserts in construction, although perhaps not in shape.

M'hencha is a strudel-like roll filled with an orangeflower-flavoured nut filling. The long roll of pastry is then coiled around and around and baked in its serpent-like coil. The name 'm'hencha' in fact means the serpent, and pastries in this coil form are known to have been made by Mediterranean and Egyptian bakers since the time of Rameses.

MIGNARDISE
(see also friandise)

Meaning a small sweet delicacy, mignardises are very similar to friandises. The only real difference between them is that friandises were served with coffee or tea and were slightly larger than petits fours, while mignardises are slightly larger again and are served between meals as a snack, or as an afternoon tea fancy.

MIKONG

This Chinese honey cake is a true form of gingerbread, lightly flavoured with ginger. It was apparently supplied in the rations of soldiers during the marauding wars of Genghis Khan and has been in existence in some form for centuries.

MILK
(see also buttermilk)

Taken from cows and other animals, milk has been used for thousands of years for drinking and for cooking. Before being used, milk undergoes many processes to ensure it is safe for consumption and prolong its life. Firstly, milk is pasteurised, which means it is heated to 75°C (167°F) and then quickly cooled, to destroy micro-organisms. At the same time, milk is homogenised, which involves passing it through minute fine nozzles to disperse the fat globules evenly and make them uniform in size. These processes enable milk to last up to 10 days if kept cool in a refrigerator. However, Ultra Heat Treatment (UHT), evaporated or condensed milk can be stored for longer.

The UHT process destroys all the micro-organisms and producing milk that has a long life even at room temperature. The process involves heating the milk to 132°C (270°C) for one to two seconds then cooling it rapidly and sealing it into packages. Once the package is opened, though, the UHT milk must be refrigerated and has a shelf life similar to that of pasteurised milk.

Cultured Milk
Cultured milks and buttermilks are made by adding special starter cultures to the pasteurised milk and allowing time for the cultures to produce the desired flavour and acidity.

Evaporated Milk
By gentle heating of thin films or droplets of milk in stainless steel evaporators, over half of the water is removed. This heat treatment destroys all bacteria and enzymes, ensuring a long shelf life. It also causes a slight browning of the milk, giving the evaporated milk its typical colour and flavour. Whole milk is evaporated down to 40% of its original volume. The evaporating is done under vacuum at fairly low temperatures.

Sweetened Condensed Milk
Another method of ensuring long shelf life for concentrated milk is to add enough sugar so that it will act as a natural preservative. Heat treatment of the milk before concentration need only be mild so that the flavour and colour are not changed. The amount of sugar added needs to be controlled carefully. Long-term stability is achieved with about 45% sugar added.

Another important part of the process involves crystallising the lactose (milk sugar). The added sugar (sucrose) competes with the lactose for the available water, causing the lactose to form crystals. This must be controlled so that numerous small crystals are obtained; otherwise, large lactose crystals may form on storage, giving a texture which is gritty rather than smooth.

Instant Milk Powders
Milk powders are produced by evaporating the water from the milk and producing a solid which is then ground into fine particles. The drying process is carried out in one of two ways: spray drying or roller drying.

In the spray drying method, milk is sprayed onto a hot plate or belt which evaporates the moisture from the finely sprayed film as soon as it hits the plate. It is then scraped off into a grinding or crushing tank.

In roller drying, the milk is poured lightly over steam-heated rollers which evaporate the moisture, leaving a fine film of powder which is scraped off the roller and crushed or ground.

MILK CHOCOLATE
(see chocolate)

Mimosa Cake (see page 184)

MILK SUGAR
(see also lactose, sugar)

Otherwise known as lactose, this is a member of the sugar family found naturally in milk.

MILLEFEUILLE
(see also allumettes, puff pastry)

Meaning 'a thousand leaves', millefeuilles are made from puff pastry. The baked pastry is cut into several layers and filled with crème Chantilly and jam (jelly) and is dusted with icing (powdered) sugar, much in the same way as its cousin, the match or matchstick.

MIMOSA

These yellow flowers from the acacia (wattle) tree have been used in baking for centuries, although now they have only limited uses: in the production of liqueurs and in fritter batters (for flavour and colour).

MIMOSA CAKE

Named for its yellow yolk interior and bright yellow marzipan decoration, this cake recalls the sunny yellow colour of Australian wattle, or mimosa.

2 cups (8 oz) cornflour (cornstarch)
1 cup (4 oz) plain (all-purpose) flour
6 egg yolks
6 eggs
½ cup (4 oz) caster (superfine) sugar
1½ tablespoons honey

To Decorate
1 quantity quick no-fuss buttercream (see page 43)
125 g (4 oz) marzipan, tinted yellow (see page 177)
icing (powdered) sugar, for dusting
60 g (2 oz) dark (plain or semi-sweet) chocolate,
melted (see page 62)

Preheat oven to 180°C (350°F). Lightly grease two 23 cm (9 in) springform cake tins with butter and line the bases with baking paper (parchment).
Mix flours and sift twice. Beat eggs yolks, eggs and sugar until light and fluffy and the mixture forms a ribbon (see page 236). Stir in honey and gently fold in the sifted flours by hand. Pour mixture into the prepared tins and bake for 40 minutes, or until the top of each cake springs back when lightly touched. Cool in tins on a cake rack. When cold, cut one cake horizontally into thirds. Spread buttercream on each layer and stack them on top of each other. Cover the top and sides with more buttercream. Roll out the marzipan into a 10 cm (4 in) circle and place in the centre of the top layer. For extra effect, texture the marzipan with a patterned rolling pin.
Cut the second cake into 2 cm (¾ in) cubes and place randomly around the marzipan and on the sides of the cake. Dust lightly with icing sugar. Decorate with piped chocolate.

See page 183

MINCEMEAT
(see fruit mince)

MINCE PIES
(see fruit mince pies)

MINT
(see also flavourings, herbs)

Mint, from the plant species mentha, is one of the most popular flavourings for pastry and desserts, and is also often used as a garnish for desserts. There are several varieties, including spearmint and peppermint, which are used for their aroma and flavour in cakes, pastries, fillings and confectionery. Mint is also ground and pulverised into a liquid for its colour.

MINT PESTO SAUCE

300 g (10 oz) fresh mint
300 g (10 oz) pine nuts
1 cup (8 fl oz) sugar syrup

Place all ingredients in a food processor and allow to blend to a fine paste. If a thinner consistency is required, thin with more syrup. Serve under sweet fritters or dumplings.
Keeps for 3–4 days refrigerated.

MIQUE

These flat dumplings originated during the Middle Ages, and are still popular in certain regions of France. The mixture is made from cornmeal, eggs, yeast and butter. It is flattened into small discs and poached. The poached dumplings are then covered with a boiled jam (jelly) sauce and dusted with icing (powdered) sugar.

MISSISSIPPI MUD CAKE

3 cups (12 oz) plain (all-purpose) flour
2 teaspoons baking powder (soda)
4 teaspoons bicarbonate of soda
½ cup (2 oz) cocoa powder
120 g (4 oz) unsalted (sweet) butter
2¼ cups (14 oz) soft brown sugar
2 eggs
150 g (5 oz) dark (plain or semi-sweet) chocolate
1 cup (8 fl oz) milk
1 teaspoon vanilla essence (extract)

To Decorate
1 quantity chocolate ganache (see page 131)

Preheat oven to 180°C (350°F).
Grease a 25 x 30 x 3 cm (10 x 12 x 1¼ in) baking tray (jelly roll pan) and line with baking paper (parchment). Sift flour, baking powder, bicarbonate of soda and cocoa powder twice. Beat butter and sugar until light and fluffy. Add eggs one at a time, beating well after each one is added. Add chocolate to the butter mixture and beat in well.

Mix in by hand the sifted flour alternately with the milk and vanilla essence. Pour into prepared tray and bake for 35–40 minutes, or until firm to the touch. Cool in the tray. Cover the top with chocolate ganache. Allow the ganache to set in the refrigerator before cutting.

MIXED PEEL
(see citrus peel)

MIXED SPICE
(see also garam masala, spices)

A mixture or blend of several types of spices. The spices, and the proportions of each used, differ from producer to producer, but the most accepted blend is one of cinnamon, nutmeg and cloves.

MOCHA
(see also coffee, flavourings)

Mocha is a variety of coffee found on the borders of the Red Sea. In pastry terms, mocha refers to the blending of coffee and chocolate to create a balanced flavour, where neither overrides the other.

MOCK CREAM
(see cream imitations)

MODELLING CHOCOLATE
(see chocolate)

MODELLING PASTE
(see gum paste and pastillage)

Monkey Faces, bottom (see page 186) and Mai Landerli, top (see page 170)

185

MODELLING TOOLS

Also known as modelling pins or marzipan modelling tools, these small instruments are used for the decoration or modelling of marzipan and other modelling pastes into artistic designs. They are made of either bone, ivory, wood or plastic and are usually sold either individually, in pairs, fours or larger sets. The tools are used for cutting, making round holes for eyes, marking feet, hooves or paws, each of the tools having a different use, or creating a different impression.

MOLASSES

(see also golden syrup, sugar, treacle)

Also known as black treacle, molasses is very dark and thick in texture, strong in flavour and rich in aroma. It is extracted during the early stages of sugar refining, when the sugar is still in its crude dark form. The molasses used in cake manufacture is almost always made from cane sugar, while molasses from beet sugar is used in animal feeds and alcohol manufacture. Molasses can be purchased either dark or light in colour, depending on how much it has been refined.

MONKEY FACES

These biscuits (cookies) are formed by joining two small fluted biscuit rounds together with jam (jelly). The top round has 3 small holes cut into it to form the monkey's face and is glazed with a lemon icing.

3½ cups (14 oz) plain (all-purpose) flour
1¼ cups (7 oz) icing (powdered) sugar
270 g (9 oz) unsalted (sweet) butter
1 egg
redcurrant jam (jelly)

Icing Glaze
1 cup (6 oz) icing (powdered) sugar
2 tablespoons lemon juice

Sift flour and icing sugar into a bowl and, using your fingers, lightly rub butter through dry ingredients until mixture resembles breadcrumbs. Add egg and continue mixing to a soft dough. Wrap dough in plastic wrap (cling film) and refrigerate for 1 hour to firm up.
Preheat oven to 200°C (350°F). Lightly grease baking sheets.
On a lightly floured surface, roll the dough out to 3–4 mm (⅙ in) in thickness. With an 8 cm (3 in) fluted round biscuit (cookie) cutter, cut out an even number of rounds.
Place half the rounds on a prepared sheet. These will form the bases of the biscuits. Using a 1 cm (½ in) fluted biscuit cutter, cut three small holes into the remaining rounds to make the monkey faces. Place on the baking sheet.
Bake both bases and faces in preheated oven for 8–10 minutes, or until lightly browned at the edges.
Remove from oven and allow only the bases to cool on the sheet. Immediately brush the faces with the icing glaze, then allow to cool and set before continuing.
Spread the bases with redcurrant jam.
Top with the iced faces.

Icing Glaze
Sift icing sugar. Mix in the lemon juice to make a thin icing. If icing is thick and stiff, add extra lemon juice or warm water.

Makes 12

See page 185

MONT BLANC

A rich dessert made of chestnut purée, Mont Blanc is named after the mountain which runs along the border between France and Italy. It is known to the Italians as Monte Bianco. The dessert is a mixture of sweet pastry, sponge and fresh fruit, covered with a high tower of sweetened chestnut purée and decorated with cream to signify the snow which features on the real thing. Alternatively, the mixture can be made into individual tartlets, the chestnut purée being forced through a potato masher or sieve to produce long strands which cover a sweet cream mixture on a tartlet pastry base.

½ (cut horizontally) chocolate génoise sponge (see page 134)
2½ cups (20 fl oz) crème Chantilly (see page 85)
1 japonaise base (see page 156)
400 g (13 oz) canned sweetened chestnut purée
8 maraschino cherries
fresh berries of the season

Cut a 10 cm (4 in) circle out of the centre of one layer of sponge and discard it. Spread a small amount of crème Chantilly on top of the japonaise base. Top with the sponge ring. Pile most of the remaining crème Chantilly on top of the ring, shaping it to form a mound around the well in the centre.
Mix the chestnut purée until smooth and creamy.
Fill a piping (pastry) bag fitted with a star nozzle with purée and pipe up the sides and over the mound to the centre.
Repeat until the cake is covered. Fill the piping bag with the crème Chantilly and pipe rosettes around the top edge.
Decorate rosettes with maraschino cherries and fill the well with fresh berries. Chill.

MONTE CARLOS

These are rich little biscuit (cookie) delights.

180 g (6 oz) unsalted (sweet) butter
⅔ cup (5 oz) caster (superfine) sugar
1 egg
1 teaspoon vanilla essence (extract)
1¾ cups (7 oz) plain (all-purpose) flour
2 teaspoons baking powder (soda)

Filling
90 g (3 oz) unsalted (sweet) butter
1 cup (6 oz) icing (powdered) sugar
1 teaspoon vanilla essence (extract)
2 tablespoons milk
strawberry jam (jelly)
icing (powdered) sugar, extra, for dusting

Preheat oven to 180°C (350°F). Lightly grease baking sheets.
Place butter and sugar in a mixing bowl and cream until light
and fluffy. Add egg and vanilla. Beat well.
Add sifted flour and baking powder and mix until combined.
Roll walnut-sized pieces of the mixture into balls.
Place on prepared sheet. Gently press down with a fork
so as to leave an impression. Bake in preheated oven
for 10–15 minutes, or until golden brown.
Remove from oven and cool on a cake rack.
Place a teaspoon of jam and a teaspoon of the prepared
filling in the centre of half of the Monte Carlos.
Top with the remaining biscuits, press together lightly,
then dust with icing sugar.

Filling

Cream butter and sifted icing sugar until light and fluffy. Add
vanilla and milk. Beat well. Cover with plastic wrap (cling
film) and store in the refrigerator until required.

Makes 18

MONTMORENCY

Any dessert or cake, be it ice cream, bombe, iced mousse,
croûte or tart, in which the predominant flavour is provided
by fresh or crystallised (candied) cherries is usually termed
Montmorency. A traditional Montmorency gâteau is a génoise
sponge which is covered, and possibly filled, with cherries
and then covered with an Italian meringue, decorated with
glacé or crystallised cherries and flamed to give it a golden
brown colour. Bombe Montmorency has a similar basis.

MONTPENSIER

A Montpensier is any cake or pastry which is baked in a tin
that is lined before baking with the ingredient which gives it
its predominant flavour. The name derives from the 17th
century Duchesse de Montpensier.

MORELLO

A variety of cherry often used in pastry cooking. The cherry
has a dark flesh colour and is mainly used in jams (jellies)
and preserves, although it is also used for sorbets and ice
cream and eaten raw.

MOULDS

Any container which can be used to hold a mixture while it is
baked or set: there is no regulation shape or depth. Many
moulds are predominantly used for baking one item in
particular, such as brioche, savarin or kugelhupf moulds,
although they can, of course, be used for many other
mixtures. Moulds can be made from aluminium, tin, glass,
porcelain or plastic.

Individual Cake or Pastry Moulds

These include dariole moulds, timbale moulds, brioche
moulds, savarin moulds and ramekins. Each has a different
shape, depth and size and can be used for an array of goods,
although each is known more commonly for one or two items.

Tray or Multiple Moulds

These include madeleine trays and langue de chat or éclair
trays. Each has a specific set of shapes according to its use
and each can be used for other items. Most come in 6-, 9- or
12-cup or hole capacity.

Chocolate and Confectionery Moulds

Made from metal, silicon or plastic, these moulds are
available in freestanding forms, in trays or as individual
moulds.

MOULDED CHOCOLATES
(see chocolate)

MOULDING PASTE
(see gum paste and pastillage)

MOUSSE
(see also avocado, banana mousse)

There are many forms of mousse, some very light, some quite
firm, but always velvety smooth in texture. Most are fruit
based, although chocolate and coffee are also very popular.
They can be lightened with a mixture of whipped cream or
whipped egg whites or, for a very light dish, both.

Mousses are a combination of fools, whips and chiffons
and can be set using gelatine; in the case of chocolate mousse,
this can be omitted as the chocolate will set it firm enough.
A good mousse should be so light as to only just hold its
shape and should have a single flavour which is crisp and
refreshing.

CHOCOLATE MOUSSE

250 g (8 oz) cream cheese
¾ cup (6 oz) caster (superfine) sugar
1 egg
2½ cups (20 fl oz) fresh cream, lightly whipped
250 g (8 oz) dark (plain or semi-sweet) chocolate,
melted (see page 62)

Place cream cheese, sugar and egg yolks in a mixing bowl
and beat until smooth — sugar may not dissolve completely.
Whip cream until stiff and return to refrigerator until
required. Quickly stir melted chocolate into smooth cream
cheese mixture and immediately fold through whipped
cream with your hand. The warmth of your hand
will enable the stiff chocolate to fold through the cream.
Any remaining sugar granules will dissolve during setting.
Spoon into glasses or cream puffs and
chill for 30 minutes before serving.
Makes enough for 6–10 individual portions,
or 1 dozen cream puffs.

MUESLI
(see also Bircher muesli)

The name muesli derives from the German word meaning
'mixture', and two main forms of muesli are available. The
first is Bircher muesli, created by Dr Bircher-Benner in

Switzerland and considered by many to be a perfect health food. It is a common sight on European breakfast buffets. The other form of muesli is the dry toasted or raw muesli of oats, wheatgerm, dried fruits, seeds and nuts.

MUESLI AND BLUEBERRY COOKIES

250 g (8 oz) unsalted (sweet) butter
1½ cups (9 oz) brown sugar
2 eggs
1 teaspoon vanilla essence (extract)
¾ cup (3 oz) plain (all-purpose) flour
½ teaspoon baking powder (soda)
5 cups (13 oz) prepared toasted muesli
250 g (8 oz) frozen blueberries

Preheat oven to 160°C (320°F). Grease a baking sheet. Cream butter and sugar until light and fluffy. Slowly add eggs and vanilla, then add all the dry ingredients. Add blueberries last; these are best if frozen rather than thawed. Using a standard ice cream scoop, place portions on prepared sheet and bake in preheated oven for about 20 minutes.

Makes approximately 30

MUFFINS, ENGLISH

In the United Kingdom, a muffin refers to the flat yeast-risen cake which is baked and eaten for breakfast or as a snack. Usually 10–12 cm (4–5 in) in diameter and 2–3 cm (¾–1¼ in) in depth, the muffin is closely related to the range of griddle cakes that date back to medieval Wales and Scotland.

15 g (½ oz) fresh compressed yeast
1 cup (8 fl oz) milk
1 tablespoon vegetable oil
1⅓ cups (6 oz) wholemeal plain
(wholewheat all-purpose) flour
1¼ cups (5 oz) plain (all-purpose) flour
⅛ teaspoon salt
1 teaspoon caster (superfine) sugar
½ cup (3 oz) polenta (cornmeal)

Dissolve yeast in the milk by whisking lightly. Then add oil. In a large bowl, place flours, salt and sugar. Add yeast liquid and mix to a firm dough. Remove it from the bowl and knead for 5–8 minutes, until smooth and elastic. Cover and place in a warm area for 30–45 minutes, until double in bulk.
Line a baking sheet with baking paper (parchment). Knock the dough back (punch it down) on a bench (counter) surface which has been lightly dusted with the polenta. Roll the dough to 1–1½ cm (½ in) in thickness and, using a 10 cm (4 in) biscuit (cookie) or scone cutter, cut out discs and place these on prepared sheet. Cover muffins and allow to double in size in a warm area for a further 30–40 minutes. Heat a frying pan (skillet) to 140°C (280°F) and grease it well.

Take two muffins at a time and place them in the frying pan. Cook for 10–12 minutes either side, until golden brown. Remove to a wire rack and eat while still warm. Test the first muffin, by breaking it open. This will tell you if the remaining muffins need extra cooking time.

Makes 6—8

MUFFINS, AMERICAN

A small, high-capped, light-textured cake, similar to a cup of queen cake, American muffins are risen using baking powder (soda) and are usually much sweeter than the English variety. Made originally by the early American settlers, they are a form of quickbread which is made by adding all the liquid ingredients at once to the combined dry ingredients and then baking them in a deep muffin pan for 15–25 minutes. They should then be served immediately.

3¼ cups (13 oz) plain (all-purpose) flour
1 tablespoon baking powder (soda)
¾ cup (4 oz) soft (light) brown sugar
½ cup (4 oz) caster (superfine) sugar
½ cup (4 oz) chocolate chips (drops)
2½ cups (8 oz) desiccated (shredded) coconut
2 large ripe bananas, lightly mashed
1¼ cups (10 fl oz) milk
125 g (4 oz) unsalted (sweet) butter, melted
2 eggs, lightly beaten
3 tablespoons caster (superfine) sugar, extra
1 teaspoon ground cinnamon

Preheat oven to 180°C (350°F). Lightly grease a muffin pan. Sift flour and baking powder. Add brown sugar, caster sugar, chocolate chips, coconut and lightly mashed bananas. Add milk, melted butter and eggs and mix through the dry ingredients until all are combined. Fill three quarters of each muffin mould with the mixture. Mix the extra caster sugar with the cinnamon and sprinkle this on top of each muffin. Bake in preheated oven for 20 minutes. When baked, cool in the tin for 5 minutes, then carefully remove each muffin from the tin and cool on a cake rack.

Makes 15

MUFFIN PAN

A tray containing six, eight or twelve deep holes ranging from 4–5 cm (1½–2 in) in diameter to 8–10 cm (3½–4 in) in diameter. Used for baking the American version of muffins and other small cakes.

MULTIPLE PASTRY WHEEL
(see also pastry)

A metal expandable frame which holds four to six sharp wheels at one end. The width between wheels can be extended as required, and the multiple pastry wheel pushed or dragged through pastries or cakes to mark or cut the product into slices or bars.

American Thanksgiving muffins

MUSCOVADO SUGAR
(see also Barbados sugar, sugar)

Used in mixtures such as gingerbreads, honey cakes and highly spiced goods, muscovado is a partially refined brown sugar which is moist and highly aromatic. It is coarser than normal brown sugar but finer than demerara.

MUSLIN CLOTH

Also known as cheesecloth, the muslin cloth is commonly used in all good kitchens for straining purées and sauces. Muslin is a loosely woven cloth which has small holes that are usually finer than any metal seive can achieve. It is thus perfect for straining impurities or seeds from liquids.

Spices or herbs are often placed in a small muslin bag, which is then dropped into boiling liquids so that the flavours can infuse. The bag can then easily be removed.

Muslin can also be used to wrap soft foods and those which need to drain slightly, such as coeur à la crème, or mousses. The muslin can be placed on the setting item and carefully removed once the dish has set, leaving a decorative fine mesh texture.

NAAN

An Indian flatbread, risen using yeast, that is baked on the sides of the tandoori ovens. The bread puffs up during baking, which takes only a few minutes. The flatbread is served with savoury dishes.

NAPOLEONS

A small French pastry produced from three layers of puff pastry that have been sandwiched together with a sweet mixture of crème pâtissière and crème Chantilly. The top layer of pastry is coated in a thickened glaze of apricot jam (jelly) and spread with fondant when this is cool. The fondant is traditionally feathered with a coloured fondant or chocolate, but can also be left plain.

NAPOLITAIN

A cake consisting of discs or rings of a sweet almond or hazelnut pastry which are layered with jam (jelly) and topped with a feathered fondant. Possibly invented by the founder of haute cuisine, Marie-Antoine Carême, the napolitain differs from the napoleon only in that it is not made with puff pastry and it is made either as a disc- or ring-shaped whole cake.

NASHI PEAR

Nashi is Japanese for pear, but it is really a cross between apples and pears. It has the texture and taste of a pear but the shape of an apple. The fruit has a yellow/green skin with a champagne-coloured, sweet, juicy flesh.

NAVETTE

From the Latin 'navis', meaning boat, the navette cake is a small cake baked in barquette moulds (from a basic buttercake recipe) and soaked in orangeflower water. While the recipe is French, it is thought that the shape and ingredients originated in Egypt, where the cake represented the boat that carried Isis, the goddess of fertility.

NEAPOLITAN SLICE

First produced in 19th century Paris and invented by the pastry chef Tortoni, neapolitan ice cream consists of three flavours — strawberry, chocolate and vanilla — either set on top of each other or moulded beside each other and then cut to give slices containing all three ice creams.

NECTARINE
(see also fruit)

A variety of peach, the nectarine is a smooth, red, thin-skinned fruit with a yellowish flesh. When ripe, it is soft and juicy, and when unripe it is firm and a green/white colour. Nectarines, like peaches, come in two varieties, clingstone or freestone: the distinction relates to how firmly the flesh is attached to the stone when cut. In pastry cooking, nectarines offer a delicate flavour to many sweet dishes, such as strudels, pies, sorbets, jams, jellies and preserves, and are also used simply in fresh fruit salad. First cultivated throughout Asia, the nectarine was so named because its its flavour and delicate aroma was cherished as being 'nectar of the gods'.

NEENISH

A small sweet pastry tartlet filled with a rum-flavoured cream and topped with vanilla and chocolate icings. Thought to have been invented by cooks in outback Australia.

NEGERKUSSE

Negerküsse are chocolate-coated biscuits (cookies) or small sponge cakes which are sandwiched together with fresh cream or buttercream.

NEIGE
(see also Boule de Neige, meringue, Oeufs à la Neige)

This French word, literally translated as 'snow', refers to egg white dishes: the light white product resulting from whisking egg whites.

NELUSKO

The name given to popular petit four consisting of a pitted cherry which is soaked in Kirsch and then dipped into fondant and allowed to set firm. The bottom is sometimes dipped into chocolate so that it has a firm flat base on which to sit.

NERO ROSETTES

A rich biscuit (cookie) piped into rosettes, which then have their bases dipped in chocolate.

300 g (10 oz) unsalted (sweet) butter
⅓ cup (1½ oz) cocoa powder
1 cup (6 oz) icing (powdered) sugar
1 egg
3 cups (12 oz) plain (all-purpose) flour
zest and juice of 1 lemon
dark (plain or semi-sweet) chocolate, melted (see page 62)

Preheat oven to 180°C (350°F).
Line baking sheets (trays) with baking paper (parchment).
Place butter, cocoa and icing sugar in a mixing bowl and
cream together until light and fluffy. Add egg and mix well.
Fold through the sifted flour and the lemon juice and zest.
Place the mixture in a piping (pastry) bag fitted with a
1 cm (½ in) star-shaped nozzle and pipe small rosettes
onto prepared sheets. Bake in preheated oven for
10–12 minutes and cool on the sheets.
Turn rosettes upside down and dip bases of each into
melted chocolate. Decorate chocolate by running a fork
through it lightly before placing it in refrigerator to set.

Makes 36

NESSELRODE PUDDING

A chilled or frozen dessert consisting of a light custard filled
with chestnut purée, glacé (candied) fruits, nuts and liqueur
which can either be set with gelatine or frozen. The
Nesselrode pudding was invented by the chef Mouy, who
cooked for Count Karl Nesselrode (1780–1862), the Russian
diplomat who negotiated the Treaty of Paris after the
conclusion of the Crimean War. The Count was living in Paris
at the time and, having an appreciation of fine food, his name
was given to many of his chef's dishes.

NEUFCHATEL
(see cream cheese)

A soft unripened cheese from the same family as cream cheese
and mascarpone. The cheese is originally from the town of
Neufchâtel-en-Bray in France, where it has been a famed
local product since the Middle Ages. The cheese is a soft
creamy colour with a mild flavour and has a fat content of
44–48%. It is used extensively for desserts and can be
substituted for cream cheese quite easily in most cream cheese
recipes.

NOCKERLN

A specialty of Salzburg, Austria, nockerln means dumplings,
but not in the usual sense. Traditionally, the Salzburg
nockerln are made from a very light soufflé mixture which
is floated above a vanilla-flavoured milk and then baked
in the oven. The result is a light, rich mixture which is served
by the 'spoonful', using a crisp cookie or a pastry piece as a
spoon.

NON-LUMPING SUGAR

Also known as icing (powdered) sugar mixture, this is a
mixture of pure icing sugar and a starch or drying substance
(such as cornflour, arrowroot, phosphate or silicate) which
prevents the finely ground sugar absorbing moisture from the
air and becoming a solid lump. The inclusion of the drying
agent does, however, prevent the mix being used in some
recipes, such as flavouring creams and some icing or frosting
mixtures. It is perfect for use in shortbread and sable recipes,
though, as these call for both starch and icing sugar in the
recipe anyway.

NOUGAT
(see also confectionery)

Nougat refers to different sweet mixtures, and has different
meanings in different countries:

(i) Molten sugar and almonds mixed together and cooled,
then ground to a paste and mixed with melted chocolate;

(ii) Molten sugar and flaked almonds mixed and poured onto
marble or baking paper (parchment) and allowed to
firm, then used crushed or rolled flat when warm for
decorations. Also known as praline/croquant/grillage;
and

(iii) A boiled sugar, honey and water mixture which is added
to whisked egg whites. Nuts and glacé fruits are then
added. It is allowed to firm in a slab or block and cut
into slices when cold. This form of nougat can be quite
sticky and is susceptible to humidity, so it is traditionally
pressed between sheets of rice paper for storage and ease
of handling.

One of the original and most famous varieties of these white
meringue-, honey- and nut-based nougats is the delicious
Nougat de Montelimar. It was first manufactured at
Montelimar, in France, and is known to have existed since the
Roman Empire.

NOUGAT DE MONTELIMAR

2½ cups (20 oz) granulated sugar
1 cup (10 oz) liquid glucose (corn syrup)
⅓ cup (4 oz) clear honey
2 egg whites
¾ cup (3 oz) flaked almonds
⅓ cup (2 oz) hazelnuts (filberts)

Preheat oven to 200°C (400°F).
Place sugar, glucose and honey in a heavy-based saucepan
and slowly bring to the boil, stirring so that sugar does not
burn on sides of pan. (There is no need to dissolve the sugar
before boiling. Simply combine the ingredients.) This mix will
be very thick and sugary. Place a sugar (candy) thermometer
in the mixture and boil to 140°C (284°F).
Place egg whites in the mixing bowl of a powerful electric
mixer and whisk until they form stiff peaks. While whites are
still whipping, begin drizzling the boiled mixture into them.
(This mixture will become very thick and stiff, so make sure
the electric mixer is on a medium speed and not
overworking.) Mix until all boiled mixture is combined.
Place almonds and chopped hazelnuts on a baking sheet
in preheated oven for 8 minutes. Fold hot nuts
and cherries through egg white mixture.
Place rice paper sheets on the base of an 18 x 28 x 2 cm
(7 x 11 x ¾ in) baking tray (jelly roll pan) so that they fit
without overlapping. Spoon mixture onto the rice paper base
and then place more rice paper over the top of the nougat.
Press firmly down on rice paper to flatten and even the
mixture. Allow to sit for 6 hours (or overnight) to set.
Cut into finger-sized slices with a lightly oiled knife.
Store in an airtight container.

See page 192

Nougat (see page 191)

NOUGATINE
(see also croquant, nougat, praline)

This is known by many names (nougat, grillage, praline or
croquant), depending on the country it is made in, but it is all
the same. Nougatine is a molten mixture of sugar to which an
equal quantity of flaked almonds is added. The hot mixture is
poured onto baking paper (parchment) and rolled to 2–3 mm
(⅛ in) in thickness, using a well-oiled rolling pin, or covering
it with a second sheet of paper. It is then cut or modelled into
any shape required.

NOZZLE
(see also piping, piping bag)

A small plastic or metal conical-shaped tube between 2–5 cm
(¾ –2 in) in length which has a wide opening at one end and a
narrow round or star-shaped opening at the other. The
nozzle is placed in the small end of a piping bag and soft
biscuit (cookie), mousse, cream or buttercream mixtures are
forced through it to create decorative shapes for baking, or
for cake decoration.

NUSSTORTE

750 g (24 oz) sweet pastry (see page 272)
2 cups (14 oz) caster (superfine) sugar
60 g (2 oz) unsalted (sweet) butter
1½ cups (12 fl oz) cream
1 tablespoon golden syrup (light treacle)
1 tablespoon honey
⅔ cup (3 oz) cornflour (cornstarch)
3¼ cups (13 oz) chopped walnuts

Preheat oven to 180°C (350°F).
Using two-thirds of the pastry, line the base and sides of a
26–28 cm (10–11 in) round flan or tart ring or pie dish (pan).
Allow this to refrigerate until filling is ready.
Place a saucepan (preferably copper, but otherwise heavy-
based) over medium to high heat and begin spooning in the
sugar, 1–2 tablespoons at a time, until it begins to melt. As it
melts, stir the sugar to ensure it does not burn (the first
amount of sugar melts quickly). Keep adding more until it is
all melted and golden in colour. Add butter and, using a long-
handled wooden spoon, add cream in a steady stream,
stirring carefully (steam can burn), until butter and cream
are combined with the sugar. Allow this mixture to cool.

Stir through golden syrup and honey. Add cornflour and
walnuts to the cold mixture and pour into pastry base.
On a lightly floured surface, roll remaining pastry to fit
over the top of the pie dish or flan ring. Seal edges well
by crimping together firmly. Bake in preheated
oven for 40–45 minutes. When cool, dust with icing
(powdered) sugar. Cool completely before serving
small slices with strong coffee.

NUTS
(see also individual entries)

Since before biblical times, nuts have been eaten for
sustenance and nutrition. They are single-seeded dry fruit
enclosed within hard shells, although the kernels of some
fruits are also called nuts. Macadamia nuts, hazelnuts,
walnuts, almonds, cashews, pecans, brazil nuts and peanuts
are but a few of the most commonly used nuts in pastry, and
are available either ground, flaked, slivered, roasted, whole,
blanched or chopped. To develop their full flavour when used
in cooking, nuts should be roasted. They are also prized for
their oils.

NUT BRITTLE

2 cups (16 oz) granulated sugar
1 cup (8 fl oz) water
30 g (1 oz) unsalted (sweet) butter
1¾ cups (9 oz) dry roasted peanuts
250 g (8 oz) dark (plain or semi-sweet) chocolate,
melted (see page 62)

Lightly oil an 18 x 28 x 2 cm (7 x 11 x ¾ in) baking tray
(jelly roll pan) and line with aluminium foil.
Place sugar and water in a saucepan and slowly bring to the
boil, stirring only to move the sugar and prevent it burning
on the base. Place a sugar (candy) thermometer in the
mixture and allow the mixture to boil to 150°C (300°F). As
the mixture boils, wash down the sides of the saucepan with a
pastry brush dipped into clean warm water, to remove any
stray sugar crystals from the sides of the pan.
Remove thermometer and add butter, stirring with a long-
handled wooden spoon until all is dissolved and combined.
Add the peanuts quickly and stir until they are all covered.
Pour the mixture into the prepared tray. Spread the peanut
mixture as smoothly and evenly as possible and
cool at room temperature until hard and cold.
Spread the top of the peanut brittle with half the melted
chocolate and place the mixture in the refrigerator for
2–3 minutes, until the chocolate is firm enough to handle.
Turn the mixture out of the tray and peel away the oiled
aluminium foil from the base of the brittle. Wipe away any
excess oil, then cover the base with the remaining half of the
chocolate. Allow this to set in the refrigerator for
3–4 minutes, then remove immediately.
Break the brittle into edible-sized pieces and store in airtight
jars at room temperature until required. Only store for
short periods of time, especially in humid conditions,
and make fresh when required.

NUT BUTTER
(see also peanut butter)

Smooth or chunky nut butters are used in the flavouring of
cakes and breads, and are also made into slices and baked
into biscuits. The best known and most widely used of these
nut butters or pastes is peanut butter, although nuts such as
pecans, pine nuts, almonds and hazelnuts can also be made
into a butter or paste.

NUTMEG
(see also spice)

A spice which grows on the nutmeg tree, which is bushy, tall,
and grows to 8 m (25 ft) in height. The nutmeg tree actually
grows two different spices at once. After nine years, the trees
grow the nutmeg, which is contained within the dried kernel
of the nutmeg fruit. The kernel has a groove down one side
and, when dried, splits open to release the nutmeg. The
outside coating, though, is ground for use and is known as
mace. The nutmeg kernel is ground or sold whole. A better
flavour is obtained when it is bought whole and ground
freshly onto foods, as it loses its flavour quickly otherwise.

NUTMEG GERANIUM BANANA CAKE

150 g (5 oz) unsalted butter
105 g (3½ oz) caster (superfine) sugar
¼ cup (1½ oz) light brown sugar
3 eggs
2 teaspoons dark rum
1 teaspoon ground nutmeg
⅛ teaspoon ground cardamom
1 tablespoon geranium leaves, chopped
250 g (8 oz) peeled and mashed bananas
1¼ cups (5 oz) plain (all-purpose) flour
2 teaspoons baking powder (soda)
150 g (5 oz) apricot glaze (see page 10)
150 g (5 oz) fresh fondant (see page 118)
½ cup (2 oz) roasted chopped almonds
raspberry coulis (see page 162), for serving

Preheat oven to 160°C (320°F).
Grease a 24 cm (10 in) springform cake tin well
and line with baking paper (parchment).
Place butter and sugars in a mixing bowl and beat until light
and creamy. Add eggs one at a time, beating well after each
one is added. Add spices, geranium leaves and banana to the
mixture. Fold through lightly until combined. Sift flour and
baking powder and add to mixture. Fold through until well
combined. Spread mixture into prepared cake tin and
bake in preheated oven for 60–70 minutes.
When baked and cool, turn the cake upside down onto a cake
rack and spread the top and sides lightly with the boiled
apricot glaze. Spread the fondant over the top and allow to
drizzle down the sides of the cake. Press the roasted nuts
around the base of the cake. Allow the fondant to set.
Cut and serve with fresh raspberry coulis.

OATCAKE

One of the original forms of unleavened bread, oatcake was a mix of oats, water and salt which was baked on a hot griddle plate over an open flame. A common form of bread in medieval Wales and Scotland, it is the predecessor of many oatcake biscuits or crackers now served with cheese.

OATMEAL

This is produced by removing the husks and separating out the grain and chaff from the oats. The oats are then ground to a powder, which can vary from coarse to fine in texture. Oatmeal is used in some breads and crackers.

OATS

A member of the cereal grass family, oats are cultivated for their seed, which is used to make cakes, biscuits (cookies) and porridge. More commonly known as rolled or breakfast oats, which are produced by heat-treating the oats and passing them through heavy rollers. The result is a flat oat which is commonly used in porridge for breakfast. It is also used in Bircher muesli and other forms of muesli.

NEW ORLEANS OAT COOKIES
125 g (4 oz) unsalted (sweet) butter
1½ cups (9 oz) soft (light) brown sugar
1 tablespoon clear honey
1 tablespoon cream
1 egg
1 cup (4 oz) plain (all-purpose) flour
½ teaspoon baking powder (soda)
1 cup (5 oz) oatmeal

Preheat oven to 180°C (350°F). Line baking trays (sheets) with baking paper (parchment).
Place butter and sugar in a mixing bowl with honey and cream until light and fluffy. Add egg and continue mixing until combined. Sift flour with baking powder and oatmeal and add to creamed mixture. Place teaspoonfuls of the mixture on the prepared sheets and bake in the preheated oven for 12–15 minutes. Remove and cool for 5 minutes on the sheets before removing to cake racks to finish cooling.

OBSTTORTE
(see also fruit tart)

The name of a Dutch fruit flan which consists of a base of sponge cake, a filling of crème pâtissière and glacé (candied) fruits. It is surrounded by a decoration of roasted flaked almonds.

OEUFS A LA NEIGE

A delicious light dessert of poached meringues which are floated on a light lemon-flavoured crème anglaise.

5 egg whites
1 cup (7 oz) caster (superfine) sugar
2 cups (16 fl oz) milk
1 vanilla bean
⅓ cup (2 oz) sugar
1 quantity lemon-flavoured crème anglaise (see page 84)

Whisk egg whites until peaks form, and slowly add the first amount of sugar while still whisking slowly. Beat until all sugar is completely dissolved and whites retain stiff peaks. Place milk, the second amount of sugar and the vanilla bean in a saucepan and bring to the boil. Reduce heat and continue to simmer. Place tablespoonfuls of the meringue into the simmering milk, turning each meringue over and over for 3–4 minutes. When the meringues have set firm, remove them carefully and place them directly on a plate or bowl of crème anglaise.

OILS, COOKING

The difference between a fat and an oil is that an oil should be liquid at room temperature. Oils can be obtained from many fruits, vegetables, seeds and nuts and are used for different purposes in different cultures and cuisines. They are divided into fat types: saturated, polyunsaturated and monounsaturated are just a few of the classes or categories. Most oils are extracted by pressing, either with or without the use of heat. Cold-pressed oils are preferred. Once the product has been pressed, the seed cake still contains an amount of oil, so a solvent is added to dissolve the oil from the seed cake. The solvent is then evaporated.

A wide variety of oils is used, but those most commonly used by the pastry chef are walnut oil, vegetable oil, olive oil, sesame oil and almond oil. Some oils are used as part of the ingredients, while others, with higher smoking points, are used for cooking items.

Sometimes oil is used as the sole fat content of a cake: hummingbird cake, carrot cake and pear cake, for example. In other instances, oils are simply sprinkled over doughs such as pizzas or focaccia to assist with cooking, add flavour and give moisture to the baked product.

OLIEBOLLEN

These rich, fried doughnuts of the Netherlands are flavoured with spices and filled with apples, fruit mince or mixed (candied) peel and other dried fruits. Traditionally served during the Christmas festive season, they are rolled in sugar or made small and served with a sweet dipping sauce.

OMELETTE
(see also eggs)

A sweet omelette is produced by first whisking egg yolks with some sugar and whisking the whites until stiff. The two mixtures are then folded together and cooked in a frying pan (skillet). When cooked, the omelette is covered with chopped fresh fruits or berries and folded in half. It is served dusted with icing sugar.

OMELETTE SURPRISE

An oval-shaped iced dessert consisting of a syrup-soaked biscuit (cookie) or sponge base topped with ice cream. The ice cream and base are covered with Italian meringue and the whole thing is dusted with icing (powdered) sugar. The omelette is baked in a hot oven for 2–3 minutes, or a small blowtorch or gas gun is used to glaze the meringue until golden brown. The shape of this traditional dessert is part of its surprise, as is the flavour of the enclosed ice creams.

ORANGE
(see also citrus)

Perhaps the most popular fruit in the world, oranges are one of the sweetest members of the citrus family. As well as being used in the pastry kitchen for their sweet juice, oranges can be skinned and slices of the bright orange flesh served as is, soaked in liqueurs or steeped in a rich caramel to make caramelised oranges.

As the flesh is divided into compartments by rows of white veins, oranges can be segmented for use on fruit tartlets, in fruit salads or as a garnish. A correctly segmented orange is a sign of the pastry chef's professionalism.

The orange flesh is tightly surrounded by a white layer of pith which is best discarded as it has no flavour and becomes bitter when cooked.

The skin of the orange, though, contains essential oils and essences. These can be removed by grating (zesting) or by rubbing a sugar cube over the surface, which will soak up the oils and flavour. The zest or rind of the orange can be used on its own, crystallised or boiled in sugar syrup and dipped in chocolate as a petit four or garnish, or left plain for serving on top of cakes or desserts.

ORANGE BLOSSOM

Orange blossoms have been used in pâtisseries throughout history. They used to be picked fresh and used in cakes, jellies and jams, but today it is a safer practice to simply use the flavour of the orangeflower water which is produced commercially from Seville orange blossom.

ORANGEFLOWER WATER

A distilled liquid from the orange blossom of the Seville orange tree, or bitter oranges, orangeflower water has been used for centuries in the manufacture of many confections, cakes and desserts, particularly in Turkey, Iran and Africa. There it is used in ice creams, sorbets, Turkish delight and sugar syrups that are poured over pastries. It was also added in small amounts to sugar to impart the flavour and aroma of orange blossom.

ORANGE JUICE

A popular drink worldwide, orange juice can be used by the pastry chef for jellies and also to soak sponges and cakes to prevent them drying out.

Make a syrup of equal parts orange juice to sugar and boil for 10–15 minutes, allowing the syrup to reduce slightly. This orange syrup can be brushed onto thin layers of cake before decorating the cake to prevent the layers going stale. Using orange juice for this purpose is cheaper than using expensive orange liqueurs or brandies.

ORANGE CAKE

1½ cups (6 oz) plain (all-purpose) flour
2 teaspoons baking powder (soda)
180 g (6 oz) unsalted (sweet) butter
⅔ cup (5 oz) caster (superfine) sugar
grated rind and juice of 2 oranges
2 eggs
½ cup (2 oz) ground almonds

To Decorate
orange frosting (see page 125)
slices of fresh orange

Preheat oven to 180°C (350°F).
Lightly grease a 23 cm (9 in) springform cake tin with butter and line with baking paper (parchment).
Mix flour and baking powder and sift twice. Beat butter and sugar until creamy, light and fluffy. Mix in orange rind and juice and beat very well. Add the eggs one at a time, beating very well after each one is added. Mix in sifted flour and baking powder and almonds by hand. Do not over mix.
Pour into prepared tin and bake for 40–45 minutes, or until a skewer inserted in the centre of the cake comes out dry and the cake has shrunk slightly away from the sides of the tin. Cool in the tin on a cake rack.
When cold, remove from the pan and cover the top of the cake with orange frosting. Decorate with slices of orange.

ORANGE STICKS

3 large oranges of a good colour
1¼ cups (10 oz) granulated sugar
1 cup (8 fl oz) water
200 g (7 oz) dark (plain or semi-sweet) chocolate,
melted (see page 62)
60 g (2 oz) unsalted (sweet) butter, melted

Orange Supreme Torte Step-by-Step

Step 1: After coating the cake with warm apricot glaze, roll out the modelling chocolate to about 3 mm (⅛ in) thick, and wide enough to cover the cake easily.

Step 2: Stretch the modelling chocolate until it is wider than the cake, and place it on the glazed surface, allowing it to fall where and how it pleases.

Step 3: When the cake is completely covered with the chocolate, carefully mould the surface by hand to make folds in the chocolate, being careful not to flatten the top. Neaten the bottom edge of the chocolate. See page 198.

Step 1: Using a set of cutters to measure from, pipe marzipan rings onto the prepared trays. The rings should go from large, to a small ball. Bake the rings until they are golden brown.

Step 2: Bake the rings until they are golden brown.

Step 3: Join the rings together with chocolate, piping it thicker at the back than the front so that the rings curve as they get higher.

Step 4: Join the rings in three piles and allow to set hard before joining them.

Step 5: Join the largest two sets of rings first and allow to set hard. See page 197.

The finished Overflodigshorn.

Wash and clean the oranges. Using a sharp knife, cut long thin strips of rind from the oranges. Make sure the rind is free of white pith and flesh. Cut the rind into thinner strips.

Place orange strips in a saucepan of boiling water for 30 seconds. Remove and allow to drain. Place water and sugar in another saucepan and bring slowly to the boil as the sugar dissolves. Place orange strips in the sugar mixture and allow to boil for 8 minutes. (If the sugar mixture is beginning to brown slightly, add another cup (8 fl oz) of water and reboil.) Remove orange strips and allow to sit on a wire rack for about 12 hours, or overnight.

Mix chocolate and butter in a small bowl. Use a fork to dip each orange strip into the chocolate and allow the strips to sit on a sheet of baking paper (parchment) until the chocolate has set. If the chocolate will not set at room temperature, place the sheet of orange sticks on a tray and refrigerate for 30 minutes.

Makes 15—18

ORANGE SUPREME TORTE

Made without flour, this torte uses the entire orange, giving it a rich and full-bodied flavour.

3 whole oranges
6 egg yolks
¾ cup (6 oz) caster (superfine) sugar
8 egg whites
1 teaspoon baking powder (soda)
2½ cups (9 oz) ground almonds

To Decorate
apricot glaze (see page 10)
modelling chocolate (see page 65)
cocoa powder, for dusting

Preheat oven to 180°C (350°F).
Lightly grease a 23 cm (9 in) springform cake tin with butter and line base with baking paper (parchment).
Place oranges in a saucepan, cover them with water and bring to the boil. Boil oranges for 1½ hours. Remove oranges from the water while still hot, place them in a food processor or blender and blend them to a pulp.
Beat egg yolks with ⅓ cup (3 oz) of the sugar, until the mixture forms a ribbon (see page 236). Beat egg whites until stiff peaks form. Gradually beat in remaining sugar, a spoonful at a time, until the sugar is dissolved. Add ground almonds and baking powder slowly to the meringue and beat mixture until it is well combined. Fold egg yolk mixture into orange pulp and then fold in egg whites. Pour into prepared tin. Bake for 50–55 minutes, or until the cake has shrunk slightly away from the sides of the tin and the top of the cake springs back when lightly touched.
Cool in the tin on a cake rack.
When completely cold, turn out and coat with warmed apricot glaze. To decorate the torte, cover it with modelling chocolate and lightly dust the top with cocoa powder.

See page 196

ORANGEAT

Also known as pearle orangeat, this is a small classical petit four made of an orange-flavoured almond paste which is filled with mixed (candied) peel and made into flat discs. These are then coated in several layers of sugar which has been cooked to the pearl degree, coated in a citrus-flavoured fondant and decorated with mixed (candied) peel.

OREILLETTES

A fried pastry fritter made and served at festivals in France. The fritters are flavoured with citrus zest and consist of a rectangular strip of yeast dough which is slit part the way down the centre. One end is pulled halfway through this slit to form a curl or knot. The fritter is fried and rolled in icing (powdered) sugar or cinnamon sugar before being eaten hot and fresh.

OTHELLO
(see also Desdemonas, Iagos, Rosalinds)

A sweet confection served for afternoon teas or, if made small enough, as a petit four. It was developed by an English pastry chef, who on seeing Shakespeare's *Othello*, selected a colour to describe each of the central characters — Othello, Desdemona and Iago. (The Moor Othello kills his wife, Desdemona, having been made jealous by Iago.) The pastry chef did likewise for the character of Rosalind, from another of Shakespeare's plays, *As You Like It*. He then made small cakes in honour of each character, using the same mixture – known as Othello sponge mixture – for all, but used a different filling for each, and covered each in a fondant of the relevant colour. The cakes are made by piping the mixture into small rounds, which puff in the oven to form semi-circles, then using the filling to join two rounds together. The circle or ball which is created is then covered in the appropriately coloured fondants to form each cake.

5 egg yolks
105 g (3½ oz) plain (all-purpose) flour
⅔ cup (5½ fl oz) water
5 egg whites
⅓ cup (2½ oz) caster (superfine) sugar
⅔ cup (2½ oz) cornflour (cornstarch)
200 g (6½ oz) apricot jam (jelly)
250 g (8 oz) fondant (see page 118), melted
30 g (1 oz) dark (plain or semi-sweet) chocolate, melted (see page 62)

Preheat oven to 160°C (320°F).
Grease and lightly flour three baking trays (sheets).
Place egg yolks, flour and water in the bowl of an electric mixer and beat at top speed for 15–20 minutes, by which time all the gluten strength of the flour should have been destroyed. Beat egg whites until stiff peaks form and beat in the sugar, a spoonful at a time, until it has dissolved and combined. Gently fold cornflour in by hand. Take a spoonful of the egg whites and mix by hand into the beaten egg yolks. Gently fold in the remaining egg whites. Pour mixture into a piping bag fitted with ½ cm (⅕ in) plain round nozzle.

Pipe small bulbs of mixture, about 4 cm (1½ in) in diameter, onto baking trays (sheets). Bake for 12–15 minutes, until light golden brown and springy to the touch. Cool on the sheets, then pair the Othellos up so that two of the same shape and size fit together. Spread apricot jam (jelly) onto the flat side and join the two together. Heat fondant until runny and smooth. If necessary, add a tablespoon of sugar syrup to help thin it down. Mix in melted chocolate. Place the filled Othellos on a cake rack then spoon the fondant over so that a very thin, smooth coating is achieved. Scrape up any drips of fondant and melt for re-use. When fondant has set, pipe a spiral of fondant onto each, starting from its centre and working out. Serve in paper cases.

OVEN

First used many centuries ago, ovens were initially used simply for cooking breads, as the open fire took care of everything else. Today we have the choice of electric, gas, microwave, and convection, to make cooking cakes, pastries and breads much easier. The oven consists of five insulated walls. In an electric oven, the top and bottom walls have elements attached to them; in a gas oven, a gas jet is located at the rear of the bottom wall. The insulated oven door forms the sixth wall, and is usually made of glass or has a glass window so that one can view the baking items. Oven temperature scales can be Fahrenheit, Celsius or the gas scale, though in many countries both gas scale and Fahrenheit are being phased out for the globally accepted Celsius scale.

OVEN MITTS

Also known as oven gloves, these are two hand-shaped mittens worn in the pastry kitchen by the ovens person, who deals with the baking of goods. In the home, towels and different-shaped gloves, mitts or mittens are used to prevent the heat from the baking tin or tray penetrating to the hands of the person removing it from the oven.

OVEN SPRING
(see also breadmaking)

This bread-baking term refers to the final lift of a bread dough once it goes into the oven and before the yeast dies (which prevents the bread rising any further). It is usually a sudden lift and is caused by the effect of the direct heat on the carbon dioxide within the dough.

OVERFLODIGSHORN
(see also wedding cakes)

Also known as cornucopia cake or corne d'abondance, meaning 'horn of plenty', this cake is a Scandinavian specialty. It is served as a wedding cake in Denmark and is traditionally made from many rings of marzipan, decorated and stuck together in the shape of a horn. The cake is set upright and an effigy of the bride and groom is placed on the tail of the horn. Gifts and sweets for the married couple run out from the large open hole.

The horn as a symbol of plenty originated in ancient Greece. When Zeus was lost, he hid in a cave and, being hungry, drank milk from a goat, filling a horn full of food for it in return. The horn or cornucopia design has remained as a sign of gratitude and as a thank you to the land for supplying food for all to eat. This is why the design also appears at American Thanksgiving.

500 g (16 oz) marzipan
1½ cups (12 oz) caster (superfine) sugar
6 egg whites, lightly beaten
250 g (8 oz) dark (plain or semi-sweet) chocolate, melted (see page 62)
marzipan flowers (see page 179), for decoration

Line two or three baking sheets with baking paper (parchment). Blend together marzipan and sugar until they are well combined and have formed a solid mass. Add sufficient egg white to make a soft paste that can be piped without losing its shape. Fill a piping (pastry) bag fitted with a plain 1 cm (½ in) nozzle with the marzipan paste and, using different-sized pastry cutters as a guide, pipe 10 rings of different sizes onto the prepared sheets. Shape some marzipan into a ball the same size as the centre of the second smallest ring. Leave the rings out to dry for 8 hours. Preheat oven to 160°C (350°F). Bake the rings for 10–15 minutes or until golden brown. Leave on the sheets for 24 hours to dry.

To Assemble
Take the smallest ring and join it to the next smallest with chocolate. Continue until all the rings are used. Secure the ball of marzipan to the top with more chocolate. The horn can either stand upright or be curved by piping more chocolate on one side of the ring than the other. A marzipan ball can support it underneath. Place the horn in a cold place, but do not refrigerate it, because the marzipan will sweat. Decorate with marzipan flowers. Fill the curved horn with petits fours.

See page 197

PAIN AU CHOCOLAT

Made from either croissant or Danish pastry dough, the 'pain au chocolat' is a rectangular or square piece of pastry which is rolled around a stick of chocolate, allowed to prove (rise) and then baked. The pain au chocolat is eaten in France at breakfast, or in the early part of the morning, with hot black coffee.

PAIN D'EPICES

Meaning 'bread of spices', this French delight is a cousin of the European gingerbreads and honey cakes. It traditionally contains both honey and mixed (candied) peel, and dates back several centuries.

1 cup (8 fl oz) water
¾ cup (6 oz) caster (superfine) sugar
¾ cup (9 oz) clear honey
2½ cups (10 oz) rye flour
2½ cups (10 oz) plain (all-purpose) flour
2 teaspoons baking powder (soda)
1 teaspoon mixed spice
½ teaspoon ground cinnamon
2 tablespoons mixed (candied) peel
4 egg yolks

Line a 30 x 28 x 3 cm (12 x 11 x 1½ in) baking tin with baking paper (parchment).
Place water, sugar and honey in a large saucepan and slowly bring to the boil, stirring continuously. Cool.
Sift flours, spices and baking powder into a large bowl and add mixed (candied) peel. Pour in the honey mixture and add the egg yolks. Stir mixture slowly until it comes together.
Pour mixture into the prepared tin and bake for 60–70 minutes. Cool. Cut into fine slices and serve.

PALETS DE DAME

This traditional French small, crisp, biscuit (cookie) style petit four is served with mousses and other soft desserts, or simply with coffee or other hot beverages. The biscuits are usually left plain, but can be flavoured with orange or lemon, or by adding mixed (candied) peel.

3 egg whites
½ cup (3 oz) icing (powdered) sugar
45 g (1½ oz) unsalted (sweet) butter, melted
⅔ cup (2½ oz) plain (all-purpose) flour

Preheat oven to 175°C (345°F). Grease two baking trays (sheets) well and dust each with flour. With your finger, mark three 7 cm (2½ in) circles on each of the floured trays. Place egg whites in a mixing bowl and whisk until they just begin to turn frothy. Continue mixing and add the sifted icing sugar and melted butter. Add the flour and mix with a spatula until the paste is smooth and lump free.
Allow the mixture to rest for 15 minutes.
Place 1 heaped teaspoonful of the mixture in each marked circle on the sheet and use a small spatula or palette knife to spread the mixture so that it fills the circle.
Bake one sheet at a time in the preheated oven for 5–8 minutes, or until the biscuits begin to brown slightly around the edges. Remove the sheet and quickly slide a palette knife underneath each cookie. Place cookies on a cake rack to cool.

PALETTE KNIFE

Flat or bent, large or small, a palette knife has a metal blade which is blunt and rounded at its tip, attached to a wooden or plastic/rubber handle. The knife is used for decorating or spreading icings and chocolate on cakes, biscuits (cookies) and most other baked goods.

PALMIER
(see also puff pastry)

Also referred to as pig's ears or donkey's ears, a palmier is made from puff pastry which is rolled thinly and then folded several times over itself, with the layers separated by sugar. Cut into thin slices, the palmier bakes to a golden colour with the puff layers spreading flat on the baking sheet. As it bakes, the sugar that is trapped between the layers turns to caramel and gives the baked product a crisp crust as well as a sweet flavour. They are traditionally made quite small and served as petits fours, but they can be made larger and sandwiched together with chocolate-flavoured mousse or whipped cream and fresh fruit.

300 g (10 oz) puff pastry (see page 228)
egg white, lightly beaten, for glazing
granulated sugar, for sprinkling

Preheat oven to 180°C (350°F). Grease a baking tray (sheet). On a lightly floured surface, roll pastry to 2–3 mm (⅛ in) in thickness and 30–40 cm (12–16 in) in width. Brush pastry with egg white and sprinkle with sugar. Fold edges of the pastry in so that they meet in the centre. Using the rolling pin, roll gently over the pastry to press the two layers together. Brush again with egg white and sprinkle again with sugar. Again bring the two edges together and then roll again to flatten. Repeat this process once more. Using a sharp knife, cut the pastry strip into 1 cm (½ in) slices and place each of these cut-side down on the prepared sheet, leaving room for spreading between them. Bake in preheated oven for 8–10 minutes, then remove. Using a palette knife, turn the palmiers over and place back in the oven for a further 10 minutes, or until golden brown.

PALM SUGAR
(see also sugar)

Obtained from the coconut palm, palm sugar or jaggery is the dark brown sugary sap of the tree and is used in place of ordinary sugar in certain recipes. It is common in Asian and Indian cookery.

PANADE
(see also soufflés)

This paste, produced using a variety of recipes, can have various consistencies. It is used as a base for soufflés. It usually has a crème pâtissière base rich with egg yolks, then has egg whites folded through it to form the soufflé.

PANARY
(see also aeration, fermentation, yeast)

Panary refers to a form of fermentation or aeration; panary action refers to doughs risen using yeast. It derives from the Latin word 'panare', which means bread.

PANCAKES
(see also crêpes)

One of the world's most popular and oldest types of cake product, having a different form in almost every culture, pancakes are made from a flat sweet or savoury batter of flour, eggs and milk. They are virtually a thick form of crêpe, known in Russia as blinis, Mexico as tortillas, North America as flapjacks, Australia as pikelets or griddle cakes, by the Jews as blintzes, and by many other names in many other places.

While some countries serve pancakes as a savoury dish, the Russians in particular being famed for their (dairy) sour cream, salmon and caviar blinis, the majority of countries serve pancakes as a breakfast or sweet dessert dish, smothered with maple syrup, whipped butter or stewed fruits, ice creams and toppings.

Pancakes are traditionally eaten before Lent or Passover, as a means of building one's strength before the long period of fasting, and also because most of the ingredients included in the pancake are forbidden during Lent. The day on which these pancakes are eaten is known as Pancake or Shrove Tuesday. It is observed in most English-speaking countries. In England, it was a tradition to hold pancake races (before eating the pancakes) in which the local housewives had to flip the morning pancake on the first toll of the church bells and then run, flipping their pancakes, to the church, trying to reach it before the last toll. The name 'shrove' derives from the word shrive, the Tuesday before Lent being the day on which the parishioners had to shrive, or confess, their sins.

2 eggs
½ cup (4 oz) caster (superfine) sugar
30 g (1 oz) unsalted (sweet) butter, melted
¾ cup (6 fl oz) milk
2 cups (8 oz) plain (all-purpose) flour, sifted
1 teaspoon baking powder (soda)

Place eggs and sugar in a mixing bowl and whisk until light and fluffy. Fold in melted butter and milk. Fold through flour and baking powder and mix until a smooth batter has formed. Pour a little of the mixture into a frying pan (skillet) which has been heated and spread lightly with a small amount of oil (use 4 tablespoons with each pancake).

Allow the pancake to cook until the top surface is full of bubbles. Using a spatula, flip the pancake over and cook the second side until golden brown in colour. The pan should be hot enough for each side of the pancake to take no more than 3 minutes. Remove pancakes from the frying pan and serve immediately with maple syrup.

PANCAKE SYRUP
(see maple syrup)

PANAMA CAKE

A beautiful fine-textured cake with a nutty flavour.

6 egg yolks
1 egg
½ cup (3 oz) icing (powdered) sugar
½ cup (2 oz) ground hazelnuts (filberts)
5 egg whites
50 g (2 oz) sponge cake, crumbed
½ cup (2 oz) ground almonds
⅓ cup (1½ oz) plain (all-purpose) flour

To Decorate
1 quantity no-fuss chocolate buttercream (see page 43)
1 cup (3½ oz) flaked almonds, roasted (see page 5)
cocoa powder

Preheat oven to 180°C (350°F).
Lightly grease a 23 cm (9 in) springform cake tin with butter and line the base with baking paper (parchment).
Beat egg yolks, whole egg and sugar until light and fluffy, and mixture forms a ribbon (see page 236). Mix in ground hazelnuts. Beat egg whites until stiff peaks form. Mix a large spoonful of the beaten egg whites into the beaten egg yolks by hand. Very gently fold in remainder of the egg whites, cake crumbs, almond and flour. Pour into prepared tin and bake in preheated oven for 45–50 minutes or until the cake has shrunk slightly away from the sides of the tin and the top springs back when lightly touched. Cool in the tin for 5 minutes before turning out onto a cake rack.
When completely cold, cut cake into thirds horizontally. Spread two layers with buttercream and stack one on top of the other. Top with remaining layer and cover the top and sides with the remaining buttercream. Press flaked almonds onto the top and sides. Dust with cocoa powder.

PANETTONE

Similar to the French brioche, the Italian panettone is a traditional festive bread. Baked in a tall cylindrical mould, the panettone is rich, buttery and filled with dried fruits. First produced in this form in Milan during the 15th century, according to one story, it is thought to have been around in some form since the 3rd century. The name derives from 'pan di toni', meaning bread of Toni, the baker who is said to have invented this famous product.

Story has it that a wealthy young Italian wished to marry the baker's daughter. However, the baker being of a poor class, it was not conventional for the two to marry, so the wealthy lad gave the baker, Toni, all the ingredients required to make a special bread. Toni made his bread, and it made him so famous and wealthy that his daughter was soon married to the wealthy lad.

PANFORTE DI SIENA

A very flat, heavy, rich cake made with honey, spices and dried fruits, panforte is traditionally served in thin slices, dusted heavily with icing (powdered) sugar, at Christmas. It is thought to originate from the honey or ginger cakes of Medieval times, but it could possibly have evolved from a sweet peppered fruit loaf brought back from Asia by merchants and traders. Although also known as Vienna cake, the panforte is most definitely Italian.

½ cup (6 oz) clear honey
¼ cup (3 oz) golden syrup (light treacle)
1⅓ cups (7 oz) soft (light) brown sugar
½ cup (2 oz) plain (all-purpose) flour
½ cup (2 oz) cocoa powder
2 teaspoons ground cinnamon
1 teaspoon mixed spice
1 cup (4 oz) dried apricots, finely chopped
½ cup (3 oz) glacé (candied) pineapple, finely chopped
1 cup (5 oz) mixed (candied) peel
1½ cups (6 oz) hazelnuts (filberts), finely chopped
1⅓ cups (5 oz) blanched almonds, finely chopped
¾ cup (3 oz) macadamia (Queensland) nuts, finely chopped
zest of 1 lemon
zest of 1 orange
1 tablespoon marmalade
icing (powdered) sugar, for dusting

Preheat oven to 160°C (320°F).
Lightly grease and line an 18 x 28 x 2 cm (7 x 11 x ¾ in) baking sheet with baking paper (parchment).
Place honey, golden syrup and brown sugar in a saucepan and slowly bring to the boil. Boil, stirring continuously, for 5 minutes. Mix the flour, cocoa, spices, fruits and nuts, lemon and orange zest and marmalade in a large mixing bowl. Pour boiled mixture over the top and stir until all are combined.
Pour the mixture onto prepared sheet and press flat, using the back of a spoon. Bake in preheated oven for 25 minutes. Remove and dust heavily with icing sugar while still hot. Cool for 40 minutes, before cutting into very thin fingers to serve.

Makes 28–30

PAPAYA
(see pawpaw)

PAPER CORNETS
(see also piping bags)

These are small paper piping bags made from silicon paper or baking paper (parchment). They are usually used where small amounts of fine piping work are required, for which nozzles are too large. The bag is disposed of after use.

PARATHA
(see also bread)

This Indian unleavened bread is generally made from wholewheat or wholemeal flour. The dough pieces are rolled flat, folded and then fried, creating thin, flaky, crisp layers. The bread can be stuffed or served plain with savoury dishes.

PARCHMENT PAPER

Generally refers to the silicon-based parchment (baking) papers available in both retail and industrial sizes. Parchment paper does not brown or weaken with heating and can be used several times for baking of goods. It is also good to use with sugar, praline and chocolate work, because these substances do not stick to the paper at all, so it can be re-used several times.

PARFAIT
(see also coupé)

In French, 'parfait' means perfect and a delicious parfait is exactly that — light, smooth and rich. It is produced from a mixture of whipped egg yolks, cream, occasionally egg whites, and a flavouring. It is frozen and then served as is.

The name actually refers to two different desserts, though, the other being a coupé-style dessert of ice cream layers, sauce, nuts and fruits, which is served in a parfait glass (a long, narrow fluted glass).

3 egg yolks
¾ cup (4 oz) icing (powdered) sugar
1½ cups (12 fl oz) cream, lightly whipped (soft peaks)
2 egg whites
6 teaspoons caster (superfine) sugar
2 teaspoons ground cinnamon
2 teaspoons cracked black pepper

Whisk egg yolks and icing sugar in a large bowl over a bain-marie until a thick and creamy sabayon (see page 243) has been achieved. Fold through the lightly whipped cream. Whisk egg whites to a soft foam and, while still mixing, slowly add sugar, until all is dissolved. Fold egg whites through the mixture of egg yolk and cream and finally add the cinnamon and black pepper. Pour the mixture into a log-shaped mould or deep tray, cover and freeze for 6 hours, or overnight. Cut into slices and serve immediately with langue de chat biscuits (cookies) or with a warm cherry compôte.

Panforte di Siena, top and Lebkuchen, bottom (see page 163)

PARIS BREST
(see also choux pastry)

This famous French gâteau was invented in 1891 as a celebration cake for the bicycle race from Paris to Brest: the large circle of choux pastry represents a bicycle wheel. In the traditional Paris Brest, the choux ring is baked, then cut horizontally, filled with fresh fruits and sweetened cream and dusted with icing sugar. The choux pastry can also have flaked almonds baked onto it.

1½ cups (12 fl oz) water
190 g (6½ oz) unsalted (sweet) butter
1½ cups (6 oz) plain (all-purpose) flour
3 eggs, lightly beaten
1 cup (3½ oz) flaked almonds, roasted (see page 5)
crème Chantilly (see page 85)
fresh fruit pieces
icing (powdered) sugar, for dusting

Preheat oven to 200°C (400°F).
Line a baking tray (sheet) with baking paper (parchment) and draw a 23 cm (9 in) circle on it.
Place water and butter in a saucepan and bring to the boil over medium heat. Remove from heat and add flour all at once, beating all the time. Return the saucepan to the heat and add lightly beaten eggs, a little at a time, until the mixture is smooth, soft and shiny. Place mixture in a piping (pastry) bag fitted with a medium to large fluted nozzle.
Pipe a thick line of choux pastry onto prepared sheet, following the outline of the circle. Sprinkle flaked almonds onto the pastry. Bake for 40–50 minutes, or until the choux pastry is a medium golden brown.
Cool on the sheet on a cake rack.
When cold, cut in half horizontally and fill bottom half with crème Chantilly and fresh fruit. Replace top and dust with icing sugar.

PARIS STICKS

These are soft French shortbreads dipped in chocolate.

250 g (8 oz) unsalted (sweet) butter, softened
½ cup (3 oz) icing (powdered) sugar, sifted
1 teaspoon vanilla essence (extract)
1 egg white, lightly beaten
2½ cups (10 oz) plain (all-purpose) flour, sifted
2 teaspoons lemon juice
210 g (7 oz) dark (plain or semi-sweet) chocolate,
melted (see page 62)

Preheat oven to 175°C (345°F). Line two baking trays (sheets) with baking paper (parchment).
Place butter, icing sugar and vanilla essence in a mixing bowl and mix until very light and fluffy and pale in colour. Add egg white and mix in thoroughly. When combined, add flour and lemon juice and mix through thoroughly and quickly. Place the mixture in a piping (pastry) bag fitted with a 1 cm (½ in) star-shaped piping nozzle. Pipe onto prepared sheets in 5–6 cm (2 in) lengths, about 2–3 cm (1 in) apart. Bake in preheated oven for 10–15 minutes, or until slightly golden brown. Cool on the tray.
When cold, dip 1 cm (½ in) of the shortbread into the melted chocolate. Place back on the lined sheet to set.

Makes 36

PARISIEN

A French cake of the 18th century, this consists of a lemon-flavoured frangipani cake with dried or crystallised (candied) fruits. The cake is masked in an Italian meringue mixture and flamed quickly to give a golden brown glaze.

PARISIEN CREAM
(see also ganache)

Invented in the late 1800s, Parisien cream is the equivalent of ganache, a mixture of boiled cream and chocolate (in varying ratios), used widely in the pastry area.

PARKIN

An early form of gingerbread made using oats, parkin is a tradition of the Scottish Highlands and the Yorkshire Lakes District, where it is traditionally served on 5 November, Guy Fawkes' Night.

150 g (5 oz) unsalted (sweet) butter
⅔ cup (8 oz) golden syrup (light treacle)
1 tablespoon clear honey
½ cup (3 oz) light brown sugar
75 g (2½ oz) caster (superfine) sugar
1 tablespoon mixed spice
2 cups (8 oz) wholemeal (wholewheat) flour
½ cup (2 oz) plain (all-purpose) flour
4 cups (12 oz) rolled (minute) oats
1 teaspoon bicarbonate of soda
1 cup (8 fl oz) milk

Preheat oven to 175°C (345°F).
Grease a 25 x 30 x 3 cm (10 x 12 x 1¼ in) baking tray (jelly roll pan) and line with baking paper (parchment). Place butter, golden syrup, honey, sugars and spice in a saucepan and place over low heat. Bring to the boil, stirring continuously so as not to burn the base. Place flour, oats and bicarbonate soda in a large mixing bowl and pour the hot liquid over the top. Using a wooden spoon, stir the mixture and begin adding the milk. Stir to a batter, then pour mixture into prepared tray. Bake for 45–50 minutes, or until firm to the touch. Remove and cool in the tray before cutting into fine slices.

PASHKA

A Russian cake served during Easter festivities, pashka is made from curd or cottage cheese, dried fruits and nuts and is moulded into a pyramid shape. The outstanding feature of the pashka is that the sides of the pyramid are decorated with dried fruits in the letters XB — the letters stand for the words 'Christ is risen'. The pashka is traditionally served with slices of warm kulich, the Russian Easter cake.

PASSIONFRUIT

The passionfruit (purple granadilla) is a vine fruit which originated in South America and is today grown in most tropical areas. Also called a granadilla or bell apple, it is a small ball-shaped fruit with a thick, dark purple to black skin which covers a moist interior of yellow/orange pulp with black seeds. The pulp and seed are sweet but slightly acidic to the tastebuds. When first seen by the Spanish while colonising South America, the passionfruit vine was only noted for its flowers. They called the flowers 'passion flowers' in their religious talks, when they were attempting to convert the indigenous South Americans. It was from this time that the fruit became known as passionfruit.

Passionfruit is used in sorbets, ice creams, cakes and biscuits (cookies), sauces, parfaits and soufflés.

PASTA

Pasta is a dough which is dried and then boiled to al dente stage. It is then served on its own or with a variety of sauces. Traditionally produced with durum wheat, due to its high gluten level, pasta is a product of the Italians, although it is thought that Marco Polo may have brought the recipe with him from his trips to China. Pasta was not produced on a commercial basis until the mid to late 1800s, but today is one of the world's biggest convenience foods.

Pasta in its many forms is now eaten all over the world and in recent times it has also been produced using a sweetened or chocolate-flavoured dough and served warm, with sauces, as a dessert.

2 cups (8 oz) strong (bread) flour
4 eggs
2 tablespoons oil
pinch of salt

Place all ingredients in the bowl of an electric mixer and beat well for 5–8 minutes. If the dough feels a little too

dry, add a small amount of extra oil.
When dough is well kneaded, remove from the bowl and
cover. Allow to rest for 20–30 minutes in a cool area.
Cut dough into four pieces and roll each as thin as possible
(or as required). Cut into the desired shapes and set in a
covered tray in a cool place until required.
Bring some water to the boil and cook the pasta
for 5–8 minutes, or until al dente
(firm but not crunchy in the centre).

PASTILLAGE
(see also centrepieces, sugar)

Pastillage is one of the most exciting mediums with which the pastry chef can work, producing designs that can be flat or shaped in almost any form imaginable. It is a sweet paste of icing (powdered) sugar, egg whites, gelatine and starch, the starch being added to help the paste dry. If the paste will not dry, additional starch is added. Once produced, the pastillage is allowed to rest and then rolled and either cut out or modelled. The piece is then allowed to sit and dry in the open air for 1–2 days before being painted or added to major designs. Large pieces of pastillage can be painted with cocoa or food colourings.

2 tablespoons gelatine powder
4 tablespoons warm water
3½ cups (21 oz) icing (powdered) sugar
1 cup (4 oz) cornflour (cornstarch)
2–3 egg whites

Soak gelatine in warm water. When firm, place the dish
containing the gelatine in hot water and allow to melt to a
clear liquid. Place icing sugar and cornflour in the bowl of an
electric mixer, add two of the egg whites plus the melted
gelatine and mix together quickly to combine all ingredients
thoroughly. If mixture is very firm, add extra egg white.
If it is too wet, slowly add more cornflour. (The mixture
should be very white, firm to the touch and not sticky.
It should not form a solid ball, but remain a firm, dry paste.)
Beat mixture for 1–2 minutes and then remove and store in
an airtight container for 24 hours. After this,
it can be used for modelling or rolling.
When working with pastillage, use only a very small amount
of cornflour to dust under a small piece of the mixture.
Do not work with too much paste, because it dries quickly.
As soon as the paste becomes too dry to use, place it in a bag.
Once you have accumulated an amount of this dry paste,
place it in the bowl of an electric mixer, add another egg white
and reduce to a paste of the same consistency.

PASTILLE
(see also confectionery)

A sugar-based confection which is said to have been invented by chef Jean Pastilla, who worked for Marie de Medici. Pastilles are small, flat, round sweets produced from a boiled sugar syrup mixture to which gum arabic has been added. The hot sugar syrup is poured into a large hand-held funnel which has a rod inserted into the small hole at the base. The rod is lifted at regular intervals so that small amounts of mixture are released and poured onto either a starch tray or silicon sheets (parchment paper) to form droplets. It is also possible to stamp out the pastilles by rolling a series of cutters over the sugar syrup mixture while still warm.

Pastilles can be either chocolate-coated or flavoured with the oils of citrus fruits or various essences (extracts).

PASTRY
(see also individual listings)

Pastries are a vital medium for the pastry cook and must be made to perfection. They are a combination of flour, fat and a liquid and usually have an egg added to combine the mixture. Choux, sweet, shortcrust, puff and croissant or Danish pastries are perhaps the most well-known basic pastries, all others being a variation of one of these, with one or more ingredients being added to or deleted from the basic recipe.

PASTRY BAG
(see also piping bag)

This bag is the larger variety, usually made of material or plastic, and is used for pastry cream and choux pastry.

PASTRY BRUSH

A tool which has many hairs or bristles attached to one end of a stick or handle, usually made of wood. Pastry brushes come in a variety of sizes and shapes and are used to spread glazes, egg wash and syrups, oils, butter and milk over pastry. They have a variety of other uses as well, including brushing flour from doughs before rolling or brushing cake crumbs from cake slices before joining them together with buttercreams.

PASTRY BLENDER

Pastry brushes are similar to whisks in appearance, but much stronger, consisting of a series of metal loops attached to a metal handle. They are used to combine fat and other ingredients into flour to produce pastry. They are really only useful for small quantities, not for large mixtures.

PASTRY CASE
(see also bouchée, vol au vents)

A case or crust of pastry, either sweet or shortcrust, puff pastry or shortbread, into which other mixtures will be placed after their baking.

PASTRY CREAM
(see crème pâtissière)

PASTRY CUTTER
(see biscuit cutter)

PASTRY MARGARINE
(see margarine)

PASTRY WHEEL
(see also multiple wheel cutter)

Pastry wheels come in many shapes and sizes and have many uses. Several wheels joined together on a collapsible frame make up the multiple wheel cutter used for cutting large trays of bars and slices, while the single wheels on wooden handles are used for cutting slices from flat cake sheets, for marking or cutting Danish and croissant doughs, and as pizza cutters. Shaped wheels (which are used to produce decorative imprints) can also be used to remove the pastry from pies or tartlet lids or to cut decorative pastry strips for the tops of pies.

PASTIE
(see also Cornish pastie)

An enclosed pie, usually containing vegetables, although meat can be used. A disc of pastry has the filling placed in its centre, then the edges are brought to the top, pinched firmly together and baked.

PATE A CHOUX

Pâte à choux is the French name for choux pastry or a dish which contains choux pastry mixture.

PATE A DECOR

Otherwise known as hippen decorating paste, pâte à decor is similar to the tuile biscuit mixture. It is used to pipe designs which are then used on desserts. When baked, it is like a thin biscuit.

PATE A FONCER

Pâte à foncer is short pastry which is used mainly for lining tarts and pies. It contains very little sugar.

PATE BOMBE

Pâte bombe is a cold sabayon which is used as a filling for a bombe or as a glaze for desserts.

15 egg yolks
2½ cups (20 oz) caster (superfine) sugar
1 cup (8 fl oz) water

Combine all ingredients in a large stainless steel mixing bowl and place over a saucepan of boiling water. Whisk the mixture continuously and allow to cook over the boiling water for 1 hour. Remove mixture from heat and strain into the bowl of an electric mixer. Whisk egg mix until light and fluffy, then pour into an airtight container and store in refrigerator until required.
When needed, mix equal parts of the pâte bombe with equal parts of whipped cream.

PATE BRISEE

Pâte brisée is shortcrust pastry made with virtually no sugar which can be stored for several weeks. It is used for savoury articles such as barquettes.

PATE FEULLETEE

Pâte feulletée is also known as puff pastry.

PATE SUCREE

Pâte sucrée is a sweet shortcrust pastry also known as sweetpaste. It is used for small items where a biscuit base is required, or to make flat round discs to be placed under cakes.

PATISSIER

This is the French word for a qualified pastry tradesperson, which translates as 'pastry chef'. The pâtissier in most major establishments is the person in charge of the pastry section, and is able to work with ease with sugar, chocolate and most decorative mediums, as well as being capable of making the basic pastries, cakes and desserts.

PATISSERIE

This term refers both to the trade of creating and producing many basic and beautiful desserts and pastry goods, and to the shop in which pastries are produced and sold. The pastry-cooking trade was first spoken of in the 13th century and since that time many famous chefs, such as Carême, the Julien Brothers, Chiboust, Stohrer and, in modern times, Le Nôtre, Ewald Notter and so on, have honoured and enhanced the trade with their sheer brilliance. They are all famed for their skills, recipes or the impact they have had on pâtisserie. Over the centuries many people have worked at giving an element of mystery and fantasy to the pastry chef's trade, the food that the pastry chef creates being sweet, wicked and almost always spectacular to the eye.

PATRANQUE
(see also French toast)

This dessert is made from stale bread soaked in milk until soft then fried on both sides until golden brown. It is similar to the original French toast, where the bread is soaked in an egg and milk mixture and flavoured with cinnamon sugar. Traditionally it takes on the flavour of a soft unripened cheese folded or stirred through the hot milk mixture.

PATTY CAKE
(see also Queen cake/cup cake)

Small individual cakes produced from a buttercake mixture, cooked in a small patty cake tin, then iced or cut in half and filled with cream or jam.

The traditional patty cake has a rounded base and differs from the cup cake or Queen cake in that it is not baked in paper cups.

PATTY PAN
(see also tins/moulds)

Theses are baking trays (sheets) which have 12–16 holes, each with a slight curved indentation of about 2 cm (¾ in) depth, in which patty cakes are baked.

Pavlova Step-by-Step

Step 1: The pavlova must be finished with its crème Chantilly and fresh fruits just before being served. Ensure that all fruits and the crème are ready beforehand.

Step 2: To decorate, cover the top surface of the pavlova with the crème Chantilly and spread evenly.

Step 3: The fruit decoration can be as exotic as you like, but have a plan before beginning! Once the fruit is on the crème, it is messy to remove. See page 208.

PAVLOVA

This dessert, named after Russian ballerina, Anna Pavlova, was first produced in 1935 in Perth, Western Australia when chef Herbert Sachse mixed egg whites with sugar. Harry Nairn, who owned the hotel in which it was created, reckoned that the marshmallow centre was as soft as the ballerina's personality, the whiteness was as white as her skin, and the sides resembled her tutu. Pavlovas are traditionally served cold with fresh cream and fruit.

8 egg whites
2½ cups (17½ oz) caster (superfine) sugar
1½ teaspoons white vinegar
vanilla essence (extract)
300 ml (10 fl oz) crème Chantilly (see page 85)
fresh fruit pieces dusted with icing (powdered) sugar

Preheat oven to 100°C (210°F). Line a baking tray (sheet) with baking parchment and draw a 23 cm (9 in) circle on it. Beat egg whites until stiff peaks form, then gradually beat in sugar, a spoonful at a time. Beat until sugar is dissolved. Add vinegar and vanilla essence and beat for one minute. Spread mixture inside the marked circle on the tray and bake for 1¾ hours. Turn off oven, open door slightly and leave pavlova in oven until completely cold. Place on a serving platter and just before serving, cover top with crème Chantilly and fruit pieces.

See page 207

PAWPAW

An oval tropical fruit commonly known as papaya. When ripe, it has a thin greeny-yellow skin. The flesh is orange and the hollow centre is filled with numerous small black ball-shaped seeds.

There are two main varieties. The first is as described above; the second is oval with a slightly longer neck at one end, and is firmer to touch. It is not as juicy and contains a flesh which is pinkish in colour rather than orange.

Pawpaw is used to make ice cream, mousse and sorbet desserts but is most commonly used in fruit salads. If used in recipes which contain gelatine, the pawpaw must be cooked — it contains an enzyme which will render the gelatine useless as a setting agent unless the pawpaw is cooked.

PAWPAW SORBET

flesh of 1 ripe pawpaw (papaya),
skinned, seeded and sliced
zest and juice of 1 orange
2 egg whites
¼ cup (2 oz) caster (superfine) sugar

Purée pawpaw flesh and when smooth mix in orange zest and juice. Place mixture in a flat container and freeze until it begins to firm.
Whisk egg whites in a large bowl until they form stiff peaks. Slowly add small amounts of sugar while continuing to whisk egg whites and whisk until all sugar is dissolved.
Remove pawpaw flesh from freezer and stir until smooth.

Fold pawpaw mixture into whipped egg whites. When combined, pour mixture into a container and freeze for 4–5 hours or overnight.

PEACH

A round stone fruit, the peach is used in many forms in pastry cooking. Its most renowned dish is Peach Melba. Thought to be a symbol of immortality by the Chinese, it has been cultivated there since 500 BC and is now cultivated throughout the world.

There are two varieties, freestone and clingstone, which mean exactly what their names imply: the flesh of the clingstone clings tightly to its central stone and the freestone flesh is easily separated. All varieties have a light coating of fuzz or fur and the thin skin is usually light orange to yellow. Peaches are best to eat when just ripe. The central stone is often cracked open revealing the kernel, which can be eaten although it is bitter. The whole kernel is often added to peach jams and jellies to add flavour. Peaches are also used for ice creams and sorbets, upside down cakes, crumbles, stewing and baking. Poach peaches lightly to remove their skin. Warm the fruit through for compôtes. They are also good for making preserves, jams and jellies.

PEACH MELBA

Created by the famed chef Auguste Escoffier, this dessert was named in honour of the opera singer Dame Nellie Melba, after Escoffier had heard her perform.

The original dish consisted of a poached peach served on a bed of vanilla ice cream, covered with spun sugar and served between the wings of a swan carved from ice.

The more appealing and common serving of the dish is with a sauce of raspberries on a bed of vanilla ice cream.

⅔ cup (5 oz) caster (superfine) sugar
2 cups (16 fl oz) water
1 cinnamon stick (quill)
2 cloves
3–4 fresh ripe freestone peaches
2 cups (16 fl oz) fresh raspberry purée (coulis)
3–4 scoops vanilla ice cream

Place sugar, water, cinnamon sticks (quills) and cloves in a large saucepan and bring to the boil. Immerse peaches in boiling liquid, turn down the heat and simmer for 10 minutes. Then carefully remove peaches.
Cool for several minutes before peeling the peach skin from the flesh with a small sharp knife. Place one scoop of vanilla ice cream into the centre of a chilled plate and, with the back of the ice cream scoop, press into centre of the ball of ice cream to make a hollow in which to set the peach.
Pour a small amount of raspberry purée (coulis) over the peach and serve immediately.

PEANUT
(see also nuts)

Peanuts are known to have existed since before the birth of Christ. They are native to South America, and were spread to Africa and around the world by traders and missionaries. Often referred to as ground nuts, peanuts are the seeds of a pod which grows below ground. When ready, the nuts are encased in a soft, thin, brown shell which, when cracked, reveals two red-skinned nuts. They are either eaten raw or roasted to remove the red skin. Once roasted, peanuts are used in a variety of biscuits and confectionery.

PEAR

For 4000 years since they were found in Asia and parts of Europe, pears have been dried, stewed, canned, puréed, made into sorbets, used in cakes and eaten raw. Members of the pome family (meaning they have separate compartments for their core and seeds), there are now over 5000 varieties. There are two major varieties: one is the small, almost round, yellow- to green- skinned Asian (also known as the nashi or Japanese) variety with a crisp flesh, while the second has the more typical rounded base which tapers to a narrow neck.

Its juice is often used as a sweetener in foods where excess sugar is not welcome, and is also used in confectionery.

PEAR CAKE

500 g (16 oz) ripe pears, peeled, cored and coarsely grated
4 cups (24 oz) soft light brown sugar
180 g (6 oz) walnuts chopped
3 cups (12 oz) plain (all-purpose) flour
4 level teaspoons baking powder
2 level teaspoons ground cinnamon
375 ml (12 fl oz) light (safflower) oil
3 eggs, beaten

To Decorate
1 quantity lemon cream cheese frosting (see page 125)
ground cinnamon

Preheat oven to 180°C (350°F). Grease a 23 cm (9 in) springfrom pan lightly with butter and line base with baking paper (parchment). Mix pears, sugar and walnuts and stand for 30 minutes. Mix flour, baking powder and cinnamon and sift twice. Mix oil and eggs into pear mixture and gently mix in sifted flour, by hand.
Pour mixture into prepared pan and bake for 1 hour, or until skewer inserted into the centre of the cake comes out dry. Cool in pan on a wire rack.
When cold, remove from pan and cover top and sides with frosting. Dust top lightly with cinnamon.
Serve with slices of fresh pear.

PEAR BELLE HELENE

Invented by Auguste Escoffier after seeing the opera La Belle Hélène, this dish is similar to his other renown creation, the Peach Melba. Both desserts consist of poached fruits covered with sauce and served with vanilla ice cream.

1 litre (32 fl oz) water
1 lemon, cut in half
1⅓ cups (10 oz) caster (superfine) sugar
1 cinnamon stick (quill)
2 cloves
4 whole ripe pears
4 scoops vanilla ice cream
2½ cups (20 fl oz) chocolate sauce

Place water, lemon halves, sugar, cinnamon and cloves in a large saucepan and simmer. Peel pears, leaving their stalks intact. Place pears in the simmering liquid and prevent them floating, using a smaller-sized lid rested directly onto the pears. Cook for 8–10 minutes.
Using a slotted spoon, remove cooked pears and set aside to cool until required.
When cool, use a melon baller to carefully remove the core of each pear, starting at the base and working only ¾ of the way to the top, so that the stalk remains.
Place a scoop of vanilla ice cream on a chilled plate and, using the back of the scoop, press into centre of the ice cream ball to make a hollow in which to place the pear. Place pear on top of ice cream, pour chocolate sauce over top and serve.

Chocolate Sauce
2½ cups (600 ml) thickened cream
250 g dark cooking chocolate
1½ tablespoons rum

Place all ingredients into a suacepan and stir over a low heat until chocolate is melted and all ingredients are combined into a smooth sauce. Serve immediately.

PECAN
(see also nuts)

Often referred to as the hickory nut, the pecan nut was first discovered by Native Americans. Explorers in the 1500s watched Native Americans crushing the nuts for soups and griddle breads in place of flour and thickening agents. These days we know it best because of the pecan pie.

There are 160 varieties of pecan nuts. They are used in some dishes instead of walnuts. The nut grows inside a brown, smooth oval-shaped shell, has a soft texture and is best when heated or roasted in its whole form, although they are available ground into meal or pre-roasted. They contain no cholesterol. Caramel-covered pecans are delicious in ice cream.

300 g (10 oz) pre-prepared sweet pastry
6 eggs
2 teaspoons ground cinnamon
¾ cup (4 oz) brown sugar
1½ cups (15 oz) maple syrup
400 g (13 oz) whole pecan nuts
210 g (7 oz) apricot jam

Preheat the oven to 180°C (350°F)
Line a 20–22 cm (8–9 in) flan tin or pie dish. Roll pastry thinly on a lightly floured surface. Whisk eggs lightly in a medium bowl and add cinnamon, brown sugar and maple

Petits fours Step-by-Step

Step 1: Weigh down the jam-spread sponge layers using a chopping board with a brick wrapped in aluminium foil placed on top.

Step 2: Cut out small-sized portions from the sponge, with the marzipan at the bottom. Then insert a fork into the base of each upturned petit four and dip it into the fondant.

Step 3: Decorate the dry petits fours with chocolate piping designs. See page 212.

Petits Fours – sec (see page 212)

syrup. Whisk together well and stand mixture for 5 minutes. Spread pecan nuts evenly over base of the lined flan or pie dish. Slowly pour liquid egg mixture over nuts. When dish is filled, place it on a baking tray. Bake for 30–40 minutes, or until the filling is solid. Remove and glaze with apricot jam, warmed in a saucepan, or serve with vanilla ice cream. This pie stores well and is delicious hot or cold.

PECTIN

Pectin is a natural gelling agent found in many fruits, such as apples, quinces, plums and citrus fruits. When heated, it causes jams and jellies to set. When fruits low in pectin (many of the berry family and pears) are being made into jam and jelly, they are often boiled in a muslin bag with the seeds and rind of citrus fruits to extract their pectin. Sometimes lemon juice is added.

Pectin is also available in powdered or liquid form — use 15–30 g per litre to set.

PEEL
(see also bread baking)

A peel is a thin metal or wooden blade attached to a staff, perhaps 2.5 m (7–8) ft long. The first ovens used in the Roman and Greek Empires were deep and could not be reached into by hand and so 'peels' were invented, to load and unload bread from the oven and move products around inside the oven.

Smaller versions are used in pizza establishments but are now rarely seen in bakeries, because this form of baking is cumbersome when compared with modern techniques.

PEEL
(see also candied peel)

Peel refers to the rind or zest of citrus fruits, which has been crystallised in sugar syrup and cut into strips or pieces for inclusion in fruit cakes, gingerbreads and puddings.

It is sometimes used as a decoration around pashka cakes.

PEPPERMINT

Peppermint is an aromatic herb of the mint family which blends with many other flavours in the pastry area. It is generally crushed to extract its essences and oils, which are then added to chewing gums, fondants and chocolates, ice creams, mousses, confectionery and sugar work and cakes. Used as a garnish in its natural form, peppermint is also the flavour in crème de menthe.

PERSIPAN
(see also almond paste, marzipan)

Persipan is the name of a substitute paste for marzipan and almond paste, but the word really is the correct name for the apricot or peach kernels used to make the paste. The kernels are ground, warmed and mixed with sugar and glucose to form a dough which looks similar to the other two products. Whilst in many countries persipan is often passed off as almond paste, because it has a strong almond essence aroma and flavour, European laws require that all products made using persipan must be clearly labelled.

PETIT-BEURRE

A French classic biscuit (cookie) similar to the sable cookie recipe, containing no eggs — simply sugar, flour and butter. Petits-beurres have a rich buttery taste and are baked slowly in the oven to draw out the butter flavour. They are almost always oblong in shape, with fluted edges, and are sprinkled with sugar before and after baking.

PETIT FOUR

It is uncertain whether one country can claim full honours as the creator of the petit four. It is more likely that petits fours evolved over many years. Even more inconclusive is the definition of a petit four. The words, according to Carême, date back to the 18th century, and suggest that petits fours either came from the name of the ovens (petits fours — small ovens) used to bake these products, or that in fact the art of baking these sweet delicacies was termed 'a petit four' — meaning to bake at a very low temperature. Frenchman La Vareene, the first person to devote a book entirely to pastry making, describes the small ovens used only by pastry chefs in small bakehouses as 'petits fours'. This seems to be the most likely definition. Others suggest the name refers to 'small bit' or 'one bite'. No matter what the definition, each is correct to a point. Therefore a petit four is 'a one- or two-bite morsel which is usually baked or flamed (browned) in the oven in some way'.

Many people mistakenly categorise every small sweet served after a meal or with coffee as a petit four, but to be correct, chocolates are termed pralinées, and petits fours are categorised into two separate types: 'sec' and 'glacé'.

'Sec' means dry and refers mainly to biscuits or pastries which are ready to eat once cooled from baking. Usually nothing is added to these once they are baked, although they may be joined together with a cream or chocolate filling.

'Glacé' means iced or glazed, and refers to any petit four which requires finishing with a glaze of fondant or boiled syrup. This category includes the most common of petits fours; the sponge-based, highly decorated delicacy.

These two types are subdivided into the following groups:

(i) cake- or sponge-based petit four;
(ii) biscuit-based;
(iii) marzipan-based;
(iv) fresh fruit petit four;
(v) chocolate-based.

PETIT FOUR GLACE

75 g (2 ½ oz) unsalted (sweet) butter, softened
¼ cup (2 oz) caster (superfine) sugar
3 egg yolks
5 teaspoons caster (superfine) sugar
6 egg whites
⅔ cup (2½ oz) plain (all-purpose) flour, sifted
extra caster (superfine) sugar, for sprinkling
⅓ cup (4 oz) apricot jam
120 g (4 oz) plain marzipan

Preheat oven to 160°C (320°F). Line four 18 x 28 x 2 cm (7 x 11 x ¾ in) baking trays (sheets) with baking paper (parchment). Place butter and first amount of sugar into a mixing bowl and cream until light and fluffy. Add egg yolks, one at a time, and continue creaming until mixture is a smooth light consistency. In a separate bowl, whisk egg whites until stiff peaks form. Add second amount of sugar gradually and whisk until combined. Fold flour through whisked egg whites, then fold egg white mixture lightly through butter mixture. Spread mixture thinly on each prepared tray. Bake each tray (or if you can fit them, all trays together) for 12–15 minutes, or until sponge mixture is light golden brown. Remove from oven and sprinkle each cake with caster sugar before turning out onto sheets of baking paper (parchment). (Sprinkling this extra sugar on top will prevent the cake sticking to the baking paper (parchment)).

When cool, remove baking paper (parchment) from both sides of cake layers. Place one cake layer on work surface and spread it thinly with apricot jam. Place second cake layer on top of the first and spread it with jam. Repeat for remaining layers. Place layered sponge in a baking tray (sheet) lined with greaseproof (waxed) paper. Place another sheet of greaseproof paper on top. Weigh down sponge using a chopping board with a brick (or cans of food) wrapped in aluminium foil. Leave in refrigerator for several hours, preferably overnight.

Remove weights, chopping boards and paper from layered sponge. On a lightly floured surface, roll marzipan into a thin sheet. Spread top of layered sponge sparingly with apricot jam, then place rolled marzipan on top. Press marzipan down firmly to ensure there are no air bubbles.

Turn complete cake over so that marzipan is face down and, using a ruler and a knife or different shaped cutters, cut the layered sponge into small portions, no bigger than 3 x 3 cm (1 x 1 in). (Cutting the layered sponge marzipan-side down will ensure clean edges for the finished petits fours.) Leave the cut pieces marzipan-side down and prepare fondant glaze.

Fondant Dipping
Fondant is available in small tubs and packets from supermarkets or in large quantities from bakeries. 300 g (10 oz) of fondant is required to glaze petits fours. Heat

fondant over a water bath (bain marie or double broiler) to between 35–37°C (95–99°F) — no hotter. Overheating the fondant results in the sugar crystallising, which gives a patchy look to the set glaze. As the fondant heats, add any flavourings or colourings, then thin it down with water to the required consistency. Stir the fondant constantly while heating to give it a fuller sheen when set.

Coating Petits Fours

There are many ways to do this and as you experiment you will find your own way. Buy a dipping fork from a specialist kitchenware store. Insert the fork into the base of the petit four. Dip it into the warm fondant and turn it right side up to dry on a wire rack.

A cheaper way is to pick up the petit four at its base with your fingers, dip it into fondant and then turn it right side up to drain and dry. Excess fondant runs off the sides of the dipped petit four and can be remelted and used again with fresh fondant as long as it is free from crumbs.

It is good practise to dip one or two petits fours and let them set before dipping all of them. This tells you if the consistency of the fondant is correct, that is, thin enough to drain away from the top of the petit four and leave a bevelled edge. The fondant takes about 5–10 minutes to dry. If the fondant does not look dry allow it to set for a few minutes more. Once the fondant is bruised or cracked, or has fingerprints on it, the petit four is ruined.

When the fondant has set, carefully slide a flat sharp knife under each petit four, separating it from the rack and removing all excess fondant. To prevent the now exposed underside of the petit four drying out, place it in a paper petit four cup. Decorate with chocolate piping designs.

Makes 20–24

See pages 210-11

PETIT POTS AU CHOCOLAT

5 eggs, separated
250g (8 oz) dark (plain or semi-sweet) chocolate,
melted (see page 62)
2 tablespoons Grand Marnier
⅓ cup (2½ oz) caster (superfine) sugar
zest of 1 orange

In a medium-sized bowl, whisk egg whites to form stiff peaks.
Add sugar slowly, whisking until sugar is dissolved.
In a separate bowl, mix egg yolks with melted chocolate, then
add Grand Marnier and orange zest and mix well.
Fold whisked egg whites through chocolate mixture.
Pour mixture into small ramekins or cups and
refrigerate for 2–3 hours, or until firm. Serve.

PETS-DE-NONNE

A French sweet delight with a name which is anything but flattering for such a delicacy. These are small balls or quennelles of choux pastry mixture, deep fried until golden brown and served hot with a raspberry (or any style of fruit) sauce. If you prefer them cool, split them in half and serve with cream or flavoured mousse and fresh fruits. From the same family as beignets and beignet soufflé, the English translation of pets-de-nonne is 'nuns' farts'. They are more commonly known as 'soupirs de nonnes' or 'nuns' sighs'.

PETTICOAT TAILS

Named in the 16th century, these are small wedge-shaped pieces of shortbread. This is the shortbread traditionally served at Hogmanay. It was originally made in large discs with an imprint of the thistle on top, but when it was decided that this was too hard to cut or break evenly, the imprint was omitted and the top of the shortbread was scored deeply before being baked into 8–12 wedge-shaped portions. When broken, the wedges resembled petticoat tails, hence the name for all shortbreads in this shape.

PFEFFERNUSSE

1⅓ cups (16 fl oz) honey
1 cup (12 fl oz) golden syrup
2 tablespoons) brown sugar
⅔ cup (5 oz) caster (superfine) sugar
1 teaspoon ground allspice
3 tablespoons (1½ oz) unsalted butter
4 cups (16 oz) plain (all-purpose) flour
1 teaspoon baking (soda) powder

Icing

1 cup (5 oz) icing (powdered) sugar
2–3 tablespoons lemon juice

Preheat the oven to 200°C (400°F). Line two
baking trays (sheets) with baking paper (parchment).
Place honey, golden syrup, sugars, butter and spice in a large
saucepan and bring to the boil, stirring continuously. Simmer
for 3–4 minutes. Remove from heat, add flour and beat until
smooth. Place teaspoonfuls of mixture on
baking trays (sheets) leaving room to spread.
Bake the trays of cookies for 15–20 minutes. Remove from
oven and place on a wire rack. While cookies are still hot,
brush lightly with lemon icing mixture (below).
Cool without touching.
Mix lemon juice and icing (powdered) sugar to make
a thin icing for brushing over cookies.

PHYLLO
(see also filo pastry, pastry, strudel dough)

These are paper-thin sheets of pastry made from flour, water, oil and egg. Greek in origin, the dough is used extensively in the Mediterranean for cooking sweets. The dough is worked extremely hard so that the gluten strands are well formed, allowing the dough to stretch considerably after resting. Strudel dough is made in the same way and is used for sweet and savoury products.

Phyllo pastry is sold in supermarkets and keeps well in the refrigerator or freezer. It must remain tightly wrapped or it will dry and become crisp.

PICANCHAGNE

A sweet rich dough containing fresh pears which is a traditional pastry in certain parts of France. It is named after the child's game 'piques comme en chane', meaning to bristle like an oak tree, referring to handstands. After playing this, the children would eat the pear-flavoured sweet bread. The brioche-style dough is rolled thinly, covered with a layer of pears and sugar and spices and then folded over and curled into a ring shape. Allowed to prove, it is baked until golden brown and then glazed with a sweet apricot glaze or fondant. It can be left plain if it is not to be eaten immediately.

PIE

A pie contains a filling and is enclosed on both base and top by pastry. The pastry may be puff pastry or shortcrust dough and the filling either sweet or savoury.

Said to have been created by the Greeks, the idea was spread by the Romans to the rest of Europe.

MEAT PIES
1 kg (2 lb) pre-prepared puff pastry
1 quantity egg wash (see page 110)
300 g (10 oz) unsalted (sweet) butter
4 cups (16 oz) plain (all-purpose) flour
¾ cup (6 fl oz) water
2 eggs
1 teaspoon salt

Chop butter into small pieces and mix with flour. Rub butter into flour until mixture resembles fresh bread crumbs, then add the lightly whisked eggs, water and salt. Work mixture until dough is formed. Work dough quickly for 2–3 minutes, kneading lightly but well. Cover dough and let it stand for 1 hour in refrigerator while you make filling.

Filling
1 lb (16 oz) minced beef
2 cups (16 fl oz) water
½ teaspoon salt
¼ teaspoon pepper
1 beef stock cube
1 tablespoon chopped chives
1 large finely chopped onion
¼ cup (1½ oz) cornflour (cornstarch)
⅓ cup (3 fl oz) water

Preheat oven to 180°C (350°F).
Heat oil in a pan and fry onion on low heat until it is clear. Add beef mince and stir well until meat begins to brown. Add water, salt, pepper, stock cube and chives and bring to the boil. In a separate bowl, mix cornflour with the extra water.
When mince boils, stir in cornflour and mix well.
Re-boil, then remove from heat and cool.
To complete pies, roll base dough on a lightly floured surface to a 2–3 mm (⅛ in) thickness. Cut out discs large enough to sit

Pies — meat and fruit mince

Pancakes (see page 201)

inside either 12 individual small pie dishes or 2–3 large pie
dishes. Line containers with the pie bottom dough and set
aside. Roll puff pastry to a 2–3 mm (⅛ in) thickness and cut
to exact size of top of pies.
Fill each pie dish with an equal quantity of mince.
Dip puff pastry lids into egg wash and place
on top of filled pie bases.
Trim edges of pastry for neatness and bake for
35–40 minutes, or until both pastries are golden brown.
Cool slightly before serving.

PIE SHELL
(see pastry case)

PIG'S EAR
(see also palmiers, puff pastry)

Another name for the famed French method of using scrap
puff pastry, more commonly known as the palmier.

PIKELET
(see also griddle cakes)

An Australian version of the pancake or griddle cake, made
no larger than 10 cm (4 in) in diameter. The batter is dropped
in tablespoon amounts onto the relatively dry frying surface
of a large frying pan and cooked till golden brown. Then it is
flipped over to cook on the reverse side. The pikelet is
flavoured with cinnamon, and traditionally served with
raspberry jam and cream.

PIN, TO

To roll pastry using a rolling pin is also known as pinning the
dough or pastry.

PINEAPPLE

This tropical fruit, named 'annanas' by indigenous South
Americans, has existed for centuries. The first recorded
discovery of a pineapple and subsequent eating was by Jean

de Lery during a voyage to Brazil in the 16th century. De Lery returned to France and introduced the fruit to Louis XV, who later grew the species in early conservatories.

Also known as a false type of fruit, it is not a solid fruit but made up of many hundreds of berries fused together. Many pineapple plants will only produce one fruit; some are left to develop up to three fruits. The stalks of the pineapples can also be planted and these produce a further one or two generations of fruit, although each subsequent fruit is much smaller than the last. When ripe, the skin is yellow to light green, depending on the variety, and the flesh is yellow and sweet. If pineapple is to be set in a mousse or bavarois, use canned or cooked, as the flesh contains an enzyme which, unless cooked, renders gelatine useless. Pineapple is used in crytallised or glacé form, preserved or fresh, and has an array of uses.

PEPPERED PINEAPPLE
60 g (2oz) unsalted (sweet) butter
2 slices of fresh pineapple
1 tablespoon brown sugar
1 tablespoon water
1 tablespoon caster (superfine) sugar
1 teaspoon cracked black pepper
1 tablespoon thickened cream

Melt butter in a frying pan. Add brown sugar, caster sugar and water and dissolve. When mixture begins to caramelise, whisk it quickly to ensure ingredients are mixed. Add cracked black pepper and freshly cut pineapple immediately. Heat slowly, making sure butter and sugar have caramelised before removing from heat. Melt one tablespoon of thickened dairy cream into sauce. Serve pineapple and sauce with ice cream or fresh brioche.

PINE NUT
(see also nuts)

The seed of the pine cone of certain varieties of pine originating on the banks of the Mediterranean, pine nuts are also known as Indian nuts. They can be caramelised, baked in cakes and breads, or used as a filling for most pastries.

PIPE
(see also chocolate piping)

With the use of a piping bag, cake and biscuit (cookie) mixtures or decorative mediums are piped into decorative shapes or designs, which vary according to the nozzle used in the bag.

PIPING BAG
(see also cornet)

Conical-shaped bags made from material, plastic or paper, into which soft mixtures such as buttercreams, mousses, cream and soft biscuit (cookie) mixtures are placed. A nozzle made from either plastic or metal is fitted into the narrow end of the piping bag. Nozzles of differing sizes and shapes, such as star, plain or fluted, create different designs in the piped mixture. Piping bags are available in small to large sizes, the smaller ones being for more intricate work, such as chocolate or royal icing.

For reasons of hygiene, many countries now require the disposable variety of piping bag (usually clear plastic) in commercial kitchens.

See page 218

PIPING GEL

Also known as piping jelly, this is a thick jelly-like substance, either clear or coloured, which is piped onto cakes, pastries and inside chocolate designs to add colour and decorative effect. It should only be used in small amounts, otherwise its bright colour can make the cake look gawdy and unappealing.

PIROSHKI

Of Russian or Polish origins, the piroshki is a small meat- or savoury-filled pastry which has become one of the world's latest fast or convenience foods. Traditionally made by the peasants of these countries, the piroshki is a yeast pastry, similar to brioche or kulich dough, which is rolled thinly, filled in the centre with a savoury meat filling and then rolled to enclose the filling. Fried or baked, the piroshki is eaten hot, much the same way as a savoury meat pie.

PISCHINGER TORTE

This hazelnut torte was named after Oscar Pischinger, a famed Viennese pastry cook and confectioner and the inventor of this delicacy.

500 g (16 oz) no-fuss chocolate buttercream (see page 43)
200 g (7 oz) praline (see page 221), crushed
2 japonaise bases made with ground hazelnuts (see page 156)
1 chocolate génoise sponge (see page 134), either whole or cut in half horizontally
400 g (13 oz) hazelnuts (filberts), halved
icing (powdered) sugar, for dusting

Mix together chocolate buttercream and praline and spread some onto one of the japonaise bases. Place génoise layer on top and spread with remaining japonaise base. If using two layers of génoise sponge, place one of the génoise layers on top of the japonaise base and spread with the buttercream and praline mixture. Repeat with the second cake layer. Top with the remaining japonaise base. Trim the edges of the torte so that the cake and meringue layers are even. Cover the top and sides with the remaining buttercream. Press halved hazelnuts into the side of the cake. Dust with icing sugar. Chill for 20 minutes.

PISTACHIO
(see also nuts)

Pistachios are thought to have first originated in the Middle Eastern regions, spreading from there over the centuries, although they did not reach the shores of the USA until late into the 19th century. The seed of a small tree, the pistachio nut is a relative of the cashew family. When ripe, the shell encasing the nut cracks open to reveal the nut inside. Eating or processing must occur quickly after this stage to ensure that the nuts do not soften. They are used in pastry recipes more often for colour than flavour (or any other reason). These attractive green nuts are ground into a paste, or chopped, or left whole for fillings, sauces, toppings, frostings, and as a simple decoration for some of the world's most famous chocolates, cakes and pastries.

PITA BREAD
(see also flatbread)

Pita bread is known by many names, the most popular of which are pocket bread and Lebanese bread, Lebanon being where the bread is thought to have originated. The bread is a leavened or unleavened bread, depending on the particular country in which it is produced, which is formed into balls, then rolled thinly and fried. During frying, both sides of the dough are kept covered in oil so that the dough puffs. When baked, the now ball-shaped bread product collapses, with a pocket remaining inside. When cut in half, the pocket is used as a place to serve a meal of meat or salad. Very popular in recent times, pita is considered to be something of a health food. Both sides of the flat bread are extremely thin and the bread requires good storage so as not to dry out.

PITHIVIER
(see also puff pastry, Twelfth Night cake)

Perhaps one of France's more well-known pastry products, the pithivier is a light delicacy often served as a Twelfth Night cake. It is closely linked to a galette. The cake originated in the tiny village of Pithiviers, and, in Twelfth Night tradition, often contains a small bean or token in the light almond cream filling. Whoever finds the token becomes King for the day, or the Bean King.

500 g (16 oz) puff pastry

Filling
100 g (3½ oz) unsalted (sweet) butter
⅓ cup (2½ oz) caster (superfine) sugar
1 egg yolk
¼ cup (1 oz) plain (all-purpose) flour
⅓ cup (1½ oz) ground almonds
egg wash (see page 110)
apricot glaze (see page 10)
½ cup (2 oz) flaked almonds, roasted (see page 5)

Preheat oven to 180°C (350°F).
Line a baking sheet (tray) with baking paper (parchment).
Roll out pastry and cut two 23 cm (9 in) circles.
Chill while preparing the filling.
Beat butter and sugar until creamy, light and fluffy.

Add egg yolk and beat for 3 minutes. Beat in flour and almonds. Place one of the pastry circles on the prepared sheet and brush a 4 cm (1½ in) border of egg wash around its edge. Place the filling in the centre, keeping it inside the egg wash border, and shape it into a mound 2 cm (¾ in) high in the middle. Top with the second pastry circle. Crimp around the edge with the fingertips. Use a small sharp knife to mark lines lightly on the top of the pastry. Brush with beaten egg wash. Bake for 45–50 minutes or until both base and top are cooked.
While hot, brush top and sides with apricot glaze and sprinkle sides with flaked almonds.
Cool on the sheet on a cake rack.

PIZZA
(see also bread, yeast doughs)

Pizza has become one of the world's greatest and most successful fast foods, but the original pizza bears little resemblance to the tasty treats served today. Invented in Naples, the pizza was a flat disc of unleavened dough which was covered with olive oil, olives and Parmesan cheese, and was a cross between what is now known as a pizza and the original focaccia breads. Baked or cooked over a fire, it was also occasionally made like a turnover, so that the filling was enclosed. Eventually the pizza had other toppings added and was cooked in a wood-fired oven on a large flat surface. Then a small amount of yeast was added to the dough, and the pizza came closer to today's modern version.

With a yeast-risen base, one can add virtually any savoury item one desires to a pizza, from meats and cheeses, to vegetables and herbs. They are now baked on pizza trays or discs in electric or wood-fired ovens.

It has also become popular over the past decade to produce sweet pizzas or dessert pizzas, which are made using a brioche base dough covered with crème pâtissière and fruits.

PIZZA DOUGH
½ cup (4 fl oz) water
¼ cup (2 fl oz) olive oil
¼ cup (2 fl oz) white wine
25 g (¾ oz) fresh compressed yeast
3 cups (12 oz) plain (bread) flour
¼ teaspoon salt
⅛ teaspoon cayenne pepper

Place water, olive oil and wine in a large bowl and add yeast. Stir or whisk to dissolve yeast. Add flour, salt and cayenne pepper and work to a dough. Knead well for 5–8 minutes. Cover dough and allow to rest in a warm area for 20 minutes.
Roll flat into a large disc and cover with tomato paste and toppings according to taste. Allow the pizza to prove (rise) for a further 20 minutes.
Preheat oven to 180°C (350°F).
Bake in preheated oven until the crust is baked, golden brown and crunchy.

PLAIN FLOUR
(see also flour)

Known in the USA as all-purpose flour, plain flour comes in two varieties, cake flour and bread flour. Bread flour has a higher protein content, which produces a strong gluten bread dough, and cake flour has a lower gluten or protein content, providing a light, crumbly texture for cake batters.

PLAITS

A form of decorative plaiting, also known as braiding, is performed on bread doughs where two, three, and up to eight strands of bread dough are rolled and then plaited together. Plaited bread must be worked together loosely; if the plaiting is too tight, the dough will split and break upon proving (rising).

PLASTIC ICING

A white, heavy icing paste which is used for covering rather than modelling or decoration, although it can be used for both of these as well. Plastic icing should be a cold icing paste, and requires airtight storage or it will crust. Often used for covering wedding, christening and Christmas cakes.

2 teaspoons gelatine powder
2 tablespoons water
1½ tablespoons liquid glucose (corn syrup)
1½ cups (9 oz) pure icing (powdered) sugar
pure icing (powdered) sugar, extra

Soak gelatine in water and allow to firm in a small bowl. Allow gelatine to melt over some warm water until it becomes a clear, golden liquid. Add glucose and stir. Place sifted icing sugar in the bowl of an electric mixer and add the liquid. Beat

Making a Piping Bag Step-by-Step

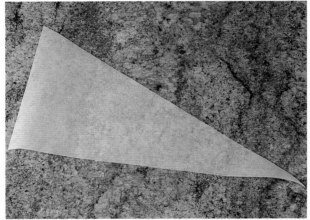

Step 1: Begin all piping bags with a triangle-shaped piece of baking paper (parchment).

Step 2: Start by taking the top corner of the paper and curling it along the longest edge.

Step 3: Pinch the point of the curl with one hand and continue curling the paper with the other.

Step 4: When all of the paper has been curled, tuck the remaining flap inside the cone. See page 216.

Step 1: Cover the base with buttercream and place the chocolate sponge layer on top. Cover with more buttercream.

Step 2: Place the second japonaise base on top of the sponge.

Step 3: Cover the whole cake with chocolate buttercream and decorate with halved hazelnuts. See page 216.

slowly until a firm paste is produced. Remove the white mixture and knead lightly on a bench (counter) surface which is dusted with the extra icing (powdered) sugar. When dough is smooth and firm enough to be rolled, cover and keep airtight until required.

PLATTAR
(see also pancakes)

Another member of the pancake family, plattar are well-known Scandinavian pancakes originating in Sweden. They are customarily served with lingonberries, hot butter and other fruit or preserves.

PLOMBIERE
(see also ice cream)

Named after the mould in which it is formed, plombière cream is made from almond milk custard with whipped cream and crystallised (candied) fruit added. It is then moulded into a pyramid shape; it was originally moulded in a plomb (lead) mould.

PLUM
(see also fruit, prune)

A stone fruit, the plum is used in sauces, compôtes, cakes and slices, sorbets, ice creams and fruit salads. There are some two hundred varieties of plum available, and they range from green to deep purple in skin colour, yellow to orange in flesh colour, as well as having a variety of shapes and sizes. Some varieties are also known as 'gage' plums such as green gage or golden gage. These are identifiable by their sweet aroma and flavour. While most plums can be eaten raw, fresh from the tree, some varieties of plum with a higher percentage of sugar are more often dried to become prunes.

PLUM PUDDING
(see Christmas pudding)

POACHED FRUIT
(see fruit, poaching)

POACHING

Poaching means cooking in simmering water (or some other liquid). Fruits, mousses and dessert products such as oeufs à la neige, (which can also be poached in milk) are poached in sugar syrups.

POLENTA
(see cornmeal)

POLKA

The Polka gâteau consists of a base of sweetcrust pastry topped with a ring of baked choux pastry filled with a mixture of crème pâtissière and fresh cream. The top of the polka is dusted heavily with icing (powdered) sugar and then a skewer which has been allowed to become red hot over the fire is laid across the top of the cake to caramelise the sugar. The caramelised lines are said to have originally followed the steps in the polka dance, hence the name.

PONT–NEUF

The pâtisserie in front of the Pont-Neuf in Paris was famed for producing a small pastry. The pastry was named after the bridge, and consisted of a sweetcrust tartlet base, filled with crème frangipane, topped with crushed macaroons and glazed with apricot jam (jelly).

POPCORN
(see also corn)

A special form of dried corn, this can either be a sweet or savoury treat depending on whether it is salted, buttered, sugared or caramelised. For something so small, the corn piece has to undergo quite a process to turn into the popped product. Basically, the starch and protein are transformed in the heating process. The heating gelatinises the starch present in the corn; the hotter it gets, the greater the pressure on the protein, until, eventually, the kernel explodes violently, exposing and expanding the internal endosperm.

Popcorn is generally sold either pre-popped and flavoured or as bags of popping corn.

POPOVER
(see also puftaloon, Yorkshire pudding)

Made and cooked in the same way as the English Yorkshire pudding, popovers are its American cousins and can be served either sweet or savoury. The batter is baked in small oil-filled containers which are very hot. The intense heat causes the mixture to puff very quickly and become light and airy. Occasionally it rises with such speed that it is said to 'pop over'.

They are served split with jam (jelly) and cream or with poultry or even meat dishes, but they must be served direct from the oven to the table.

POPPY SEED

Originating in Asia, the poppy seed is produced from the opium poppy. It is very popular in European cooking, and is known to have been used in the Egyptian culture as well as throughout Ancient Roman and Greek times and as far back as 15–1200 BC. Very small and black in colour, the poppy seed has a slightly nutty flavour and is commonly used on the crusts of bread products, as well as being made into cakes and puddings.

SWEET POPPY SQUARES

210 g (7 oz) unsalted (sweet) butter
½ cup (3½ oz) caster (superfine) sugar
6 egg yolks
1½ cups (8 oz) poppy seeds
1 teaspoon ground cinnamon
1 cup (4 oz) plain (all-purpose) flour
6 egg whites
½ cup (4 oz) caster (superfine) sugar, extra
1 quantity lemon cream cheese frosting (see page 125)

Preheat oven to 180°C (350°F).

Grease a 25 x 30 x 3 cm (10 x 12 x 1¼ in) baking sheet (tray) and line with baking paper (parchment). Place butter and sugar in a mixing bowl and cream until light and fluffy. Slowly add egg yolks and mix until well combined. Add poppy seeds, ground cinnamon and flour and mix well. Whisk egg whites until stiff peaks form, then slowly add sugar until all is dissolved. Carefully fold whisked egg whites through the poppy seed mixture, so as not to knock out all the air. Spread mixture onto prepared sheet and bake for 35–40 minutes, or until the top springs back when lightly touched. Remove and cool. Spread the top of the slice with lemon cream cheese frosting.

Makes 30–35 squares.

GERMAN POPPYSEED CAKE

If you cannot find ground poppy seeds for this splendid cake, lightly roast whole seeds for a few minutes and pulverise them in a coffee grinder or with a mortar and pestle.

Base
¾ cup (3 oz) plain (all-purpose) flour
½ cup (3 oz) icing (powdered) sugar
65 g (2 oz) unsalted (sweet) butter, cut into small pieces
1 egg

Filling
2¼ cups (12 oz) ground poppy seeds
200 g (7 oz) sponge cake crumbs
⅔ cup (5 fl oz) milk
2¼ cups (18 fl oz) milk, extra
⅔ cup (2½ oz) custard powder
3 egg yolks
1 cup (7 oz) caster (superfine) sugar
½ cup (3 oz) sultanas (golden raisins)

Topping
⅓ cup (2½ oz) caster (superfine) sugar
1¾ cups (7 oz) plain (all-purpose) flour
150 g (5 oz) unsalted (sweet) butter
icing (powdered) sugar, for dusting

Base
Place the flour and icing sugar in a bowl. Add the butter and lightly rub into the flour and icing sugar until the mixture resembles fresh breadcrumbs. Add the egg and mix thoroughly. Turn the mixture onto a lightly floured surface and knead lightly to form a dough. Wrap in plastic wrap (cling film) and chill for 30 minutes.

Filling
Mix the poppy seeds, sponge cake crumbs and milk in a bowl and soak for 15 minutes. Blend a little of the extra milk with the custard powder and egg yolks and put to one side. Place the remaining milk and the sugar in a saucepan and bring to the boil. When the mixture boils, pour slowly onto the custard powder and egg yolk mixture, beating all the time. Remove from the heat and pour over the poppy seed mixture. Add the sultanas and mix thoroughly.

Topping
Place all the ingredients in a bowl and rub in the butter until the mixture resembles coarse breadcrumbs.

To Assemble
Preheat oven to 180°C (350°F). Lightly grease a 23 cm (9 in) springform cake tin with butter and line the base with baking paper (parchment).
Roll out the pastry into a 23 cm (9 in) circle and place in the prepared tin. Pour in the poppyseed filling and sprinkle on the topping. Bake for 45 minutes. Dust thickly with icing sugar while still hot. Cool in the tin on a cake rack. When cold, dust again with more icing sugar.

PORK PIES

The pork pies of Melton Mowbray, a small market town in the English Midlands, are almost legendary. These pies actually originated as the result of a by-product of another of the town's famous products, Stilton cheese. In producing the cheese, a lot of whey was made, which, not being required, was fed to the pigs. The farmers tried everything to sell the quality pork produced from the fat healthy pigs, one farmer making pork pies, which have been in demand ever since.

The pork pie is made from a hot water crust pastry and seasoned fresh pork mince, and is round in shape. When cooked and cooled, the top of the pie has a small funnel placed in it and the pie is filled with aspic.

POTATOES

The potato is one of few vegetables or food products which grow in cold climates and in most soil types, hence its cheapness and availability to the poor, who have been the primary inventors of potato-based foods. Potatoes have long been used in recipes, especially in European and Irish kitchens, where bread doughs such as focaccia or pratie bread were made. Yeast was also originally made from potatoes, as was vodka, a drink often served chilled with desserts. Potatoes can basically be used in any recipe which calls for flour. They help keep cakes moist. Those not used for cooking can also be dried and ground to make potato flour (which is used in many recipes), and even a potato glaze that is still used for the tops of gingerbread products throughout Europe.

POUND CAKES

An English cake which follows a very easy recipe, using one pound of each of the major ingredients — sugar, butter and flour.

PRALINE
(see also croquant)

Praline is one of many recipes which originated from a mistake in the kitchen. The chef to César de Choiseul, Comte de Plessis-Praslin, saw one of his kitchen hands eating the remains of caramelised sugar with almonds. This gave him the idea of combining the almonds with the caramel. Initially the mixture was used in a crumbed or crushed form, and folded through recipes such as crèmes, including crème beau rivage, or on the outside of cakes for garnish. It has since been made with flaked and slivered almonds, rolled finely and used for decorating or as a treat in itself.

1½ cups (12 oz) granulated sugar
2½ cups (11 oz) flaked almonds

Line a baking sheet (tray) with baking paper (parchment). Heat a heavy-based saucepan on medium heat. Slowly sprinkle sugar into the pan. Allow to melt before adding more. As it melts, stir sugar to ensure it does not burn. Keep slowly adding the sugar, stirring all the time. Heat until all the sugar has melted and is a dark golden brown colour. Immediately stir in flaked almonds. To make individual treats, take tablespoonfuls of the mixture and place on prepared sheet. When the sheet is full, allow the pieces to set and cool at room temperature before serving.

To make a cake decoration for a square or oblong cake, line an 18 x 28 x 2 cm (7 x 11 x ¾ in) baking tray (jelly roll pan) with aluminium foil and oil lightly. Pour the hot mixture into the tray and spread it so that it covers the entire surface evenly and smoothly. Using an oiled rolling pin, roll gently over the top of the mix to flatten it. Allow the mixture to sit for several minutes, until it firms slightly, then remove it from the tray with the aluminium foil still attached and peel the foil from the back of the praline. Place a lightly oiled cylindrical object, or small rolling pin, on one corner of the praline and roll the corner back and over the object.

Allow the mixture to cool in this position. When hard, remove the cylinder and decorate the praline sheet before placing it on top of a cake.

To make a decoration for a round cake, lightly oil the surface of a flat metal or marble bench, and set a round cake or tartlet ring on the surface. Pour the hot praline mixture into the centre of the ring and press out, using an oiled spoon, so that it covers the area evenly and smoothly. Cool slightly and remove the ring. Carefully slide a sharp knife or scraper under the cooling disc to loosen it and then, using a lightly oiled pizza cutting wheel or a large sharp knife, mark the disc into eight portions, but not marking the outer 2 cm (¾ in). When marked, cut through the portions, taking care that the outer 2 cm (¾ in) edge is not cut or broken. Fold the cuts up from the centre towards the outer edge so that a hole is created in the centre. Place a bowl or small dish in the centre to hold the folded back portions out. Decorate with white chocolate or royal icing or leave plain.

Sit on top of a round cake to serve.

See page 226

PRALINEE

Pronounced in exactly the same way as the French praline, pralinee is a caramel mixture which contains almonds. The German pralinee refers to small bite-sized chocolates or confections which are served with coffee after a meal or sold on their own or in packages from confectionery stores or Konditorei.

125 g (4 oz) unsalted (sweet) butter
300 g (10 oz) dark (plain or semi-sweet) chocolate,
melted (see page 62)
¼ cup (2 fl oz) Kirsch
cocoa powder, for rolling

Line a baking sheet (tray) with baking paper (parchment). Place butter in a mixing bowl and cream until almost white and very light. Add melted chocolate to butter and then the Kirsch, mixing until ingredients combine into a smooth paste. Place the mixture in a piping (pastry) bag fitted with a 1 cm (½ in) plain round nozzle. Pipe small straight towers about 3 cm (1¼ in) in height onto the prepared sheet. When all the mixture has been piped, place in refrigerator for 2 hours to allow the pralinees to set hard. Remove and roll each lightly in the sifted cocoa powder. Refrigerate until ready to serve.

PRATIE BREAD
(see also bread)

A quickbread from northern Ireland, this is also known as Tatie bread and is made using cold mashed potatoes. It is a fried bread which is made slightly thicker than pancakes and leavened using baking powder (soda). As the Irish have always used potatoes in all forms of cookery, the bread was made for breakfast to use up the leftover cold potato from dinner the previous night.

PREMIX

Premix refers to a mixture that has been mixed prior to use. This saves time for the pastry chef by deleting the small weighing of certain ingredients and deletes the worry of mistakes. Most premix products require the addition of either water, or water with eggs, or occasionally a raising agent for them to produce the finished products. Premix is available for every type of cake mix imaginable, bread and most yeast doughs and icings.

Because of time constraints and today's higher wages, many products which were once prepared by the pastry chef are now professionally manufactured ready for use. This new industry has evolved to offer various semi-finished products to the pastry chef, such as marzipan, fondant, nougat paste, praline paste, gianduja and glazing jellies.

PRESERVING
(see fruit)

PRESERVING JAR

A large clear jar which usually holds 1–2 litres (32–64 fl oz) of fruit and syrup. The jar may be screwtop, but more commonly is a large, wide-necked bottle on top of which sits a

Chocolate Pretzels Step-by-Step

Step 1: Take both ends of the sausage shape and draw them up towards you so that the ends meet in the middle.

Step 2: Cross the two ends over each other.

Step 3: Draw them back into the base of the shape. See page 224.

rubber ring, a metal lid and metal clips, so that the jar will remain airtight. The preserving jar must be washed in boiling water and allowed to drip dry before the fruit and preserving syrup are added, to prevent the growth of bacteria.

PRETZEL

Pretzels can be one of two items: a thick, looped, bread-like dough mass or a fine, crisp and crunchy biscuit-like product. Both are eaten as snacks and are traditionally sprinkled with rock salt before being baked.

The breaded pretzel has been produced since the early 14th century, when monks made the bread doughs in looped shapes to resemble their hands when praying. 'Pretzel' derives from the word pretiola, which means little gifts, and this is exactly what they originally were used for — gifts for the locals after prayer sessions. This form of pretzel, also known as 'bretzel', is still produced in vast quantities around the world today. A popular breakfast bread of Germany, the traditional shape of the intertwined loops is now used in all forms of pastry, from puff pastry, sweet pastry and shortcrust pastry pretzels to biscuit and cookie doughs, which are shaped in the same way and baked, then dipped into chocolate or fondant.

The second form of pretzel — the crisp biscuit style, eaten with drinks or as a snack — is said to have been invented by a Pennsylvanian baker's apprentice. The apprentice was left to tend the ovens and fell asleep. When he awoke, he relit the ovens and, without realising, double-baked the pretzels, making them shrink in size and become crisp.

CHOCOLATE PRETZELS
2 tablespoons boiling water
¼ cup (1 oz) cocoa powder
125 g (4 oz) unsalted (sweet) butter
¼ cup (2 oz) caster (superfine) sugar
1 egg
½ teaspoon vanilla essence (extract)
2 cups (8 oz) plain (all-purpose) flour
390 g (13 oz) dark (plain or semi-sweet) chocolate,
melted (see page 62)

Preheat oven to 170°C (340°F).
Line baking sheets (trays) with baking paper (parchment).
Place boiling water in a cup and stir in cocoa powder until a smooth paste is formed. Place butter and sugar in a bowl and cream together until the mixture is light and fluffy.
Add egg and mix until well combined. Add vanilla and cocoa paste to the creamed mixture and mix until all ingredients are combined. Sift flour and add to the mixture.
Work to a soft dough. Wrap in plastic wrap (cling film) and place in the refrigerator for 1 hour.
Lightly knead chilled dough so that it is soft enough to roll by hand. Taking small amounts of the dough at a time, roll ½ x 15 cm (⅕ x 6 in) sausage shapes. Place on prepared sheet and lay flat. Taking both ends in your hands, draw them up towards you so that they meet in the middle. Cross the two ends over each other and then draw them back through the loops to form a pretzel. Continue until all the dough is used.
Bake in preheated oven for 8–10 minutes. Cool on the tray.

Dip the cold pretzels in the melted chocolate and place on a cake rack to drain before returning them to the lined sheet to set in the refrigerator.

Makes 18

See page 223

PRINCESS CAKE

This Danish cake includes many of the features Scandinavians love in their desserts — sponge cake, cream, custard and marzipan.

Filling
1 cup (8 fl oz) cream (single or light)
1 cup (8 fl oz) milk
1 cup (8 oz) caster (superfine) sugar
¼ cup (2 fl oz) cream (single or light), extra
¼ cup (2 fl oz) milk, extra
75 g (2½ oz) custard powder
2 eggs
4 drops yellow food colouring
1 vanilla génoise sponge (see page 134)
200 ml (7 fl oz) crème Chantilly (see page 85)

To Decorate
500 g (16 oz) marzipan, tinted green (see page 177)
100 g (3½ oz) marzipan, tinted yellow (see page 177)
dark (plain or semi-sweet) chocolate, melted (see page 62)

Line the sides and base of a 23 cm (9 in) springform cake tin with baking paper (parchment). Place cream, milk and sugar in a saucepan and bring to the boil over low heat. Blend together the extra cream, extra milk, custard powder, eggs and food colouring and add to the heated cream mixture. Cook over low heat until the mixture boils and thickens, stirring constantly. Divide filling in half. Chill one half.

To Assemble
Cut the sponge in half horizontally. Place one layer in the prepared tin and spoon on the unchilled filling. Top with the second layer of sponge. Chill the cake for 40 minutes. When the filling is completely cold, remove the rim of the tin. Gently fold crème Chantilly into the chilled filling to make a smooth, stiff cream. Cover the sides of the cake with the cream and place a mound of cream on the top in the centre. Shape the mound to form a dome. Chill for 15 minutes. Roll out the green marzipan thinly and drape it over the chilled cake, moulding to fit. Drizzle melted chocolate over the top. Decorate with yellow marzipan flowers and green marzipan leaves.

See page 226

PRINCE REGENT TORTE

1 quantity japonaise base, uncooked (see page 156)
1 quantity dobos torte filling (see page 101)
250 g (8 oz) marzipan (see page 177)

To Decorate
*400 g (13 oz) dark (plain or semi-sweet) chocolate,
melted (see page 62)
whole hazelnuts (filberts)*

Preheat oven to 180°C (350°F).
Line 6 baking sheets (trays) with baking paper
(parchment) and draw a 23 cm (9 in) circle on each.
Spread the japonaise mixture into the circles on the prepared
sheets and bake for 15–20 minutes.
Cool on baking paper (parchment) on a cake rack.

To Assemble
Cover each japonaise base with Dobos torte filling and stack
one on top of the other. Cover the top and sides of the torte
with the filling. Roll out the marzipan thinly and cover the
whole torte. Spread melted chocolate smoothly and evenly
over the marzipan. When chocolate is set, cut the torte
into wedges with a hot, sharp knife and decorate
each wedge with whole hazelnuts.

See page 227

PROFITEROLE
(see also choux pastry, cream puff, croquembouche)

Made of feathery light choux pastry, a profiterole is a small ball of baked choux dough filled with cream or ice cream and served as a snack or as a dessert. Profiteroles, being bland in flavour, lend themselves well to any flavoured cream, mousse or ice cream, and any flavoured sauce. Profiteroles filled with crème pâtissière are the basis of the croquembouche, the traditional French wedding cake, as well as being part of the decoration for Gâteau St Honoré.

The name 'profiterole' is said to derive from profit, a French word meaning small gift, which is just what the profiterole is; a small sweet gift with a surprise filling.

PROVE
(see also breadmaking, fermentation)

Also known as proof, the word simply means to allow to rise. This is done either by sitting a yeast dough in a warm area or placing it in a proofing/proving cabinet which is steam heated and run by gas or electricity. When doughs are proving (rising), they should be surrounded by moist steam or covered loosely with a soft, light cloth or oiled plastic wrap. If the covering material is too heavy, the dough will not rise, and if it does not cover the dough well enough, the dough will form a crust, which will also prevent it rising.

During the proving process, the idea is to warm the yeast dough so that it will ferment, causing the release of carbon dioxide and alcohol to fill the dough like a balloon. It should double its volume before being baked. The best temperature for proving is around 24–32°C (70–90°F). If bread or brioche dough has not risen sufficiently, it remains heavy and solid; if proving goes on for too long, the dough becomes acid.

In general, the first rising of the dough takes longer than the second, as there are more yeast cells present for the second fermentation.

PROVER

A cabinet for proving (rising) dough. It can be either small or large, depending on how much dough requires proving. The cabinets in small pastry sections and bakeries are usually stand-up closets with tight-fitting doors. At the bottom of the cabinet is a small gas or electric burner which heats a bain marie of water to produce warm, moist steam. Provers can be quite cheaply put together by placing a wire rack over a simmering frying pan (skillet) of water and placing a box over this to trap the steam and warmth.

PRUGELKUCHEN
(see also baumkuchen)

Prugelkuchen belong to the family of tree cakes more commonly known by the name of baumkuchen. They were the traditional cake of this type made by peasants and farming communities, and were served at feasts and weddings or celebrations. Like the baumkuchen, they were originally cooked on a turning shaft over an open fire. They differed from the baumkuchen in that as the batter from which they were made was poured and baked, its drips and irregularities were not cleaned up as for the baumkuchen, so that they baked in different and quite fantastic shapes every time. When cut, though, they still showed the rings, which looked like the growth rings of a tree. They were also baked on a tapered roller or shaft to assist with removal, whereas the baumkuchen were baked on a straight shaft.

When cool, prugelkuchen are either left plain or dusted with icing (powdered) sugar before being served in thin slices. If the cake is to be kept for any period, it is glazed with a boiled apricot glaze and can be iced with fondant or covered in chocolate.

PRUNE
(see also plums)

The prune is a dried plum, dried either through mechanical dehydration or naturally in the sun. Once it has ripened on the tree, the fruit is washed, spread over drying trays and passed through drying tunnels. After 18 hours of temperature-controlled drying, you have sweet prunes. Good quality prunes are dark brown or black in skin colour and should have a dark but moist flesh. Prunes can be semi-rehydrated by being soaked in hot tea or a hot sugar syrup solution and can be used in cakes, biscuits (cookies) and slices. They may also simply be dipped into boiled sugar syrups or melted chocolate and used for petits fours. The most popular variety is produced from the French d'Agen plum, which is dried into the d'Agen prune.

PUDDING
(see also individual listings)

The word 'pudding' refers mainly to sweet dishes. Originally, though, the word referred to a dish which was covered in a complete outer crust or dough of pastry or bread. Such puddings included suet puddings, summer puddings and steak and kidney puddings. Today, however, the word also refers to many other desserts of different varieties. The most common are:

Praline (see page 221)

Pumpkin pie (see page 228)

(i) Milk puddings: dishes such as junket;
(ii) Iced puddings: parfaits, bombes and frozen marquises, all of which must have an outer coating of sponge or biscuit;
(iii) Steamed puddings: light sponge cake based puddings;
(iv) Cottage puddings: dishes such as cobblers, brown betty and crumbles;
(v) Batter puddings: crêpes, waffles, blinis and fritters;
(vi) Egg puddings: treats such as Eve's pudding, diplomat pudding, bread and butter pudding, brulées and crème caramels, to name but a few; and
(vii) Cold-set puddings: mousses, jellies and bavarois.

Many other puddings exist that do not even fall into these categories, and there are new puddings being produced daily by pastry chefs around the world, although these are often simply different uses of old methods and styles.

PUFF PASTRY
(see also butter puff pastry, lamination, pastry)

Puff pastry is one of the most frequently used pastries in pâtisserie: pie lids, pie crusts, palmiers, vol-au-vents, fleurons, millefeuilles, bouchées, crescents and many other dishes, both savoury and sweet. Puff pastry can be made in several different ways and in a number of forms, from butter puff pastry, which is regarded as the best, to rough puff and flaky pastry. All use the process of lamination to gain their actual puff when baked. Lamination involves rolling the fat between the dough layers and then layering the pastry repeatedly on top of itself via a series of folds.

While many ascribe the invention of puff pastry to the French chef Feuillet, it seems that he might simply have given rebirth to an older pastry, as it was around long before his time. Records show that a pastry similar to puff pastry was used as early as the early 14th century. Indeed, the chef who is more often accredited with the invention of the puff pastry is Frenchman Claude Gellee. Inventing a cake for his ill father, Gellee placed a lump of fat inside a piece of dough and rolled the dough thinly, then folded it and rolled it again several times. As he placed the dough in the oven, his master insisted he was wasting time and money on the experiment as the butter would be so fine it would melt out and ruin his oven. To the surprise of both, the layers separated and puff pastry was born in its modern form. In 1622, Gellee moved to Paris and continued work on his creation. Over the next few years he perfected his recipe. Gellee died in 1682, having spread the puff pastry idea through several European countries.

When making puff pastry, one must ensure that the dough and fat are of the same consistency. A tough dough on soft butter will force the butter from within, and if the butter is harder than the dough, the dough will tear. On being rolled for the first time, the dough and fat must be allowed to rest for at least 20 minutes before further rollings or the dough will become wild as a result of overstretching.

When rolling puff pastry, never roll from closed side to closed side; this will destroy the pastry layers. Puff pastry must always be rolled from open end to open end until the very last rolling, when it may be rolled in both directions if necessary to gain more width.

BOOK FOLD: Roll out the pastry into a rectangle shape, turn both ends in so that they meet a little off centre, then fold in half as illustrated.

SINGLE FOLD: Roll out the pastry into a rectangle shape and fold into three as illustrated.

PUFTALOON
(see also popover, Yorkshire pudding)

Also known as a popover, the puftaloon is a small scone or biscuit which is fried in a gem iron in which each hole is filled with hot oil. If made correctly, it will flip over as it cooks, hence its other name, popover. It is served as a sweet dish with treacle or icing (powdered) sugar and butter.

PULLED BREAD
(see also rusks, zwieback)

The soft, inner white part of the bread loaf which is pulled from the loaf, dipped in milk and placed on a tray and baked until golden brown. When crisp, the bread is also known as zwieback, or 'twice baked' bread.

PUMPERNICKEL
(see also bread)

An extremely dense and dark-coloured rye bread which originated in Germany during a 16th century famine. It is made from rye flour, rye grains, rye meal and spices, and is traditionally steam baked, resulting in a strong, slightly acidic flavour in the finished bread. Pumpernickel bread is sliced extremely thinly and is served as the base for canapés, hors d'oeuvres and Danish open sandwiches.

PUMPKIN
(see also vegetables)

This vegetable has earned a well-recognised place in pastry cooking for its contribution in the American pumpkin pie and pumpkin scones.

PUMPKIN PIE

In order to qualify as a traditional Thanksgiving pie, the pumpkin pie must have a rich, spicy flavour.

Base
105 g (3½ oz) plain (all-purpose) flour
3 tablespoons icing (powdered) sugar
60 g (2 oz) unsalted (sweet) butter
1 egg yolk

Filling
1 cup (8 fl oz) cream (single or light)
2 eggs
2 cups (16 oz) cooked pumpkin
1¼ cups (7 oz) soft (light) brown sugar
½ teaspoon ground cinnamon
½ teaspoon ground ginger

Preheat oven to 175°C (345°F). Lightly grease a 22 cm (9 in) pie dish (plate).

Place flour and sugar in a bowl. Add butter and rub into flour until the mixture resembles dry breadcrumbs. Add egg yolk and mix thoroughly. Turn the dough onto a lightly floured surface and knead lightly. Press the mixture into the prepared dish and around the sides. Bake in preheated oven for 8–10 minutes, or until lightly golden brown. Maintain the oven temperature. Pour the filling into pre-baked base. Return to oven and bake for a further 40–45 minutes, or until an inserted knife comes out clean. Cool slightly before serving hot, or refrigerate and serve cold.

Filling

Place all the filling ingredients in a blender or food processor and blend or purée until smooth.

See page 227

PUNCH TORTE

This torte takes its name from the punch-like syrup used to soak the slices of génoise sponge.

Base

¾ cup (3 oz) plain (all-purpose) flour
¼ cup (1½ oz) icing (powdered) sugar
60 g (2 oz) unsalted (sweet) butter, softened
1 egg
2 teaspoons water

Syrup

⅔ cup (5 fl oz) dark rum
2 cinnamon sticks
1 cup (7 oz) caster (superfine) sugar
¼ cup (2 fl oz) water
100 ml (3½ fl oz) orange juice
2 tablespoons apricot jam (jelly)
1 vanilla génoise sponge (see page 134)
½ cup (5 oz) apricot jam (jelly), extra

To Decorate

apricot glaze (see page 10)
225 g (7½ oz) marzipan
150 g (5 oz) white chocolate
60 g (2 oz) dark (plain or semi-sweet) chocolate,
melted (see page 62)
1¾ cup (7 oz) flaked almonds, roasted (see page 5)

Place flour and icing sugar in a bowl and very lightly rub in butter until the mixture resembles coarse breadcrumbs. Add egg and sufficient water to make a firm dough. Wrap the dough in plastic wrap (cling film) and chill for 1 hour. Preheat oven to 180°C (350°F). Lightly grease the base of a springform tin with butter. Roll out chilled dough to fit the prepared base. Bake for 5–10 minutes, or until the top is a light golden brown. Cool.

Syrup

Place rum, cinnamon sticks, sugar, water, orange juice and apricot jam in a saucepan and bring to the boil. Cook for 10 minutes. Cool and strain.

To Assemble

Spread the cooled pastry base with warm apricot jam. Cut the sponge into quarters horizontally. Stack each layer of sponge on top of the pastry base, spreading each with cooled syrup and jam. Coat the top and sides with warm apricot glaze. On a lightly floured surface, roll out the marzipan into a 23 cm (9 in) circle. Pour white chocolate over the marzipan. Pipe dark chocolate on top of the white chocolate. Use the feathering technique (see page 113) to decorate. When set, use a hot, sharp knife to cut the marzipan and chocolate circles into 12 wedges. Place on topof the cake and press flaked almond around the sides.

See page 230

PUREE
(see also coulis, sauces)

The raw or cooked flesh of fresh fruit which is reduced to a smooth sauce or liquid by being liquidised in a food processor and strained through a sieve to remove seeds. The fluidity of the sauce depends on the particular fruit and its water content. A purée should not have any sugar or sweeteners or sugar syrup or water added to thin it down or change its flavour; then it is called a coulis.

PURE ICING SUGAR

Pure icing sugar is the pure form of sugar crushed until it is fine enough to be icing sugar. It is known as powdered sugar in the USA. When starch is added to icing sugar it becomes a product known as non-lumping icing sugar or icing sugar mixture.

PURI
(see also bread)

An Indian deep-fried bread and also a leavened sourdough bread made along the shores of the Black Sea. The puri of India is a flat disc of unleavened or slightly leavened wholemeal dough which is rolled thinly and fried. As it cooks, it should puff considerably to become a pocket bread. A puri is made from atta or roti flour and served as an accompaniment to Indian savoury dishes.

The puri of the Georgia region is a long loaf of leavened sourdough bread which is baked on the sides of the tandoor oven and should also puff to become a pocket bread.

2 cups (8 oz) wholemeal flour
45 g (1½ oz) unsalted (sweet) butter
1 teaspoon fresh compressed yeast
1 cup (8 fl oz) warm water
vegetable oil, for deep-frying

Place flour, butter and yeast in a mixing bowl and lightly rub ingredients together until they resemble breadcrumbs. Add half the water, stirring into the dry ingredients, then slowly add more water until a fairly firm dough is achieved. (It is better to have a dough that is too soft than too hard.) Knead dough for 5–8 minutes or until smooth and elastic. Place dough in a bowl and cover.

Punch Torte Step-by-Step

Step 1: Brush each of the four layers with syrup and jam. Stack the sponge layers on top of the pastry base. Coat the top and sides of the cake with apricot glaze.

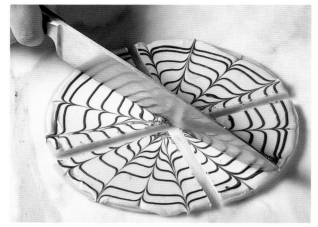

Step 2: Use a hot, sharp knife to cut the firm chocolate and marzipan top into 12 portions. Place on the surface of the cake. See page 229.

Step 1: Cover strip with the chocolate filling and place the next strip on top. Cover this with filling. Continue adding cake strips and chocolate filling until the stack is about 7 cm (2¾ in) high. Chill for 30 minutes.

Step 2: Place the chilled stack on the very edge of the workbench and place a ruler along the top edge of the cake furthest from you. Cut diagonally along the bottom edge nearest you with a clean serrated knife. The ruler and the benchtop edge are used as the guide for the knife.

Step 3: Join the triangles together with a thin layer of the chocolate mixture to form a pyramid, ensuring that all layers are running in the same direction. See page 232.

Place in a warm area for 40 minutes.
Cut dough into 14 pieces and roll each piece into a ball.
On a lightly floured surface, roll each ball to
15–16 cm (6–6½ in) in diameter.
Heat the oil to around 180°C (350°F).
Place one puri at a time in the hot oil. (The others should
remain covered until fried.) The puri will begin to puff up
immediately. Use a pair of tongs or a slotted spoon to keep the
puri under the oil for the first minute it cooks. Keep covering
the puri with oil and fry on each side until golden brown.
When fried and puffed, remove the puri from the oil and
allow to sit on absorbent (kitchen) paper
for several minutes. Serve fresh with meals.

PYRAMID CAKE

This is a visually striking cake with its thin layers of cake and
chocolate in the shape of a pyramid.

¼ cup (2 oz) plain (all-purpose) flour
¼ cup (2 oz) cornflour (cornstarch)
150 g (5 oz) unsalted (sweet) butter
⅓ cup (2½ oz) caster (superfine) sugar
60 g (2 oz) marzipan (see page 177), finely chopped
7 egg yolks
3 egg whites
⅓ cup (2½ oz) caster (superfine) sugar, extra
¼ cup (1 oz) ground almonds

Filling
200 ml (7 fl oz) cream (single or light)
20 g (¾ oz) unsalted (sweet) butter
600 g (20 oz) dark (plain or semi-sweet) chocolate, chopped
cocoa powder, for dusting

Preheat oven to 180°C (350°F).
Line three 28 x 20 cm (11 x 8 in) baking sheets (trays)
with baking paper (parchment).

Mix the flours and sift twice. Beat butter, sugar and marzipan
until creamy, light and fluffy. Add egg yolks one at a time,
beating very well after each one is added. Beat egg whites
until stiff peaks form, then add the extra sugar, a spoonful at
a time. Beat until sugar is dissolved. Gently fold in the sifted
flour and ground almonds by hand, then add the beaten
marzipan mixture. Spread the mixture onto prepared
trays and bake for 15–20 minutes, or until
the top of each cake springs back when lightly touched and
the cakes have shrunk slightly away from the sides of the
sheets. Cool on the sheets for 5 minutes before
turning out onto cake racks to cool.

Filling
Place cream and butter in a saucepan and bring to the boil.
Remove from heat and quickly stir in chopped chocolate. Stir
until chocolate is melted. Chill. Stir occasionally so that no
lumps form. Do not allow the filling to become too thick. It
must remain easy to spread.

To Assemble
Cut the cakes into 7 cm (2¾ in) strips and spread thinly
with the chocolate. Stack on top of each other until the pile is
7 cm (2¾ in) high. Chill for 30 minutes.
Place the chilled cake on the very edge of the bench (counter)
top. Place a ruler along the top edge of the cake furthest from
you and cut diagonally through to the bottom edge nearest
you with a clean serrated knife. When cut, you will have two
triangles of cake. Stand the triangles so that the layers of cake
run vertically. Join the triangles to make a pyramid shape
with a thin layer of chocolate mixture.
Cover the two sloping sides with the chocolate mixture and
chill for 30 minutes. Dust with the cocoa powder.

See page 231

QUANDONG

A peach-like fruit harvested in the southern regions of Australia and often referred to as Australia's native peach. Quandongs change from green to bright red when ripe and fresh and have a similar flavour to lightly spiced peaches. They can be eaten fresh, but are normally dried for later use and rehydrated using apple or grape juice. They are used in cakes, pies and sorbets, and made into jams (conserves).

QUARK
(see cream cheese)

Similar to cream cheese, quark can be substituted for cream cheese in almost all recipes. Quark is used extensively in cheesecakes, cremes, mousses and parfaits throughout Europe. The production of quark comes from the addition of rennet to the leftover milk from cheese making. This separates the whey and thus the quark is produced.

QUEEN CAKES
(see also cup cakes, patty cakes)

The English name for small, round, light buttercakes so named because they were enjoyed by a Queen of England. Queen cakes are usually dusted with icing (powdered) sugar and accompanied by whipped cream. They should not be cut, iced or filled with anything.

QUEENSLAND NUT
(see macadamia)

QUEEN OF PUDDINGS

An egg-based custard dessert which is said to have been invented for a Queen of England, who liked the traditional pudding, but wanted it much sweeter, although still very light. The egg custard is poured over bread or sponge crumbs and baked. It is then glazed with strawberry jam (jelly) and topped with a feathery, light topping of meringue.

1 cup (60 g) fresh bread or sponge,
cut into cubes (1 cm/½ in)
2 eggs
1¼ cups (10 fl oz) fresh milk
1 cup (8 fl oz) single cream
¼ cup (2 oz) caster (superfine) sugar
2 tablespoons strawberry jam (jelly)
1 egg white
2 tablespoons caster (superfine) sugar

Preheat oven to 150°C (325°F).
Sprinkle bread or sponge crumbs in the base of a large ramekin dish or pie dish. Whisk together eggs, milk, cream and sugar in a large mixing bowl. Pour the liquid mixture over the bread or sponge and bake in preheated oven until golden brown, and the custard is firm.
Spread the top of the set custard with the jam. Place egg white in a clean bowl and whisk until light and fluffy, and it holds stiff peaks. While still beating, slowly add sugar, until all is combined and dissolved. Spread the meringue over the top of the jam-topped custard and return to the oven for 5 minutes, or until the meringue has a golden glaze.

QUEEN OF SHEBA

A light round chocolate cake which is said to be the chocolate version of the American favourite, angel's food cake. It is lightened by whisking the egg yolks to a sabayon and the egg whites to a meringue. The two are then folded together and the chocolate or cocoa folded through with the cornflour (cornstarch). This very light cake rises in the oven and sinks slightly when cooled. It should be served warm with crème anglaise.

QUENELLE

Originally, a quenelle was a small dumpling boiled or poached in stock or sugar syrup, depending on whether it was to be sweet or savoury. Eventually the word came to mean the shape of the dumpling, and is now used to describe mixtures ranging from potato to thickened creams and ice creams, all of which have the quenelle shape, formed by scooping the mixture between two spoons and forming a dumpling shape with three oval sides, almost like an egg. Quenelles of cream and ice cream make an attractive garnish for desserts.

QUICHE
(see also savoury pastries)

Once made using a base of yeast-raised dough, this 16th-century dish of French origin is a savoury open-faced flan which is filled with a cream or custard of cream and eggs flavoured with bacon, cheese, onions and certain vegetables.
The art of good quiche-making is in ensuring the base has been properly blind baked so that it is solid enough for the liquid filling to cook. If the base is not blind baked or is not

baked well enough, the base may not cook through once the liquid filling has been poured in; this finished article will have a soggy or wet base.

QUICKBREAD
(see also bread, damper, scones, soda bread)

Known by more common names such as damper, scones or biscuits, quickbreads are those bread products which are risen using baking powder (soda). They are usually flavoured with sour milk or buttermilk, which helps make them light. Quickbreads form the basis for many of the world's most famous and oldest bread products, which are still greatly enjoyed today.

QUILTERS' CAKE

An American farmland cake, this delight was baked for the quilters' meetings. During working bees, the men would work together on the farm to help each other out and during this time the women would sit inside and make quilts. Cakes and refreshments would be served, and the most popular of these cakes soon became known as the quilters' cake. Known to have originated around 1875, the quilters' cake was a pound cake made with farm fresh butter, cream and eggs.

4 cups (16 oz) plain (all-purpose) flour
2 teaspoons baking powder (soda)
375 g (12 oz) unsalted (sweet) butter, softened
2 cups (10 oz) light brown sugar
5 eggs
1 cup (8 fl oz) milk
1 teaspoon vanilla essence (extract)
1 cup (5 oz) walnuts, chopped

Preheat oven to 180°C (360°F).
Grease well a 25 x 30 x 5 cm (10 x 12 x 1¼ in) loaf tin.
Sift flour and baking powder. Place butter and brown sugar in the bowl of an electric mixer and cream until fluffy.
Beat in the eggs one at a time, beating well after each one is added. Add the flour mix, alternating with the milk.
Blend well and stir in vanilla essence and walnuts.
Pour into prepared tin and bake in preheated oven for 50-55 minutes. Leave in the tin until cool. Remove from the tin and dust with icing (powdered) sugar.
Cut into slices to serve.

QUINCE
(see also fruits)

This unusual fruit has been used for many centuries in perfumery, cookery and confectionery, and was seen as a symbol of love and fertility in ancient Greece. Its use in the pastry kitchen dates back to the early Greeks and Romans,. The Greeks were known for their peeled quinces stuffed with a sweet nutty filling and baked in a sweet pastry casing. However, quinces have never seen a huge demand or great popularity. They simply have fleeting bursts of stardom on occasions when young chefs reintroduce this delicately flavoured fruit. Its greatest rise of popularity was probably in the 14th century, when it was mentioned in the journals of several of the leading pastry chefs of the time.

Looking like a large misshapen pear or apple, quinces are a yellow-skinned and yellow-fleshed fruit. The ripe fruit is covered with fine, soft down or fur and the fruit should still be quite hard to the touch. Far too bitter and sour to eat raw, the yellow flesh is usually stewed in water or sweetened syrups, where it turns a light soft pink colour.

Due to its high pectin content, the fruit is also a popular addition or flavour for jams, jellies and marmalades, its pinkness being an unmistakeable attribute and harmonising perfectly with the pleasant fresh aroma. One of the most popular sweetmeats made from quince is the Spanish dulce de membrillo, a thick paste made from the dried quince paste and rolled into fine sheets.

QUINCE SNOW

2 large quinces, peeled, cored and thinly sliced
½ teaspoon ground cinnamon
¾ cup (6 fl oz) water
3 egg whites
½ cup (4 oz) caster (superfine)

Cook quinces and cinnamon with water until quite soft. Purée through a sieve or in a blender. Cool. Beat egg whites until stiff peaks form. While the whites are still whipping, slowly add the sugar, a little at a time, to form a solid meringue mixture. Gradually fold in the quince purée until smooth and well mixed. Chill and serve.

RABOTE
(see also bourdelot, baked apple, talibur)

A rabote (ball) is a small pastry dessert in which the apple or pear is enlosed within a casing of puff or shortcrust pastry. A specialty of different provinces within France, this dessert is served warm or cold with a sweet crème anglaise.

RAISIN
(see also dried fruits)

Raisins, dried black grapes, are used in cakes, desserts, fruit mince and wherever dried fruits are required.

Sun dried or dehydrated through machines, raisins are known in the USA as sultanas, and sultanas are referred to as seedless raisins.

RAISING AGENT
(see also aeration, baking powder, yeast,
bicarbonate of soda)

A raising agent is any substance or process which when added to (or carried out upon) a food will cause that food to expand upon heating so that it rises, increasing in volume, and making the internal structure somewhat lighter.

The most common raising agents are processes such as whisking, laminating and steam, or products such as baking powder and yeast.

RASPBERRY
(see also berries)

A member of the rose family, and known as the king of berries, the raspberry is firm red and juicy. The myth is that raspberries, cultivated since the Middle Ages, were always golden until the nymph Ida pricked her finger on the berry bush whilst collecting food for Jupiter. Ever since, her blood has stained the fruit. (A golden raspberry is still grown.)

Each raspberry is slightly conical in shape and consists of a cluster of many tiny stone fruits. When picked, the raspberry actually pulls off from the core, leaving a hollow space in its centre. Raspberries are used in jams, sorbets, cakes, pie fillings, ice cream and sauces.

RASPBERRY JAM

1 kg (2 lb) fresh raspberries
1 kg (2 lb) caster (superfine) sugar
3 lemons, rind and juice
1 teaspoon cinnamon
5 cups (40 fl oz) water

Place all ingredients in a large saucepan or stock pot and slowly bring to the boil.
Rapid boil for 5–8 minutes, stirring. Turn down heat and simmer for a further 30–35 minutes. Pour jam mixture into sterilised jars and cool before sealing.

RATAFIA BISCUITS

A form of the original macaroon recipe, with the rice giving a special texture and flavour to the biscuit (cookie).

4 egg whites
1¾ cups (13 oz) caster (superfine) sugar
210 g (7 oz) ground (minced) almonds
45 g (1½ oz) ground rice

Preheat the oven to 180°C (360°F).
Line two baking trays (sheets) with baking paper (parchment).
Place sugar, almonds and rice in a saucepan and add egg whites. Combine mixture with a wooden spoon.
Place pan over gentle heat and warm to around 30°C (60°F)
Remove from heat and cool slightly.
Place mixture in a piping bag fitted with a plain 1 cm (½ in) nozzle and pipe mixture onto baking trays (sheets) in discs of 2–3 cm (¾ in–1¼ in) diameter.
Bake for 15–18 minutes. Remove and cool.

Makes 24

RAW SUGAR
(see also coffee sugar)

A small, light brown sugar crystal. Raw sugar is also available in darker brown crystals which have a deeper flavour. The colour and flavour comes from the coating of molasses on the sugar.

REDCURRANT
(see also berries)

The redcurrant is similar to the black and white currants, and grows in small clusters on bushes. Scandinavians use it for dishes such as rodgrod and grits but elsewhere it is used for redcurrant jelly, desserts (summer pudding) and sorbets. Redcurrants are sometimes eaten raw, with a little sugar.

RENNET
(see also junket)

Obtained from the stomach of calves, rennet is a substance which, when mixed with milk, turns it into a soft but digestible clotted substance. Rennet is most commonly sold as junket tablets.

REST

A settling period for pastry. Once made, pastry needs to allow the gluten to mellow in a refrigerator. If this does not happen, the gluten structure begins to form and the result is tough pastry.

RETARDATION
(see also bread making)

This is the action of a yeast dough when the fermentation process is stopped or slowed to such an extent that it does not begin producing alcohol and carbon dioxide. When dough is refrigerated or frozen, the yeast action is suspended by the cold. The amount of salt in a dough and the temperature of the water or other ingredients also play a role in retarding the fermentation process.

RHUBARB

Rhubarb is a vegetable from the celery family and grows with thick red to pink stalks with green leafy inedible fronds at the end. The ouside skin of the stalk is removed before cooking, because it is fibrous and tough.

The stalks are washed, cut and stewed or sweated in a small amount of liquid to make them soft enough to eat.

For centuries rhubarb was used for medicinal purposes. Then the British used it as a general cooking ingredient in pickles, sorbet, ice creams, crumbles, cobblers, sauces, jams and dessert pies. Commonly mixed with apple, rhubarb also blends well with quinces and pears, and is tasty when served sweetened on its own with custard.

RHUBARB CRUMBLE

½ cup (4 oz) caster (superfine) sugar
½ cup (3 oz) light brown sugar
½ cup (4 fl oz) water
60 g (2 oz) unsalted (sweet) butter
4 cups chopped, destringed rhubarb
zest of 2 lemons
zest of 1 orange
2 quinces, cooked
1 tablespoon unsalted (sweet) butter, extra

Crumble Topping

1 cup (4 oz) plain (all-purpose) flour
½ cup (2 oz) toasted muesli
90 g (3 oz) unsalted (sweet) butter
2 tablespoons brown sugar
2 tablespoons caster (superfine) sugar
1 teaspoon ground cinnamon
icing (powdered) sugar, for dusting

Preheat oven to 180°C (350°F).
Dissolve sugars in the water and butter over medium heat to make a syrup. Bring to the boil, then add rhubarb and lemon and orange rind. Cover and simmer for 5 minutes, or until rhubarb is tender but not mushy.
Turn into a stainless steel bowl to cool.
To cook quinces, remove conical shape from top

and bottom with a sharp knife. Fill both ends with a teaspoon of butter and wrap in foil.
Set quinces on a bed of rock salt on a tray and bake for 2 hours. Cool.
Chop quinces and add to stewed rhubarb.
Spoon mixture into ramekins or serving dishes.

Crumble Topping
Place flour, toasted muesli, cinnamon and sugars in a bowl.
Rub the butter through until mixture resembles fresh breadcrumbs.
Sprinkle top of each ramekin with the crumb-like mixture and bake for 15–20 minutes, or until golden brown on top.
Dust lightly with icing sugar and serve.

RIBBON STAGE

This stage of any mixture is achieved when a dribble of the mixture, from the whisk or a spoon, will form an impression of itself on top of the mixture and remain there for at least the count of 8.

RICE

A popular starchy Asian dish for centuries, rice is also used in such famous desserts as English rice pudding, the French riz à l'Imperatice or the riz à la Condé.

The raw product is crushed to make rice flour, used in cakes and rice paper and in confectionery (nougat Montelimar). It is also used as a weight in the centre of pastry cases when blind baking the pastry.

RICE FLOUR
(see also flour)

Rice is crushed and milled very finely and used in many sweet cakes, batters and biscuit (cookie) doughs. It adds a slight gritty texture to the cake mixture. Rice flour is also a common thickening agent, used to thicken milk- and syrup-based puddings and sauces.

RICE PAPER
(see also rice, nougat)

A white sheet of rice paper resembles paper in all aspects except that it is edible.

A form of unleavened bread, it is made from finely ground rice flour, water and (possibly) salt. The mixture is spread in fine sheets across hot irons, dried or cooked until firm, then dried before being storing.

It is used in pastry for decorations; they are painted or printed using edible dyes then cut into shapes and placed directly on cakes to be eaten.

Some moist biscuit (cookie) mixtures are baked onto rice paper and eaten along with the paper. Rice paper is commonly used on both sides of nougat, which is otherwise quite sticky. Rice paper is readily available from health food stores.

RICOTTA

Ricotta is an Italian curd cheese (soft and unripened) produced from the whey by-product of other cheeses. Slightly sweet and grainy in texture, ricotta cheese is used in many pastry preparations such as cheesecakes and cassata alla Siciliana.

RIGO JANCSI

Famed throughout the USA, Rigo Jancsi is named after an 1800s gypsy who broke the hearts of young ladies, serenading them with his brilliant playing of the violin. It is not known why this cake was named after him; perhaps because he had a love for the sweeter things in life!

3 eggs
1 egg yolk
1 cup (7 oz) caster (superfine) sugar
1 cup (4 oz) plain (all-purpose) flour
1 teaspoon baking (soda) powder
½ teaspoon ground cinnamon
¼ cup (1 oz) cocoa powder
⅓ cup (3 fl oz) milk

Filling
390 g (13 oz) dark (plain or semi-sweet) chocolate, chopped
2 cups (16 fl oz) thickened cream
zest of 1 orange
2 tablespoons Grand Marnier

Icing
⅓ cup (4 oz) liquid glucose (light corn syrup)
2 tablespoons hot water
30 g (1 oz) unsalted (sweet) butter
450 g (15 oz) dark (plain or semi-sweet) chocolate, melted

Preheat oven to 180°C (350°F).
Line a 28 x 30 x 3 cm (11 x 12 x 1¼ in) baking tray (sheet) with baking paper (parchment).
Place eggs, egg yolk and sugar in an electric mixer bowl and whisk until mixture reaches the ribbon stage or is very thick.
Sift flour, baking powder (soda), cinnamon and cocoa together and add to egg mixture. Add milk and fold ingredients together. Pour mixture into prepared tray and spread evenly.
Bake for 20 minutes, or until just cooked. Remove and cool.

Filling
Place cream in a saucepan and bring to the boil.
Add chopped chocolate, orange zest and Grand Marnier.
Take off the heat and stir until chocolate is completely melted, and the mixture is smooth and thick.
Cool mixture in referigerator for 2–3 hours.

Icing
Place the glucose (corn syrup), butter and water in a saucepan and heat slowly until butter is melted. Raise the heat slightly and bring to the boil, stirring. Add chocolate to mixture, take of the heat and stir until combined.
Cool slightly.
To assemble, whip orange-flavoured chocolate cream until stiff using an electric mixer. Cut cake in half horizontally, creating two even sheets.
Remove top sheet and spread base sheet of cake with all the chocolate cream. Place second half of cake on top and press down lightly to ensure it is sitting on the cream. Refrigerate cake for 1 hour. When chilled, pour cooling chocolate mixture over top of cake and spread evenly. Refrigerate for a further 1–2 hours. Using a hot knife, cut cake into 12–16 even portions. Serve with whipped cream or raspberry coulis.

RIGODON

This is a French regional pudding specialty which consists of spiced brioche dough mixed with nuts and dried fruits, soaked in milk or cream and baked. It is usually served with a berry or fruit compôte.

RIND
(see also zest, citrus)

Rind is the outer skin of citrus fruits. It is grated for flavour into cakes and biscuit doughs or cut into strips for crystallising or garnishing.
It contains essential oils which can be also removed by rubbing the rind with sugar cubes.
Rind also refers to the outer crust of cheeses such as brie or camembert.

RIOLER

A French term for the placement of pastry strips across a dish to create a patterned (usually criss-cross) effect. The term 'à la rioler' refers to use of this method with marzipan on alkazar cake or slices, or linzer paste on the top of a linzer torte.

RIZ A LA CONDE

One of several dishes which were named after the great French General Condé.
This is a cold dessert made from milk, rice, poached fruit and gelatine, set in a fruit purée sauce to serve. Produced in a ring shape or savarin mould, it traditionally uses poached apricots and is served with a fruit sauce flavoured with Kirsch.

1 litre (32 fl oz) milk
1 cup (7 oz) caster (superfine) sugar
1⅓ cups (7 oz) long grain rice
4 egg yolks
90 g (3 oz) unsalted (sweet) butter
1 cup (8 fl oz) thickened cream

Preheat the oven to 180°C (350°F).
Place milk and sugar in a pan on the stove top and bring to the boil. Add rice to boiling liquid and continue to stir as mixture returns to the boil. Cover baking tray with a lid (or foil) and bake for 1–1½ hours, or until the rice is tender; stir rice occasionally and cook until all the liquid has been absorbed.
Remove rice to a large bowl and cool slightly. Add egg yolks

and butter while rice is still quite hot, stirring quickly.
Cool mixture. When rice is cold, whisk cream stiffly
and fold through rice mixture.
Use rice Condé as required, or place in individual containers
or a large savarin ring and allow to refrigerate for
2–3 hours, before serving with a fruit sauce.

RIZ A L'IMPERATICE
(see also rice)

Translated, riz a L'Imperatice means 'rice in the Empress
style'. This dish is named after the Napoleon III's consort
Empress Eugènie. It is traditionally served plain or with
raspberry coulis or sauce.

8 leaves gelatine
300 ml (10 fl oz) crème anglaise (see page 84)
500 g (16 oz) rice Condé mixture (before setting — see above)
75 ml (2½ fl oz) Kirsch
¾ cup (6 fl oz) cream, lightly whipped
100 g (3½ oz) mixed glacé (mixed) fruits
(pineapple,cherries,apricot, pear), chopped finely

Soak gelatine in cold water until soft. Add gelatine to the
freshly cooked crème anglaise while it is still warm, and stir
until the gelatine is melted. Stir Kirsch in.
Allow the crème anglaise to cool slightly and then fold through
the rice mixture. Fold cream in, then the glacé fruits.
Mould mixture into a 23–24 cm (9–9½ in) savarin ring and
refrigerate for 2–3 hours, or until set.
Serve with fresh fruits and whipped cream.

ROASTED FLAKED
ALMONDS

Simple and quick to make, flaked or slivered almonds are a
great side decoration for any cake.

250 g (8 oz) flaked or slivered almonds

Preheat oven to 180°C (350°F). Spread almonds thinly on a
baking tray (sheet) and bake for 4 minutes. Remove tray
and use a fork to turn almonds over. Bake for a further
4 minutes. Remove and turn again. Continue this process
until almonds are golden brown. Cool on the tray.
When cold, press the almonds around the sides of a
cake covered with glaze or cream. Makes sufficient
to cover the sides of one 23 cm (9 in) cake.
Roasted almonds can be stored in an airtight
container for up to 2 weeks.

ROCHER

This is a traditional almond-based petit four. It is irregular in
shape, with almonds either sugar-coated or crystallised in an
icing (powder) sugar then coated with a liqueur and baked in
the oven. The crystallised almonds are then broken into
pieces, cooled, coated thinly with chocolate and set in small
pieces.

2 cups (7½ oz) slivered almonds
¾ cup (4 oz) icing (powdered) sugar
30 ml (1 fl oz) Cointreau or orange liqueur
210 g (7 oz) milk chocolate, melted

Preheat oven to 180°C (350°F). Line a baking tray (sheet)
with baking paper (parchment). Place almonds, icing sugar
and Cointreau in a small bowl. Stir until combined and
mixture is slightly moist. Spread mixture onto a baking
tray (sheet) and place in oven. Remove mixture every
3–4 minutes and turn with a palette knife so that it is
evenly coloured and cooked.
After 20 minutes, icing sugar should lose its powdery look and
begin to crystallise around the almonds. Leave almonds in the
oven for a further 10 minutes to brown evenly. Remove tray
and turn mixture occasionally, to allow almonds to cool.
Once cooled, break mixture into bite-sized pieces and
place in bowl. Pour in melted chocolate and stir so it
completely covers almond mixture. Spoon small
amounts of mixture onto lined baking tray. Set chocolates
firm in refrigerator before serving with coffee.

ROCK CAKE
(see also shortcakes)

This small dry biscuit has the texture of a cake and is similar
to a shortcake or drop scone. A rockcake may be plain,
sweet, spicy or filled with dried fruits. Serve hot or cold.

ROCK SUGAR
(see also sugar work)

A decorative sugar produced when a boiling sugar syrup is
quickly poured into and mixed with a quantity of royal icing.
The mixture is poured into shapes and allowed to set. The
cold product is broken into pieces and can be left plain or
coloured to suit.The open texture of these rock sugar gives a
textured appearance that is similar to some kinds of rocks
and corals.
  Rock sugar is created by heat expanding air that is
trapped within royal icing. The albumen in the egg white of
the royal icing sets and the liquid is evaporated by the heat,
allowing the resulting sugar to crystallise before setting firm.

ROCKMELON
(see also melons)

This member of the melon family is also known as a
cantaloupe.
  The rockmelon has a sandy textured skin with hints of
orange. The internal flesh is bright orange and the centre of
the rockmelon is hollow, but full of pips or seeds which are
scraped away before the fruit is eaten.
  Rockmelon is often used in cold fruit soups as a purée, in
ice creams and fruit salad, or it can be served on its own as a
breakfast meal.

RODGROD

Otherwise known as grits, this is a jelly-like product made
from the crushings of red berries and fruit. When heated, the

Rocher Chocolates Step-by-Step

Step 1: Spread the almond, icing sugar and Cointreau mixture into a baking tray.

Step 2: Break the cool almond mixture into bite-sized pieces.

Step 3: Stir the pieces in the melted chocolate so it completely covers the almond mixture.

liquid is thickened with potato flour or arrowroot and allowed to cool. More commonly the pulp is sieved so only the clear juices remain. The cold dish is served with whipped cream.

ROLL
(see also bread)

A small bun or piece of bread dough made into an individual size and shape and baked for individual consumption. More commonly referred to as a bread roll.

ROLLING PIN

A cyndrical instrument used to roll pastry into the required thicknesses.

A rolling pin can be made from wood, metal, marble, plastic or glass and may have revolving handles, or may be simply a straight shaft used for rolling.

Certain varieties of rolling pin are also hollowed, and need to be filled with ice or cold water to keep the pastry cool and to add weight to the rolling pin.

While a rolling pin traditionally has a smooth surface, the cylinder can also come in textured surfaces such as basket weave, fluted, patterned or with sharp grooves for cutting strips or different shapes (such as for croissants and Danish pastries).

ROLY-POLY

This is a traditional British pudding consisting of a suet pastry crust covered with jam (jelly) or other toppings, rolled up like a Swiss roll and tied in a moist floured towel and boiled or steamed. The roly-poly may also be baked on a baking tray (sheet) in a dry oven. The most common fillings are jam (jelly) and dried fruits, but it is often rolled with a sugar filling and served with golden syrup.

ROMANOFF

This is a style of dessert invented in the 19th century and dedicated to the Russian Imperial family. It consists of fresh fruits, such as strawberries, raspberries, cherries, peaches and similar fruits, folded through an orange-flavoured sweetened cream (made with either fresh orange juice with sugar, Curaçao, or Cointreau).

ROSALINDS
(see also Othellos, Desdemonas, Iagos)

Rosalind is one of four characters from plays by William Shakespeare who have been immortalised in confectionery. Rosalind was a character from *As You Like It*. These small pastries are made by joining two Othello sponges together with raspberry jam (jelly) and coating them with a pink, cherry- flavoured fondant.

ROSCA DE REYES
(see also Twelfth Night Cakes)

Rosca de Reyes means the ring of Kings' Day and the cake named in honour of this occasion is a sweet yeast-raised bread dough served on 6 January (Epiphany, or Twelfth Night). It is the Mexican version of the Twelfth Night or Epiphany cake or galettes. As with the European galette, a small bean or ceramic baby doll representing the baby Jesus is baked into the sweet yeast dough and whoever receives the bean or baby doll is the King. This person must then hold a party on Godparents or Candelmas Day (2 February).

ROSE
(see also flowers)

Roses are used in pastry for their decorative appeal as well as their flavour. The perfume is often commented on but few Westerners use the perfume to its fullest effect. This delicacy has been used throughout the Middle East for centuries.

Rose petals are now used in salads, jams (jellies) and syrups, and also in mousses, cakes, confectionery and sauces.

When rose petals are dipped into egg white, then sugar, and allowed to dry, they can be used as decorations on plates or on cakes (as frosted rose petals).

ROSE HIP

Rosehips are the fruit of the wild rose or dog rose and are small, red or orange berries. With the removal of the top and tails of the hip they can be boiled and puréed. With the addition of sugar, they are then used to produce jams, jellies and desserts, and to make rosehip tea.

ROSETTE

A decorative swirl of a mixture such as cream, ganache or biscuit paste produced by piping the mixture through a star-shaped nozzle. Rosettes are used as decorations on top of cakes, or to make shaped biscuits: if they are piped from biscuit paste, the baked biscuit retains that shape through and after baking.

ROSEWATER

Rosewater is a fragrant and aromatic liquid produced by distilling rose petals. It is used frequently in Middle Eastern cooking for sweet dishes where a syrup is used, or for confections such as Turkish delight.

Available in liquid form from health food stores and chemists, rosewater is a pleasant addition to light cakes or creams where its flavour and aroma is going to be appreciated.

ROTHSCHILD

The name given to several desserts by famous chefs who worked for the Rothschilds, a famous and wealthy banking family. The most celebrated of these chefs was Carême, who invented the equally celebrated soufflé. The most successful and well-known of these is the Rothschild soufflé, perhaps because of its use of crystallised (candied) fruits soaked in goldwasser, a liqueur which contains small pieces of gold.

ROTHSCHILD SOUFFLÉ

75 g (2½ oz) crystallised (candied) fruit,
cut into very small pieces
¼ cup (2 fl oz) Goldwasser
1 cup (8 fl oz) milk
⅓ cup (2½ oz) caster (superfine) sugar
4 egg yolks
⅓ cup (1½ oz) plain (all-purpose) flour
6 egg whites
icing (powdered) sugar, for dusting

Preheat oven to 180°C (350°F).
Grease 4 soufflé ramekin dishes with butter and line
with sugar. Steep crystallised fruit in the Goldwasser
for 1–2 hours.
Place milk in a saucepan and bring to the boil. Place sugar,
two egg yolks and flour in a mixing bowl and whisk together.
Pour scalded milk over the egg yolk mixture, whisking
continuously. Place the whisked liquid in the saucepan and
return to the heat. Stir till the mixture thickens, then allow it
to cook for 2 minutes, stirring continually. When thick,
remove from the heat and quickly stir in the remaining two
egg yolks. Allow this mixture to cool slightly.
Whisk egg whites in a clean bowl until they form stiff peaks.
Fold the steeped fruit into the custard mixture and then
carefully fold the egg whites through the mixture.
Pour the mixture into the prepared dishes and quickly place
these in the oven. Bake for 20 minutes, or until risen.
Remove from oven, dust the top with icing
(powdered) sugar and serve immediately.

ROUGH PUFF PASTRY
(see also puff pastry)

Made using the second method of producing puff pastry, the
chop-in method, this puff pastry obtains its name because of
the rough-looking nature of the dough. Instead of being made
into a slab and rolled immediately into the dough, the fat
content of rough puff pastry is chopped into pieces and
pressed into the dough of flour and water. It is then rolled out
and folded 3–4 times, as for normal puff pastry. The fat will
still be quite adequately laminated within the dough. This
quick method of puff pastry is used for sausage rolls, pie
tops, pies, pasties and for puff pastry sheets where the quality
of the puff does not matter too much.

ROULADE
(see also Swiss roll)

The French word for 'roll', a roulade may be either sweet or
savoury. The sweet version is very similar to a Swiss roll. It is
made using much thinner sponge sheets, has more rolls and is
usually much smaller in circumference. It is also richer than a
Swiss roll and is therefore served in much smaller slices.

ROUT BISCUITS
(see also marzipan)

England is the home of rout biscuits (cookies), although
European countries have special marzipan treats very similar

in style. These are simply a mixture of marzipan, sugar and
egg whites. They must contain real marzipan (66% almonds
and 34% sugar being the perfect ratio) or the mixture will
boil instead of simply drying out. The same will occur if too
much sugar is added, if any egg yolk should be left with the
whites or if too much egg white is added. Other than these few
rules, rout biscuits are a simple, quick, effective and tasty
petit four for coffee or light snacks.
It is thought that the original idea for the rout biscuit came
from the home of marzipan, Italy, where similar delights were
produced using ground almonds, sugar and egg whites, and
flavoured with rosewater or orange blossom.

550 g (18 oz) marzipan
1½ cups (12 oz) caster (superfine) sugar
3 egg whites
210 g (7 oz) dark (plain or semi-sweet) chocolate,
melted (see page 62)
glacé (candied) cherries, for decoration
chopped nuts, for decoration

Preheat oven to 200°C (400°F). Line a baking sheet with
baking paper (parchment). Place marzipan and sugar
in a bowl and mix until they form a solid mass. Slowly
add egg whites until a nice piping consistency is formed.
The amount of egg white needed will depend on
the brand of marzipan used.
(The mixture is better too stiff than too runny.)
When the mixture is ready, place in a piping (pastry) bag
fitted with a 1½ cm (¾ in) star-shaped nozzle or a 1 cm (½ in)
round nozzle. Pipe the mixture onto prepared tray in various
shapes. Bake in preheated oven for 10–12 minutes. Cool on
the tray. Remove the paper and spread bases with chocolate.
Decorate with glacé cherries and chopped nuts.
Wrap the biscuits in plastic wrap (cling film) and
store in the freezer. Remove 1 hour before eating.

ROYAL ICING

A sweet icing made from whisked egg whites and pure icing
sugar, with the occasional use of lemon juice or acetic acid to
help with the setting of the icing. Royal icing is used for fine
piping work, for decorating wedding cakes or Christmas
cakes and for decorations where a firm, fine icing is required.
It is also used in floodwork designs and to make rock sugar.

1 egg white at room temperature
2 cups (12 oz) pure icing (powdered) sugar, sifted
1 to 2 drops acetic acid or lemon juice

Place egg white in a small glass bowl. Add two spoonfuls of
icing sugar and beat for 2 minutes by hand. Beat in the rest of
the sugar, a teaspoonful at a time, beating well after each
amount is added. Add acetic acid (or lemon juice) and
continue to add icing sugar, a teaspoonful at a time, until the
mixture reaches a 'soft peak' stage. The 'soft peak' stage is
for writing and lattice work. Add more icing sugar for the
'firm peak' stage; icing for shell borders and piped flowers.
Place icing in a plastic bag, then seal in a small plastic
container to prevent the icing drying out and setting.

To cover a cake with royal icing, it should first be covered with a thin coating of marzipan. Cakes with royal icing should be eaten within a few days or the icing becomes too hard. For cakes that are stored for a long period, simply remove the decorations of royal icing before storage (or eating).

RUB-IN

A method of incorporating ingredients, usually referring to the incorporation of fat into dry ingredients. The fingertips are used to rub the butter, lard or fat lightly into the flour and other dry ingredients until the butter is in fine particles. Depending on the amount of fat used in a recipe, the mixture may resemble fine, powdery breadcrumbs, or coarse, fresh breadcrumbs (if a high proportion of fat is used). This method is used mainly in the production of pastries which require little or no kneading.

RUIFARD

The French ruifard is a cousin of the German hefeteig and of the yeast streusel slices of Austria. It is an open tart with a yeast dough base, filled with sliced apples and quinces. The fruit is placed on before the dough is proved (risen), covered with a light crumble or streusel mixture and sprinkled with sultanas. The top is then dotted with butter, and when baked, it is glazed with apricot glaze. It can be served warm or cold, as individual slices or as a dessert.

RUM
(see also spirits)

A fermented spirit, rum is produced from a mixture of sugar cane and molasses which is fermented, distilled, diluted and aged. There are two major types of rum: white rum, a clear transparent liquid, and dark rum, a more highly flavoured brown rum, having had caramel added for colour and been aged in wood casks. Known as arrack since around 800 BC, rum is a precious flavouring to the pastry chef, as it blends well with many other ingredients (nuts, fruits, chocolate and even coffee).

RUM SAUCE

3 egg yolks
1 cup (6 oz) sifted icing (powdered) sugar
½ cup (4 fl oz) dark rum
1 cup (8 fl oz) thickened cream

Place egg yolks and sugar in a large mixing bowl and, using a hand whisk, beat until light, white and fluffy. Slowly add rum, whisking well to combine thoroughly. Whip cream until very stiff, then fold through the rum mixture.
Serve the rum sauce in a jug (pitcher).

RUN-OUTS

The term run-out refers to a prefabricated decoration made from royal icing. These are made for and used in cake decorating, usually for wedding or christening cakes. A picture or design is chosen and a sheet of parchment paper or silicon paper is placed over the design. Using a thick mixture of royal icing, the design's outlines are drawn and allowed to set firm. When firm, thinner mixtures of coloured royal icing are piped into or 'run-out' into the different areas within the outline. These in turn are allowed to dry and set firm. This usually takes 1–2 days. The design is then peeled from the parchment paper and stuck onto the cake when required.

Run-outs are often called floodwork pieces, and can also be made using chocolate; dark chocolate for the outlines, white and plain (milk) chocolate for the colours (or the white chocolate is coloured, using oil-based colourings).

RUSKS
(see also pulled bread, zwieback)

Popular in many European countries as a snack made from slightly sweetened breads, rusks are served with dips, on their own or as nibbles to have with drinks. A rusk is a piece or slice of bread which has been rebaked in the oven until it is golden brown, dry and crisp. They were originally made as a means of preserving breads which were required on long travels or sea voyages. They are commonly given to children who are teething.

RYE
(see also flour)

Rye is a popular flour or grain for bread production throughout Europe. In Britain it is popular for its role in whisky making. It is used mainly for the production of dark breads or rye breads (also known as black breads) such as pumpernickel, which have good keeping properties. However, due to the low gluten content of rye flour, it produces a heavy, close-textured bread.

Rye is a widely grown cereal grass, the flour being made from its seeds or grains. It has been in cultivation for less than two thousand years, making it a relative newcomer to the grain family.

RYE BREAD
(see also bread)

Rye bread is popular throughout Europe, where the heavy dense loaves are served in thin slices or used in Danish open sandwiches. This bread does not rise well, because of the lack of gluten in the rye flour, but this can be remedied by adding wheat flour and gluten flour to the dough. Rye bread loaves are traditionally small, blunt-ended baton shapes or large flat rounds, traditional shapes from the times when they were baked on hot stones or griddle plates over open fires.

Some dark rye breads use a sourdough starter, which assists the rye and gives the dough a familiar flavour. Light ryes tend not to use the starter, having white wheat flour mixed with the rye to give it lightness.

SABAYON
(see also weinchaudeau, zabaglione)

Sabayon is the name of the French version of the Italian zabaglione or Austrian weinchaudeau. It is a mixture of egg yolks and sugar whisked (over a bain-marie or hot water bath) with champagne until light and pale and triple its volume. Sabayons are traditionally spiced with cinnamon or mixed spices. Although the egg mixture being whisked requires heat to form a stable sabayon, the temperature must never reach or exceed 45°C (113°F), as this will cook the egg mixture. When whisked to optimum volume the mixture should be further whisked over ice or iced water until cool, for greater stability. It can be served over fresh fruits and glazed under a salamander or on its own as a dessert, with langue de chat biscuits, or as a type of sauce with hot puddings.

When making sponges or other pâtisserie items using egg/sugar mixtures, the mixture is said to be at sabayon stage, also referred to as ribbon stage, once it has been whipped until it is light and fluffy, and has tripled in volume.

BASIC SABAYON RECIPE
5 egg yolks
¾ cup (6 oz) caster (superfine) sugar
1 cup (8 fl oz) champagne

Place all ingredients in a large bowl over a bowl or saucepan of simmering water and, using a large balloon whisk, whisk for about 10 minutes, or until the mixture is thick, white and creamy. Place the bowl over iced water and whisk for a further 3 minutes or until the sabayon is cool.
Serve immediately.

SABLE

The French name for a classic shortbread biscuit (cookie), Sable means 'sand' and refers to the light crumbly texture of the sable biscuit. Traditionally flavoured with lemon zest, sables consist of three ingredients (flour, sugar and butter), which are rubbed together lightly until a dough is formed. Also used as the base for fresh fruit tartlets, sable dough is traditionally moulded into a round log and rolled in sugar

before being refrigerated or frozen until firm. When firm, 2–3 mm (⅛ in) slices are cut from the log and placed flat on a baking sheet. The centre of each is then dotted with apricot jam (jelly). When baked, the biscuits should be golden brown around the sugar crust, with a white biscuit and a golden centre of jam.

2 cups (8 oz) plain (all-purpose) flour
¾ cup (4 oz) icing (powdered) sugar
pinch salt
180 g (6 oz) unsalted (sweet) butter
zest and juice of 1 lemon
caster (superfine) sugar, for rolling
200 g (7 oz) apricot jam (jelly)

Preheat oven to 200°C (400°F).
Line baking sheets with baking paper (parchment).
Sift flour, icing sugar and salt into a bowl and add the butter. Using your fingertips, lightly rub butter through the dry ingredients until the mixture resembles fresh breadcrumbs. Add lemon zest and juice and work mixture into a dough. Divide dough into 3 even pieces and roll each piece into a sausage shape 2 cm (¾ in) thick. Sprinkle caster sugar evenly over the work surface and roll the sausage shapes in the caster sugar. Wrap each roll carefully in plastic wrap (cling film) and freeze for 2–3 minutes.
Remove dough from the freezer and roll in the sugar once more before cutting the sausage shapes into even 3 mm (⅛ in) rounds. Place each round on the prepared sheet. Pipe a small dot of apricot jam onto the centre of each. Bake in preheated oven for 8–10 minutes, or until the edges are just turning golden brown. Remove immediately and cool on the sheet.

Makes 48

SACCHARIN
(see also sugar, sweeteners)

With many people now following special diets, pastry chefs need to be familiar with substitutes for foods they are used to using. One such substitute is saccharin, which is a sweetening substitute for sugar and is used by diabetics. This white powder in crystal form is 400 times stronger than sugar and can only be substitued in such dishes as sauces, confectionery and jams, jellies and mousses. It cannot be used in cake mixtures, where the butter and sugar mixture not only gives bulk but is an integral process of making the cake.

SACCHAROMETER
(see also Baume, sugar)

This instrument is used to measure the specific gravity of sugar syrups. It works on the principle that an object immersed into a heavy syrup will displace its own body weight by volume. Thus the amount of sugar syrup displaced is how heavy the syrup is. In more simple terms, a saccharometer measures the density of the sugar syrup. It works better on cold syrups which have been allowed to thicken slightly, but it will work on syrups up to the soft crack stage (129–135°C/265–275°F). It is used when making sorbets and ice creams and when crystallising (candying) fruits.

SACHER TORTE

Invented by Franz Sacher, Prince Metternich's pastry chef, in 1814 for the Congress of Vienna, Sacher torte was originally a rich light chocolate cake covered with apricot glaze and a thin rich chocolate glaze. The cake was enjoyed so much that it took pride of place in Franz Sacher's hotel in 1832, where it became famous because of its lightness and luscious chocolate flavour.

When Sacher died and the Hotel Sacher was taken over by Eduard, a seven year law suit ensued over the fact that Demels, an opposition pastry shop, was serving Sacher torte and claiming theirs to be the original recipe. The Hotel Sacher may have won the battle, but Demels continued serving a rich chocolate cake in similar style, using the name 'Ur Sacher' or original Sacher. Whatever the truth, the court battle certainly served to make the cake famous, and it remains so today. While it is said that the descendants of the Sacher family still have the original recipe, the pastry chefs of the world are now left to battle it out over what is a true Sacher: is it cut into slices and covered with jam and then iced, or is the whole cake simply iced and left uncut?

1¼ cups (5 oz) plain (all-purpose) flour
3 tablespoons cocoa powder
180 g (6 oz) unsalted (sweet) butter
⅓ cup (2½ oz) caster (superfine) sugar
7 egg yolks
⅓ cup (1½ oz) ground hazelnuts (filberts)
7 egg whites
⅔ cup (5 oz) caster (superfine) sugar, extra

To Decorate
apricot glaze (see page 10)
¾ cup (8 oz) apricot jam (jelly)
1 cup (8 fl oz) Sacher torte glaze
dark (plain or semi-sweet) chocolate,
melted (see page 62), for piping
Preheat oven to 180°C (350°F).

Very lightly grease a 23 cm (9 in) springform cake tin with butter and line base with baking paper (parchment).
Mix flour and cocoa and sift twice. Beat butter and sugar until creamy, light and fluffy. Gradually add egg yolks and beat well. Gently fold in by hand the sifted flour and cocoa, and the hazelnuts. Beat egg whites until stiff peaks form and gradually add the extra sugar, a spoonful at a time. Beat until sugar is dissolved. Take a quarter of the beaten egg white and gently mix it by hand into the mixture. Very gently fold in the remaining egg whites. Pour the mixture into the prepared tin and bake for 45–50 minutes, or until the top of the cake is firm and springs back when lightly touched. Cool in the tin for 5 minutes before turning out onto a cake rack.
When cold, cut into quarters horizontally. Spread the apricot glaze on each layer and stack one on top of the other. Boil the apricot jam until thickened and spread evenly over the top and sides of the cake. Cool, then coat with slightly warmer Sacher torte glaze. Decorate with piped melted chocolate.

Sacher Torte Glaze
½ cup (3½ oz) caster (superfine) sugar
100 g (3½ oz) dark (plain or semi-sweet) chocolate, chopped
⅓ cup (2½ fl oz) water

Place all the ingredients in a saucepan and very slowly bring to the boil. Using a sugar (candy) thermometer, cook to 115°C (240°F). Cool slightly.

See page 246

SACRISTAIN

A classic French pastry petit four made using leftover scraps of puff pastry. The puff pastry is pinned thinly (2–3 mm/ ⅛ in) and is cut into 10 x 2 cm (4 x ¾ in) lengths. These are brushed with egg wash, held at either end and twisted, then covered with flaked almonds and cooked. When cooked, they are sprinkled liberally with sugar and served as an accompaniment to coffee or tea, or with sabayons, ice creams and mousse-style desserts.

SADDLE OF VENISON
CAKE TINS

Used for making Rehruken (deer's back) cake, the saddle of venison cake tin is a rectagular tin with a round base, and many ridges along the base and sides. It is also useful for giving a decorative appearance to other cakes and breads. These tins are normally made from aluminium or copper.

SAFFRON
(see also Cornish Saffron cake)

Saffron is the brightly coloured yellow orange dried stamen of the crocus flower. In use since before Biblical times, saffron is renowned as the world's most expensive spice, some 80 000 blossoms (or 250 000 individual stamens) being required to produce just 500 g (1 lb) of saffron. Enjoyed in recipes for its colour, flavour and aroma, it should be infused in a hot liquid for up to one hour before being used in a recipe.

Saffron is said to have magical powers. It was introduced into almost all styles of food during the medieval period, although as it became expensive, it was more rarely used. It is not often used in pastry nowadays, but does make the wonderful Cornish Saffron cake. Phoenician traders who travelled to Cornwall in search of tin apparently left this recipe as a legacy, having traded their saffron and culinary ideas for the tin.

SAGO

A seldom used commodity today, sago is the small dried starch granules obtained from the pith or marrow of the sago palm tree. Sago is used in pastry work as a thickener and in puddings, cakes, confectionery and fritters.

SAGO PLUM PUDDING

¼ cup (1 oz) sago
1 cup (8 fl oz) milk
¾ cup (4 oz) raisins
¾ cup (4 oz) sultanas (golden raisins)
⅓ cup (2 oz) currants
2 tablespoons mixed (candied) peel
⅓ cup (3 oz) caster (superfine) sugar
1 teaspoon ground cinnamon
⅛ teaspoon ground cloves
1½ cups (3 oz) fresh breadcrumbs
1 egg
1 teaspoon bicarbonate of soda
60 g (2 oz) unsalted (sweet) butter, melted

Soak sago in milk for 24 hours.
Lightly grease a large pudding basin or bowl.
Place raisins, sultanas, currants, mixed peel, sugar, spices and breadcrumbs in a large mixing bowl. Mix until well combined. Pour sago and milk and the egg over the other ingredients and combine well. Dissolve bicarbonate of soda in melted butter and add to the other ingredients. Mix well.
Place the pudding mixture in the prepared pudding bowl, cover tightly with greaseproof (waxed) paper or the pudding basin lid and steam for 2½–3 hours.

SAINT HONORE
(see also choux pastry, gâteaux)

Invented in 1846 by French pastry chef Chiboust, this gâteau is named after the patron saint of pastry cooks and chefs, Saint Honoré. Chiboust, who is also famous for the crème Chiboust filling that this gâteau contains, was possibly inspired to name his gâteau as he did because his shop was located in the rue St Honoré. The gâteau consists of a flat pastry base and a ring of choux pastry filled with fresh fruit and crème Chiboust. It is topped with profiteroles which have been dipped in caramel.

Base
¾ cup (3 oz) plain (all-purpose) flour
⅓ cup (2 oz) icing (powdered) sugar
70 g (2½ oz) unsalted (sweet) butter, cut into small pieces
1 egg, lightly beaten

Choux Pastry
1¼ cups (10 fl oz) water
150 g (5 oz) unsalted (sweet) butter
1¼ cups (5 oz) plain (all-purpose) flour
5 eggs, lightly beaten
egg wash (see page 110)

To Decorate
apricot glaze (see page 10)
375 g (12 oz) crème Chiboust (see page 85)
fresh fruit pieces
crème Chantilly (see page 85) for piping
½ cup (4 fl oz) caramel (see page 49)

Base
Preheat oven to 180°C (350°F). Very lightly grease the base of a 23 cm (9 in) springform cake tin with butter. Place flour and icing sugar in a bowl. Add butter and very lightly rub into flour until the mixture resembles fresh breadcrumbs. Add egg and mix to a firm dough.
Wrap in plastic wrap (cling film) and chill for 30 minutes. Roll out to fit the prepared base and prick all over with a fork.
Bake for 10–12 minutes, or until very lightly browned. Cool the pastry on the base on a cake rack.

Choux Pastry
Preheat oven to 200°C (400°F).
Line a baking sheet with baking paper (parchment). Place the water and butter in a saucepan and bring to the boil over medium heat. Remove from the heat and add the flour all at once, beating all the time. Cook until the mixture leaves the sides of the saucepan, stirring all the time. Remove from the heat and add the eggs, a little at a time, until the mixture is smooth, soft and shiny. Place the mixture in a piping (pastry) bag fitted with a star-shaped nozzle and pipe a 23 cm (9 in) doughnut-shaped ring and twelve 3 cm (1¼ in) mounds onto the prepared sheet. Brush with a little beaten egg wash and bake for 25–30 minutes, or until the profiteroles are puffed, brown and crisp. Cool the profiteroles on the sheet on a cake rack.

To Assemble
Slide the cooled pastry base onto a serving dish and cover the top and sides with a thin layer of apricot glaze. Place the choux pastry ring on top. Spoon the crème Chiboust into the centre of the ring and smooth. Cover with fresh fruit pieces. Fill a piping (pastry) bag fitted with a nozzle with crème Chantilly and pipe decoratively over the fruit. By lightly scoring the crème with a knife, divide the gâteau into 12 wedges. Dip the profiteroles in lukewarm caramel and place around the edge of the ring, one profiterole per portion. Decorate with extra fruit pieces.

See page 247

SALAMANDER

Named after a legendary animal who was impregnable by fire and lived deep in the earth, a salamander today is a type of open-doored oven, usually heated by gas (electric versions are also available). Using a top heating element only, salamanders are used for keeping food warm or for glazing, browning or caramelising dishes such as crème brulées or sabayon mixes on fruit.

SALAMMBO

This cake was invented and named in the late 1800s, after a famous opera by Reyer. The Salammbo is a large choux pastry puff which is filled with an orange-flavoured crème and covered with thick caramel. Each end of the caramel topping is dipped into finely chopped pistachio nuts, leaving a central line of caramel.

Sacher Torte Step-by-Step

Step 1: Remove glaze from the heat and allow it to cool before pouring it evenly over the cooled cake.

Step 2: After pouring the chocolate glaze, make sure no air bubbles form on the surface of the cake. Allow the excess to run down the sides of the cake and drip through the wire rack. When cold, remove from the rack and serve. See page 244.

Step 1: Place the choux pastry ring on the pastry base and fill with the crème Chiboust.

Step 2: Cover the crème Chiboust with fresh fruits and crème Chantilly before placing caramel-covered profiteroles around the edge of the gâteau. See page 245.

SALLY LUNNS

The Sally Lunn was first made in Bath, England during the 1700s. It is a light fruited tea cake which is served warm with butter. Whether it was named after the pastry chef, one of the guests (which seems more likely), as a distortion of the street cry heard at dusk, 'Soleil lune', or because the round shape of the bun and its dark top and light base look remarkably like the sun and moon is not clear.

SALT

Otherwise known as sodium chloride, salt is not used much by the pastry chef. It can be used in salt doughs that are used in decorating, and a pinch of salt will assist with the development of egg whites when whisking. It can also be added to cake batters to help bring out the flavour. However, it is in bread and yeast doughs that salt is particularly helpful. Salt assists in the development of the gluten structure in yeast doughs, assists with the fermentation process, adds flavour to the dough and assists with the crust colouring, as well as helping to retain moisture in the baked product. The salt, however, should never come in direct contact with the yeast itself as it has a retarding effect on the yeast if the two are in contact for long.

SALT DOUGH

This has been produced for centuries by farmers, who originally increased the salt content in their loaves of bread as they found it prolonged the life of the bread. The salt was increased to the point of inedibility and the result was a firm dough which would dry out and could be used for decorations and artwork. This form of artwork has been used by the Chinese and other civilisations since the 15th century, small presents and decorations and earrings being made from the dough.

2½ cups (10 oz) plain (all-purpose) flour
1 cup (7oz) salt
¾ cup (6 fl oz) water
½ teaspoon glycerine

Place flour and salt in a mixing bowl and mix well. Add water and glycerine and work to a dough. Knead dough for 6–8 minutes, as it must be well worked. At this stage, check the dough's consistency; it should be firm, but also smooth and elastic, and most certainly should not be dry or crumbly. If the dough is too dry, add a small amount of water until it softens. After kneading, the dough should be wrapped in plastic wrap (cling film) and allowed to rest overnight. Once rested, the dough can be made into any shape desired, by being rolled, cut, modelled or moulded.

Drying

Once decorated into shapes, the objects should be dried for 2–3 days at room temperature (18–25°C/64–77°F). The objects then have to be baked at 180°C (350°F) for about 2 hours (depending on the thickness of the object). For a golden brown colour, the temperature should be 200°C (400°F). Before removing the object from the oven, make sure it is baked through.

Colouring

The finished objects can be painted, the most suitable paints being water-based paints which have had a little alcohol added to assist with drying. Other paints can also be used, but be careful not to wet the object too much during painting.

Varnishing

Once the object has dried, it must be varnished in order to prevent moisture penetrating it. You can use shiny or silky lacquer, but for objects used for food decoration, food lacquer must be used.

Storage

The objects should be stored in dry not too cold places. If by chance the object becomes soft again, it can be baked again.

SALZBURG NOCKERLN

4 egg yolks
zest and juice of 1 lemon
¼ cup (1 oz) plain (all-purpose) flour
8 egg whites
pinch salt
¼ cup (2 oz) caster (superfine) sugar
icing (powdered) sugar, for dusting

Preheat oven to 180°C (350°F). Generously butter a large round pie dish (pan) or large baking dish or tray.
In a mixing bowl, whisk egg yolks, lemon zest and juice and flour until combined. In another bowl, whisk egg whites with a pinch of salt until they form stiff peaks. Slowly add the sugar and beat until sugar is completely dissolved and whites are still forming stiff peaks. Slowly and carefully fold the egg whites into the yolk mixture. Pour the mixture carefully into the prepared dish and bake in preheated oven for 15–20 minutes, or until light golden brown on top but soft inside. Remove from oven. Dust with icing sugar and serve immediately.

SAMOSAS

Samosas are savoury fried pastries of Indian origin. The samosa paste is quite firm and is rolled thinly and made into conical shaped containers into which a meat filling is placed. The base of the cone shaped-pastry is then folded over and pinched tightly to enclose the filling.

SAND CAKE

A light cake so named because it should have a slight grittiness on the palate. For this reason it often contains a small amount of ground rice in the mixture.

Base

1¾ cups (7 oz) plain (all-purpose) flour
½ cup (3 oz) icing (powdered) sugar
135 g (4½ oz) unsalted (sweet) butter, cut into small pieces
1 egg, lightly beaten
2 tablespoons water

Cake

1½ cups (6 oz) plain (all-purpose) flour
1¼ cups (5 oz) cornflour (cornstarch)
3 level teaspoons baking powder (soda)
250 g (8 oz) unsalted (sweet) butter
1¼ cups (8 oz) caster (superfine) sugar
4 eggs
200 g (7 oz) sour black cherries, pitted
⅔ cup (2½ oz) ground almonds
icing (powdered) sugar, for dusting

Base

Place the flour and icing sugar in a bowl. Add the butter and very lightly rub into the flour until the mixture resembles fresh breadcrumbs. Add the egg and enough water to make a firm dough. Knead very lightly and wrap in plastic wrap (cling film). Chill for 1 hour.

Cake

Preheat oven to 160°C (320°F).
Lightly grease a 23 cm (9 in) springform cake tin with butter and line base with baking paper (parchment). Mix the flours and baking powder and sift twice. Beat butter and sugar until creamy, light and fluffy. Add eggs one at a time, beating very well after each one is added. Mix in the sifted flours and baking powder by hand.

To Assemble

Roll out the chilled pastry into a 35 cm (14 in) circle. Gently ease the pastry into the tin. Cover the pastry with the cherries and ground almonds. Top with the cake mixture. Bake for 45–60 minutes, or until a skewer inserted into the centre of the cake comes out dry. Cool in the tin on a cake rack. Lightly dust with icing sugar and serve warm.

SANDWICH
(see also bread)

The pastry chef is not often asked to produce this, unless the main kitchen is extremely busy. But the pastry chef or baker will have produced the bread for them, so he/she may as well understand the background of them. The sandwich was created by John Montague, fourth Earl of Sandwich, who, being a keen gambler, found it hard to put his cards down to eat. He therefore asked that his cold meat be placed between two slices of bread, thus making it easier to eat while playing. The bread for sandwiches may be of any flavour although the traditional white and brown (wholemeal) breads are most commonly used.

SANDWICH LOAF
(see also bread)

A sandwich loaf refers to those loaves of bread made precisely for use as sliced bread for sandwiches. Instead of the dough for the loaf being laid directly into its tin, the long sausage-shaped piece of dough is cut into four even pieces, and the cut pieces are laid together so that the cut sides face the sides of the tin. When proved (risen) and baked, this results in a loaf of bread with finer crumb and a closer texture, giving it strength to hold the fillings of a sandwich.

SAPOTE

This fruit is the natural chocolate mousse. It resembles an avocado and is also called black pudding fruit in reference to its dark chocolate-coloured flesh. Cream and sugar can be added to make a tasty chocolate mousse dish. A tropical fruit, it was first discovered in Central America and is now cultivated in many tropical countries. The fruit may be puréed, stewed, made into jam and jelly, bavarois or light crèmes.

SAUCES
(see also coulis, crème anglaise, purée)

Sauces in pastry cooking can either be cream-based, fruit-based or syrup-based and can be produced to enhance and complement any flavour imaginable.

Sauces made from puréed fruits are thinned by the addition of stock syrup and a sweetener, or can be served still tart in flavour to offset the sweetness of some dishes. Fresh cranberry or raspberry purée is often served with sweet apple fritters because of its tartness.

Cream-based sauces including anglaises are made from cream, sugar and eggs, which is heated until they thicken. In the same line, custards are also used as sauces, as too are mixtures of chocolate and cream and cream by itself.

Syrup-based sauces are usually the sweetest and can be a pure stock syrup enhanced with citrus peelings or infused with herbs or spices.

Thickened sauces include fruit juices which are thickened with cornflour (cornstarch) and sweetened slightly.

SAUSAGE ROLLS
(see also savoury pastry)

A cousin of the Chateaubriand, a sausage roll is a length of minced meat enclosed in a puff pastry casing. The filling may be pork, beef or chicken, or any combination of these or other meats, with flavourings of fresh vegetables and herbs.

4 slices white bread, crusts removed
¾ cup (6 fl oz) warm milk
1 kg (2 lb) sausage mince
1 egg
½ onion, finely diced
1 carrot, finely grated
½ stick celery, finely diced
1 teaspoon chopped rosemary
1 teaspoon chopped parsley
1 teaspoon salt
500g (16 oz) butter puff pastry (see page 41)
egg wash, for glazing

Preheat oven to 200°C (400°F). Line baking sheets with baking paper (parchment). Break up bread into small pieces in a mixing bowl. Pour milk over bread and allow to soak for 1 hour. After soaking, drain bread slightly by lightly squeezing. Place all the other ingredients in a large mixing bowl and mix in the soaked bread. On a lightly floured surface, roll the puff pastry to a thickness of 2–3 mm (⅛ in) and to at least 30 x 25 cm (12 x 10 in) in size. Place the sausage mince mixture in a piping bag fitted with a 2 cm (¾ in) plain round nozzle or without a nozzle at all. Lightly brush the puff pastry all over with milk.

Starting at the top and on the longest edge, pipe a length of the mince across the pastry. When piped, roll the puff pastry over the mince so that the puff pastry slightly overlaps underneath. Cut along this edge to free the first strip. Pipe the mince along the new edge and repeat the above procedure. Continue to do this until the remaining mince mixture has been piped. You should obtain three rows. Place each of the long sausage roll strips side by side and, using a fork, prick the pastry down each length. Cut the lengths every 5 cm (2 in) and place each of the sausage rolls onto prepared baking sheet. Brush the tops with egg wash and bake in preheated oven for 25–30 minutes, or until the puff pastry is well risen and golden brown. Remove and serve immediately, or cool and freeze.

SAUTERNE
(see also dessert wines)

A sweet or sticky dessert wine which is served chilled with pastry and dessert dishes.

SAUTERNE CAKE

250 g (8 oz) unsalted (sweet) butter
1 cup (7 oz) caster (superfine) sugar
3 egg yolks
2 tablespoons sauterne
zest of 1 lemon
1 cup (4 oz) chopped walnuts
2 cups (8 oz) plain (all-purpose) flour
1 teaspoon baking powder (soda)
1 teaspoon bicarbonate of soda
1½ cups (12 fl oz) sour cream
3 egg whites

Syrup
¼ cup (2 oz) caster (superfine)
1 tablespoon orange juice
½ cup (4 fl oz) sauterne

Preheat oven to 180°C (350F°). Lightly grease a 22 cm (9 in) springform cake tin and line with baking paper (parchment). Cream the butter and sugar until light and fluffy. Add egg yolks one at a time, beating well. Add the sauterne, lemon zest and walnuts. Sift flour, baking powder and bicarbonate of soda together. Fold through the mixture alternately with the sour cream. In a clean bowl, whisk egg whites until they form stiff peaks. Lightly fold through the mixture. Pour into prepared cake tin and bake in preheated oven for 45–55 minutes.

Place syrup ingredients in a saucepan and heat gently. When the cake is baked, remove from ovenand turn upside down onto a plate. Brush the wine syrup over the cake as it cools. While still warm, serve the cake with cinnamon-flavoured whipped cream.

SAVARIN

A light ring-shaped yeast cake which is soaked in a sweet syrup and served cold, filled with mousse, ice cream, cream, berries or fresh fruits.

The Savarin was invented by Auguste Julien, one of three brothers who owned a pâtisserie in Paris during the 19th century. The Savarin, like the famous creation of the Julien brothers, the Trois Frères, was based on similar principles.

Auguste invented the Savarin in 1850 after having worked with French gastronome Brillat-Savarin, after whom he named the cake. Savarin gave him the sweet syrup recipe; the yeast dough base was based on the baba recipe invented by Polish pastry chef Stohrer only 14 years earlier. The major difference between the two cakes is that babas contain sultanas (golden raisins) and are baked in a dariole mould while Savarins are made of plain dough and are baked in their characteristic ring moulds.

The Savarin is soaked in syrup and is then drained slightly while still warm. It is allowed to cool and then glazed with an apricot glaze to prevent it drying out or going stale.

4 cups (16 oz) bread (strong white) flour
¼ teaspoon salt
30 g (1 oz) fresh compressed yeast
(or 3 tablespoons active dry yeast)
½ cup (4 fl oz) lukewarm milk
6 eggs, lightly beaten
6 teaspoons caster (superfine) sugar
250 g (8 oz) unsalted (sweet) butter,
cut into 2.5 cm (1 in) cubes

Syrup
2 cups (16 fl oz) water
1¼ cups (10 oz) caster (superfine) sugar
1 cup (8 fl oz) white (light) rum
cinnamon stick
5 whole cloves

To Decorate
fresh fruit pieces
icing (powdered) sugar, for dusting

Preheat oven to 180°C (350°F). Very lightly grease a 23 cm (9 in) savarin tin (ring mould) with butter. Mix flour and salt and sift twice. Dissolve yeast and milk in a large mixing bowl. Add eggs and sugar and beat in the sifted flour and salt. Knead for 5 minutes. Place butter on top of the dough and cover with a damp cloth. Leave the covered dough in a warm place to prove (rise) for 20 minutes. Beat in butter. Place dough in prepared tin in a warm place and cover with a damp cloth for 30 minutes, or until the dough has risen to the top of the tin. Bake for 45–50 minutes, or until a skewer inserted in the centre of the cake comes out dry. Turn out onto a cake rack to cool.

Place all ingredients for the syrup in a saucepan and bring to the boil. Simmer for 20 minutes. Place the cooled Savarin in a bowl and pour on the warm syrup. Leave until all the syrup has been absorbed by the Savarin. To serve, fill the centre with fresh fruit pieces and dust with icing sugar.

SAVOIARDI
(see sponge fingers)

SAVOURY PASTRY

While a pastry chef does not usually cook savouries, some savouries do come under his or her area of expertise. It is common, though, that while the pastry chef will make the savoury dishes and their pastries, the main kitchen usually prepares the fillings, such as for savoury meat pies.

The most commonly used pastries for savoury pastries are choux pastry, puff pastry and shortcrust pastry, although croissant doughs, savoury brioche doughs, pizza doughs and other pastries are used on occasion. The savouries prepared by the pastry section usually only include finger foods such as barquettes, bouchées, mini ham and cheese croissants and savoury tartlets, although the section is also in charge of making the sausage rolls, meat pies, quiche pastries and pizza bases, along with focaccia and pasties.

SAVOURY FILLING
(for choux pastries or for piping onto barquette tartlets)

180 g (6 oz) unsalted (sweet) butter
270 g (9 oz) meat or ham paste
2 tablespoons brandy
1 teaspoon finely chopped spring onion
⅛ teaspoon cayenne pepper
salt and pepper

Place all ingredients in a food proccessor and reduce to a smooth paste. Pipe the mixture directly into the savoury tartlet, or barquettes, or into small profiteroles.

SAVOY CAKES

Also referred to as savoy sponges, these extremely light cakes are a more stable mixture than the French génoise sponge. The Savoy cake was first made in the 14th century, when it was made as a special treat for Amadeus of Savoy by the court chef. Savoy cake mixture was the basis for Josef Dobos's famous Hungarian Dobos torte.

To make the cakes, the yolks and whites are separated. Both are whipped into light foams, folded together with flour and cornflour and then baked.

¾ cup (4 oz) icing (powdered) sugar
zest of 1 lemon
8 egg yolks
8 egg whites
¾ cup (4 oz) icing (powdered) sugar, extra
¾ cup (3 oz) plain (all-purpose) flour
¾ cup (3 oz) cornflour (cornstarch)

Preheat oven to 180°C (350°F). Lightly grease and line a 23 cm (9 in) springform cake tin. Beat sugar, lemon and egg yolks until thick and creamy. Whisk egg whites until they hold stiff peaks. While still whisking, slowly add icing sugar and continue whisking until all sugar is dissolved. The egg whites should still be holding stiff peaks. Fold egg whites under the yolk mixture at the same time as adding the flour and cornflour. Fold in lightly and, when combined, pour into prepared mould. Bake in preheated oven for 35–40 minutes.

SAXONY PUDDING

A light, moist, rich sponge pudding named after the Saxons, as it was allegedly first made in Saxony.

90 g (3 oz) unsalted (sweet) butter
¾ cup (3 oz) plain (all-purpose) flour
¾ cup (6 fl oz) milk
zest of 1 lemon, finely grated
1 egg
3 egg yolks
5 egg whites
75 g (2½ oz) caster (superfine) sugar
raspberry purée (see page 162), for serving

Preheat oven to 180°C (350°F).
Lightly butter and breadcrumb 12 dariole moulds.
Place butter in a saucepan and allow to melt. Slowly add flour and work the mixture to a roux. Cook gently for 2–3 minutes over the heat.
Heat milk with lemon zest in a separate saucepan. Allow to come to the boil. Slowly add milk to the roux, whisking quickly while the roux mixture is still over the heat. When all the milk is added, quickly whisk in the the whole egg and the egg yolks until completely combined and the batter is smooth. Whip egg whites in a clean bowl until they are light and fluffy and hold stiff peaks. Slowly and gently fold egg whites through the roux mixture. Divide the mixture evenly among the 12 dariole moulds and place them in a baking dish. Half fill this with hot water and place the whole thing into preheated oven. Bake the puddings for 30–35 minutes, or until cooked. Unmould and serve immediately with a raspberry purée.

SCALD

Usually referring to milk or cream, to scald is to bring a liquid to the boil rapidly.

SCANDINAVIAN CHRISTMAS COOKIES

250 g (8 oz) unsalted (sweet) butter
1 cup (7 oz) caster (superfine) sugar
¼ cup (3 oz) golden syrup (light treacle)
1 tablespoon honey
¾ cup (3 oz) flaked almonds
3 teaspoons ground cinnamon
3 teaspoons ground cardamon
3 teaspoons ground ginger
1 teaspoon bicarbonate of soda
1 tablespoon water
4 cups (16 oz) plain (all-purpose) flour

Preheat oven to 180°C (350°F).
Line baking sheets with baking paper (parchment).
Place butter, sugar, golden syrup, honey, almonds and spices in a saucepan and heat gently until butter melts, stirring at all times. Allow the mixture to come to the boil then remove from heat, still stirring. Dissolve bicarbonate of soda in the water and add to the boiling mixture. Add flour and work into a dough. (This may require more or less flour, depending on whether the dough is sticky or dry.) Lightly knead the formed dough and then divide it into two portions. Shape both pieces of dough into long square blocks no wider than 5 x 5 cm (2 x 2 in). Wrap both in plastic wrap (cling film) and refrigerate for 2 hours. Remove and cut into very fine slices, a maximum of 2 mm (⅛ in) thick.
Place each biscuit (cookie) on the prepared sheet, allowing room for spreading. Bake for 10 minutes. Remove and cool on the sheets. Serve plain, or dusted with icing sugar.

SCHLOTFEGER

Made from a tuile mixture which contains marzipan or a hippen paste, this is a rectangular-shaped petit four which is baked until golden brown and then rolled around a wooden spoon handle or a round cylinder. When cold, the cylindrical biscuit (cookie) is left plain and served as a petit four with coffee, or dipped completely in chocolate, filled with chocolate mousse, whipped cream or lighter-style mousses, and served as a dessert.

SCHWARZWALDER TORTE
(see Black Forest gâteau)

SCONES
(see also biscuits, drop scones, griddle scones)

Known to the Americans as biscuits or soda biscuits, and served as a savoury cake with soups and Southern fried dishes or sweet toppings, a scone is a cousin of the Scottish bannock, which was made from a similar dough and formed into a round large flat disc which was baked on a griddle plate. To assist with baking, it was eventually marked into 4 and then 6 even triangles and baked this way to make it easier to turn the large disc and to ensure even baking. A wise cook then had the idea of cutting the dough into small pieces and baking each separately, and so the scone was born.

Scones are light cakes of flour, butter, water and a leavening agent (usually baking powder (soda)). They are quick to make as there are only a few ingredients in the recipe, but they offer pastry chefs quite a challenge, as all too often scones turn out heavy and doughy and not the light soft cakes they should be. The butter should always be rubbed into the dry ingredients lightly — the dough should not be overworked — and should not be kneaded at all. It should be rested well before baking. Scones should be placed closely together on the baking sheet to assist with rising and to help keep their shape, and should always be cooked in a hot oven.

A good scone should be of uniform colour and size, lightly golden brown on the base and top, but with white sides. The interior should be light, soft and white. Scones come in many flavours and varieties, but the plain scone is still served as part of a Devonshire tea with clotted cream and jam (conserve) in England.

1 cup (4 oz) plain (all-purpose) flour
⅛ teaspoon salt
½ teaspoon baking powder (soda)
3 teaspoons caster (superfine) sugar
30 g (1 oz) unsalted (sweet) butter
½ cup (4 fl oz) milk
jam (jelly), for serving
Cornish clotted cream, for serving

Preheat oven to 200°C (400°F). Lightly grease a baking sheet.
Place flour, salt, baking powder, sugar and butter in a large mixing bowl and rub butter into the dry ingredients until they resemble fine breadcrumbs. Add milk to the mixture and, using a knife, chop mixture without overworking the dough. Tip the dough out onto a lightly floured surface and knead only lightly to ensure all the ingredients are well combined. Roll dough out to 2 cm (¾ in) in thickness and, using a 4 cm (1½ in) scone cutter, cut out the scones. Place them side by side on the prepared sheet. Cover and allow to rest for 10 minutes. Bake in preheated oven for 3 minutes and then reduce the temperature to 180°C (350°F) for a further 15 minutes. Remove and serve immediately with jam and Cornish clotted cream.

SCORE

This means to lightly mark the top of pastry using a sharp knife, but without cutting it. It is preferable to score using the back of a knife or fork prongs. This is done to pastries, slices and pie tops, to give a decorative effect.

Apples are also scored, using the sharp blade of a knife, to prevent them splitting due to the heat when baking.

SCOTTISH SHORTBREAD
(see also shortbread)

Another Hogmanay festival treat, Scottish shortbread is a fine mixture of flour, butter and sugar which is usually rolled or pressed into moulds. The traditional shape is a large disc of shortbread which is marked with a knife into 12 triangular portions. When baked and cooled the shortbread is broken into what are known as petticoat tails.

4 cups (16 oz) plain (all-purpose) flour
345 g (11 oz) unsalted (sweet) butter
⅔ cup (5 oz) caster (superfine) sugar

Preheat oven to 175°C (345°F).
Line baking sheets with baking paper (parchment).
Place all ingredients in a mixing bowl. Lightly rub butter through the dry ingredients or mix slowly until the mixture resembles fresh breadcrumbs. Scrape mix down and form a dough. Knead the dough lightly and shape into two balls of equal size. Flatten the balls by hand onto the prepared baking sheet to form circles 1 cm (½ in) thick. Pinch the edges of each disc to give a decorative frilled edge. Using a knife,

lightly score the top of both discs. Mark out each into 8 wedge-shaped portions. Bake in preheated oven for 20 minutes, or until golden brown around the edges. Remove from oven and sprinkle with extra caster (superfine) sugar while still very hot. Cool on the sheet. When cold, sprinkle with sugar again.

SCROLLS

A pastry scroll, also known as a cinnamon scroll, is usually made from Danish dough or puff pastry and is rolled up into a Swiss roll shape with a filling of custard or ground cinnamon. The rolls are cut into fine slices and these slices baked flat on sheets. When baked, they are glazed with apricot glaze, or fondant or both.

Chocolate scrolls are fine rolls of chocolate removed either from a marble slab or chocolate block using a large scraper, and are known as caraque.

SELF-RAISING FLOUR
(see also flour)

This flour was invented in the USA, and known either as self-rising flour or pancake flour. In England and Australia, self-raising flour is flour which already contains a percentage of baking powder (soda). It is not popular in commercial kitchens, as chefs and pastry chefs feel they have no control over the recipe when baking.

SEMIFREDDO
(see also ice cream)

Meaning semi frozen or semi cold, this iced dessert contains such a high proportion of sugar that the dessert does not freeze solidly and therefore seems not to be as cold as most iced desserts.

SEMOLINA
(see also flour)

Semolina is a gritty coarse flour rich in gluten, obtained from the milling of durum wheat at the point when the wheat is halfway between wheat and flour. Its high gluten content makes semolina popular for pasta products, although in other goods it takes a long time to cook. It has, however, been made into puddings successfully. Semolina is often dusted onto baking sheets when baking English muffins and is also used on the base and crusts of bread doughs to give them a crisp firm crust. The normally creamy yellow semolina can also be purchased with saffron added, which turns it bright yellow.

SESAME SEEDS
(see also tahini)

This small seed, the fruit of a tropical herb bush, is mostly used by Mediterranean countries. Tahina or tahini, a paste of roasted sesame seeds, is used in Lebanese, Turkish and Greek cooking, while the raw sesame seed, which has a sweet nutty flavour, is also used in halva, breads and confections. A fine flour made from sesame seeds is also available in some countries. Sesame seeds are used in many recipes, the most common of these being pancakes. Thoughout Europe, roasted sesame seeds are set into chocolate-dipped products, especially fruits, to provide a delicious, crunchy base. They are also often sprinkled on top of bread doughs and buns, as the sesame seeds are delicious when roasted.

SHAVINGS
(see chocolate)

SHERBERT
(see also sorbet)

Sherbet differs from sorbets and water ices in that it contains milk. Sherbert derives from the word 'sharbart', a drink made with fruit juice or purée, sugar and milk and sometimes spices. Like sorbet, the drink was frozen one day, and sherbert was invented. Different countries have differing laws but in the USA, for example, manufactured sherberts must have a minimum of 2% butterfat.

SHERRY
(see also spirits)

A member of the fortified wine family, sherry was invented in the Spanish town of Jerez, whence it obtains its name. Sherry is available either dry or sweet: this is determined by which grapes are used in production, the container in which the sherry is stored throughout the fermentation process and the length of fermentation and ageing. Sherry is not often used in pastry, although sherry trifle is widely enjoyed. Sherry is also used in sabayons, zabagliones and served with cakes and pastries for afternoon or high teas.

SHOE SOLES
(see also puff pastry)

These are scraps of puff pastry which are rolled thinly, then rolled in icing (powdered) sugar or caster (superfine) sugar, so that when the pastry bakes the sugar caramelises. The shoe soles are turned over halfway through baking so that both sides have an even coating of caramel. They are served with parfaits, mousses and zabagliones. They can also be dipped into chocolate and served individually, or as two, sandwiched together with chocolate mousse or fresh cream.

SHOO-FLY PIE

An American dessert pie consisting of a biscuit crumb crust which is filled with molasses, brown sugar and spices.

SHORTBREAD

A light, easily broken biscuit (cookie) which should melt in your mouth. There are numerous recipes for shortbreads throughout the world, each containing the basic ingredients of sugar, flour and butter, and possibly a flavouring. The ingredients are combined until they form a dough, which is then flattened or rolled. Baking should be long and slow so as to not burn or overheat the shortbread and also so that the full flavour of the butter is baked through. A true shortbread should be the colour of light straw on the top and base.

PIPED ENGLISH SHORTBREAD

270 g (9 oz) unsalted (sweet) butter
⅓ cup (2½ oz) caster(superfine) sugar
2¼ cups (9 oz) plain (all-purpose) flour
⅓ cup (1 oz) cornflour (cornstarch)
caster (superfine) sugar, for dusting

Preheat oven to 180°C (350°F).
Line baking sheets with baking paper (parchment).
Place butter and sugar in a mixing bowl and cream together
until light and fluffy and almost white in appearance.
Sift together flour and cornflour and add this to the well
creamed butter. Ensure that the sides of the mixing bowl are
scraped down and that all the butter is mixed into the flour.
When well combined but not overmixed, place the mixture
in a piping (pastry) bag fitted with a 1 cm (½ in) star nozzle.
Pipe small rosettes onto the prepared baking sheet.
Bake in preheated oven for 8–10 minutes, or until the shortbreads are just turning golden brown around the edges.
Sprinkle with caster sugar immediately and cool.

SHORTBREAD MOULD

A shortbread mould is traditionally made of wood and has a
thistle carved into its base to show that shortbread is truly
Scottish. The mould is lightly dusted with flour, cornflour
(cornstarch) or icing (powdered) sugar and the shortbread
dough is pressed in firmly. Excess dough is cut from around
the edge and then a baking sheet is placed over the top. When
inverted, the shortbread is released from the mould onto the
baking sheet. These moulds are only suitable for use with the
rolled or firm shortbread mixtures of Scottish origin, not for
the piped soft shortbread mixtures from England.

SHORTCAKE
(see also rock cake)

Very quick and simple, shortcakes are American in origin.
They consist of a short mixture of butter, flour, baking
powder (soda), sugar, and a liquid (eggs, milk and/or water).
The mixture is simply dropped onto the baking sheet. Only
lightly baked, they should be short and light, with a texture
somewhere between cakes and biscuits (cookies). They are
split, either warm or cold, filled with fresh fruits or custards
and dusted with icing (powdered) sugar.

STRAWBERRY CHOCOLATE SHORTCAKES

4½ tablespoons cocoa powder
1 tablespoon instant coffee granules/powder
1¼ cups (5 oz) plain (all-purpose) flour
⅓ cup (2½ oz) caster (superfine) sugar
1½ teaspoons baking powder (soda)
½ teaspoon bicarbonate of soda
100 g (3½ oz) unsalted (sweet) butter
½ cup (4 fl oz) thickened cream
200 g (7 oz) white chocolate, melted (see page 62.)
200 g (7 oz) strawberries, washed and sliced

Preheat oven to 200°C (400°F).
Line baking sheets with baking paper (parchment).

Sift all dry ingredients into a mixing bowl. Add butter and
lightly rub through the dry ingredients until the mixture
resembles fresh breadcrumbs. Add cream and combine well.
Drip tablespoonfuls of the mixture onto prepared baking
sheets. Bake for 8–10 minutes, or until cooked.
Cool on a cake rack. Drizzle melted white chocolate
over the top of each cake, and allow to set.
Cut each shortcake in half and fill with sliced strawberries.
Serve with fresh whipped cream.

Makes 6—8

SHORTCRUST PASTRY
(see also pastry)

A pastry used for savoury pies, tartlets and some sweet goods,
shortcrust pastry is so named because it gives a short
(crunchy) eating quality and will break easily, either in the
hand or in the mouth. Most shortcrust pastry recipes consist
of a ratio of 50% or more of butter or shortening to flour.
Small amounts of liquid, such as water, egg or milk, are then
used to make the mixture form a dough. Shortcrust pastries
should be made using a soft flour, worked lightly and rested
well, so that the gluten content of the flour is not overworked.
There are three main methods of making shortcrust: rubbing
the butter into the flour, using a hot water crust, or using a
creaming method.

SHORTENING
(see also fats)

This can be butter or margarine or any fat or oil which acts
as a shortening agent on the gluten in cakes and biscuits.
When whisked with sugar until light and fluffy, shortenings
also add a degree of leavening to a mixture.

SHREWSBURYS

These small shortbread biscuits (cookies) of English origin
had quite a different form from the one they have now when
originally produced in the 16th and 17th centuries. They
began as spiced shortbreads flavoured with cinnamon and
eaten with jam (jelly). This led to somebody sandwiching two
shortbreads together with the jam. Eventually the top of the
two shortbreads had the centre cut from it, and this, apart
from a dusting of icing sugar, is how they remain today. The
shortbreads, named after the town in which they were baked,
should be well flavoured.

3½ cups (14 oz) plain (all-purpose) flour, sifted
1½ cups (9 oz) icing (powdered) sugar, sifted
270 g (9 oz) unsalted (sweet) butter
1 egg
200 g (7 oz) redcurrant (or similar berry) jam (jelly)
icing (powdered) sugar, extra, for dusting

Place sifted flour and icing sugar in a bowl and, using your
fingertips, lightly rub butter through the dry ingredients
until the mixture resembles fresh breadcrumbs. Add egg
and continue mixing to a soft dough. Wrap dough in

plastic wrap (cling film) and refrigerate for 1 hour.
Preheat oven to 200°C (400°F). Lightly grease baking sheets.
Cut two rounds for each Shrewsbury with a 5 cm (2 in)
diameter fluted round biscuit (cookie) cutter. Take one round
from each pair and, using a 1 cm (½ in) fluted round biscuit
cutter, cut a hole in the centre. Place on prepared sheet.
Bake in preheated oven for 8–10 minutes or until lightly
browned on the edges. As the shortbreads will be fragile,
cool on the sheet before continuing. When cool, spread
the bases with redcurrant jam and dust the tops
with icing sugar. Place the tops on the bases.

Makes 48

SIENA CAKE
(see panforte di Siena)

SIEVE
(see also dredger, strainer)

A useful piece of equipment in the pastry kitchen, used to
remove foreign objects and lumps from dry ingredients such
as flour and icing (powdered) sugar. Sieves are available in a
variety of sizes, shapes and styles, but all consist of a frame,
which holds a fine sieve mat through which the ingredients
pass. The sieve mat can be made of finely woven wires of
mesh or silk, attached to a plastic, wood or metal frame.
Sieves are also used to incorporate air and lighten ingredients
for cake batters and to remove lumps and seeds from sauces
and purées.

SIMNEL CAKE
(see also fruit cake)

A traditional English Easter fruit cake baked with a central
stream of marzipan and also decorated with marzipan. There
are many stories as to the origins of both the cake and its
name, although it seems that 'simnel' is a derivation of the
Latin words simila or simnellus, meaning flour and a festive
breaded loaf respectively. Another likely alternative is that
the word comes from the Anglo-Saxon symel, meaning a feast.

On the more romantic side, it is said that in the 15th
century a Lambert Simnell and Richard Symonds were
captured by enemy forces in England. Symonds was executed
but Simnell survived. On being pardoned, he was employed in
the King's kitchens as royal baker. In honour of the king who
had pardoned him, he produced a cake full of fruit and with
an almond paste mixture in the centre. The cake was
apparently decorated in the shape of a crown, and the King,
liking both the appearance and the taste of the cake, named it
after its creator. This is contrary, however, to the modern
belief that the twelve balls or egg-shaped marzipan pieces
which traditionally surround the top of the cake were in
honour of the twelve disciples of Jesus, Judas being excluded.
In any case, a simnel cake should be rich and full of fruit,
with a high-grade marzipan or almond paste used in the
centre to enhance its wonderful flavour.

2½ cups (10 oz) plain (all-purpose) flour
2½ teaspoons baking powder (soda)
2 teaspoons ground cinnamon
275 g (9 oz) unsalted (sweet) butter
1 cup (7 oz) caster (superfine) sugar
5 eggs
¼ cup (2 fl oz) orange juice
grated rind of 1 orange
1¼ cups (4 oz) ground almonds
1 cup (5 oz) currants
1 cup (5 oz) sultanas (golden raisins)
⅓ cup (2 oz) seedless raisins
500 g (16 oz) marzipan
90 g (3 oz) dark (plain or semi-sweet) chocolate,
melted (see page 62), for piping
tinted marzipan, for eggs

Preheat oven to 170°C (340°F). Very lightly grease a 23 cm
(9 in) springform cake tin with butter and line the sides of the
pan with 5 layers of baking paper (parchment), bringing the
level of the paper 2.5 cm (1 in) above the top edge of the tin.
Mix flour, baking powder and cinnamon and sift twice.
Beat butter and sugar until creamy, light and fluffy. Add eggs
one at a time, beating very well after each one is added.
Mix in sifted flour and cinnamon, orange juice and rind,
almonds and dried fruit, by hand. Spoon half the
mixture into the prepared tin and smooth out.
Roll out half the marzipan into a 22 cm (9 in) circle.
Place the marzipan on top of the cake mixture in the tin.
Spoon on the remaining cake mixture. Bake for 2 hours,
or until a skewer inserted in the top comes out clean.
Cool in the tin on a cake rack.
When cold, remove from the pan and cover the top of the
cake with a second circle of marzipan. Crimp the edges
of the marzipan and decorate the top of the cake with the
marzipan eggs, or write the name simnel in chocolate
across the top, or do both. Serve in small slices.

See page 256

SIMPLE FACTOR

The 'simple' factor is a number used by leading baker
tradesmen and depends upon the air temperature and
climate. When this number is subtracted from the flour
temperature, it gives the water temperature for a dough,
so an ideal temperature is achieved for bread and dough
production: flour temperature – simple factor = water
temperature.

SIMPLE SYRUP
(see stock syrup)

SINGAPOUR

A decorated génoise sponge which has been cut and filled with
syrup-soaked fresh fruits. The cake is decorated with
crystallised (candied) fruits which are glazed with an apricot
glaze. This rich cake is served in thin slices with fresh cream.

SIROPER

A French term referring to the soaking of pâtisserie items such as rum babas or savarins in a syrup. The product must be completely soaked, either by ladling the syrup over the goods several times or by completely immersing the product in the syrup.

SKIMMING

The careful removal of scum or other unwanted matter such as fat or dirt from liquid substances such as syrups or sauces using a tea strainer, spoon or ladle.

SLICE

An English term referring to the small bar-shaped pieces of cake or other mixtures which are cut from a full tray of the mixture.

SMORRESBROD
(see also sandwich)

Meaning buttered bread, 'smorresbrod' is the Danish word for open sandwiches. These sandwiches are usually made of a delectable variety of toppings which are decoratively presented on open slices of buttered rye bread. They can be eaten as finger food or served on plates.

SNOW FLAKE

An American starch product containing cornflour (cornstarch), which can be boiled.

SNOW PUDDING

This is made from a warm gelatinised fruit jelly or cream which has a lot of egg white folded through it and is then allowed to set firm. The most traditional snow puddings are lemon and apple snow.

SOCKERSTRUYOR

Swedish in origin, sockerstruyor are flower-shaped fritters made by dipping a shaped iron into a thin batter and then placing this into deep-frying fat until the sockerstruyor is cooked and lifts away from the iron.

SODA BISCUIT
(see scone)

SODA BREAD
(see also damper, quickbread, scones)

Known also as damper, griddle scone, soda biscuit or scones, soda bread is a traditional quickbread of Ireland leavened with baking powder (soda). Depending on the recipe and its use, it may be baked on a griddle, in the oven or even in camp ovens in outback areas. Soda bread has more of a cake consistency than a bread consistency.

Simnel cake (see page 255)

SOFT-DOUGH DANISH

30 g (1 oz) fresh compressed yeast
60 g (2 oz) unsalted (sweet) butter
¼ cup (2 oz) caster (superfine) sugar
3½ cups (14 oz) plain (all-purpose) flour
⅛ level teaspoon salt
¼ cup (1 oz) milk powder (non-fat dry milk)
lukewarm water
210 g (7 oz) brown nougat (hazelnut) paste
⅔ cup (3 oz) currants
2 tablespoons mixed (candied) peel
1 quantity apricot glaze (see page 10)
250 g (8 oz) fresh fondant or stiff water icing
(see page 118 or 288)
½ cup flaked almonds, roasted (see page 5)

Place yeast, butter, sugar, flour, salt and milk powder in the bowl of an electric mixer fitted with a dough hook. Blend for 1 minute. Gradually add water in small amounts until the ingredients come together to form a soft dough. Add a little more water if necessary. Mix for 5 minutes. Cover, and leave in a warm area to prove (rise) for 20 minutes. Preheat oven to 180°C (350°F). Lightly grease a 25 x 30 x 3 cm (10 x 12 x 1¼ in) baking tray (jelly roll pan) with butter and line the base with baking paper (parchment). Gently knead the dough for 30 seconds to expel the air. Roll out the dough into an oblong, 30 x 40 cm (12 x 16 in). Carefully and evenly, spread the top of the dough with the nougat or hazelnut paste. Sprinkle currants and mixed peel over this. Starting at the longest side the furthest from you, roll dough up tightly like a Swiss roll. When the dough is completely rolled into a log shape, cut it, using a sharp knife, straight down the centre, into halves which both reveal the internal rolls. Press both ends of each half together and plait them or twist them together tightly. Press the ends of the plait together and place the dough (on prepared baking tray), covered, in a warm place for 35–40 minutes, or until double in size.

Bake in preheated oven for 35–40 minutes. When baked, glaze the Danish with the apricot glaze and drizzle the top with either the fondant or the stiff water icing. Sprinkle the top with roasted flaked almonds. Cut into thin slices to serve.

SOFT FLOUR
(see also flour)

A soft flour, or cake flour, is one which contains little gluten (usually only 9%), and is used for products which do not require a solid gluten structure, such as shortbreads, light cakes and biscuits. It can be made by mixing one part cornflour (cornstarch) with two parts plain (all-purpose) flour.

SOFT PEAKS

Whisked egg whites reach the soft peak stage when the peaks slowly fold back on the count of four.

SORBET
(see also ice cream, sherbert)

Traditionally served between meals as a refresher course, a sorbet is a light ice of water, fruit or vegetable which is folded through Italian meringue and churned till frozen. The freezing point will depend on the amount of water, meringue or sugar syrup in the recipe.

The sorbet derives not only from prehistoric water ices made of snow and honey, but from the Chinese, Persians and Arabians as well, who all enjoyed similar ice treats. It was the Italians, though, who folded meringue through the ice to make the sorbet as we know it today.

SOUFFLE
(see also iced soufflés)

A French dessert, the name of which is taken from the word 'souffler' — to blow or to breathe. A sweet or savoury dish, the soufflé is almost revered in the dessert world. Although not too hard to make, the dish can easily fail. A soufflé is a feather-light dessert comprised of a base of whisked egg white folded through a thickened panade, which can be crème pâtissière or a blond roux mixture and which contains the egg yolks. The air trapped within the whisked egg whites heats during baking and expands to lift the soufflé above the soufflé dish or ramekin in which it is baked.

The perfect soufflé is not a stiff meringue but a light egg white mixture which looks almost liquid when going into the ramekin. It should be levelled off at the top of the dish. The hardest part of soufflé-making is ensuring that someone is on hand to take the soufflé to the table the second that it is baked, as it will begin to fall as soon as it cools.

Soufflés can be flavoured with spices, liqueurs, finely diced fruits (as in the Rothschild soufflé), and even thick fruit purées. The traditional way of making fruit soufflés is to cook a sugar syrup until crack hard, then add the purée and return the mixture to a soft ball stage. This is allowed to cool before being added to the whisked egg whites.

SOUFFLÉ PANADE
150 g (5 oz) unsalted (sweet) butter
1 cup (8 fl oz) milk
1 egg
1 egg yolk
⅓ cup (2½ oz) caster (superfine) sugar
⅔ cup (2½ oz) plain (all-purpose) flour
5 egg yolks

Place butter and milk in a saucepan and bring to the boil. In a separate bowl, mix egg and egg yolk with sugar. When whisked together, pour the boiled milk mixture into it. Whisk well to combine. Add flour and continue whisking until smooth. Return mixture to the saucepan and allow to come to the boil while whisking continuously. Cool slightly, then whisk into the other egg yolks.

To Make Soufflé
2 tablespoons soufflé panade
3 egg whites

Preheat oven to 180°C (350°F). Lightly grease a soufflé dish or ramekin. Whisk egg whites in a bowl. Fold in the cooled panade mixture and a little spice or liqueur. Place in prepared dish and bake for 12 minutes in preheated oven. Remove. Dust with icing sugar and serve immediately.

FRUIT SOUFFLÉ
1¼ cups (10 oz) caster (superfine) sugar
1¼ cups (10 fl oz) water
1¼ cups (10 fl oz) fruit purée
3 egg whites

Bring ingredients to the boil and boil to the soft ball stage at 116–118°C (240–245°F). Cool.

To Make Fruit Soufflé
Preheat oven to 180°C (350°F). Grease a soufflé dish or ramekin with butter and line with sugar. Whisk egg whites in a bowl. Fold 2 tablespoons of the purée through the whisked egg whites. Place the mixture in prepared dish and level off at the top of the dish. Bake for 12 minutes in preheated oven. Remove. Dust with icing sugar and serve immediately.

SOUR
(see sour dough)

SOUR CREAM
(see also cream)

A thickened cream mixture produced by adding a bacterial culture or lactic acid to fresh cream. The (dairy) sour cream is naturally thickened by this process.

SOUR CREAM CAKE

2 eggs, lightly beaten
1¼ cups (10 fl oz) (dairy) sour cream
1⅓ cups (10 oz) caster (superfine) sugar
3 cups (12 oz) plain (all-purpose) flour, sifted
1 teaspoon bicarbonate of soda
1½ teaspoons ground ginger

Preheat oven to 180°C (350°F). Grease a 20 cm (8 in) springform cake tin and line with baking paper (parchment). Place eggs, sour cream and sugar in a large mixing bowl and combine. Add flour, bicarbonate of soda and ginger and whisk to a smooth mixture. Pour mixture into prepared tin. Bake in preheated oven for 1½ hours, or until a skewer inserted into the centre of the cake comes out dry. Cool completely in the tin before unmoulding onto a plate. Serve in thin slices.

SOURDOUGH
(see also bread)

Used mainly in the production of breads, especially rye and sourdough breads, a sourdough, or sour, is a fermented mixture of flour, water and yeast, usually obtained by mixing some leftover bread dough into a slurry with fresh water and leaving it to sour naturally.

SOURDOUGH BREAD
(see also sour dough)

Famous both in Europe and San Francisco for its flavour, a sourdough bread has a crunchy crust and should be soft-crumbed, with a delicious aroma and flavour on the inside. It is produced from a sourdough starter, which provides the leavening agents and also gives the bread its distinctive aroma and flavour. This is said to be the oldest form of bread making, originating in Egypt some 5000–6000 years ago. The process spread to Europe and then to the USA and the gold fields, where the only ferment or leavening agent available to make bread was a sourdough.

It is said that some of the sourdoughs in several of the more traditional bakeries of Europe are up to several hundred years old, as the sourdough-making process can be repeated endlessly.

SPANISH CREAM

Similar to a crème Chiboust, a Spanish cream consists of a light custard containing gelatine which has whisked egg whites folded through it and is then allowed to set firm. It is usually served as a pouring cream with fresh fruits.

SPANISCHE WINDSTORTE

A Viennese specialty, the windstorte is made predominantly of meringue, rings of meringue being joined together with flavoured creams.

SPATULA

A hand-held utensil with a plastic or wooden handle and a large flat plastic end, used to scrape down the sides of bowls when beating ingredients together.

SPECULAAS

These delicious thin spicy wafer biscuits (cookies), rich in butter, are a well-known specialty of Holland. Flavoured with honey or brown sugar and sprinkled with flaked almonds, the thin speculaas are served for Christmas Eve and are made in the shape of St Nicholas.

125 g (4 oz) unsalted (sweet) butter
¾ cup (4 oz) brown sugar
1½ cups (6 oz) plain (all-purpose) flour
2 teaspoons baking powder (soda)
½ tablespoon ground cinnamon
½ teaspoon ground cloves
½ teaspoon mixed spice (apple pie spice)
¼ teaspoon salt
¼ cup (2 fl oz) milk
1 tablespoon brandy

Preheat oven to 180°C (350°F).
Lightly grease a baking sheet with butter.
Place the butter and sugar in a mixing bowl and beat until light and creamy. Sift flour and baking powder and place with cinnamon, cloves, mixed spices and salt and brandy, in the butter mixture. Work the ingredients until well combined and keep mixing until they form a dough. Knead dough on a well floured surface, then roll to a thickness of 2–3 mm (⅛ in). Using a sharp knife, cut the rolled dough into rectangular shapes 5 x 10 cm (2 x 4 in). Carefully place these on the prepared sheet. Bake in preheated oven for 10–12 minutes, or until golden brown. Cool before storing in airtight containers.

Makes 24

SPICE
(see also individual listings)

These flavourings used in cooking are obtained from the roots, bark or dried seeds, buds, fruits or flowers of plants. Spices differ from herbs in that they tend to be used dried and powdered rather than fresh. They have strong, aromatic flavours and should be used sparingly in food. They include cinnamon, nutmeg, ginger and many more.

SPIRITS

Spirits refer to all those alcoholic liquids produced by the distillation of plant parts. They are often used (in small doses!) to flavour creams, sauces and cakes. As alcohol is evaporated with heat, they should not be combined with the cake batter but should be poured over the cake when it is baked and cooling instead. Most spirits are expensive, and are also available in concentrated form. Where the alcoholic volume is above 50%, only a very small amount is required. The most commonly used spirits are listed below.

CLASSIC PATISSERIE SPIRITS

Calvados	an apple brandy; light brown colour comes from its storage for 1 year in oak casks	used in sorbets, ice creams, syrups, jellies, confectionery, sabayons and mousses of either apple or pear base
Vodka	colourless and tasteless, vodka is distilled from wheat or rye	limited use in pâtisserie as it has no flavour or taste; often served in a glass, ice-chilled, with certain cakes
Brandy	may refer to a distillation of fruit or wine; French brandy refers to a distillate of wine and is called cognac	marries well with chocolate and berries and is used in liqueur-filled chocolates; can be expensive, so not usually used in large quantities
Armagnac	similar to French cognac; a rich, reddish-brown colour, assisted by its storage in chestnut wood barrels	cakes, soaking syrups, with fresh berries, sauces, chocolate- and coffee-based desserts
Arrack	distilled from coconut palm juice	fillings for petits fours
Rum	sugar cane distillation; caramel added for colour and flavour	chocolate-based desserts, savarin syrups and praline-flavoured crèmes
Kirsch	distilled from cherries; clear in colour	used in Black Forest gâteau, sauces, sorbets, and as a steeping liqueur for berries

SPIRIT LAMP
(see also sugar pulling)

A small lamp filled with methylated spirits used to assist with the joining of sugar pieces in sugar work.

SPONGE
(see also génoise, savoy)

A very light cake made of three basic ingredients (eggs, sugar and flour), which are whisked and folded together to form a light framework, the lightness depending on the amount of whisking and the light-handedness of the chef. There are two basic methods of making sponge: the first is typified by the génoise sponge, and requires very light work, and the second by the savoy sponge, a much more stable mixture. Sponge mixtures form the basis of many products in pâtisserie, including angels' food cake, sponge fingers and savoiardi.

SPONGE DOUGH
(see also bread making)

Used to produce a loaf of bread with impeccable flavour, a sponge dough is one where the majority of the yeast and sugar in the recipe is mixed with some of the warm liquid, and, occasionally, some of the flour. This mixture is made into a soft batter and then allowed to ferment in a warm area until the mixture is more than double its size and is full of bubbles. This is the sponge. The mixture is then dropped (knocked back or punched down), and, depending on the type and style of bread being made, it may be allowed to rise several more times before being mixed with the remaining liquids and ingredients and made into a bread dough.

SPONGE FINGERS

Light, finger-shaped sponge-based biscuits (cookies), otherwise known as savoiardi or lady fingers, which are used around the outside of charlottes or served with sabayons or light mousses (as part of the dessert).

²⁄₃ cup (3 oz) cornflour (cornstarch)
⅓ cup (2½ oz) caster (superfine) sugar
5 egg yolks
75 g (2½ oz) caster (superfine) sugar, extra
1–2 drops vanilla essence (extract)
2 egg whites
²⁄₃ cup (2½ oz) plain (all-purpose) flour

Preheat oven to 180°C (350°F). Line baking sheets with baking paper (parchment). Combine cornflour and caster sugar. Use half the mixture to lightly dust the lined baking sheets. Reserve the remaining cornflour/caster sugar mixture. Place egg yolks, extra caster sugar and vanilla essence in a mixing bowl and whisk to the ribbon stage (see page 236). Place egg whites in a clean bowl and whisk until they form stiff peaks. Fold flour through the egg yolk mixture, then lightly fold egg whites through this mixture. Place mixture in a piping (pastry) bag fitted with a ½ cm (⅕ in) plain nozzle and pipe 10 cm (4 in) straight lengths onto prepared sheets. Bake in preheated oven for 10–12 minutes, or until the sponge fingers are lightly golden brown. While they are still hot from the oven, dust the tops of the fingers with the remaining cornflour/caster sugar mixture.

Makes 36

SPONGE SANDWICH

Two light sponges which are joined together with cream and jam (often strawberry, raspberry or apricot), and dusted with icing sugar. They are traditionally served with morning or afternoon teas.

SPRINGERLE

A lemon and aniseed Christmas biscuit (cookie) which is baked or pressed into decorative moulds. It is lightly flavoured and quite thin, and is made throughout Europe.

SPRINGFORM TIN
(see cake tins)

SPRITZKUCHEN
(see also choux pastry)

Fried choux pastry balls rolled in icing sugar and filled with crème pâtissière.

SPUMONE

Spumone is basically the frozen version of zabaglione, but, depending on the region in which it is made, it can be very similar to or quite different from the original dish. A spumone has an outer layer of ice cream covering a filling of semifreddo or zabaglione. This Italian Christmas dessert is traditionally made in a log-shaped tin or terrine mould and served in wedges.

SPUMONE ZABAGLIONE
2 teaspoons water
3 tablespoons caster (superfine) sugar
½ cup (4 fl oz) Marsala or similar sweet wine
3 egg yolks
¾ cup (6 fl oz) cream

Place water, sugar and dessert wine in a saucepan and bring to the boil. Allow the mixture to cool slightly. Place egg yolks in a large mixing bowl and whisk slightly to break them up.

Pour in the cooling wine liquid, whisking to ensure all ingredients are well combined. Whisk well until mixture is frothy and slightly thickened. Continue whisking until it is cool. Whisk cream in a clean bowl until it forms stiff peaks, then fold it through the mixture. Pour mixture into a terrine mould or loaf tin, cover with foil and freeze for 24 hours.

To serve, cut thin slices and then cut these into wedges.

Serve wih fresh fruits.

SPUNCHADE
(see also sorbet)

Another name for a sorbet, a spunchade dessert is made by simply adding Italian meringue to a fruit purée which has been boiled with sugar syrup.

SPUN SUGAR
(see also candy floss, sugar)

A decoration which is also commonly known as angel hair, spun sugar is made by boiling a sugar syrup until it just reaches caramel stage and then allowing it to cool down slightly. At this stage, a fork or a whisk with the rounded ends removed is placed in the caramel. It is then removed and whisked or shaken very fast to produce wispy, thin lines of sugar. Being so fine, these cool quickly, becoming firm almost as soon as they leave the end of the spinning utensil.

Spun sugar is used as a decoration on many cakes and especially on large buffet pieces. It is also used as a plate decoration for individual desserts or to form a plate itself upon which all number of desserts, especially ices and sorbets, can be served.

In cooler climates, spun sugar can be produced in advance. However, in humid and tropical climates, the sugar threads may very quickly begin to dissolve, so they need to be produced as each dessert goes out.

ST JACOB'S BREAD
(see carob)

STAR FRUIT
(see carambola)

STARCH
(see also arrowroot, cornflour, cornstarch, sago, tapioca)

Starch is used almost exclusively in pastry cooking for thickening products such as sauces, custards and so on. It is produced from potatoes, corn, tapioca, sago, rice, wheat and arrowroot. When heated in a liquid above 55–60°C (131–140°F) a starch will begin to thicken, the thickness depending on how much starch has been added to the liquid. Starches are usually prepared by first adding a small amount of the liquid to be thickened to the starch and forming a paste. This is then added to the boiling liquid, be it water, milk or wine, so that it thickens smoothly and quickly and without lumps.

As a general guide, depending on the result desired, starches should be added in the following ratios:

SAUCES: 30–45 g (1–1½ oz) per litre;
THICK SAUCES AND CUSTARDS: 45–80 g (1½ oz–3 oz) per litre;
CUT-OUT STAGE: 80–120 g (3–4 oz) per litre.

STEAMED PUDDING

A soft pudding which is quite open in texture and is steamed rather than baked. Virtually any flavour or combination of flavours can be achieved from the one basic recipe. Steamed pudding dishes should be well greased before the mixture is added, and should be tightly sealed so that water does not get in. When covering and sealing the steamed puddings room should be allowed for the pudding to expand, otherwise a heavy, close-textured pudding will result. A folded crease can be put in the top of the paper or foil which is going over the dariole mould or pudding basin so that the crease can open up as the pudding rises higher.

BASIC STEAMED PUDDING MIXTURE
This mixture is perhaps quicker and more successful if made in a large food processor.

3 cups (12 oz) plain (all-purpose) flour
1 tablespoon baking powder (soda)
250 g (8 oz) unsalted (sweet) butter
1 cup (8 oz) caster (superfine) sugar
4 eggs
¼ cup (2 fl oz) milk

Grease a large steamed pudding basin well, greasing the lid as well. Make a sheet of paper (with a crease across its centre) large enough so that it covers the inside area of the bowl and hangs over the edge by 2–3 cm (1 in) all round.

Sift flour and baking powder together. Cream butter and

Stollen Step-by-Step

Step 1: Use a rolling pin to form a deep depression along the centre of the oval-shaped dough, then place the marzipan sausage in the depression.

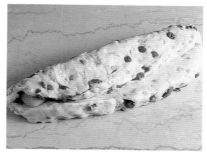

Step 2: Fold one side of the stollen over the marzipan to meet the other side.

Step 3: Once baked, glaze with melted butter before dusting heavily with icing sugar. See page 262.

sugar in a large food processor until light and well combined. Add eggs one at a time, mixing well after each one is added. Add flour and baking powder and flavourings as required. Add milk and process until a smooth batter is produced. Pour the mixture into the prepared pudding basin. Place the sheet of creased paper on top of the basin and the lid on top. Steam for 45–55 minutes, or until firm to the touch on top. This mixture can also be baked in individual greased ramekin or dariole moulds. It makes 8 individual portions.

Ginger and Sultana (Golden Raisins) Pudding
Add 1 teaspoon ground ginger or 1 tablespoon freshly grated ginger and ⅓ cup (2 oz) sultanas (golden raisins) to the basic mixture.

Chocolate Pudding
Mix 2 tablespoons of cocoa with the milk to make a paste and add to the mixture in place of the plain milk. Serve with chocolate sauce (see page 209).

Golden Syrup (Light Treacle) Pudding
Add 3 tablespoons of golden syrup (light treacle) to the basic mixture. Serve with a pot of warmed golden syrup.

Butterscotch Pudding
Serve the basic pudding with butterscotch sauce (see page 45).

Orange Pudding
Add the grated zest of 2 oranges to the basic mixture. Serve with orange-flavoured crème anglaise (see page 84).

Lemon Pudding
Add the finely grated zest of 2 lemons to the basic mixture. Serve with lemon-flavoured crème anglaise.

Coffee Pudding
Add 2 teaspoons instant coffee to the basic mixture. Serve with mocha (coffee/chocolate) sauce.

Cinnamon and Brown Sugar Pudding
Use brown sugar instead of white sugar in the mixture and add 1 teaspoon ground cinnamon. Serve with vanilla crème anglaise.

STEEP
(see also macerate, marinade)

To steep is to soak or marinate in a hot or cold liquid. It usually refers to alcohols or spirits being poured over a product which is then covered and allowed to steep for 1–2 hours, or overnight.

STENCIL

Also known as templates, these can be metal, plastic or paper cut-out designs which are placed over the food, plate or cake which is to be decorated. A powder such as icing (powdered) sugar or cocoa is dusted over the stencil and when the stencil is carefully lifted from the article, the cut-out shape remains. Stencils can be bought or made using a sharp knife and a sheet of paper or plastic.

Stencils and templates are also used for making some tuiles or products made from hippen paste. The stencil or template is placed on the baking sheet and the biscuit paste spread over the template. When the template is lifted the design remains on the baking sheet. The paste is then baked and served as a dessert or as a decorative element with a dessert.

STEWED FRUIT

Another means of poaching or boiling fruits. Stewed fruits, though, tend to be cooked in their own juices with only a little sugar and water added, and become a pulp mixture with very few firm pieces of fruit remaining.

STIFF PEAK

The stiff peak stage of egg whites is reached when the peaks hold their shape indefinitely.

STOCK SYRUP
(see also sugar syrup)

A mixture of sugar and water boiled together to become a thick syrup used for sauces, sorbets, brushing over sponge layers, softening fondant and pouring over fresh fruit salads. Its name derives from the fact that it should always be kept in stock to be used as the basis for many other recipes.

1 cup (8 fl oz) water
1¼ cups (8 oz) caster (superfine) sugar
2 teaspoons liquid glucose (corn syrup)

Place all ingredients in a clean saucepan and slowly bring to the boil. When boiling, skim the surface with a tea strainer to remove impurities. Once cleaned, remove the mixture from the heat and cool before storing in the refrigerator until required.

STOHRER

Stohrer was the famous pastry chef/confectioner who invented the rum baba in 1835. Stohrer introduced his creation to Paris when he opened his own shop on the Rue Montorgueil in Les Halles.

STOLLEN

A traditional German Christmas bread which is firm and dry and filled with fruits and nuts, and has a central vein of marzipan. Stollens are thought to have been made since as early as the 13th century, and the Dresden stollen, which is considered by many to be the best, is recorded as having first been made in 1438.

If the stollen is made at home, it is a German tradition to make two loaves: one to give to your neighbours or friends and the other for the family. One of the things that makes stollens so delicious is that the baked loaf is basted with butter. More experienced pastry cooks can start the basting process 20 minutes after the stollen has begun baking and should continue basting it until just before dredging the baked loaf heavily with icing sugar.

1 cup (8 fl oz) warm water
45 g (1½ oz) fresh compressed yeast
¼ cup (2 oz) caster (superfine) sugar
4 cups (16 oz) plain (all-purpose) flour
1 egg
¾ cup (3 oz) plain (all-purpose) flour, extra
210 g (7 oz) unsalted (sweet) butter, softened
⅔ cup (3 oz) sultanas (golden raisins)
⅔ cup (3 oz) currants
⅓ cup (2 oz) slivered almonds
⅔ cup (2 oz) mixed (candied) peel
zest of 1 large lemon
210 g (7 oz) marzipan

Topping
180 g (6 oz) unsalted (sweet) butter, melted
1 cup (6 oz) icing (powdered) sugar, for dusting

Preheat oven to 180°C (350°F).
Line a baking sheet with baking paper (parchment).
Place water in a small bowl and stir in yeast and a tablespoon of sugar until dissolved. Rest this mixture in a warm place for 15–20 minutes, or until the mix begins to froth. Place flour in a large mixing bowl, along with the remaining sugar, eggs, lemon rind and the yeast mixture. Work the mixture into a dough and knead for a further 10 minutes. Place in a bowl and cover. Leave in a warm place for 40 minutes.
Work the extra flour and butter into the dough by hand until all the ingredients are well combined. Add currants, sultanas, mixed peel and almonds and work into the dough. Cover dough again and allow to rest in a warm place for 25 minutes. Remove the dough from the bowl and knead lightly to knock out all the air. Roll dough into an oval shape about 30 cm (12 in) long. Using a rolling pin, press down along the centre of the dough to form a deep depression. Roll the marzipan into a 25 cm (10 in) long sausage shape and place along the depression. Fold one side of the stollen over the marzipan to meet the other side. Place the stollen on the prepared tray and sit it in a warm place for 25 minutes.
Place the risen stollen ino the preheated oven and bake for 40–50 minutes. Remove when baked and immediately glaze the top with the melted butter. Dust heavily with the icing sugar. Cool. Cut into thin slices and serve with coffee.

Makes 1 large or 2 small stollen

See page 261

STRAWBERRIES
(see also berries)

Third behind lemons and oranges in the most popular fruit stakes, strawberries add a refreshing sweet flavour to mousses, soufflés, bavarois, sauces and jams (jellies), lend colour and flavour to fruit salads and Bircher muesli, and are delicious served in a chocolate basket.

Strawberries are members of the Rosaceae family and are 85–90% water. They differ in size from area to area and can be almost as large as a golf ball or as small as a thumb nail, the larger strawberries usually not having as much flavour. Strawberries have also been in cultivation since the beginning of the 14th century.

STRAWBERRY GLAZE
250 g (8 oz) strawberry jam (jelly)
¼ cup (2 fl oz) water
2 teaspoons lemon juice

Place all ingredients in a saucepan and stir until thoroughly blended. Cook over high heat for 5 minutes and force through a fine wire strainer. Brush over the cake while still warm and cool before finishing the decoration.

STRAWBERRIES ROMANOFF

This dessert can in fact be made using any berries or fruit, but its flavour best suits strawberries and raspberries. The Romanoff was created at the beginning of the 19th century and were dedicated to the Russian Imperial family.
Strawberries Romanoff simply consists of chopped strawberries soaked in orange liqueur or orange juice and then folded through a sweetened cream and served in a champagne glass or chocolate basket.

300 g (10 oz) fresh strawberries, finely chopped
⅓ cup (2½ fl oz) orange liqueur or orange juice
⅓ cup (2 oz) icing (powdered) sugar
1 cup (8 fl oz) cream, freshly whipped

Steep strawberries in orange liqueur for 2–3 hours.
Fold icing sugar into whipped cream and allow to stand in refrigerator for 1–2 hours, covered.
Fold strawberries and the steeping liquid through the sweetened cream. Pour into glasses or chocolate baskets to serve.

STREUSEL
(see also brown betty, cobbler, crumble)

The German version of the English crumble mixture, which is sprinkled over fruit dishes and pastries. Streusel has much more butter than a crumble mixture and is traditionally made into a firm dough, then grated when still hard. It is prepared in a basic ratio of 2 parts flour, 2 parts butter and 1 part sugar. This is either mixed to a dough, or the mixture is used once large clumps begin to form while rubbing the butter through the ingredients.

STRONG FLOUR
(see also flour)

Also known as bakers' flour and bread flour and, in some countries, hard flour, strong flour has a high protein or gluten level: 11–13%. This type of flour is used in breads and pastries, being of most value in pastries. It is able to absorb more liquid than weaker flours. The liquid being converted into steam during the baking process helps puff pastries and choux pastries achieve their large puff.

STRUDEL

This pastry gained its fame as a Viennese invention, but is in fact Hungarian in origin. The Viennese no doubt gained recognition for it because they were the better bakers.

The Hungarian pastry chefs took the pastry for their strudel from the Middle Eastern filo (phyllo) pastry used for baklava, but pulled the pastry thinner, then spread it with butter, fried breadcrumbs, apples and dried fruits. They then rolled the dough and baked it until crisp and golden brown and served it covered with icing (powdered) sugar. In Vienna, their beautifully light rendition is served covered with a rich vanilla bean anglaise and whipped cream.

Strudels are either made using a strong or hard flour or have gluten flour added to ensure a strong dough with plenty of elasticity. As well as a variety of sweet and fruit fillings, strudels can be made with savoury fillings. Apple is the most traditional filling, but other sweet fillings include apricot, peaches, sour black cherries, quince and rhubarb, as well as sweet cream cheese or quark fillings.

In addition to the traditional wafer-thin pastry of the Viennese strudel, there are two other versions of strudel made by the pastry chef. The German strudel is made using a fine puff pastry base which is spread with custard and fruit and then covered with a puff pastry top, which can be latticed. The Danish strudel is a fruit-filled yeast dough which is glazed and coated with fondant.

Dough
2½ cups (10 oz) plain (all-purpose) flour
or strong (bread) flour
⅛ teaspoon salt
1 egg
¾ cup (6 fl oz) water
1 tablespoon vegetable oil

Filling
250 g (8 oz) unsalted (sweet) butter, melted
1¼ cups (5 oz) dried breadcrumbs
⅔ cup (4 oz) sultanas (golden raisins)
⅔ cup (5 oz) caster (superfine) sugar
1 teaspoon ground cinnamon
5 fresh apples, peeled, cored and finely sliced
icing (powdered) sugar, for serving

Preheat oven to 180°C (350°F). Grease a baking sheet. Sift flour and salt into a bowl. Beat egg in a small bowl and add water and oil. First with a knife, then with one hand, mix water and the egg into the flour, adding more water if necessary to make a soft dough. Beat the paste until smooth and elastic. Place dough in a clean lightly floured dish and cover. Leave in a warm place for 15 minutes. Place dough on a large floured tablecloth or sheet and, beginning from one edge, pull dough and stretch slowly until the edge becomes thinner. Beginning from the centre and, using the back of your hands, lift up and pull and stretch slowly until the dough becomes paper-thin all over. When dough is as thin as it will become, brush thoroughly with melted butter. Sprinkle buttered dough with breadcrumbs, sultanas, sugar and cinnamon and sliced apples. Fold the sides of the pastry in toward the centre and, using the cloth or sheet to assist, roll the strudel up tightly. Tip strudel from cloth onto prepared baking sheet and coat with melted butter. Bake for 30–35 minutes. When cooked, dust with icing sugar and serve immediately.

SUCCES (LE)

Le succés consists of layers of cake-like almond meringue filled and covered with chocolate buttercream and coated with chopped hazelnuts.

5 egg whites
1 cup (7 oz) caster (superfine) sugar
1 cup (3½ oz) ground almonds
⅓ cup (1½ oz) cornflour (cornstarch)
¼ cup (2 oz) icing (powdered) sugar

Filling
1 quantity no-fuss chocolate buttercream (see page 43)

Topping
2½ cups (13 oz) hazelnuts (filberts), chopped, for decoration

Preheat oven to 180°C (350°F).
Line 4 baking sheets with baking paper (parchment) and draw a 23 cm (9 in) circle on each. Beat egg whites until they form stiff peaks and gradually add sugar, a spoonful at a time. Beat until sugar is dissolved. Fold in ground almonds, cornflour and icing sugar by hand. Place a quarter of the mixture in the centre of each circle and spread out evenly to the edges. Bake for 30 minutes. Cool on the sheets on a cake rack. When completely cold, spread buttercream thinly on each layer of cake and stack one on top of the other. Coat the top and sides smoothly with the buttercream. Chill for 40 minutes. Press hazelnuts onto the top and sides. Chill for 1 hour before serving.

SUEDOISE

Suédoise is a simple fruit-based dessert made from a purée of fresh stone fruits such as peaches or apricots, to which a small amount of sugar and gelatine are added. The mixture is set in a small mould until firm, then decorated before serving.

SUET

A hard fat taken from around the kidneys of cattle and sheep which is used in pastries and puddings and fruit minces. A good suet should be odourless, dry to the touch and quite hard or firm, if fresh. Any blood clots, membranes and sinew remaining in the suet needs to be pulled away from the fat before it is crumbled or grated into the pastry mixture. Suet is an older style of fat and, due to the many vegetarians in today's society, has become unpopular, although it is still used in traditional desserts such as spotted dick, some other puddings and some fruit mince recipes.

SUET CRUST PASTRY

Made using suet, this light pastry can be used not only as a crust but also as a dessert on its own if sweetened and served with a sauce or custard. Suet crust pastry can be baked, boiled or steamed and should be served immediately as it does not store.

SUGAR

One of the most important ingredients in the pastry kitchen, sugar is used to sweeten cakes, biscuits and sauces, as well as being boiled into syrups and confectionery and used raw as a decorating medium. Made from sugar beet or sugar cane, it is extracted by boiling the beet or cane and then purifying the sugar solution which is obtained. Several by-products are obtained during this process, and once the sugar has been cleaned and produced into the familiar sugar crystals, it can be turned into a variety of different forms of sugar for different uses.

Sugar is found naturally in many products, including flour, but extra sugar is required in recipes to produce tenderness, moistness, sweetness and to enhance the colour within a batter or dough through caramelisation.

Sugar type	Characteristics	Uses
Brown sugar (light /dark brown)	refined sugar from which not all of the molasses has been removed; strong flavour	gingerbreads, fruit cakes, honey cakes
Beet sugar	a natural form of sugar from which sugar is processed	no direct use in pastry; only from its processed products
Brown lump sugar	made by forcing or pressing brown sugar into cubes	used for extracting flavours from limes, oranges and lemons by rubbing over their skins, and in sauces and honey cake
Barbados sugar	dark brown soft sugar which is almost black in colour	gingerbreads, fruit cakes
Candy sugar	large lumps of yellow sugar which is processed from either cane or beet sugar	for making candies and confectionery
Cane sugar	the natural form of sugar from which all sugar derivatives are processed	can be chewed and sucked for its sweetness; no other uses, as it is unprocessed
Caster sugar	simply white sugar which has been more finely ground	used in cakes, biscuits and pastries where quick dissolving sugar is a benefit
Superfine sugar	American name for caster sugar	as for caster sugar
Cube sugar	produced by pressing caster sugar into cubes	used in boiling sugar syrups because it is considered the cleanest form of sugar
Coffee sugar (crystals)	large brown sugar crystals	used only as decoration and rarely in recipes
Raw sugar	in various shades of brown; similar to coffee crystals and with a distinct flavour	used sparsely in recipes but more as decoration on top of cakes and biscuits
Demerara sugar	most popular of the brown sugars; raw sugar which contains molasses	used in many recipes for its flavour: cakes, pastries and biscuits and cookies
Fondant	a pure white paste made from sugar used in all forms of pastry and confectionery	used in buttercreams, petits fours, confectionery and decorating
Glucose	called corn syrup in the USA; a thick clear pure form of sugar	used in all forms of sugar boiling and fondant making as well as in modelling pastes
Honey	a thick natural syrup obtained by bees; available in a variety of flavours	used in nougats, gingerbreads and other confectionery products
Golden syrup	a by-product of refining; filtered and concentrated leftover syrup	in buttercreams, confectionery and (for flavour) in cakes and biscuits and sauces
Treacle	made by diluting and filtering molasses and then concentrating it	for flavour in cakes, and sauces
Non-lumping sugar	icing or powdered sugar to which starch has been added to keep it dry and prevent lumps	biscuits, icings and buttercreams
Pure icing sugar (or powdered or confectioners' sugar)	pure sugar which has been reduced to powder	icings, buttercreams and where instant dissolving is required of sugar
White sugar (granulated sugar)	normal white sugar available in varying degrees of refinement	everywhere sugar is required
Rock sugar	produced from sugar syrup mixed with royal icing	decorations
Molasses	dark black liquid from the sugar refining process	pies, flavouring in cakes
Muscovada	partially refined dark brown sugar, with a high molasses content	in rich desserts for flavour

Caramelised Sugar
(see caramel)

Cast Sugar
(see also sugar work)

Boiled sugar syrups which are poured into moulds or flat plastic mats for casting. Many separate pieces are usually cast, then stuck together with fresh sugar and decorated with royal icing.

Pulled Sugar
(see also sugar work)

A carefully measured mixture of water, sugar and glucose syrup, which is boiled to a syrup, poured onto an oiled marble slab and allowed to cool slightly. It is then worked into a solid mass and pulled with the fingers before completely cooling. The sugar is pulled in this manner continuously until it is silken and shiny. It is then cut and immediately pulled into the desired shapes or stored until ready to pull.

Pulled sugar is used for making ribbons and many other decorations for centrepieces, cakes and petits fours, or for blown sugar.

Rock Sugar
(see also sugar work)

A sugar mixture which is produced from a boiled sugar solution mixed with royal icing and then poured into a container to cool and harden. When hard, it is broken into pieces and used in decorations and centrepieces.

Spun sugar
(see also candy floss)

A sugar mixture boiled to around 145°C (293°F), at which point it is spun into a web of fine sugar threads which are used to decorate cakes, desserts and centrepieces. It is so fine that it is called Angel Hair as well. It is not as fine as when spun using a machine; then it is called candy or fairy floss.

SUGAR CAGE
(see also caramel)

A fine cage or dome of caramel which is used to serve over the top of desserts.

SUGAR CANE

A member of the grass family, sugar cane has been cultivated since at least 1000 BC and was first processed from 500 BC when it was learnt that by pressing the sugar from the cane and boiling the syrup, crystals would form and these could be used as a sweetening and cooking medium. At this stage in its history, though, it was still a brown sugar mass. With advances in processing and purification, the first sugar factory opened in the Barbados in 1641, and since this time, sugar factories have opened in many areas where the sugar cane grows.

Sugar cane can also be served in its raw state as a strange type of petit four, one which the guests chew and suck.

SUGAR NIBS

These are small pieces of solid sugar of differing shapes and sizes which closely resemble almond nibs. An accumulation of sugar crystals, nibs are sprinkled on top of biscuits (cookies) sweet buns and rolls and certain cakes for decoration. They are available in three grades — small, medium and large.

SUGAR SYRUP

1⅓ cups (9 oz) caster (superfine) sugar
1¼ cups (10 fl oz) water

Place sugar and water in a saucepan and gently bring to a gentle simmer. Skim the surface with a tea strainer to remove impurities. Boil syrup for 2–3 minutes, remove from heat and cool. If infusing the syrup, add the herb, spice or flavouring while warm. Cool before using mixture.

SUGAR TEMPERATURES

The following list indicates the termperatures to which sugar should be boiled for the various boiled sugar products:

SMALL THREAD: 101°C (214°F)
LARGE THREAD: 102–103°C (215–217°F)
SMALL PEARL: 103–105°C (217–221°F)
LARGE PEARL: 107–109°C (224–228°F)
SOFT BALL: 116–118°C (241–244°F)
HARD BALL: 121–124°C (250–255°F)
SOFT CRACK: 129–135°C (265–275°F)
HARD CRACK: 149–150°C (295–300°F)
LIGHT CARAMEL: 151–160°C (302–325°F)
DARK CARAMEL (BLACK JACK): 161–170°C (326–338°F)

SUGAR THERMOMETER

A thermometer which is marked with the temperatures at which changes occur in sugar. Also known as a candy thermometer, it usually starts at 100°C (212°F) and goes as high as 180°C (350°F).

SUGAR WORK

Sugar for Pulling, Pouring or Blowing
A good sugar for pulling and blowing needs to be elastic, pliable and have a silky sheen. Having only a few basic rules, sugar boiling can hardly be called an art, but it is still not possible to give a foolproof recipe, as the raw materials vary in their quality and composition and can, in interaction with each other, give differing results.

Pour 2 cups (16 fl oz) of cold water into a pan and add 4 cups (2 lb) of sugar. Dissolve the sugar over low heat, stirring constantly. It is important to be attentive about stirring, as the crystals are more obstinate than they might look in water. Also, any sugar splashes on the side of the pan should be washed down quickly with a wide, flat brush dipped in cold water, to prevent them caramelising or reverting to crystals and making the sugar impure. If using gas, it is important that the flame does not come up too high on the sides of the pan, as this will increase the rate of caramelisation and crystallisation of any sugar that splashes up the sides of the pan.

The scum begins to froth up shortly before simmering point, as impurities such as chalk remain and plant proteins separate from the sugar. The amount of scum is an indication

Sugar Pulling Step-by-Step

MAKING A RIBBON

Step 1: Place the coloured strips together.

Step 2: Pull out the sugar.

Step 3: Cut the strip in half and place together symmetrically.

Step 4: Pull out for the final length.

Step 5: Shaping the ribbon.

MAKING A BOW

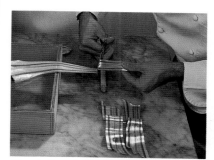

Step 1: Cut pieces of ribbon.

Step 2: Form the loop by curling the piece of sugar around a stick of dowel or a wooden spoon handle.

Step 3: Form the lower circle by heating the tips of each piece and pressing them together.

Step 4: Carefully form the second row.

Step 5: Position the centre loop.

Step 6: The finished bow.

All photographs courtesy of Ewald Notter, School of International Confectionery Arts, USA.

267

of the quality of the sugar. Each time the sugar comes to the boil, remove any impurities and skim the surface of the syrup with a tea strainer several times. (Once the syrup boils, there is no further opportunity to skim the sugar and the impurities are boiled into the mixture.)

Once the sugar has been skimmed and boiled, add 20% of the weight of sugar in glucose to the mixture. For example, for 5 cups (2½ lb) of caster (superfine) sugar, add 1 cup (8 oz) of glucose. Bring slowly back to the boil. A better result is achieved if the sugar crystals have dissolved slowly before the glucose is added. (The glucose is added to prevent recrystallisation of the sugar.) The sugar can be finished off directly if you require, but it is better to give the crystals time to dissolve well. The simplest method is to cover the hot pan (clean the sides first!) with plastic wrap (cling film) so that it is airtight, and leave it standing for 24 hours. If left uncovered, the water evaporates, and crystallisation will start on the surface of the syrup. If it is airtight, the plastic wrap (cling film) rises when first placed over the pan, as the trapped warm air expands. Condensation forms on the plastic wrap (cling film), and as the air contracts, the film becomes concave.

Finishing the Syrup

The syrup must be boiled quickly after storage so that it does not become yellowish. However, if using gas, ensure that the flame remains under the pan and any splashes are regularly washed down from the sides of the pan. At this point it is possible once again to remove any impurities from the syrup using a tea strainer.

Acid is added to the sugar at this stage to make it elastic enough to pull and blow. Acid also helps prevent crystallisation. Allow the sugar to boil to 125°C (258°F), and then add 15 drops of acid to 4 cups (2 lb) of sugar. Continue to boil the syrup until it reaches 154°C (309°F), at which point the syrup should be removed from the heat.

From Syrup to Pulled Sugar

From this hot molten sugar we now want to produce an elastic sugar mixture with a silky sheen that can be stored for later use or pulled and blown immediately for decorations.

Empty the sugar out of the pan onto a cold, oiled marble slab and wait a moment until the mixture cools a little around the edges. The aim is for the sugar to cool quickly and evenly on the cold marble. To achieve this, slide a spatula under the outside edges of the sugar and fold them into the middle. Allow the sugar to flow out again and repeat. Try to move the sugar onto colder areas of the marble as you work, so that it does not stick onto the warmer area where it was initially poured.

Note: Any sugar that sticks to the marble or spatula should not be mixed back into the main batch. Remove these pieces and throw them away!

As the sugar cools, it thickens. Once this occurs, use a spatula to lift the sugar from the table and then fold it in half, cold sides together. Continue to repeat this process. Once the sugar has cooled enough to not spread any more, it can be folded with the finger tips instead of the spatula, but take care, because the sugar is still very hot! The quicker the sugar cools, the better the end result will be.

At this stage, you can use the sugar for decorations immediately, or store it for later use. However, without pulling air into the sugar, it will have a glassy appearance rather than the silky sheen which gives show pieces a shine like that of mother of pearl.

As soon as the sugar has stopped spreading, pulling can begin, to incorporate air into the sugar. The more experience you have, the later you can begin to pull. When you handle and work with the sugar for the first time you should be very aware that it is very sensitive to temperature and handling, as opposed, for example, to marzipan. Sugar should be pulled quickly and slackly.

Remove any surplus oil from the table with a clean, dry paper towel. Take the sugar in both hands and pull apart, twisting at the same time to trap air. Pull first towards the left-hand side, holding the end of the sugar with the palm of the right hand and lifting the sugar up off the table with the left hand. Twist and fold together. Repeat this procedure, this time pulling towards the right-hand side. Continue this process, alternating from one side to the other. Try not to hold the sugar for too long, as your hands can cool the sugar unevenly. The sugar should slowly become lighter and develop a silky sheen. Once lighter stripes are visible, you can begin to pull the sugar flat, ready for cutting and storage. At this stage, continuing to pull the sugar will not make it any shinier; in fact, it will become dull instead.

Storing the Sugar

A piece could be pulled or blown immediately from the freshly boiled sugar, but it is better to rest sugar for a least one day before use. It is much more efficient and time saving in the long run if you boil the sugar in larger quantities in advance. The portioned colours can then be kept at hand and used as needed. Correctly stored, sugar can be kept for up to one year.

Rewarming the Sugar

To work the sugar pieces, they have to be warmed to a working temperature: until they become soft and pliable. The best way to do this is to use a warming lamp, preferably infrared, as this is the least dazzling. A warming case, comprised of 3 sides of perspex, an infrared lamp with a cable and a wooden frame covered with a soft PVC sheet, can be used for this purpose. If you only work occasionally with sugar, a silicon mat or a frame of stretched silk is quite sufficient as a working surface. In an emergency, a lightly oiled tray in an open oven will do.

Sugar Pouring

Sugar pouring is the quickest and simplest technique used for the creation of a show piece. Impressive decorations can be made with just a few materials and little expense.

Poured sugar is used in show pieces in a number of ways:

(i) as a base plate for blown and pulled pieces;
(ii) as a support for unstable decorations; and
(iii) as a background.

Ribbons

Ribbons and bows are an important feature in many show pieces. They may be used for dressing figures, as well as for covering the handles of baskets and decorating flower arrangements.

Ribbons are produced by placing even strips of sugar together. This creates a silky sheen, since the light is reflected off the ribbon in many directions. Using a lot of colours together does not necessarily produce a better ribbon — two or three colours are quite enough. The ribbon should largely be made up of light colours and then, for example, a single strip of darker sugar may be used for contrast. Using various shades of a single colour, or combinations that contain clear unpulled sugar, can also be very attractive.

Warm the colours needed and cut away short, finger-width strips. Place the strips together side by side. (In the example illustrated, there are, from left to right: 1 strip clear sugar, 2 white, 2 pink, 1 red, 1 black and 2 white.) Using both hands, pull the assembled sugar out lengthways to about 15 cm (6 in). Halve the sugar and then place the halves together, rotating one piece so that the ribbon is symmetrical. Now, in a continuous motion, pull out a strip of ribbon to the required length, remembering to allow for any unevenly ended pieces, which will need to be cut away. Cut and shape the ribbon immediately and leave to cool.

Bows

It is important that a bow has the same colour combination as the ribbon it accompanies. The individual loops must be made evenly and in the correct shape so that they can be assembled to form a perfect bow.

Approximately 13 loops are needed to make a bow. To do this, pull a long length of ribbon as previously described. Cut 6 cm (2½ in) strips from the ribbon, and lay each piece over the round handle of a wooden spoon. Press the cut ends together and pull down away from the handle so it forms a triangular shape which runs to a point. This shape allows the loops to be assembled easily. Slide the loop off the handle and lay it on the marble.

Divide the 13 loops into groups according to their size, reserving the most perfect loop for the centre of the bow. Six or 7 of the larger loops are needed for the lower circle. Warm the pointed ends over a burner and place them side by side, with the points all facing into the centre to form a compact circle.

If 6 loops are used for the lower circle, then 4 are needed for the second row. If 7 loops have been used for the lower circle, then 5 are needed for the second row.

Warm the tips of the smaller loops to be used for the second tighter row, and set them into the circle at a slight angle. Once this row is complete, the loop reserved for the centre can be set in position in the middle of the bow, at a point slightly higher than the second row. When you look at the bow from above, it should form a circle, and from the side it should form a semi-circle. If the shape needs to be altered slightly, this can be done while the bow is still warm.

Blowing Sugar

To make the larger voluminous parts of show pieces, the technique of sugar blowing is used. The sugar must be formed quickly into the shape needed while it is being blown: it is very difficult to rewarm a piece once it is shaped. When blowing sugar, it is particularly important to have a firm grasp of the basics before moving onto the more complicated exercises. But even the beginner can create delightful pieces just from a ball and a cone shape. Those at a more advanced stage can tackle a natural figure made up of many individual parts. Animals blown from one piece of sugar should only be attempted by those who are very well practised at sugar blowing.

Preparing for Blowing

To blow sugar you need to following equipment:

A GAS STOVE TOP is preferable, since heat is quickly and easily controlled. A hot plate may also be used.

A GOOD QUALITY HEAT-CONDUCTING PAN for boiling sugar. Traditionally, these are made out of copper, but aluminium or steel pans will suffice.

A TEA STRAINER to remove impurities from the sugar before boiling.

A WIDE, FLAT AND SPOTLESSLY CLEAN BRUSH to wash down the sides of the pan and remove crystals which splash up onto the pan.

A WARMING CASE WITH AN INFRARED LAMP. This is a three-sided cabinet with a perspex lid. In the lid is a slit which allows the infra red lamp to be raised or lowered depending upon how much heat is required on the sugar. Most sugar cabinets are collapsible.

A BURNER FILLED WITH SPIRIT ALCOHOL to heat or melt sugar to attach to another piece. Do not used a lighter as this gives off black soot.

A HAIRDRYER WITH A COLD OR COOL SETTING to cool pieces.

A RUBBER HAND PUMP WITH A VALVE to allow air to pass through in one direction.

The basic technique of sugar blowing and the starting point of all blown sugar pieces is the blown ball, explained here in detail.

Fold the sugar 2 or 3 times, so that it has an even temperature and consistency. Using your hand, begin to form a ball with a completely smooth surface. Using scissors, separate the ball completely from the main piece of sugar. Take the ball carefully in your hands and push a short hole into the cut side with your thumb. If necessary, warm the hole a little over the burner. Slide the tubing attachment a short distance into the ball of sugar. Press the sugar firmly onto the tube, so that the air does not escape at the sides. Take the tube in one hand and the pump in the other in preparation for blowing.

Blowing a Ball

During the whole blowing process, the blowing tube and the sugar should be held in front of you with one hand. Air is pumped into the sugar and the shape corrected using the other hand. The blowing tube should be rotated while working, to keep the ball under control on all sides.

Commence pumping the air very slowly and carefully into the ball of sugar. The ball will expand more readily where the sugar is warmer, resulting in an uneven shape and thickness: these areas must be cooled using your hand. The temperature of the sugar is 60–70°C (140–158°F), so the temperature of your hand will be enough to cool the sugar down.

After having blown a little and corrected the shape, pull the ball away from the tube a little so that a short air channel forms. This will be severed later. The ball should take its shape from about 1 cm (½ in) above the tubing attachment.

Continue to blow carefully, turning and correcting with the hands. As far as possible, the sugar should be kept at an even thickness and not be allowed to become too thin.

As soon as the desired shape and size has been reached, use the hairdryer to cool it evenly. Keep your eye on the sugar ball while you are cooling it, otherwise it could burst or become irregular in shape. Corrections can only be made while the sugar is still warm.

A fine example of blown sugar (courtesy Ewald Notter).

Home-grown sugar crystals (courtesy Ewald Notter)

Once the ball is cold, place it over the burner and rewarm the air channel directly in front of the tubing. Rotate the ball at the same time, so that the sugar warms evenly.

As soon as the sugar is pliable, cut through the rewarmed sugar with the back part of the scissors. The stump of the air channel remaining on the ball will be needed later when assembling the pieces.

Once the basic ball shape has been mastered, the same rules and techniques can be used to produce many other shapes and designs.

ROCK SUGAR

Rock sugar can be used in combination with fish and shellfish show pieces to create a deep sea atmosphere. The porous structure is ideal to represent corals and sponges, or even chipped rocks.

The shape of the rock sugar is determined by the shape of the containers into which it is poured, so before you start, select containers of the desired shapes. Line these well with aluminium foil and oil the foil.

Place sugar and water in a saucepan and bring to the boil. For 3 cups (24 oz) of caster (superfine) sugar, add 1 cup (8 fl oz) of water: a ratio of 3:1. Boil the syrup to 148°C (298°F).

While the sugar is boiling, make a stiff royal icing from egg white and icing sugar and 2−3 drops of lemon juice or tartaric acid (see page 241). If you wish to colour the rock sugar by adding colour to the royal icing rather than spraying the finished product, add 2−3 drops of your chosen colour.

Once the sugar syrup has reached the correct temperature, quickly plunge the pan into cold water. Add 1 teaspoonful of royal icing and beat it into the syrup very quickly. The sugar rises up and collapses while stirring. Place the saucepan back on the heat until the mixture rises again, then quickly pour into the prepared containers. The rock sugar usually collapses to about two-thirds its original volume. Allow the sugar to cool for about ½ hour.

Cut the rock sugar into pieces in the sizes needed. Use a grater to define the porous structure. (The grater roughs up the surface.) Then spray the rock sugar with colour, using an air-brush or atomiser. The best results are obtained by shading the rock sugar with various colours. Alternatively, the colour can be incorporated into the rock sugar by colouring the royal icing. Spraying creates a more attractive effect.

Crystals

A home-grown sugar crystal is something very special, whether it be used in an ice landscape, a mountainscape, as a cocktail mixer or as a decoration for a dessert. All that's needed is patience and the right recipe.

Prepare a super-saturated sugar solution. For example, add 12 cups (6 lbs) of sugar to 4½ cups (36 fl oz) of water, and boil without glucose. Use a saccharometer to determine when the solution has reached a baume of 33−35°. When this is reached, pour the syrup into a suitable container, as described below. The container should be very clean to ensure that the crystals do not begin to grow on the inner walls but only concentrate on the 'seed' that is hung in the solution.

For cocktail mixers, dip toothpicks or longer wooden sticks into the sugar syrup and then sprinkle with granulated sugar. Allow to dry for 1 day, then push the tip of the sticks into a piece of polystyrene. This is then turned upside down so that the sticks hang in the solution, with the polystryene forming a lid.

To achieve the forms and shapes of mountain crystals, attach a piece of marzipan to a clean thread. This is then hung in a container that has a lid with a hole in it. The thread is passed through the hole and knotted on the outside.

An ice-landscape is created by pouring syrup into a large container which is lined with aluminium foil. The syrup should be about 5 cm (2 in) deep. The surface can be sprinkled with granulated sugar so that the crystals also grow from above.

Allow the crystals to grow undisturbed for 1–2 weeks. If the container is moved or the solution is checked too often, only small crystals will grow, not the larger sizes required. If, after 2 weeks, you wish the crystals to continue growing, the solution can be renewed.

SULTANA
(see also dried fruit)

Known in the USA as a golden raisin or seedless raisin, the sultana is the golden-coloured dried fruit of the small seedless grape. It is used in fruit cakes, baked cheesecakes, puddings, sweet chutneys and fruit mince, and has a sweet but slightly acidic taste.

SUMMER PUDDING

This is another well-known English pudding. To make the pudding, line a pudding bowl with fresh bread slices which have had the crusts removed and fill the centre of the pudding with a lightly poached and sweetened fresh berry mixture. The top is then covered with pieces of fresh bread and the whole pudding is weighted down and refrigerated to allow the bread to soak up the berry syrup. When cool and soaked the pudding is unmoulded.

Summer pudding can contain any amount of fresh berries of any types: blueberries, blackberries, raspberries, strawberries or loganberries, for example.

1 kg (2 lb) redcurrants, blueberries,
blackberries or raspberries
½ cup (4 oz) caster (superfine) sugar
¼ cup (2 fl oz) sauterne
10 slices fresh or day-old bread with crusts removed

Place berries in a saucepan with sugar and sauterne.
Heat slowly, then gently simmer for 5–6 minutes, until berries begin to soften and break down. Do not allow them to turn to a pulp, though. When the fruit has softened, remove from heat and allow mixture to cool.
Line the insides of a pudding bowl or basin of 1.5 litre (3 pint) capacity or more with the bread slices, cutting them so that they form a firm side and base. Cover the entire bowl or the pudding will fall apart. Reserve 2–3 slices of bread for the base. Carefully spoon the cooled fruit mixture into the bread-lined bowl. Do not allow much liquid into the bowl. Press down to fit all the fruit in. Cover the top with the reserved bread slices, cutting them to fit if necessary. Pour the reserved juices over the pudding. Allow them to soak slowly into the bread and fruit. Pour the rest of the juice over, then place a sheet of baking paper (parchment) and a flat plate or lid on top of the pudding and weigh it down using a rock covered in aluminium foil, some food tins or a 1 kg (2 lb) weight. Place the pudding in refrigerator and leave for 2 days.
Remove from refrigerator, and remove the weights and flat plate or lid. Run a thin knife around the outside edge of the pudding, then invert it onto a large plate. Give the bowl a sharp shake if the pudding will not come out.
Serve the pudding with fresh cream.

SUNDAES

Exactly the same as the classical coupé and served in a similar glass coupé bowl, the sundae is the American (and slightly sweeter) version of this classic dish. The sundae was so named when American laws prohibited ice cream soda being served on a Sunday: it was seen as an offence against God. An enterprising American invented the sundae simply by omitting the soda. Ice cream, whipped cream, nuts, grated chocolate and a fruit or flavoured sauce were what remained.

SURPRISE (EN)

This literally means to surprise someone with the dish being presented to them. The outside of such a dish is usually coated in such a way that it is impossible to tell what the inside flavours or texture will be. Many bombes are said to be bombes 'en surprise' because their meringue outer coating hides what lies inside them. Another sweet dessert dish termed 'en surprise' is made of fruits such as oranges, lemons or grapefruit. They have a lid removed or cut from their top and their pulp or flesh is scooped out and replaced by a mousse, ice cream or sorbet. The lid is placed back on the fruit and the dish when presented at the table is a surprise to eat.

SOME POPULAR VARIETIES OF SUNDAES

Name	Ice Cream	Fruit Base	Sauce	Decoration
Osborne	vanilla	sliced banana	maple syrup	whipped cream, maple syrup and chopped dried fruits
Peach Royal	vanilla	fresh diced peaches	fruit purée	whipped cream, nuts and chocolate filigree
Temptation	chocolate, strawberry and vanilla	strawberries	chocolate	whipped cream and pistachio nuts
Tutti Frutti	lemon, mango and pineapple	diced glacéd (candied) fruits	raspberry purée	whipped cream and strawberries
Viennese or Café Liègois	coffee ice cream softened with sweet strong black coffee	—	chocolate	whipped cream, grated chocolate and coffee bean

SWANS
(see choux paste)

SWEETS
(see also confectionery)

This name refers both to the nickname or slang terminology for desserts or puddings, and also to sugar-based confectionery. Sweets, in the sense of a pudding or dessert, can be anything from pancakes to puddings or from cakes to fine pastries that are served on a plate at the end of a meal.

The first full-scale factory production of confectionery sweets began in the USA in the late 19th century, although pâtisseries and private sweet shops had been involved in the large-scale production of sweets for many hundreds of years before this.

In general, the term sweets best describes the mass-produced non-professional tradesman's products sold en masse, whereas confectionery and confections refers to the more exclusive and labour-intensive range of sugar products which are usually only produced by the confectioner.

See page 271

SWEETEN

To add a sweetener such as sucrose (commonly known as sugar) or an artificial sweetener to a product, to either make it more palatable or remove a tart, acidic or pungent flavour.

SWEETENERS
(see also saccharin, sugar)

This term is usually used to refer to artificial sweeteners such as saccharin, a chemically produced substance that has 400 times the intensity of natural sugar. Sweeteners are commonly used by those experiencing diet-related problems and by diabetics, for whom eating natural sugar is not possible.

SWEET PASTRY

A quick and simple no-fault pastry which is used to make French fruit tarts, tart shells, cake bases or biscuits (cookies), also known as pâte sucrée.

2½ cups (10 oz) plain (all-purpose) flour
½ cup (4 oz) icing (powdered) sugar
155 g (5 oz) unsalted (sweet) butter
1 egg
juice of ½ lemon

Sift flour and icing sugar and place in a bowl with the butter. Using the fingertips, rub butter into the dry ingredients until the mix resembles coarse breadcrumbs. Add egg and lemon juice and continue to mix until the mixture forms a dough. Lightly knead dough before wrapping and storing in the refrigerator to rest for 20–30 minutes. On a lightly floured surface, roll the pastry to the required size and shape.

Makes about 600 g (20 oz)

SWEET CHOCOLATE PASTRY

2 cups (8 oz) plain (all-purpose) flour
¼ cup (¾ oz) cocoa powder
½ cup (4 oz) icing (powdered) sugar
155 g (5 oz) unsalted (sweet) butter
1 egg

Sift flour, cocoa and icing sugar and place in a bowl with the butter. Using the fingertips, rub butter into the dry ingredients until the mixture resembles coarse breadcrumbs. Add egg and allow the mixture to form a dough. Lightly knead dough, then wrap in plastic wrap (cling film) and refrigerate for 20–30 minutes. On a lightly floured surface, roll dough out to the required size and shape.

Makes about 600 g (20 oz)

SWEET POTATO
(see also vegetables)

A sweet-flavoured, tuberous potato-like vegetable which, due to its flavour, can be served either sweet or savoury. Although so named, the sweet potato is not in fact a potato, belonging instead to the morning glory family. It was spread from South America to other parts of the world by traders and merchants. It is also known as kumera.

It usually has an orange to red skin, and the flesh can be either orange or yellow. When cooked, the flesh has a slight floury consistency and is somewhat similar in texture to cooked pumpkin. The most popular dishes for which the sweet potato is known are sweet potato pie and sweet potato cakes, which can be flavoured with either citrus, coffee or chocolate to complement the natural chestnut flavour of the sweet potato.

SWEET POTATO CHOCOLATE CAKE

150 g (5 oz) unsalted (sweet) butter
⅔ cup (5 oz) caster (superfine) sugar
2 eggs
1 cup boiled and finely mashed sweet potato (kumera)
1¼ cups (5 oz) plain (all-purpose) flour
3 teaspoons baking powder (soda)
¼ cup (1 oz) cocoa powder
1 teaspoon ground cinnamon
⅓ cup (3 fl oz) milk
15–20 fine slices sweet potato
6 teaspoons caster (superfine) sugar, extra
1 teaspoon ground cinnamon, extra
icing (powdered) sugar, for dusting

Preheat oven to 180°C (375°F). Grease a 22 cm (9 in) springform cake tin. Cream butter and sugar until light and fluffy. Add eggs one at a time, beating well after each one is added. Stir in sweet potato. Add sifted flour, baking powder, cocoa and cinnamon, alternately with the milk and beat lightly until the mixture is smooth. Spread the mixture into prepared cake tin and cover the top of the cake with the fine slices of sweet potato. Mix the extra sugar and cinnamon together and sprinkle this over the top of the sweet potato. Bake for 50–55 minutes in preheated oven, or until a skewer inserted into the centre of the cake comes out dry. Cool on a cake rack. Dust with icing sugar before serving.

SWEET WINE CAKES

These firm little cakes are somewhat similar in shape and style to the modern scone (biscuit). This recipe dates back to the Roman invasion of Britain in 43 AD and has changed little since then, although the texture and tastes will have altered because we now have processed flours, butter, cheese and better quality wine.

2 cups (8 oz) plain (all-purpose) flour
60 g (2 oz) unsalted (sweet) butter
1 tablespoon honey
¼ cup (1 oz) grated mild cheese
zest of 1 lemon
¼ cup (2 fl oz) sauterne
1 egg, beaten

Preheat oven to 200°C (400°F). Grease a baking tray (sheet). Place flour in a mixing bowl with the butter. Lightly rub in butter until the mixture resembles fine breadcrumbs. Add honey, cheese, lemon zest, egg and sauterne and mix to a dough. Cut mixture into 12 evenly sized pieces and mould into flat ball shapes. Place on prepared sheet and bake in preheated oven for 30 minutes, or until baked. Eat with jam.

SWISS ROLL
(see also roulade)

An English specialty, the Swiss roll is similar to a roulade, except that the sponge base is thicker and there are fewer rolls in a Swiss roll. Nor is it as rich as a roulade, making it possible to enjoy a slice or two with coffee or tea. Traditionally, Swiss rolls are flat sheets of sponge coated in jam and then rolled up into a log, but they can also have a cream or mousse filling.

caster (superfine) sugar
⅔ cup (2½ oz) plain (all-purpose) flour
⅔ cup (2½ oz) cornflour (cornstarch)
10 egg yolks
100 g (3½ oz) marzipan, softened
10 egg whites
1 cup (7 oz) caster (superfine) sugar, extra
¾ cup (8 oz) strawberry jam (jelly), warmed
icing (powdered) sugar, for dusting

Preheat oven to 200°C (400°F). Very lightly grease a 23 x 20 x 1 cm (9 x 8 x ½ in) Swiss roll tin with butter and line with baking paper (parchment). Sprinkle a large sheet of greaseproof (waxed) paper with caster sugar. Sift the flours twice. Place egg yolks in a mixing bowl and crumble marzipan into them. Beat until mixture is stiff, white and foamy. Beat egg whites until stiff peaks form and gradually add the extra sugar, a spoonful at a time. Beat until sugar is dissolved. Take a spoonful of egg white mixture and mix by hand into the marzipan mixture. Very gently fold in the sifted flours and remainder of the egg whites. Pour into prepared tin and bake for 35–40 minutes, or until the top of the sponge springs back when lightly touched and the sponge has shrunk slightly away from the sides of the tin. Turn the sponge out onto the sugared greaseproof paper and trim the crusty edges. It is important to work quickly. Spread the sponge with jam. With a short side nearest you, start rolling the sponge tightly toward you. Place the roll, seam side down, on the greaseproof paper and roll the greaseproof paper over the Swiss roll. Using a scraper, further tighten the roll. Dust with icing sugar and serve in thin slices.

SYLLABUB

Although often thought to be a member of the zabaglione or sabayon styles of dessert, the syllabub does not contain eggs. It is made using sweet dessert wines and is a lightly flavoured and spiced foam of liquids. Syllabub was very popular during the reign of Queen Elizabeth I, as it was a favourite of hers. It is served with langue de chat biscuits or in a tuile basket.

⅔ cup (5 fl oz) sauterne
2 tablespoons Benedictine
2 cloves
2 cinnamon sticks
zest of 1 lime
zest and juice of 1 lemon
⅓ cup (2½ oz) caster (superfine) sugar
1½ cups (12 fl oz) thickened cream

Place sauterne and Benedictine in a saucepan with cloves and cinnamon and bring slowly to the boil. Remove immediately. Add lime and lemon zest and lemon juice to the mixture and allow to stand overnight. Strain the sauterne liquid then stir in sugar until dissolved. Add cream to the mixture and, using a balloon whisk, whisk until light and foamy. It should hold soft peaks. Pour the mixture immediately into long or fluted glasses. Chill for 2 hours before serving with langue de chat, tuiles, shortbread biscuits, or fine slices of toasted sweet brioche.

Serves 4–6

T

TAHINI
(see also sesame seeds)

Otherwise known as tahina, this thick, smooth paste of ground sesame seeds has a sweet, nutty flavour. Tahini is used in cooking and as a dip in many Mediterranean countries. It is mainly used by pastry chefs in bread doughs and to give a delicate flavour to sweet pastes or an unusual flavour to mousses and crèmes, custards and sauces.

TALIBUR
(see also bourdelot, baked apple, rabote)

This is very similar to the French bourdelot and the rabote, and consists of apple stuffed with almonds, dried fruit and spices, then wrapped in a square of puff pastry. When baked, it is glazed with apricot jam (jelly) and a Calvados-flavoured fondant. It can be eaten hot or cold as either a substantial snack or a main dessert. The basic difference between the talibur, bourdelot and rabote is the fillings and the pastries used (sweet, shortpaste (shortcrust) or puff pastry).

TALMOUSE

A French savoury pastry from the Middle Ages, the talmouse was first invented for the Archbishop of Paris and consisted of puff pastry filled with soft cheese.

TAMALE
(see also cornmeal)

A well-known sweet or savoury Mexican steamed cornmeal cake. A tamale is a thick paste of cornmeal spread onto a banana leaf and topped with a sweet or savoury filling. It is wrapped up and tied, then steamed until cooked. This type of cake has been produced in Mexico for many centuries.

TANK LOAF
(see bread)

TAPIOCA
(see also thickeners)

A form of starch which is extracted from the roots of the cassava plant, a small shrub of which there are some 2000 varieties. Cassava, also known as manioc, grows in tropical regions, and is a native of Asia and South America. During the 1800s Spanish explorers took it to the East Indies. It soon spread from there to Africa and other tropical regions.

The tapioca is drawn from the root of the plant, which becomes stringy when mixed with water. The sap is extracted and dropped onto hot plates, where it gelatinises into the characteristic white balls of starch. Tapioca is used as a thickener and in puddings. It swells and becomes very clear when boiled in a liquid, making it perfect to use in milk and milk-based puddings or thickened desserts.

TART
(see also flan, pie)

A tart means different things depending on the region in which it is being cooked. It is also known as a pie or as a flan, although there are certain differences between the three. A tart normally has both a pastry base and a lid. It can be any size and filled with virtually anything: fruit mince or stewed fruits, for example. A tartlet is a miniature tart.

TART RINGS
(see flan ring)

TARTA PASIEGA

A Spanish cheesecake which is traditionally served at Easter and is flavoured with rosewater or orange blossom (orangeflower water) and honey. The recipe dates back to medieval times, when honey was the main product used as a sweetener.

TARTE TATIN

A French legend in the dessert world, tarte Tatin was the inspiration behind the American upside down cake. It consists of caramelised apples under a crust of pastry, which is inverted once cooked and served apple side up, to reveal the rich caramelised pieces of fruits. Tarte Tatin was invented by a Madame Tatin, one of two sisters who ran a hotel in the early 1900s, and who made the famous apple dish as a way of using leftover pastry. The pastry base can be sweet pastry, puff pastry or even shortcrust pastry. The tarte is usually made in a deep copper frypan. The depth is required to hold the cut apples and the copper is a good heat conductor, ensuring that the apples are caramelised by the time the pastry is baked.

45 g (1½ oz) unsalted (sweet) butter
¼ cup (2 oz) caster (superfine) sugar
10–12 large red delicious apples, peeled, cored and cut in half
210 g (7 oz) puff pastry (see page 228)

Melt butter in a heavy-based pan which is 5–7 cm (2–2 ¾ in) deep and 20–25 cm (8–10 in) in diameter. Ensure that you use sufficient butter to form a 2–3 mm (⅛ in) layer of melted butter. Sprinkle with sugar until totally absorbed by butter. Place apples upright in the pan, wide-end down and as close together as possible. Over a low heat, cook the apples on the

Tarte aux fruits

stove for 22–25 minutes, until they are caramel brown (shake pan occasionally during this process). As the apples brown, add extra pieces of apple where space allows.

On a lightly floured surface, roll the pastry out to the same size as the diameter of the pan and prick heavily with a fork or docker. Cover the apples with the pastry, tucking it in at the edges. Preheat oven to 200°C (392°F) and bake for a further 30–40 minutes. Remove from the oven and allow the tarte Tatin to rest for several minutes. Turn out onto a platter and serve warm or cold with fresh cream.

TARTE AUX FRUITS
(see also Obsttorte)

A rich custard-filled flan pastry case (pie shell) topped with a selection of fruits (or one type of fruit) and glazed with sweet thickened glazes.

The first fruit tart or flan could quite possibly have been produced by the chef of a nobleman who saw it as an easier, less messy and more flavoursome way of presenting his lord with his daily fruits. A sweet or shortcrust pastry base is lined with chocolate to stop the pastry from softening and is filled with a thin layer of crème pâtissière. It is then topped with segments or slices of fruit and glazed using any number of glazes: arrowroot glaze, fruit jellies, a strawberry or apricot glaze, or in today's pastry kitchen, perhaps a manufactured gelatinised glaze.

1¾ cups (7 oz) plain (all-purpose) flour
½ cup (3 oz) icing (powdered) sugar
155 g (5 oz) unsalted (sweet) butter
2 egg yolks
½ quantity crème Chantilly (see page 85)
selection of fresh fruits
icing (powdered) sugar, extra, for dusting

Preheat oven to 180°C (350°F). Grease a tartlet tin (12–14 moulds). Sift flour and icing sugar in a bowl. Rub butter into the dry ingredients until the mixture resembles fresh breadcrumbs. Add egg yolks and continue mixing until a dough is formed. Wrap dough in plastic wrap (cling film) and refrigerate until firm. Remove dough and knead until pliable. Roll the dough to 2 mm (⅛ in) or as thin as possible. (Take care or the dough may crumble.) Using a 4–5 cm (1½–2 in) plain round biscuit (cookie) cutter, cut discs from the dough and press them into the tartlet moulds. Bake in the preheated oven for 12 minutes, then cool in the tin. No more than 1 hour before serving, fill each tartlet with a teaspoon of the crème Chantilly and garnish with small pieces of your favourite fruit. Dust lightly with icing sugar.

The fruit will shine from the glaze created by the icing sugar mixing with the fruit's natural juice.

Makes 12–18

275

TARTLET

A smaller version of a tart, a tartlet is usually made from sweet or shortcrust pastry, although puff pastry tartlets can also be made. Served with either a sweet or savoury filling, tartlets are usually open faced, but can have a lid, depending on the filling and the individual recipe.

TEA — AFTERNOON

Afternoon tea or high tea can mean slightly different things, depending on the country in which it is served, but it is generally accepted that it is served at 4 pm and is a light but substantial meal of finger sandwiches, a selection of fine but small pastries, a beverage of tea or coffee and a nip of Madeira, port or sherry. Afternoon tea is particularly popular throughout England, where tea is the drink served. The food served should be small, very flavoursome and usually in an abundance. It is not uncommmon for the afternoon tea to include a pastry trolley or selection board of fruit cake, fresh fruit tartlets, Battenberg, Swiss roll or a strawberry frangipane tart. In some places, one would enjoy the Devonshire tea, a light meal of fresh scones, jam and clotted cream served with tea.

TEA CAKE

Traditionally, a yeasted bun flavoured with dried fruits and, when baked, dusted with a cinnamon-flavoured sugar or sugar syrup wash, or both. Intended as an accompaniment to tea, tea cakes are cut open and served with jam and cream. The buns are light and buttery and can also be served in slices. The modern day high tea cake is more often served these days as it requires less preparation time and there is no proving time for a dough. It is buttery and rich and is usually sprinkled on top with a cinnamon sugar, much as its yeasted cousin.

2½ cups (10 oz) plain (all-purpose) flour
2½ level teaspoons baking powder (soda)
100 g (3½ oz) unsalted (sweet) butter
1½ cups (12 oz) caster (superfine) sugar
2 eggs
1 cup (8 fl oz) milk
⅔ cup (2 oz) desiccated (shredded) coconut
4 level teaspoons ground cinnamon
¼ cup (2 oz) caster (superfine) sugar
100 g (3½ oz) unsalted (sweet) butter, extra

Preheat oven to 180°C (350°F).
Lightly grease a 23 cm (9 in) springform cake tin with butter and line base with baking paper (parchment). Sift flour and baking powder twice. Beat butter and sugar until creamy, light and fluffy. Add eggs one at a time, beating very well after each one is added. Add sifted flour and baking powder alternately with the milk. Do not over mix. Pour into prepared tin and bake for 40–45 minutes, or until a skewer inserted into the centre of the cake comes out dry. Cool in the tin for 5 minutes before turning out onto a cake rack.

Mix coconut, cinnamon and sugar. Spread extra butter over the top of the cake and sprinkle on the coconut mixture. Serve immediately.

TEMPER
(see also chocolate)

A process by which chocolate is heated, cooled and then warmed again to bring the cocoa butter crystals in alignment so that the couverture or pure chocolate may set firm, crisp and with a high glossy sheen.

TEMPLATES
(see stencils)

TERRINE

Usually oblong in shape, a terrine can be either sweet or savoury and consists of an outer coating or covering of pastry filled with a meat filling or a pastry or cake layer filled with a sweet mousse or crème filling. The savoury terrine is baked and, when cooled, can have gelatine or aspic poured into the top of the crust to fill any space left after the filling has cooked. Sweet terrines are set in the refrigerator or, occasionally, baked in a water bath before being cooled and set.

Terrine moulds can be metal, cast iron or ceramic and are about 10 cm (4 in) wide by 30 cm (12 in) in length and 5–10 cm (2–4 in) in depth.

TERRINEE

A French rice-based dish consisting of rice, milk, sugar, cinnamon, cloves and ginger which is poured into a large pie dish or ceramic dish and baked very slowly in the oven for several hours. The resulting dessert has a sweet crust of moist, soft and flavoursome rice which can be served hot or cold.

TETE DE NEGRE

Tête de negre is a French petit four or small pastry made up of two dome-shaped white meringues which are sandwiched together with chocolate buttercream, then coated in the buttercream and rolled in grated chocolate. The chocolate buttercream should be richly coloured and flavoured, buttery but light and soft. The two completely different consistencies, the rich dark chocolate and the snow white meringue, marry to create a delicious bite.

THERMOMETER
(see also bakers' thermometer)

Thermometers measure heat, as their name implies. They usually consist of a metal backing board marked with the degrees Fahrenheit or Celsius and a glass vial filled with either alcohol or mercury. When the thermometer is placed into a hot or warm substance, the alcohol or mercury expands in response to the heat and is forced up the glass vial. The chef can see how far up it has travelled and check the temperature by looking at the marked gauge beside the vial.

Treatment of thermometers is important as air bubbles can enter the mercury and alcohol if the thermometer is roughly handled. Always keep the thermometer spotlessly clean, as any dirt or old mixture can affect the liquids currently boiling, especially if they are sugar solutions. When using a thermometer, wash it under warm water, making it increasingly hotter, and then sit the thermometer into hot water until it is required to check the boiling liquid. This warming of the thermometer in advance ensures that the change in temperatures is not so great that it adversely affects the mercury or alcohol.

When the boiling liquid has reached its measured temperature, place the thermometer in the warm water again to avoid a shock of temperatures. Boiling sugar solutions will also help dissolve anything stuck to the thermometer.

Different thermometers, offering differing ranges of degree scale, are available for measuring the temperatures of chocolate, sugar and confectionery, and bread doughs.

THICKENERS
(see also arrowroot, cornflour, custard powder)

Cornflour, arrowroot, manufactured custard powder and gelatine are all thickeners used by the pastry chef. As well, plain flour, tapioca or sago, and a myriad of other ingredients, do roughly the same job, different ones being used for different recipes. Cornflour and arrowroot can be used instead of modern custard powder, and can also be used to thicken sauces; arrowroot gives a clearer finish, however. Gelatine is more aptly described as a setting agent, but does thicken crèmes and mousses in the process of setting them.

Sago and tapioca are little used commodities in today's kitchen, and although plain (all-purpose) flour is often used as a thickener in savoury dishes, it is not commonly used in pastry cooking as it produces a milky cloudy sauce and leaves a floury taste if not cooked correctly.

TIFFANY CAKE
(see also Bishop's cake)

Also known as American fruit cake, stained glass christmas cake and Bishop's cake, this cake contains so much crystallised (candied) fruit and is so rich that it is only served in thin slices. If held to the light, a slice should look like a stained glass picture.

¾ cup (3 oz) plain (all-purpose) flour
1 level teaspoon baking powder (soda)
¾ cup (3 oz) cocoa powder
70 g (2½ oz) glacé (candied) ginger
100 g (3½ oz) glacé (candied) pineapple
1½ cups (8 oz) glacé (candied) cherries
¾ cup (4 oz) seedless dark raisins
1½ cups (8 oz) pitted dates
1¼ cups (7 oz) mixed (candied) peel
1¾ cups (6 oz) walnut halves
¾ cup (6 oz) caster (superfine) sugar
4 eggs, lightly beaten
6 egg yolks, lightly beaten
1 tablespoon vanilla essence (extract)

Preheat oven to 130°C (265°F). Lightly grease a 23 cm (9 in) springform cake tin with butter. Line the base and sides with two layers of baking paper (parchment).
Sift flour, baking powder and cocoa powder. Reserve two handfuls of the best whole fruit and nuts for the topping and set aside. Place ginger, fruit and nuts in a bowl. Mix sifted flour and sugar into the fruit and nuts, then add the beaten eggs and vanilla essence. Spoon the mixture into prepared tin and press the reserved fruit and nuts into the top. Bake for 2 hours or until a skewer inserted into the centre of the cake comes out dry. Cool in the tin on a cake rack.

TIPPALEIVAT

This Scandinavian May Day favourite is a yeast-raised fried batter. Piped into a cruller shape in the frying oil, the batter is cooked to crisp golden brown and then rolled in sugar.

TIPSY CAKE
(see also zuppa Inglese)

An English treat, this cake consists of light layers of sponge filled with custard and sherry and decorated with whipped cream or custard. There are two stories as to its name. The first is that the cake was originally made for the local priest of a small town by one of his parishoners, who had so overdone the sherry that the cake was named tipsy parson's cake and later just tipsy cake. The other is that the cake is so laden with sherry and custard that it always tipped to one side.

TIRAMI-SU

There are two major varieties of the Italian tirami-su: one is the traditional soft mascarpone (Italian cream cheese) dessert and the other is a modernised cake of japonaise and coffee-flavoured mascarpone filling. The name means pick-me-up, and refers to the reviving effect of the coffee that pervades the dessert.

TIRAMI-SU CAKE
7 level teaspoons gelatine
¼ cup (2 fl oz) water
½ cup (4 fl oz) coffee liqueur
½ cup (4 oz) caster (superfine) sugar
1 cup (2 oz) instant coffee
500 g (16 oz) mascarpone (Italian cream cheese)
3 eggs
1 cup (8 oz) thickened cream, lightly whipped
2 japonaise bases (see page 156)
cocoa powder, for dusting

Place gelatine and water in a small bowl and stand it in a pan of hot water to dissolve. Place coffee liqueur, sugar and instant coffee in a saucepan and bring to the boil. Stir in dissolved gelatine. Place mascarpone in a mixing bowl and beat in the eggs and coffee mixture. Gently fold in the whipped cream. Place one of the japonaise bases in the bottom of a 23 cm (9 in) springform pan and pour in the mixture. Top with the second base and press down lightly. Chill for 2 hours. Remove from the tin and dust the top with cocoa powder.

TIRAMI-SU DESSERT

2 tablespoons instant coffee granules
2 tablespoons coffee liqueur or brandy
½ cup (4 oz) caster (superfine) sugar
5 egg yolks
125 g (4 oz) mascarpone (Italian cream cheese)
or plain cream cheese, softened
2 cups (16 fl oz) cream, lightly whipped
12–14 savoiardi biscuits

Place coffee granules and liqueur or brandy in a small bowl and stir until dissolved. Dip the base of each savoiardi biscuit into the coffee mixture and place them directly on the base of a pie dish.
Place sugar and egg yolks in a bowl and whisk together until light and creamy. Add the mascarpone and fold into the egg mixture until smooth. Add lightly whipped cream and fold through gently. Pour the mixture over the coffee-soaked biscuits and refrigerate for 4 hours before serving.

TOFFEE
(see also confectionery)

From a Creole word for a mixture of molasses and sugar, toffee, or taffy as it is sometimes called, is a mixture of sugar, water and glucose (corn syrup), and occasionally golden syrup or molasses. The mixture is boiled and cooked until it turns a golden brown or until it reaches 155°C (300°F), at which stage it is poured into greased paper cases or a lined or greased baking sheet. Once it has cooled, the sheet of toffee is broken into pieces for eating.

Toffee apples are the most popular confection to be made from toffee and are the perfect combination, the apple counteracting the intense sweetness of the toffee.

Toffee can also be used for decorative effects and can be made into many shapes. If neither golden syrup nor molasses is used in its production, it can be coloured by adding a water-based colouring to the molten sugar mixture. that has a tight-fitting lid. Storing the syrup in this way helps all the sugar crystals to dissolve. Store the syrup in the container for 12–24 hours.

TOFU

This white-coloured product made from soy bean curd has no particular flavour of its own but absorbs and takes on flavours of other food easily. It is available in fresh, canned and powdered form. The fresh tofu is produced by crushing, grinding and filtering the soybean and then extracting a mixture from this, which is heated to 75–80°C (167–76°F). Coagulants are then added to assist in the production of a soy curd and whey, the curd being pressed, washed and cooled to form tofu.

Tofu is often used in ice creams and other dessert dishes but is not overly popular for use in the pastry area. It can be coated in sweet crumbs, fried and served with a light cream sauce or anglaise, or it can be grilled and served with fresh fruits, or steamed or boiled and served with fruits, fondue and biscuits.

TOLLHOUSE COOKIES

A well known American cookie, otherwise known as a chocolate chip cookie, the Tollhouse was invented in the early 1930s when the chef of the Tollhouse restaurant had the idea of adding large chocolate chips of chocolate to a basic cookie dough.

180 g (6 oz) unsalted (sweet) butter
1 cup (5 oz) soft (light) brown sugar
¾ cup (5 oz) caster (superfine) sugar
2 eggs
2½ cups (10 oz) plain (all-purpose) flour
1 teaspoon baking powder (soda)
1¼ cups (10 oz) dark chocolate chips
1 cup (8 oz) milk chocolate chips

Preheat oven to 180°C (350°F).
Line baking sheets with baking paper (parchment).
Place butter and both sugars in a mixing bowl and whip until light and fluffy. Add eggs one at a time and mix well after each one is added. Sift flour and baking powder and add to butter mixture with both amounts of chocolate chips. Stir until well combined. Take tablespoonfuls of the mixture and place on the prepared sheet, leaving enough room for spreading. Bake for 15–20 minutes, or until biscuits are golden brown and firm to the touch. Remove and cool on the sheet.

Makes 2–3 dozen

TOMATO BREAD

3¾ cups (15 oz) bread flour
1 teaspoon gluten flour
1 teaspoon salt
6 teaspoons fresh compressed yeast
3 teaspoons caster (superfine) sugar
¼ cup (1 oz) milk powder
2 tablespoons unsalted (sweet) butter
⅓ cup (4 fl oz) tomato paste
1 cup (8 fl oz) water
2 tablespoons chopped chives

Grease a baking sheet.
Place all dry ingredients in a bowl and lightly rub through the butter and the yeast until mixture resembles breadcrumbs. Add chives then add the tomato paste and water together — add only enough liquid to the mixture to form a firm dough. Knead the dough for 5–10 minutes or until dough is smooth.
Cover dough and allow to sit for 10 minutes.
Knock back (punch down) the dough and scale into desired sizes. Allow the dough to sit, covered, in a warm place for 30 minutes.
Roll into desired shapes and place on prepared sheet.
Leave in a warm area to prove (rise) for 40 minutes.
Preheat oven to 190°C (375°F).
Bake in preheated oven for 20–25 minutes, or until golden brown.

TONKINOIS

A French almond cake which, when cool, is cut and then filled and masked with a praline-flavoured buttercream. Refrigerated until the buttercream is firm, the cake is covered with an orange-flavoured fondant and dusted liberally with finely grated roasted almonds or with shredded and roasted coconut.

TORTA DI RICOTTA

A rich Italian ricotta cheese mixture baked into a fine crust of sweet pastry which can be served with fresh fruits.

375 g (12 oz) sweet pastry (see page 272)
750 g (24 oz) ricotta cheese
⅓ cup (2½ oz) caster (superfine) sugar
¾ cup (3 oz) ground almonds
grated zest of 2 lemons
grated zest of 2 oranges
⅛ teaspoon ground cinnamon
5 eggs

Tollhouse Cookies and Viennese Shortbreads (seee page 286)

FAMOUS TORTES

NAME	BASE	FINISH
Dobos torte	multiple discs of Baumkuchen sponge, chocolate custard and caramel	cake layers separated with chocolate custard, masked with custard and sides covered with flaked almonds; top sponge layer covered in buttery caramel
Mimosa torte	two honey sponges, buttercream and marzipan	one sponge layered with buttercream; second cake cut into small squares which are placed around edge of cake; centre has yellow marzipan disc
Dutch apple torte	sweet pastry, sponge, apples and fondant	sweet pastry-lined cake tin; sponge base, then filled with apple mixture; topped with sweet pastry and when baked glazed with fondant
Pischinger torte	two japonaise bases, chocolate génoise, buttercream and hazelnuts	japonaise base, buttercream, sponge, then more buttercream and then last japonaise disc; masked in buttercream and sides covered in hazelnuts
Truffle torte	two japonaise bases, chocolate cream and cocoa powder	japonaise bases filled with chocolate cream and masked with it when set firm; the word 'Truffle' is written in cream across the top, which is then dusted in cocoa
Fraisier torte	vanilla sponge, strawberries, fresh cream and green marzipan	vanilla sponge square cut in half; bottom half topped with fresh cream and halved strawberries around outside edge; topped with second half of sponge, which is topped with green marzipan; name piped across top
Japonaise torte	japonaise bases, buttercream and almonds	japonaise bases joined with buttercream and masked with almonds, dusted with icing sugar; traditionally centre has large dot of fondant
Dual torte	flaked almonds, chocolate meringue mixture and vanilla almond cake mixture	loaf tin greased and covered in flaked almonds; chocolate meringue mixture spread around sides of tin and almond cake mixture placed in centre; when baked turned upright to serve
Sacher torte	chocolate hazelnut cake and chocolate fondant or boiled glaze	chocolate hazelnut cake covered in boiled apricot glaze and chocolate fondant or boiled glaze; name written in chocolate across centre of top
Linzer torte	linzer paste, raspberry or cranberry jam (jelly) and fondant	linzer paste lined cake ring; spread with jam (jelly) and then covered in criss-cross fashion with remaining dough; baked and glazed with fondant when cool
Frangipane torte	sweet pastry, crème frangipane and fondant	sweet pastry lined cake tin filled with crème frangipane and baked; glazed with fondant when cool

Preheat oven to 180°C (350°F). Grease a 26 cm
(10 in) pie dish.
Roll out dough and use to line the prepared pie dish.
Place ricotta cheese, sugar, almonds and the lemon and
orange zest in a bowl and mix together lightly. Whisk in eggs
one at a time and pour the mixture into the pastry-lined pie
dish. Bake in preheated oven for 40–45 minutes, or until
firm to the touch. Cool and serve with fresh fruits.

TORTE

A large, highly decorated cake containing cream and other
rich ingredients such as fruit or nuts. Tortes are decorated in
one piece either by decorating a base cake or adding the
decoration before baking and, when the torte is removed
from the oven, simply glazing it. A list of famous tortes is on
page 279.

TORTEIL
(see also brioche)

One of numerous varieties of Twelfth Night cakes, this citrus-
flavoured brioche dough is shaped like a crown and
traditionally flavoured with aniseed, rum and dried fruits. It
is decorated with sugar crystals before baking.

TORTILLA

A flat unleavened bread of Mexico and South America. Made
from a white cornmeal paste, the tortilla is traditionally a soft
cake made by cooking the paste on a griddle. If a crisp form is
required, this soft dough is then fried. The tortilla hase been
used for centuries, not only as a dish in itself, but also as a
serving base for many other dishes. The topping can be
turned into a filling by rolling up the tortilla.

TORTILLON
(see also puff pastry)

A thin strip of puff pastry which is held at either end and
twisted before baking. It is then glazed with an egg wash and
sprinkled with a mixture of finely ground almonds, flaked
almonds and parmesan cheese. The sticks are baked and then
served with savoury fondues or with a cheese board or
platter. A sweet version of the tortillon is also made for petits
fours by using exactly the same procedure but sprinkling with
ground and flaked almonds and sugar crystals.

TORTONI

A rich Italian iced dessert made from cream and crushed
macaroons which are spooned into small custard cups, or
soufflé dishes, decorated with fruit chocolate and nuts, then
frozen.

¾ cup (3 oz) crushed macaroons
2 cups (16 fl oz) cream
¼ cup (2 fl oz) Madeira
⅓ cup (2 oz) icing (powdered) sugar, sifted
100 g (3½ oz) finely grated dark (plain or semi-sweet)
chocolate

Place crushed biscuits and half the cream into a bowl with
Madeira and icing sugar. Combine all ingredients
and allow to sit in the refrigerator for 1 hour.
Whip remaining cream to firm, but not stiff, peaks and fold
through the first mixture. Pour mixture into 6–8 ramekins or
small soufflé dishes and cover with the grated chocolate.
Freeze for 2 hours before serving.

TOSCANER

Base
1¼ cups (5 oz) plain (all-purpose) flour
⅓ cup (2 oz) icing (powdered) sugar
90 g (3 oz) unsalted (sweet) butter
1 egg
1 tablespoon cold water

Filling
150 g (5 oz) unsalted (sweet) butter
⅔ cup (5 oz) caster (superfine) sugar
1 egg
⅓ cup (1½ oz) plain (all-purpose) flour
1⅓ cups (5 oz) ground almonds

Topping
105 g (3½ oz) unsalted (sweet) butter
½ cup (4 oz) caster (superfine) sugar
2 tablespoons honey
1 cup (3½ oz) flaked almonds

Base
Place flour and icing sugar in a bowl and very lightly rub in
butter until the mixture resembles coarse breadcrumbs.
Add egg and water and work to a firm dough. Wrap dough
in plastic wrap (cling film) and chill for 1 hour.
Preheat the oven to 180°C (350°F).
Grease a 25 x 30 x 3 cm (10 x 12 x 1¼ in) baking tray
(jelly roll pan) and line with baking paper (parchment).
On a lightly floured surface, roll the pastry
to fit the base of the prepared sheet.

Filling
Place butter and sugar in a mixing bowl and
beat until creamy, light and fluffy.
Add egg and beat for 3 minutes. Beat in sifted flour and
ground almonds. Spread the mixture over the pastry-lined
baking tray and bake for 40–45 minutes or until
brown and firm to the touch. Cool in the tray.

Topping
Place all the topping ingredients in a saucepan and slowly
bring to the boil. Boil for 2 minutes, or until the mixture
begins leaving the sides of the pan. Using a lightly oiled
palette knife, spread the topping mixture over the baked
base. Return the whole slice in its tray to the oven for
10 minutes, then cool thoroughly before cutting.

See page 282

TOT-FAIT

A tea cake made from a pound cake mixture that is flavoured with mixed (candied) peel. It is served in slices on its own or cut in half horizontally and the base covered with poached fruits and lightly spiced whipped cream. The top is placed on the filling and the cake is liberally dusted with icing sugar.

Tot-fait is also the name of an egg dish made from sugar, flour, butter and whisked eggs, lightly baked in a ramekin dish. The dish rises like a soufflé and then collapses soon after being removed from the oven.

TOURIER

The paste handler in the pastry section is known as the tourier. He or she usually produces all the pastries and sometimes the fermented doughs as well. Normally the tourier will simply make the doughs, preparing them to finished dough stage and leaving the pâtissier or other pastry chefs to make the finished doughs into sweet delicacies. If the pastry section is busy, however, the tourier may be required to blind bake pastries and prepare some of the basic doughs for baking. A tourier is usually only ever employed in very large or very busy establishments. Having a tourier is the best way of ensuring 100% consistency in doughs: if a pastry dough is made by whoever needs it, there will be a lack of uniformity in dough products and the flavours and textures of pastries.

TRAGACANTH

Used to produce decorating icing pastes, tragacanth or gum tragacanth, as it is known, is produced from a Middle Eastern plant. The tragacanth is extracted from the plant, dried and crushed to a powder. To use tragacanth, it is mixed with water in the proportions of 125 g (4 oz) tragacanth for every litre (32 fl oz) of water. The gum is also used in confectionery items and jellies.

TREACLE
(see also golden syrup, molasses, sugar)

A sweet, dark by-product of the sugar-refining process, treacle is the liquid which remains after processing has taken place. It is known also as golden syrup in some countries; golden syrup is the lighter form of treacle, and dark treacle is sweeter, with a more intense colour and a stronger flavour. Both styles are used in exactly the same way to give colour and flavour to gingerbreads and honey cakes, as well as puddings, sauces and confectionery.

TRIFLE

The perfect dessert for using leftovers. A traditional pudding of the United Kingdom made from a base of stale leftover cake crumbs lightly soaked in alcohol (port or fortified wines, usually) then covered with fresh fruits and topped completely with a thin sweet custard. Further decoration or layers can be made using whipped cream.

TROIS-FRERES

The trois-frères (three brothers) is a dessert based on the Savarin, the invention of Auguste Julien. Invented by the three Julien brothers in the 19th century, this dessert is baked in a savarin mould and consists of a light mixture of butter, eggs, rice flour, sugar and maraschino cherries. When baked, it is turned out onto a disc of sweet pastry or sable paste which has been lightly baked. It is then glazed with boiled apricot jam (jelly) and decorated with angelica or cherries.

TRUFFLE

A truffle is a small bite-sized petit four, usually made from chocolate and ganache, to which a flavouring has been added. Truffle mixtures can be piped into ball shapes or long strands, cut and rolled into balls or set in a large dish. A melon baller can be used to produce perfect balls. The firm balls are then rolled in cocoa powder, icing sugar or melted chocolate or flaked almonds. Truffle fillings can be any flavour and are often enhanced by adding natural oils or essences, or alcohol or liqueur.

BRANDY PASTE TRUFFLE
¾ cup (6 fl oz) thickened (double or heavy) cream
105 g (3½ oz) unsalted (sweet) butter
440 g (14 oz) dark (plain or semi-sweet) chocolate, melted (see page 62)
⅓ cup (2½ fl oz) brandy
2⅔ cups (8 oz) chocolate drinking powder

Line a baking sheet with baking paper (parchment). Place cream and butter in a saucepan and bring slowly to the boil. Add melted dark chocolate and stir to a smooth liquid, free of any lumps. Add brandy and mix in well. Pour the mixture into a mixing bowl and place in refrigerator. Stir every few minutes until mixture becomes smooth and thick enough to pipe. Place the truffle mixture in a piping (pastry) bag fitted with a 1.5 cm (½ in) star-shaped nozzle. Pipe star or rosette shapes onto prepared baking sheet. When the tray is full, place in the refrigerator and allow the truffles to set hard. Remove from refrigerator and dust each truffle with chocolate drinking powder. Serve immediately, or place in an airtight container and store in refrigerator until required.

Makes 36

TRUFFLE TORTE

Filling
⅔ cup (5½ fl oz) milk
⅔ cup (5½ fl oz) cream (single or light)
530 g (17 oz) milk chocolate, chopped
300 g (10 oz) unsalted (sweet) butter
2¾ cups (19 oz) caster (superfine) sugar
1 cup (8 fl oz) water
8 egg whites
½ cup (4 oz) caster (superfine) sugar, extra

Base
2 japonaise bases (see page 156)
cocoa powder, for dusting

Toscaner (see page 280)

Place milk and cream in a saucepan and bring to the boil. Remove from heat, add chocolate and stir until melted. Cool, but do not refrigerate. When set, cream with the butter until the mixture is light and has increased in volume. Place sugar and water in a saucepan. Bring to the boil and heat to 120°C (250°F). Test this, using a sugar (candy) thermometer. Beat egg whites in a bowl until stiff peaks form. Add sugar.

When sugar syrup reaches the correct temperature, pour slowly onto the beaten egg whites, beating all the time until the filling is cool. Mix a small amount of the filling into the cooled mixture. Very gently fold in the remaining meringue by hand. Spread three quarters of the filling onto one of the bases and top with the other base. Press gently on the top to spread the filling evenly. Spread the remaining filling on the top, reserving sufficient to pipe 'Truffle' across the top of the torte. Chill for 2 hours before serving.

Dust with cocoa powder.

TUILE

Translated, 'tuile' means tile. These thin baked biscuits (cookies) are the shape of a traditional French roofing tile. Made from a liquid paste of eggs, flour and icing sugar, tuiles are easy to make with a good recipe. They are brittle and smash easily and do not hold up too well to changes in humidity, so it is much better to prepare them each time they are to be served than to try to store them.

Tuiles can be made in the traditional biscuit (cookie) shapes, or into small baskets — drape the baked flat tuiles over a jar or bowl and chill them in this shape.

ALMOND TUILES
¾ cup (4 oz) icing (powdered) sugar
1 cup (4 oz) plain (all-purpose) flour
3 egg whites
90 g (3 oz) unsalted (sweet) butter, melted
1⅓ cups (5 oz) flaked almonds, for decoration

Preheat oven to 180°C (350°F).

Lightly grease baking trays (sheets).

Sift icing sugar and flour into a bowl. Lightly whisk egg whites and add to icing sugar and flour. Stir until well mixed and no lumps of dry ingredients are present. Stand, uncovered, for 5 minutes. Pour melted butter over top of mixture and stir until a smooth paste has formed. Rest for a further 5 minutes.

Take dessertspoonfuls of mixture and place on prepared sheet, using the back of a spoon to spread them into a large circle. Spread very thinly and sprinkle a few flaked almonds on the top of each tuile. Bake in preheated oven for 8–10 minutes, or until just turning golden brown around edges. (The tuiles may take more or less time, depending on their thickness.) Remove from oven and, using a flat clean palette knife or spatula, very carefully and quickly remove each tuile before it sets hard. Press over a rolling pin or any utensil which will give a curved shape. Cool over the rolling pin and then store in an airtight container until required.

Makes 12—18

TURKISH DELIGHT

Invented centuries ago in the Middle East, this gelatinous, confection is usually dusted in cornflour (cornstarch) or icing (powdered) sugar, or a combination of both. Traditionally it is made either red or clear and flavoured with rosewater or citrus rinds.

2 cups (16 oz) granulated sugar
100 ml (3½ fl oz) water
grated zest of 1 orange
⅔ cup (2½ oz) cornflour (cornstarch)
½ cup (4 fl oz) orange juice
2 tablespoons gelatine powder, soaked in
3 tablespoons cold water
2–3 drops red (cochineal) food colouring
⅔ cup (2½ oz) cornflour (cornstarch)
½ cup (3 oz) icing (powdered) sugar

Lightly oil an 18 x 28 x 2 cm (7 x 11 x ¾ in) baking tray (jelly roll pan).

Place sugar, water and orange zest and juice in a large saucepan over gentle heat. Stir until sugar has dissolved, then increase heat and bring to the boil. Add the first amount of cornflour to orange juice and mix to a paste. Quickly whisk the paste into the boiling liquid and allow the mixture to reboil. Add soaked gelatine and stir to ensure all ingredients are well combined. Add red food colouring. Boil the mixture for 10 minutes, stirring continuously to ensure mixture does not burn. Pour mixture through a fine sieve into prepared tray. Refrigerate for 12–24 hours before

cutting into squares with a sharp hot knife. Combine the second amount of cornflour and icing sugar and sift to ensure they are evenly mixed. Drop squares of Turkish delight into the powdery mix and coat each piece well.

Serve immediately or store in an airtight container in the refrigerator.

Makes 36—40

TURNOVER
(see also chocart)

Made with either sweet or savoury fillings, a turnover is usually a disc of puff pastry which is filled in the centre with a fruit filling. Then the edges are brushed with egg yolk, one side is brought over to join the other and the edges are pinched together. The whole turnover is brushed with egg yolk or egg wash, sprinkled with sugar crystals and baked until golden brown. Upon removal from the oven, European turnovers are glazed with apricot jam (jelly) and washed with a thin fondant glaze.

TURNTABLE

A moveable round disc usually set onto ball bearings that allows a cake to be turned smoothly and easily in order to be decorated with royal icing, creams and other toppings.

TUTTI-FRUTTI

Tutti-frutti is an Italian expression referring to the use of many fruits in one dish. Traditionally it also refers to the use of crystallised (candied) fruits, a combination of which are used in tutti frutti ice creams, cakes, custards and fillings or for tutti frutti bombe.

TWELFTH NIGHT CAKE
(see also galette, pithivier, rosca de reyes)

The arrival of the three wise men to see the Baby Jesus is celebrated on the January 6, also known as Epiphany, King's Day or Bean King Day. This day is celebrated throughout Europe by the giving of special Twelfth Night cakes, which vary according to the country. In Italy the panettone is given, in France it is the galette de rois, while in Mexico it is the rosca de reyes. Traditionally, the cakes must be baked with a bean or small china token inserted within them, and whoever finds this bean in their slice becomes the Bean King of the Day or the King or Queen of the Twelfth Night. It is from this tradition that the practice of inserting coins into the original Christmas pudding originated. Twelfth Night cakes can be made from pastry, cake or yeast doughs in the shape of a crown, while in some countries pithiviers and galettes have been used for Twelfth Night celebrations.

U

UNBLEACHED FLOUR
(see also flour)

Normally flour is bleached using a whitening agent such as benzol peroxide, which improves the colour and quality of the flour. Unbleached flour has a slight yellow or creamy colour.

UNLEAVENED BREAD
(see also flatbreads and individual listings)

Unleavened bread is a flatbread which has not had any leavening agents added to it, so it will not rise.

UPSIDE DOWN CAKE
(see also tarte Tatin)

An American adaptation of the classic French dessert dish tarte Tatin, which consists of caramelised apples which are topped with pastry and inverted when cooked. The American version uses cake batter rather than pastry to cover the fruit base. This allows finer slices to be cut.

2 cups (8 oz) plain (all-purpose) flour
2 level teaspoons baking powder (soda)
6 canned pineapple rings
6 glacé (candied) cherries
90 g (3 oz) unsalted (sweet) butter
⅔ cup (5 oz) caster (superfine) sugar
2 eggs
100 ml (3½ fl oz) milk
apricot glaze (see page 10)
2 cups (8 oz) flaked almonds, roasted (see page 5)

Preheat oven to 180°C (350°F).
Lightly grease a 23 cm (9 in) springform cake tin with butter and line the base with baking paper (parchment).
Sift flour and baking powder. Place pineapple rings in prepared tin and decorate with cherries. Beat butter and sugar until creamy, light and fluffy. Add eggs one at a time, beating well after each one is added. Add sifted flour, baking powder and milk and pour the mixture over pineapple rings. Bake for 40–45 minutes, or until a skewer inserted into the centre of the cake comes out dry and the cake has shrunk slightly away from the sides of the tin. Let stand for 5 minutes before turning out onto a serving platter. Brush with apricot glaze and decorate around the edge with flaked almonds.

V

VACHERIN
(see also meringue)

Named after a cheese of the same shape and colour, a vacherin is a high-sided meringue-based dessert. It is formed either by piping the mixture into rings and then stacking these upon each other, or by piping the mixture continuously over itself to make a dish or basket from the meringue. In some varieties of vacherin a lid is also piped, and when the vacherin is filled with cream, mousse or fresh fruit, the lid is placed on top.

VANDYKE

To vandyke fruit or vegetables is to create V-shaped cuts or a zigzag effect around the edge of the fruit or vegetable. This decorative effect is normally used when creating fruit platters.

VANILLA

Vanilla was introduced into Europe after Cortés travelled to Mexico, where the Aztecs had been using vanilla pods in the production of their chocolate. The vanilla pod is the fruit of a Mexican climbing orchid and grows 12–20 cm (5–8 in) in length. It is picked while still green, then cured and dried to become black and aromatic. Once dried, the vanilla pods must be kept in airtight jars to retain their flavour. Vanilla essence is an extract from the vanilla pod which is mixed with alcohol and does not have the intensity of flavour that the pod has. Vanilla pods are used in sauces and crèmes by being boiled with the milk or cream and allowed to infuse for some time. Once the pods have been infused, they can be removed and washed for re-use or split open and the vanilla beans scraped into the sauce, creating a characteristic look of black spots throughout. This is the only way of indicating that real vanilla has been used.

VANILLA SUGAR

Sugar in which a vanilla pod has been stored so that its flavour permeates the sugar. Alternatively, vanillin can be added to the sugar. It is used in recipes in the same way as normal caster (superfine) sugar, but imparts a stronger flavour.

VANILLIN
(see also vanilla)

A substance found naturally in various plants and barks and responsible for the aroma in vanilla pods. Vanillin can also be synthetically produced and should be used sparingly. Natural vanilla is preferred by pastry chefs.

VATROUCHKA
(see also cheesecake)

A traditional Russian cheesecake made with curd cheese and dried fruits and baked onto a sable biscuit base. The cheesecake is covered with latticed sweet pastry and dusted with icing (powdered) sugar before serving.

VATROUCHKI

These turnovers are a traditional Russian dessert and are made from a rich brioche dough. Balls of the dough are pinned thinly, filled with curd cheese and fruit and then pinched together. Once they have proved (risen), the turnovers can be either fried or baked.

VETTALAPAM

A national dish of Sri Lanka consisting of palm sugar, coconut and coconut cream. If coconut cream is unavailable, it can be replaced by ordinary milk in which desiccated (shredded) coconut has been soaked.

3 cups (9 oz) desiccated (shredded) coconut
1⅔ cups (13 fl oz) milk
¾ cup (6 oz) palm sugar
¼ cup (2 fl oz) water
4 eggs
¼ teaspoon ground cardamom
¼ teaspoon ground cinnamon
¾ cup (3 oz) chopped peanuts

Preheat oven to 160°C (320°F).
Grease or oil a savarin ring well.
Bring milk to the boil and add desiccated
(shredded) coconut. Allow it to sit until cool.
Heat water and palm sugar in a saucepan and stir until
dissolved. Add eggs to milk/coconut mixture and then stir
through the palm sugar mixture along with
the spices and the chopped nuts.
Pour the mixture into prepared tin and bake in preheated
oven for 35–45 minutes, until the custard has set firm.
When the mixture is set, refrigerate until cold, then turn
out onto a serving dish.

VEGETABLES

A number of different vegetables have been used in cakes and pastries for centuries. Carrots are used in carrot cake or biscuits (cookies), pumpkin in the traditional American

Thanksgiving pie, beetroot in beetroot cake and zucchini in cakes and muffins. Sweet potato or kumera, swede, cabbage and many other vegetables have been made into cakes, but these haven't gained the popularity of the carrot cake or pumpkin pie.

VICTORIA SANDWICH

Unlike traditional sponges, this is made using equal quantites of flour, fat, sugar and eggs. Two sponges are sandwiched together with jam and cream to produce a Victoria sandwich. This famous English cake was named after Queen Victoria in the late 19th century. The same sponge mixture is used for trifles, Swiss rolls and many small pastries and petits fours.

VIDELER

The French terminology for decoratively pinching the edge of a pie or pastry crust to give it a neat, even, stylish border.

VIENNA CAKE
(see panforte di Siena)

VIENNESE SHORTBREADS

These shortbreads are made to exactly the same recipe as Paris sticks (see page 204), except that they use 2 teaspoons of vanilla essence and have no lemon juice at all. As well as having one half dipped in chocolate, they have the other half dusted with icing (powdered) sugar.

VINEGAR
(see also acetomel)

Vinegar is an acidic by-product of the production of wines and the fermentation of grains and certain fruits. It varies in flavour and intensity according to what it is made from. Vinegars are used in cooking for their flavour, for pickling and, in some instances, to replace lemon juice.

VISITANDINE

First made in French and Italian monasteries during the 16th century by the monks to reduce their surplus of egg whites, visitandines are small boat-shaped cakes with pastry bases. Barquette or boat-shaped moulds are lined thinly with sweet pastry, then filled with a mixture of ground almonds, egg whites, butter and sugar. When baked, they are glazed with apricot glaze and brushed with a very thin Kirsch-flavoured fondant. Visitandines are served with coffee.

VOILER

Meaning to cover pastries, cakes and desserts with a fine mesh of sugar threads. The sugar is cooked to hard crack stage and a whisk-like tool is whisked rapidly over the top of the pastries to create fine threads as the sugar pulls away from the tool and cools.

VOL-AU-VENT
(see also puff pastry)

Invented by Carême, these puff pastry cases are today famous throughout the world. Carême is said to have invented these from puff pastry only after having served a similar dish from sweet pastry for years. Finding the sweet pastry too hard and too heavy for his desserts, he made the vol-au-vent, which translates as 'it flew away in the wind' (il volait au vent).

They are made by placing a disc of puff pastry on a baking sheet, glazing the top of the pastry and then placing another disc, which has had its centre removed, on top of the first disc. A third disc, with its centre removed, may be place on top of this. The vol-au-vents are then baked and the puff pastry rises to leave a central core free for filling with mousse, fresh fruit, or savoury fillings. The smaller version of the vol-au-vent, called a bouchée, is only 4–5 cm (1½–2 in) in diameter whereas a vol-au-vent should be 10–12 cm (4–5 in) in diameter.

batter is formed. Slowly and gently fold whisked egg whites through the batter so that all the air is not knocked out. Spoon 2–3 tablespoonfuls of the mixture onto heated waffle iron. Close the lid and wait for 1–2 minutes, or until the batter is golden brown on both sides before removing. Serve immediately or freeze and toast when required.

WAFFLE IRON

While most waffle irons today are electric, the traditional waffle iron consisted of two discs of iron which were hinged together. The two facing sides were marked into ridges or ribs. These two discs were attached to two long handles with wooden hand grips. The discs were heated over the open fire, then lightly oiled and the batter poured in. The waffle iron was closed again and placed over the flames until the waffle was baked. Crudely shaped waffle irons have been found dating back to the early 12th century. Waffle irons have been found from the 15th century with gold handles, religious insignias and coats of arms adorning the waffle plates.

WALNUT
(see also nuts)

Native to the Asian region, walnuts are the most commonly consumed nuts in the world. They were used for trade in the Persian Empire, and many cultures held that the consumption of walnuts made couples fertile. Yet other cultures believed they warded off evil spirits and bad luck.

Walnuts grow on the walnut tree inside green pods which turn brown and almost woodlike when they dry. Walnuts are delicious eaten plain and are ground, chopped or used whole in cakes, pies, pastries and slices.

WALNUT BREAD

4½ cups (18 oz) plain (all-purpose) flour
1 teaspoon salt
½ cup (3 oz) soft (light) brown sugar
1 tablespoon fresh compressed yeast
60 g (2 oz) unsalted (sweet) butter
1 cup (8 fl oz) milk
4 tablespoons water
½ cup (2 oz) walnuts, chopped

Place flour, salt and sugar into a bowl and rub through with the fingers to combine. Crumble yeast into flour mixture. Place butter into a saucepan and allow to melt, then brown slightly. Cool. Add milk and water to the flour and work mixture into a dough. Knead well for 5 minutes or until smooth and elastic. Place dough back into the mixing bowl and work through butter and walnuts and again form into a dough. Place, covered, in a warm area for 30–40 minutes, or until double in size. Preheat oven to 200°C (400°F). Grease a baking tray (sheet). Cut dough into 24 small pieces and roll these into small balls. Place the balls on prepared sheet and leave in a warm area for 30–40 minutes or until double in bulk. Bake the bread for 20–25 minutes or until golden brown.

WAFER

A very thin mixture of eggs, flour and sugar which is traditionally baked into long flat sheets. When baked, it is rolled into cigarettes, made into fans, rolled into cones or cornets for ice creams or left as flat discs.

WAFFLE
(see also batters)

Waffles have been in existence since early in the 12th century and belong to a large group of desserts produced from batters, including pancakes, blini and more.

A good waffle should be light and airy and about 1 cm (½ in) thick. Waffle batter is made either sweet or plain and is risen using baking powder (soda) and occasionally yeast. The major difference between a waffle and a pancake is that a waffle mixture is traditionally poured into a flat iron called a waffle iron which is ribbed on the inside and has a second side that closes over the first once the mixture is inside. The waffle is turned over in the flames to bake to a golden brown colour, and when the waffle iron is opened, the shaped waffle drops out. Waffles can be served with either sweet or savoury toppings, although traditionally they simply have lemon juice poured over them and are then sprinkled with sugar.

2 cups (8 oz) plain (all-purpose) flour
½ teaspoon baking powder (soda)
1½ cups (12 fl oz) milk
2 egg yolks
2 egg whites
¼ cup (2 oz) caster (superfine) sugar
60 g (2 oz) unsalted (sweet) butter, melted
2 tablespoons cold water

Sift flour and baking powder together. Whisk milk and egg yolks together in a bowl. Place egg whites in a bowl and whisk until stiff peaks form. Slowly add sugar, a little at a time, whisking continuously. Whisk until all sugar is combined. Add melted butter, water and sifted flour and baking powder to the milk mixture and stir until a smooth

WALNUT PIE

⅓ cup (4 fl oz) maple syrup
⅔ cup (5 oz) caster (superfine) sugar
1 teaspoon mixed spice (apple pie spice)
100 ml (3½ fl oz) water
125 g (4 oz) unsalted (sweet) butter, melted
2 eggs, lightly beaten
2¼ cups (7 oz) walnut halves
1 x 28 cm (11 in) sweet pastry case (pie shell) or
300 g (10 oz) sweet pastry (see page 272)

Preheat oven to 200°C (400°F).
Place maple syrup, sugar, spice, water and melted butter in a bowl with eggs and lightly whisk together. Sprinkle walnuts onto the base of the pastry case, then pour the liquid mixture over the top of the nuts. Place the pie on a baking sheet and bake in preheated oven for 15 minutes. Then reduce the temperature to 175°C (345°F) and bake for a further 25–30 minutes. Remove and cool slightly. Serve warm or cold.

WALNUT LOGS

1 cup (8 oz) caster (superfine) sugar
2½ tablespoons golden syrup (light treacle)
125 g (4 oz) unsalted (sweet) butter
⅓ cup (4 oz) liquid glucose (corn syrup)
410 g (13 oz) sweetened condensed milk
1 tablespoon instant coffee granules dissolved in
⅓ cup (3 fl oz) hot water
2½ cups (10 oz) chopped walnuts
375 g (12 oz) dark (plain or semi-sweet) chocolate,
melted (see page 62)

Lightly grease an 18 x 28 x 2 cm (7 x 11 x ¾ in) baking tray (jelly roll pan).
Place sugar, golden syrup, butter, glucose and condensed milk in a large heavy-based saucepan. Stir continuously and slowly allow the mixture to come to the boil. Continue boiling mixture until it becomes thick and a light golden brown colour. Keep stirring mixture at all times or it will stick to the saucepan and burn very quickly. Add coffee mixture.
Remove saucepan from the heat and pour mixture into prepared sheet. Refrigerate until firm (overnight if possible). When firm, cut into 6 strips, cutting across the breadth of the baking sheet. Remove the strips from the sheet and quickly roll them into round logs on a clean surface. Once rounded, roll the logs in the chopped walnuts to coat them completely. Place the walnut-covered logs on a flat tray and freeze for 30 minutes.
Pour melted chocolate into an 18 x 28 x 2 cm (7 x 11 x ¾ in) baking tray (jelly roll pan). Remove the logs from the freezer and place them in the chocolate one at a time. Roll them so that they are completely covered. Once covered, remove the chocolate logs to a baking sheet lined with baking paper (parchment) and allow to stand until the chocolate has set firm. If required immediately, simply cut the logs into slices

using a hot knife. If being stored, wrap each log individually in plastic wrap (cling film) and refrigerate until required.

Makes six 18 cm (7 in) logs which are each cut into 12 pieces

See page 290

WASH
(see also bun wash, egg wash, glazes)

To glaze a product once it has been baked with fondant, sugar syrup or bun wash.

WATER BISCUIT
(see also cracker)

A thin crisp biscuit (cookie) made of flour and water (and little else!) and served with cheese platters or savoury toppings. Known as a water cracker in the USA.

3¾ cups (15 oz) plain (all-purpose) flour
3 tablespoons poppy seeds
60 g (2 oz) unsalted (sweet) butter
1 cup (8 fl oz) milk

Preheat oven to 180°C (350°F).
Lightly grease 2 baking trays (sheets).
Place flour and poppy seeds together in a bowl and rub through butter until the mixture resembles coarse breadcrumbs. Add milk and mix through until a soft but not sticky dough is formed. (If the dough is too stiff, add a little more milk; if the dough is too sticky, add a little flour.) Knead for 4–5 minutes, or until dough is smooth. Cover with plastic wrap (cling film) and set aside for 5 minutes.
On a lightly floured surface, roll dough out as thinly as possible. Cut into 4 cm (1½ in) squares or rounds using a plain biscuit (cookie) cutter. Place the crackers on the prepared sheets and bake in the preheated oven for 10–12 minutes, or until the crackers are a light golden brown around the edges. Cool on the trays. When cold, wrap immediately in plastic wrap (cling flim) in batches of 12 and store in an airtight container until required.

Makes 36

WATER CRACKER
(see water biscuit)

WATER ICE
(see sherbert, sorbet)

WATER ICING

3 cups (15 oz) pure icing (powdered) sugar
warm water

Place icing sugar in an bowl and add sufficient water to make an icing thick enough to leave a trail when it is swirled over itself. It has to remain thin enough to spread.

Makes about 600 g (20 oz), enough to cover one 23 cm (9 in) cake.

WATERMELON
(see also melon)

Watermelons have been grown in Italy for many centuries and are now grown in the Americas, Australia and throughout Asia. They are large round or oval fruits which have a thick green skin that contains a sweet pink to red flesh.

The seeds of this fruit, which also contain an edible oil, are spread throughout the pink flesh. Consisting mostly of water, watermelon flesh is very soft and thirst-quenching; it does not last long once ripe. The flesh is used mainly in fruit salads, although sorbets and bombes have been made using it.

WATTLE SEED

The seeds of the wattle tree are picked by the Australian Aborigines and roasted and ground to look like coffee grounds. The wattle seeds, with their nutty flavour, can be made into a form of coffee or used in biscuits (cookies) or cakes and pastries for added flavour.

WAXED PAPER
(see greaseproof paper)

WEDDING CAKE
(see also croquembouche, Overflodigshorn)

A wedding cake is to some the most important fixture at a wedding ceremony. Throughout the world, there are different traditional forms of wedding cakes: France has the croquembouche, Denmark the Overflodigshorn. In the USA any cake can be used as a base and decorated with creams, icings, frostings and fresh flowers or flowers made of icing, while the English tradition is to have a fruit cake of several layers formally iced and decorated with delicate pastillage flowers.

WEINCHAUDEAU

This is the Austrian equivalent of the sabayon or zabaglione, but it is a slightly more delicate recipe and should be used immediately, as it will not hold. It can be used as a sauce or as a dip for langue de chat or fresh fruits.

4 egg yolks
1 egg
⅓ cup (3 oz) caster (superfine) sugar
1 cup (8 fl oz) chardonnay wine

Place egg yolks, egg and sugar in a large mixing bowl and stir together until sugar and eggs are creamed.
Pour in white wine and place the mixing bowl over a saucepan of simmering water. Using a large balloon whisk, whisk egg/wine mixture for 5–8 minutes, or until the mixture becomes light, fluffy and is double its original volume. Remove mixture from the simmering water and whisk for several minutes over ice. Serve immediately.

WHEAT
(see also flour)

Evidence indicates that wheat was used some 4000 years before the birth of Christ and has probably been in use since human beings first walked on earth. The Egyptians were among the first civilised people to mill wheat into flour. They then added water and salts to the flour to make a flat batter or dough which they baked on hot flat stones.

Hard wheats are those which contain the highest gluten contents and are best used for pasta and bread making, where gluten development is critical to the success of the recipe. Soft wheats contain the least gluten and are used for cakes and unleavened breads. Local millers can inform you of the strength of their flours on request. In some countries the strength is marked on the flour bag or sack.

WHIP

A dish consisting of fruit purée, whipped cream and egg white folded together and served as a dessert in chocolate baskets, tuile baskets or bowls.

To whip is to lighten an ingredient or mixture of ingredients by hand, using a wooden spoon, paddle or fork, or using a machine. An ingredient is whipped to aerate it or the mixture, in order to increase their volume.

WHISK

An instrument used to lighten egg whites, creams and other soft ingredients. It is made of fine wires joined together at a handle. The whisk incorporates air into products as it is being passed quickly through the ingredient or mixture.

To whisk is to lighten an ingredient or mixture of ingredients by incorporating the maximum amount of air possible using a whisk.

WHITE CHOCOLATE
(see also chocolate)

Made using milk solids, cocoa butter, milk fat and about 50% sugar, white chocolate is used in the same way as ordinary chocolate in pastries and desserts.

WHITE CHRISTMAS

2½ cups (2 oz) rice bubbles (crispies)
¼ cup (1 oz) desiccated (shredded) coconut
½ cup (1½ oz) slivered almonds
⅓ cup (2 oz) icing (powdered) sugar
⅓ cup (1½ oz) currants
1 tablespoon mixed (candied) peel
1 tablespoon chopped glacé (candied) cherries
¼ cup (1 oz) dried apricots, chopped
150 g (5 oz) copha (white coconut shortening)

Lightly grease and line an 18 x 28 x 2 cm (7 x 11 x ¾ in) baking tray (jelly roll pan) with baking paper (parchment). Place rice bubbles, coconut, milk powder and slivered almonds in a bowl and sift icing sugar over them. Place currants, mixed peel, cherries and apricots on top and combine well. Place copha in a saucepan

289

Walnut Logs Step-by-Step

Step 1: When firm, cut the mixture into strips across the breadth of the baking tray.

Step 2: Roll the logs of chilled mix in the chopped walnuts.

Step 3: Roll the logs in chocolate. See page 288.

White Christmas (see page 289)

and melt over gentle heat. Pour copha over the dry ingredients and fruit and stir until all are combined. Do not overmix or crush the dried fruits. Spread the mixture into prepared tray and smooth over. Place in refrigerator for 1 hour before cutting into fingers and serving.

Makes 20 slices

WHOLEMEAL
(see also flour)

A flour which is made up of the whole grain of wheat, having nothing removed after the milling process. Wholemeal or wholegrain doughs tend to soak up more liquid, and therefore require more water. It is also difficult to perform a gluten test on wholemeal or wholegrain products as the germ or grain splits the dough as soon as it becomes too fine.

WHOLEMEAL BREAD

5¼ cups (21 oz) plain wholemeal flour
3 teaspoons gluten flour
3 teaspoons salt
4 teaspoons caster (superfine) sugar
30 g (1 oz) fresh compressed yeast
30 g (1 oz) unsalted (sweet) butter
2 cups (16 fl oz) lukewarm water

Preheat oven to 200°C (400°F). Lightly oil 2 loaf tins. Place flour, salt and sugar in a mixing bowl and combine. Add butter and yeast and combine thoroughly until the mixture resembles fine breadcrumbs. Add enough water to form a firm dough and knead well. Knead for 5–10 minutes, or until the dough becomes smooth and elastic. Rest the dough, covered, in a bowl for 35–45 minutes. Knock back (punch down) the dough and form into

two equal portions. Allow to prove (rise), covered, for a further 20 minutes. Knock back (punch down) the dough and roll into loaf shapes to fit the prepared tins. Place on a tray and allow to stand in a warm area for 30–40 minutes, or until doubled in size. Bake for 20–25 minutes.

WIENERBROD
(see Danish pastries)

WIENER WAFFELN

270 g (9 oz) unsalted (sweet) butter
¾ cup (6 oz) caster (superfine) sugar
2 egg yolks
zest of 1 lemon
6 teaspoons ground cinnamon
3 cups (12 oz) plain (all-purpose) flour
1⅓ cups (5 oz) ground hazelnuts (filberts)
½ cup (5 oz) redcurrant jelly
210 g (7 oz) apricot glaze (see page 10)
125 g (4 oz) fondant (see page.118)

Place butter and sugar in a mixing bowl and cream until light, fluffy and pale in colour. Add egg yolk, lemon zest and cinnamon and beat until all are well combined. Add flour and ground hazelnuts and work the mixture to a dough. Cover dough in plastic wrap (cling film) and refrigerate for 1 hour. Preheat oven to 175°C (345°F). Lightly grease a 19 x 28 x 2 cm (7½ x 11 x ¾ in) baking tray (jelly roll pan). Knead dough lightly. Roll half the dough thinly to fit the base of the tray. Trim the edges to neaten and spread redcurrant jelly over the base. Roll out the other half of pastry and place firmly over the top. Trim to neaten. Bake in preheated oven for 12–15 minutes. Remove from oven and allow to cool in the baking tray. When cool, brush with apricot glaze and fondant. Cut into squares.

Makes 24

WINE CREAM

Used in recipes such as men's torte, wine cream was invented in Germany during the 18th century as a means of using up leftover wine. The wine is thickened and sugar added to it and a sweetened thick custard made from it.

Wine cream is a good and inexpensive way of using up a restaurant's leftover wine supply or incorporating sauternes or dessert wines in recipes. It can replace custard in any recipe and is truly delicious when used in trifles.

WUCHTELN

A popular Austrian dessert consisting of a buttery rich yeast dough filled with plums or plum jam. When proved (risen) and baked, the small buns are served with a crème anglaise or light custard.

YEAST

(see also aeration, bread, fermentation,
leavening agent, raising agent)

Yeast, or *saccromycies cerevisae*, is a form of plant life, a single-celled living organism which, under certain favourable conditions, will grow and multiply.

Used as a leavening agent for breads and other doughs and batters, yeast in its fresh compressed form can be yellow, grey or white and is quite pliable. In its dried form it consists of small beads that range from sand-coloured to yellow and as it is stronger than fresh compressed yeast, only one third the amount is required.

When mixed into the doughs, and in the presence of warmth, moisture and food, yeast breaks down the sugars present in the dough to simple sugars and then to carbon dioxide. The proccess of fermentation also mellows the gluten strands held within the dough. As the carbon dioxide gas is given off by the fermenting yeast, the gas is trapped within the gluten strands and the dough rises, making it lighter, higher and tastier.

Although the yeast requires sugars to feed upon and the dough requires salt for development of the gluten, these two ingredients must never come into direct contact with the yeast as they can retard the effects of the yeast and slow or kill fermentation.

Yeast is affected by temperature in the following way:

(i)   Below 10°C (50°F) yeast action is retarded but not in danger;

(ii) At 10°C (50°F) yeast action is slowed;

(iii) At 32°C (90°F) yeast is at its optimum temperature for fermentation;

(iv) Above 40°C (104°F) yeast action is slowed and retarding; and

(v)   Above 55°C (131°F) yeast is being killed and no further fermentation will take place.

YEAST DOUGH

Any dough which contains yeast as a leavening force. Danish pastry, croissant, soft dough Danish and brioche are types of yeast-raised doughs.

YEAST FOOD

(see also ascorbic acid, bread improver)

Yeast foods are combinations of ingredients mixed in certain proportions; a small amount added to a yeast dough assists and encourages healthy yeast growth and fermentation. They are likely to contain a combination of ammonium salts, bromate, salt and simple sugars and minerals.

YOGHURT

Yoghurt was possibly produced by mistake by Arabic shepherds who boiled some milk and then left it in their canvas water bottle for several days. It is a specialty which originated in Turkey and is still produced there in exactly the way described above, either cow, ewe or buffalo milk being reduced over heat, placed in a canvas water container and allowed to ferment naturally until the yoghurt forms.

Today yoghurt is a fermented milk product produced as a result of the actions of two species of bacteria, these being *streptococcus thermophilus* and *thermobacterium bulgaricum*, both strains of which were discovered by Metchnikoff, Louis Pasteur's Russian assistant.

In simple terms, the milk is homogenised and heated to 90°C (194°F) then cooled to 45°C (113°F), at which point the two bacterial starters are added. When they begin reacting with each other, this reaction turns the lactose in the milk into lactic acid, which gives the yoghurt its distinctive taste and flavour, and the milk begins to thicken naturally. The flavour, thickness, texture and aroma of the yoghurt can be adjusted by varying the amounts of the two bacteria used.

Yoghurts are traditionally only served for breakfasts but mousses, ice creams, sorbets, cakes and pastry fillings can also be produced using the different types of yoghurt available, with their varying flavours.

YORKSHIRE PUDDING

(see also batters, popover, pudding)

One of the simplest batter mixtures in the world, the perfect Yorkshire pudding is nonetheless very elusive. Yorkshire pudding is a basic batter of water, eggs and flour which is baked in small containers filled with hot fat or oil. It should be baked until golden brown, light and crisp and then set beneath the turning spit roast to catch the juices and dripping from the meat. This practice was dropped during the 19th century, when the Yorkshire pudding began being served as a sweet as well as a savoury item. Usually a large batch would be made for Sunday lunch and any leftovers would be served for Sunday dinner dessert with hot jam (jelly), icing sugar, golden syrup (light treacle) or thickened cream.

YULE LOG

(see also Buche de Noël, Swiss roll)

An English Christmas cake, this is a decorated Swiss roll log covered with buttercream to look like a felled tree log. Buche de Noël and the yule log are the same cakes, invented by a British pastry cook working in France around 1874. Apparently he had seen the German Baumkuchen and on returning to Paris wanted to create something similar, so he decorated a traditional Swiss roll with buttercream to form its bark and used sugar paste to create holly leaves.

Z

The zest is also grated or peeled and chopped finely or removed with a zester and used as garnish or decoration for plates and desserts. As well, it can be made into petits fours by boiling it in sugar syrup and then drying it and coating it in chocolate.

ZESTER
(see also canneller)

A small hand-held utensil used for removing the zest of citrus fruits or for making decorations in the sides of soft vegetables such as carrots and cucumbers.

Zesters can range from having one metal groove (these tend to be called cannellers) to having five small sharp grooves. By holding the handle of the zester and pressing the grooves up against the fruit and dragging down, the fruit zest is peeled away quite finely.

ZITRON

A true Swiss classic — a small, sweet pastry tartlet filled with a rich, smooth and tangy lemon butter and topped with a fine layer of lemon yellow fondant. The decoration the pastry has on top depends on which side of the country you buy it in. In the German sector it is decorated with a chocolate Z for 'Zitron', while in the French areas the decoration is the letter C or the entire word 'Citron'.

2½ cups (10 oz) plain (all-purpose) flour
1 cup (6 oz) icing (powdered) sugar
¼ cup (1 oz) ground almonds
150 g (5 oz) unsalted (sweet) butter
1 egg
1 tablespoon water

Lemon Butter
3 eggs
zest and juice of 2 lemons
½ cup (3½ oz) caster (superfine) sugar
250 g (8 oz) unsalted (sweet) butter

Icing
1 cup (6 oz) icing (powdered) sugar, sifted
2 tablespoons lemon juice
1–2 drops yellow food colouring
125 g (4 oz) dark (plain or semi-sweet) chocolate,
melted (see page 62)

Line baking sheets with baking paper (parchment). Place flour, icing sugar, almonds and butter in a bowl and lightly rub butter through until the mixture resembles coarse breadcrumbs. Add lightly beaten egg and water and work to a dough. Wrap in plastic wrap (cling flim) and place in the refrigerator for 30 minutes.
Preheat oven to 180°C (350°F).
Remove dough and knead until ready to roll. On a lightly floured surface, roll to 2–3 mm (⅛ in) in thickness. Using a 5 cm (2 in) diameter round biscuit (cookie) cutter, cut out two discs of dough for each zitron and place directly on the prepared sheets. Bake in preheated oven for 8–12 minutes, or until lightly golden brown. Remove and cool on a cake rack.

ZABAGLIONE
(see also sabayon)

The word comes from the Neapolitan 'zapillare' which literally translates as foam. It is a perfect whisking of egg yolks, sugar and wine which is stabilised by the warmth created by whisking the mixture. This mousse-style whipped and airy dessert or foam is traditionally poured into glasses and eaten while still warm using langue de chat biscuits (cookies) or a similar style of sweet biscuits. It may also be ladled over hot or cold puddings as a sauce or frozen in a log tin and served as a frozen slice, similar to a very light sorbet. The foam of the zabaglione can also be set using a small amount of gelatine.

Traditionally, zabaglione is produced using Marsala, a fortified wine. However, many variations have been made over the centuries and dessert wine and champagne are quite often added nowadays.

6 egg yolks
¾ cup (6 oz) caster (superfine) sugar
¾ cup (6 fl oz) Marsala

Place egg yolks and sugar in a large mixing bowl and stir using a large balloon whisk. Add the marsala. Place the bowl in a bain-marie or over a pan of hot water and whisk vigorously and continuously, keeping the sides of the bowl clean. The zabaglione is sufficiently set when it clings to the whisk when raised from the bowl. Carefully pour into glass goblets and refrigerate until served or pour into a loaf tin to freeze.

ZEST

This is the rind of citrus fruits and in pastry terms refers mainly to orange, grapefruit, lemon and lime zest, as these are the most widely used. The zest of these fruits is used in a crystallised or candied form for cakes and pastries and in fruit minces. When finely chopped, it is boiled with the flesh and used in marmalades, jams and jellies. As well, when still on the fruit, it has sugar rubbed over it to extract the oils and colour; the sugar is then dissolved in sauces and mixtures.

Zitron Step-by-Step

Step 1: Place one of the iced cookies on top of a base and press together.

Step 2: Pipe a decorative Z on the top of each cake. See page 293.

Lemon Butter

Whisk eggs well in a mixing bowl. Add lemon, sugar and butter to eggs and stir. Place the bowl over a pot of boiling water and whisk continuously for 15–20 minutes or until mixture is thick. Cool, then refrigerate for 1 hour.

Icing

Place icing sugar and lemon juice in a bowl and mix until smooth and lump free. Stir in several drops of yellow colour but keep it to a pastel shading.

To Assemble

Dip the tops of half the discs into icing mixture and allow to set on a cake rack. Spread a small amount of lemon butter on remaining discs (these will form the base). Place one of the iced biscuits (cookies) on top of the base and press lightly together. Place melted chocolate in a piping (pastry) bag and pipe a decorative Z on top of each biscuit. Allow to set and harden before serving.

ZUCCHINI CAKE

2 cups (8 oz) plain (all-purpose) flour
1 teaspoon bicarbonate of soda
1 teaspoon ground cinnamon
⅓ cup (2 oz) poppy seeds
2 eggs
⅔ cup (5 fl oz) vegetable oil
300 g (10 oz) zucchini, grated
½ cup (3 oz) hazelnuts (filberts), chopped

Preheat oven to 180°C (350°F).
Grease and line a 20 cm (8 in) springform cake tin.
Sift flour, bicarbonate of soda and cinnamon into a large bowl with the poppyseeds. Add lightly whisked eggs, with oil, zucchini and hazelnuts and combine. Pour batter into cake tin and bake for 50–55 minutes, or until the top springs back when lightly touched in the centre. Remove from oven when baked and cool in the tin.

ZUCCOTA

A Tuscan specialty, the zuccota is a dome-shaped ice cream cake which consists of an outside crust of sponge and a rich chocolate fruit ice cream centre. It is decorated with whipped cream and grated chocolate.

ZUG TORTE

This Kirsch-flavoured cake is named after the historic Swiss town of Zug.

1 cup (7 oz) caster (superfine) sugar
100 ml (3½ fl oz) water
¾ cup (6 fl oz) Kirsch
1 vanilla génoise sponge (see page 134)
2 japonaise bases (see page 156)
1 quantity Italian buttercream (see page 43)
12 maraschino (candied) cherries, for decoration

Place sugar and water in a saucepan and bring to the boil. Cook slowly for 15 minutes. Remove from heat and add Kirsch. Chill for 1 hour.
Cut the sponge horizontally 3 cm (1¼ in) from the top and 3 cm (1¼ in) from the bottom. Discard top and bottom layers. Pour cooled syrup on the middle layer.
Place a japonaise base on a serving dish and spread thinly with a little of the buttercream. Top with the soaked sponge and spread with buttercream. Top with remaining japonaise base. Press lightly to spread the filling and cover top and sides of the cake with the remaining buttercream. Decorate with cherries.

ZUPPA INGLESE
(see also tipsy cake)

A rich Italian cake which is not what its name ('English soup') implies. It is an Italian cake not unlike the English tipsy cake. It consists of a liqueur-soaked sponge layered with a rich custard and covered with an Italian meringue which is glazed under the salamander or in a hot oven until golden brown.

ZWIEBACK
(see also bread, pulled bread, rusk)

Meaning 'twice baked', zwieback is simply bread which has been baked twice to make it firm, crisp and crunchy and to prolong its life. Otherwise known as pulled bread or rusks, zwieback is made by simply breaking pieces of any sweet type of bread off the loaf and baking them in the oven until golden brown. Remove and serve with dips or eat as a snack.

Bibliography

That's Sugar, Ewald and Susan Notter, 1991;

The Book of Ingredients, Philip Dowell and Adrian Bailey (Mermaid, 1990);

Reader's Digest Complete Guide to Cookery, Anne Willan (Ecole de Cuisine La Varenne, 1990);

The Penguin Dictionary of Cookery, Rosemary Hume and Muriel Downes (Penguin, 1966);

Food and Cooking in 19th Century Britain, Maggie Black;

Food and Cooking in 16th Century Britain, Peter Breares;

Food and Cooking in 17th Century Britain, Peter Breares;

Food and Cooking in 18th Century Britain, Jennifer Stead;

Food and Cooking in Medieval Britain, Maggie Black;

Food and Cooking in Roman Britain, Jane Renfrew;

Food and Cooking in Pre-Historic Britain, Jane Renfrew;

Food, Waverley Root (Simon & Schuster, 1980);

Dictionary of Food Ingredients, 2nd edition, Robert S. Igoe;

International Dictionary of Food and Cooking, Ruth Martin;

The Book of Ingredients, Bailey, Ortiz and Radecka (Michael Joseph, 1980);

The Great Book of French Cuisine, John Fuller (Collins, 1967);

The Food of the Western World, Theodora Fitzgibbon (Hutchinson, 1976);

Encyclopaedia Americana No. 3 (Grolier);

Cakes, Tortes & Gateaux of the World, Aaron Maree (HarperCollins, 1991);

Biscuits, Cookies and Slices of the World, Aaron Maree (HarperCollins, 1992);

Chocolate Cookery, Aaron Maree (Bay Books, 1992);

Real Food, Anne Willan (PaperMac, 1988);

English Food, Jane Grigson (Macmillan, 1974);

Betty Crocker's International Cookbook (Random House, 1980);

Hungarian Cooking, Ruth Kershner (Hamlyn, 1979).